Marriages and Families in a Diverse Society

Marriages and Families in a Diverse Society

Robin Wolf

Diablo Valley College

HarperCollins*CollegePublishers*

Acquisitions Editor: Alan McClare
Developmental Editor: Carol Einhorn
Project Coordination, Text and Cover Design, Art Coordination: York Production Services
Cover Photograph: Tony Freeman
Photo Researcher: Kelly Mountain
Manufacturing Manager: Helene G. Landers
Electronic Production Manager: Christine Pearson
Electronic Page Makeup: Graphic Express
Printer and Binder: R.R. Donnelley & Sons Company
Cover Printer: New England Book Components, Inc.

For permission to use copyrighted material, grateful acknowledgment is made to the copyright holders on pp. 553–554, which are hereby made part of this copyright page.

Marriages and Families in a Diverse Society

Library of Congress Cataloging-in-Publication Data
Wolf, Robin.
  Marriages and families in a diverse society / Robin Wolf.
    p. cm.
  Includes bibliographical references and index.
  ISBN 0-06-047185-9
  1. Family--United States.   2. Marriage--United States.   3. United States--Social conditions--1980-
I. Title.
HQ536.W58 1995
306.8--dc20   94-42089
                                                                            CIP

95 96 97 98   9 8 7 6 5 4 3 2 1

Brief Contents

Contents

This book was born out of my own pedagogical needs during the past 25 years in which I have taught courses on the family. In my own classes, I have used a variety of textbooks combined with supplementary readings to expose students to the breadth of family themes and issues that excite me. These themes include:

* the linkages between interpersonal dynamics and social structure,
* multi-ethnic and cross-cultural perspectives from both within and outside the United States,
* the family experience within a context of recent social change,
* gender issues, and
* the application of social theory to real-life situations.

Coordinating many different readings with a textbook left me feeling that the effort was somewhat fragmented, and so began my project to create one accessible book that could incorporate these various approaches. *Marriages and Families in a Diverse Society* is the fruit of that project.

Themes

Interpersonal Dynamics and Social Structure

In a society of changing families, it is important for students to have a societal overview of families and also to understand interpersonal dynamics within families. In this book, a strong effort has been made to integrate these two perspectives in each chapter so that students can be exposed to both levels of significance. A perspective that examines interpersonal dynamics allows students to gain information that can be helpful in understanding their own relationships. For example, this book presents useful information on the process of communication, the life cycle experiences of couples, interpersonal issues in dating, sexuality, cohabitation, and styles of childrearing, including stepparenting.

In addition, an effort is made to connect the personal experiences of individuals in the family with social structural issues. Structural material on social class, poverty, gender and employment, and the change to a post-industrial economy is presented. In Chapter 10, "Social Class and Poverty," I look at single mothers struggling to raise their children in the inner cities. In Chapter 12, "Parents and Children," I examine parenting styles and their impact on children, the rise in one-parent families since 1960, the relationship between single parents and their extended kin, and the "sandwiched generation" of adult children caring for elderly parents. Chapter 11, "Pregnancy: Experiences and Choices," addresses the joys, anxieties, and marital relationship during pregnancy as well as the rise in teen pregnancy and nonmarital childbearing. In Chapter 3, "Gender," I discuss the acquisition of gender roles, the income disparity between men and women, and the question of whether or not societies that exhibit gender equality exist. Even Chapter 13, "Communication and Conflict," contains a social structural element, looking at the influence of social roles on communication patterns.

In spite of the concerted effort made to link interpersonal dynamics to a societal overview, some chapters will be of more interest to those who emphasize interpersonal relationships or a human development approach that examines families over the life cycle. These chapters include Chapter 3, "Gender"; Chapter 4, "Falling in Love: Sexuality and Dating"; Chapter 5, "Patterns of Mate Choice and Cohabitation"; Chapter 7, "Marriage and Partnerships: Interpersonal Relationships"; Chapter 11, "Pregnancy: Experiences and Choices"; Chapter 12, "Parents and Children"; Chapter 13, "Communication and Conflict"; Chapter 14, "Family Abuse and Violence"; and Chapter 16, "Looking Forward: Emerging Trends and Future Potentials," which has substantial sections on stepparenting and adult children who return to live in their parents' home.

Those who emphasize a societal overview will be particularly interested in Chapter 1, "Perspectives on the Family," which asks "What is a family?" and presents an overview of demographic change; Chapter 2, "Research Methods and Social Theories," which includes sample questions from a sexuality survey; Chapter 3, "Gender," which examines issues of gender inequality; Chapter 8, "Marriage, Work, and Power"; Chapter 9, "Racial and Cultural Diversity Among Families"; Chapter 10, "Social Class and Poverty"; Chapter 14, "Family Abuse and Violence"; and Chapter 16, "Looking Forward: Emerging Trends and Future Potentials," which contains a substantial section on families caring for AIDS patients and a look at AIDS worldwide.

A social structural perspective is also found in portions of each of the other chapters, relating to such topics as date rape (Chapter 4), trends in cohabitation (Chapter 5), AIDS in the United States (Chapter 6), gay and lesbian relationships (Chapter 7), and one-parent families (Chapter 12).

Racial and Cultural Diversity

Marriages and Families in a Diverse Society presents a cross-cultural perspective in several ways. First, there is a special chapter entitled "Racial and Cultural Diversity" (Chapter 9), which focuses on American subcultural groups. Throughout the text, the family experiences of African Americans, Hispanics, Native Americans, and Asians in the United States are explored. We look at working wives among Mexican immigrants, Vietnamese immigrant parents raising children in American society, Native American views on gender, African American extended kin networks, and many other family experiences. A number of graphs in the book depict the racial and ethnic diversity in American family trends, including divorce, childbearing, poverty, and parenting. Finally, from a broader perspective, families from around the world are discussed in a series of World Perspective Boxes. (See "Features," below, for a more complete description of these.)

Gender Issues

The construction of gender—and its impact on our lives—is explored throughout this book. Some of the issues covered that touch on the influence of gender include sexuality in dating, combining employment and family life, domestic violence, divorce and the economic well-being of one-parent families, and AIDS. Furthermore, I strove to achieve gender balance so that the family experiences of both men and women are presented. Single-father families as well as single-mother families are described. Dating and questions of sexuality are discussed in interviews giving both the male and the female perspectives.

Applied Theory

Students need to be familiar with major social theories, but theories are often presented in a dry, abstract manner. I tried to avoid this problem by discussing theories and then applying them to concrete situations in families. Thus, after I present theories, I then use them to explain a personal interview or to illuminate a specific study. For example, in the chapter on mate choice, interviews with a couple are discussed from three different theoretical perspectives. While exchange theory and conflict theory receive particular attention, structural-functional theory, systems theory, and symbolic interaction theory are also discussed.

Student-Oriented Book

In writing this book, high priority was given to selecting examples and studies that not only represent solid research but also will engage students' interest. Students can imagine themselves in many of the situations presented, while at the same time gaining information about research on family life.

Features

On a more structural level, several features have been designed to make *Marriages and Families in a Diverse Society* more useful and more interesting for students.

Chapter Opening Vignettes: Every chapter opens with a vignette, frequently based on my own research interviews, which illustrates some of the major concepts in the chapter. The text then refers back to the opening interview when major ideas are discussed in the chapter. These interviews are used to illustrate either social theories or the findings of specific studies. The one exception to this pattern is Chapter 2, "Research Methods and Social Theories." This chapter opens with a survey on sexuality, which is used to illustrate research methods.

Boxed Features: Three types of boxed inserts have been developed to provide students with high-interest complements to the main text reading:

World Perspectives: These inserts allow students to view contemporary family life around the world. For example, in Chapter 8, "Marriage, Work, and Power," the World Perspectives box looks at women and work in Japan. In the pregnancy chapter, a box on the couvade describes pregnancy symptoms in men in a variety of cultures. Childrearing among the !Kung of the Kalahari desert is discussed in Chapter 12, "Parents and Children." Through World Perspectives boxes, students may gain insight into the variety of ways in which family life can be organized.

Social Issues: So many aspects of marriage and family life lie at the center of heated debate, and I believe it is important for students to be exposed to the different opinions that comprise that debate. Therefore, in almost every chapter, Social

Issues boxes present the current range of views on such controversial topics as date rape (Chapter 4), the feminist split over marriage issues (Chapter 8), polygyny (Chapter 9), the criminalization of illegal drug use during pregnancy (Chapter 11), and family consent for abortion (Chapter 11). These Social Issues inserts cover subjects that are of deep importance to American families.

*A Closer Look: Some of these inserts elaborate on in-text topics with more detail, as in "Gender and Participation in the Labor Force" (Chapter 1), "Mexican-American Mate Choice" (Chapter 5), and "Anatomy and Reproduction" (Chapter 6). Others depart briefly from the text coverage to address a relevant issue, for example, "Do Men and Women Have Different Love Styles?" (Chapter 4), "Challenging the Myth: Births to Unmarried Older Women" (Chapter 11), "Suggestions for Negotiating a Solution to a Conflict" (Chapter 13), and "What's a Stepfather to Do?" (Chapter 16). As a group, the A Closer Look boxes provide interesting highlights to a wide-ranging discussion on marriage and the family.

Special Chapters and Topics: Chapter 9, "Racial and Cultural Diversity Among Families," presents the family life of Appalachian white families and fundamentalist Mormon families practicing plural marriage, as well as Vietnamese, African American, and Hispanic families. Chapter 10, "Social Class and Poverty," allows students to relate the economic insecurity that they observe in families they know to a changing economy and social class structure. Two substantial sections on AIDS appear in the book (in Chapters 6 and 16); these bring in new information on women with AIDS and families nursing AIDS patients. Nonmarital parenting, including teen parenting, appears in the pregnancy chapter (Chapter 11) and again in the chapter on parents and children (Chapter 12). These topics are not covered in a number of books on marriage and families but I believe are essential to a well-rounded understanding of contemporary marriage and family life.

Appendices: Four segments at the end of the book offer important, practical information at a level of detail that would overload the relevant text chapters. These appendices are:

Appendix 1 Sexually Transmitted Diseases
Appendix 2 Contraception
Appendix 3 Pregnancy and Childbirth
Appendix 4 Sexual Dysfunction

These should be valuable reference sections, to be read either in conjunction with the related text material or on their own.

Attention to Key Terms and Concepts: Key terms and concepts are introduced in *bold type* so that students can identify them as central to the chapter they are reading. Concepts are defined at this first usage to encourage students to build a social science vocabulary. These words are also listed at the end of the chapter in a Key Words section, reminding students to review what they have learned. A glossary at the end of the book also provides a comprehensive set of definitions.

Recent Research: Topics are discussed by presenting up-to-date research that is both quantitative and qualitative. Studies using national samples are utilized along with studies involving in-depth interviews in which individuals describe family life in their own voices.

Midchapter Review Questions: An entire text chapter can contain a challenging amount of information for a student to absorb. Therefore, I have inserted Review Questions after each major subject section of text, typically two or three times per chapter. These questions should encourage students to think about what they have just read and test their mastery of the key concepts in that material before reading on.

Resources: At the end of each chapter, a Resources section lists organizations that either provide information on family topics, lobby congress, organize a network of self-help groups, or provide some useful family service. Addresses and phone numbers are given so that students seeking information for a term paper or a personal issue can contact the organizations. Some hotlines are listed for families in crisis.

Annotated Bibliography: Often the bibliography is an element of a textbook that is scanned by instructors but ignored by students. I wanted the bibliography to be yet another part of *Marriages and Families in a Diverse Society* that students could really use, both during their Marriage and Family course and afterward. Toward that end, I created a system of marginal annotations that organize citations into several central themes or areas, namely, Race and Ethnicity, Gender, Fatherhood, Homelessness, Poverty, Aging, and Sexuality. I hope this will aid students in preparing research papers for this course and even for courses they take in the future.

Supplements Package

Instructor's Manual/Test Bank: Written by Robin Wolf, each chapter of this manual contains a chapter outline; a class activity, including a handout suitable for photocopying; critical thinking questions for major topics covered in the chapter; at least 30 multiple-choice test questions; and tables for analyzing from the student survey.

Study Guide: To assist students in their review and comprehension of the text material, Lawrence Basirico of Elon College has created this workbook for students, which includes detailed student projects, journal exercises, and essay and research paper suggestions.

Computerized Test Bank: A computerized version of the test question bank is available for both IBM compatible and Macintosh computers.

Acknowledgments

The effort of many people goes into creating a textbook. I am especially appreciative of the help and encouragement given to me by Alan McClare, Acquisitions Editor for Sociology at HarperCollins. Alan reacted to ideas for the book with delight while at the same time offering suggestions for their further development. It was indeed a pleasure to work with him. It is impossible to express how valuable the counsel of Carol Einhorn, Developmental Editor at HarperCollins, was in helping to give this book direction and focus. She provided both challenges and emotional support as the book developed. Her insights helped solve knotty problems and her suggestions contributed to a more interesting book. I am very grateful to have worked with such an enthusiastic and knowledgeable person. I also want to thank Larry Basirico for putting together a creative student study guide, Tom Kulesa for his help with the Instructor's Manual, Angela Gladfelter, of York Production Services, for her attention to detail as Production Coordinator, Elsa Peterson for handling permissions, and Lorraine Ferrier for careful copyediting.

A number of people sent articles and gave references to me while I was writing this book, and I am grateful for their interest and help. I appreciate members of the Sociology–Social Science–Anthropology Department at Diablo Valley College who provided me with opportunities to discuss ideas for the book. I also want to thank my students who eagerly gave me feedback on class exercises that now appear in the Instructor's Manual and who commented on the Student Survey that is found in both the textbook and the Instructor's Manual. Special accolades are due to the very helpful Diablo Valley College Library staff and to the Government Documents Library staff at the University of California at Berkeley. I am also grateful to Diablo Valley College for providing me with a sabbatical leave during which part of this book was written. I would like to thank Keith Farrington for inviting me to conduct a teaching workshop at the 1994 meeting of the Pacific Sociological Association. I would also like to thank Reed Geertsen for inviting me to participate in a round table on teaching sociology at the 1994 meetings of the American Sociological Association. Likewise, thanks to Hal Charnofsky for asking me to give a round table at the California Sociological Association on a multicultural approach to teaching a marriage and family course and to Scott Coltrane for inviting me to share some class exercises that I have developed at a round table at the 1994 meeting of the Pacific Sociological Association.

This textbook has also benefited enormously from several rounds of constructive critique from many instructors across the country who teach courses in the family. For their thorough and insightful comments, I am grateful to the following colleagues: Karen Baum, Mira Costa College; John Bedell, California State University at Fullerton; Michael Breci, St. Cloud State University; Lois Bryant, University of Missouri at Columbia; Margaret Cassidy, University of Wisconsin at Eau Claire; Peter Chroman, College of San Mateo; Rebecca Clark, Arizona State University; Marilyn Coleman, University of Missouri at Columbia; Robert Deverick, John Tyler Community College; Bette Dickerson, American University; Mark Eckel, McHenry County College; Henry Fischer, Millersville State University; Becky Glass, State University of New York at Geneseo; Rachel Kahn-Hut, San Francisco State University; Gary Lee, University of Florida; Cynthia Negrey, University of Louisville; Christa Reiser, East Carolina University; Robert Salt, University of Wisconsin at Stout; Jay Schvaneveldt, Utah State University; Constance Shehas, University of Florida; Jerry Shepperd, Austin Community College; David Wemhaner, Tulsa Jr. College; and Les Whitbeck, Iowa State University of Science and Technology.

My historian husband, Tom, was a loving friend and colleague during the writing of this book. He continually engaged me in provocative conversations and raised issues concerning family change. I also appreciate the encouragement and tolerance from my children Jim, Bob, and Jennifer; my brother, Buck, who always asked about my progress; my mother-in-law, Ocky, and my sister-in-law, Margaret, who provided a comfortable place for me to work in on weekend visits; my friends Joe and Dorothy Simmons, who were so helpful while I was doing research in Arizona; my cousins Bruce and Valerie for their encouragement; and, especially, my mother, Jane, who continually cheered me on as this book developed.

Robin Wolf

Preface to the Student

The Marriage and Family Course and Your Life

I hope that this book will help you think in new ways about family life. The issues and ideas in the book are relevant to your own personal life, and you can also use your experience with families to illuminate concepts in the book. In addition, the book allows you to become acquainted with families around the world that are different from the families you know on a day-to-day basis.

Many of my students find it useful to know where they can find information on personal problems or find references for a term paper. The Resources section at the end of each chapter provides a helpful list of organizations that either send out information on request, lobby Congress, or coordinate a set of self-help organizations.

In addition, the annotated bibliography at the end of this book can be helpful in writing papers for a family course and for other courses that you may take in the future. Notations next to certain bibliographic references indicate that a particular reference pertains to such topics as Gender, Fatherhood, Homelessness, Poverty, Race and Ethnicity, Aging, and Sexuality. Many of the articles and books in the bibliography were published in the 1990s and can provide you with current references to look up for writing papers.

Be sure to fill out the Student Survey that follows. Questions in the Student Survey are keyed to ideas in each chapter. By participating in this survey, you can compare your experience to trends and patterns in the United States that are discussed in this book. After you fill out the Student Survey, transfer your answers to the Code Sheet that appears after the Student Survey. The Code Sheet consolidates answers into a single page and provides you with privacy when the survey results are examined. Do not put your name on the Code Sheet. Your professor may want to gather the information in the Student Surveys to present a picture of class attitudes. He or she may ask you to carefully cut out the completed Code Sheet and turn it in. The professor can then shuffle the code sheets and pass them out to the class. Then you can let the class know how the person whose code sheet you are holding answered a particular question. You could ask your professor to query the class about how the members answered specific questions related to the chapter that you are currently reading.

In this Student Survey exercise, you will be participating in a sociological survey, a research method explained more thoroughly in Chapter 2 of this book. I have been doing survey research with my students for more than 20 years, and I hope that you find it as interesting as I do. My students found this survey to be fun and helpful in clarifying issues and values in their own lives. Since the survey questions are keyed to concepts in each chapter, participating in the survey will help to reinforce important ideas in the book.

If you would like to contact me about this survey and let me know how it is working for you, or if you would like to make comments on the book, you can reach me on E-mail at rwolf@viking.dvc.edu or write me at: Robin Wolf, Diablo Valley College, Pleasant Hill, California 94523. Have a good semester.

Robin Wolf

Instructions for Using the Student Survey and Code Sheet

1. The Student Survey: Have your students fill out the Student Survey at the end of the Preface to the Student. An additional copy of the Student Survey and Code Sheet are found in the Instructor's Manual on perforated pages for easy reproduction.

2. The Code Sheet: Ask students to transfer their answers for the Student Survey to the Code Sheet, that is located after the Student Survey in their textbooks. Students circle the letter code on the Code Sheet that matches the letter code of the answer that they chose in their Student Survey. The Code Sheet consolidates answers into a single page and provides students with privacy when the survey results are tabulated. Ask the students not to put their names on the Code Sheet. Ask students to carefully cut out or tear out the Code Sheets and turn them in to you.

3. Tabulating Results: Shuffle the code sheets and pass them out to the class at random so that most people are holding a Code Sheet filled out by someone else. Then draw a table on the blackboard and tabulate answers by calling for a show of hands. You could ask the students to raise their hands if the Code Sheet that they are holding has a particular answer. It is especially interesting to compare the answers of men and women in your class. You could ask students to raise their hands if they hold a female Code Sheet (Question 1, Answer F) on which "P" is circled for Question 11 (people of the opposite sex push too hard to have sex). Examples of interesting tables are given in the Instructor's Manual. You may want to bring a calculator to class to work out percentages, but I have found that someone in class always has a calculator and is glad to work out the percentages for me.

4. Comparing Your Class to National Data: At the end of the semester, PLEASE SEND THE CODE SHEETS TO ME so that I can provide you with combined data from a variety of colleges and universities around the country. I will send the results back to you right away so that next semester you can compare your class to aggregate data from other classes. My address is: Robin Wolf, Diablo Valley College, Pleasant Hill, California 94523, E-Mail: rvwolf@viking.dvc.edu

<u>Directions</u>: Choose only <u>ONE</u> answer for each question. If you are asked about your partner and you have no current partner, answer for a previous relationship.

1. Your gender:
____ male (M)
____ female (F)

2. Your age:
____ 19 and below (19-)
____ 20 to 24 (20-24)
____ 25 and above (25+)

3. Your marital status:
____ never married (NM)
____ divorced, not remarried (D)
____ widowed, not remarried (W)
____ married (M)

4. Three years from now, I expect to be
____ married (M)
____ living with a romantic partner (L)
____ neither married nor living with a partner (N)
        (Chapter 1, Perspectives)

5. If all of the following forms of marriage were legal, the form of marriage that I would prefer for myself is
____ polygyny, the marriage of one husband to two or more wives (PG)
____ polyandry, the marriage of one wife to two or more husbands (PA)
____ group marriage, two or more husbands married to two or more wives (G)
____ monogamy, the marriage of one husband to one wife (M)
____ I do not ever intend to marry (NM)
        (Chapter 1, Perspectives)

6. Do you agree or disagree with the following statement? People are basically rational in their choice of a romantic partner.
____ strongly agree (SA)
____ mildly agree (MA)
____ mildly disagree (MD)
____ strongly disagree (SD)
        (Chapter 2, Research and Theories)

7. Do you agree or disagree with the following statement? It is important for me to have power or influence in my marriage or romantic partnership.
____ strongly agree (SA)
____ mildly agree (MA)
____ mildly disagree (MD)
____ strongly disagree (SD)
        (Chapter 2, Research and Theories)

8. If I were distressed about something, I would be more likely to discuss it with a
____ male relative (M)
____ female relative (F)
        (Chapter 3, Gender)

9. Do you agree or disagree with the following statement? In general, I think that men and women have equality in this society.
____ strongly agree (SA)
____ mildly agree (MA)
____ mildly disagree (MD)
____ strongly disagree (SD)
        (Chapter 3, Gender)

10. If you had to choose ONE, which of the following would you consider most important in a romantic relationship?
____ passion, sexual attraction (P)
____ commitment, the decision to remain with the partner. (C)
____ emotional intimacy, having someone you can easily talk to (I)
        (Chapter 4, Love, Dating, Sexuality)

11. I often think that people of the opposite sex
____ push too hard to have sex (P)
____ have an attitude toward sex that I am comfortable with (C)
____ withhold sex too often (W)
        (Chapter 4, Love, Dating, Sexuality)

12. In a romantic relationship, which type of love style best describes you?
____ Ludis: playful, uncommitted love (L)
____ Pragma: practical mate choice (P)
____ Storge: love as companionship (S)
____ Mania: jealous, emotional love (M)
____ Agape: selfless, altruistic love (A)
____ Eros: erotic, romantic love (E)
        (Chapter 4, Love, Dating, Sexuality)

13. In general, how important is it to you for your family (parents, brothers, and sisters) to approve of your partner?
____ very important (V)
____ somewhat important (S)
____ not important (N)
    (Chapter 5, Mate Choice)

14. If two people met, fell in love, saw each other every day, married after one month, and then remained happily married, would you find the fact that their marriage was intact and happy
____ not surprising (N)
____ somewhat surprising (S)
____ very surprising (V)
    (Chapter 5, Mate Choice)

15. How much, if at all, do you worry about contracting HIV, which causes AIDS?
____ I worry a great deal (G)
____ I worry somewhat (S)
____ I hardly ever worry about it (H)
    (Chapter 6, Sexuality)

16. If my spouse or live-in partner had a sexual affair with someone else, I would probably
____ remain in the relationship and probably not bring up the subject (NT)
____ talk to find out why it happened and probably be forgiving (TF)
____ express my anger or hurt feelings but not split up (AH)
____ split up (SU)
    (Chapter 6, Sexuality)

17. Do you approve or disapprove of homosexual romantic relationships?
____ strongly approve (SA)
____ mildly approve (MA)
____ mildly disapprove (MD)
____ strongly disapprove (SD)
    (Chapter 6, Sexuality)

18. In general, I feel that marriage is
____ harder for the wife (W)
____ equally hard for the husband and wife (E)
____ harder for the husband (H)
    (Chapter 7, Marriage and Partnerships)

19. Do you agree or disagree with the following statement? People of the opposite sex are difficult to understand.
____ strongly agree (SA)
____ mildly agree (MA)
____ mildly disagree (MD)
____ strongly disagree (SD)
    (Chapter 7, Marriage and Partnerships)

20. Would you approve or disapprove of legislation that allowed homosexual couples to legally marry?
____ strongly agree (SA)
____ mildly agree (MA)
____ mildly disagree (MD)
____ strongly disagree (SD)
    (Chapter 7, Marriage and Partnerships)

21. Assuming that my spouse or live-in partner and I had children, I would prefer that my partner be
____ employed full-time (F)
____ employed part-time (P)
____ not employed (N)
    (Chapter 8, Marriage, Work, Power)

22. In a marriage in which the couple has children and both partners are employed full-time, who do you think should have responsibility for housework?
____ Mainly the wife (W)
____ A 50–50 split between husband and wife (50–50)
____ Mainly the husband (H)
    (Chapter 8, Marriage, Work, Power)

23. How often do you get together with your extended kin (grandparents, aunts, uncles, cousins)?
____ once a week or more (W)
____ once or twice a month (M)
____ less than once a month (L)
    (Chapter 9, Diversity)

24. How important do you think it is for people to retain their ethnic identity?
____ very important(V)
____ somewhat important (S)
____ not important (N)
    Chapter 9, Diversity)

25. Do you think that AFDC (welfare) payments should be
____ increased (I)
____ remain the same (S)
____ decreased (D)
  (Chapter 10, Social Class and Poverty)

26. If your partner was a steady worker, did not drink, was not violent, and brought home a good income, how important do you think it would be for you to be able to bring up grievances about the relationship?
____ not very important (N)
____ somewhat important (S)
____ very important (V)
  (Chapter 10, Social Class and Poverty)

27. Do you agree or disagree with the following statement? The most important thing that children should learn is to follow directions and obey parents.
____ strongly agree (SA)
____ mildly agree (MA)
____ mildly disagree (MD)
____ strongly disagree (SD)
  (Chapter 10, Social Class and Poverty)

28. What do you think is the ONE most important thing that the federal government should do about homelessness?
____ provide housing for homeless people who enter drug and alcohol treatment programs (T)
____ provide additional permanent housing without treatment program requirements (PH)
____ provide more homeless shelters for temporary housing(S)
____ not increase spending for the homeless (N)
  (Chapter 10, Social Class and Poverty)

29. If you could know the future and you found out that you would have a child but not be married, how would you feel?
____ disappointed (D)
____ neither disappointed nor glad (N)
____ glad (G)
____ I already have a child (HC)
  (Chapter 11, Pregnancy)

30. During childbirth, how important do you think it is for the husband to be with the wife during labor and delivery?
____ not very important (N)
____ somewhat important (S)
____ very important (V)
  (Chapter 11, Pregnancy)

31. Who do you think should be the major decision maker in a parent-child relationship involving an 8-year-old child?
____ primarily the parent (P)
____ 50–50 split with parent and child having equal influence (50–50)
____ primarily the child (C)
  (Chapter 12, Parents and Children)

32. Do you agree or disagree with the following statement? Single teenage parents should be required to live in the household of a responsible adult, such as their own parent (the infant's grandparent), to be eligible for public assistance.
____ agree (A)
____ disagree (D)
  (Chapter 12, Parents and Children)

33. When you and your partner get into a disagreement, which ONE of the following BEST describes how YOU generally respond?
____ I'm silent or leave the room (S-NA)
____ I tend to agree with the partner to avoid further hassles (A-NA)
____ I tend to tell my partner that his or her ideas are stupid (AG)
____ I try to state my objections or feelings (AS)
  (Chapter 13, Communication)

34. Which ONE of the following bothers you MOST in a relationship?
____ when a partner says that I am being too sensitive or overreacting (IV)
____ when a partner hints at what he or she wants without being direct (ID)
____ when I hear contradictory things from my partner and don't know what he or she wants (D)
____ when I suspect that my partner has an ulterior motive and wants something from me (M)
  (Chapter 13, Communication)

35. When you and a partner get into an argument, what is your partner's response?
____ it often ends with my partner slapping or hitting me (ES)
____ once in a while my partner slaps or hits me (OWS)
____ my partner has only slapped or hit me once (SO)
____ my partner has never slapped or hit me (N)
    (Chapter 14, Family Abuse and Violence)

36. When disciplining children,
____ children can benefit from a good spanking (BS)
____ an occasional mild spanking is sometimes necessary (OS)
____ children should never be spanked (N)
    (Chapter 14, Family Abuse and Violence)

37. Do you agree or disagree with the following statement? Marriage is a risky business because so many marriages end in divorce.
____ strongly agree (SA)
____ mildly agree (MA)
____ mildly disagree (MD)
____ strongly disagree (SD)
    (Chapter 15, Divorce)

38. Do you agree or disagree with the following statement? If I were to divorce after having children and did not get along with my ex-spouse who had child custody, I would probably avoid seeing my ex-spouse even if it meant spending less time with my children
____ strongly agree (SA)
____ mildly agree (MA)
____ mildly disagree (MD)
____ strongly disagree (SD)
    (Chapter 15, Divorce)

39. If you were a mid-life parent of an adult child, how would you respond if that adult child got a divorce and returned to live with you?
____ happy to share my home (HS)
____ somewhat reluctant to share my home but willing to do it (RS)
____ I would not share my home (N)
    (Chapter 16, Future)

40. Do you think that government spending on AIDS research should be
____ increased (I)
____ remain the same (RS)
____ decreased (D)
    (Chapter 16, Future)

41. If you were to become a stepparent, how would you feel about it?
____ enthusiastic (E)
____ willing but not enthusiastic (W)
____ reluctant (R)
    (Chapter 16, Future)

42. How often, if ever, do you attend religious services?
____ once a year or less (Y)
____ about once a month (M)
____ about once a week (W)

43. Your parent's annual income. (If you live with a single parent, use that parent's income. If you do not know the amount, give an estimate.)
____ below $25,000 (24-)
____ $25,000 to $49,000 (25-49)
____ $50,000 to $74,999 (50-74)
____ $ 75,000 and over (75+)

44. What is your annual income?
____ below $25,000 (24-)
____ $25,000 to $49,000 (25–49)
____ $50,000 to $74,999 (50–74)
____ $75,000 and over (75+)

45. What is your racial or ethnic background?
____ Asian or Pacific Islander (A-P)
____ African-American (AA)
____ Hispanic-American (H)
____ Native American NA)
____ Non-Hispanic white (W)
____ Other, please specify (O)_____
    _____

46. What is your religious preference?
____ Catholic (CA)   ____ Mormon (M)
____ Fundamentalist Christian (FC)
____ Protestant (P)   ____ Jewish (J)
____ Islamic (I)   ____ Hindu (H)
____ Buddhist (B)   ____No religion (N)
____ Atheist, do not believe in God (A)
____ Other, please specify (O) _____
    _____

CODE SHEET

Directions: Carefully circle the letter code that corresponds to the letter code (printed on the questionnaire) for the answer that you chose.

1. Gender
   M   F

2. Age
   19-   20-   24   25+

3. Marital Status
   NM   D   W   M

4. Three years from now
   M   L   N

5. Form of marriage
   PG   PA   G   M   NM

6. People basically rational
   SA   MA   MD   SD

7. Want power or influence
   SA   MA   MD   SD

8. Discuss distress with
   M   F

9. Men and women have equality
   SA   MA   MD   SD

10. Most important in romantic relationship
    P   C   I

11. People of opposite sex
    P   C   W

12. Your love style
    L   P   S   M   A   E

13. Family approve partner
    V   S   N

14. Marry after one month
    N   S   V

15. Worry about AIDS
    G   S   H

16. Spouse extramarital affair
    NT   TF   AH   SU

17. Homosexual romance
    SA   MA   MD   SD

18. Marriage harder for
    W   E   H

19. Understand opposite sex
    SA   MA   MD   SD

20. Homosexual marriage
    SA   MA   MD   SD

21. Partner's employment
    F   P   N

22. Household labor
    W   50-50   H

23. Get together with extended kin
    W   M   L

24. Retain ethnic identity
    V   S   N

25. AFDC payments
    I   S   D

26. Bring up grievances
    N   S   V

27. Children obey
    SA   MA   MD   SD

28. Homelessness
    T   PH   S   N

29. Unmarried parenthood
    D   N   G   HC

30. Husband at birth
    N   S   V

31. Parent-child relationship
    P   50– 50   C

32. Teenage parent
    A   D

33. Disagreements
    SNA   ANA   AG   AS

34. Bothers you
    IV   ID   D   M

35. Partner's response to argument
    ES   OWS   SO   N

36. Spanking children
    BS   OS   N

37. Marriage is risky
    SA   MA   MD   SD

38. Spend less time with children
    SA   MA   MD   SD

39. Adult child moves in
    HS   RS   N

40. AIDS research spending
    I   RS   D

41. Becoming a stepparent
    E   W   R

42. Attend religious services
    Y   M   W

43. Your income
    24-   25–49   50–74   75+

44. Parent Income
    24-   25–49   50–74   75+

45. Race and Ethnicity
    AP   AA   H   NA   W
    O (other, please specify)
    _____

46. Religious preference
    CA   M   FC   P   J
    I   H   B   N   A
    O - other-please specify
    _____

Robin Wolf received her Ph.D. from the University of California at Berkeley and has taught marriage and family classes at Diablo Valley College for 25 years. In addition, she teaches classes in gender, social psychology, research methods, and critical thinking about social and cultural issues. She is involved in the effort to increase the recognition of undergraduate teaching as an important endeavor and represents community colleges on the council of the Undergraduate Education Section of the American Sociological Association. Robin Wolf is also actively involved in the Pacific Sociological Association and the California Sociological Association. She lives with her husband and three children in Oakland, California.

Marriages and Families in a Diverse Society

Part One

Marriage & Family: An Overview

1

Perspectives on the Family

When Ryan asked Yvette to move into his apartment, Yvette was pleased. She assumed that if they got along well, they would soon marry. When Yvette met Ryan she was struggling to raise her three-year-old daughter, Lara, while holding down a full-time job. Now Ryan picks up Lara from day care and looks after her until Yvette comes home from the restaurant where she works as a waitress. Over the past year Ryan has become attached to Lara and enjoys taking her with him in the late afternoons when he goes into town on errands. Yvette and Ryan have discussed marriage, but Yvette does not want to press the issue because she thinks that it would be a big step for Ryan to take on a ready-made family. However, Ryan is beginning to feel "settled-in" and already considers Yvette and Lara to be part of his family. He would like eventually to get married and have a child with Yvette. Their use of birth control has been somewhat sporadic, and Yvette now suspects that she might be pregnant. When she told Ryan of her suspicions, he seemed startled, then smiled and put his hand on her stomach, halfway hoping to feel some sign of a new life. Ryan feels ambivalent about working mothers, and he has told Yvette that he thinks young children are better off if they have a mother at home with them. Yvette points out that the parent at home could just as easily be the father, but Ryan chuckles and asks how she could support a family on the salary of a waitress, when he earns a great deal more as an electrician. On the other hand, Ryan's feelings are mixed and he is reluctant for Yvette to become a full-time homemaker. Marriage seems like a major step to him, and the financial burden would be less if Yvette would continue working after the birth of the baby, at least part time. Yvette's income makes the difference between a lean lifestyle and having some money for recreation, an occasional weekend get away, and perhaps being able to purchase a second car. The prospect of marriage is a little unsettling for Ryan, with so many of his friends getting divorces. But the idea of a family has a powerful pull for him; and now in his late twenties, he feels like he is ready to make a commitment. (Interviews by author.)

Ryan and Yvette are caught up in the trends that are shaping the modern family. The high divorce rate, the rise in cohabitation, and the increasing employment of married women are factors that affect the lives of this couple, as well as many others. American families have become complex and diverse during the second half of the twentieth century as the number of one-parent families, stepfamilies, and cohabitors has grown. These developments have led to a raging debate over how to define the family, as well as a debate over whether or not the family is in a state of decline. In this chapter we explore these issues as we examine the meaning of recent trends in family patterns. However, let us first turn to a brief overview of the book.

In this book we look at families as they struggle to adapt to the changing world of the late twentieth century. We will explore changes in dating patterns, delayed marriage, evolving sexual patterns, changing gender roles, changing work patterns that have led to changes in family life, the increase in divorce and cohabitation, the AIDS crisis, family patterns of new immigrants, and a number of other aspects of family life that have emerged in a changing world. We also look at the increasing diversity of American families. Structural diversity, or diversity in the organization of the family, is explored as we examine cohabitation, two-earner families, one-parent families, stepfamilies, same-sex partnerships, and extended families. Cultural diversity among families in the United States is also examined in many chapters; Chapter 9 is devoted to ethnic and racial diversity among families. Moreover, "World Perspectives" boxes give us a glimpse of families from an international perspective. As we explore these varied topics, gender is a theme that runs throughout the book, with a number of chapters addressing such gender issues as work, child care, dating and sexuality, family violence, and economic issues involved in divorce and employment.

The family is the most basic form of social organization, and the urge to form families is strong. Yet some social scientists argue that we have entered an era in which criticism of the family is so intense that it amounts to "family bashing" (Schvaneveldt and Young 1992). As we discuss family change, it is important to keep in mind that family life provides gratification, intimacy, and a sense of well being for many adults. The vast majority (85%) of married respondents in a Gallop poll said that they were "very satisfied" with their marriages (Tiesel and Olson 1992). That is not to say that families are trouble free. As in any intense relationship, the potential for conflict is always present, particularly as the society around us is changing. However, families have proven to be resilient in the face of social change. Strong families whose members display commitment, appreciation for each other, togetherness, good communication, and problem-solving skills provide enormous satisfaction and benefits to their members (Schvaneveldt and Young 1992; Stinnett and DeFrain 1989). In this book we look at changing trends in the family without loosing sight of the importance of interpersonal relationships, communication and conflict resolution, and positive parenting in producing a rewarding family life. We therefore look at the family on both the societal and interpersonal levels.

Let us turn now to the theme of this chapter, Perspectives on the Family, and begin with the debate over what relationships constitute a family.

What Is a Family?

Do Yvette and Ryan, who were described above, constitute a family? The definition of a family has become a topic of heated controversy over the last few years. There are two major sides in this debate: One position supports a definition of the family that emphasizes tradition and stability, and the other position argues that the definition of the family should stress diversity and social change.

Traditional Definition of the Family

Beutler and his colleagues (1989) present a traditional definition of the family. They argue that families are formed through childbearing and the central core of the family is a parent–child relationship that links two generations through adoption or birth. Beutler makes a sharp distinction between marriage and family, arguing that married couples do not become a family until they have a child. Under this traditional definition, Yvette and her daughter would constitute a family and Ryan would join that family when he marries Yvette and becomes a stepparent.

Beutler maintains that family ties are unique and need to be strengthened in modern society. He argues that the family realm differs from other spheres of life—such as employee–employer relationships—in that family relationships emphasize permanence; involve the total person; and are expected to be nurturing, emotionally intense and altruistic.

Expectation of Permanence. The relationship between a parent and a biological or adopted child is not easily legally severed. This relationship and the relationships between siblings tend to endure.

Total Person. Nonfamily relationships, such as business relationships, often have a particular goal. Such relationships are often temporary and convenient. Families, on the other hand, are interested in the welfare of the total person. Being with a family member can be rewarding in itself and does not depend on accomplishing a particular goal.

Nurturing. Because having children is seen by Beutler as central to family formation, families involve nurturing dependent children as well as nurturing other family members.

Emotional Intensity. Family relationships are some of the most emotionally intense relationships we experience. We are not expected always to be cool and rational in the family setting. For example, sibling relationships are often fraught with alternating feelings of love and hostility.

Altruism. Family members tend to be concerned about each other's welfare. Unlike business relationships, which are supposed to be motivated by self-interest, family relationships are often characterized by generosity and altruism.

The family is universal; it is found in all societies in one form or another. Most people gain important life satisfaction from their family relationships. The urge to form warm, nurturing, intimate family relationships is perhaps one of the most

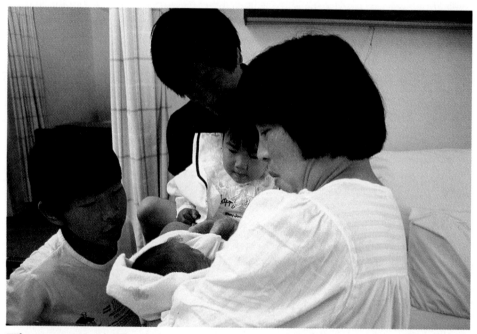

What constitutes a family? Today we recognize that the family exists in many different forms. Pictured here and on the next page are two of those forms: a nuclear family of two parents with their biological children and a single mother with both biological and adopted children.

basic motivations in human behavior. Beutler should be commended for emphasizing the importance of providing a nurturing environment for raising children and fostering intimate relationships. However, there are some problems with Beutler's traditional definition of the family.

Critique. Beutler has been criticized for creating a view of the family that excludes much of the diversity and complexity of modern families (Edwards 1989). Critics argue that today families come in a variety of forms, such as voluntarily childless married couples. Berardo (1990) argues that the family has been described as "chameleonlike" because it has adapted to social change by taking on a variety of forms.

Next we turn to the definition of the family used by the U.S. Bureau of the Census; this is the definition used for most of the data collected on families. This definition provides a somewhat broader view of families. As we look around us we see voluntarily childless couples, two-earner families, one-parent families, and step-families with children from different backgrounds as part of the diversity among families.

U.S. Bureau of the Census Definition of the Family

Federal government agencies that collect data on families use the U.S. Bureau of the Census definition of the family. According to this definition, a family includes two or more people related by blood, marriage, or adoption who share a common residence (U.S. Bureau of the Census 1994b). By this definition a grandparent and child living together constitute a family, as do two sisters who share a residence. Let us consider the example at the beginning of this chapter of Yvette, a divorced mother who shares a household with her child and her cohabiting partner. The U.S. Bureau of the Census would count Yvette and her child as a single parent family. Yvette and her partner, Ryan, would be considered heterosexual cohabitors, but not a family. The U.S. Bureau of the Census

Nurturing Nonbiological Fathers Redefine the Family

Jeff Jones of California made news when he sued for custody of the two children whom he had raised but who were not related to him biologically. Jones, who is sterile, thought that his wife had sought artificial insemination, when in fact she was impregnated twice by a lover. Jones helped to raise the children and developed a strong paternal bond. When the Jones' marriage dissolved, his wife and the children's biological father planned to marry and move from southern to northern California with the children. Jeff Jones sued for custody even though he has no genetic link to the children. His attachment to the children is strong. He describes crying from happiness at the birth of the children, and he has spent $150,000 in legal fees for his custody battle. His effort was successful, and in 1992 an Orange County Superior Court declared Jones to be the children's legal father. The judge granted shared custody of the children to Jones and his ex-wife. The biological father was determined to have no legal rights over the children. The California court followed a trend set by the U.S. Supreme Court, referred to as "grasping the opportunity" of parenthood. That is, the family is coming to be defined in the law in terms of establishing a nurturing and committed relationship with children, and these social ties sometimes take precedence over genetic ties.

In another case, Larry McLinden thought that he was the biological father of four-year-old Larry McLinden, Jr., who was born to a woman to whom he was not married. He helped to raise the child as if it was his own, and later he discovered that another man was the child's biological father. McLinden was granted primary custody of his son even though he has never been married to the mother and has no genetic relationship to the child. As family ties are increasingly defined by the courts in terms of nurturing and committed relationships, some nonbiological fathers are claiming and winning legal custody of the children they have raised (Klein 1992).

---

definition of the family is useful in separating cohabitation from other family forms and allows us to chart the rise in cohabitation and the decline in families based on marriage among young adults. Nonetheless, this official definition of the family has some problems.

Critique. Demographer Larry Bumpass and colleagues (1991), who study trends in marriage and cohabitation, have criticized the definition of the family used by the U.S. Bureau of the Census. Bumpass would classify Yvette and Ryan as a family. He writes that "cohabitation is very much a family status" (Bumpass et al. 1991:926). Moreover, excluding cohabiting couples from the definition of families represents a form of bias: Low-income couples are more heavily represented among cohabitors than are middle-income couples, and divorced persons typically cohabit prior to remarriage. Cohabitation is increasingly becoming a family lifestyle, and in our example Ryan fills a father role for Yvette's daughter, Lara (Bumpass et al. 1991).

Social Change Definition of the Family

Some social scientists have revised the traditional definition of the family and thus broadened criteria for classifying a relationship as a family. They have produced a definition of the family that emphasizes social change. John Scanzoni (1989) and others (Aldous and Wilfried 1990:1137) consider families to include partnerships based on a long-term intimate sexual relationship. This perspective includes oppo-site-sex and same-sex cohabitors as families. Thus Ryan, Yvette, and her child, Lara, would be considered a family. Under this broad definition of the family, the quality of the relationship, not its legal standing, is the key criterion in determining whether or not a couple qualifies as a family. With this new focus on "close rela-tionships which endure over a considerable length of time" (Scanzoni 1987:407), marriage is no longer considered to have a privileged status that sets it off from other committed and intimate sexual relationships. For a perspective that views the family in terms of commitment and nurturance see Box 1.

Critique. Scanzoni makes a good point when he says that cohabitors are playing an increasingly important role in American society. However, defining the family in terms of the quality of the relationship could make it difficult to conduct research on the family. It would be hard to know whom to include and whom to exclude from family studies because an investigation into the duration and quality of the relationship would have to precede the decision to place a particular couple in the sample of couples to be studied.

Defining the Family in This Book

There are two major situations in which we need a definition of a family. First, we need to define the family in order to specify the kinds of relationships family specialists study. In describing the field of family studies, it is useful to use a loose definition of the family that is broad enough to include heterosexual cohabitors, voluntarily childless couples, two-earner families, homosexual cou-ples, one-parent families, as well as traditional two-parent families. For the pur-pose of deciding what kinds of relationships to study, we use a definition of the family that includes the U.S. Bureau of the Census definition and adds Scan-zoni's category of couples in a long-term intimate sexual relationship. Thus fam-ilies consist of *two or more people related through blood, marriage, adoption, legal custody, or an ongoing sexual relationship who share a common residence.*

The second situation in which we need a definition of the family is when we are using statistics and following demographic trends in marriage, divorce, and cohabitation. Here we need a standard, widely agreed upon definition so that we can examine trends in family behavior. When we use demographic data from the U.S. Bureau of the Census or other government agencies, the definition of the fami-ly will be more narrow and will refer to *two or more people related through blood, marriage, or adoption who share a common residence.* This traditional definition of the family counts cohabitors separately from families. If we were to alter this definition of the family, we would render useless this wealth of demographic data.

Having examined how to define a family, let us turn to the question of defining marriage.

What Is Marriage?

Unlike the controversy over how to define a family, there is far less debate over how to define marriage. We define *marriage* as a sexual relationship between two adults who cooperate economically, which is marked by a ceremony or ritu-al that is publicly recognized as changing the social status of the partners involved. There are four basic forms of marriage: monogamy, polyandry, polygyny, and group marriage; these are discussed below.

Monogamy

Although the dominant form of marriage in the United States is *monogamy*, the marriage of one man and one woman, there is a decreasing tendency to have only one marriage partner during one's lifetime. Because half of marriages end in divorce and three-fourths of these divorced persons remarry, many Americans practice *serial monogamy*. In serial monogamy, a person has more than one marriage partner in sequence, so that monogamy is practiced at any one time. However, not every society considers monogamy the most desirable form of marriage. In addition to monogamy, there are three forms of "polygamy," or plural marriage: polyandry, polygyny and group marriage.

Polyandry

The marriage of one woman to two or more men is known as *polyandry*. This extremely rare form of marriage has been known to exist in only ten societies. Polyandry is considered the *ideal marriage* form, or preferred form of marriage, in only three societies: among some Tibetans, the Toda of India, and the Marquesians of the Polynesian Islands. In these three societies the majority of fami-

Monogamy, the marriage of one man to one woman, is the form of marriage that is most universally accepted throughout the world. In the United States, where 50 percent of marriages end in divorce, many men and women practice serial monogamy.

lies practice polyandry. In the other seven societies, polyandry is allowed to co-exist along with other forms of marriage, but only a minority of families actually practice polyandry (Cassidy and Lee 1989). Box 1.2 examines polyandry among the Toda.

Polygyny

The marriage of one man to two or more women is known as *polygyny*. Three-fourths of the world's societies have allowed polygyny, with this form of marriage being particularly popular in the Middle East, Asia, and Africa (Wyatt, Gary, 1989). Polygyny is still found in the United States among some fundamentalist Mormons who live in rural areas along Utah's boarders with Arizona and Colorado. See Chapter 9 for a more complete discussion of polygyny in the United States.

Group Marriage

The marriage of two or more men to two or more women is called *group marriage*. Group marriage requires a minimum of four people. Like polyandry, group marriage is rare. Group marriage tends to be found in societies in which plural marriage in the form of either polygyny or polyandry already exists. When group marriage occurs it is often initiated as a solution to a family problem, as is the case of group marriage among the Toda described in Box 1.2.

Next we turn to family life in the United States and look at major demographic change in families over the last three decades.

Is The Family in a State of Decline?

The debate over how to define the family, which we discussed earlier, is closely linked to an argument over whether or not the family is in a state of decline. This debate has two primary positions: the family decline perspective and the family change perspective.

The Family Decline Perspective

Those who use the family decline perspective argue that the family is under siege as it endures social change, and that it is in a state of decline (Gill and Grandom 1993; Glazer 1991; Popenoe 1988, 1992). This group of social scientists argues that the family has been weakened by the rise in the divorce rate, the sexual revolution, the growth of one-parent families, and the employment of mothers (Popenoe 1988, 1992). Many traditionalists trace these trends to changing family values. They cite studies indicating that fewer people today subscribe to traditional values that emphasize self-sacrifice and commitment in family relationships (Berardo 1990; Gill 1993; Kahn and London 1991). Today's couples are more likely to exhibit values that stress individualism with an emphasis on independence and self-development (Simon, Eder, and Evans 1992, Swidler

BOX 1.2   W o r l d   P e r s p e c t i v e s

The Polyandrous Toda of India

The Toda are buffalo herders who live in the hills of a remote part of southern India that is not suitable for agriculture. Their relative isolation in the high country has made it possible for the Toda to retain their culture. Among the Toda, when the eldest brother marries, his wife automatically becomes the wife of all his brothers. This form of marriage is called *fraternal polyandry,* which means the marriage of a set of brothers to one woman. The Toda practice "infant marriage," with parents typically arranging their daughter's marriage when she is age two or three. When the daughter reaches age fifteen or sixteen, her husband, who is the eldest brother in his family, comes for her and takes her to his home. There is no other marriage ceremony. The bride becomes the wife not only of this man but also of his younger brothers. In addition, any brothers born after the marriage become cohusbands of the wife. However, younger brothers must reach physical maturity before they may exercise their sexual rights. The Toda are remarkably free of jealousy and sexual competition over the wife. In fact, both husbands and wives are allowed to take lovers outside the marriage as extramarital affairs. Perhaps this sexual outlet keeps the level low of sexual jealousy between brothers.

When the wife gives birth, the biological father of child is unknown. However, the Toda are uncon-cerned about biological fatherhood and instead stress "social fatherhood." When the wife becomes pregnant with her first child, the eldest brother claims paternity and becomes the "social father" by giving the pregnant wife a bow that symbolizes his willingness to teach the child to hunt with a bow and arrow if the child is a boy. Paternity is not a problem in polyandrous societies. Husbands who share the same clan pass on that clan membership to all their children. In traditional societies, placing the child in a kinship group is often far more important than identifying a specific biological father. After two or three children are born, the second eldest brother claims paternity for future children.

The Toda utilize "patrilocal residence," in which the bride moves in with the husband and his family. Each family typically occupies a single-room 8-by-10-foot hut for part of the year and migrates with the herds during the rest of the year. The Toda live at subsistence level, producing only enough food to feed their families without any surplus. Polyandry maximizes the ratio of productive adults (the cohusbands) to dependent children. On marginal land it may take four cohusbands working together to support a single set of children (Cassidy and Lee 1989:5). Patrilineal clans, in which descent and inheritance pass through the male line, own buffalo and grazing land. Polyandry allows a set of brothers to produce a single

1980). From the family decline perspective this change in values is undermining the foundation of the American family.

The Family Change Perspective

On the opposite side of the argument is the family change perspective. This position maintains that the family is not crumbling, but instead is becoming more complex and diverse (Cherlin 1993; Scanzoni et al. 1989; Skolnick 1991). Arlene Skolnick (1991) points out that discussions of family decline refer to a traditional form of the family that was prominent in the 1950s: the two-parent family with a mother who is a full-time homemaker. From the family change perspective, two-earner families, childless couples, extended families, one-parent families, and cohabitors are part of the rich variety of family forms. This group of social scientists sees strength in the ability of the family to change its form and adapt to social change.

set of children who then inherit their fathers' clan membership and right to herd buffalo on clan land. It takes a great deal of land to herd and feed buffalo, and the land would not support a large population. If each brother were to marry a separate wife and each of those wives produced a set of children, the local resources could not feed the population.

The Toda practice *female infanticide,* the killing of female infants. Female infanticide, which reduces the number of childbearers, is used by a number of traditional societies to keep the population size in balance with the food supply. In many other traditional societies these female deaths are balanced by deaths of young males in warfare. However, the Toda are rarely at war because their land is considered undesirable by their neighbors. The result is a lopsided sex ratio among the Toda in which men outnumber women. The practice of polyandry provides a wife for brothers who otherwise would have no marriage partners.

There is a natural tendency for polyandry to occasionally develop into group marriage. The Toda of India began to practice group marriage on an increasing scale when the Indian government declared infanticide illegal. The number of females in the Toda population rose, changing the sex ratio. As a result, some young women ended up without a husband. This situation created opportunities for younger brothers to break the social norms, which gave preference to polyandry, and enter into monogamous marriages. The deviant monogamous couple typically left the community and lived in another village in the surrounding Hindu culture.

However, it was often not long before the wayward brother became homesick for his own culture with its unique customs, religion, and lifestyle. Usually the runaway brother returned home with his new wife to live again with his brothers. The acceptance of the returning brother created a group marriage. The set of brothers shared the elder brother's wife as well as the wife of the newly returned younger brother (Queen et al. 1985). Because of the exposure to people outside their community, disease has ravaged the Toda community; today only a small number of Toda remain alive. The Toda culture flourished in the early twentieth century, when their population numbered 500 or more members.

In their review of the ten polyandrous societies, Cassidy and Lee (1989) identified three characteristics shared by polyandrous societies: marginal economy, sexual freedom, and female infanticide. All of these elements are present in Toda society. However, some social scientists have been critical of the attempt to explain the reason for the existence of polyandry. These critics argue that social observers feel a need to explain polyandry because they assume that males have a need for sexual exclusivity in their partners and therefore consider polyandry unnatural. On the other hand, if polyandry were considered part of the normal diversity found in family forms, then there would be less pressure to explain how polyandrous marriage could possibly exist (Cassidy and Lee 1989).

The two sides of this debate over family change have different interpretations of recent *demographic trends.* A demographic trend is a change in population characteristics. The family decline perspective views the recent demographic trends discussed below as evidence that the family is crumbling; the family change perspective looks at the same trends more optimistically.

Divorce

The divorce rate has doubled over the last two decades, and now over half of all marriages end in divorce (U.S. Bureau of the Census 1994b), as shown in Figure 1.1 in Box 1.3. Both sides of the family debate, the family decline perspective and the family change perspective, agree that divorce often results in serious economic hardships for women and children. Both sides favor strict enforcement of the requirement that noncustodial parents pay child support (Cherlin 1993;

13

BOX 1.3 | A Closer Look

Hints on Reading Figure 1.1

Look for the overall trend, the recent trend, and the most dramatic change.

1. The overall trend: The overall trend in divorce is definitely upward: The divorce rate has more than doubled between 1960 and the present.

2. The recent trend: The divorce rate declined slightly during the 1980s and levelled off in recent years. This slight reversal of the upward trend could be an encouraging sign indicating that the divorce rate has stabilized. This finding is comforting to those who feared that a continuous rise in the divorce rate might mean that someday almost all marriages would end in divorce.

3. The most dramatic change: The 1970s was the decade during which the divorce rate took the greatest leap upward. This was also the decade in which women's participation in the labor force grew at a rapid pace. The rising divorce rate and rate of

Increase in the U.S. Divorce Rate

female participation in the labor force are related. The economic independence of women makes alternatives to marriage possible.

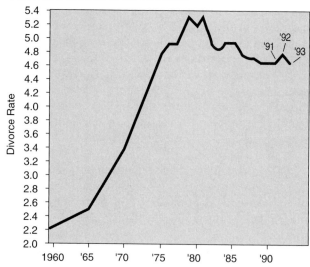

Figure 1.1
U.S. Divorce Rate 1960 to 1993.

Sources: U.S. Bureau of the Census 1993a, *Statistical Abstract of the United States, 1993,* Table 91, page 73, Washington, D.C.: U.S. Government Printing Office.

Centers for Disease Control and Prevention 1994, National Center for Health Statistics, *Monthly Vital Statistics Report,* Vol. 42, No. 13, Oct. 11, p. 4. Washington, D.C.: U.S. Government Printing Office.

Gill 1993). However, there is a great deal of debate over the impact of the high divorce rate on the American family in general.

The Family Decline Perspective

The family decline position argues that the United States has become a *high-divorce-rate society* and that in this kind of society, commitment to marriage declines. According to this argument, divorced couples are not the only people affected. In a high-divorce-rate society families in general, including intact families, are weakened (Gill 1993). When divorce is "ubiquitous, socially acceptable, and easily available," it becomes harder for couples "to commit themselves wholeheartedly to the marital union . . . " (Gill 1993:86). Over the last three decades, surveys that track attitudes toward marriage have found a decline in the expectation that marriage will be permanent (Glenn 1991). To some extent the expectation of divorce becomes a self-fulfilling prophecy in that lower commitment to marriage results in increased marital break-ups (Gill 1993).

Impact on Children. The family decline perspective points out that divorce is hard on children, who experience a decline in their standard of living. Three-fourths of divorced mothers are awarded child support (U.S. Bureau of the Census 1993a, Table 611); however, only half of these received full child support payments in 1990. Another one-fourth received partial payment, and the last fourth received no payments (Ahlburg and DeVita 1992). In addition, children often experience strain after their parents divorce, particularly when conflict between divorced parents is ongoing (Schvaneveldt and Young 1992). Moreover, divorce creates one-parent families, in which levels of discipline and guidance for adolescents are generally lower than in families with two parents (Amato 1987; Gill 1992; Glazer 1991; Popenoe 1992; Wilson 1993). Children in one-parent families tend to receive less help with their homework than children in two-parent families, primarily because help from the father is missing. When income is held constant, teenagers in one-parent families still have a greater level of high school noncompletion than children in two-parent families (Astone and McLanahan 1991).

The Family Change Perspective

The family change perspective argues that the negative impact of divorce on the family has been exaggerated.

Divorce as a Transition. Divorce often ends unacceptable relationships, including those that include domestic violence, irresponsible behavior, alcoholism, and drug abuse. In such a case, divorce creates a "new beginning." Divorce is increasingly considered to be a transition in the normal family life cycle rather than an end point. Most divorced persons remarry, and 40 percent of the marriages in recent years have been remarriages (Coleman and Ganong 1990). The large number of remarriages indicates that divorced persons may be unhappy with their former partners, but most are not disillusioned with the institution of marriage. Divorce and remarriage can be viewed as evidence that Americans value marriage highly and seek satisfying marital relationships (Ahlburg and DeVita 1992). As a result, stepfamilies are becoming an increasingly important part of American society.

The Process of Conflict. From the family change perspective it is marital conflict, both before and after divorce, not the divorce itself, that has a negative effect on children. Some studies have found that many of the behavior problems exhibited by children which had been attributed to divorce, actually predate the divorce and began while the family was intact and the parents were in conflict (Cherlin 1993; Cherlin et al. 1991). Whether or not divorce brings emotional distress to children is to a large extent determined by the parents' ability to put their conflicts aside and cooperate in childrearing. There is an increasing tendency for states to require parenting classes for divorced parents; these classes stress the need to exclude the child from any parental conflict.

One-Parent Families. The family change perspective sees positive signs as well as drawbacks in one-parent families. One-parent families grant children more autonomy than two-parent families. That is, they allow children to make more decisions and have more control over their lives. This autonomy can have negative consequences when a teenager decides to put activities with peers ahead of studying (Amato 1987; Dornbusch et al. 1985). However, one-parent families also require responsibility for household chores from children of all ages. Children in one-parent families perform more housework than children in two-parent families. It has been suggested that single parents make an unspoken trade-off in which personal autonomy is granted in return for help in running the household (Amato 1987; Weiss 1979). Moreover, children in one-parent families tend to be more androgynous than children in two-parent families, in that they learn aspects of both traditional male and traditional female roles (Amato 1987). Boys often learn to cook, and it is not unusual for teenage girls to work on Saturdays to earn spending money. These characteristics—household responsibility and androgyny—which one-parent families tend to foster in children can be viewed as positive adaptations to new circumstances.

Another demographic trend that traditionalists have interpreted as indicating family decline is the entry of married women, particularly mothers, into the labor force.

Review Questions

1. How does Beutler, who is a traditionalist, define the family? What does Beutler see as the primary characteristics of the family? What are the problems with Beutler's traditional view of the family?

2. How does the U.S. Bureau of the Census define a family? What are the problems with this definition?

3. How does John Scanzoni define the family? What are the problems with this definition?

4. In what way does the author of this text broaden the definition of the family used by the U.S. Bureau of the Census in defining the field of family study?

5. Why is it necessary to retain the U.S. Bureau of the Census definition of the family in looking at demographic data on family trends?

6. What is marriage? What are the four forms of marriage?

7. What does the family decline perspective say about the recent rise in the divorce rate?

8. What does the family change perspective say about the rise in the divorce rate?

Married Women and Employment

As Table 1.1 in Box 1.4 shows, married women's rate of participation in the labor force has doubled since 1960. The *labor force* is those who either are employed or are looking for work (U.S. Bureau of the Census 1994a, p. 392). Unlike in the 1950s, when most mothers were full-time homemakers, the typical family today is the two–earner family. In fact, there are currently twice as many two-earner families as there are traditional single-earner families with a full-time homemaker (Ahlburg and DeVita 1992). Mothers of young children are enter-

BOX 1.4   A Closer Look

Table 1.1 compares labor force participation by gender and marital status.

Hints on Reading the Table

1. The greatest increase: The group with the greatest increase in participation in the labor force since 1960

Gender and Participation in the Labor Force

was married women. Women's role as a traditional homemaker has changed substantially over the last three decades.

2. Opposite trends: As the participation of married women increased, the participation of married men in the labor force declined slightly. When a man has a working wife, he often has the option to change jobs and be "in between employment" for short periods while the wife brings in the family income. Many husbands of employed wives also have the opportunity to take an early retirement.

3. The lowest rate: The lowest rate of participation in the labor force occurs among divorced, widowed, or separated women. This rate is affected by the fact that many widows are elderly and not in the labor force.

Labor Force Participation of Men and Women

Percent in the Labor Force

Year	Married		Single		Divorced, Widowed, Separated	
	Men	Women	Men	Women	Men	Women
1960	89.2	31.9	69.8	58.6	63.1	41.6
1970	86.1	40.5	65.5	56.8	60.7	40.3
1975	83.0	44.3	68.7	59.8	63.4	40.1
1980	80.9	49.8	72.6	64.4	67.5	43.6
1985	78.7	53.8	73.8	66.6	68.7	45.1
1990	78.2	58.4	74.9	66.9	68.3	47.2
1993	77.3	59.4	74.2	66.4	67.4	47.1

Note: Labor force participation refers here to men and women age sixteen or over who are either employed or looking for work.

Source: U.S. Bureau of the Census 1994, *Statistical Abstract of the United States, 1993*, Table 631, page 399.

ing paid employment in increasing numbers. Over half (60 percent) of women with children under age six were in the labor force in 1993 (U.S. Bureau of the Census 1994a, Table 402). Two-thirds of these mothers were employed full time (Ahlburg and DeVita 1992). Half of married women return to the labor force within one year of giving birth (U.S. Bureau of the Census 1989a, p. 17). The traditional family with a full-time homemaker is becoming less common.

The Family Decline Perspective

From the point of view of traditionalists, the primary function of the family is to raise the next generation of children (Gill and Grandom 1993). Therefore, those who adopt the family decline perspective look at the employment of young mothers with alarm. They are concerned that the family may transfer even more of the function of nurturing young children to day-care centers (Wilson 1993).

In particular, there is some concern that infants who spend long hours (more than twenty hours per week) in institutionalized day care during the first year of life are at risk for forming insecure attachments to their parents (Belsky 1988; 1990). Although traditionalists would like to see children cared for by a parent in the home, some point out that the person responsible for child care could be either husband or wife (Gill 1993).

Conflict between Work and Family. Traditionalists argue that two-earner families experience substantial conflict between work and family, and that this conflict has put strain on marriage and family life. During the 1970s and 1980s, when married women substantially increased their participation in the labor force, the level of happiness reported by married women to social researchers declined (Glenn and Weaver 1988). Using the General Social Science Survey, which is based on a nationally representative sample of Americans, Lee and his colleagues (1991) found that young married women in the 1980s reported lower levels of happiness than young married women in the 1970s. The greatest decline in happiness appears to have occurred among employed mothers (Greeley 1989). Women often expect equality in marriage and feel disillusioned when they must juggle household chores, child care, and employment (Lee et al. 1991).

The Family Change Perspective

Andrew Cherlin (1993) says that it sounds like traditionalists would like mothers to quit their jobs and return to the home. Yet he questions whether or not it is fair to ask women to give up paid employment. One of the strongest cases in favor of diverse family structures is made by feminists who see benefits in the two-earner family. Feminists argue that traditional breadwinner–homemaker marriages make women dependent on the economic support of a man (Allen and Baber 1992). Economic dependence reduces the wife's influence in marriage and brings her economic hardship in the case of divorce (Ferree 1990; Thompson 1992). Therefore, the two-earner family is seen as an important change that has the potential to make marriage more equitable.

Faludi (1991) argues that academics and media have created a "backlash" against feminism by focusing attention on the conflict women often experience when combining employment and family. The implied message of the "backlash" is that the quest for equality has caused women trouble and that women would be happier if they returned to the home. However, according to Faludi, a solution could be found in egalitarian marriages. The work–family conflict experienced by employed wives could be reduced by greater sharing of child care and household chores by marriage partners. In addition, businesses could be more accommodating to working parents by allowing flexible schedules, job sharing, and extended leaves of absence for both husbands and wives.

Family Stability. There is already some evidence that husbands recognize the importance of the wife's income. The leveling off the divorce rate in the 1980s may signal a new attitude toward both marriage and the employment of married women. Now that many married men have come to depend on the income of their wives, female employment may be discouraging divorce. The higher the wife's income and the greater the percentage of family income she provides, the lower her chance of divorce (Greenstein 1990). As attitudes begin to change, female employment may be encouraging marital stability.

Next we turn to a trend that traditionalists have found particularly disturbing: cohabitation.

Cohabitation

Cohabitation refers to two people living together in a sexual relationship without marriage. Two decades ago cohabitation was rare. In 1970 only 11 percent of people who married for the first time had prior experience with cohabitation. Today, almost half of people who enter first marriages have previously cohabited (Bumpass et al. 1991). The U.S. Bureau of the Census estimates that today there are 5 million cohabiting couples in the United States: 3.5 million opposite-sex couples and 1.5 million same-sex couples. Of the cohabiting couples, 1.2 million have children under age fifteen living with them (U.S. Bureau of the Census 1994b, Table 8).

The conflict between work and family does put a strain on married life, but it can encourage married partners to develop greater sensitivity to each other and greater equality.

The Family Decline Perspective

Those who adopt the family decline perspective argue that the increase in cohabitation has meant a decline in committed relationships (Gill 1993; Wilson 1993). In support of this position, evidence shows that growth in the popularity of cohabitation has paralleled a decline in the marriage rate (Bumpass et al. 1991). Even researchers such as Larry Bumpass, who argue that cohabitation should be considered a family form, point out that cohabitors typically have less committed relationships than married couples. Bumpass (1991) and his colleagues examined data from the National Survey of Families and Households, a nationally representative sample, and found that a number of cohabitors view marriage as more restrictive of personal freedom than cohabitation. One-third of cohabiting men and one-sixth of cohabiting women reported that they thought they would be worse off in terms of "freedom to do what they want" if they were to marry their cohabiting partners.

The Family Change Perspective

Those who adopt the family change perspective argue that the rise of cohabitation should not be viewed as a sign that Americans are rejecting family life. Although cohabiting couples may be postponing marriage, they are nonetheless choosing to enter intimate relationships (Arcus 1992). Many heterosexual couples, especially those who have been divorced, cohabit as a transitional stage between dating and marriage. Often these relationships include children that women bring with them from a previous relationship. Cohabitation can have a positive effect on the economic well-being of divorced women and their children. In a national study, three-fourths of cohabiting men and women believed that they would be no better off economically if they were to marry their partners (Bumpass et al. 1991).

For others, cohabitation has become an alternative to marriage. This is particularly the case for low-income women with children, who often want to marry but do not have the opportunity because both they and their partners lack the job skills necessary to support a family (Wilson 1987). People who cohabit are seeking to form an intimate relationship with a partner and, in that sense, demonstrate a desire to form a family (Scanzoni et al. 1989). In Chapter 5 we explore heterosexual cohabitation, and in Chapter 7 we look at same-sex partnerships.

Explaining Demographic Trends

The United States is not the only country to have experienced a rise in the divorce rate, an increase in the employment of married women, and growing cohabitation. All industrialized nations with the exception of Japan have undergone a similar set of changes since the 1960s (Sorrentino 1990). Let us look at explanations for these dramatic changes in the family.

From Industrial to Postindustrial Society

The United States changed from an industrial society based on factory production, which had its heyday in the 1940s and 1950s, to a postindustrial society in the 1960s that is organized around information processing, advanced technology, and services jobs. A number of factors associated with this change altered American families.

Female Employment. The expansion of service jobs drew married women into the work force. Female employment and financial independence made divorce possible for a greater number of people.

Delayed Marriage. In modern society, well-paid jobs for both men and women require higher education. Extended education is incompatible with early marriage, so three decades ago the marriage age began to rise. This encouraged cohabitation and premarital sexual expression.

The Sexual Revolution. Attitude change associated with the sexual revolution of the 1960s and 1970s encouraged cohabitation and probably also contributed to the rising divorce rate by making sexual relationships outside of marriage more acceptable. In addition, the oral contraceptive and legalized abortion separated sexual pleasure from reproduction (D'Emilio and Freedman 1988).

Life Cycle Change. During the twentieth century the life cycle changed as life expectancy increased, fertility declined, and the number of years that women spent raising children also declined. This made it possible for more married

BOX 1.5   S o c i a l   I s s u e s

The Welfare Debate

Currently there is a heated public debate over future welfare policy. Approximately five million families in 1995 were receiving Aid to Families with Dependent Children, also known as welfare. This includes over two million white women, one and a half million African American women and 800,000 Hispanic women (McLeod 1995). Many Americans would like to eliminate AFDC (Aid to Families with Dependent Children) arguing that welfare benefits should not be an entitlement. Furthermore, they maintain that public policy affects human behavior, and welfare policy has weakened the institution of the family by encouraging childbearing outside of marriage. Today 30 percent of all births in the United States are to unmarried mothers (U.S. Department of Health and Human Services 1993a).

Giving birth out-of-wedlock increases the likelihood that a woman will go on welfare. Two-thirds of women who receive AFDC were unmarried when they had their first child. Many of these women were young when they first entered the welfare program; half of mothers receiving AFDC were age 20 or younger at their first birth (McLeod 1995). The connection among poverty, single parenthood, and public assistance is a strong one. Ninety-three percent of children in poverty who live in a single-mother family receive some form of public assistance, either cash benefits in the form of AFDC or another benefit such as a public housing subsidy (U.S. Bureau of the Census 1993d).

Charles Murray (1993) argues that ending the welfare program would reduce the incidence of never-married motherhood. He maintains that nonmarital childbearing can only be discouraged when it carries a strong social stigma. Ending AFDC would mean that young women who become pregnant would set an example of hardship for their peers to observe. Murray maintains that if the AFDC program no longer existed, parents would take extra steps to oversee the behavior of their teenagers and discourage teen pregnancy. Murray envisions the establishment of orphanages and additional group homes to care for children who are not able to be supported financially by a parent or grandparent.

On the other side of the debate, supporters of the Aid to Families with Dependent Children program point out that two-thirds of the 15 million people receiving AFDC are children. These children, who are impoverished while receiving public assistance, would be even more destitute if funds for AFDC were cut off (Whitman 1995). Ending welfare would amount to punishing children for the actions of their parents. Defenders of the AFDC program maintain that welfare does not cause poverty. The vast majority of mothers receiving AFDC were poor before they became pregnant (Wilson 1987). Some social scientists argue that because over half of AFDC recipients are nonwhite, the outcry against welfare has racial overtones (Quadagno 1994).

Whether AFDC is increased, maintained, or eliminated, the decision about this program is a controversial one—one that is of great concern to both the taxpayers who finance this public assistance and the people who receive it.

Finally, a number of social scientists would like to see welfare benefits increased. They argue that the low monthly income provided by AFDC discriminates against divorced and never-married single mothers. Widowed mothers whose income benefits are provided through the social security program receive a much higher monthly payment that places them and their children above the poverty line (Gordon 1994). Besides, orphanages or group homes, which have been advocated by some reformers, are an impersonal and expensive way to raise children.

---

women to seek paid employment and probably also contributed to the rise in the divorce rate. It is a challenge to choose a mate with whom to share a half century of married life (Skolnick 1991).

Changes in Technology: Changes in technology made divorce and the employment of married women easier. Washing machines, fast food restaurants, microwave ovens, and prepared frozen entrees freed women to enter the labor force (Nye 1988). Antibiotics and vaccinations reduced the time women spent caring for children with childhood diseases (Nye 1988).

All of the factors discussed above contributed to the growing employment of married women, the rising divorce rate and willingness to enter a period of independent living following divorce, and the rise in cohabitation. Was the era before these changes took place a "golden age" for families?

Was There a Golden Age?

Traditionalists observe these social changes and look nostalgically back at the family of the 1950s in which the mother kept house and looked after the needs of the children and husband. However, social observers in every era look at family change, lament the discomfort it causes, and long for an earlier golden age when family life seemed more appealing (Skolnick 1991). In reality, all periods of history challenge family members with problems and troubles. In the so called "golden age" of the 1950s, many wives felt frustrated by their inability to develop their talents in activities outside the home. It would probably be a mistake to judge the health of a family by the presence or absence of family tensions. Rather, the hallmark of a strong family is its ability to cope with difficult situations.

As we observe family change in this book, we will also examine the dynamics of interpersonal relationships. It is through strong family relationships that we are best able to cope with a changing society. In Chapter 13 we examine communication and conflict resolution, which are important in building intimate partnerships. In Chapter 4 we look at love relationships, and in Chapter 7 we delve into the interpersonal dynamics of marriage and partnerships. In times of rapid social change, it is important to look at ways in which strong and satisfying relationships can be fostered.

Harbor Not Haven

The family has traditionally been viewed as a "haven" or retreat from a harsh world (Lasch 1977). However, it is probably expecting too much of families to assume that they can satisfy all of the personal needs of their members. Schvaneveldt and Young (1992) suggest that it is more useful to view the family as a "harbor" rather than a "haven." A safe harbor provides its members with rest and security, but they can also set sail into the outside world and experience themselves as independent people. Marriage is coming to be seen as an institution that combines intimacy with autonomy, or self-direction. This image of the family is particularly useful for two-earner marriages and for stepfamilies in which children must relate to a complex array of family members in several nuclear families. Social change associated with the shift from an industrial to a postindustrial society often appears chaotic. Yet family change may represent a normal adjustment to new economic realities. Also, family change may, in part, reflect the attempts of family members to find a balance between autonomy on one hand and commitment and self-sacrifice on the other. In these changing times, it is not surprising that we have a growing diversity of family forms.

Structural Diversity among Families

Families in the United States are becoming increasingly diverse in their structure. One-parent families, stepfamilies, two-earner families, and families with extended kin are becoming increasingly important. These family forms have increased in number in response to the recent social change discussed earlier.

One-Parent Families

Thirty percent of all families with children are one-parent families (U.S. Bureau of the Census 1994b, page XI). Moreover, one-parent families are often a transitional state between first and second marriages, so that the number of people who have lived in one-parent families is far greater than the number who currently reside in one. It is estimated that over one-half of all children born in the early 1980s will live in a one-parent family before they reach age eighteen (Astone and McLanahan 1991). One-parent families make up a significant portion of all families: one-fifth of white families, one-third of Hispanic families, and six-tenths of African American families. The loss of well-paid blue-collar (manual labor) jobs in the postindustrial era has hampered the ability of many men, particularly men of color, to support a family. The result has been a rising divorce rate and an increasing number of nonmarital pregnancies.

As Box 1.5 shows, between 1960 and 1993 the percent of children in one-parent families who were living with a never-married mother grew from 4 percent to 35 percent. In fact, the 5 million children living with never-married mothers in 1993

Families must change in response to new environments and new economic realities, but they may retain important rituals and traditions. Here, a Laotian family eats dinner in the traditional Laotian fashion in their New York City apartment.

BOX 1.6   A C l o s e r L o o k

The Impact of Non-marital Childbearing and Divorce

A *pie chart* takes a specific population and breaks it down into its component parts. A *population* is the total group of cases studied. The population described in the pie charts of Figure 1.2 is children living in one-parent families.

parent families tripled from 5 million in 1960 to 17 million in 1993. This increase has resulted from rises in both divorce and nonmarital births (U.S. Bureau of the Census 1992b, Table F; U.S. Bureau of the Census 1991b, Table 5).

Hints on Reading the Pie Charts

1. Pie chart with the most recent data: In 1993 most children in one-parent families had divorced or separated parents. However, one-third of children in one-parent families lived with a never-married parent.

2. Comparing the two pie charts: Between 1960 and 1993 children became increasingly likely to have a never-married parent. In 1960 only 4 percent of children in one-parent families lived with a never-married parent. By 1993 this proportion had grown to 35 percent. Likewise, children were more likely to live with a divorced parent in 1993 than in 1960. Meanwhile, when we look at one-parent families, the percentage of children living with a widowed parent declined between 1960 and 1993. Why did this happen? As the total number of children in one-parent families grew, children with a widowed parent became a shrinking component of this group.

3. The totals: The total number of children in one-

Figure 1.2
Children Living in One-Parent Families in 1960 and 1993: What Was the Marital Status of the Parent?

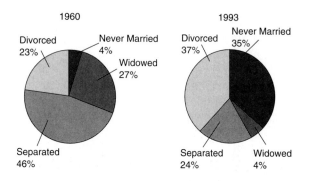

The total number of children in one-parent families in 1960 was 5 million and in 1993 was 17 million.

Sources: U.S. Bureau of the Census 1991b. Current Population Reports, P20-450, *Marital Status and Living Arrangements, March 1990,* Table F, page 6, Washington, D.C.: U.S. Government Printing Office.

U.S. Bureau of the Census 1994b. Current Population Reports, P20-478, *Marital Status and Living Arrangements: March 1993,* Table 5, page 31, Washington, D.C.: U.S. Government Printing Office.

equaled the total number of children living in all one-parent families in 1960. Among low-income persons, non-marital parenthood, sometimes combined with cohabitation, has become an important family form (O'Hare et al. 1991; Testa 1989).

Recently, the make-up of one-parent families has undergone a small but interesting change. Over the last two decades the number of one-parent families headed by fathers has tripled, so that father-headed families now make up 13 percent of all one-parent families (U.S. Bureau of the Census 1994b, Table 5). Fathers are becoming more likely to seek custody of their children, particularly when those children are older boys.

In Chapter 15 we look at divorce, and in Chapters 11 and 12 we cover one-parent families.

Stepfamilies

Stepfamilies are becoming an increasingly important family form. Half of all divorces involve a child under age eighteen (Ahlburg and DeVita 1992). Three-fourths of divorced persons remarry, often bringing children with them. It has been estimated that one-third of all children will live in a stepfamily at some time before they reach age eighteen (Coleman and Ganong 1990). Many of the traits that children exhibit in one-parent families are carried over into stepfamilies, such as taking responsibility for household chores. However, the autonomy that adolescents typically experience in one-parent families tends to disappear in stepfamilies. Children in stepfamilies are generally more closely supervised than those in one-parent families. The high school completion rate of children in stepfamilies is higher than that of children in one-parent families (Amato 1987; Astone and McLanahan 1991).

Although stepfamilies experience a good deal of stress as family members adjust to new roles in the family, most couples who remarry report that they are satisfied with their marriages (Amato 1987). Moreover, some aspects of stepfamily life that were previously considered to be social problems, such as low cohesion (which refers to loose emotional connections between stepparents and stepchildren), are now considered to be a creative adaptation to the demands of relating to two families (Pill 1990). See the section on stepfamilies in Chapter 16.

Two-Earner Families

The typical married couple today forms a two-earner family. In addition, cohabitors are most often found in a two-earner partnership. The working mother has become the norm even in families with young children. Because the purchasing power of wages earned by men declined after 1973, only with the entry of wives into the labor force have families been able to maintain their standard of living (Ahlburg and DeVita 1992). Even families from traditional cultures, in which the wife was expected to remain at home to care for the family, tend to undergo change when they immigrate to the United States. Mexican-American wives and Southeast-Asian wives often find it necessary to seek employment in order to help support the family (Rodriguez 1988; Kibria 1990). For more information on two-earner families, see Chapter 8, Marriage, Work, and Power.

Families That Include Extended Kin

In American society, life in many families is organized primarily around the *nuclear family*. A nuclear family is made up of parents and their children and spans only two generations. In contrast, traditional societies consider the *extended family* to be of primary importance. The extended family includes those kin who extend outward from the nuclear family, such as grandparents, aunts, and uncles. Extended kin relationships have always been central in immigrant families, which were coping with a new environment, but have diminished in importance among white middle-class families. However, today extended kin relationships are once more growing in importance (Sorrentino 1990). Families are increasingly likely to provide housing to extended kin who have fallen on financial hard times. One-third of African-American families and one-fourth of white families include other adults in the household (O'Hare et al. 1991). Most often this other adult is a relative.

By focusing on intergenerational bonds, we can see a good deal of strength in families (Stack 1974). Today an increasing number of mid-life couples are providing housing to unlaunched adult children (see Chapter 16). In addition, the number of *subfamilies* is on the rise. Subfamilies are families housed in the dwelling of another family. Two million mother–child subfamilies live in the household of the mother's parents (Wetzel 1990). In the past, when a grandparent lived with children, the home typically belonged to the younger generation. Today, with high rates of divorce and nonmarital childbearing, the grandparent is more likely to supply the home and invite the younger generation to move in (Ahlburg and DeVita 1992). African-American children are more likely than others to live with a grandparent: 12 percent of African-American children, 6 percent of Hispanic children, and 4 percent of white children share a household with a grandparent (O'Hare et al. 1991). The presence of another adult in the household has been shown to improve the well-being of children in one-parent families (Kellam et al. 1982).

Cultural Diversity among Families

The study of the family would not present an accurate picture of the United States without taking into account racial and ethnic diversity (Arcus 1992). By the year 2001, one-third of the American population will consist of people of color (Tiesel and Olson 1992). Currently, the largest minority group is African Americans, rep-

One-quarter of white American families and one third of African-American families include adult extended kin in their households.

resenting 31 million people, 12 percent of Americans. Hispanics make up the second largest and fastest growing minority group, with 24 million people (U.S. Bureau of the Census 1994a). Yet African-American and Hispanic families are over-represented among the poor. The changing world economy has placed many minority families at an economic disadvantage during the last three decades as opportunities for factory employment have diminished (Smith and Ingoldsby 1992).

It is not possible to study one version of "the family" in the United States as if it represented all families. Marital patterns and household composition vary with race and ethnicity, as does the meaning of "the family" (Smith and

Ingoldsby 1992). For example, multiple roles have traditionally been the norm in African-American marriages, with women being wives, mothers and employees (Taylor et al. 1990). In addition, the extended family is likely to be far more important to the functioning of African-American, Hispanic, and Asian families than to white families of European extraction. The economic marginality of many minority families means that they must rely on extended kin for security, for information on how to adjust to residence in a new country, and for such services as child care. Because family experiences of racial and ethnic groups vary, an examination of families in the United States would not be complete without taking into account ethnic and racial variation.

Biculturalism

Biculturalism is a distinctive feature that sets minority families apart from white families. Biculturalism refers to living in two distinct cultures. Ethnic and racial minority families live in two separate worlds, often separated by language, custom, and ethnic or racial identity (Arcus 1992; Smith and Ingoldsby 1992). Members of minority groups often have "double vision" (MacDermid et al. 1992). Minority families participate in dominant American society, but they also view mainstream society from the unique perspective of the minority culture. Thus it is important to view family life from the perspective of those who experience it. Racial and ethnic diversity among families appears throughout this book; in Chapter 9 we examine this diversity in more depth. In Chapter 10 we look at family variation by social class. In addition, World Perspective boxes in each chapter present examples of family diversity around the world.

In this book we look at modern families and the challenges they face as they undergo social change. Demographic trends, diversity among families, interpersonal relationships, gender issues, and the growing complexity of families and family relationships are examined in the chapters that follow.

Review Questions

1. What arguments does the family decline perspective present to show that the growing employment of married women, especially mothers, indicates that the family is in a state of decline?

2. What arguments does the family change perspective present to show that the negative aspects of female employment have been exaggerated and the positive aspects have been overlooked?

3. How does the family decline perspective interpret the growing popularity of cohabitation?

4. How does the family change perspective interpret the growing popularity of cohabitation?

5. What are the characteristics of the postindustrial family?

6. Was there a "golden age" of the family? In what sense can the family be seen as a harbor rather than a haven?

7. How common are one-parent families, stepfamilies, two-earner families, and families with extended kin? What are the strengths of these family forms?

8. Why is it important to study cultural diversity among families?

Summary

1. There is a debate over how the family should be defined. In a traditional definition of the family, marriage and childbearing or adoption are the central components of the family. The U.S. Bureau of the Census defines the family as two or more people related through blood, marriage, or adoption who share a common residence. For those social scientists, such as Scanizoni, who emphasize social change, long-term sexual relationships that involve emotional intimacy and a shared residence also qualify as a family.

2. There are four types of marriage: monogamy, polyandry, polygyny, and group marriage.

3. The family decline perspective views the family as being in a state of decline, as evidenced by the high divorce rate; the employment of married women, especially mothers; and the rise in cohabitation.

4. The family change perspective sees the family as becoming more diverse and complex, not weaker.

5. Since the 1960s the United States and other industrialized countries, with the exception of Japan, have entered a postindustrial era that encourages the employment of married women, a rise in divorce, and an increase in cohabitation. Other changes have helped to reshape families: the sexual revolution, delayed marriage, a decline in fertility and increase in life expectancy, and technological advances that made men and women less dependent on the domestic services and income of each other.

6. Some of the structural diversity among families includes one-parent families, stepfamilies, two-earner families, and families that include extended kin.

7. Every era looks back to an earlier "golden age" of the family. Perhaps today it is more useful to think of the family as a harbor than a haven.

8. It is important to study cultural diversity among families. Members of minority families experience biculturalism and often have a perspective on family life that is somewhat different than that of white families of European heritage.

Key Words

Family	Marriage
Ideal Marriage Form	Monogamy
Serial Monogamy	Polyandry
Demographic Trend	Polygyny
Labor Force	Group Marriage
Industrial Society	High-Divorce-Rate Society

Family Wage
Independent Living
Nuclear Family
Subfamilies
Extended Family

Cohabitation
Postindustiral Society
Global Economy
Sexual Revolution
Biculturalism

Resources

At the end of each chapter appears a set of resources. These resources are private and public organizations and some self-help groups whose work is related to one of the topics covered in the chapter. Some organizations collect data and provide information to the public. These organizations might be useful to those who have a personal interest in that information and who are writing term papers. Some organizations lobby Congress as advocates of particular family issues, and would be useful if you who want to increase your political involvement. Other organizations provide personal advice, support, or information to people who are experiencing a particular family problem but do not send out printed information. Still other organizations coordinate national networks of self-help groups that provide support in coping with a particular personal or family problem. The resources for Chapter 1 are as follows:

National Council on Family Relations
3989 Central Ave. N.E., Suite 550
Minneapolis, MN 55421
(612) 781-9331
Disseminates information and research on family life in a multidisciplinary fashion. Publishes: *Family Relations,* journal; *Journal of Marriage and the Family.*

American Family Society
5013 Russett Rd.
Rockville, MD 20853
(301) 460-4455
Encourages quality time with children and presents the Great American Family Recognition Award to families with traditional values. Publishes *Guidelines for Great American Family Recognition.*

Research Methods and Social Theories

Shana, Lamont, and Juanita sat around a table in the college cafeteria discussing the class project just assigned to them. Their task was to study sexual attitudes and behavior among college students. Shana suggested that they could interview ten of her friends. "My friends are pretty open about sex and wouldn't mind filling out a questionnaire," she volunteered. Lamont wondered aloud if ten people were enough to reflect the range of attitudes and behaviors among students. They decided to increase the number of people to be interviewed and turned their attention to the questions they would ask.

"I'd like to know if people are practicing safe sex," ventured Juanita. Lamont added "I wonder if students worry about contracting AIDS?" Shana broke in with, "Good ideas, but first we need to find out if they have had intercourse. If we ask students whether or not they practice safe sex, they might answer 'yes' even though they have never had intercourse." Juanita chimed in, "That could throw off our results because we would think that some people were more sexually experienced than they actually are." Lamont frowned and said, "You know, we can ask about condom use, but there is more to safe sex than using condoms. Condoms can break or leak, and people who have casual sex also risk contracting AIDS. We need to know whether or not students are having sex with people they hardly know." The other two agreed, and then Shana spoke up, saying, "I'd like to know what people think about virginity. Does anyone still think that it's important?" Juanita interrupted, "That's why we can't just interview your friends, Shana. Your friends are likely to think that virginity is old-fashioned, while my friends think that it is important." Lamont commented, "Shana, your friends might not be typical of the student body. We need to include people with a whole range of attitudes in our study." Shana suggested, "What if we stand outside the bookstore and ask every tenth person who walks by to fill out a questionnaire?" The other two nodded their agreement.

Many of us wonder about the thoughts and activities of other people, especially when the topic is something as interesting to us as sexuality. By using a social survey, Shana, Lamont, and Juanita were employing the most widely used method of gathering information in the social sciences. Social surveys allow us to look at the attitudes and behaviors that shape social life. Typical survey questions that Shana, Lamont, and Juanita could ask appear in Box 2.1 in Sexuality Survey A. This survey contains questions similar to those professional social scientists have found useful in measuring sexual attitudes and behavior.

In this chapter we explore the process of conducting social research and the snags that can arise. In the first part of the chapter we discuss research methods, including the scientific method, questions concerning accuracy in research, and methods of collecting data. However, research results are only as good as the methods used. Problems can occur in conducting a study. The questions in Sexuality Survey B in Box 2.1 have some serious problems that would be likely to lead to inaccurate study results. In this chapter we discuss some of the things that can go wrong in conducting social research, including the problems with the questions in

Sexuality Survey B. In the second part of this chapter we look at social theories that attempt to explain social behavior. It is not enough simply to conduct research; we must also attempt to put our findings in a theoretical perspective that sheds light on the causes of human behavior.

The Scientific Method

If Shana, Lamont, and Juanita were to follow Shana's initial suggestion and interview only Shana's friends, they might have a problem. If these student researchers were to assume that the rest of the people on campus felt the same way as Shana's friends, they would probably obtain a distorted view of sexual attitudes on campus. Because friends tend to have similar attitudes, interviewing only Shana's friends might not show the variety of sexual attitudes and behavior that exists on the college campus. In order for research to produce valid results, scientists, including social scientists, use the scientific method. The *scientific method* is a procedure for designing a study, systematically collecting data, and analyzing results. The aim of the scientific method is to maximize the accuracy and objectivity of the study. Using the scientific method involves the following steps:

1. **Formulate a research question.** The first step in conducting social research is to formulate a research question. For example, social researchers Kahn and London (1991) wanted to know whether or not experience with premarital sex affects the risk of divorce. They asked the question: Do women who are virgins at marriage have a higher or lower risk of divorce than nonvirgins?

2. **Specify independent and dependent variables.** A *variable* is something that can change and have more than one value. There are two primary types of variables, dependent and independent variables. The *dependent variable* is the variable the study hopes to explain. In the Kahn and London study, the dependent variable is the "risk of divorce." The *independent variable* is the explanatory variable. That is, an independent variable is a factor that influences the dependent variable and explains a change in the dependent variable. In the Kahn and London study, the independent variable was "premarital sexual experience," or, to be more specific, virginity status at marriage. This study of virginity and divorce also has a *constant*, which is a factor that does not change in the study. Gender was a constant in the Kahn and London study because only women were interviewed.

3. **Develop a hypothesis.** A *hypothesis* is a prediction about how two or more variables are related. In their study of virginity and divorce, the researchers hypothesized that women who were virgins at marriage would have a lower risk of divorce than women who were nonvirgins. The researchers chose this hypothesis, reasoning that people who are dating may mistake physical intimacy for compatibility. Therefore, people who are sexually active prior to marriage may make worse choices in marital partners than those who are not sexually active. In addition, because nonvirgins have had sexual experiences with people other than the spouse, they may have high expectations for personal fulfillment in marriage and therefore be vulnerable to disappointment.

BOX 2.1   A C l o s e r   L o o k

Sexuality Surveys

Sexuality Survey A: Typical Survey Questions

These are the kinds of questions researchers often ask in sexuality surveys.

1. Which of the following represents the most intimate sexual experience you have had?
   a. breast fondling
   b. genital fondling
   c. vaginal intercourse
   d. none of the above

2. How often, if ever, during the last year have you felt upset or angry because your partner withheld sex?
   a. frequently
   b. occasionally
   c. seldom
   d. never

3. If you had sexual intercourse during the last three months, about how often did you use condoms?
   a. all of the time
   b. about three-fourths of the time
   c. half of the time
   d. about one-fourth of the time

   e. never
   f. I have not had sexual intercourse during the last three months.

4. Among the people with whom you had sexual intercourse during the last year, how familiar were you with the person who was *least close* to you?
   a. just met
   b. casual acquaintance
   c. friend
   d. really liked
   e. in love with the person
   f. engaged
   g. I have not had sexual intercourse during the last year.

5. Have you ever had sexual intercourse when you did not want to for any of the following reasons? (You may choose more than one if appropriate).
   a. because you were overwhelmed by your partner's arguments or pleading
   b. because the partner was in a position of authority over you, such as a boss, camp counselor, or supervisor
   c. because you felt sorry for the partner

The researchers could have used an alternative and opposite hypothesis. They could have hypothesized that premarital intercourse would decrease the risk of divorce. This hypothesis would be based on the assumption that physical intimacy could provide a way to test compatibility and weed out unsatisfying relationships. After considering the two possible hypotheses, the researchers chose the first one.

4. **Operationalize the variables.** To *operationalize a variable* is to find a concrete procedure for measuring it. To measure virginity status at marriage, respondents were asked about the date at which they first experienced sexual intercourse. Then they were asked the date of their marriage. If a woman first had sexual intercourse during the month of her marriage or after that time, she was considered to be a virgin at marriage. Notice that the researchers avoided asking directly whether or not a woman was a virgin at marriage. Such a question might lead to dishonest answers due to embarrassment because it might imply that the researchers are making a moral judgment about premarital sex.

5. **Select a population to study.** The *population* is the entire category of people

d. because you felt obligated to the partner

e. because your partner threatened you or used some physical force (such as holding you down)

f. other reason, please specify: _____

g. I have never had sexual intercourse.

h. I have never had sexual intercourse when I did not want to.

6. How important do you think it is for a woman to be a virgin at marriage?
   a. very important
   b. somewhat important
   c. not very important

7. How important do you think it is for a man to be a virgin at marriage?
   a. very important
   b. somewhat important
   c. not very important

Sexuality Survey B: Problem Survey Questions

The following survey questions have some problems. What do you think the problems might be? What problems could result from using these questions in a survey? These questions are answered in this chapter.

1. Do you agree or disagree that abortion should be legal only during the first trimester of pregnancy?
   a. strongly agree
   b. mildly agree
   c. mildly disagree
   d. strongly disagree

2. Do you think that the killing of a fetus by abortion should be legal or illegal?
   a. illegal
   b. legal

3. Do you think that the government should be able to take away a woman's right to abortion?
   a. Government should not be able to take away abortion rights.
   b. Government should be able to take away abortion rights.

4. How important do you think it is to use condoms?
   a. very important
   b. somewhat important
   c. not very important

(Adapted from Buss 1989)
(Adapted from Baldwin and Baldwin 1988.)
(Adapted from Koss et al. 1987.)

being studied. In our example, the population was women in the United States who were married between 1965 and 1985.

6. **Select a sample.** It is generally impossible to interview or observe the entire population because of the expense and time involved. Therefore, a sample is selected. A *sample* is a limited number of cases selected from the population. Kahn and London (1991) used data from the 1988 National Survey of Family Growth, a nationally representative sample. A *representative sample* is one in which the characteristics of the population are accurately reflected in the sample. For example, in a representative sample we would expect that the age distribution, the rural–urban mix, and income distribution of the sample would match that of the population from which the sample was drawn.

Random sampling provides the best chance of ending up with a representative sample. A *random sample* gives each respondent in the population an equal chance of being selected in the sample. Random sampling was used in the National Survey of Family Growth, which produced the data used in Kahn and London's study of virginity status and divorce.

BOX 2.2   S o c i a l   I s s u e s

How Useful Are Convenience Samples?

There has been debate over the usefulness of convenience samples. Because it is not always possible to use a random sample, researchers sometimes use convenience samples. A convenience sample consists those people who are readily available either because they volunteer, because they have been referred to the researcher (often by other people in the sample), or because the researcher works with this group of people (such as clients of therapists). Convenience samples are used when financial resources for a study are limited or when the group to be studied, such as those with a sexual dysfunction, are difficult to locate. In addition, students who are learning the process of constructing and administering surveys and analyzing results often use convenience samples because of time limitations. Because we have no way of knowing whether or not a convenience sample is representative of the population being studied, convenience samples are not useful for describing population characteristics. That is, we would not use a convenience sample to describe the percentage of virgins in the college population. However, as long as the limitations of the sample are noted, a convenience sample can be used to investigate the relationship between two variables, for example, the relationship between participation in religious activities and sexual behavior.

The limitations of convenience samples can be seen in the studies of sexual dysfunction, in particular in studies of hypoactive sexual desire, or diminished sexual desire. This is one of the fastest growing forms of sexual dysfunction (Goleman 1990; Spector and Carey 1990). Much of our knowledge of hypoactive sexual desire comes from samples of patients seen by marriage counselors and other therapists. In these studies, sexual dysfunction appeared to be related to problems in the couple's relationship or in the individual's family history (Richgels 1992). These patients often responded positively to treatment that focused on improving the marital relationship or on changing stringent self-demands for sexual performance (Ellis 1992).

Our overall view of sexual dysfunction began to broaden when different kinds of convenience samples were used. Samples of medical patients turned up a connection between diminished sexual desire and various physical conditions. For example, certain medications used to treat hypertension turned out to be related to reduced sexual desire (Weiss 1991). In another study, (Goleman 1990) diminished androgen in midlife men was related to diminished sexual desire.

Studies of desire disorders sometimes try to link emotions with sexual arousal. One such study (Meisier and Carey 1991) subjected participants to mood elevating and depressing situations. Then the subjects were shown erotic films. This study found that depression increased the length of time it took for the subject to become sexually aroused. Studies of sexual arousal such as this one, which provide us with important information about hypoactive sexual desire, often require intrusive assessment procedures. In this type of study subjects are hooked up to equipment that measures sexual arousal in the genitals. These studies draw their convenience samples from volunteers, and thus, the samples may not be representative of the larger population. A case in point is a study (Nirenberg et al. 1991) of males who were inpatients at an alcohol treatment program that used a convenience sample made up of volunteers. The researchers then compared those subjects who volunteered for the study to the other patients who declined to participate. The volunteers turned out to be more interested in sex, reported less satisfaction with their sexual experiences, and had been more frequently diagnosed with cocaine and cannabis (marijuana) dependence than those in the inpatient program who did not volunteer for the sexual dysfunction study.

The results from studies using convenience samples can be generalized only to a population with characteristics similar to those of the people who were drawn into the sample. Nonetheless, studies conducted with convenience samples have added to our knowledge of sexual dysfunction. When the studies are viewed together, they reveal that a variety of both medical and social factors are related to hypoactive sexual desire. Each study that used a convenience sample was valuable in that it added to our overall understanding of sexual dysfunction.

7. **Response rate.** Usually not every one who is drawn into a sample agrees to participate. Generally, the higher the *response rate*, the more faith a researcher can have that the sample accurately reflects the population studied. The *response rate* is the percentage of people in the sample who agree to participate in the study. Studies of sexual behavior present special problems in selecting a sample. Some people who are not sexually active may be so traditional that they refuse to participate because they feel that the questions are an invasion of their privacy. Others will refuse to participate because they are very sexually active and embarrassed to admit how active they are. The social scientist who is conducting the study tries to make sure that those who refuse to participate are doing so for a variety of reasons that balance each other out. The researcher hopes that the refusals do not represent one particular point of view that will then be underrepresented in the sample. One way to check on the representativeness of the sample is to find out whether or not those who refused to participate have the same social characteristics as those in the sample. If low-income participants have dropped out of the sample, then the researcher must be careful to generalize the study results only to more affluent people. A discussion of types of samples appears in the next section.

8. **Collect data.** Data can be collected through a variety of methods, including surveys, experiments, demography, and unstructured observation, all of which are discussed in this chapter. The Kahn and London study used a survey.

9. **Analyze results.** After data are collected, the results need to be analyzed and explained to the community of social scientists so that the study can be discussed and criticized. Kahn and London found that women who were vir-

Social scientists tailor the designs of their research studies according to many variables, including the topic being researched and the types of individuals being studied. What special issues might arise in collecting data from this sample?

gins at marriage had a lower risk of divorce than nonvirgins. That is, there is an association between virginity status and risk of divorce. An *association* exists when two variables vary together. When one variable changes, the other one changes.

Causality. In order to say that a causal relationship exists between two variables, three conditions must exist (Sullivan, Thomas J. 1992). First, the two variables must be related so that a change in the independent variable brings about change in the dependent variable. Second, there must be a temporal order in which change in the independent variables precedes change in the dependent variable. Third, the relationship between the independent and dependent variables must not disappear when a third variable is introduced. Kahn and London tested the causal relationship between virginity status and risk of divorce by introducing a third variable described below.

Introducing a Control Variable. Kahn and London introduced a control variable, traditional values, in order to see what effect this variable had on the relationship between virginity status and risk of divorce. In other words, they controlled for traditional values. A *control variable* is a third variable which is introduced in order to see whether or not it explains the relationship between the first two variables. Kahn and London found that traditional values encourage virginity. Virgins were more likely than nonvirgins to come from intact families, to have gone to church regularly as teenagers, and to have grown up in a household with strict rules, all of which tend to produce traditional values. The same background factors were related to a low risk of divorce. The researchers reasoned that it was traditional values, rather than virginity, that led to the low divorce rate. That is, traditional values caused both the tendency to be a virgin at marriage and the tendency to avoid divorce (see Figure 2.1). Therefore, virginity status and divorce had a *spurious relationship*. A spurious relationship exists when two variables are related but one did not cause the other; a third variable caused the relationship to exist. A woman with nontraditional values who had no opportunities for sexual activity and married as a virgin would not reduce her risk of divorce by being a virgin at marriage. It is a system of tradi-

Figure 2.1
Casual Relationship; Spurious Relationship

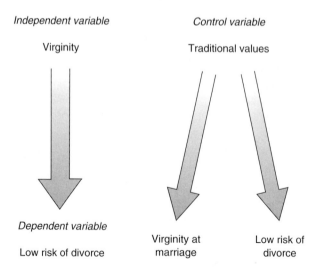

tional beliefs, rather than virginity, that leads to the low risk of divorce.

39
Chapter 2
Research Methods
and Social Theories

Another factor researchers need to be concerned about is maximizing the accuracy of their research, the topic of the next section.

Aiming for Accuracy

In order produce accurate results in research, we need to be concerned about validity and reliability.

Validity

Validity refers to the accuracy of measurement. Research has validity to the extent that it measures what it set out to measure (Sullivan, Thomas J. 1992). For example, a group of students who constructed a social survey discovered problems with validity when they used the following survey question: "Do you agree or disagree that abortion should be legal only during the first three months of pregnancy?" This question appears in Box 2.1 in Sexuality Survey B, "Problem Questions." While conducting interviews, the students discovered that almost all of their respondents, both those who were pro-life and those who were pro-choice, tended to disagree with the statement. Pro-life advocates disagreed because they did not think that abortion should be legal during any portion of pregnancy. In addition, many pro-choice advocates disagreed with the statement because they did not want to place time restrictions on the availability of abortion. As a measure of pro-choice and pro-life sentiment, the question lacked validity. It was not able to measure what it set out to measure.

Social scientists also need to be concerned about reliability.

Reliability

Reliability refers to the ability of a measuring device to produce consistent results in more than one measurement on the same person. Error that results from problems in the measuring device is referred to as "noise." Noise involves random error and has been likened to the error in a bathroom scale that has been calibrated accurately (Katzer et al. 1991). Even with accurate calibration, each time a person steps on the scale it is likely to give a slightly different reading, even though the readings are all taken within a few minutes of each other and may involve only a narrow range of error, such as one-sixteenth of a pound. If approximately half of the readings are above the actual weight and half are below, then the error is random and is known as noise.

Noise, or low reliability, is created when survey questions are vague and open to different interpretations by respondents. For example, the following question, which appeared in Box 2.1 in Sexuality Survey B, "Problem Questions," has some problems with reliability:

How important do you think it is to use condoms?

   a. very important

   b. somewhat important

   c. not very important

In answering this question on one occasion, respondents may think of people in general and answer in terms of what they think others should do. On another occasion this question could be interpreted more personally as asking how important respondents consider condom use to be in their own lives. On a third occasion, respondents may interpret the question as asking whether or not they currently use condoms. Two less vague and therefore more reliable questions could ask:

Attitude Question: "How important do you think it is for you, personally, to use condoms?

Behavior Question: "On the most recent occasion when you had sexual intercourse, did you use a condom?

Another important concern of the researcher is the method of collecting data, which is discussed below.

Methods of Collecting Data

There are a number of methods of collecting data for social research. Three of the major methods are discussed here: surveys, experiments, and demography. (A fourth method, unstructured observation, is presented in the World Perspectives Box 2.3.) Each of these methods has advantages and disadvantages, and no one method is better than the rest in all circumstances.

Surveys

A *survey* is a set of standardized questions asked of a sample of people. The people interviewed are known as *respondents*. The emphasis in survey research is on making the questions uniform so that answers can be compared. There are two main tools in survey research: questionnaires and interviews. A *questionnaire* is written set of questions that the respondents answer by writing down or marking off their answers. In contrast, in an *interview* the researcher asks the questions and records the respondent's answers. Questionnaires have the advantage of privacy and use a standardized set of questions. Interviews emphasize the development of rapport and trust between the interviewer and respondent. As the interview proceeds, the interviewer can ask follow-up questions to gain clarification and elicit more complete information. Interviewers are usually instructed to ask neutral follow up-questions, such as, "Tell me more about that."

Constructing Survey Questions. The wording of a survey question can have an important influence on how respondents answer the question. For example, respondents have been far more willing to say that they approve of the government funding programs that "help poor people" than they are to approve of the government funding "welfare programs" (Sullivan, Thomas J. 1992).

Bias. In constructing survey questions, it is important to avoid *bias*. Bias refers to systematic error, that is, an error that is consistently in the same direction. For example, in studying attitudes about abortion, a researcher would want to avoid the following question, which appears in Box 2.1 in Sexuality Survey B, "Problem Questions": "Do you approve or disapprove of killing a fetus through abortion?" The word "killing" implies that the researcher disapproves of abortion. In answering this question, pro-choice respondents may be too uncomfort-

Unstructured Observation of World Cultures

Sociologists and others who study the family have been influenced by the field methods of anthropologists. In puzzling over how to study the diverse cultures of the world with integrity, anthropologists have relied heavily on a method called *unstructured observation.* While other social scientists focus primarily on people living in the United States, they have benefited greatly from this method, which evolved in international fieldwork. Carol Stack's (1974) research, described in this chapter under "Exchange Theory," utilized unstructured observation to learn about low-income African-American families.

Unstructured observation requires researchers to immerse themselves in the social situation being studied. The anthropologist becomes a *participant observer* who lives with or interacts with a group of people, observing their behavior in an intensive way. A participant observer becomes part of the group even though the group typically knows that the participant observer is conducting research. During a private moment, the participant observer writes down *field notes,* which are a record of the conversations and other behavior the researcher has witnessed.

Unstructured observation typically uses *unstructured interviews.* Unlike surveys, which use a standardized set of questions, in unstructured observation there is flexibility in the topics covered by the questions, in the wording of the questions, and in the selection of people to interview. The person interviewed, called an *informant,* explains the behavior and rituals of the group to the participant observer. In these interviews the researcher can make up questions on the spot and is not limited by a standardized questionnaire. A series of World Perspectives Boxes in this book rely strongly on anthropological research using the techniques of unstructured observation. In addition, the discussion of Vietnamese-American families in Chapter 9, Racial and Cultural Diversity among Families, draws largely on Nazli Kibria's (1990a,b) field work using this method.

The use of unstructured observation has become hotly debated among feminists. Some feminist researchers feel strongly that the issues they study cannot be quantified and require the openness and sensitivity of a qualitative method, such as unstructured observation. An example of a quantitative method is a questionnaire survey in which the researcher counts the number of people who answer a question in a certain way. In contrast, anthropologists and sociologists using a qualitative method describe the behavior and some of the conversations they observe. Some feminists have complained that the quantitative methods used in some studies of domestic violence, which count the number of wives and husbands who hit their spouses, do not accurately portray the battered woman's situation in the family. For a more complete discussion of this issue, see Chapter 14, Family Abuse and Violence. Other feminists who espouse quantitative research argue that no method is feminist and the need to quantify our experiences is a fundamental tenet of social science research (Thompson 1992).

---

able to reveal their attitudes. Likewise, the question, "Do you feel that the government should be able to take away a woman's right to abortion?" would be slanted in the pro-choice direction. A neutral question would simply ask if the respondent approved or disapproved of abortion. It is important to ask neutral, or unbiased, questions so that the survey results reflect the attitudes of the respondents rather than the attitudes of the researcher.

Advantages and Disadvantages. Surveys have both advantages and disadvantages. Because survey questions can be standardized and self-administered, a large number of people can be studied. Surveys provide various participants' responses which are easy to compare because no new questions are added during the course of the interview. Follow-up questions in surveys are usually limited to neutral probes for additional information. On the other hand, survey researchers have the disadvantage of not being able to follow an interesting lead by spontaneously inventing a new set of questions on the spot. This disadvantage is overcome in unstructured observation, which is discussed in World Perspectives Box 2.3.

Experiments

Experiments involve manipulating one variable while attempting to control, or hold constant, as many other variables as possible. The researcher typically uses two groups, an *experimental group* and a *control group,* which are matched in social characteristics, such as age and income. Ideally, the two groups should differ only in the experimental variable. Nelson and Levant (1991) conducted an experiment in order to discover whether or not training in communication skills would improve relationships between stepparents and their stepchildren. The experimental group consisted of fourteen families who received the experimental treatment, which consisted of training in communication skills. Parents in the experimental group were encouraged to make a conscious effort to listen to children and to express empathy with children's feelings. These parents were also taught to express their feelings and to negotiate conflict. The control group of twenty stepfamilies received no training in communication skills. Stepparents in the experimental group significantly improved their communication skills in the area of listening to children and expressing their own feelings. They also reduced their level of physical punishment and yelling. However, in addition to these desirable changes, the experimental parents continued to use undesirable communication patterns that they had used prior to the study, such as ignoring children, threatening, and preaching.

In follow-up interviews, the stepparents in the experimental group revealed that they felt resistant to the new focus on listening and responding to the child's feelings because they felt that they had given as much as possible to the stepparent–stepchild relationship. They now wanted to express their anger, gain some control, and bring order to the household. As a result, stepchildren did not report any perceived improvement in the relationships with stepparents. The researchers concluded that intervention involving communication skills training is needed early in stepparent–stepchild relationships, when signs of distress first appear. Later intervention, such as that in this study, which occurred after the stepparents had accumulated substantial anger over stepparenting problems, did not appear to be very effective. In late intervention, parents retain unfavorable communication patterns and children do not perceive an improvement in relationships with stepparents.

Advantages and Disadvantages. Experiments have the advantage of focusing on only one variable and observing the effect of that variable while other variables are controlled. However, the disadvantage is that the researcher can never be sure that all of the important variables have been controlled. In addition, experiments are somewhat artificial in that the researcher influences the behavior of those in the experimental group. Therefore, experiments are less natural than unstructured observation.

In the next section we look at demography, a far less personal and more statistical method of studying the family which allows generalizations to large groups of people.

Demography

Demography gathers statistics on major milestones in the lives of people, such as births, deaths, marriages, and divorces. Demographic data are often called "structural data" because they show us the overall organization of families and households by measuring such things as the number of children per family, family income, participation of women in the labor force, and the percentage of families headed by single mothers. Demographic data are collected by public agencies, such as the U.S. Bureau of the Census, the National Center for Health Statistics, and university demography centers. Demography has been important in tracking such trends as the growing number of mother-headed families and the increasing tendency for single mothers and their children to live in poverty.

Advantages and Disadvantages. The advantage of using data collected by government agencies is that these agencies continuously conduct surveys utilizing random sampling techniques that produce highly accurate, nationally representative data. These data allow us to generalize to large groups of people and to follow long-term trends, such as divorce trends.

The disadvantage of demographic data is that although the data tell us about behavior, such as female employment, demographic data do not reveal attitudes and motivations that cause behavior. Therefore, it is useful to use demography in combination with information from attitude surveys and other research methods in order to show why the demographic trends are taking place.

The methods of collecting data discussed above and in Box 2.3 represent some, but not all, of the research methods employed by social scientists. Some other meth-

Demographic data, gathered by large public institutions, may be very useful for tracking trends among large groups, such as single mothers, rural families, or college students. To understand thoroughly the personal experiences of those groups, however, a researcher would have to rely on additional data gathered through observation or interviews.

ods include the case study, which is an in-depth description of one person or one family, and the focus group, in which a group leader asks interview questions to a group of approximately ten people and generates group discussion to reveal cultural attitudes.

Having examined social research methods, we now turn to an exploration of social theory that helps guide the design of social research and aids in putting the findings of social research into a larger explanatory context.

Review Questions

1. What are the steps in using the scientific method in social research?

2. What are independent and dependent variables? What is a hypothesis? What hypothesis did Kahn and London test? What is the difference between a population and a sample? What is a representative sample and why is it important to use a representative sample?

3. In analyzing study results, what relationship did Kahn and London find between the independent and dependent variables? Why was the relationship between virginity status and risk of divorce a spurious relationship?

4. What is validity? What is reliability? What type of survey questions are likely to have a low level of reliability?

5. What are four major ways to collect data for a study? What are the advantages and disadvantages of each method? What is bias? What aspects of experiments were illustrated by the stepparent–stepchild communication experiment?

What Is a Social Theory?

When people casually discuss family life, they may be using the perspective of a social theory without realizing it. All descriptions of social life are "inherently theory-laden" (Lavee and Hollahite 1991:361). Whether families are viewed as inevitably fraught with conflict or as striving to maintain harmony depends on the theoretical perspective used. Likewise, whether we view people as making rational choices or as controlled by strong social forces also depends on the theoretical perspective used. However, unlike casual discussions in everyday life, *social theories* attempt to make their assumptions explicit. A social theory explains how societies operate by providing a set of *concepts* that label behavior. For example, structural-functional theory, which is discussed below, utilizes the concepts of "structure" and "function." A concept is an abstract term that describes certain aspects of reality. When concepts are combined in a social theory, they allow us to explain human behavior.

There are many social theories, and some of them will be introduced in the following chapters. Here we concentrate on four major social theories: structural-functional theory, conflict theory, exchange theory, and systems theory. All of these social theories are useful in some situations, and thus all are valuable tools in studying social life. Each theory also has limitations. Family situations that are easily explained by one theory may be difficult to explain using other theories. Therefore, it is important to know the strengths and weaknesses of a social theory when using it to explain social behavior.

Structural-Functional Theory

Structural-functional theory, developed by Emile Durkheim (1966, original 1897) and Bronislaw Malinowski (1922), views society as a set of structures with each structure performing a function important to the maintenance and stability of society. From this perspective, society is seen as being similar to a biological organism, which also has structures and functions. In a biological organism, the heart and lungs are structures that perform such functions as pumping blood and oxygenating blood. These functions contribute to the stability and survival of the living organism. Transferring this analogy to human societies, the *structures* of society are its social institutions and behavior patterns. The term *social institutions* refers to social organizations such as the family, churches, synagogues, schools, businesses and corporations, and government agencies. Each social institution performs *functions,* tasks contributing to the maintenance and continuation of society. When society is working properly, each structure performs important functions and the society tends to achieve an equilibrium or stability. However, sometimes a *dysfunction* occurs in which a social institution fails to fulfill its social functions (Merton 1968). For example, today's schools often fail to prepare young people, particularly those in the inner cities, for jobs. According to structural-functional theory, dysfunctions produce strain, which tends to lead to adjustments in society, such as educational reform.

For example, in family life, the old-order Amish family tends to perform most of the functions necessary for the survival of Amish culture.

Application: The Old-Order Amish Family

The old-order Amish family came to the American colonies from Switzerland, Germany, and Holland in the 1600s, settled in Lancaster County, Pennsylvania, prospered, and established additional communities in the midwestern United States (Redekop 1989). The Amish are farmers with a "horse and buggy" culture whose primary characteristic is resistance to social change (Hostetler 1989). The Amish have rejected industrialization, and with it they have rejected electricity, automobiles, modern indoor plumbing and heating, and appliances (such as radios, televisions, and microwave ovens). One of the few concessions the Amish have made to modernization is the use of modern medical services for serious illnesses and for eyeglasses.

The Amish community has a simple social organization in which the family and church, as the main *social institutions,* perform most of the *social functions* necessary for the community to survive. These functions are discussed below.

Economic Production. Most of what the Amish eat is home-grown. Tobacco, the basic cash crop of the Amish, provides money to purchase land so that newly married sons can begin farming. The Amish family provides a stable unit of economic production because the Amish do not approve of divorce, and

Observation has shown that the Amish live life as though industrialization had not occurred. They do not make use of modern technology, and they grow most of the food they need to live, bartering for the rest. And the family is still the center of Amish social life.

commitment to one's spouse is considered second only in importance to commitment to God (Schwieder and Schwieder 1975).

Sexual Reproduction. Couples do not use contraception and raise an average of eight children, who are valuable farm workers, (Schwieder and Schwieder 1975). Sexuality is regulated by the family, and children are almost always born within marriage. Young people are allowed to marry a mate of their choice as long as the partner is Amish and parental permission to marry is obtained. Young people are secretive about their courtships, and the young man sometimes visits the girl whom he is courting by sneaking into her home at night after the family is asleep (Kephart 1987).

Social Cohesion. Both the church and the family play an important role in supporting community beliefs and enforcing social norms, or social rules, thereby providing *social cohesion*. Social cohesion is the sense of unity among the members of a group. Amish churches are intertwined with the family; there are no church buildings, and church meetings are held in family homes on a rotating basis. A church district consists of the number of families that can fit into a farmhouse for a church meeting. The church district oversees the behavior of its members and imposes social control on errant members by voting *meidung,* or shunning (Kephart 1987). Once voted against a person, meidung is enforced by both the family and the community and the shunned person is ostracized. Other members of the community cannot talk with, eat with, or do business with that person. The spouse cannot have sexual relations with the shunned person. Shunning is often temporary and is revoked when the person repents and is accepted back into the community. Shunning provides a powerful means of social control. Children are allowed a good deal of leeway, but once they are baptized at age fifteen to eighteen, they can be shunned for violating the social norms (Schwieder and Schwieder 1975).

Socialization. The family is the primary source of *socialization* for children. Socialization refers to passing on the beliefs and knowledge of a community. The family provides occupational training in farming but shares the socialization function with Amish schools, which are private religious schools, typically housed in a one-room school house. Amish formal education ends after eighth grade. Lessons are presented in German, the native language of the Amish, and taught by an Amish teacher with an eighth-grade education.

Mutual Aid. The Amish strongly value mutual aid and offer help to kin and neighbors who need it. For example, when a barn burns down, the community comes together and raises a new barn over a weekend. The Amish also depend on the family for elder care. Amish families leave their farm to the youngest child, whether male or female, who then cares for the aging parents.

Recreation. Because modern entertainment such as televisions and radios are lacking, the Amish look to their families and churches for recreation. The church provides entertainment for young people in the form of the "Sunday Sing," or hymn singing, which is held on Sunday evening at the home of the family that hosted church services. After a young couple marry, they spend their honeymoon visiting the homes of friends and relatives rather than retreating from family and friends as is typical of the mainstream American honeymoon. Visiting kin is a major form of entertainment for adults and children alike.

Critique of Structural-Functionalism

Structural-functional theory has been criticized for emphasizing social integration and cohesion while downplaying conflict and power in society. There is an emphasis in structural-functionalism on seeing how social institutions meet social needs, rather than focusing on how social institutions allow one group to dominate and exercise power over another group. Structural-functionalist theory tends to focus on explaining the status quo, or things as they currently exist, and tends to view society as being in a state of equilibrium, or balance. Even the concept of dysfunction implies that strains in the society will eventually produce beneficial change. Thus, societies and families are viewed as moving in the direction of harmony. The structural-functionalist perspective de-emphasizes inequality and the exercise of social power in relationships between parents and children, husbands and wives, and between social classes. In the next section we explore conflict theory, which assumes that social relationships are less harmonious than structural-functional theory would portray them.

Conflict Theory

Conflict theory assumes that life rarely runs smoothly and conflict is a natural part of social relationships. Conflict is particularly likely to develop in close interpersonal relationships. According to conflict theory, marital disputes are a normal part of family life (Coser 1956). On a broader societal level conflict theory examines how one group exercises power over another group. Conflict theory emphasizes competition over scarce *resources.* The most important resources are economic resources, including income and wealth, such as the ownership of property and businesses. The ownership of economic resources provides a person with *power,* or the ability to influence other people (Engels 1973, original 1884; Marx 1967, original 1867). Because resources tend to be distributed unequally in society, the *dominant groups,* which have a greater share of the society's income and wealth, exercise power over less affluent *subordinate groups.* According to conflict theory the institutions of society, such as schools, courts, corporations, and families, play an important role in perpetuating *inequality* by providing economic advantages to the dominant group. For example, wealthy families are able to send their children to elite private colleges. The graduates of these colleges tend to be recruited into important government and corporate jobs that carry a good deal of power. Conflict theory also maintains that the economic system produces a *superstructure of ideology,* which is a set of values that supports and justifies the superior power position of the dominant group (Engels 1977 reprinting). For example, one such ideology blames the poor for their condition of poverty by suggesting that personal choices, such as early pregnancy or early marriage, are responsible for poverty rather than explaining poverty in terms of limited job opportunities.

Application: Social Class and the Definition of the Family

The middle and upper classes control a large percentage of the income and wealth in American society and thus hold a good deal of power or influence. As a result, the social definition of the "normal family" mirrors the middle-class and upper-class ideal of an intact two-parent family. Lower-class families, which are often mother-headed single-parent families, frequently with children born out of wedlock, are defined as deviant. From this perspective, the problems of the lower class come to be seen as growing out of a single-parent family structure and a welfare system that is out of control. Conflict theory argues that such an ideology is a smoke screen that conceals the economic conflict between upper-class and lower-class families. Factories have closed and moved overseas, diminishing the number of jobs available to the fathers of children on welfare (Wilson 1980, 1987). As corporations relocate to seek cheap labor, the benefits of moving factories overseas fall to the upper-middle-class and upper-class families who own stocks and bonds. Corporation executives who command high salaries also benefit when the corporation shows a profit after the move. However, lower-class families are disadvantaged by the flight of industrial production to third-world countries. Factory jobs have traditionally provided the first rung on the ladder for poorly educated men to climb out of poverty and earn enough money to support a family. As factories in the United States close and factory jobs dry up, an impoverished group of mother-headed families develops. According to conflict theory, the ideology that blames welfare mothers for the ills of American society but ignores the need for employment of lower-class men grows out of conflict between the upper and lower classes.

Critique of Conflict Theory

Conflict theory has been criticized for overemphasizing the economic aspects of social life and paying too little attention to social values and cultural attitudes as causes of social behavior. For example, the Amish family is guided by a strong set of social values, and these values are more than a superstructure of ideology that arises out of the economic system. It is true that Amish parents act in their own economic interest in retaining their farm and giving it to their youngest child, who in return will support the parents in their old age. However, conflict theory is not able to explain the latitude given to children in mate choice and the secrecy with which young people approach courtship. We have to look to cultural beliefs and attitudes to explain these practices. In addition, conflict theory has been criticized for placing too much emphasis on social conflict and the differing interests of people while overlooking the harmony in society. For example, the way the various parts of society fit together often makes some societies, such as the old-order Amish, look like the interlocking pieces of a puzzle. Furthermore, conflict theory views people as acting out of their own economic self-interest. Thus conflict theory diminishes the importance of other motivations, such as altruism, which probably plays a part in the development of poverty programs.

Unlike conflict theory, exchange theory does not consider economic motivation to be the primary explanation for human behavior.

Exchange Theory

One of the most frequently used theories in the study of the family is *exchange theory*. Exchange theory maintains that behavior is influenced by the cost and benefits of taking a particular action. In addition, the attractiveness of alternative choices influences the decisions people make (Ballard-Reisch and Weigel 1991). People tend to remain in relationships when they perceive that the benefits outweigh the costs and when the alternatives are not appealing. The benefits of a relationship are the *resources* a person receives. Unlike conflict theory, which concentrates primarily on examining economic resources, exchange theory considers *personal resources* also to be important. Personal resources include such things as companionship, sex, affection, and services such as cooking and child care. (Safilios-Rothschild 1970).

Personal relationships are based on a *system of exchange* (Blau 1964, 1974). In an exchange, resources, such as companionship or a cooked meal, are given as gifts and the giver hopes that the favor will be returned at some later date. For example, the wife gives affection to the husband in expectation that he will give her in the future something that she values, such as companionship and help with child care. The gift provides the giver with credit by obligating the partner to reciprocate in the future. However, the commodity to be returned and the date of the repayment are not specified. The receiver of the gift determines when and how to make a repayment. This system of exchange is built on trust, with each partner making the assumption that the gift will be reciprocated (Curtis 1986). When the resources a person provides cannot be readily gained from an alternative source, commitment to the exchange system increases (Safilios-Rothschild 1970; Surra 1990). For example, poor people, such as those discussed below, often depend on an exchange system because they have so few alternative ways to gain resources.

Application: Lower-Class African-American Families

Carol Stack (1974) in *All Our Kin* reported on her experiences as a participant observer living among low-income African-American single-mother families in a midwestern small town. She described an elaborate system of exchange in which mother-headed families "swapped" goods and services. When one family was in economic crisis, kin offered food and shelter. The women added close friends to the exchange network by making them into *fictive kin* and giving them an honorary title, such as "Aunt." By providing child care, sharing a meal, or even giving a piece of furniture, the giver obligated the recipient to offer aid sometime in the future. In fact, a simultaneous exchange of goods was rare because the debt would be paid off and no obligation would be created (p. 41). The exchange system operates as a kind of social insurance that provides a cushion against hard times in the future. In fact, Stack pointed out that low-income families could not afford to stand aside from the exchange system because they were likely to need help later on.

According to Stack's study, local values supported the exchange system. The community valued generosity and sacrifice, and residents sometimes bragged about help they provided to others. In addition, those residents who received goods or services but failed to reciprocate were judged harshly and were avoided by the people in the exchange network. In this economy no one had a chance to acquire surplus goods, so the limited supply of scarce items was redistributed through the exchange system in a continuous flow of goods and services. As Carol Stack put it, "What goes round comes round" (p. 32). The values of this lower-class African-American culture, which emphasizes cooperation and mutual aid, sharply contrasts with middle-class culture, which values individualism and competition. The cooperative exchange system among poor families represents a creative adaptation to poverty.

Critique of Exchange Theory

Exchange theory has been criticized for emphasizing rational decision-making processes in human behavior. Critics argue that people do not always have a mental balance sheet on which they keep track of exchanges they have made. Exchange theory de-emphasizes people's irrational motives, which operate at a low level of consciousness. The next theory we examine, systems theory, attempts to take into account this less conscious motivation for behavior.

Systems Theory

Systems theory views society as a social system made up of a set of interdependent parts. In a social system, a change in one part of the system has an impact on the the other parts of the system (Parsons 1964). Systems theorists rarely discuss causality, and when they do, causality is viewed as circular (Madanes 1984).

We can think of the family as one element in a system of social institutions or as its own social system.

For example, social institutions, such as the family, the economy, the political system, and religion, all influence each other. On a smaller scale the family also operates as a social system. In the family system, the social roles family members play constitute the components of the system. These roles act "like chips in a kaleidoscope" in that the social interactions among family members form patterns (Minuchin 1984:3). As family theorist Salvador Minuchin (1984:3) puts it, a family system becomes "more than the sum of its parts"; a family is more than a collection of family members. The social roles enacted by the family members fit together into a pattern that affects everyone in the family.

An important characteristic of a system is *homeostasis*, or the stability of the system. Homeostasis renders a system resistant to change. That is, when the behavior of one family member changes, disrupting the pattern of family interaction, the other family members often subtly encourage that member to resume his or her former role in the family (Bratter and Forrest 1985). Systems theorists examine how the interpersonal relationships among family members work to maintain the system over time (Madanes 1984).

Application: Families with an Alcoholic Parent

Alcoholism has an impact that extends beyond the chemically dependent family member. The other family members become caught up in the addiction process in their attempt to cope with the chaotic family life that alcoholism produces. The alcoholic is known as the "dependent" because he or she is dependent on a chemical substance. The spouse typically takes on the role of the "enabler" (sometimes called "co-dependent") who tries to help the alcoholic and thereby unwittingly engages in behavior that allows the alcoholic to continue drinking. The enabler attempts to save the alcoholic from experiencing the consequences of addictive behavior (Iber 1991). For example, if the alcoholic is drunk or hung over and does not show up at a family barbecue attended by extended kin, the enabler will make excuses for the alcoholic and might say that the alcoholic has the flu. Thus the alcoholism is kept secret and the alcoholic is protected from the anger of relatives.

Sharon Wegscheider (1981) identified four predictable roles that children in alcoholic families tend to play: hero, scapegoat, lost child, and mascot. These roles are not necessarily distinct; one child may exhibit behavior that incorporates the elements of several of these roles. The role of *hero* is often played by the eldest child, who functions as a surrogate parent to the other children and becomes involved in trying to prevent the alcoholic from drinking. The *scapegoat* receives the anger that would otherwise be directed toward the alcoholic if the alcoholism were to be discussed openly. The scapegoat often misbehaves and deflects family attention from the problems of alcoholism and marital tension. The *lost child* avoids making demands on the family and appears to be an independent loner. However, the lost child receives very little nurturing or attention in childhood and often has low self-esteem. The *mascot* is entertaining and provides comic relief, distracting the family's attention from its problems. The efforts of children enacting these roles are directed toward avoiding a family crisis and coping with a confusing family situation, rather than toward developing an individual and separate sense of self (Bepko 1985).

According to psychologist Virginia Satir and her colleague, healthy, or functional, family systems promote open communication as a basis for problem solving (Satir and Baldwin 1983). However, families with an alcoholic parent often keep the alcoholism a secret by developing an implicit rule that no one will discuss the parent's drinking problem. Thus some family members may not recognize or identify alcoholism as the source of the family's problems. One job of the family therapist is to find the messages the family is hiding and help create avenues for open discussion (Satir and Baldwin 1983). Alcoholic families also develop boundary problems. The boundaries between members of an alcoholic family often become blurred as one family member begins to feel overly responsible for other family members (Minuchin 1984).

As the alcoholic gives up drinking and enters recovery, the homeostasis, or stability, of the family system is disrupted and family members often resist change. When the alcoholic was drinking, the enabler took charge of family finances and child rearing. Thus, while the alcoholic was an underfunctioning member of the family, the enabler took an overfunctioning role (Bepko 1985; Black 1982). As the alcoholic recovers and begins to reassert control over these areas of family life, the enabler is likely to feel resentful over the loss of control and resist change. Moreover, while the alcoholic parent was drinking, one child typically became elevated to the role of friend and confidant to the nonalcoholic parent. Thus, the normal hierarchical structure in which parents exercise authority over children became disrupted (Minuchin 1984). As the alcoholic enters recovery, the marital subsystem becomes reestablished and the marriage provides increased companionship. In addition, the recovering alcoholic parent reasserts parental authority, often in a harsh manner (Bepko 1985). The child who previously enjoyed a special status and unique privileges as friend to the nonalcoholic parent is now demoted to the position of child once again. Thus the recovery of the alcoholic parent often generates hostility and even rebellion on the part of one or more children (Zuska and Pursch 1988). These reactions form a feedback loop through which family members resist change in the family system.

Critique of Systems Theory

Systems theory has given rise to the growing and useful practice of family therapy. However, family therapy has been criticized for applying systems theory in a "one size fits all" manner. That is, systems theory is applied to a variety of family and individual problems. There is a need to evaluate the efficacy of family therapy in different situations in order to determine which problems are best treated by family therapy. For example, systems theory may be more useful in addressing alcoholism than schizophrenia, and yet it is used to treat both disorders. The focus of systems theory is on interpersonal interaction, and less attention is given to intrapersonal factors, which take place within the individual. Thus, individual psychological conditions are sometimes overlooked and the genetic or biological basis for a disorder is often de-emphasized in family therapy (Searight and Merkel 1991).

Another criticism is that family therapy may prevent the individuation and successful separation of some individuals from the family. This is particularly the case for young adults who may have struggled to gain independence and then become once again enmeshed in family problems when the family enters family therapy. Thus systems theory has been criticized for placing the needs and goals of the system (such as the goal of sobriety for the alcoholic family member) above the needs of the individual. The spouse, as an individual, may desire separation or even divorce rather than remaining in the family system (Searight and Merkel 1991). Critics do not advocate doing away with systems theory or family therapy, but rather suggest limiting the scope of problems and families to which systems theory and family therapy are applied.

Review Questions

1. What is a social theory? What is meant by the statement that all descriptions of family life are inherently "theory-laden"?

2. What is structural-functional theory? What are the basic concepts of structural-functional theory? What is the critique of structural-functional theory?

3. How do the Amish family and Amish society illustrate structural-functional theory? What social functions does the Amish family fill?

4. What assumptions does conflict theory make about social behavior? What are the basic concepts in conflict theory? What is the critique of conflict theory?

5. How would conflict theory explain the view of poverty that says the poor are responsible for their condition?

6. What are the assumptions of exchange theory? What are the basic concepts in exchange theory? What is the critique of exchange theory? How does

Carol Stack's study of impoverished African-American families illustrate exchange theory?

7. What are the assumptions of family systems theory? What are the basic concepts in family systems theory? What is the critique of systems theory?

8. What roles do members of alcoholic families typically enact? How does the alcoholic family illustrate homeostasis?

Summary

1. Following the scientific method produces the best chance for objective, accurate research results.

2. Random sampling is the method most likely to produce a representative sample.

3. The dependent variable is the factor the researcher is trying to explain; the independent variable is the explanatory variable.

4. Validity refers to accuracy in measurement, and reliability refers to consistency of measurement.

5. Researchers using surveys attempt to minimize bias by constructing neutral survey questions.

6. In unstructured observation the researcher often acts as a participant observer, living with the group to be studied.

7. Experiments apply the experimental treatment to the experimental group but not to the control group.

8. Demography shows long-term trends in the milestones of family life, such as marriage and divorce.

9. Four major theories that explain social behavior and family life are structural-functionalism, conflict theory, exchange theory, and systems theory.

10. Structural-functionalism examines the functions filled by society's structures, or social institutions such as the family. In Amish society the family and church fill most of the social functions necessary to maintain the society.

11. Conflict theory views power relationships in society as based on the ownership and control of economic resources. An ideology develops to justify the position of the dominant group. For example, one current ideology blames the poor for their disadvantaged economic position.

12. Exchange theory views personal relationships as a system of exchange in which the partners provide valued resources to each other and thereby obligate each other to reciprocate in the future. In Carol Stack's study of low-income mother-headed families, an exchange system provided a buffer against economic crisis by obligating others to offer aid in hard times.

13. Family systems theory focuses on the way interpersonal relationships and family roles fit together so that change in any one family member affects the lives of other family members. Alcoholic families, like other social systems, resist change. The spouse often plays the role of the enabler, while children's roles include hero, scapegoat, lost child, and mascot.

Key Words

Scientific Method
Independent Variable
Population
Representative Sample
Association
Validity
Surveys
Unstructured Observation
Demographic Data
Structural-Functional Theory
Dysfunction
Dominant Group
Superstructure of Ideology
Personal Resources
Homeostasis

Dependent Variable
Hypothesis
Sample
Random Sample
Spurious Correlation
Reliability
Bias
Experiment
Social Theory
Social Function
Conflict Theory
Subordinate Group
Exchange Theory
Systems Theory

Resources

The following associations conduct research on families and family matters and make their findings available in various publications.

Family Research Council
601 Pennsylvania Ave. N.W., Ste 901
Washington, DC 20004
(202) 393-2100

Collects data on families, teen pregnancy, welfare, child development, and the elderly. Publishes a bimonthly minimagazine, *Family Policy,* and a bimonthly newsletter, *Family Research Today.*

Center for Demography and Ecology
University of Wisconsin, Madison
4412 Social Science Bldg.
1180 Observatory Dr.
Madison, WI 53706
(608) 262-2182

Publishes working papers on demographic trends.

Consumers Union of the United States
256 Washington St.
Mount Vernon, NY 10533
(914) 667-9400

Conducts consumer product testing and publishes *Consumer Reports* monthly as well as annual buying guides.

National Student Consumer Protection Council
College of Commerce and Finance
Villanova University
Villanova, PA 19085
(215) 645-4374

Conducts seminars on wise purchasing and investments for later life and publishes *Consumer Affairs,* weekly.

Chapter 3

Gender

Dan has a genuine affection for children. He has attempted to break out of rigid gender roles by taking a job as the only male teacher in a day-care center. On Wednesdays his shift begins at 1:30 in the afternoon. He made the following comments about his job:

> *When I arrive at work on Wednesdays, I look around the empty play yard and ask myself, "Why hasn't one of the other teachers taken some of the kids outside?" But I know the answer. Since I am a man, they leave outdoor activities to me. As soon as I walk in the door one of the other teachers calls to the children, "Dan is here! It's time to go outside now!" With this announcement some of the children will run up to me and start pulling on my clothes, asking, "What are we going to play today?" My day has begun instantly. Then one of my co-workers will say to me, "I'm glad you're here now. They need to get outside and use up some of their energy." I can see a look of relief on the faces of the other teachers.*
>
> *This situation bothers me because the other teachers act as if a man is necessary so that the kids can learn sports. However, on days when I don't work, the women teachers will take the children outside and start games for them. In a sense the female teachers are saying: It's okay for a woman to teach children sports if there is not a man around to do it, but it is better if a man teaches children about sports because that's more "natural." (Interview by author.)*

By working with preschool children, Dan is trying to break away from traditional gender-role expectations. A *gender role* is a set of social expectations associated with the male or female sex. There is an important distinction between *gender* and *sex*. Sex denotes a person's biological maleness or femaleness. In contrast, gender refers to the nonbiological, culturally learned behavior associated with a particular sex (Lips 1988). Dan is dealing with a problem of gender when he feels pressured by his co-workers to perform his preschool teaching job in a manner consistent with the male gender role. Dan senses that the female teachers expect him to be athletic, to prefer the outdoors, and to like rough-and-tumble rather than quiet play. Yet Dan told the interviewer that he would prefer to begin his workday by calmly helping children with artwork or another quiet activity. Although Dan resents the division of labor between the traditional male and traditional female roles, he is reluctant to speak up in protest because he still feels some obligation to fulfill male role expectations. Here, as in so many situations, gender roles have a powerful influence on behavior.

In this chapter we explore traditional gender expectations, including the process by which children acquire gender roles. We then turn to gender and work and the division of household labor. Finally, we look at theories that attempt to explain inequality between men and women in the family.

Traditional Gender Roles

The traditional gender roles are the male instrumental role and the female expressive role. The male *instrumental role* emphasizes rationality, aggression, goal-orientation, and competitiveness. In contrast, the female *expressive role* stresses nurturance, peacemaking, and emotional expression. Traditional gender roles take human experience and divide it in half, presenting male and female character as opposites. Ferree (1990) points out that traditional gender roles are *bipolar* in that they assume that males and females represent "polarized dichotomies" of reason versus emotion and aggression versus nurturance. The social expectations associated with traditional gender roles ignore the similarities between men and women as well as the variation in behavior within each gender (Ferree 1990).

Traditional Male Role

The influence of the traditional male gender role becomes evident when we look at child care, sexual relationships, and health issues.

Men and Child Care. The source of a husband's identity has traditionally been his work outside the home. Men have fulfilled their parental and spousal obligations primarily through providing financially for the family (Biernat and Wertman 1991). This traditional male gender role has been reinforced by the income differential between husbands and wives, by the wife's involvement in pregnancy and lactation, and by the failure of many employers to accomodate working parents (Hawkins et al. 1993). However, as women enter the labor force, men are expected to take up some of the slack by increasing their share of child care and household duties. This shift in gender roles has led to mixed reactions from men. Some non-traditional men, such as Dan, at the beginning of this chapter, welcome the opportunity to explore the nurturing parts of themselves. In fact, the modern male role is beginning to include the image of the nurturing father (Ahlburg and DeVita 1992). However, more traditional men often feel uncomfortable with the new demands made on them. A number of studies have found that, because the traditional man's identity is not closely tied to child care or home management, some men feel resentful about doing household chores and child care (Biernat and Wertman 1991; Crouter, et al. 1987). Fathers who are active in child care report considerable role conflict and stress in attempting to combine work and family responsibilities (Volling and Belsky 1991). Yet some of the awkwardness that some fathers feel with children stems from lack of practice. Fathers who actually participate in child care feel more competent as caregivers than do fathers who avoid caring for young children (Crouter et al. 1987).

African-American men have traditionally been actively involved in child care (Lewis 1989; McAdoo 1981). This situation reflects the different economic opportunities that have been available to African-American men and women. Jobs have been more readily available for African-American women than for African-American men. As a result African-American families have traditionally had marital roles that emphasize equality, with men doing some of the cooking and cleaning and child care (Ross 1987; Taylor et al. 1990). This pattern has existed regardless of whether the partners were married or cohabiting (Lewis 1989). Nonetheless, as African-American men have entered the middle class, they have developed a gender role pattern similar to that of white men. The ability to provide economically for the family is a central part of African-American male identity. This emphasis on career development among middle-class African-American men still leaves middle-class African-American women with primary responsibility for child care and other

Fathers who are actively involved in child care feel more competent as parents and more involved with their families.

household duties (Broman 1991; Taylor et al. 1990).

While some men feel stressed by child care, others view relationships with children as an important part of a changing male gender role.

Men and Sexuality. Sexuality is another area in which traditional gender roles have an important impact on behavior. Men, particularly teenage and college-age men, tend to be more sexually liberal than women in that they engage in less cautious sexual behavior. Men tend to have more sexual partners and are more likely than women to engage in casual sex. In contrast, teenage and college-age women are more likely than young men to prefer sex within an ongoing, emotionally expressive relationship (Baldwin and Baldwin 1988; Hendrick et al. 1985). In addition, a growing body of research that examines attitudes toward contraception points out that a number of teenage males take a dominant position in sexual relationships, object to condom use, and hold their female partners responsible for contraception (Nix et al. 1988; Pleck et al 1988).

In marriage, the lingering effect of the traditional male instrumental role and the female expressive role can be seen in the sexual relationships of distressed couples. In a national study of married couples, Flowers (1991) found that in unhappy marriages, husbands tended to be far more satisfied with marital sex than wives. Apparently, the men were able to be goal-oriented in sexual matters and achieve sexual satisfaction. In contrast, the wives' attitudes toward their sexual experiences were affected by the emotional quality of the marital relationship. Husbands, but not wives, were able to enjoy sex regardless of whether or not the couple was currently getting along.

Men and Health. The male tendency to shy away from emotional expression has led to what Jourard (1971) called the "lethal aspect of the male role." Men often ignore the "all is not well signals" in their bodies and are less likely than women to seek medical treatment in the early stages of an illness (Gerzon 1982). In addition, feelings of discomfort, anxiety, and depression are often brushed aside by the traditional male. Men will often continue in a stressful way of life until an illness-producing breakdown, such as a heart attack, occurs (Coombs 1991). The male tendency to die at a younger age, on average, than women may result in part from the male tendency to ignore both emotional and physical internal signals.

Strain in the Traditional Male Role

Mark Gerzon (1982) points out that the requirements of the male provider and protector role are difficult to fill. Men are expected to be ultimately responsible for the family's financial support. In addition, men are expected to fight wars and to endure pain with bravery; they are taught that it is their patriotic responsibility to sacrifice their lives if necessary. All of these cultural demands create stress. Because the social expectations associated with gender roles can create discomfort, some cultures provide the option of an alternative gender role. Native American cultures of the American plains offered socially accepted alternative roles for individuals who were more comfortable with the behavior associated with the opposite sex. The Plains Indians had the social role of the "berdache" for males who preferred cooking and the artistic pursuit of pottery making to warfare. The berdache dressed and behaved as a woman. He held a sacred position among Native Americans on the plains and was well respected because of his performance of important ceremonial functions in these societies (Crapo 1990).

The traditional male role is not the only gender role that can produce strain, as we will see when we examine the traditional female role.

Traditional Female Role

The traditional female role emphasizes nurturance and caregiving. In addition, because the traditional female role is considered to be an emotionally expressive one, the mother is typically at the center of the family's communication network.

Nurturance and Caregiving. Nurturing children and caring for a family is a valuable contribution to society. In addition to caring for children, women are far more likely than men to be caregivers to elderly relatives (Walker and Pratt 1991). The nurturant, caregiving aspects of the traditional female role lead many women to put the needs of their partners and families before their own needs (Ferree 1991; Miller, Jean Baker, 1976). The woman provides domestic services, such as cooking and laundry, for the husband to free him to concentrate on his career. In fact, the ideology of love encourages women to value self-sacrifice (Cancian 1987; Cancian and Grodon 1988). Meanwhile, women tend to give their own personal development low priority. This puts women at a disadvantage when they must support themselves.

Communication Hub. Gender affects the pattern of communication in the family. Men and women differ in the extent to which other family members confide in them. The wife–mother, who is generally perceived as the expressive parent, is typically at the hub of family communication and is expected to be a good listener. Children of both sexes reveal more information about themselves to their mothers than to their fathers (Pearson 1989). Mothers tend to receive a broad range of information, covering social topics, such as dating and friendships, and task-oriented topics, such as information on grades. Fathers, on the other hand, tend to hear from children mainly about task-oriented topics, such as academic progress. Children report that they tend to select the mother to hear personal information because they perceive mothers as more interested in having a conversation with them (Pearson 1989).

In the Mexican-American immigrant family, the wife is often the hub or clearinghouse for information for family members. This position increases her influence and importance in the family. Mexican-American immigrant women become part of an information network, gathering knowledge about publicly funded social services, such as child care, Women, Infants, and Children (WIC) food subsidies, and health care services. Women gain power by acquiring and controlling information on subsidy programs. Family documents necessary for entry into these programs are carried and stored by women (Chavira 1988).

As children reach school age, Mexican-American immigrant wives begin to attend meetings at their children's schools or health care facilities. Husbands usually object to their wives being involved with "public" activities outside the home, but their objections are typically limited to scolding their wives rather than attempting to prevent them from attending (Rodriguez 1988). The Mexican-American wife's position as an important collector and distributor of information is recognized by her husband and thus her activities outside the home are tolerated, which provides her with increased independence (Chavira 1988).

Strain in the Traditional Female Role

Women who have adhered to the caregiving aspect of the female role over a period of years may lose touch with their own needs. At this point such women experience a feeling of *loss of self,* an inability to recognize one's own inner wants and desires (Maltas 1991). Some women feel so compassionate that they often ignore their own needs in order to meet the perceived needs of the partner. Strain can occur not only in marital roles but also in caregiving roles with elderly relatives. Wives who care for ill or disabled husbands often become homebound and isolated from friends and relatives (Hoyert and Seltzer 1992).

Next we examine the way in which children acquire gender roles.

Acquiring Gender Roles

How do men and women come to behave according to gender expectations? Three explanations for the acquisition of gender roles are social learning theory, cognitive development theory, and identification theory, all of which are explained below.

Social Learning Theory

The key elements of social learning theory are *observation, imitation,* and *reinforcement* (Mischel 1970; 1966). Children observe and imitate a wide range of behavior in a trial-and-error fashion, including the actions of both males and females (Maccoby and Jacklin 1974). The three-year-old boy is likely to help his mother make cookie dough, then later pick up a shovel and insist on helping his father plant a tree. As long as these behaviors receive *positive reinforcement,* they are likely to continue and become part of the child's gender role. Positive reinforcement consists of social rewards that communicate approval, such as parental delight, smiles, hugs, and encouraging statements such as, "Look at how far Jimmy hit the baseball!" Children soon learn to maximize their social rewards by imitating same-sex persons.

Parents reveal their attitudes about gender roles to their children in a variety of ways that, in turn, affect children's views of gender (Katz and Boswell 1986). The socialization of children into male and female roles begins early in life. From birth, parents tend to respond to male and female infants differently (Kagan 1964; Sidorowicz and Lunney 1980). Parents tend to touch infant girls more and handle them gently, as if they were more delicate than male infants (Weitzman 1975). Parents also talk more to their daughters, encouraging verbal expressiveness, while they play in a rough manner with their sons, encouraging physical assertiveness (Tauber 1979).

The toys and games parents choose for children also reflect gender stereotyping (Miller, C.L., 1987). Parents also communicate their gender expectations to children through the clothing styles they choose for them. Often parents are unaware that they are communicating cultural expectations about gender to children when they select clothing. Boys tend to be dressed in loose, functional, and durable clothing, ideal for running and climbing trees. This clothing supports a physically active lifestyle. Girls are often dressed in delicate, restrictive clothing that gives the appearance of neatness and hampers female movement:

> Imagine yourself as an infant trying to crawl while wearing a skirt. You're likely to find the skirt caught under your knee and your nose hitting the floor. The nonverbal message is clear: don't do too much of something that gets you a sore nose. (Bate 1988:119)

The symbols of culture, including clothing, present children with messages that guide gender behavior in directions the culture deems appropriate. Parents also influence their children's attitudes toward gender in subtle ways by modeling behavior. Barak, Feldman, and Noy (1991) interviewed 113 five- and six-year-old children and their parents and discovered that mothers with nontraditional occupations (such as managers) tended to have both sons and daughters who preferred nontraditional occupations. On the other hand, the sons and daughters of mothers with traditional occupations (such as secretaries) tended to have traditional occupational preferences. Through observation, imitation, and reinforcement children receive parental messages about gender-appropriate behavior.

Critique. From the conditioning perspective, parents and others in the environment

Parents may be unconsciously gender stereotyping their children when they dress boys in loose, functional clothing and girls in outfits that are more delicate or restrictive.

shape the behavior of the child. In this process the child is a passive learner. Critics have argued that children are much more active in the learning process than social learning theory assumes.

The next perspective, cognitive development theory, gives children a more active role in choosing the way they will play their gender roles.

Cognitive Development Theory

According to cognitive development theory, the process of learning gender roles is influenced by the child's stage of *cognitive development*. Cognitive development refers to the way children process information at each stage of maturation (Kohlberg 1966, 1969). Therefore, age is important in the process of learning gender expectations. Children begin to form gender identity by first forming two mental categories, male and female. By age two children have discovered that there are two genders, but they are not sure to which one they belong. At this age, gender is seen as a changeable characteristic. If an adult asks, "Are you a boy or a girl?" the two-year-old is likely to answer "a boy" at one time and "a girl" when the question is repeated. This is also the age at which children ask such questions as, "Mommy, were you a boy when you were little?" Between the ages of three and five the child develops *gender constancy*. Gender constancy refers to the recognition that gender is a permanent characteristic, not subject to change. As gender constancy develops, children are able to form a firm gender identity.

The gender identity of children becomes clarified as they actively seek out information on behavior that is considered gender appropriate. This is accomplished by choosing same-sex *role models* to observe and imitate. A role model is someone with whom a person identifies and whose behavior is imitated. By age six, children can give detailed descriptions of behavior considered appropriate by their culture for a boy and a girl. Around age six or seven, children have a rigid view of gender roles and make a sharp distinction between male and female behavior. As children mature, they begin to see gender roles as more flexible and find it more acceptable for male and female behavior to overlap (Kohlberg 1966; Vogel et al. 1991).

Gender Schemas. As children observe role models and imitate behavior, they build a gender schema (Bem 1981, 1985). A *schema* is a mental structure through which a person processes information. A *gender schema* is a set of general characteristics that the child sees as being central to a particular gender. Psychologist Sandra Bem described the struggle her four-year-old son, Jeremy, experienced in trying to discover which characteristics separated males from females. One day Jeremy insisted on wearing a barrette in his hair when he went to nursery school.

> Several times that day, another little boy told Jeremy that he, Jeremy, must be a girl because "only girls wear barrettes." After trying to explain to this child that "wearing barrettes doesn't matter" and that "being a boy means having a penis and testicles," Jeremy finally pulled down his pants as a way of making his point more convincingly. The other child was not impressed. He simply said, "Everybody has a penis; only girls wear barrettes." (Bem 1983:612)

In the above example, both Jeremy and his playmate had developed two mental categories of male and female and searched for information to fill these categories, but the boys had come up with different content for their cognitive categories. As is typical of their age, both boys had focused on concrete criteria for determining gender. As children mature, their gender schemas include more abstract characteristics, such as neatness, power, or strength. A gender schema can be thought of as a map that gives a broad general outline of behavior deemed appropriate for a male or female. For example, a child who notices that the father's word is final in the household may develop a gender schema in which men are seen as dominant and powerful and women are seen as submissive. This gender schema becomes the filter through which the child processes information, incorporating those pieces of information that fit this schema and rejecting information that does not mesh.

If a girl's gender schema depicts women as peacemakers, she may make an effort to be agreeable and submissive, and she may view women who speak out and stand up for themselves as "troublemakers." A girl with this gender schema would typically reject the strong, assertive woman as a role model. Likewise, the boy who sees his father become emotional and then abruptly leave the room may draw the conclusion that emotions are acceptable for women but frightening and unacceptable for men. Later, when the boy sees another man express sadness or hurt feelings, the child may define this man as weak and unmasculine, rejecting him as a role model. Through this process of filtering information, children structure their gender identity.

Next we turn to identification theory.

Children rehearse for adult gender roles by imitating their role models. As they gather information about what is considered male and what is considered female, they form gender schema.

Identification Theory

Early identification theorists argued that children identify with the same-sex parent (Freud 1960, original 1924; 1974, original 1925). In contrast, contemporary sociologist Nancy Chodorow argues that in early childhood both boys and girls identify with their primary caretaker, who is typically the mother. *Identification* is a strong emotional attachment to another person and a desire to be like that person. Chodorow emphasizes that in most societies, the caretaker of very young children is the mother. Regardless of the social organization of the society, the father is usually away from the home, engaged in hunting, warfare, farming, or office employment. All of these activities are ill-suited for the very young who are left behind as the father works. In this situation the girl experiences a continuous identification with the mother throughout childhood and will later grapple with the *issue of separation*. As an adolescent, the girl faces the problem of separating her identity from that of her mother. According to Chodorow, the teenage girl's need for separation results in feelings of competition with and hostility toward her mother. Resolving the separation issue is a major task of female development.

The Male Identification Shift. In contrast to girls, who have a continuous identification with the mother, boys make a major and traumatic *identification shift* around age six or seven. Having previously identified with the mother, the boy must switch his identification to the father. The girl never faces this necessity. The boy's traumatic and sudden identification with the father occurs when the boy realizes that he and his mother are different sexes and it is no longer appropriate to identify with her. Almost all traditional societies recognize age six or seven as a special point of change in the young male's life. In agricultural societies seven-year-old boys leave their mothers and go out into the fields to begin learning farming side-by-side with the father. In traditional, craft-oriented societies, young boys become the father's apprentice around age six or seven, learning the father's trade, such as leather working or carpentry.

Rejection of Feminine Culture. In order to make the identity shift from feminine to masculine, Chodorow argues, the young male must reject activities associated with the mother and considered feminine. The boy "defines masculinity negatively as that which is not feminine and/or connected with women. . . " (Chodorow 1978:174). In many cultures male puberty initiation ceremonies in adolescence serve to further distinguish male identity from the world of women.

The puberty initiation ceremony is a *rite of passage* marking the young person's change in status from childhood to adulthood. Going through a rite of passage grants the young male full entry into adult male culture, including admission to the men's ceremonial meeting rooms, from which women are typically restricted. Exclusively male social groups and organizations reinforce the establishment of male identity by the rejection of femininity. For example, in American culture young boys often set up "males only" clubhouses, and adult men's clubs and male hunting or fishing trips reinforce the distinction between men and women.

Rigid Male Gender Role. The transition for young males from feminine to masculine identification is easier in traditional than in modern societies. The young male in modern society rejects behavior defined as feminine but does not have a readily available male model to imitate. Because the American father spends a good deal of time outside the home, the young male "must attempt to develop a masculine gender identification and learn the masculine role in the absence of a continuous and ongoing personal relationship to his father" (Chodorow 1978:176). Thus the young boy tends to identify with a cultural stereotype of masculinity, suggested by his mother and his teachers and portrayed in the mass media. This stereotyped view of masculinity has been likened to a vague road "map showing the major outline but lacking most details, whereas the mother as a model for the girl, might be thought of as a detailed map" (Lynn 1966:466). The necessity of identifying with vague demands of the masculine role leads to male anxiety. The young male fears social rejection for not properly filling the masculine role. This anxiety leads to his rigid adherence to his stereotyped view of masculinity (Lynn 1966). The modern boy is missing the complex male role model provided by the farm father who patiently took care of his son and taught him the family trade.

Inner-City Males. We could use Chodorow's theory to understand the establishment of gender identity among young lower-class, inner-city males. Children in the inner city are likely to be raised by an unmarried mother. These mothers receive little, if any, financial support from the unemployed or intermittently employed fathers of their children, who have little education and few job skills. Some of the boys grow up in households in which few adult male role models are present. Middle-class males fled the inner city in the 1950s and 1960s, and now there are few employed male role models in the ghetto for a young boy to emulate. Those men with whom the boy has contact are often disparaged by females as "triffling," a term that refers to the lower-class male's inability to support his children. When the young urban male shifts his identification from his mother to a male role model, he turns to his peers for examples of male gender role behavior. This identification with peers results in a growing tendency toward inner-city gang activity (Cottingham 1989).

Rubin: Male Rejection of Emotions. Sociologist Lilian Rubin (1983) builds on Chodorow's gender theory by using the male identification shift to explain male discomfort with emotions. She traces the discomfort some men have with intimacy to their painful identification shift to the father in childhood. Many men feel uncomfortable expressing emotions other than anger or impatience. Rubin argues that the male process of shifting identification to the father in childhood and rejecting the mother leaves the boy with a profound sense of hurt and loss. He represses his longing for a close emotional attachment to the mother, pushing these feelings into his unconscious mind. At the same time, he rejects emotions in general because they are seen as too threatening. Experiencing feelings might bring to consciousness the early pain of rejecting the nurturing relationship with the mother.

Next we examine how gender roles which the culture holds up for children to follow have changed.

Review Questions

1. What do we mean when we say that the traditional male role is instrumental and the traditional female role is expressive?

2. What is meant by gender roles as "polarized dichotomies"?

3. What are the characteristics of the traditional male gender role and the traditional female gender role?

4. How does social learning theory explain the process by which children learn gender roles?

5. In what way does clothing give symbolic gender messages to children?

6. How does cognitive developmental theory explain the acquisition of gender roles?

7. According to Chodorow, how do boys and girls acquire gender roles?

8. What special problems do boys face in establishing their gender identity?

Changing Gender Roles in Society

Gender roles have changed over the course of American history. A number of historians have argued that the division between the male instrumental role and the female expressive role did not develop until the nineteenth century. Colonial farm families of the eighteenth century required husbands and wives to be both instrumental and expressive. Fathers played an important part in child care and occupational training for sons. When a boy reached age seven, he spent his days in the fields with his father, who became his primary caretaker. Mothers had instrumental tasks to accomplish in preserving food and making clothing. Children did not receive intensive nurturance because mothers and older siblings cared for young children at the same time that they were performing chores (Filene 1986; Skolnick 1991).

With the advent of industrialization around 1830 and the separation of the workplace from the home, male and female roles became more specialized (Gerzon 1982). In the industrial era, it was the job of the traditional wife–mother to make the family run smoothly by attending to the emotional needs of others. The family became separate from the economic sphere and was considered "a haven in a heartless world" (Lasch 1977). Men specialized in the instrumental, breadwinning role; females took over nurturing children.

Work and Gender

Recently gender roles have changed to encompass greater androgyny and equality. *Androgyny* refers to choosing and combining traits associated with male and female roles. Gender roles in the family are becoming more androgynous as husbands and wives return to shared breadwinning and shared childrearing. Today three-fourths of women age twenty-five to fifty-four are in the labor force, and the typical family is the two-earner family (U.S. Department of Labor 1992a, Table 3). Androgynous gender roles benefit both men and women. Because men no longer bear alone the burden of financially supporting a family, a number of men have been able to change careers with the help of an employed wife. In addition, men can share in the special relationship that women have had with children. At the same time, women can develop their talents and put them to use in the world outside the home.

Although gender roles have become similar in that both husbands and wives are expected to work outside the home, gender expectations still influence a person's choice of occupation. Because 98 percent of preschool and kindergarten teachers are women, Dan, the preschool teacher described at the beginning of this chapter, has chosen a nontraditional occupation (U.S. Bureau of the Census 1993a). As Table 3.1 shows, there is a good deal of *gender segregation* in employment. Gender segregation by jobs refers to the tendency for males and females to be separated into different occupations. By choosing to be a preschool teacher, Dan has to accept a relatively low rate of pay. The wage of the typical preschool teacher is only slightly above the minimum wage. Dan's choice of a female-dominated occupation means that he, together with many women, experiences the disadvantages of *gender stratification*. Gender stratification refers to a social system that evaluates and rewards the work of males and females unequally. Women tend to be concentrated in jobs, such as preschool teaching and secretarial services, that pay less and have fewer opportunities for advancement than occupations typically held by men. Table 3.2 shows that within each broad occupational category, women are typically found in the lowest-paying jobs.

The pattern of male-dominated and female-dominated occupations persists even though women have greatly increased their participation in the labor force.

Percent of Workers in Each Occupation Who Are Men and Women		
Male-Dominated Occupations	*Men*	*Women*
Construction trades	98%	2%
Mechanics and repairers	97	3
Engineers	92	8
Dentists	90	10
Transportation workers	89	11
Architects	82	18
Lawyers	77	23
Physicians	78	22
Mathematical and computer scientists	68	32
Female-Dominated Occupations		
Cashiers	22	78
Elementary school teachers	14	86
Sewing machine operators	14	86
Registered nurses	6	94
Preschool and kindergarten teachers	2	98
Dental hygienists and assistants	1	99
Secretaries, stenographers, typists	4	96

Source: U.S. Bureau of the Census, 1994a, *Statistical Abstract of the United States, 1994*, Table 637, pages 407–409. Washington, D.C.: U.S. Government Printing Office.

	Median Annual Income for Full-Time Workers by Sex and Occupation		
	Men	*Women*	*Women's Earnings as a Percent of Men's Earnings*
Total: all occupations	$30,358	$21,440	70%
Executive, administrators, and managerial	42,509	27,495	64
Professional specialty	44,051	31,261	71
Administrative support, including clerical	27,186	20,321	75
Skilled laborers	28,923	19,045	66
Unskilled laborers	18,793	14,522	77
Service workers, except private household	20,656	13,195	64

Source: U.S. Bureau of the Census, 1994a, *Statistical Abstract of the United States, 1994,* Table 667, page 431. Washington, D.C.: U.S. Government Printing Office.

Women have only recently begun to enter highly paid professions such as law and medicine. Strict quotas limited the number of female admissions to medical, law, and other professional schools in the first half of the twentieth century (Deckard 1983:297). Furthermore, women who have recently attempted to enter some well-paid male-dominated blue-collar occupations, such as the construction trades, have sometimes faced *sexual harassment* in the form of sexual advances, as well as practical jokes and even threats of violence (Colwill and Colwill 1985). Today, only 2 percent of construction workers, such as carpenters, are women.

Implications for Divorce or Widowhood

Of men and women who are year-round, full-time workers, women earn only 70 cents for every dollar earned by men (U.S. Bureau of the Census, 1994a, Table 667). Table 3.2 shows that service occupations are at the bottom of the pay range; that is where we find the bulk of female workers, who are waitresses, cashiers, and counter clerks. This pay differential has an important negative effect on the well-being of women who become divorced, separated, or widowed (Thompson 1992). Women whose marriages dissolve face a substantial drop in their standard of living. The new no-fault divorce laws that have been adopted by almost all states assume that after divorce both the husband and wife will be self-sufficient and support themselves financially (Weitzman 1990). Divorced women typically have custody of their children and try to support them on a substantially decreased income (Weitzman 1990). The growing divorce rate and an increasing out-of-wedlock birth rate have led to the *feminization of poverty.* The feminization of poverty refers to the growing number of families that are headed by women and that live in poverty. The ranks of the poor are increasingly filled with mother-headed families. In addition, the earning differential between husbands and wives produces a powerful incentive for many women to make concessions to their husbands and try to make the marriage work.

Next we turn to an examination of life in two-earner families.

Gender Roles in Two-Earner Families

In modern two-earner families, there is pressure for the marriage relationship to undergo change. Most husbands and wives report that they believe husbands should engage in more household labor when the wife is employed (Thompson 1991). In recent decades the husband's role has undergone a modest alteration, with the greatest shift coming in the increased time that husbands spend in child care (Ferree 1991). As the behavior of husbands has changed, the image of the nurturing father has become increasingly popular (Alburg and DeVita 1992). However, traditional gender roles continue to assign women primary responsibility for cleaning, cooking, and doing laundry. Hochschild and Machung (1989) point out that an employed wife actually holds down two jobs, one job for which she receives an income and a *second shift* of unpaid labor in the home. Overall, wives in modern two-earner families do approximately two-thirds of the housework (Thompson 1991).

A group that has traditionally had relatively egalitarian gender roles are African-Americans.

African–American Families

African-American marriages tend to be more egalitarian than white marriages. Although African-American women have primary responsibility for household chores, marriage involves more sharing of housework and child care in African-American families than in white families (Broman 1991; McAdoo 1981). African-American women with a supportive male partner report less strain in

Gender roles have shifted in modern two-earner families, with wives pursuing professional careers and husbands participating more in child care. However, traditional gender roles remain influential: Wives in two-earner families do approximately two-thirds of the housework.

BOX 3.1   W o r l d   P e r s p e c t i v e s

Immigrant Families from Mexico

When Mexican men immigrate to the United States, they are often unable to bring their wives and children with them. Even though many husbands send money home for their family's support, wives must seek employment in Mexico to help support their children. Thus, when the Mexican wife joins her husband in the United States, a significant shift in gender roles and work patterns has already taken place (Rodriguez 1988). The husband in the United States has learned to cook and do laundry. The wife in Mexico has learned how to function as the unofficial head of the family. In addition to supporting a family and arranging child care with relatives, wives often have to travel to distant cities in order to obtain formal papers for their own immigration or for a visit (which turns into illegal immigration). All of these tasks require the wife to gain a measure of independence and self-sufficiency.

Reuniting Families

Unfortunately, it is too expensive for most Mexican wives to immigrate with their children. Before coming to the United States, the immigrant wife must talk reluctant Mexican relatives into raising her children until she can afford to send for them. By leaving her children, the mother faces criticism from her relatives in Mexico as well as from her husband when she arrives in the United States. These sturdy and determined Mexican wives seek employment soon after entering the United States so that they can save money and reunite their families. It is difficult to send for all of the children at once. Thus, many Mexican American families become *binational families* in which some children are born in the United States and have siblings in Mexico whom they have never met (Rodriguez 1988). Saving money to reunite the family is difficult because Mexican-American women are some of the most poorly paid workers in the United States. They are heavily represented among domestic servants and seasonal agricultural workers, who earn minimum wage (Melville 1988). After gaining employment in the United States, Mexican women are expected to take primary responsibility for child care and household chores. However, the husband's experience of taking care of the household before the wife arrived encourages him to assume some of the household chores (Rodriguez 1988).

Economic Pressures of Migration

The economic pressures of migration sometimes lead to family disruption. Among undocumented migrants, those who viewed their employment as permanent were more likely to have spouses and children with them, whereas workers who viewed their jobs as temporary tended to live as single adults (Chavez 1988; Vega 1990). The Mexican family has adapted to the strains created by migration by relying on extended kin to provide housing, job referrals, and emotional support. In second-generation Mexican-American families the wife's mother frequently helps her employed daughter by taking care of her daughter's children, bringing cooked food to her daughter's family, and occasionally coming to clean her daughter's house (Ybarra 1988). The extended family appears to view upward mobility as a collective effort.

Husband's Reaction to the Wife's Employment

The traditional female gender role in Mexico does not include employment outside the home. Hispanic husbands typically object when their wives enter paid employment. However, immigrant women often need to work outside the home in order for the family to survive. Unlike the more financially secure Cuban women in Miami, who tend to enter the labor force for short-term employment and then leave the labor force when living conditions improve, Mexican women who migrate to the southwestern United States usually need to remain continuously employed (Kelly and Garcia 1989; Vega 1990). When Mexican women do enter the labor force their marriages go through a period of adjustment. The wife must justify her employment to her husband, and marital conflict is common. This conflict can take a toll on the wife, and there is also some evidence that married Hispanic working women are more vulnerable to depression than married Hispanic homemakers (Vega 1990). Nonetheless, both spouses usually agree that the wife's employment is essential in order to reunite the family in the United States. Thus, traditional gender roles in Mexico become altered when Mexican families migrate to the United States.

their parental role than single women (Lewis 1989). The expectation of role sharing in marriage arose during slavery and continued after the Civil War (Broman 1991; Genovese 1974). Black men have experienced limited employment opportunities, low wages, and frequent unemployment; therefore, unemployed men played an important role in child care and taking care of the home. Sharing household chores was considered natural in low-income African-American families. Meanwhile, employment was usually available for black women, who could work as domestics (Broman 1991).

Nonetheless, whether a family is white, Mexican-American, or African-American, women still do the majority of the housework and child care. For a more complete discussion of the division of household labor, see Chapter 8, Marriage, Work, and Power. In the next section we look at explanations for gender inequality.

Review Questions

1. In what way does gender affect occupation and income?
2. What is gender stratification and how has it contributed to the feminization of poverty?
3. How do men and women differ in their contribution to household labor?
4. How do African-American two-earner marriages differ from white two-earner marriages?

Gender Inequality

Although some American couples have managed to forge egalitarian relationships, in which husband and wife have equal influence in marriage, a good deal of gender inequality remains. Women still earn less on average than men and are more likely than men to live in poverty. Women have primary responsibility for household labor even when they are employed (Ferree 1991). A number of women are victims of domestic violence (Straus and Smith 1990). In addition, it is usually the husband's job, rather than the wife's, that determines whether or not the family will migrate to another city (Shihadeh 1991). Why is it that husbands tend to have so much influence in the family? Social scientists have attempted to determine the factors that provide one partner with more power than the other in a marriage. Some explanations for gender inequality are discussed below. These theories include structural-functional theories, Ortner's "women as part of nature" argument, conflict theory, and feminist theory.

Structural-Functional Theory

Structural-functional theory examines social relationships and asks how they contribute to the maintenance and survival of society. Parsons and Bales (1955) argue that male dominance is a natural and inevitable outgrowth of living in families. They maintain that any small group, such as the family, tends to develop two specialized roles, an instrumental role and an expressive role. The instrumental role, typically taken by the husband, involves leadership and is the role that exercises decision-making power. The expressive role, concerned with emotional expression and maintaining smooth relationships, is typically taken by the wife.

Parsons and Bales contend that the development of an instrumental and an expressive role is natural and appears in all small groups. Furthermore, they consider this role specialization to be *functional*. A behavior pattern that is functional meets social needs. Parsons and Bales see the division into instrumental and expressive roles as meeting the needs of the family because decisions need to be made and emotional well-being needs to be fostered. They state that "the problem with respect to the family is not *why* it [the instrumental-expressive differentiation] appears [in the family] . . . but why the man takes the more instrumental role [and] the woman the more expressive role" (p. 23). The answer to this question, as they see it, lies in a woman's biological nature. The woman's close relationship with children gives her the expressive role, and the husband, by default, takes the instrumental, decision-making, role. Thus a woman's subordinate position in the family grows out of her biological function of childbearing.

Critique of Structural-Functional Theory. The structural-functionalist perspective of Parsons and Bales provides some insight into gender roles, but they make the highly questionable assumption that male dominance is natural and inevitable. The basic problem in their theory lies in the assumption that the instrumental, or decision-making, function must be concentrated into a single social role. In fact, decision-making can involve both parties in an egalitarian relationship. In this case the instrumental function is shared by the husband and wife. Furthermore, the lopsided relationship in which the wife alone specializes in emotional expression makes marital communication difficult and is frustrating for both husband and wife. Such frustration could be reduced by male–female relationships in which the expressive function is shared by the husband and wife. Moreover, parent–child relationships would benefit from a male role that emphasizes expressiveness and communication skills.

In some societies, women's abilities to menstruate, give birth, and breastfeed children have caused them to be dismissed as weaker and less fully competent than men. Other societies, including many Native American tribes, celebrate these characteristics of women. Here, a White Mountain Apache girl participates in a puberty ceremony.

Women as Part of Nature Argument

Sherry Ortner and Harriet Whitehead (1981) argue that male dominance and female subordination are found in all societies. They trace this assumed universal inequality

BOX 3.2   S o c i a l   I s s u e s

Do Egalitarian Societies Exist?

Do any societies exist that grant equality to men and women? One egalitarian society is the Hopi, who live high on top of mesas, or flat-topped mountains, in a remote desert reservation in northern Arizona. The relative isolation of the Hopi villages has allowed them to retain a great deal of their traditional culture. Theirs is a horticultural society in which men farm with a sacred digging stick, rather than a plow, and families live at the subsistence level (Lisitzky 1966; Queen et al. 1985). The Hopi have a "mother right society" in which women own the farm land and kinship is *matrilineal*, with family name, property rights, and inheritance passing through the female line, from a mother to her children. Families are organized into "matrilineal clans," which consist of a group of relatives who trace their family line back to a common female ancestor. Sons may use clan land but have no ownership rights and cannot pass that land on to their children. Nothing of any great importance is inherited from a person's father (Euler and Dobyns 1971). The importance of women in Hopi society is reflected in the Hopi religion, in which Spider Grandmother, an eternal female deity, is believed to be the female creator of the universe (Allen 1986).

A man also inherits his right to participate in religious ceremonies and to belong to religious societies from his mother's clan. Women own the sacred masks their sons wear in religious ceremonials to portray kachinas, which are religious spirits (Geertz and Lomatumay'ma 1987). There is a balance of power between the genders in Hopi society: Clan heads are women, and the equally important religious societies are headed by men. Women own the houses in Hopi society, and the Hopi practice *matrilocal residence*, meaning that at marriage the groom moves in with the bride and her family (Euler and Dobyns 1971). Female ownership of houses makes divorce easy for women. Women can effect a divorce either by asking the husband to leave the house or by putting his belongings outside on the doorstep. When the husband returns home and sees his belongings, he realizes that he has been divorced and returns home to his mother's house.

Women are granted important courtship rights in Hopi society. A young women can propose to a man by offering him a sweet corn bread, called *qomi*, at a religious ceremonial. If the young man keeps the bread he has accepted her proposal. Women can also acquire a husband through the courtship practice of *dumaiya*. Young women are expected to grind corn at night in the family's storage room while the rest of the family sleeps. *Dumaiya* translates as "night crawling," and refers to secret night visits by the young man who crawls past the window of the girl's mother at night in order to get to the corn-grinding room to see the young woman (Aberle 1951). Unmarried women typically take several lovers with whom they have sexual relations on different nights. When a girl becomes pregnant, she chooses her favorite lover, names him as the father of her child, and they marry (Queen et al. 1985).

It is unusual for a young man to refuse to marry a woman after she has designated him the father of her child. However, such resistance occurs on a rare occasion. When this happens, the young woman continues with the pregnancy and bears the child out of wedlock. In this case there is no disgrace for her because it is the woman, not the man, who legitimizes the child and grants the child clan membership. Her relatives readily accept the child as part of the family. When she later marries, as she almost invariably will, her new husband accepts the child as if it were his own (O'Kane 1970).

In his wife's home a man has little, if any, authority. Important family decisions are made by the wife and her brother. Likewise, fathers have little say in the upbringing of their children. Female children are disciplined by their mother and male children by their mother's brother, who shares their clan membership. This does not mean that men are without influence. The same man who feels powerless as a husband and father in his wife's home will help make important decisions in the home of his mother and sister.

We see that gender behavior takes a wide variety of forms across cultures. The Hopi of the American southwest are an egalitarian society that grants great respect and influence to women but also places great importance in men's role as mother's brother.

between the sexes to women's biological reproductive functions. Only women menstruate, become pregnant, experience childbirth, and breastfeed children. According or Ortner and Whitehead, males find it natural to subordinate women because the reproductive functions of women cause them to be associated with "animal-like nature" and male activities of hunting, clearing land, and growing crops represents mastery over and taming of nature.

The Menstrual Hut. Drawing on the work of anthropologist Robert Lowie, Ortner maintains that in all cultures women have less social honor and value than men because their menstrual cycles lead them to be stigmatized as polluted. As evidence of universal male dominance and female subordination, she points out that most traditional societies confine women to a menstrual hut during their periods. Among the Native American Crow, menstruating women were thought to bring harm to a wounded warrior or to men about to enter a war party. Thus women were seen as a threat to the highly valued practice of warfare.

Critique. Although a large number of societies, especially agrarian societies, view women as polluted and subordinate to men, it is important not to *overgeneralize* by assuming that male dominance is found in all societies (Lerner 1986). To *overgeneralize* is to assume that behavior and attitudes found in one group can also be found in groups with different social characteristics. Observers often impose upon the menstrual hut interpretations that are different from the meaning attached to the practice by the culture being studied (Bataille and Sands 1984). Most discussions of the menstrual hut give the impression that women are banished there by men who are dominant and who devalue women as contaminated. Paula Gunn Allen (1986), a Keres Native American and anthropologist, offers an alternative explanation for the widespread existence of the menstrual hut. Among Native Americans menstruation was associated with the spiritual power of women. During menstruation, this female spiritual power became so strong that it could easily overwhelm and nullify a man's power. Vulnerable men who had been wounded or who would be exposed to battle were not strong enough to withstand this spiritual force and could be harmed, not because women were polluted but because of their spiritual strength. Women were not banished to the menstrual hut against their will. Rather, they took seriously their responsibility for protecting the weaker members of their community from their power. A woman's power at menstruation could be harmful to healthy men as well (Niethammer 1977). A Native American woman was believed to be able to paralyze a man by stepping over him and allowing menstrual blood to fall on his body. Women were sometimes known to use the threat of such action to get what they wanted from male relatives.

Menstruation came infrequently in Native American society because women were often pregnant or lactating, both of which suppress ovulation and menstruation. Women often viewed the four-day stay in the menstrual hut as a vacation because it freed them from the normal chores and child care. In fact, there are cases of Native American women sneaking off to the menstrual hut for a rest when they were not having their periods (Niethammer 1977).

Native Americans typically treated a woman's first menstruation as a time for rejoicing. The Papago honored a young woman who returned from the menstrual hut on her first menstruation with a celebration of feasting and all-night dancing. Thus, women are not universally devalued because of their biological functions.

Conflict Theory

According to conflict theory, power and privilege are derived from the *resources* a person possesses. *Power* is the ability to influence the lives of others. Classical conflict theorists considered economic resources, such as income and property, to be the primary source of power. In his book, *The Origins of the Family, Private Property and the State* (1973, original 1884), Frederick Engels argued that the economic system forms the basis for power in social relationships. He maintained that the basis for male dominance over women in the family lies in the male's control over economic resources, property and wages, in the larger society. In fact, Engels argued that *patriarchy,* or male dominance, has not always existed. Patriarchy arose in European society along with the development of private property and *patrilineal* family systems, in which inheritance passed through the male line. Male control over female behavior, particularly over female sexuality, arose as a way of making sure that children of the wife were produced by the husband and were thus rightful heirs to his property. Family systems that existed at the subsistence level, such as hunting and gathering societies, had little or no property to pass on to children and therefore no need for a strong system of male dominance to control property and inheritance. Engels argued that these simple societies are far more egalitarian than either societies with advanced agriculture or industrialized societies, both of which are organized around property ownership and wages.

Since the time of Engels, the concept of resources has been expanded to include the same resources that place a person in the social class system—namely, income, educational attainment, and occupational status (Blood and Wolfe 1960). According to conflict theory the partner with the most resources holds the greatest power. Because men tend to marry women who are younger, less educated, and earn less than themselves, they are often able to translate these resources into influence in marriage.

Critique. Conflict theory has been criticized for defining resources too narrowly and placing too much emphasis on economic resources as sources of power. Conflict theory tends to overlook personal resources, such as sex, love, and companionship, which can also provide a partner with influence in a relationship (Safilios-Rothschild 1976, 1970). Conflict theory has also been criticized for overlooking social beliefs as a causal factor. Traditional love ideology can be a causal factor that reduces a woman's influence in a romantic relationship. Traditional love ideology values self-sacrifice on the part of women. This ideology can lead women to defer to men regardless of their economic circumstances (Cancian 1987).

Conflict theory also overlooks much of the impact of gender roles on male and female behavior. Yet gender roles can be a powerful influence on behavior regardless of a partner's income. Gender roles hold up ideals for men and women to live up to, and these gender expectations and images can also motivate behavior (Ferree 1991). Conflict theory would argue that the unequal division of household labor between husbands and wives is an outgrowth of economic inequality between the sexes in the larger society. However, housework is also influenced by gender roles, and having a pleasant home is frequently tied to female identity as a "good wife" and homemaker. Women are sometimes living up to their own self-ideals when they perform housework (Bergen 1991). Gender roles as well as values and ideologies are important influences on behavior. (For a discussion of gender role theory see Chapter 8, Marriage, Work, and Power.)

The feminist perspective combines conflict theory with a study of gender roles and social values and thus takes a broader view of social causation than classical conflict theory.

Feminist Theory

Osmond and Thorne (1993) have identified five basic elements of feminist theory:

1. *Gender is fundamental:* Feminist theory takes the position that the social relationships between women and men are a fundamental aspect of social life. From this perspective gender is an organizing theme in society.
2. *Experiences of women:* Feminist theory focuses on the experiences of women and points out that the everyday experiences of women are important, such as women's experiences with child care and the division of household labor.
3. *Inequality:* Feminist theory illuminates inequality between men and women in the family and in the larger society. From the perspective of feminist theory, the subordination of women in the family is found in such experiences as wife battering, an unequal division of household labor, and the sexual abuse of female children. In the larger society, gender inequality appears in the occupational segregation of women, low pay for women, and the high level of poverty in mother-headed families.
4. *Social change:* Feminist theory argues that it is acceptable, even necessary, to bring personal values and political action into social science. Feminist theorists are generally interested in confronting female subordination and bringing about social change.
5. *Social images:* Feminist theory examines the social images of women and men in society. In particular, feminist theory is interested in cultural beliefs that exaggerate male–female differences and then use these differences to legitimize the subordination of women. From this perspective, images of women and men are socially constructed in that they primarily reflect social beliefs about men and women rather biologically based differences.

Much of the terminology of conflict theory has been adopted by feminist theorists (Ferree 1991, 1990). Feminist theorists argue that women are underrepresented in power positions in the larger society, such as seats in Congress and the Senate and executive positions in corporations. From the perspective of feminist theory, this lack of societal power is reflected in the low level of power held by many women in families. Feminists examine the distribution of economic resources between men and women and point out that the median income for employed women is only two-thirds of the median income for men (Thompson 1992). Women also face some discrimination in the workplace in the form of sexual harassment and gender discrimination in hiring and promotion. The earning differential between men and women places women at a disadvantage in the case of divorce or desertion (see Chapter 15, Divorce) (Weitzman 1990). A growing divorce rate and an increasing nonmarital birth rate have led to the "feminization of poverty," which is discussed in Chapter 10, Social Class and Poverty. Feminists also study families in which violence is used as a resource to control the behavior of a spouse (see Chapter 14, Family Violence and Abuse). Gender is explored throughout this book, and gender issues are examined in more depth in upcoming chapters.

Critique. Some critics argue that feminist theory puts too much emphasis on power in male–female relationships and not enough emphasis on the gratification that male–female relationships provide. Some other social scientists prefer to focus on social exchanges in which men and women provide each other with rewards, such as affection, sexual satisfaction, and companionship, as they build intimate relationships (Safilios-Rothschild 1976).

The debate over theory is a healthy one that leads to changes and adjustments in the perspectives we use to analyze family life. Social science is vigorous when the debate over social issues, including gender issues, is lively.

Review Questions

1. How does structural-functional theory explain gender inequality? What is the critique of this theory?
2. What is the basis of Ortner's argument that male dominance is universal? What aspects of Native American culture lead us to challenge Ortner's argument?
3. How does conflict theory explain gender inequality? What is the critique of this theory?
4. What are the basic elements of feminist theory? What issues are feminists concerned with? What is the critique of this theory?

Summary

1. Gender has an important impact on the way we lead our lives. The traditional female expressive role tends to involve placing the needs of the husband above those of the wife. Traditional gender roles affect attitudes toward child care, sexuality, health, and communication. Women tend to be the communication hub of the family.

2. Three major theories that explain how children acquire gender roles are social learning theory, cognitive development theory, and identification theory.

3. Social learning theory explains the acquisition of gender roles through observation, imitation of parents, and parental reinforcement of gender behavior.

4. Cognitive development theory holds that children form mental categories of "male" and "female" and then actively seek out information on gender behavior to fill these categories.

5. Chodorow's identification theory argues that children of both genders identify first with the mother; young boys must subsequently make an identification shift to identify with the father.

6. The workplace is characterized by a tendency toward gender segregation of men and women into separate jobs.

7. Gender stratification results in the concentration of women in a small number of low-paid occupations that lack opportunities for advancement. As a

result women are economically disadvantaged in the case of divorce or widowhood.

8. Married African-American women have traditionally been in the labor force. African-American men gain a sense of identity from the provider role.

9. The major theories that attempt to explain dominance and subordination in male–female relationships include structural-functional theory, which argues that male dominance develops naturally in the family; the women as part of nature argument, which maintains that women are less valued than men because of their reproductive functions; conflict theory, which holds that power derives from the control over economic resources (namely, property and wages); and feminist theory, which not only explains dominance and subordination in male–female relationships but also advocates social change.

Key Words

Instrumental Role	Expressive Role
Bipolar Gender Roles	Loss of Self
Social Learning Theory	Positive Reinforcement
Cognitive Development Theory	Cognitive Development
Gender Constancy	Role Model
Gender Schema	Identification
Issue of Separation	Male Identification Shift
Rite of Passage	Androgyny
Gender Segregation	Gender Stratification
Sexual Harassment	Feminization of Poverty
Two-Earner Family	Second Shift
Structural-Functional Theory	Women as a Part of Nature
Overgeneralize	Conflict Theory
Power	Resources
Patriarchy	Patrilineal Family
Matrilineal Family	Feminist Theory

Resources

National Organization for Women (NOW)
1000 16th St. N.W., Ste. 700
Washington, DC 20036
(202) 331-0066
Engages in lobbying, education, and litigation to promote women's issues in employment, medicine, law, religion, and labor unions and seeks to reduce prejudice and discrimination against women. Publishes *NOW Times*, bimonthly newsletter.

National Organization for Men
381 Park Ave. South
New York, NY 10016
(212) 686-MALE

Promotes men's equal rights in alimony, child custody, battered husbands, affirmative action, educational benefits, and veterans' benefits. Publishes *The Quest,* bimonthly newsletter.

National Congress for Men
2020 Pennsylvania Ave. N.W., Ste. 277
Washington, DC 20006
(202) FATHERS
Promotes fathers' rights, divorce rights for men, and equality in child custody and emphasizes the role of fathers in child development. Makes recommendations to Congress and runs educational programs. Publishes *Fathers for Equal Rights Newsletter.*

Women for Racial and Economic Equality
198 Broadway, Room 606
New York, NY 10038
(212) 385-1103
A multiracial organization working to reduce race and sex discrimination in employment, child care, and wages. Promotes awareness of issues concerning feminism, homelessness, and world peace. Publishes *Women of the Whole World,* quarterly.

Male Liberation Foundation
701 N.E. 67th St.
Miami, FL 33138
(305) 756-6249
Organization that disapproves of men paying the expenses of dating and argues that working women are equally or more financially able to pay their share. Believes there is discrimination against men in employment and parental leave policy.

Part Two

Forming Partnerships

4

Falling in Love: Sexuality and Dating

He Says . . .

I had been dating Sarah a few weeks. We were at a party at a friend's house and had gone to my friend's bedroom. At first she seemed willing to have sex. She didn't say anything—there was just a lot of body language. The combination of her perfume and the wine coolers led me to start making strong advances. I told her that we really seemed to connect and that this [sex] would only make our bond stronger. She got upset because I had never tried anything like that before with her. She pulled away acting tense and said, "I don't believe this. I thought you were such a nice guy!" I felt insulted and said, "Well, I guess you were wrong then!" I became silent for a while and then drove her home. As I drove away from her house, I felt depressed because she didn't consider my feelings. I wish she had been more willing.

Afterwards, when I was at home, I asked myself questions about why this happened: Was I too aggressive? Was she a tease? Was she experiencing PMS? Am I a jerk? I felt a little embarrassed about maybe being a little too pushy about sex. I just wanted to have fun, but she was so serious. I could have done without sex, but the way she reacted shocked me into reacting like a cold stone.

Later, after I thought about it I realized that it probably wouldn't be too much longer before we could go all the way. I was even more attracted to her since nothing had happened. About a month after that we had sex for the first time, and we are still dating. (Interview by author.)

She Says . . .

Paul and I had been dating for a few weeks when his parents went away for the weekend and Paul decided to have a party. The party was noisy, and Paul suggested that we go to his bedroom to talk. We sat down on his bed and he started touching me. I ignored his advances and tried to distract him with semi-normal conversation. Then he laid back on the bed, pulling me down with him. I tried to remain calm and said that maybe we should join the party outside. He ignored what I said, and I went along with his advances for a while. Then, I tried to stop him when I thought he wanted intercourse. I pulled away and told him that I had to get home. He said, "It's not late. You don't have to be home. Come on. It's okay." I told him that I liked him a lot but I wasn't ready for this. He said that he thought that I was ready and that I owed it to him for getting him so "turned-on." I became nervous and told him that things were moving too far, too fast—that I didn't know him well enough. He said that we did know each other well and that I was special, that I wasn't like other girls. "Besides," he said, "there is nothing wrong with sex. It's totally natural. It will make us closer and help us to know each other better." When I repeated that I wasn't ready, he became angry and threatened our relationship, saying that if we didn't have sex, he wouldn't see me any more. I said, "Don't threaten me. Do you think that will help me be in a sexual mood!" I pushed him away and got up *and went back to the party. Later, when I was at home I felt guilty for denying him sex and wondered if I had ruined the relationship. We went out again the next weekend and had sex soon after that. (Interview by author.)*

I n this chapter we examine aspects of falling in love including sexuality and dating. We explore changing patterns of sexual attitudes and behavior, the conflict between dating partners over whether or not to begin intercourse, gender differences in the interpretation of sexual behavior, sexuality and dating among divorced persons, romance and love, and social networks that support or detract from love relationships. In dating, sexual situations can either promote personal intimacy or wind up being a tug-of-war that produces resentments. In the midst of social change, sexual communication can often be problematic, as it was for the two people whose interviews appear above. Let us turn now to changing sexual attitudes and behavior.

Sexual Attitudes and Behavior

A good deal of the confusion surrounding sexual situations occurs because the sexual revolution has left us with few, if any, firm guideposts for sexual behavior.

The Sexual Revolution

Sexual attitudes and behavior have changed dramatically over the last half century. In 1953 Kinsey and colleagues found that only one-fourth (23 percent) of the women he interviewed had experienced coitus by age twenty. A decade later, in the 1960s, the sexual revolution was underway, with its emphasis on sexual experimentation. The introduction of the birth control pill in the mid-1960s separated sex from reproduction and encouraged more liberal sexual behavior (D'Emilio and Freedman 1988). By the early 1970s women were twice as likely to have experienced premarital intercourse as they had been in the Kinsey study (Zelnick and Kantner 1972). The legalization of abortion in 1973 further sep-

Although the sexual revolution of the 1960s brought widespread acceptance of sexual activity outside of marriage, both men and women still prefer partners with limited sexual experience.

arated sex from the consequences of pregnancy and childbearing. As married women entered the labor force and higher education became a goal of both genders, young adults delayed marriage. This extended dating period provided increased opportunities for sexual activity.

Sexual Attitudes and Behavior Today

The trend toward increasing participation in premarital sex has continued. Today the average age at first intercourse for women is between the ages of sixteen and seventeen, with the majority of high school students becoming sexually active before they graduate (Miller and Heaton 1991). African-American women begin intercourse one year earlier than white women; Hispanic women are in between (Day 1992). Looking at those colleges for which data on sexual behavior is available, the percentage of women students who have experienced intercourse ranges from 60 percent at a private East Coast university (Williams and Jacoby 1989) to 81 percent at a southern California university (Baldwin and Baldwin 1988)

Unmarried Americans are having intercourse within less committed relationships than was the case in the 1950s, when Kinsey's study was conducted. In the 1950s the majority of sexually active women were engaged to be married to their sexual partners (Wyatt, Gail Elizabeth 1989). In contrast, social norms today sanction intercourse within "serious relationships" that fall short of commitment to marriage. Sprecher and her colleagues (1988) studied undergraduate students at a midwestern university and found that almost three-fourths (72 percent) of those interviewed approved of sexual intercourse for couples who were seriously dating, compared to only one-fourth (28 percent) who approved of having intercourse on a first date (see Figure 4.1). However, the definition of a serious relationship tends to be fuzzy. As we saw in the interviews at the beginning of this chapter, modern sex-

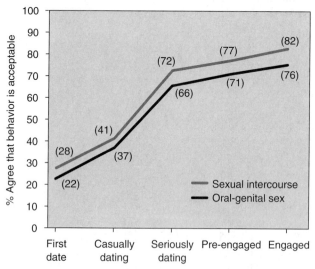

Figure 4.1

Acceptance of Sexual Activity by Relationship Stage

Source: Susan Sprecher, Kathleen McKinney, Robert Walsh, and Carrie Anderson, 1988. "A Revision of the Reiss Premarital Sexual Permissiveness Scale." *Journal of Marriage and the Family*, 50, Figure 1, page 825.

ual relationships tend to be defined in terms of vague concepts such as "knowing each other well enough to have sex" or "being ready for sex." Under these circumstances, arguments and clashes of expectations between partners are bound to arise. Yet in spite of these difficulties, sexual attitudes are exhibiting more gender equality than they did in the past.

The Double Standard

The double standard of the 1950s, which allowed male sexual promiscuity while requiring female virginity, has faded. Modern attitudes uncovered in the Sprecher study include a good deal of gender equality. Respondents felt that the acceptable timing of male intercourse was approximately the same as the acceptable timing of female intercourse. In other words, those who approved of intercourse on a first date for college men also approved of the same behavior for college women. However, one important gender difference did show up in Sprecher's study: Males tended to feel that it is acceptable for both genders to have intercourse early in the relationship, while females would prefer to have both men and women delay intercourse.

Some aspects of the old double standard still exist. Men are still expected to initiate the sexual encounter, and women are expected to appear less interested than men in sex (Muelhenhard and Hollabaugh 1988). At ages fifteen and sixteen, males are twice as likely as females of the same age to have had intercourse (Furstenberg et al. 1987a). In addition, women, but not men, are still expected to limit their number of sexual partners. Both male and female subjects studied by Sprecher and colleagues (1988) thought that it was more acceptable for men than women to have multiple sexual partners (ten or more) prior to marriage. Furthermore, it is still considered more acceptable for men than for women to engage in casual sex (Hendrick et al. 1985). Murstein and his colleagues (1989) found that 12 percent of college males had their most recent intercourse experience with a stranger or casual acquaintance. This was three times the rate of casual sex among college women.

The Selfish Standard

In spite of the fact that college students tend to expect both men and women to be sexually active, when it comes to picking a marriage partner for themselves, they become quite conservative. College men and women both prefer marriage partners who are without previous experience in either coitus or oral–genital sex (Williams and Jacoby 1989). This holds true regardless of the respondent's own level of sexual experience. Those respondents who had previously experienced intercourse desired partners who had gone no farther than genital fondling. Meanwhile, respondents who had engaged in genital fondling but not intercourse preferred partners whose experience was limited to breast fondling. This modern preference for a marriage partner less experienced than oneself has been called the *selfish standard* (Jacoby and Williams 1985). In other words, both men and women prefer virginal marriage partners while allowing themselves to be sexually active.

The selfish standard is interesting in light of the widespread approval of intercourse among those who are seriously dating. It appears that college students are ambivalent in their sexual attitudes. When looking at their current relationship, college students tend to approve of sex, but when looking toward the distant future and marriage, they tend to fantasize about an inexperienced marriage partner. Perhaps college students tend to feel that a sexually inexperienced marriage partner would exercise a good deal of self-control and remain sexually faithful in the marriage. Some people have attempted to deal with these marriage preferences by having oral–genital sex instead of sexual intercourse.

Oral–Genital Sex

Dating partners who have a strong motivation to avoid intercourse and retain their virginity sometimes use oral–genital sex as a substitute for coitus. In a study of high school students, almost half of sixteen-year-olds who had experienced oral–genital sex had never experienced coitus (Newcomer and Udry 1985). The same behavior has been found among college students who want to avoid intercourse (Williams and Jacoby 1989). College students with a high level of religious belief are particularly likely to use oral–genital sex as a substitute for coitus (Gagnon and Simon 1987; Williams and Jacoby 1989).

Deciding whether and when to begin intercourse with a partner can be problematic because of the divergence between liberal and conservative attitudes among college students. While one-fourth of the college students in Sprecher's (1988) study approved of sexual intercourse on a first date, at the other end of the spectrum, one-fifth felt that intercourse should be reserved for marriage. This wide range of sexual attitudes makes for difficulty and confusion in communication when dating partners attempt to define the sexual situation.

Review Questions

1. What changes took place in sexual attitudes and behavior during the sexual revolution of the 1960s and 1970s and why did these changes occur?
2. In what type of relationship do college students tend to consider sexual intercourse acceptable?
3. In what way has the double standard changed, and in what way has it remained the same?
4. What is the selfish standard?
5. What are some of the reasons why oral–genital sex is popular among college students?

Sexual Communication in Dating

Both men and women have difficulty letting their dating partners know what sexual activities they feel are appropriate and inappropriate. Women often

communication to thwart sexual advances (Murnen et al. 1989). The female college student whose interview appears at the beginning of this chapter reports being uncomfortable with a sexual situation before voicing her objections. Men also have communication problems and tend to have difficulty interpreting verbal and nonverbal cues in sexual encounters (Shotland and Craig 1988). The male college student whose interview also appears at the beginning of this chapter reports that he thought his partner was sexually willing, yet his sexual assertiveness angered her. To clarify some of the confusion over sexual communication, some researchers have explored gender differences in interpreting behavior.

Interpreting Behavior

Behavior that women interpret as neutral or "friendly" is often interpreted by men as exhibiting "sexual interest." In one study (Muehlenhard, Friedman, and Thomas 1985) men interpreted a woman's willingness to go to a man's apartment as a sign that she wanted to have sex, whereas women viewed this behavior in a more neutral way. Adolescent males, but not females, often perceive a female who wears short skirts or low-cut clothing as someone who "wanted sex" (Shotland and Craig 1988). Furthermore, when a woman asks a man out on a date, males but not females tend to interpret the invitation as exhibiting an interest in sex. Even if a woman hints that she is available for a date, such as letting it be known that she is not doing anything on Saturday night, males are

---

BOX 4.1 — A Closer Look

Love at First Sight: Showing Sexual Interest

Many people wonder how they can tell whether or not someone else is sexually attracted to them. Shotland and Craig (1988) discovered that when people first meet a person in whom they are sexually interested, they exhibit a particular pattern of behavior. In their study, pairs of male and female college students who had just met were videotaped having a conversation. Afterward, the researchers asked the subjects whether their interest in the other person had been sexual or just friendly. The researchers then matched reports of sexual interest to specific behaviors in the videotapes. They found that behaviors that exhibit sexual interest include long eye contact; playing with inanimate objects; asking questions; giving long answers; discontinuing eating; drinking; or reading; being the first to speak after a pause; doing most of the talking; and especially mentioning that one has noticed the other person before this meeting. Although these behaviors, such as asking questions, also tend to occur when a person has only a friendly interest in the partner, they occur to a greater degree when sexual interest is present. When the interest is simply friendly rather than sexual, eye contact is briefer; fidgeting is less; answers to questions tend to be shorter; and the person tends to continue eating, drinking, or even reading when the other person is present. However, because friendly and sexually interested behavior fall at two ends of a continuum and the difference between them is a matter of degree, interpreting behavior can be difficult.

BOX 4.2   S o c i a l   I s s u e s

The Date Rape Debate

A debate is raging over what constitutes date rape. This debate focuses on where to draw the line that separates persuasion from sexual coercion on a date. Date rape is the most common form of acquaintance rape, in which the victim and perpetrator know each other. Koss and her colleagues (1987) define "date rape" as a situation in which a man obtains sexual intercourse by exerting physical force, such as holding a woman down or twisting her arm, by threatening to use force, or by giving a woman alcohol or drugs. In a nationally representative sample of college students, Koss found that 15 percent of all women had had an experience that met this definition of rape on a date and one-fourth (27 percent) had experienced either date rape or attempted date rape. In addition, Koss reports that one-fourth of the women in her sample experienced sexual coercion by verbal pressure. They answered yes to the question, "Have you given in to sexual intercourse when you didn't want to because you were overwhelmed by a man's continual arguments and pressure?" Koss points out that sexual coercion is more common than has previously been assumed.

The act of rape treats the victims as if they have no human rights, physical boundaries, or control over their bodies (Burt and Katz 1987). As a result, rape victims are likely to suffer *rape trauma syndrome,* symptoms of which include changes in sleeping patterns, nightmares, fear of being home alone, and insecurities concerning sexual attractiveness (Davis and Friedman 1985). Victims tend to blame themselves for the rape and often behave in a withdrawn and constricted manner after the incident. More than one-third (42 percent) of the women who experienced date rape in the sample of Koss and colleagues (1987) were "hidden victims" who never told anyone about the incident for fear of being embarrassed or of not being taken seriously. Rape victims also report increased difficulties in heterosexual relationships, including difficulty affirming their dignity and exercising influence in dating relationships (Koss and Burkhart 1989; McCahill et al. 1979). The sexual coercion of men by women has also been documented (Muehlenhard and Cook 1988). Sometimes this coercion takes the form of threats made by a woman in a position of power over the man, such as an employer. These men undergo symptoms similar to those of the rape trauma syndrome but are afraid to tell others about their experiences for fear of not being believed (Smith, Pine, and Hawley 1988).

A number of men report that they have acted aggressively in sexual situations. Koss and her colleagues (1987) found that 7 percent of the college men in their study reported that they had engaged in behavior that Koss defined as date rape or attempted date rape and 25 percent had engaged in sexually aggressive behavior. In interviews conducted by Malamuth and Cook (1984), one out of three college men indicated that in a hypothetical situation they would be likely to force sex with an unwilling woman if they could be guaranteed not to be caught or punished. Stets and Pirog-Good (1989) point out that date rape represents more than simply a desire for sex. It also shows a desire on the part of the perpetrator to dominate and control the victim in cases where a disagreement over sex has occurred. Social scientists, such as Koss, are attempting to point out that women are taken advantage of in sexual situa-

more likely than females to view the woman as interested in sex (Muehlenhard et al. 1985). Shotland and Craig (1988) conducted a study in which pairs of male and female college students engaged in a casual discussion. Other students viewed these conversations and specified whether they considered the behavior to be friendly or sexually interested. Behavior that male viewers saw as exhibiting sexual interest tended to be perceived by females as friendly behavior. The difficulty men sometimes have in distinguishing between female friendliness and sexual interest can lead a male to press for sex when the female would rather

Date rape is more difficult to prove than other forms of rape because, to many people, the context of a date implies a consent to sexual activity. In 1992, William Kennedy Smith was tried for date rape that allegedly occurred during a party at his family's Palm Beach estate.

woman had sexual intercourse when she didn't want to because a man gave her alcohol or drugs. He maintains that sexual encounters are complex and that many social scientists, such as Koss, do not allow for "emotional confusion, ambivalence, and vacillation" that people often feel in "the initial stages of intimacy" in a relationship.

Social scientists who argue that the incidence of date rape is exaggerated put more responsibility on the woman for avoiding sex, particularly in situations in which no strong physical force is used. Shotland and Goodstein (1983) interviewed college students and found that they tend to decide whether or not a sexual incident constitutes rape by trying to discover the degree of sexual desire on the part of the woman and the stage in the sexual encounter at which she objects to sex. For example, the researchers found that if a woman becomes fully disrobed before she says "no" to sex, both female and male college students tend to see her as responsible for precipitating sexual intercourse even though she objects to sex at that point. These researchers maintain that many sexual incidents fall in that fuzzy area where it is difficult to tell whether persuasion or coercion is being used.

tions far more often than has previously been assumed.

On the other side of the date rape debate are those social scientists, such as Gilbert (1991), who refer to date rape as a "phantom epidemic." Gilbert acknowledges that sexual assault on dates is a serious problem but maintains that the incidence of date rape presented by Koss (1987) and others (Russell 1984) is exaggerated by their use of too broad a definition of rape. He refers to Koss's date rape figures as "advocacy numbers," used create a public awareness of the problem and "to influence social policy for a good cause" (Gilbert 1991;64). Gilbert objects to including in the date rape count cases in which the

avoid or delay it. This problem is exacerbated by the tendency of some females to offer token resistance to sex.

Token Resistance

American society is often described as having developed "sexual scripts" in which the woman's role is to behave in a resistant manner when the man makes sexual overtures, while the man's role is to disregard her protest and persuade her to give in. Muehlenhard and Hollabaugh (1988) set out to see if this script is actually followed by women and if so, which women use this script. In a study of 610 female college students, one-third (39 percent) of the women said that they had engaged in *token resistance* to sex at least once, even though they had been willing to engage in intercourse at the time. The women who were most likely to make token protests were those who felt a moderate amount of guilt over sexual activity. In contrast, those females with high levels of sex guilt were likely to say no to sex and mean it. Women with low levels of sex guilt tended to avoid token resistance to sex. These were women with liberated sexual attitudes who were not afraid to show an interest in sex. Furthermore, women who offered token resistance to sex tended to believe that token resistance was a common behavior among women.

Muehlenhard and Hollabaugh (1988) argue that the double standard in American culture encourages a number of women to engage in token resistance. The double standard expects that men will be more interested in sex than women and encourages social disapproval of sexual initiative in women. Women acquire a stigma when they violate these social norms and are likely to be labeled "promiscuous," or "an easy lay." In this context, Muehlenhard and Hollabaugh maintain that token resistance is a rational action that some women take in order to avoid being chastised for their sexual behavior. Muehlenhard is not suggesting that all female resistance to sex is dishonest. It is important to keep in mind that Muehlenhard and her associates studied ritualized sexual behavior under conditions in which both partners found sex to be desirable. This study did not ask women about situations in which they wanted to avoid sex.

Unwanted Sex

Both men and women report that they have felt pressured to engage in unwanted sex. Muehlenhard and Cook (1988) interviewed 507 college men and 486 college women and found that over 90 percent of both men and women reported that they had at some time engaged in unwanted sexual activity ranging from breast fondling to intercourse. Unwanted sexual activity was defined as unwanted kissing, petting, or intercourse when the respondent would rather have avoided it. Almost half of the women interviewed (46 percent) and 63 percent of the men reported having experienced unwanted intercourse (Muehlenhard and Cook 1988:58). A major factor encouraging both men and women to engage in unwanted sex is traditional gender roles.

Traditional Gender Roles

There are important gender differences in the way in which men and women view the initiation of a sexual relationship. Males tend to encourage sexual intercourse, whereas females are more inclined to delay it (McCormick 1979; Rodgers and Rowe 1990). Unmarried students at a large midwestern university were asked what things their partners did to make them upset, irritated, hurt, or angry. Women tended to express anger and upset over male demands for sexual intimacy, whereas men expressed upset and anger over female sexual withholding and sexual rejection (Buss 1989). Because women suffer more direct consequences from pregnancy, they are motivated to delay sexual encounters.

Traditional Female Gender Role

Traditionally, women have played the role of the "gatekeeper" who is expected to set limits in sexual situations. Yet, in spite of the woman's gatekeeping position, the traditional female gender role sometimes inhibits women from dealing effectively with unwanted sexual advances. Traditional feminine traits such as passivity, nurturance, helpfulness, and submissiveness often lead the woman to defer to the man's decisions. In addition, female socialization encourages women to place the needs of others, especially those of a man, above their own needs in importance (Murnen et al. 1989). In the interview at the beginning of this chapter, the female college student refused to have sex and then later felt guilty for not meeting her partner's sexual needs. Because women are taught to be kind and compassionate, refusing sex can be awkward (Muehlenhard and Cook 1988). In addition, the tendency for women to blame themselves for unwanted sexual activity arises out of the female "gatekeeping" role. Women are most likely to blame themselves when they knew the man well and when he used verbal persuasion rather than physical force to obtain sex (Murnen et al. 1989).

Traditional Male Gender Role

Men are socialized to have a more favorable view of casual sex than women (Carroll, Volk, and Hyde 1985). Males tend to view a hypothetical situation in which a stranger of the opposite sex touches "their sexual area" to be more pleasant than do females (Heslin, Nguyen, and Nguyen 1983). Nonetheless, men often feel pressured by the male gender role to pursue sex even when they would rather avoid it. The American image of masculinity depicts the man as perpetually interested in sex. This image makes it difficult for men to turn down sexual advances, or perceived sexual advances, from women. A number of college men report that they fear their female partners will think they are homosexual if they refuse a sexual advance. Furthermore, men worry that if they refuse a sexual advance from a woman she will think they do not consider her attractive (Murnen, Perot, and Byrne 1989).

The traditional male gender role sets up expectations that promote adversarial sexual encounters (Murnen, Perot, and Byrne 1989). Males are socialized to be dominant and sexually assertive and to initiate sexual advances. Men tend to view male virginity as a personal problem and are motivated to gain sexual experience. In one study, college men reported that they sometimes engaged in sex when they would rather have avoided it because of peer pressure and the desire for popularity (Muehlenhard and Cook 1988). Males who score high on measures of traditionality tend to interpret a woman's protests against having sex as part of a "game" or ritual rather than as a genuine objection (Shotland and Craig 1988). Traditional males are more likely than egalitarian males to agree with the statement, "Sometimes the only way to get a cold woman to turn on is to use force" (Burt 1980). When force is used to obtain sex, traditional males are more likely than egalitarian males to blame the victim and feel that the woman precipitated the incident by being a "tease" and getting the man excited, or by indicating an interest in sex through her nonverbal behavior (Shotland and Goodstein 1983). In contrast, males with egalitarian attitudes tend to see men and women as having an equal say in whether or not to have sex.

Next we turn to dating and sexual behavior among divorced persons.

Dating and Sexuality After Divorce

Until recently, only a few studies were available describing sexuality among divorced persons (Hunt 1974; Kinsey and Gebhard 1953). Today, new studies have raised questions about the sexual image of divorced people presented by these early studies (Stack and Gundlach 1992).

Is the Sexually Liberated Divorced Person a Myth?

The social image of divorced people over the last two decades has depicted them as sexually liberated. One classic and frequently cited study by Hunt (1974) found that divorced people had a variety of sex partners and had sex at least two times a week. However, this image of the sexually active divorced person has been challenged. A more recent study of sexuality among divorced persons by Stack and Gundlach (1992) revealed that divorced people are far more sexually conservative than previously thought. Three-fourths of divorced persons in the 1992 Stack and Gundlach study had either one sex partner or no sex partners, and divorced people had sex an average of twice a month. The presence or absence of children had no effect on the number of sex partners a divorced person had. Both parents and nonparents tended to be sexually conservative (Stack and Gundlach 1992).

There are two possible explanations for the large discrepancy in sexual activity reported in the Hunt study in 1974 and the Stack Gundlach study in 1992. These explanations are discussed below.

Flawed Sample. The sample used in the earlier Hunt (1974) study may have been flawed: 80 percent of the respondents refused to participate. Perhaps only those who were comfortable with their sexuality and who were more sexually active were willing to be interviewed. The more recent study by Stack and Gundlach (1992) used the General Social Survey based on a nationally representative sample. This survey sandwiched sexuality questions among other, more general, questions and had a much higher response rate. Therefore, the more recent study is probably more accurate.

Changing Sexual Behavior. The second possible explanation for the discrepancy between the 1974 and 1992 studies is that sexual behavior could have become more conservative over the last twenty years. The rising concern over sexually transmitted diseases, including AIDS, could have led to less casual sex. In addition, the increased social acceptance of cohabitation could have encouraged more monogamous sexual relationships among divorced people.

Divorce, Dating, and Stress

Divorce is one of the most stressful life events a person can experience (Gove and Shin 1989). African-American families tend to provide greater levels of social and emotional support in dealing with this stress than do white families, and there is less stigma attached to divorce in the African-American community than in the white community (Cherlin 1981; Gove and Shin 1989). In addition to relying on kin to ease the strain associated with divorce, many divorced people of both races look for support from a romantic partner. However, the difficulty of navigating the dating world and dealing with sexual issues can create additional strain. Clinicians have pointed out that sexual tensions in dating are an important factor contributing to anxiety, depression, and low self-esteem among divorced persons (Fisher, B., 1987; Stack and Gundlach 1992). Much of the tension associated with divorce and being in the dating arena is reduced when a divorced person finds a compatible partner and enters into cohabitation. Divorced persons who are cohabiting report a higher level of life happiness than noncohabiting divorced persons. In addition, cohabiting divorced persons report greater physical health than other divorced people (Kurdek 1991a). Cohabitation also reduces stress by improving the economic position of most divorced persons.

Courtship Prior to Remarriage

Since over half of all divorces involve children, a large number of divorced people in the dating world are parents. Montgomery and her colleagues (1992) used a representative national sample to study the pattern of courtship among divorced mothers who had remarried. Again, in this study, sexual behavior among divorced people appeared to be conservative. The women typically dated between three and five men before meeting their future spouse, and half of the women dated no other man after meeting the future marriage partner.

The courtship pattern that Montgomery and her colleagues uncovered among divorced mothers typically progressed through the following three stages before remarriage:

1. *Dating:* The first stage involved dating while living separately and lasted an average of five months.
2. *Partial cohabitation:* In the second stage the couple maintained separate residences but stayed together several nights a week. The duration of part-time cohabitation was typically four months, and over 90 percent of the women cohabited with their future husband at least part time before remarriage.
3. *Full-time cohabitation:* In full-time cohabitation the couple set up housekeeping together. This stage lasted approximately nine months before the couples married.

For those divorced people who are custodial parents, children play an important role in the courtship process. These parents use the dating process to try out future family roles. Over half of remarried mothers report that while dating their future husband, they and their partners included the children in their recreational activities at least once a week (Montgomery 1992).

Review Questions

1. Looking at the study by Shotland and Craig, in which conversations between male and female pairs were observed by other students, in what ways do men and women tend to interpret behavior differently?
2. What is token resistance to sex, and why do some women engage in this behavior?
3. How frequently does unwanted sex occur?
4. In what way does the traditional female gender role influence sexual behavior?
5. In what way does the traditional male gender role influence sexual behavior?
6. Is the image of the sexually liberated divorced person more myth or reality? What pattern does courtship usually take among divorced mothers?

From Romantic Love to Companionate Love

Sexual behavior, which we have been examining, often takes place within the context of romance. In the remainder of this chapter we look at different types of love, including romantic love, which involves a strong sexual attraction. Love has been described in a variety of ways and does not lend itself to a single definition. However, social investigators have identified two important types of love, romantic love and companionate love, which are explored in this section. Dorothy Tennov (1980) and other social scientists (Hatfield 1988; Jankowiak and Fischer 1992) maintain that love usually progresses through two stages: romantic love followed by companionate love. *Romantic love* is an intense, erotic attraction and yearning that idealizes the partner (Jankowiak and Fischer 1992). The fire and passion of romantic love tends to be replaced gradually by *companionate love,* a strong and enduring affection that is more peaceful and comfortable than romantic love (Hatfield 1988; Jankowiak and Fischer 1992; Tennov 1980).

Characteristics of Romantic Love

Dorothy Tennov (1980) interviewed over 1,000 college undergraduates and other adults; most of these respondents reported that their love relationships began with romantic love (which Tennov called "limerence"). The characteristics of romantic love that Tennov described are given below.

1. *Intrusive thoughts:* In romance, intrusive thoughts invade the lover's mind, interfering with concentration and productive work. This persistence of uninvited thoughts can give the lover a sense of being out of control.
2. *Mood Swings:* The emotional state of the lover becomes dependent on the perceived reactions of the loved one. Romance is experienced as an emo-

tional roller coaster of highs and lows, in which the feelings of the lover rise to heights of ecstasy when the loved one appears to respond with romantic interest.

3. *Idealization:* Romance involves a tendency to idealize the partner, viewing the partner as the romantic lover would like the partner to be. Idealization involves focusing attention on the positive characteristics of the partner and exaggerating those desirable traits. Conversely, unattractive traits that the individual would find offensive in anyone else are minimized.

4. *Exclusivity:* Exclusivity refers to the desire to have the romantic partner all

---

BOX 4.3   W o r l d   P e r s p e c t i v e s

Is Romantic Love Universal?

For decades, social scientists thought that romantic love was a product of modern Western culture. It was believed that romantic love arose along with modernization, free mate choice, and the belief in individualism. The elite classes of some non-Western cultures experienced romantic love, but this occurred primarily outside of marriage as extramarital affairs. Among the peasant classes, romantic love was thought to be absent except in the West.

Recent evidence challenges the assumption that romantic love is a Western development. In fact, it appears that romantic love may be a human universal, or near-universal, in that it is experienced by some individuals in all, or nearly all, societies. Jankowiak and Fisher (1992) examined ethnographies from 186 societies in order to find those in which romantic love was present. They distinguished between lust and romantic love. Lust was motivated by a desire for temporary sexual fulfillment. Romantic love, on the other hand, was an intense attraction that idealized the lover and that was expected to continue over time. In each society, the researchers looked for evidence of romantic love in such things as love songs, folklore describing romantic love, accounts of personal anguish and longing, and elopement motivated by mutual affection.

Romantic love was found in 89 percent of the societies examined. In the other 11 percent, the ethnographers made no mention of romantic love. However, this does not mean that romantic love was absent from these societies, because until a decade ago, ethnographers were not trained to look for indications of romantic love.

One example of romantic love came from the !Kung, a hunting and gathering society in the Kalihari desert of sub-Saharan Africa. A woman named Nisa described her romantic love for her lover as having "hearts on fire." However, she said that after a while "the fire cools." In contrast, Nisa described her love for her husband as "rich, warm, and secure" (Jankowiak and Fisher 1992: 152).

Jankowiak and Fisher (1992) found that stories similar to that of Romeo and Juliet are found in the folklore of many cultures to warn young people about the dangers of romantic love. Romantic love is potentially disruptive to the established social order. In most traditional societies, parents choose mates for their children and marriage is considered an agreement between two extended families. Romance as a basis for marriage would constitute a significant threat to the authority of kinship groups. However, it appears that in some traditional societies men are allowed more leeway than women to act on feelings of romantic love. In a recent study of four villages in Indonesia, men reported that they had a good deal of input into the selection of their marriage partners even though the marriages were arranged by parents. Women perceived themselves as having far less say in the matter of mate choice. When parents arranged a marriage, they often took the son's romantic wishes into account (Williams 1990).

BOX 4.4 A Closer Look

Do Men and Women Have Different Love Styles?

Lee (1973) interviewed people from a variety of backgrounds about their orientation toward love relationships. He identified the following six styles of love:

1. *Eros:* The erotic lover is passionate and emotionally intense, but not possessive or jealous. Sexual attraction is an important aspect of eros, but eros also involves a desire to get involved quickly by talking endlessly and openly. The eros lover usually has self-confidence and high self-esteem (Hendrick and Hendrick 1992).

2. *Mania:* The manic lover also seeks an emotionally intense relationship, but the love relationship is colored by the manic lover's insecurity. Manic lovers tend to be jealous, possessive, and worried about the loss of the relationship. Mania is characterized by highs and lows and physical symptoms of distress (Hendrick and Hendrick 1992).

3. *Agape* (pronounced a-GAH-pay): The agape lover is selfless or altruistic; agape is the rarest of Lee's styles of love. The agape lover is willing to make personal sacrifices for the partner and for the relationship. The agape lover views love in primarily spiritual rather than sexual terms (Hendrick and Hendrick 1992).

4. *Pragma:* Pragmatic lovers are practical in choosing a mate and know the characteristics, such as occupation, religion, or income, that they are looking for in a lover. For example, the pragmatic lover would try to avoid falling in love with someone who would not make a desirable marriage partner (Hendrick and Hendrick 1992; Laner 1989).

5. *Storge:* Storge is a slowly developing love based on friendship, companionship, and shared interests. Having a partner with similar attitudes and values is important to the storge lover. Storge love is secure and trusting, but unexciting and uneventful (Hendrick and Hendrick 1992; Laner 1989).

6. *Ludus:* Ludus describes the lover who is playful and "cool" rather than intense and "hot." Ludic lovers tend to think of love as a game for mutual enjoyment of the partners, and they enjoy sex as fun rather than as part of a committed relationship. Ludic lovers avoid becoming serious and often have multiple partners. The ludic lover typically states the "rules of the game" early in the relationship and has no intention of hurting the partner (Hendrick and Hendrick 1992).

Hendrick and colleagues (1984) developed a questionnaire based on Lee's six styles of love and found that all of Lee's love styles are found among both men and women. However, men and women report leaning toward different styles of love (Hendrick and Hendrick 1992). Men are much more approving of ludus (game-playing uncommitted love) than women. Women, on the other hand, reported

to oneself, a desire that gives rise to jealousy. The lover tends to see friends and activities outside the relationship as an interference with the romantic bond.

5. *Fear of rejection:* Fear of rejection appears to be an important element in the tension and anxiety associated with romance. Obstacles to the love relationship, such as doubts concerning the loved one's feelings, tend to intensify the feeling of love (Tennov 1980:46).

These five characteristics of romance—intrusive thoughts, mood swings, idealization, exclusivity, and fear of rejection—do not all have to be present for a state of romance to exist. Rather, a cluster of some or all of the traits are frequently present in the early stage of romantic relationships. However, these traits appeared so consistently in Tennov's interviews concerning romantic love that she said her

that they tended toward storge (friendly love), mania (insecure and possessive love), and pragma (practical mate choice) (Davis and Latty-Mann 1987; Hendrick et al. 1986, 1992). Women are socialized to be practical in their search for a mate who will also be an economic provider, and women also tend to be more concerned than men about combining love and friendship. In addition, women display more characteristics of manic love in that they report more physical symptoms associated with a love relationship than men. Hendrick and Hendrick (1992) suggest that perhaps women are more willing than men to admit their feelings of manic love.

In a study of love styles and life satisfaction among college students, additional gender differences appeared. Agape (selfless) love was associated with high levels of life satisfaction in women who used this love style. However, the use of an agape love style by men failed to produce this high level of life satisfaction. In contrast, men who engaged in manic (possessive) love and ludic (uncommitted game-playing) love tended to be very satisfied with life. The researchers point out that a double standard in love exists in which a number of men are comfortable with possessive or manipulative expressions of their love while women tend to be comfortable when they are making personal sacrifices. This double standard sometimes puts women at a disadvantage in love relationships (Yancey and Berglass 1991).

The style of love a person uses also affects satisfaction with marital relationships. Experiencing eros (intense romantic and sexual love) tends to be associated with high levels of marital satisfaction (Hen-

drick and Hendrick 1992). In addition, the style of love used by the wife influences a man's marital satisfaction. In one study of married couples, wives who expressed agape (selfless) love tended to have husbands with high marital satisfaction. In contrast, wives whose love style was categorized as mania (possessive love) tended to have husbands who were dissatisfied with the marital relationship. Surprisingly, the style of love used by husbands was unrelated to the wife's marital satisfaction (Martin et al. 1990). Perhaps wives have a greater tendency to make adjustments to accommodate the love style of the spouse.

Ethnic differences also influence love styles. Asian students tend to endorse pragma (practical love) and storge (friendly love). Hendrick and Hendrick (1992) point out that traditional Asian culture puts more emphasis on the group than on the individual "self" and tends to emphasize the less emotional expressions of love. Like Anglos, Mexican-American men tend to approve of ludus (game-playing uncommitted love) much more than Mexican-American women. Mexican-American men often expect to be the first sexual lover of the woman they marry but also expect to establish their masculinity through multiple sexual relationships. On the other hand, Mexican-American women, particularly those who have recently arrived in the United States, need to be pragmatic in choosing a mate and family breadwinner (Hendrick and Hendrick 1992).

research task was a simple, straightforward one, namely, to record the consistent themes which she found.

Does Romance Have a Biological Basis?

Psychologist Stanley Schachter, in his *two-component theory of emotions,* maintains that when a person experiences any emotion, including romantic love, two components of the emotion are present. First, the person experiences physiological arousal, and second, the person applies a label to the physiological response (Berscheid and Walster 1974). Some biologically oriented anthropologists and psychologists have suggested that the experience of romantic love is probably related to a biochemical response in the brain (Fischer, H., 1987; Jankowiak and Fischer 1992; Leigh 1990; Perper 1985). The chemical phenylethylamine (PEA), a compound similar to amphetamine, has been associated with the feeling of romantic love (Jankowiak and Fischer 1992; Liebowitz 1983). PEA has a mood-elevating effect, bringing about a feeling of giddiness, euphoria, and optimism. PEA may also be responsible for the extra energy often felt by romantic lovers (Jankowiak and Fischer 1992). The crash that lovers feel after a break-up may be related to amphetamine withdrawal (Hatfield and Rapson 1987). If the feeling of romantic love turns out to be related to a biochemical response in the brain, then the ability to experience romantic love would be present in the members of all societies, even though the society may suppress or channel the love experience (Fisher, H., 1987; Jankowiak and Fischer 1992; Leigh 1990).

Characteristics of Companionate Love

Over time, the excitement of romantic love tends to give way to a calmer *companionate love* (Hatfield 1988; Jankowiak and Fischer 1992; Tennov 1980). Tennov (1980) found that people who experienced companionate love were not burdened with intrusive thoughts and had their minds clear so that they could concentrate on productive work. The companionate love relationship was more emotionally even than romantic love because it lacked the mood swings from ecstasy to despair that characterize romance. Also missing in companionate love was the intense need for exclusivity. People involved in companionate love tended to have friendships and activities outside the love relationship. The idealization of the partner typical of romance gave way to a more realistic assessment of the partner's character in companionate love. Lastly, companionate love tended to generate greater feelings of security and acceptance than romantic love produced (Tennov 1980).

Sternberg's Triangular Theory of Love

Love is a combination of erotic attraction and deep, enduring affection.

Robert Sternberg (1986) rejects Tennov's (1980) assumption that there is an inevitable progression in which romantic love becomes transformed into companionate love. He argues that it is possible to maintain over time love relationships that contain the passion of romantic love as well as the comfort of companionate love.

In his *triangular theory of love,* Sternberg combines elements of both romantic love and companionate love into a single description of love. According to Sternberg (1986), love has three components: passion, intimacy, and commitment.

1. *Passion:* Passion is the erotic or motivational component of love, which involves physical attraction and physiological arousal.

2. *Intimacy:* Intimacy refers to the emotional component of love, which includes feelings of closeness, connectedness, and support. Intimacy gives rise to feelings of warmth in the relationship.

3. *Commitment:* Commitment is the cognitive component of love, which involves thought and decision making. Sternberg defines commitment as a decision to maintain the love relationship.

According to Sternberg (1986), all three components of love—passion, intimacy, and commitment—must be present in order for love to be complete. When only one element is present, we do not have genuine love. When a person feels only passion, the experience is one of infatuation. Intimacy by itself produces liking. Commitment without either passion or intimacy is empty love.

Sternberg (1986) has explored what happens when one of the three components of love is missing. He argues that romantic love contains passion and intimacy but lacks commitment. This lack of commitment creates anxiety and makes romantic love volatile. Sternberg also views companionate love as having a missing component. Companionate love contains commitment and intimacy, but passion has gone out of the relationship. Companionate love is comfortable and close, but does not arouse excitement. The third type of incomplete love is *fatuous love,* which involves commitment and passion without intimacy. An example of fatuous love is a couple who meet and become engaged two weeks later. They make a commitment based on passion before intimacy can develop.

Passion is the component of love that is least under conscious control and that is most difficult to maintain over time. Sternberg (1986) suggests that one way to help retain passion is to assess whether or not the love relationship is meeting individual needs. Then each partner can make an effort to meet the needs of the other. In contrast, commitment is the component of love that is most under conscious control. Sternberg argues that expressing passion and maintaining intimacy by communicating thoughts and feelings helps to keep commitment strong.

Reiss's Wheel Theory of Love

Both Sternberg and Tennov attempted to define the characteristics of love. Sociologist Ira Reiss (1980) takes a different approach and describes the process of developing a love relationship. Reiss's *wheel theory of love* maintains that a person goes through four stages when falling in love: rapport, self-revelation, mutual dependency, and intimacy need fulfillment.

1. *Rapport:* The process of developing a love relationship begins with the first meeting in which the couple attempt to establish *rapport.* In this stage each person assesses whether or not he or she feels at ease and free to talk to the other person. Reiss refers to rapport as the "first door" that must be opened in order for love to develop.

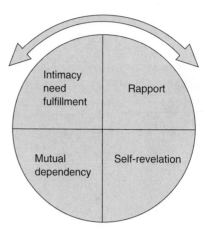

Figure 4.2
Reiss's Wheel Theory of Love

Source: Adapted from Figure 5.1 page 129 in Ira L. Reiss, 1980, *Family Systems in America,* Third Edition. New York: Holt, Rinehart and Winston.

2. *Self-revelation:* When rapport is established and people feel trusting and relaxed enough, they begin to engage in *self-revelation,* which involves sharing personal information about themselves. Throughout this and the other stages of falling in love, the sociocultural background and social roles of the couple influence the course taken by the love relationship. For example, through self-revelation the couple may discover that they have very different views of male and female gender roles. If the woman holds egalitarian beliefs about gender roles and the man has a traditional view of gender roles, the relationship may break off in the self-revelation phase. For a more complete discussion of self-revelation, see Chapter 7, Marriage and Partnerships: Interpersonal Relationships.

3. *Mutual dependency:* If all goes well, the couple progresses to the *mutual dependency* stage, in which the partners cooperate in doing things together and come to depend on each other. For example, each partner needs the other as an audience for jokes, as a companion for going to the movies, and often as a partner in sexual experiences. Sociocultural background is also important here. If one partner perceives the joint activities as objectionable, he or she may pull away from the relationship.

4. *Intimacy need fulfillment:* Finally, the couple enters the stage of *intimacy need fulfillment.* This stage is the result of the processes that occurred in the first three stages (rapport, self-revelation, and mutual dependency). Intimacy need fulfillment involves having a partner in whom to confide and who listens. Intimacy consists of a feeling of closeness and the desire for some privacy in the relationship.

Reiss's wheel of love, depicted in Figure 4.2, can turn in either direction. The relationship can move in the direction of greater or lesser love. For example, partners who are becoming less engaged with each other move from the stage of intimacy need fulfillment to a stage of mutual dependency with less intimacy. Therefore, Reiss's wheel theory presents a dynamic picture of the love relationship.

Love Relationships and Social Networks

Because love rarely develops in a vacuum, we now turn to the social networks that influence love relationships. The kind of relationship a person has with her or his *social network* of friends and relatives tends to change when that person falls in love. A social network is a group of people with whom a person interacts on a face-to-face basis. Catherine Surra (1990) reviewed research that has tested two major hypotheses in the area of romance and social networks: the withdrawal-integration hypothesis and the Romeo and Juliet hypothesis. These two hypotheses are discussed below.

Withdrawal-Integration Hypothesis

The *withdrawal-integration hypothesis* states that as people fall in love, they tend to withdraw from their social network of friends. Then as they begin to detach from the love relationship, people become reintegrated with friends. The research on social networks supports this hypothesis. The average number of friends in a person's social network tends to decrease as the couple becomes more committed to the romantic relationship. As the love relationship develops, it consumes an increasing amount of the lovers' emotional energy. Nonetheless, lovers do not typically shy away from all friends. People in a romantic relationships generally withdraw from their less close friends and add some of the

lover's close friends and family to their social network. However, even with these new additions, there tends to be an overall decrease in the size of a lover's social network. The reverse occurs when people begin to detach from the romantic relationship. As partners become less involved with one another, they typically become reintegrated into their network of family and friends (Surra 1990).

Romeo and Juliet Hypothesis

There is considerable interest in the degree to which family mem-

In texts as old as the Bible, lovers have been portrayed as desirous of the "forbidden fruit." The love of Romeo and Juliet only became stronger when their parents objected to their union. In real life, this trend is found in accelerated romances; relationships that progress slowly generally require the support of the social network.

bers can successfully interfere with a romance. The Romeo and Juliet hypothesis states that when parents express opposition to a romance, the romance grows stronger. Surra (1987) found that the Romeo and Juliet hypothesis was supported only in cases in which couples experienced an accelerated romance, moved quickly to commitment, and then lost momentum. Apparently, for these couples the opposition of family and friends initially strengthened the romance and later had the opposite effect, weakening the romantic relationship.

However, most romances progress more slowly, and the Romeo and Juliet hypothesis was not supported for these slowly developing love relationships. In most romances, involvement with the dating partner declines when the social network attempts to interfere with the love relationship. The type of social networks most likely to oppose the romance of one of their members are tightly knit networks of family and friends. Such tightly knit social networks are often reluctant to share their members with outsiders. Conversely, loosely knit social networks are less resistant when members begin romantic relationships (Surra 1990).

Approval of Social Networks

In most cases the approval of the social network is an important factor in a person's decision to continue a romantic relationship. Romantic involvement tends to be strengthened when a person's social network approves of the relationship. More specifically, measures of love, commitment, and time spent with the partner increase when the social network is supportive of the romantic relationship. Thus the Romeo and Juliet hypothesis is not valid for most relationships (Surra 1990).

Review Questions

1. What does Tennov see as the characteristics of romantic love? What does Tennov see as the characteristics of companionate love?
2. What are the three components of Sternberg's triangle of love? What problem does Sternberg describe with romantic love and companionate love?
3. What are the four stages of Reiss's wheel theory, which explains the process by which love relationships develop?
4. In studying social networks, what is the withdrawal-integration hypothesis? Does research support or refute this hypothesis?
5. What is the Romeo and Juliet hypothesis? Under what conditions is the Romeo and Juliet hypothesis supported? Under what conditions is the Romeo and Juliet hypothesis not supported?

Love Ideology

We now examine how love ideology influences the behavior of people who fall in love. A *love ideology* is a set of beliefs or cultural ideals related to love. We tend to judge our experiences with romantic love by holding those experiences up to a cultural ideal that specifies what love should be like (Cancian and Gordon 1988).

Defining Love by Its Feminine Expression

Love ideology throughout the twentieth century has assigned women the primary responsibility for maintaining love relationships. Underlying this aspect of love ideology is the belief that women understand love better than men and are better at expressing love. Men and women often show love in different ways. Women tend to be *expressive* in love relationships, emphasizing the verbal expression of love and emotional closeness. Men, on the other hand, tend to show their love in *instrumental* ways by providing economically for the family and through having sex. American culture places greater value on the female style of demonstrating love while the male style is devalued. Therefore, women tend to be viewed as more skilled than men at love relationships (Cancian 1987; Simon et al. 1992). This assumption can be frustrating to men, who sometimes feel criticized for not adequately expressing their love.

The feminine emphasis in love ideology also creates stress for women by assigning them the primary responsibility for making the love relationship run smoothly. Cancian and Gordon (1988) point out that women's magazines often contain articles explaining how a woman can change her behavior in order to improve the love relationship. In contrast, men's magazine articles on romantic relationships tend to focus either on sexual fantasies or on methods of attracting women. Because love tends to be defined by its feminine expression, women, more than men, are expected to make changes in their behavior in order to make a relationship work (Cancian and Gordon 1988).

Traditional love ideology views love as self-sacrifice.

Traditional Love Ideology: Love as Self-Sacrifice

Romantic love during the first half of the twentieth century stressed commitment, self-sacrifice, and dependence; these expectations were applied more to women than to men. Women were expected to put their needs aside and concentrate on fulfilling the needs of the partner. This ideology of *love as self-sacrifice* was captured very well in Cuber and Harroff's (1966) description of *vital marriage.* In the 1960s vital marriage was considered an ideal form of marriage that couples were urged to emulate (Marks 1989). Vital marriage was characterized by "heroic sacrifices" for the benefit of the partnership and a consuming interest in the romantic relationship so that thoughts of the partner dominated the person's attention. In the vital marriage, activities were "flat and uninteresting" if they did not include the partner (Cuber and Harroff 1966:56).

Reaction Against Love as Self-Sacrifice

The ideology of love as self-sacrifice has been widely criticized by modern social scientists for two reasons. First, Marks (1989) argues that the quality of a love relationship is diminished when one partner focuses attention almost entirely on the partnership and ignores activities, hobbies, and friends outside the partnership. The dependency of one partner often creates strain in the relationship (Marks 1989). Second, the ideology of love as self-sacrifice has been criticized for encouraging an unequal distribution of power in love relationships (Cancian and Gordon 1988). Because the love as self-sacrifice ideology applied primarily to women, this belief system tended to place men in a position of superior power in the love relationship. The man's needs were considered to be more important than the woman's needs, and women were encouraged to show a loving attitude by putting their own needs aside (Cancian and Gordon 1988), for example, (1) by giving up close ties to family, friends, and co-workers and agreeing to migrate when the husband has an attractive job offer; (2) by spending time with his friends if he objects to hers; (3) by taking an interest in his hobbies, such as attending the stock car races, while letting her own interests slide; and (4) by giving up some of her career aspirations in order to have the time to provide domestic support services, such as cooking and cleaning, which free him to concentrate on his career.

Modern Love Ideology: Love as Self-Development

As women entered the work force in increasing numbers in the 1960s and 1970s, the ideology of love began to change. Modern love ideology emphasizes self-development and individualism for both partners (Simon, et al. 1992; Swidler 1980). However, the most profound shift has taken place in attitudes women are expected to have toward love relationships (Cancian and Gordon 1988). The ideology of *love as self-development* urges women to seek their own personal fulfillment in education and a career rather focus solely on emotionally supporting the husband in the development of his career and hobbies. However, Cancian (1987) maintains that the new ideology of love reflects an interdependence between husband and wife, rather than the wife's independence from the husband and family.

In this time of social change, couples continue to seek satisfaction in their love relationships; this is the topic of the next section.

Love and Relationship Satisfaction

The last aspect of love that we examine is satisfaction with love relationships. Two of the explanations for love satisfaction come from exchange theory and the theory of the three-cornered self.

Exchange Theory

Exchange theory maintains that people weigh the rewards and costs of a relationship (Surra 1990). According to exchange theory, people tend to be satisfied with a love relationship when they perceive that the rewards they receive are equal to the rewards they provide to the partner. Partners offer resources to each other, and these resources constitute rewards in the relationship. Resources offered can be such things as companionship, affection, sex, or domestic services. Partners tend to be content when they perceive that the resources they offer are equivalent to the level of resources they receive (Hatfield et al. 1985; Sprecher 1992). Conversely, when a person perceives inequity in a relationship, feelings of distress are produced (Sprecher 1992).

Overbenefitted and Underbenefitted Partners. Sprecher (1992) interviewed a sample of over 500 undergraduate college students in order to test exchange theory. She presented college students with a hypothetical situation in which they were told that they underbenefitted from a love relationship. Respondents were told, "You feel that you are contributing more (in love, effort, time, emotions, tasks) than your partner is. . . . You feel that you are getting a worse deal than your partner." Students were asked what action, if any, they would take in a love relationship in which they underbenefitted. Gender had an important influence on the responses. Women in an underbenefitting relationship reported that they would expect to ask their partners to increase what that partner contributed to the relationship. Likewise, in an overbenefitting relationship in which they received more benefits than they provided to the partner, women reported that they would restore equity by increasing what they contributed to the relationship. Men, on the other hand, said that they were likely to do nothing in both cases of inequity.

These answers were consistent with the respondents' descriptions of their actual love relationships. Women reported that in past romantic relationships they, rather than their male partners, typically brought up discussions of equity in the relationship. The women either adjusted their own behavior or asked the partner for changes in his behavior.

Another perspective on satisfaction in love relationships is provided by Marks's theory of the three-cornered self, which is the topic of the next section.

People in a love relationship are generally happiest when they feel that what they give and what they receive are equivalent.

Marks's Theory of the Three-Cornered Self

Marks (1989) depicts the "self" as a triangle in which each of the three corners represents a separate identity within the individual. The partnership corner refers to a person's identity as part of a couple. The outside corner represents that part of a person's identity which is derived from such things as a job, hobbies, sports, and friends other than the partner. The inner corner represents a person's feelings, past history, inner experience, and thoughts. Marks maintains that the way an individual builds an identity within the love relationship helps to determine that person's satisfaction with that relationship.

Relationship Satisfaction. According to Marks, relationship satisfaction is highest when both partners give attention to all three corners of the self (see Figure 4a). Conversely, when too great an emphasis is focused on any one identity, relationship satisfaction is reduced. Marks points out that an uncomfortable situation develops when one partner identifies strongly with the partnership corner and the other partner identifies primarily with the outside corner. This situation is illustrated in Figure 4.3b. The person identified with the partnership corner seeks to merge with the partner, while the other partner seeks independence and separation within the relationship. People who see themselves primarily as part of a couple often begin to live through the partner, taking on the partner's interests and hobbies, talking a great deal about the partner in conversation with others and thinking about the partner when the partner is not around. In the sample of respondents interviewed by Marks, it was rare for both partners to identify strongly with the relationship corner to the near exclusion of the other

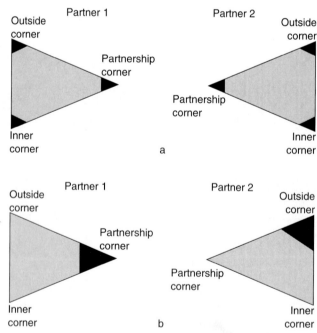

Figure 4.3a,b
Marks's Three-Cornered Self

(A) Identities that Foster Relationship Satisfaction. (B) Identities that Inhibit Relationship Satisfaction.

two corners. When one partner was strongly identified with the partnership corner, the second partner's identity was likely to be based on experiences outside the relationship, in work, friendships, and hobbies.

When one person's identity becomes fused with the partnership corner, a dynamic tension develops in which the dependent person pursues the partner, trying to get the partner's attention and trying to please the partner. Meanwhile, the other partner seeks emotional distance from the relationship. In Marks's sample, wives were more likely than husbands to identify with the partnership corner and seek the approval and attention of the spouse. Husbands in Marks's sample tended to pull away from the relationship and attempt to gain some emotional distance. As this happens, power becomes more and more skewed in the husband's direction because the person who is backing away emotionally has more power in the relationship. Meanwhile, the partner who is pursuing the relationship complains of receiving "emotional crumbs" because of the other partner's scant attention to the partnership (Marks 1989:19). Although this focus on the partnership corner tended to be typical of the wife, it could occur in either partner.

Dependence versus Autonomy. Any relationship faces some tension between dependence and autonomy (Marks 1989). If a partner moves too far in the direction of dependence, there is a risk that his or her identity can be overwhelmed by the relationship. On the other hand, with too much *autonomy*, or independence and self-direction, the danger exists that a person can become so involved in job, children, friends, or hobbies that the partnership suffers. Ammons and Stinnett (1980) found that satisfaction with love relationships tended to be high when the "self" is autonomous and also has an active participation in the partnership. Marks (1989) also found relationship quality to be high in people whose attention regularly made the rounds to all corners of the identity triangle. Such people would be actively involved with their identity as a partner, with their identity derived from outside interests, and with their inner self. Such people avoid having their identity fuse with any one corner and, instead, keep all three identities active.

Review Questions

1. What does Cancian mean when she says that love is defined by its feminine expression? What is meant by the ideology of love as self-sacrifice? To which gender did this love ideology apply? When was this love ideology the dominant viewpoint on love?

2. What is meant by love as self-development?

3. According to exchange theory, what determines satisfaction in love relationships? How do women typically respond when they are in a love relationship in which they are underbenefitted? How do men and women differ in their responses to inequity?

4. What are the three corners, or three identities, of Marks's three-cornered self? What happens when one partner focuses on the partnership corner and the other focuses on the outside corner of the self? According to Marks, what produces satisfaction with the love relationship?

Summary

1. Shotland and Craig's study of conversations between men and women found that behavior interpreted as sexually interested by men was often interpreted as friendly by women.

2. The women who are most likely to engage in token resistance are those with a moderate amount of sex guilt.

3. The traditional female gender role makes women vulnerable to unwanted sex. The traditional male gender role can also influence male sexual behavior.

4. Divorced people are probably more sexually conservative than previously thought. Remarried mothers followed a three-stage courtship process that includes partial cohabitation and full cohabitation.

5. Tennov sees love as developing in two stages: from romantic love to companionate love. Romantic love includes intrusive thoughts, mood swings, idealization, exclusivity, and fear of rejection. Companionate love is more emotionally even.

6. Sternberg views love as having three components: intimacy, passion, and commitment. Sternberg argues that romantic love and companionate love are incomplete because romantic love lacks commitment and companionate love lacks passion.

7. Reiss's wheel theory of love maintains that people go through four stages when they fall in love. First comes rapport, then self-revelation, mutual dependency, and intimacy need fulfillment.

8. In studies of social networks, the withdrawal-integration hypothesis has been supported. The Romeo and Juliet hypothesis has been supported only for couples who rapidly commit to a relationship and then lose interest.

9. Love has traditionally been defined by its feminine expression, making women responsible for maintaining love relationships. Recently, love ideology has shifted from an emphasis on self-sacrifice to an emphasis on self-development, particularly for women.

10. According to exchange theory, people weigh the costs and benefits of love relationships, and women are more likely than men to seek change in a relationship they perceive as inequitable.

11. Marks's theory of the three-cornered self holds that relationship satisfaction is highest when a person pays attention to all three corners of the self.

Key Words

The Sexual Revolution	The Double Standard
The Selfish Standard	Token Resistance
Traditional Female Gender Role	Traditional Male Gender Role
Romantic Love	Companionate Love
Two-Component Theory of Emotions	Phenylethylamine (PEA)
Sternberg's Triangular Theory of Love	Passion
Commitment	Intimacy
Reiss's Wheel Theory	Rapport

Self-Revelation
Intimacy Need Fulfillment
Withdrawal-Integration Hypothesis
Love Ideology
Instrumental Demonstration of Love
Love as Self-Development
Exchange Theory
Autonomy

Mutual Dependency
Social Networks
Romeo and Juliet Hypothesis
Expressive Demonstration of Love
Love as Self-Sacrifice
Vital Marriage
Marks's Theory of the Three-
Cornered Self

Resources

Planned Parenthood
810 Seventh Ave.
New York, NY, 10019
(212) 541-7800
Offers information on contraception, abortion, sexual health, and infertility. Operates 900 centers with family planning services nationwide.

National Gay and Lesbian Task Force
1517 U St., N.W.
Washington, DC 20009
(202) 332-6483
Advocates the elimination of prejudice based on sexual orientation; lobbies for gay rights and legislative reform. Publishes *National Gay and Lesbian Task Force Report,* quarterly.

Sex and Love Addicts Anonymous
P.O. Box 119, New Town Br.
Boston, MA 02258
A national network of self-help groups for people addicted to love and sex, who form desperate attachments to another person. Uses an adaptation of the twelve-step program of Alcoholics Anonymous.

Sex-N-Addiction
P.O. Box 759
Willimantic, CT 06226
(203) 423-2344
Addresses emotionally addictive, self-destructive love relationships that jeopardize emotional and physical well-being. Publishes *Self-Help Starter Packet.*

Samaritans
500 Commonwealth Ave.
Kenmore Square
Boston, MA 02215
Members volunteer to spend time with depressed and suicidal people. Publishes booklets.

Patterns of Mate Choice and Cohabitation

Michael was attracted to Julie's shoulder-length auburn hair and hazel eyes when they met in a Humanities class. Julie noticed Michael's friendliness and warm smile. As they became better acquainted, they talked about their dreams and what they wanted out of life in discussions that went late into the night. Michael admired couples who had an equal partnership, and he encouraged Julie in her plans to teach second grade. Julie was impressed with Michael's future career possibilities in his field of math and computer science. They both considered family and children to be important, and they seemed perfectly suited to each other.

Nonetheless, Michael was beginning to develop some doubts about Julie. She had dropped two classes this semester, frequently mentioned marriage and children, and had insisted that they spend last Saturday afternoon taking her eighteenth-month-old niece to the park. He wondered how they could have an equal relationship if she did not seem serious about finishing college and obtaining her teaching credential. He wanted a wife who would help save money for a down payment on a house and who would make a stimulating conversationalist and companion. On the other hand, he liked her support for his career. He was pleased that she stayed up all night to type his term paper last week, even though it meant that she had to turn her own paper in late.

Julie was also developing doubts about Michael. After talking about the importance of family and children, he pouted and complained when they took her niece to the park. She was beginning to wonder what kind of father he would make. She was also a little irritated because he went out drinking with his friends last week and left her to type his term paper. But she chalked his behavior up to college exuberance and blowing off steam. She was sure that he would settle down once they were married. Besides, he had such high potential for success in his career. (Composite interviews by author.)

As Michael and Julie discovered, relationships have both advantages and disadvantages that makes choosing a partner a complex and sometimes confusing task. In this chapter we explore some of the theories that explain the process of mate choice. In addition, we look at demographic patterns in mate choice, including the marriage squeeze, the trend toward delayed marriage, interracial marriage, and teen marriage. Finally, the strong trend toward cohabitation is examined, along with the characteristics of cohabitors, explanations for cohabitation, and the risk of divorce among those who have formerly cohabited.

Theories of Mate Choice

Social scientists have long been interested in the factors that lead men and women like Michael and Julie to choose each other as romantic partners and mates in marriage. Many theories attempt to explain the process of mate selection. Three of these are discussed below: exchange theory, stimulus-value-role theory, and systems theory.

Exchange Theory

Exchange theory (Homans 1961) focuses on the social assets and liabilities that each partner brings to a relationship. According to exchange theory, the choice of a partner depends on the perception that the assets and liabilities of the partner are roughly equivalent to one's own assets and liabilities. Michael sees Julie's assets as her attractiveness and her support for his career. However, he is not certain that she will finish college, and he sees her low level of commitment to her classes as a liability. Michael doesn't want to complain, however, because he feels lucky to have Julie as a girlfriend. He thinks that other women would probably find him boring because he is a math major. On the whole, he feels that the assets he and Julie have to offer each other are in balance.

According to exchange theory, both partners seek mates who will maximize their rewards from marriage. A person does not wind up with an ideal mate, but rather with a reasonable choice given the person's own assets and liabilities. It has been said that only people with a great number of assets freely choose each other, while those with substantial liabilities settle for each other (Murstein 1980:786).

Exchange theory has been useful in describing a society with traditional marital roles in which the male is a breadwinner and the woman either stays home and raises children or has a low income. In that case, marriage is viewed as an exchange between a woman's social characteristics, such as beauty, sociability, and domestic services, and a man's economic resources. When a forty-five-year-old executive marries his attractive twenty-eight-year-old secretary who has been longing to quit her job and stay home to raise children, an exchange of assets has taken place. Exchange theory would hold that he has traded his economic status and ability to support a family for her youth and beauty. Today, women bring economic assets into the mate selection process in the form of their current or future earning power.

Although exchange theory is built on an economic model, the social exchange that takes place in mate selection differs from a purely economic exchange (Blau 1964). In an economic exchange, the items being exchanged are clearly specified. However, in a social exchange a person offers a characteristic such as helpfulness or sociability as a gift and the exact item expected in return is not stated. When Julie offers support for Michael's career by typing his paper, she does not require that Michael agree to give her something specific in return. "Since the recipient is the one who decides when and how to reciprocate for a favor, or whether to reciprocate at all, social exchange requires trusting others . . . " (Blau 1974). For the relationship to continue, exchange theory holds that each person must feel that the overall assets and liabilities exchanged by the partners are roughly equivalent.

A Test of Exchange Theory. Support for exchange theory was found by Schoen and Wooldredge (1989) in their review of marriage records in North Carolina and Virginia. The researchers reasoned that in selecting a mate, women would be concerned with a male's potential earning power. It is still primarily the male's income that places the couple in a social class position and gives the couple status in the community. Male educational attainment is closely related to his occupation and earning power. Therefore, the researchers used information on the educational attainment of grooms, as recorded on marriage records, as an indicator of male earning power.

Schoen and Wooldredge found a strong tendency for an exchange to be made between a man's higher educational attainment and a woman's younger age among

BOX 5.1   A Closer Look

Mexican American Mate Choice

The traditional pattern of mate selection among Mexican Americans in south Texas during the 1920s and 1930s followed customs similar to those in Mexico. Traditional Mexican-American culture did not allow dating. However, young men and women did meet and get to know each other through school, church activities, and family events. When a young man was ready to marry, his family sent a *portador* to visit the girl's parents to convey the young man's interest in marriage. A portador was a go-between or marriage broker who was often the young man's godparent or uncle. The use of the portador protected the family's reputation; it would be embarrassing for the groom and his family to have the marriage proposal directly turned down in a face-to-face meeting. The portador spoke primarily with the girl's father, but afterward the husband and wife consulted with one another and the daughter's opinion was sought. The girl's family then took some time to evaluate the young man's moral character and his ability to be a good provider. If the young man was considered unsuitable, the girl's parents would often communicate their disapproval indirectly by postponing their decision. When the portador and the boy's family became discouraged while waiting for an answer, they began to look elsewhere for a bride. That way, the man's family did not suffer the humiliation of being directly rejected.

When the girl's parents accepted a marriage offer, the prospective groom and his parents visited the girl's family. With this second visit, "la segunda visita," the girl was considered to be betrothed. She had a new social status, and her family became even more protective of her. She could no longer go out with her friends. The couple still could not date but met at the girl's house under the watchful eye of a family chaperon.

Weddings were large and served the function of bringing the kinship group together and reaffirming extended family ties. Relatives and close friends helped pay the costs of the wedding. The couple had a number of sponsors who bought items that would be used at the wedding. The main sponsors, "los primeros padrinos," who were usually kin or close family friends, bought the wedding cake and later would give the couple advice when marital conflict arose. Other sponsors provided the "lazo," a rosary that was placed around the bride and groom during the wedding to symbolize their oneness and lifelong commitment. Thirteen coins were provided by another sponsor. The priest blessed the coins during the wedding ceremony to symbolize the husband's

white marriage partners. In other words, white men tended to marry younger, less educated white women. It is possible that the men were trading their superior earning power for the women's admiration and submissiveness, derived from their more precarious economic position.

Among nonwhite marriage partners, Schoen and Wooldredge found a different pattern. For example, among African Americans the exchange between a man's greater education and a woman's younger age did not hold. African-American women tend to marry less educated African-American men. Schoen and Wooldredge explain this pattern by pointing out that the exchange process is influenced by the *field of eligibles*. The field of eligibles is the pool of people available for marriage. Educated African-American women have a field of eligibles with relatively few well educated African-American men (Goldman et al. 1984). Thus, African-American women tend to marry African-American men with less education.

The reasons for the shortage of African-American males available for marriage are complex. Racial discrimination has led to a high unemployment rate among young African-American men, which runs twice the rate of white male unemployment. The lack of employment opportunities in the ghetto leads to a high level of

Modern Mexican-American Mate Choice

Today couples have more freedom to see each other outside the family setting and come to the decision to marry with very little parental intervention. The portador is no longer used, and the young man personally visits the girl's parents either to announce the marriage or to ask for permission to marry, which is mainly a formality. Parental authority in Mexican-American mate choice has been eroded over the last thirty years.

Parental approval of the marriage is still important. Couples who marry in a civil ceremony suffer a stigma because civil ceremonies usually mean that either the parents disapproved of the match or the girl was pregnant. Catholic priests are reluctant to marry a couple when the girl is pregnant, although some priests will respond to pressure from the parents and perform the wedding ceremony even when a pregnancy is involved. The wedding reception has been shortened to a few hours rather than an entire day and no longer represents the bringing together of a large kinship group. Fewer extended kin are willing to travel long distances to the wedding than in the past. In the middle class of business and professional families, today there are often more friends than family at weddings.

A wedding provides an opportunity for the extended Mexican-American family to come together, reinforcing the social bonds within what is often a very large group.

provider role and to express the hope that the future family would not be without money. Women in the bride's family cooked food and served it after the ceremony at a cerebration that lasted all day. Weddings provided entertainment and promoted the integration and solidarity of the extended kin group.

Source: Summarized from Norma Williams 1990. *The Mexican American Family: Tradition and Change.* Dix Hills, New York: General Hall, Inc.

frustration and an attraction to the illegal but lucrative drug trade (Norton 1985). Many teenage African-American males become derailed from the path toward a college education and upward mobility by drug abuse and gang involvement (Staples 1985). In response to these harsh inner city conditions, a large number of African-American males join the military after high school in order to escape gang recruitment and drug pressures as well as to save money for college (Hauser and Anderson 1989; Lemann 1986). Nonetheless African-American men attend college in fewer numbers than African-American women (Staples 1985). The number of African-American women seeking a partner with stable employment outnumbers the available supply of steadily employed African-American men. When African-American women marry African-American men, they tend to exchange their higher educational status for the companionship, stability, and affection of marriage (Schoen and Wooldredge 1989).

Interracial marriage, on the other hand, follows the same pattern as marriage involving two white partners. Schoen and Wooldredge found that when an African-American male marries a white female, the African-American male is likely to be the better educated partner. The researchers argue that the African-American

119

husband's education is exchanged for the white female's racial status. Because African-American men are twice as likely as African-American women to marry interracially, the problem of finding a suitable African-American mate is exacerbated for African-American women (Glick 1988b). African-American women often complain that women of other races further narrow their field of eligibles. Non–African-American women enter the African-American woman's marriage market and marry better educated African-American men.

Critique of Exchange Theory. Criticism of exchange theory centers around the rational and calculated manner in which exchange theory views romantic attachment. Exchange theory in mate selection is modeled on economic exchange and implies that dating takes place in a marketplace in which a person shops for a partner and examines assets. Some critics of exchange theory argue that interracial marriage reflects the mutual interests and affection of the partners rather than an exchange of educational assets for a partner's racial status. Exchange theory tends to be mechanical and overlooks both the emotional aspects of romantic love and the interpersonal dynamics by which romantic attraction is developed. A theory that takes a more dynamic view of the mate selection process is the stimulus-value-role theory, discussed below.

Stimulus-Value-Role Theory

Bernard Murstein's (1987, 1986, 1970) stimulus-value-role theory maintains the basic premise of exchange theory. According to stimulus-value-role theory, people are drawn toward potential mates who have overall assets and liabilities equivalent to their own. However, Murstein's stimulus-value-role theory is also a filter theory that views courtship as a series of stages. Courtship begins with acquaintanceship and moves toward commitment either to marriage or to living together. In this filter theory, the couple must successfully pass through one stage before they can move on to the next stage. Otherwise, they become "filtered out" and the courtship ends. Couples pass through the stimulus stage, then the value stage, and finally the role stage as they progress toward a committed relationship. In each of these three stages a particular issue emerges as the central focus of attention. These issues are physical attraction in the stimulus stage, value comparison in the value stage, and role compatibility in the role stage.

Stimulus Stage. The stimulus stage, the physical attraction stage, begins with the couple's first meeting. They are attracted to each other by readily observable characteristics, such as physical appearance, voice, dress, and reputation. In the interviews at the beginning of the chapter, Michael is attracted to Julie's shoulder-length hair and hazel eyes, while she likes his friendliness and warm smile. The information on which the potential partner is evaluated in this stage is easily obtainable. The partners may have mutual friends and therefore have some knowledge of each other's socioeconomic class and activities on campus. If the partners are satisfied that their assets, such as appearance, social class, and reputation, are equivalent, they are likely to continue on to the value stage of courtship.

Value Stage. In the value stage the couple describe their likes and dislikes, talk about their values, and discuss what they want out of life. *Values* are broad, vague, ideological positions such as a commitment to career, political ideology, religious beliefs, or the importance of family and children. The value stage relies primarily on conversation and sometimes results in long discussions that go into the night. The couple may discuss their attitudes toward personal ambition and achievement, abortion, parental approval, nuclear war, politics, honesty, sexual fidelity, and a whole range of other value-laden issues. Michael and Julie both value achievement, and they value her support for his career. They have also agreed that they value family, children, and equality in a relationship.

The value stage involves more than a comparison of already formed values. The couple may influence each other; each partner may change personal values in order to bring them closer to those of the mate. If the couple decide that they have compatible values, they move to the the role stage of the courtship. However, some people decide at this stage that they are "perfect for each other" and marry before going through the last courtship stage, the role stage. Such a decision is unfortunate because it places the most stressful part of the courtship process, the role stage, in the early part of marriage. Murstein assumes that for the mate selection process to go smoothly, all three stages of mate selection must be experienced prior to a decision to marry.

The Role Stage. In the role stage the focus of attention shifts from stated values to a search for role compatibility. Partners begin to observe how their mates perform their social roles, such as boyfriend, girlfriend, student, employee, friend, and son or daughter, in order to see how compatible they would be in husband or wife roles. Whereas the value stage focused on listening to the partner's words and evaluating the partner's values, the role stage involves observation of the partner's actions. The task of the individual shifts from a discussion of abstract values to observation of the partner's concrete behavior. Individuals who lie to friends, steal money from parents, or appear casual about an accident caused by their drunken driving may cause their partners to question their ability to perform marital roles responsibly. When Michael observed that Julie dropped two of her college classes, he worried about whether Julie would be a stimulating intellectual companion who would also share the breadwinning role as a spouse. When Julie saw that Michael was withdrawn when they took her niece to the park, she wondered whether Michael would be a devoted father to their future children. If the partners do not feel that role compatibility exists, they are likely to break off the relationship.

Another task of the role stage is to compare the partner's actual behavior to that partner's stated values. People expect the behavior of a partner to be consistent with that partner's stated values. In the role stage, Michael noticed that although Julie talked about an equal relationship, her behavior did not indicate a commitment to college or to contributing financially to a future family. Likewise, Julie noticed some discrepancies between Michael's stated values and his behavior. He talked about achievement and commitment to a career, but he went out drinking with friends when his paper needed to be typed. A person feels disturbed when the partner does not live up to the values he or she has stated. If the role behavior of the partner is unacceptable, the relationship usually breaks off. On the other hand, those who are satisfied with the partner's role behavior tend to move along toward a commitment either to cohabit or to marry.

Critique of Stimulus-Value-Role Theory. Most of the support for Murstein's theory has come from studies conducted by Murstein himself 1986, 1976, 1970). Criticism of Murstein's theory centers around the order in which the courtship stages fall (Leigh, Holman, and Burr 1984; Stephen 1985). Critics have questioned whether the role stage actually follows or precedes the value stage. Murstein has countered the criticism by pointing out that stimulus, value, and role issues operate at all three stages of courtship. What distinguishes one

Figure 5.1

Murstein's Stages of Mate Choice.

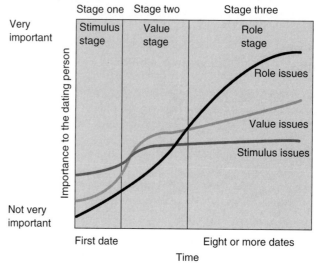

Source: Bernard I. Murstein 1987. "A Clarification and Extension of the SVR Theory of Dyadic Pairing." *Journal of Marriage and the Family,* 49, page 931.

stage from another is the prominence of a particular issue at each stage. As Figure 5.1 shows, in the value stage, stimulus attributes, such as physical beauty, still operate as attractive factors and role compatibility is noticed. However, the central focus of attention is on value comparison during the value stage. This continuous operation of stimulus, value, and role factors makes it difficult to design a questionnaire that can locate individuals in a particular stage of courtship and test this theory.

Both stimulus-value-role theory and exchange theory assume a good deal of rationality in mate selection. Neither theory takes into account the effect of emotions and romantic love. In systems theory, discussed below, the less rational aspects of mate selection are thought to have an important influence on the choice of a partner.

Systems Theory

Systems theory maintains that there is a connection between the social roles people play in their family of origin and the kind of mate they select in adulthood (Beattie 1987; Bepko 1985; Iber 1991; Satir and Baldwin 1983; Zuska and Pursh 1988). In order to understand this position, we need to take a closer look at social systems. Systems theory, which has been used in family therapy, views the family as a *social system* in which the relationships among family members form patterns (Bateson 1971; Satir and Baldwin 1983). A social system is made up of a set of interdependent parts, or social roles. Each person in the family influences all the other family members, so that one person's role in the family has an impact on other family roles (Minuchin 1984, 1974). According to systems theory, the choice of a romantic partner is not based on a rational decision concerning what is good for a person. Instead, systems theory holds that people tend to gravitate toward partners with whom they can reenact their childhood family roles (Iber 1991; Beattie 1987; Bepko 1985; Iber 1991; Zuska and Pursch 1988).

BOX 5.2   W o r l d   P e r s p e c t i v e s

Dowry Deaths in India

India has experienced a rash of "dowry deaths" in recent years. In a dowry death, the wife is murdered by her in-laws because she did not bring a dowry considered adequate by the groom's family. Dowry death is typically perpetrated by the wife's in-laws, with the mother-in-law and husband dousing the wife with kerosene and setting her on fire. The death is typically reported to the authorities as a kitchen accident (Muller 1990). In 1989 more than 4,000 dowry deaths were reported, amounting to the deaths of ten wives per day. Dowry deaths are reminiscent of the ancient practice of "suttee," in which a surviving widow was expected to throw herself on the funeral pyre of her dead husband and be immolated with him.

In India, marriages have traditionally been arranged by parents, with the bride's family contributing a dowry and the bride moving in with her husband's family. The *dowry* is gifts given by the bride's family to the groom and his family at marriage. Because the amount of the dowry is not usually agreed upon prior to the wedding, there can be considerable disagreement between the two families as to whether or not the amount of money in the dowry is adequate. In addition, in India's Hindu culture, the dowry payment does not end at the wedding. The bride's family is expected to give dowry gifts to the groom's family at religious occasions each year, making the dowry obligation an ongoing one.

In 1961 the Dowry Prohibition Act, which made the giving of a dowry illegal, was passed in India.

Nonetheless the custom persists; the law has not been able to deter families from demanding and receiving a dowry (Teays 1991). The low status of women in Hindu society, combined with a desire for consumer goods, has fueled the rising trend in dowry deaths. As India modernizes, the dowry has become an important means for the groom's family to improve their standard of living. Desired dowry items include motor scooters, propane hook-ups for wood-burning stoves, refrigerators, and the electrification of a home, all of which are very expensive. It is difficult for Indians to gain access to these consumer goods by changing jobs and acquiring additional income. The caste system persists, even though the Indian government has declared it illegal (Ramu 1991). Castes are religious and occupational groups, and the Hindu religion envisions punishments in the next life for those who try to leave their caste and enter the occupation of another caste. With upward mobility for the most part blocked both by the widespread poverty in India and by the caste system, families look to the dowry to supply consumer goods.

The strain families are under to pay dowry payments has led some middle-class families to attempt to avoid bearing and raising daughters. Ultrasonic tests allow determination of the gender of unborn fetuses. There has been a recent rash of abortions of female fetuses (Gargan 1991). In addition, female infanticide, traditionally practiced in India and Asia but now outlawed by the Indian government, is still practiced (*Commonweal* 1991).

Most of the research on systems theory and mate choice has taken place within the field of substance abuse. Adult children of alcoholics have a high probability of either marrying an alcoholic or becoming an alcoholic (Bepko 1985). In addition, people who divorce an alcoholic mate have a high probability of marrying another alcoholic (Iber 1991). According to systems theory, these mate choices occur because the social roles children learn in the family are carried over into adulthood.

Systems theory avoids seeing causality as a linear process in which the actions of person A cause the behavior of person B. In family systems, family roles are interdependent and causality is viewed as circular (Bratter and Forrest 1985). In line with this approach, systems theory focuses on the pattern of family interaction. Of particular importance is the development of complementary and symmetrical relationships within the family (Bateson et al. 1956; Bepko 1985). In a complementary relationship, two family members enact opposite roles that "fit together." Examples of complementary relationships are dominant and submissive roles, and the underresponsible and overresponsible roles typically found in families of alcoholics. In contrast, symmetrical relationships exist when two people enact similar roles, for example, when a husband and wife both believe in equality or when the husband and wife allow themselves to be both responsible and dependent on the partner.

In a family with an alcoholic parent, rigid complementary roles frequently develop (Bepko 1985; Bratter and Forrest 1985). As the alcoholic becomes underresponsible and stops paying bills, working in the yard, doing household maintenance, and attending children's school functions, the spouse and usually one or more of the children become overresponsible and perform these tasks. In addition, overresponsible behavior extends to the area of emotional functioning. In their effort to prevent a drinking binge by the alcoholic, the nonalcoholic spouse and some of the children come to feel responsible for the alcoholic's emotional health and try to anticipate the needs and feelings of the alcoholic. Thus when the alcoholic becomes depressed, the overresponsible family members feel anxiety and a need to alleviate the alcoholic's emotional distress in order to control his or her drinking behavior. The overresponsible role is referred to as the role of the "enabler" or "codependent" (Coleman 1983; Iber 1991). The more responsibility the enabler takes, the less responsibility the alcoholic exhibits. Thus, the enabler unwittingly makes it possible for the alcoholic to continue to drink and engage in underresponsible behavior.

The overresponsible and underresponsible roles become rigid and generalize to other relationships within the family (Bepko 1985). Thus the nonalcoholic parent often acts in an overresponsible manner toward one or more of the children, creating an additional overresponsible–underresponsible relationship. This underresponsible child is at risk for becoming an alcoholic as an adult and will tend to gravitate toward a mate who is overresponsible. In contrast, overresponsible adult children of alcoholics have a high probability of marrying an alcoholic. When the pressures of overresponsibility become too great, the overresponsible adult may also turn to drinking to alleviate the pressure.

Alcoholic families with rigid complementary roles, such as the overresponsible–underresponsible role relationship, have been referred to as *dysfunctional families*. Dysfunctional families exhibit rigid social roles and label certain topics, such as alcoholism, as taboo. In addition, the children's need for nurturance is often inadequately met because the alcoholic is disabled by substance abuse and the enabler is overly focused on the alcoholic. In contrast, *functional families* allow for flexible, shifting roles that change to meet the demands of the situation. Functional families also provide avenues for open communication and meet the needs of family members (Bepko 1985; Bratter and Forrest 1985; Satir and Baldwin 1983).

Julie, who was described at the beginning of this chapter, behaved in an overresponsible manner when she stepped in and typed Michael's paper while he was drinking with his friends. Michael behaved in an impulsive and underresponsible manner when he decided to go out the night before his paper was due. Julie's overresponsible behavior may have been learned in her family of origin when she stepped in and took care of an underresponsible parent who was at times emotionally disabled by substance abuse or emotional instability. Systems theory maintains that childhood roles and role relationships continue to influence us as adults.

Critique of Systems Theory. Unlike exchange theory, which assumes a good degree of rationality in evaluating a mate, systems theory focuses on aspects of mate selection that operate at a low level of consciousness. This theory looks at the seductive pull exerted on individuals by familiar family roles. One criticism of systems theory rests on its questionable applicability to the general population of courting couples (Searight and Merkel 1991). Most work with systems theory has been conducted by therapists working in the treatment of substance abuse or mental illness. To generalize their findings to the general population may result in *overgeneralization*. Overgeneralization refers to using theories developed on a limited population, such as substance abusers, to explain the behavior of people in a broader and in some ways different population to whom the theory may not apply. For this reason we must to be cautious in assuming that systems theory can explain the mate selection process of the average American. For the typical American, mate choice is probably the product of both conscious choice and forces that operate at a low level of consciousness. A realistic view of mate selection would note that any one theory has difficulty explaining mate selection in all situations. In addition, more than one theory can often shed light on the process by which two people select each other as mates.

The theories we have reviewed examine the interpersonal dynamics of mate selection. In the next section we use a societal perspective to examine demographic changes in society that impact mate choice.

Review Questions

1. According to exchange theory, what is the basis on which people choose mates? What support for exchange theory did Schoen and Wooldredge find in their study of marriage records? What is the field of eligibles and how can it affect mate choice for African-American females? What is the criticism of exchange theory?

2. According to Murstein, what are the three stages of mate selection and what tasks must be accomplished in each stage in order for the courtship to proceed? What is the criticism of stimulus-value-role theory, and what is Murstein's response to that criticism?

3. What do we mean when we say that the family is a social system? In what way do the roles people play in alcoholic families as children influence their choice of a mate as an adult? What is the criticism of family systems theory as an explanation for mate choice?

Patterns of Mate Selection

In this section we explore patterns of mate selection of interest to both casual observers and social scientists. These include the marriage squeeze, delayed marriage, and interracial marriage.

After a decrease in births during the Great Depression and World War II, couples like this one began having more children and contributed to the post-World War II baby boom.

The Marriage Squeeze

The marriage squeeze was first identified in 1963 (Glick, Heer, and Beresford 1963), when the baby boomers who were born following World War II began entering marriage age. A *marriage squeeze* exists when one gender experiences a shortage of potential marriage partners of the appropriate marriage age. Although about the same number of males and females are born in any one year, young people do not tend to marry a partner of exactly the same age. American women tend to marry men approximately three years older than themselves. Therefore, when the birth rate is either rising or falling, a marriage squeeze occurs. During World War II, from 1941 to 1945, the birth rate was low in the United States while men were away fighting in Europe and Asia. When they returned home, they made up for lost time by getting married and having children. The birth rate began to rise dramatically. The large group of women born immediately following the war looked for marriage partners among the slightly older, very small, group of men born during the war. These women were placed in a marriage squeeze. As the birth rate continued to rise during the 1950s, women faced a continuing shortage of male partners, and some of these women did not marry. The marriage squeeze is thought to have given some impetus to the women's movement, as unmarried baby boomer females entered the labor force and graduate schools, demanding economic and educational opportunities equal to those of males (Glick 1988b: 866). The mar-

Figure 5.2
Average Number of Years Groom Was Older than Bride in the United States.

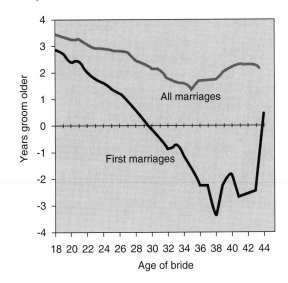

Source: Valerie K. Oppenheimer 1988. "A Theory of Marriage Timing." *American Journal of Sociology,* 94, Page: 579.

riage squeeze following World War II with its surplus of eligible females, may also have fueled the rising divorce rate as "young men with unsatisfactory marriages sought divorces with the assurance that they had a good chance of finding a partner willing to marry or with whom to cohabit" (Glick 1988b).

The tendency to marry a man approximately three years older than themselves is a strong pattern among eighteen-year-old-women, as Figure 5.2 shows. However, the scarcity of available males in the socially appropriate age range has led older women to make an adjustment in their mate selection pattern. Women who wait until age thirty to marry tend to marry men of the same age. Women whose first marriage takes place in their mid-thirties tend to marry men approximately two years younger than themselves. By considering younger men for marriage, women in their mid-thirties increase the pool of eligible male partners. Middle-aged women have made an adjustment to the marriage squeeze by altering what they consider to be the desirable age for male partners, thereby expanding their field of eligibles.

Since 1980 the marriage squeeze appears to be in a stage of reversal (Glick 1988b). The young people entering marriageable age now were born during an era of a falling birth rate. From now until the turn of the century there will be a marriage squeeze for men. In other words, men will be experiencing a shortage of marriage partners several years younger than themselves.

People who experience a marriage squeeze tend to delay marriage, which is the topic of the next section.

Delayed Marriage

Young couples do not appear as eager to plunge into marriage as they were two decades ago. It is becoming increasingly common for men and women to remain single into their late twenties. As Figure 5.3 shows, the proportion of women aged twenty-five to twenty-nine who have never married has tripled since 1970. Likewise, over the last two decades, the average age at first marriage increased by three years for both men and women. In 1993 the median age for first marriage was 26.5 years of age for men and 24.5 years for women (U.S. Bureau of the Census 1994b, page VII). A *median* is a midpoint; therefore half the American men who entered their first marriage in 1992 were aged 26.5 or over and half were aged 26.5 or under. This raises an important question: Why are young men and women today putting off marriage?

Delayed marriage has been encouraged by the changing job structure, the increasing participation of women in the labor force, the sexual revolution, and the rising divorce rate.

Changing Job Structure. Over the last three decades the United States has undergone economic change that has altered the job structure. By job structure, we mean the types of jobs available. Teenage marriage was not nearly so problematic when the United States had an industrial economy that relied heavily on factory production. Factory jobs required little formal education, and job training could be acquired at the workplace. A man could marry immediately after high school and often make as much money as his father, who had held a similar job in the same factory for twenty years. In the industrial era, a man could expect to marry young and still be able to support a family.

However, during the 1960s and 1970s the United States entered the postindustrial age and became part of a global economy in which goods were produced and sold in world markets. American factories began closing down and relocating overseas to take advantage of cheap labor. The United States became a technologically advanced society with a need for highly educated workers. The major source of employment shifted from factory production to service jobs, which involved information processing in insurance, banking, and commerce. No longer could a couple marry right after high school and find economic well-being. As a result, young people delayed marriage in order to continue their education and prepare for employment. In this economic environment, some young people who desired an intimate relationship without early marriage began to experiment with cohabitation.

Although the romantic pull toward marriage is strong during the teenage years, young marriage carries a substantial economic risk in modern America. People who marry in their teens often experience severe economic strain. A study comparing the economic position of males who married in their teens to that of those who married after age twenty found that

Figure 5.3
Percent Age 25 to 30 Who Have Never Married.

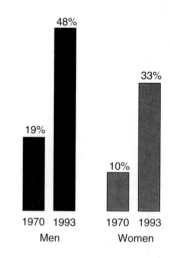

Source: U.S. Bureau of the Census 1994b, Current Population Reports, P20-478, *Martial Status and Living Arrangements, March 1993*, Figure 2, page IX. Washington, D.C.: U.S. Government Printing Office.

adolescent grooms completed fewer years of education, attained lower-status occupations, and earned less income than same-age males who married as adults. This held true for both black and white males. Furthermore, even after thirty years of marriage, teen grooms did not catch up with the economic position of their age mates who had married as adults (Teti, et al. 1987). Women who marry in their teens are twice as likely to divorce as women who marry after age twenty-two (Martin and Bumpass 1989). This finding holds true for both black and white women (Menken et al. 1981) and for women in Great Britain as well as in the United States. In Great Britain, for every year that the age of marriage decreases, the divorce rate increases (Murphy 1985). The price of early marriage is a high one in modern society.

Women in the Labor Force. The growing participation of women in the labor force since the 1960s has also contributed to delayed marriage. Throughout the nineteenth and twentieth centuries unmarried women often worked outside the home prior to marriage. However, once a woman married, she was expected remain at home and raise children. Married women did not enter the work force in large numbers until World War I in 1917 and again during World War II in 1941. Even then, married women made up a *reserve labor force* who were drawn into employment when there was a shortage of male workers. Women helped produce armaments in the war effort, but as soon as the soldiers came home, married women returned to their homemaking roles. However, by the 1970s the number of married women in paid employment was surging upward. This trend has continued, so that today most married women are expected to contribute to family income. As women prepare for future employment, they are spending more time in education and delay marriage.

Sexual Revolution. The sexual revolution of the 1970s encouraged delayed marriage by making sexual relationships outside of marriage more socially acceptable. In addition, changes in birth control technology and court decisions regarding abortion have contributed to the rise in the age at first marriage over the last thirty years. Oral contraceptives, mass marketed in the mid-1960s, provided a reliable means of preventing unwanted pregnancies. In 1973 the U.S. Supreme Court legalized abortion in all 50 states in its historic *Roe v. Wade* decision. These changes separated sex from reproduction, making it possible for teenagers and adults to have a sexual relationship while delay marriage.

Rising Divorce Rate. As divorce became more widespread, it contributed to delayed marriage by encouraging greater caution in marriage decisions. Today one out of every four children under age eighteen in the United States lives with a single parent, compared to only one out of eleven in 1960 (U.S. Bureau of the Census 1994b, pXI; 1991b, Table E). As young people watch their parents divorce, they become less anxious to leap into marriage. Evidence from an Australian study reveals that parental separation or divorce tends to influence the attitudes of children toward marriage. Using data from a national representative sample of Australians between the ages of eighteen and thirty-four, Amato (1987) compared adults whose parents divorced while they were still children to adults from intact families. Both groups thought marriage was desirable and expected to marry. However, adult children of divorced parents had less idealized views of marriage and were more willing to accept the possibility of divorce. This group was more aware of the limitations of marriage and held more negative attitudes toward the families in which they grew up than did adults from intact families. Furthermore, adult children of divorce found the alternatives to marriage, such as single parenting and living as a single adult, more acceptable than did those from intact families.

In addition to delayed marriage, modern marriage patterns are changing in the direction of increasing interracial marriage, which is discussed below.

Interracial Marriage

Interracial mate selection is on the rise. There were 2 1/2 million people in interracial marriages in the United States in 1992, representing 2 percent of all marriages. This is almost four times the number reported two decades earlier, in 1970 (U.S. Bureau of the Census 1992b, Table F). The United States is still characterized by a pattern of racial endogamy. *Endogamy* is the tendency to marry within one's own social group. *Racial endogamy* is to the tendency to marry within one's own race. However, racial endogamy is beginning to break down to a small extent as America blends cultures and races through marriage. Currently 2 percent of all marriages involving a white person, 7 percent of all marriages involving a black person, and 38 percent of all marriages involving an Asian or Pacific Islander are racially mixed (U.S. Bureau of the Census 1992b, Table F; 1990c, Table 13). Looking at a more specific breakdown by national origin, in 1980 one-half of Native American and one-fourth of Filipino marriages were racially mixed. Likewise, 40 percent of marriages involving a Japanese wife were interracial (Glick 1988b). A small but significant trend toward racial exogamy is developing. *Exogamy* is the tendency to marry outside one's own social group. *Racial exogamy* is the tendency to marry outside one's own race.

Dating between Asian women and Caucasian men on the University of California campus at Berkeley, where 40 percent of the enrollment is Asian, has become so common that local newspapers have carried articles on the subject, describing the resulting strains. This pattern has caused Asian men to experience a marriage squeeze. Asian men tend to marry within their own race and are finding a shrinking pool of eligible partners. The scarcity of Asian women as dating partners is a subject that Asian men report having discussed with family, friends, and in Asian-American studies classes. These students feel that the mass media portray Asian males as villains rather than as desirable marriage partners. A Japanese male college student described his feelings about Asian women engaging in interracial dating:

> If a Japanese-American man wants to preserve his culture, his choices are becoming increasingly limited. . . . It wouldn't be as bad if white women were dating Asian men, but they aren't. . . . So it's pretty upsetting. . . . It's like your turf is being invaded." *(Walsh 1990:14)*

The marriage squeeze at west coast college campuses is also experienced by white women, who watch many of their potential white male partners date Asian women. As the Japanese-American college student quoted above observed, the shortage of partners could be diminished if more white women dated Asian men.

Marriages involving blacks are also becoming more exogamous, but to a lesser extent than those of other races. Even though the percentage of black marriages that are interracial is small (7 percent), interracial marriage involving African

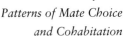

Social norms no longer limit mate selection to one's own racial or ethnic group.

Americans represents an important development. Black husband–white wife marriage occurs twice as often as white husband–black wife marriage (U.S. Bureau of the Census 1992a, Table F). In addition, black husband–white wife marriages have a lower divorce rate than white husband–black wife marriages (Glick 1988b). Perhaps the black husband has better success in integrating his white wife into his extended kinship group and circle of friends than the white husband has integrating his black wife into his extended family and group of friends. If this is the case, then racial discrimination may play a role in the lower success rate for interracial marriage involving a black wife. Next we explore one of the most prominent demographic trends today, the growing tendency toward cohabitation.

Review Questions

1. What is the marriage squeeze, and why did it occur for females born after World War II? How do middle-aged women adjust to the marriage squeeze?

2. Describe the pattern of delayed marriage and explain why it has occurred.

3. In what ways is the pattern of interracial marriage in the United States changing? What strains are resulting from interracial marriage?

Cohabitation

The popularity of cohabitation has grown rapidly in recent decades. *Cohabitation* refers to two unmarried adults who are living together in a sexual relationship. In 1993, 3.5 million couples of the opposite sex and 1.5 million of the same sex shared households (U.S. Bureau of the Census 1994b, Table 8). The U.S. Bureau of the Census does not ask couples whether they have an ongoing sexual relationship. However, the Bureau of the Census uses the term "unmarried couple household" to indicate cohabitation and has found that roommates who are living together for convenience but are not cohabiting generally do not classify themselves as an "unmarried couple" (U.S. Bureau of the Census 1994b, page VII). Because three-fourths of both opposite-sex couples and same-sex couples who share a common residence are age 25 or over, it is likely that the vast majority are cohabitors rather than young roommates not sexually involved.

Opposite-sex cohabitation in the United States has increased dramatically since 1950. In that year, there were only 50,000 unmarried couples of the opposite sex residing together (Glick 1988b). That number grew more than sixty-fold by 1993. By age thirty over 40 percent of Americans have cohabited in an opposite-sex relationship at some time in their lives (Bumpass and Sweet 1989a). Comparable historical figures are not available for same-sex relationships. (For a discussion of same-sex relationships see Chapter 7, Marriage and Partnerships: Interpersonal Relationhips.)

Who Are the Cohabitors?

Social scientists have sought to discover the social characteristics that distinguish people who cohabit from those who either are married or have other living arrangements. Below are some traits that characterize people who cohabit.

Social Class. We tend to conjure up visions of young professionals when we think of cohabitation, yet the majority of cohabitors have incomes too low to place them in the middle class (Tanfer 1987). Cohabiting couples are typically white, urban and have a lower income and a higher unemployment rate than married couples (Glick and Spanier 1980; Spanier 1983). As the United States moves from an industrial society to a postindustrial one that depends on formal education and technical training, an underclass of poorly educated, impoverished persons is left behind economically. For this group, the idea of marrying and taking on the responsibility for family support can be overwhelming. Among the poor, cohabitation is becoming increasingly common.

Single Parents. One-third (35 percent) of opposite-sex cohabiting couples and 10 percent of same-sex cohabiting couples have a child in the household. (U.S. Bureau of the Census 1994b, Table 8). In fact, unmarried women who have a child are almost twice as likely to cohabit as unmarried women who are childless (Tanfer 1987). Perhaps women with children are at a disadvantage in the marriage market because they have a ready-made family. Cohabitors are not only likely to be single parents but also to have grown up in a single-parent home. American women who spent their formative years in a single-parent family are more likely to cohabit than women who grew up in intact homes (Tanfer 1987).

Cohabitors are more likely than noncohabitors to have borne a child out of wedlock. Unwed mothers appear two and a half times more frequently among cohabitors than among those who have never cohabited. Female cohabitors are more likely than noncohabitors to be sexually active and therefore have a greater exposure to pregnancy. Among never-married women in their twenties who were interviewed by Tanfer (1987:488), all of the currently cohabiting women and 80 percent of the women who had previously cohabited had experienced intercourse within the four weeks prior to the interview. In contrast, only 42 percent of the single women who had never cohabited had had intercourse during that period. Therefore, women who are currently cohabiting or have previously cohabited have a greater exposure to pregnancy and are more likely than noncohabitors to become unmarried mothers.

Gender Roles. A number of studies have found that cohabitors are more likely than noncohabitors to subscribe to nontraditional gender roles (Khoo 1987). For example, cohabitors are more likely than married persons to approve of males performing domestic chores, such as ironing and cleaning (Bennett et al. 1988). Although cohabitors tend to hold more egalitarian attitudes, their behavior appears to be similar to that of noncohabitors. Cohabitors are about the same as married couples in their actual division of housework (Stafford, et al. 1977).

Religious Orientation. Cohabitors tend to be less religious than those who marry without cohabitation (Clayton and Voss 1977). People with live-in partners are less likely than noncohabitors to attend religious services. When asked about their attitudes toward religion, cohabitors are less likely than noncohabitors to say that religion is important in their lives (Bennett et al. 1988:128).

Next we turn to explanations for the increasing popularity of cohabitation.

Explanations for Cohabitation

The trend toward increasing cohabitation between opposite-sex partners may represent a cautious tendency to engage in trial marriage, a disillusioned rejection of marriage as an institution, or simply convenience (Bennett et al. 1988; Cherlin 1981). These three explanations for cohabitation are discussed below.

Cohabitation as Trial Marriage

According to the trial marriage explanation, cohabitation does not indicate a rejection of marriage. Instead, it represents a new stage in the mate selection process located between dating and marriage which allows couples to test their compatibility before marriage (Cherlin 1981). Margaret Mead (1966) was one of the first social scientists to advocate trial marriage. She envisioned *marriage in two steps,* with the first step involving marriage without children. This stage was not necessarily expected to be permanent and could be easily dissolved. If a couple turned out to be compatible, they would move on to the second step of marriage, childbearing. Margaret Mead saw the first stage of marriage as a screening process that would weed out incompatible relationships so that only the more successful partnerships would survive and move on to raise children. There is an important difference between trial marriage and modern cohabitation. Mead's two stages of marriage were legally binding, whereas modern cohabitation is not. However, the general principle of trying out a relationship by living together in an easily dissolved union is the same. Mead predicted that trial marriage would lead to greater stability in the second stage of marriage.

Margaret Mead's discussion of trial marriage grows out of the functionalist perspective. As we discussed in Chapter 2, *functionalism* looks for the ways social patterns, such as cohabitation, contribute to the stability of the larger society. Margaret Mead saw cohabitation as a useful courtship stage that increased the success and stability of subsequent marriage. Building on Mead's theory, other social scientists have argued that cohabitation is functional because it provides an opportunity for important developmental tasks to take place before marriage. From the functionalist perspective, cohabitation contributes to realism, role adjustment, and freedom from childbearing pressures (White 1987:645–646).

Realism. Realism is promoted as each partner gains a more realistic view of the other. While living together, idealization of the partner tends to give way to a realistic assessment of the partner's character.

Role Adjustment. Role adjustment is fostered because cohabitors have a chance to adjust to the role expectations of the partner and work out an acceptable division of household labor.

Avoidance of Childbearing Pressure. Couples who want to finish college and begin a career gain an intimate relationship through cohabitation without pressure to have children. Parents and friends are more likely to pressure a couple to marry, as a next step in the courtship process, rather than encourage them to bear children while cohabiting. In a society that emphasizes technical jobs requiring advanced training, cohabitation allows a couple to delay marriage and focus on education and career development.

Cohabitation is a stage in the mate-selection process that allows couples to test their compatibility before marriage. However, cohabitation does not reduce the risk of divorce.

Cohabitation and Divorce

In spite of Margaret Mead's prediction that trial marriage would lead to marital stability, evidence reveals a strong relationship between cohabitation and subsequent divorce. A Swedish government study of 4,300 women in Sweden between the ages of twenty and forty-four indicates that cohabitation does not reduce the risk of divorce. Swedish women who lived with their partners prior to marriage had a divorce rate almost twice as high as those who married without cohabiting (Bennett et al. 1988:127). Furthermore, extended periods of cohabitation in which the couple came to know each other well actually appeared to increase the probability of divorce in Sweden. Women who lived with their partners for three years before marriage had a higher divorce rate than women who cohabited for shorter periods of time. A similar situation was found in Canada. Canadian former cohabitors had a higher divorce rate than couples who simply married without ever cohabiting (Balakrishnan et al. 1987; Burch and Madan 1986). Thus, cohabitation does not appear to increase the stability of subsequent marriage.

The Marriage Disillusionment Explanation

The marriage disillusionment explanation for cohabitation holds that people cohabit because they have become disillusioned with the idea of marriage and so cannot commit to it (Macklin 1978).

In discussing Swedish cohabitation, Bennett and colleagues (1988) attribute the high divorce rate for Swedish cohabitors to a self-selection process. They argue that couples with traditional values, who are more likely to be committed to marriage, tend to move right into marriage without first cohabiting. On the other hand, those who have difficulty making a commitment to marital relationships are more likely to cohabit. Later, when problems arise in marriage, these less-committed former cohabitors are more willing to break up their marriages than are the traditional couples who have never cohabited. In other words, if the two groups, former cohabitors and those who have never cohabited, experience the same level of marital unhappiness, the former cohabitors are more willing to opt for divorce.

A similar study in France supports the marriage disillusionment explanation for cohabitation. Carlson (1986) compared eighteen- to twenty-nine-year-old cohabitors to married couples of the same age in France and found that cohabitors held more negative views of marriage. French cohabitors tended to think that people married because of social pressure rather than because they wanted to add something special to their relationships. Furthermore, French cohabitors had a pessimistic attitude toward the future of marriage, with many predicting that marriage would gradually diminish in importance and eventually disappear. In other words, cohabitors in France showed a lack of confidence in the institution of marriage.

Cohabitation as Convenience

A third explanation for cohabitation holds that many people enter into cohabitation simply as a matter of convenience, without any particular philosophy about marriage. Their motivation for living with a partner comes neither from disillusionment with marriage nor from a desire for a trial marriage. They cohabit because they are able to share living expenses and gain a convenient sexual arrangement in which they do not have to get up and go home after having sexual relations.

When two partners have different motives for cohabitation, frustration and misunderstanding can result. This is particularly true if the intentions of each partner are not clearly discussed before cohabitation begins. One study of American college students who were cohabiting revealed that men and women viewed cohabitation differently. College men tended to see cohabitation as a convenient sexual arrangement, whereas college women tended to view cohabitation as trial marriage (Arafat and Yorburg 1973). Because cohabitation may represent a trial marriage to one person, disillusionment with marriage to another, and merely convenience to a third, it is essential for couples to communicate openly before living together. A young woman, Sandra, looks back on her former live-in relationship and describes both her desire to discuss her expectations for cohabitation and her reluctance to bring up the subject:

> My boyfriend and I wanted to live together. There were many things that we needed to discuss, like who would do the laundry, who would pay the bills, whether or not he would want me to sit home while he went out with friends in the evening, and most importantly (at least to me), defining our relationship. I rationalized that we could deal with these issues as they came up, so I never mentioned them before we moved in together. I said to myself, "A man needs to feel trusted," and I thought that he might feel insulted that I didn't automatically trust him on these things. We moved in together and after a number of bitter arguments, I eventually moved out. (Interview by author.)

As Sandra learned, couples who state their expectation clearly are more likely to avoid disappointment after cohabitation begins.

American Cohabitation

Although people cohabit for a variety of reasons, in some respects cohabitation in the United States resembles trial marriage. American unions that do not end in marriage last only eighteen months on the average. Apparently, if the relationship does not look like it will result in marriage, it tends to break up. Furthermore, American cohabitors are just as likely as noncohabitors to report that they expect to marry, meaning that cohabitors tend to see living together as a stage in courtship rather than a substitute for marriage (Tanfer 1987).

American cohabitation also exhibits elements of marriage disillusionment. The growing tendency for unmarried cohabiting couples to bear children makes cohabitation appear to be an alternative to marriage for some couples. With regard to those couples who cohabit and then marry, American couples resemble Swedish couples in that couples who cohabit before marriage have a higher divorce rate than couples who marry without first living together. (Bumpass and Sweet 1989a). It appears that Americans who cohabit and then marry have a lower level of marital commitment than those who simply marry without first living together. In other words, cohabitation in the United States contains elements of both marriage disillusionment and trial marriage.

Review Questions

1. How frequently does cohabitation occur? What are the characteristics of cohabitors? What are the differences between cohabitors and married persons in their attitudes toward gender roles and in their gender role behavior?

2. In what way does cohabitation in the United States exhibit elements of trial marriage, marriage disillusionment, and cohabitation as convenience? In what ways is cohabitation said to be functional? In what ways does Bennett's study of Swedish cohabitation support the marriage disillusionment explanation for cohabitation? What evidence from France supports the marriage disillusionment explanation for cohabitation?

3. What is the relationship between cohabitation and risk of divorce?

Summary

1. Exchange theory holds that people seek out partners whose assets and liabilities are equivalent to their own assets and liabilities. The evaluation of the partner is made in a fairly rational manner.

2. Murstein's stimulus-value-role theory sees mate choice as a three-stage process. The stimulus stage is based primarily upon physical attraction. In the value stage the partners compare their verbally stated values, discussing what they want out of life. The last stage, the role stage, involves observation of the partner's behavior in order to see if role compatibility exists.

3. Systems theory holds that our childhood experiences with family roles influence mate choice. According to systems theory we gravitate toward mates with whom we can reenact our familiar family roles. This theory has been applied mainly to adults who grew up in families of alcoholics.

4. A marriage squeeze occurs when there are not enough partners of the appropriate marriage age available as mates. A marriage squeeze is faced by African-American women and all women who first marry in their thirties.

5. There is a modern trend toward delayed marriage. Factors that have contributed to delayed marriage include a changing job structure, participation of married women in the labor force, the sexual revolution, and the rising divorce rate.

6. Interracial marriage is becoming increasingly popular, particularly among Asians. When black–white marriage takes place, it generally includes a black husband and a white wife.

7. Women who cohabit tend to be white, lower-class or lower-middle-class, and they are often single parents who have grown up in single-parent homes. Cohabitors are more likely to approve of nontraditional gender roles and are less likely than married people to be religious.

8. Cohabitation is becoming increasingly popular. There are three major explanations for the growing trend toward opposite-sex cohabitation. Cohabitation can be a form of trial marriage; it can represent disillusionment with marriage; or it can be entered into simply as a matter of convenience.

Key Words

Exchange Theory
Stimulus-Value-Role Theory
Systems Theory
Marriage Squeeze
Racial Endogamy
Racial Exogamy
Trial Marriage
Median Age at First Marriage

Field of Eligibles
Value
Overgeneralization
Endogamy
Exogamy
Cohabitation
Functionalism

Resources

National Chastity Association

P.O. Box 402
Oak Forest, IL 60452

Organization for people who believe in abstaining from sex before marriage, desire to marry their best friend, and want a spouse who is faithful and honest. Facilitates contact between members. Publishes a national membership list.

Parents without Partners

8807 Colesville Rd.
Silver Spring, MD 20910
(301) 588-9354

Has 145,000 members and 750 local groups. Holds social events for both male and female single parents and promotes acceptance of single parents by wider society.

Interracial Family Alliance

P.O. Box 16248
Houston, TX 77222
(713) 454-5018

Promotes acceptance of interracial families and solutions to problems unique to interracial families. Publishes: *Interracial Family Alliance—Communique,* quarterly.

National Association of Christian Singles

1933 W. Wisconsin Ave.
Milwaukee, WI 53233
(414) 344-7300

Provides emotional support for divorced, widowed, and never married people and seeks to eliminate discrimination based on marital status. Publishes *Today's Single Newspaper,* periodical.

P.O. Box 18131
Washington, DC 20036
(301) 774-7446

Committee for the handicapped that compiles and disseminates information on physically challenged persons.

Chapter 6

Sexuality

When Maria Elena and Robert first married, sex was a vibrant and exciting part of their lives. At work Robert sometimes had to catch himself when he began daydreaming about an evening with Maria Elena. She also looked forward to their time together. Now, six years and one child later, they find that they have to make an effort to find time for sex. Robert is often up late at night going over paperwork from his managerial position in an engineering firm. Maria Elena finds that when she stays up with him, she is too tired in the morning to give adequate attention to three-year-old Joey, who wakes up at 6 A.M. Moreover, when Robert and Maria Elena try to make love in the morning, they are sometimes interrupted by Joey as he pushes open the door and bounds across the bedroom into their bed. Maria Elena jokingly says that if Joey wants to have a little sister, he will need to learn to sleep later. At times Robert is too stressed from work to be romantic at home, and Maria Elena often feels exhausted from the combination of a part-time job and raising an energetic three year old. Recently, Robert and Maria Elena have begun to leave Joey with Robert's mother twice a month for an overnight stay with "Gram." On Joey's first overnight Robert and Maria Elena felt awkward, and much of their conversation centered on speculation about how Joey would handle being on his own. Later Robert wryly told a friend that maybe he and Maria Elena should look for a manual on how to be a couple again, and then he laughed. Yet he also felt a bit of sadness over the difficulty he and his wife found in maintaining a romantic sexual relationship. Nonetheless, Joey continued his visits to his grandmother, and several months later Robert and Maria Elena felt relaxed enough to experiment sexually. Trying new ways of having sex was sometimes frustrating, but often their time together left them feeling an inner glow that carried over into the next day. Robert thought that there is comfort in having having sex with Maria Elena in a familiar, sometimes playful, and sometimes romantic way.

I n this chapter we examine a number of aspects of sexuality including the human sexual response, contraceptive behavior and attitudes, sexuality in marriage and midlife, extramarital sexual affairs, sexuality in gay and lesbian relationships, the influence of alcohol and drugs on sexual behavior, and high-risk sexual behavior and the AIDS crisis. Sexual involvement is both an emotional and a physiological experience. We first look at the physiological process of sexual excitement; then we turn to the social aspects of sexuality.

The Human Sexual Response

In their classic study of human sexuality, Masters and Johnson (1986) identified four phases of the human sexual response: excitement, plateau, orgasm, and resolution. These stages correspond to levels of sexual arousal in both heterosexual and homosexual relationships. Although there are some individual differences, most people go through these four stages of sexual response.

BOX 6.1   A C l o s e r L o o k

Human Sexual Anatomy

Male Genitalia

Many men believe the myth that a large penis produces greater sexual pleasure in women. Actually, the size of the penis has little to do with sexual sensation in women. The vagina accommodates itself to the size of the penis. The length of the penis has little importance because the cervix and portion of the vagina near the cervix have only a few sensory nerve endings (Masters, Johnson, and Kolodny 1986).

Female Genitalia

Female genitalia are known collectively as the vulva. During the plateau stage in the human sexual response, the clitoris withdraws under the clitoral hood and remains there during orgasm.

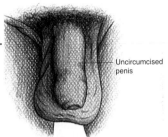

Figure 6.1
Male Genitals:
Variation in Appearance.

Uncircumcised penis

Figure 6.2
Female Genitals.

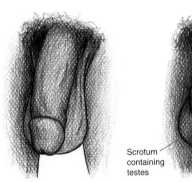

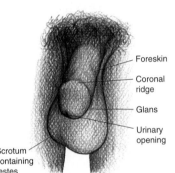

Foreskin

Coronal ridge

Glans

Urinary opening

Scrotum containing testes

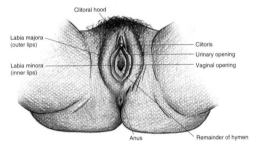

Clitoral hood

Labia majora (outer lips)

Labia minora (inner lips)

Clitoris

Urinary opening

Vaginal opening

Anus

Remainder of hymen

Source: Adapted from William H. Masters, Virginia E. Johnson, and Robert C. Kolodny 1986. *Masters and Johnson on Sex and Human Loving.* Boston: Little Brown and Co.

Excitement

In the *excitement stage* the person experiences increasing sexual arousal. Sexual excitement produces two important physiological changes: vasocongestion and neuromuscular tension. The first change, *vasocongestion,* occurs when the penis and testes of the man and the clitoris and breasts of the woman become engorged with blood. The female *clitoris* is a small nub containing sensitive nerve endings; it is located on the edge of the *labia,* or lips of the vagina. As a result of vasocongestion, the penis, the clitoris, and often the nipples experience *erection,* in which they become firm and enlarged. Vasocongestion also produces vaginal *lubrication* when glands lining the vagina emit fluid. Some men make the mistake of thinking that vaginal lubrication means that the woman is ready for intercourse and near orgasm when, in fact, the onset of lubrication can occur at a low level of sexual arousal. In men a small amount of *pre-ejaculatory*

BOX 6.2   A   C l o s e r   L o o k

Figures 6.3 and 6.4 show the stages of the human sexual

The Human Sexual Response Cycle

response cycle: excitement, plateau, orgasm, and resolution.

Figure 6.3
The Male Sexual Response Cycle.

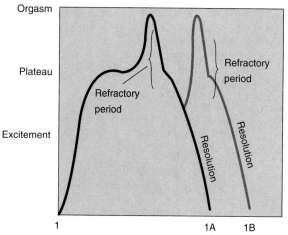

1A, orgasm and resolution; 1B, orgasm, refractory period, second orgasm, and resolution.

Figure 6.4
The Female Sexual Response Cycle.

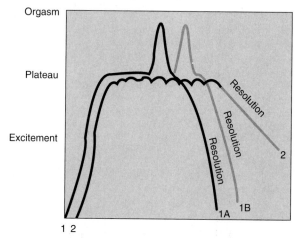

1A, orgasm and resolution; 1B, two orgasms and resolution; 2, plateau without orgasm and resolution.

Source: Adapted from William H. Masters, Virginia E. Johnson, and Robert C. Kolodny 1986. *Masters and Johnson on Sex and Human Loving.* Boston: Little, Brown and Co.

---

fluid from the Cowper's gland is likely to be emitted from the penis. This pre-ejaculatory fluid often contains live sperm and accounts for some accidental pregnancies that occur when couples use withdrawal as a method of contraception. The second physiological change of the excitement stage is an increase of *neuromuscular tension,* in which energy or tension builds up in the nerve endings and muscles throughout the body. The entire body begins to appear tense. In the excitement stage a man's erection may diminish for a period of time, but the increasing neuromuscular tension in the rest of his body indicates that sexual arousal is building to the plateau stage.

Plateau

If sexual stimulation continues, the individual moves to the *plateau stage,* in which the body prepares for orgasm. Masters and Johnson (1986) found that for many women an extended and leisurely plateau stage can be as satisfying as orgasm, even if she does not reach the orgasm stage (see Figure 6.4, female pattern 2). The plateau stage is characterized by a sensation of heart pounding, heavy breathing, and elevated blood pressure. An *orgasmic platform* is created in the vagina as the vagina experiences vasocongestion and narrows. The sensitive *clitoris* withdraws under the *clitoral hood*. In the plateau stage over half of women and one-fourth of men experience a *sex flush* in which their skin reddens, resembling measles.

Orgasm

In the *orgasm stage* sexual tension rises to a peak and is discharged. This, the shortest stage, lasts for several seconds. Muscle contractions in the man occur in the penis, prostate gland, seminal vesticles, urethra, and anus. Some of these contractions result in the release of semen. Parallel muscle contractions in the woman during orgasm occur in the vagina, uterus, clitoris, and anus.

Resolution

During the *resolution stage* sexual intensity gradually subsides and muscle tension is replaced by relaxation. Males and females differ in their sexual response during the resolution stage. Men experience a *refractory period* during which

---

BOX 6.3   A C l o s e r L o o k

The Physiological Changes that Accompany Orgasm

As Figures 6.5 and 6.6 show, orgasm is accompanied by contractions throughout the sexual anatomy.

Figure 6.5
Male Orgasm.

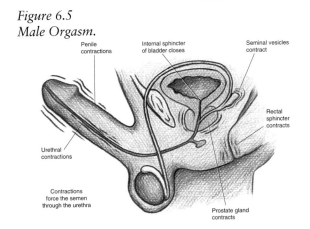

Figure 6.6
Female Orgasm.

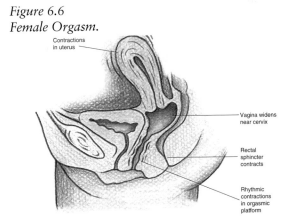

Source: Adapted from William H. Masters, Virginia E. Johnson, and Robert C. Kolodny 1986. *Masters and Johnson on Sex and Human Loving.* Boston: Little, Brown and Co.

BOX 6.4   S o c i a l   I s s u e s

Are We as Sexually Liberal as We Think?

The portrayal of sexuality in advertisements, movies, and television would lead us to believe that casual sex with many partners is common among Americans. And, in fact, many people compare their own sex lives with these media images and feel that they are missing out on something. This picture of the sexually liberal American has been challenged by a major University of Chicago study conducted by Robert Michael, John Gagnon, and their colleagues titled *Sex in America, A Definitive Survey* (1994). This survey is considered the most important study of American sexual behavior since the Kinsey reports in 1948 and 1953 (P. Robinson 1994) The researchers used a nationally representative sample of approximately 3,400 Americans ages 18 to 59, giving us a picture of American sexual behavior that is considered quite accurate. The findings are startling: Americans are far more sexually conservative than we had previously assumed.

How Many Sex Partners Do Americans Have?

The typical American has had an average of three sex partners since age 18. When we examine sexual experience over the last year, Americans appear to be even more sexually conservative. Four out of five (83 percent) people surveyed had only one sex partner or no sex partners within the past year; this includes 77 percent of men and 89 percent of women. Moreover, the vast majority of people in each racial and ethnic group were sexually monogamous. The percent having one sex partner or no sex partners within the last 12 months was 84 percent of whites, 73 percent of African Americans, 80 percent of Hispanics, 93 percent of Asians, and 88 percent of Native Americans. These high levels of sexual monogamy can be accounted for by the fact that most people in the study were either married or cohabiting. Marriage is a powerful social institution and when Americans marry, they tend to settle down with a single sex partner. This appears to be the case regardless of a person's past sexual experiences. Ninety-four percent of married people reported that they had sex only with their spouse during the previous year.

How Often Do Americans Have Sex?

Sex occurs far less often than many of us would imagine. Approximately 60 percent of married people have sex a few times a month or less. Does this mean that married people are avoiding unpleasant or boring marital sex? Not at all. The vast majority of married couples report that they are physically and emotionally satisfied with their sex lives. Nonetheless, the pressures of raising children, running a household, and meeting job demands often leave them too rushed, hassled, or tired to have sex. Single adults have sex even less often than married couples. Three-fourths of single, noncohabiting Americans have sex a few times a month or less. The only group with an extremely active sex life is cohabiting couples. Over half of them have sex two or more times a week. Since cohabitation often precedes marriage, perhaps this reflects the sexual exuberance typical of a relatively new "live-in" relationship.

Who Has Many Sex Partners?

People with many sex partners during the last year are extremely rare. Only 3 percent of respondents (5 percent of men and 2 percent of women) had five or more sex partners during the last twelve months. Most of those who had multiple sex partners were young adults who were neither married nor cohabiting. When we look at sexual experience during adulthood the percent with many sex partners increases. About one out of ten respondents (9 percent) reported having had 21 or more sex partners since age 18. In this group of extremely sexually active adults, there were only minor variations by race and ethnicity: 9 percent of whites, 11 percent of African Americans, 9 percent of Hispanics, 3 percent of Asians, and 5 percent of Native Americans reported having 21 or more sex partners in adulthood. However, we do find an important gender difference: only 3 percent of women but 17 percent of men had 21 or more sex partners since age 18. This represents almost 11 million men and 2 million women. The researchers found that these were the people most likely to have contracted one or more sexually transmitted diseases during their lifetimes (Michaels et al. 1994).

another erection and orgasm are impossible. This period of nonerection can last for several minutes to several hours. As men age, this refractory period after orgasm becomes longer. In contrast to men, some women can experience multiple orgasms within a short period of time.

Next we turn to the social aspects of sexuality, starting with contraceptive use in dating and in marriage.

The Use of Contraception

Contraception is particularly problematic for people who are dating and are in the process of becoming sexually active. Most people do not plan for contraception in their first sexual encounter. Half of all women report using no form of contraception whatsoever at their first experience with premarital intercourse (Mosher and Bachrach 1987). Most females are reluctant to bring contraceptives with them on a date and rely on male-managed methods of contraception such as condoms and withdrawal when they first become sexually active. Those who are least likely to use contraceptives at first intercourse are those with high levels of *sex guilt*. People who feel guilty about having sex often don't want to acknowledge their interest in having intercourse and tend not to plan ahead for contraception (Gerrard 1987). In addition, adolescent males who have never had intercourse expect to be embarrassed by discussing condom use with a partner and by putting on a condom in front of a partner (Pleck et al. 1990).

Race, Ethnicity, and Social Class

Race and ethnicity are associated with contraception use. Jewish women are the most likely to use contraceptives at first intercourse, and Hispanic women are the least likely to use them. Overall, white women are more likely than African-American women to use contraceptives at first coitus. However, this difference between whites and African Americans is almost entirely accounted for by the greater willingness of white males to use withdrawal as a contraceptive method (Mosher and Bachrach 1987). The higher the income and educational level of parents, the more likely a person is to have used contraceptives at first coitus.

Stage in Dating

As dating relationships evolve from short-term nonmonogamous acquaintance-ships to "monogamous" dating partnerships, the contraceptive method used tends to change. Monogamous dating relationships are those in which the couple dates only each other. The condom is popular in nonmonogamous dating relationships, whereas monogamous dating couples tend to rely on the birth control pill (Murray et al. 1989). This pattern of contraceptive use can be traced to male and female attitudes about contraception.

Male Preferences. Murray and his associates (1989) found that men tend to hold conflicting attitudes about contraception. Males express a preference for contraceptive methods that can be used by women, rather than one of the two male-controlled methods, the condom and withdrawal (Murray et al. 1989;

| TABLE 6.1 | Contraceptive Use by Women Aged Fifteen through Forty-Four | | | |

Contraceptive Method	Percent Using Each Method			
	All Women	Never Married	Married	Divorced or Widowed
	(n = 57,900)*	(n = 21,058)	(n = 29,147)	(n = 7,695)
Users of Contraception	60%	44%	71%	57%
Pill	17	22	15	13
IUD	1	0.4	1	1
Diaphragm	2	0.3	3	0.5
Condom	11	13	10	6
Spermicidal foam	1	1	1	5
Rhythm	2	1	2	0.4
Other methods (Withdrawal)	1	1	2	0.1
Contraceptive sterilization	25	5	37	31
Non-Users of Contraception	40%	56%	29%	43%
Pregnant or seeking pregnancy	9	4	14	4
Not sexually active	16	39	0.6	19
Sexually active nonuser	8	11	6	6
Sterile for other reasons	7	2	9	14
Totals	100%	100%	100%	100%

*Numbers in thousands.

Source: U.S. Department of Health and Human Services 1995. Vital and Health Statistics,

Pleck et al. 1988). Side by side with this attitude is another set of attitudes that tend to promote condom use in nonmonogamous relationships. Men in short-term relationships report that they like using a coitus-dependent contraceptive method, which means that the method is used only at the time of intercourse. Apparently, men feel reassured about pregnancy prevention when they are able to observe the use of contraception in short-term relationships. In addition, both men and women indicate some concern over contracting a sexually transmitted disease in a nonmonogamous relationship (Murray et al. 1989).

As a relationship develops into a monogamous dating partnership, the sexually active couple tends to switch from the condom to the birth control pill (see Table 6.1). The pill fits the male's desire to use a female-dominated method of birth control. However, the birth control pill offers no protection against sexually transmitted diseases and, in fact, can increase the woman's risk of contracting a sexually transmitted disease from an infected partner by reducing acidity in the vagina (Nofziger 1976). Nonetheless, sexual monogamy is an important factor in reducing some of the risk associated with intercourse.

Female Preferences. College women tend to prefer contraceptive methods that do not interfere with sexual spontaneity and that are easy to use. More specifically, women tend to dislike contraceptive methods that must be inserted before intercourse and removed afterwards (Murray et al. 1989). Methods in this category are the diaphragm, the sponge, the cervical cap, and spermicidal foams and gels (foams and gels must be inserted but not removed). The diaphragm, sponge, and cervical cap may be inserted six hours before intercourse and are typically not detectable by either partner during intercourse. However, each of these methods must be left in place for six hours following intercourse and then removed. In contrast, spermicidal foam and gel must be inserted immediately before intercourse, which many women feel is disruptive to the sexual encounter. These feelings, combined with the high level of effectiveness of the oral contraceptive in preventing pregnancy, lead many women to choose the birth control pill after they become secure in a relationship. However, many women consider the birth control pill an unpleasant necessity rather than a good solution to contraception. In a study of one birth control clinic, Cobliner (1988) found that women using the birth control pill frequently complained about having to prevent pregnancy by putting into their bodies chemicals that could cause side effects. This complaint was often expressed with resentment toward their male partners, whom they felt had placed the responsibility for birth control on the woman. For further information on contraception see Appendix A.

Marriage and Contraception

As Table 6.1 shows, the number-one choice of contraception among married couples is surgical sterilization. One partner has undergone this procedure in one-third of all marriages. After completing their families, it is a relief for married couples not to have to worry about birth control. In fact, the majority of married couples (62 percent) do not deal with contraception on a day-to-day basis because one partner is surgically sterile, sterile for another reason, the wife is pregnant or seeking pregnancy, or the couple is not using contraception. Of the nonsterile couples who use contraception, female-managed methods are popular and the oral contraceptive is the most popular choice. This puts the oral contraceptive in second place, right behind surgical sterilization, in contraceptive preference among married couples.

Half of all married people rely on either surgical sterilization or the oral contraceptive as a means of birth control. Although surgical sterilization and the oral contraceptive are the two most reliable forms of contraception, they offer no protection against acquired immune deficiency syndrome (AIDS) and other sexually transmitted diseases (STDs). An extramarital affair could result in an STD being introduced into the marriage. A national survey found that one-third of married people suspect that their partners are having an extramarital sexual affair (Patterson and Kim 1991). However, as Table 6.1 shows, only 11 percent of married couples use condoms, the contraceptive method offering the best protection against sexually transmitted disease. Perhaps it is difficult to insist on condom use because contraception is tied up with the delicate issues of trust and intimacy in a marriage.

Sexuality is an important part of the marriage relationship, and we now turn to an examination of other aspects of sexuality in marriage.

Review Questions

1. What are the four stages of the human sexual response, and what are the characteristics of each stage?

2. What kind of contraceptive practices are typical of a first-intercourse experience? How can you explain the widespread tendency to avoid contraception at first intercourse?

3. How does contraceptive practice change as dating relationships change from nonmonogamous to monogamous? What are the contraceptive preferences of dating men? What are the contraceptive preferences of dating women?

4. What type of contraception is chosen by married couples?

Sexuality in Marriage and Midlife

Sexuality is closely related to marital quality. Couples who are satisfied with their marital relationship and communication tend also to be satisfied with their sexual relationship (Banmen and Vogel 1985; Schenk et al. 1983). Couples tend to develop a more comfortable sexual relationship as they age. Over the years, the frequency of intercourse tends to decline, but satisfaction with sexual activity in marriage tends to increase (McCann and Biaggio 1989). Overall, the majority of married Americans are satisfied with their sex lives (Patterson and Kim 1991).

Communicating about whether or not one wants to have sex helps keep a relationship intimate.

Sexual Initiations

To better understand sexuality in long-term relationships, including marriage and cohabitation, it is important to examine the process of initiating and responding to sexual advances. Byers and Heinlein (1989) asked married and cohabiting men and women to keep an on-going record of each time either they or their partners tried to initiate sex. Participants then recorded the response to sexual initiations. In addition, each person kept tract of the times they considered initiating sex but refrained from doing so. In general, men showed more interest in sex than women. Men initiated sex more often and also thought about initiating sex more often than women. Almost all (93 percent) of the respondents reported at least one sexual initiation during the week that resulted in intercourse, and positive responses to sexual overtures were most often nonverbal.

When sexual initiations were met with a negative response, women were more often in the position of restricting sexual activity. However, women and men tended to have the same reasons for refraining from sex, with the main reasons being fatigue and lack of time. Most couples were satisfied with the way disagreements over whether or not to have sex were resolved. Couples felt more accepting of negative responses when the sexual initiation was verbal (rather than nonverbal) and when the partner's refusal was also verbal. Apparently, explaining one's reasons for not wanting to have sex helps to smooth over the incident (Byers and Heinlein 1989).

Outlook on Life and Sexual Satisfaction

The quality of a marital sexual relationship is closely bound up with a person's overall outlook on life. Husbands and wives who have developed a purpose in life, or feel that their life has a mission, tend to have a satisfying sex life (McCann and Biaggio 1989). Husbands who feel that their lives have meaning tend to be "mate directed" and interested in their partner's sexual pleasure. There appears to be a feedback loop in which the partner who observes the mate's sexual pleasure experiences heightened arousal. In contrast, egocentric partners, who are overly focused on their own sexual arousal, tend to be dissatisfied with marital sex (McCann and Biaggio 1989).

Gender Differences in Sexuality

A number of sexual difficulties and complaints grow out of gender differences in attitudes toward sexuality. A frequent complaint among both married and single midlife men is that sex does not occur often enough. Men tend to equate what they see as an inadequate amount of sex with rejection by the partner. Midlife men also report that they would like to experience more oral sex (Patterson and Kim 1991).

The most common sexual complaint of both married and single midlife women is inadequate amount of sexual foreplay. For women, sex often happens too quickly. In addition, women often complain of a lack of afterglow. After sex the man tends to roll over and go to sleep when the woman wants to snuggle and experience the afterglow of sex in a companionate manner (Patterson and Kim 1991).

In sexual matters women tend to have a sensuous focus whereas men tend to focus on orgasm. Problems often result in sexual relations when men become genitally oriented and move quickly toward orgasm. This goal-directed attitude leaves little time to enjoy sensuous touching. In contrast, a number of women have a sensuous focus, in which they place more emphasis on cuddling than moving toward orgasm (Steinem 1992:203).

Recently men have been urged to move away from a genital focus and to pay attention to the sexual needs of their partners. As a result, many men have begun to evaluate their sexual performance in terms of their partner's sexual pleasure. This male performance orientation creates anxiety and leads many men to feel that they have failed when their partners do not experience an orgasm. In fact, the partner may have enjoyed sex without an orgasm. As we discussed at the beginning of this chapter, many women greatly enjoy an extended plateau stage of sexual response even though they do not experience an orgasm. In addition, the female gender role places emphasis on meeting the needs of others and can lead women to miss out on some of the pleasure of sex because they overlook their own sexual needs.

Sexual Disenchantment

Even though the majority of married couples report that they are generally satisfied with their sex lives, some couples complain of *sexual disenchantment,* or boredom with the sexual relationship (McCann and Biaggio 1989). In sexual disenchantment, passion and excitement go out of sex. Sarrel and Sarrel (1984) identified three factors that can lead to sexual disenchantment: decline of intense love, stress, and habituation.

Decline of Intense Love. Cultural myths associate happiness with being in love. Our definition of love often includes visions of emotional excitement and being "swept off our feet." When the euphoria of love wears off, some people despair and adhere to the myth that sex is worthwhile only when love is intense. In con-

Who said romance is for the young? Perhaps they meant for the young at heart. Many older partners enjoy deeply satisfying sexual relationships.

trast, many married or cohabiting couples who avoid this myth settle into a relaxed, comfortable kind of love with very satisfying sex lives (Sarrel and Sarrel 1984).

Stress. Stress has been called the "antiaphrodisiac" (Sarrel and Sarrel 1984). The illness of a relative, job pressures, concerns about a promotion, feeling pressured in raising children, moving to a new apartment or house, feeling tired and hassled at the end of the day can all have a negative impact on sexual response.

In their book *The Second Shift* (1989), Hochschild and

Machung argue that wives who juggle employment and family responsibilities often experience stress, which can create tension in sexual relationships. Working mothers are typically tired at the end of the day and want to spend time with their children. It is not unusual for the wife to fall asleep with her child in the evening. Husbands often respond by feeling displaced and left out. Hochschild argues that employed wives tend to feel resentful when they do housework in the evenings while their husbands watch television or read the newspaper. This resentment is sometimes expressed, unconsciously or consciously, in sexual withdrawal.

Habituation. Over the course of a marriage the frequency of sexual intercourse tends to decline. The novelty wears off, and sex can become boring. At this point extramarital affairs may tempt one of the partners because of the *novelty effect*, in which sexual interest rises with a new experience (Sarrel and Sarrel 1984). However, partners can create the novelty effect in their own marriage by trying new sexual positions, discussing their fantasies, and finding out from each other what kind of sexual behavior would be exciting to each of them in their relationship.

Sexual Fantasies

Both men and women fantasize about situations that would bring them more sexual pleasure. The most frequent sexual fantasies of both men and women concern two forms of oral–genital sex: cunnilingus and fellatio (Patterson and Kim 1991). *Cunnilingus* is oral–genital sex in which the partner uses the lips and tongue to stimulate the female clitoris and outer portion of the vagina. *Fellatio* is another type of oral–genital sex in which the penis is licked or sucked. Couples tend to experience fantasies about oral–genital sex more often than they experience oral–genital sex in actual practice. The second and third most frequent sexual fantasies for both men and women involve having sex with a famous person, and having sex with multiple partners, in that order (Patterson and Kim 1991). Although the subjects of sexual fantasies are similar for men and women, men are far more likely than women to report that they experience sexual fantasies. In fact, three-fourths of men report that they fantasize about having oral sex, compared to approximately one-third of women (Patterson and Kim 1991). When asked which fantasies they have actually acted out; both men and women are most likely to say oral sex and anal sex (Patterson and Kim 1991).

Next we look at extramarital sexual affairs.

Extramarital Sexual Affairs

Married Americans tend to be remarkably sexually faithful to their spouses. Ninety-four percent of married people reported that they had sex only with their spouse during the previous year. When we look marriage over time, 75 percent of husbands and 90 percent of wives report that they have never had an extramarital sexual experience (Michael et al. 1994). This sexually conservative behavior may be a relatively new development. The incidence of extramarital sex rose over the last forty years due in part to the sexual revolution, improved contraceptive technology, and the increased opportunities to meet potential partners created by divorce and by the growing number of women in the workplace (Lampe 1987; Leigh, Julia Hood, 1990). However, the trend toward an increasing number of extramarital sexual affairs may now be reversing. During the second half of the 1980s, sexual attitudes took a conservative turn, with attitudes toward extramarital sex becoming more disapproving. This shift in attitudes has been attributed to the growing concern about AIDS and to the resurgence of religious fundamentalism in the New Christian Right (Smith, Tom Wo, 1990).

Gender Differences in Extramarital Sex

Gender has an important impact on the pattern taken by extramarital sexual behavior. Men engage in extramarital sex earlier in marriage than women, and men have more extramarital sexual partners than women (Glass and Wright 1992; Lawson 1988). Men who have had extramarital sexual affairs tend to separate sex from emotional involvement. They justify the extramarital sexual experience as a quest for sexual excitement or sexual novelty (Glass and Wright 1992). The majority of men who are currently having an extramarital sexual affair report that they like their wives better than their lovers (Patterson and Kim 1991). In contrast, women are more likely than men to become emotionally involved with their extramarital sexual partners. Those women who have experienced extramarital sex tend to feel that falling in love provides justification for the sexual affair (Glass and Wright 1992). Women who are currently having an extramarital sexual affair generally report that they like their lovers better than their husbands (Patterson and Kim 1991:94–95). This gender difference goes along with the female gender role's emphasis on emotional expression while the male gender role stresses instrumental, goal-oriented behavior.

Relationship with the Extramarital Partner

Most people who engage in extramarital affairs do not plan to marry their extramarital partners (Leigh 1990; Patterson and Kim 1991). However, for many people the extramarital sexual affair is more than a casual one-night fling. In a national survey, Patterson and Kim (1991) found that the average affair lasts for approximately a year. Three-fourths of those currently having a sexual affair said that they have no plans to end the extramarital relationship. Despite the tenacity with which people hold onto their extramarital sexual relationships, those who are having a sexual affair tend not to view the lover as a potential replacement for their spouse. Fewer than 10 percent of those currently having a sexual affair said that they plan to marry their extramarital partner (Patterson and Kim 1991).

Motivation for Extramarital Sexual Affairs

There are a variety of motivations for extramarital sexual affairs, some of which are given below.

Seeking Romance. Some marriage partners are disappointed when they find that their marriages have settled down into a routine of childrearing, running a household, and fulfilling daily obligations. These partners sometimes seek to regain passion and romance through an extramarital affair (Lawson 1988; Leigh, Julia Hood, 1990).

Sexual Curiosity. Many people, particularly men, report that they are satisfying their sexual curiosity and their desire for sexual variety through an extramarital affair (Glass and Wright 1992).

Avoiding Intimacy. It has been suggested that some marriage partners use extramarital affairs to avoid emotional intimacy with the spouse and to defend against a feeling of being engulfed by the love relationship in marriage (Leigh, Julia Hood, 1990).

Deprivation in Marriage. Some marriage partners report that problems in their marriages have led them to seek comfort in a sexual relationship elsewhere (Glass and Wright 1992).

Self-Development. Still others who pursue extramarital affairs are seeking self-development. They find marriage confining and argue that they gain important insights into themselves and their relationships through extramarital sexual affairs (Lawson 1988; Smith, Tom Wo, 1990). People having extramarital affairs often report enhanced self-esteem (Glass and Wright 1992).

Extramarital Sexual and Emotional Affairs

Critics of extramarital studies have complained of a male bias that leads researchers to define extramarital affairs as sexual involvement and to overlook affairs that are built solely on emotional involvement. Women are more likely than men to have affairs characterized by emotional but not sexual involvement. In fact, when we add this new category of nonsexual emotional involvement, women are as likely as men to have an extramarital affair (Glass and Wright 1992).

Having examined heterosexual sexuality, we turn to an exploration of sexuality in same-sex partnerships.

Same-Sex Relationships

Social scientists acknowledge that sexual attraction comes in a diversity of forms, and there is a growing body of research on couples whose sexual orientation is toward same-sex partners. *Sexual orientation* is the preference for same-sex or opposite-sex partners. The pattern of sexual experiences with same-sex partners differs for gay male partners and female lesbian couples.

Gay Male Relationships

In a survey using a nationally probability sample, 2.7 percent of men and 1.3 percent of women reported having sex with a same-sex partner within the last year. A larger percentage of men (6.2 percent) and women (4.4 percent) said that they were sexually attracted to people of the same sex (Michael et al. 1994). In another national study, 3 percent of men reported that they were either gay or bisexual (Harry 1990).

BOX 6.5   World Perspectives

Ritual Homosexuality among the Sambia of New Guinea

Anthropologist Gilbert Herdt (1987) lived among the Sambia in New Guinea and discovered that adolescent males practice a form of ritualized homosexuality that is associated with acquiring manhood and warrior status. Once manhood has been obtained, the men become heterosexual for the remainder of their lives. This temporary but important experience with homosexuality is associated with puberty initiation ceremonies, a rite of passage in which participants enter as boys and through ritual obtain a new adult status.

Homosexuality plays an important part in male initiation. The Sambia believe that young males who engage in oral copulation and ingest semen from older males will grow and gain strength. The older males are thought to pass on the characteristics of adult masculinity through their semen. After the male initiates mature, they gain the status of "bachelors" who donate semen for younger fellators during initiation ceremonies.

When a man matures, he marries a woman brought in from another village and becomes bisexual. Young married men continue to participate in homosexuality during initiation ceremonies. Homosexuality continues until a man becomes a father; at that time he is expected to give up homosexuality and remain heterosexual for the remainder of his life. As men age and become elders, custom requires them to sit apart from the area where open homosexuality takes place at initiation rites. It is not considered proper for a boy to engage in homosexuality in front of either his father or an elder. Thus, men go through a cycle that begins with homosexuality, adds heterosexual sex with one's wife, then gradually removes homosexual practice, and eventually prohibits any close observation of homosexual behavior. However, the elders play an important role in urging young boys to ingest semen often so that they will grow strong.

The Separation of the Sexes

The Sambia puberty initiation ceremony separates young males from society and places them in seclusion. At this time the boys are ritually sacred and powerful. The seclusion of young initiates is part of a larger pattern of separation of the sexes. At the first initiation, boys are forcibly separated from their mothers while both shed tears. After a boy's first initiation, he ceases to live in his mother's house and moves into the men's culthouse, the men's ceremonial house. Here, secretive homosexuality takes place during the boy's adolescence. This is the period during which a boy becomes a warrior. He will remain in the men's culthouse even after marriage and go to live with his wife only after she has experienced her first menstruation, sometime after marriage.

The distinctions between maleness and femaleness are strong around the time of initiation. Adult married males are not allowed to participate in sexual intercourse with their wives for at least a month prior to an initiation ceremony. It is believed that women's influence can hamper a boy's growth. Married men who have recently had sex with their wives can carry this female influence to young boys and indirectly stunt their growth. The emphasis in the male initiation ceremony is on masculinity and the removal of young men from any power or influence of women. Initiation ceremonies begin with dances at which women and children form the audience. However, as the days pass, the initiation ceremonies move into the forest, where a new temporary men's culthouse is built in a secluded area, far removed from women and children. It is here that ritual homosexuality takes place. The practice of homosexuality, a closely guarded secret, constitutes secret knowledge that the men keep from women.

Several decades ago, the norms in gay communities sanctioned having multiple sexual partners. In an attempt to avoid the stereotype and demands of heterosexual relationships, most gay couples rejected sexual exclusivity (Davidson 1991). Gay male sexual relationships fall into four major types. First, a number of gay men have no special lover living with them or separately from them, and instead seek sexual experiences with a variety of male partners. Half of the gay and bisexual men in Harry's (1990) national sample reported that they did not have a regular male sex partner. Second, a number of gay men have a regular lover, even though they live separately (Jay and Young 1979). The last two types of gay male sexual relationships involve live-in partners. Looking at gay men who have a live-in partner, Dell and Weinberg (1978) identified two types of gay relationships: closed-coupled and open-coupled. *Open-coupleds* live with a special sexual partner but also have sexual experiences outside that relationship. Even in relatively permanent gay male relationships, sexual exclusivity is viewed as something to be negotiated rather than taken for granted. In contrast, *closed-coupleds* limit sexual experiences to their live-in partner and resemble happily married heterosexual couples (Davidson 1991).

Partly in response to concern over AIDS, gay men have been limiting their number of sexual partners and reducing high-risk sexual practices (Berger 1990; Zimmerman 1988). In addition, closed-coupled relationships are becoming more popular and new norms that support sexual exclusivity are developing in some subgroups of gay communities (Berger 1990). The trend toward sexually committed gay-couple relationships is reflected in advertisements in the personals section of *The Village Voice* newspaper in New York City. Many of these advertisements now stress sexual exclusivity as a condition for beginning a sexual relationship (Davidson 1991). This new trend toward exclusive relationships has taken place primarily among those who live in urban centers with a sizable gay community.

Female Lesbian Relationships

Sex among lesbians tends to be more closely bound up with emotional involvement and love than is the case with gay men (Peplau and Gordon 1983). Sexual relationships among lesbians often grow out of friendship, with emotional attachment preceding the sexual union. In contrast, gay men tend to move quickly into sexual encounters and are more likely than lesbians to have sex with recent acquaintances (Leigh, Julia Hood, 1989). Two generations ago lesbian relationships often used the butch–femme model, patterned after dominant–submissive sexual roles among heterosexual couples (Reilly and Lynch 1990). This model was rejected during the women's movement of the 1960s in favor of more

Like heterosexual women, lesbians tend to seek committed sexual relationships.

egalitarian sexual relationships. Reilly and Lynch (1990) interviewed seventy lesbian couples who had lived together for at least one year and found that almost all (90 percent) of the couples believed that lesbian relationships should be egalitarian, especially in sexual matters. Today, lesbians appear to have loosely defined sexual roles. However, in most lesbian relationships studied by Reilly and Lynch one partner often emerged as sexually dominant. In only one-fifth of the lesbian couples did both partners agree that they were equal in the frequency with which they initiated sex.

Blumstein and Schwartz (1983) found that lesbians have a lower frequency of sexual activity than either heterosexual or gay male couples. Because lesbians are also friends, moving from a friendly to a sexual encounter can be a difficult transition. In addition, lesbian sex tends to be affected by the traditional female gender role. Lesbian women are socialized into a female role in which the woman is expected to be the more passive partner who waits for her mate to initiate sex. Blumstein and Schwartz found that often both lesbian partners are uncomfortable with the aggressor role and are reluctant to initiate sex. As a result, the lesbians in this study reported that they had sex less frequently than they would like.

In the next section we explore the impact of alcohol and drugs on sexual behavior.

Review Questions

1. In what ways is marital quality related to satisfaction with marital sex? In Byers and Heinlein's study of sexual initiations and refusals, how did men and women differ in these behaviors?

2. In what way is a marriage partner's outlook on life related to his or her satisfaction with marital sex?

3. What are some gender differences in marital sexuality? What factors can lead to sexual disenchantment? What are the most frequent sexual fantasies?

4. How do men and women differ when it comes to extramarital affairs? What are some common motivations for having an extramarital sexual affair?

5. In what way are the norms of the gay community changing? What is the difference between closed-coupled and open-coupled gay male relationships? What other forms do gay male relationships take?

6. How does sexuality among gay male couples differ from sexuality among female lesbian couples? How successful have lesbian couples been in achieving sexual equality? How do you explain the finding that lesbian partners report having sex less often than they would like?

Alcohol, Drugs, and Sex

People who use alcohol or illicit drugs are more likely than nonusers to engage in high-risk sexual behavior. Heterosexuals are likely to avoid the use of contraception while drinking alcohol heavily or using illicit drugs (Yamaguchi and Kandel 1987). Among gay men, the use of alcohol or drugs, particularly cocaine, is associated with a high rate of anal intercourse without condoms (Leigh, Barbara C., 1990). This association between alcohol and drugs and unprotected sex probably reflects the diminished ability to consider consequences while intoxicated. Use of crack cocaine is strongly associated with another high-risk sexual behavior, a form of prostitution in which sex is exchanged for drugs. Although trading sex for drugs occurs in all social groups, a large number of those who engage in this behavior are teenagers (Holmes et al. 1990).

Alcohol, Drugs, and the Onset of Sexual Intercourse

The use of alcohol and drugs and the onset of sexual activity are closely associated. Among both college students and young adolescents, those who use alcohol and illegal drugs are far more likely to have engaged in sexual intercourse than those who do not (Jessor and Jessor 1977; Murstein et al. 1989; Rodgers and Rowe 1990; Yamaguchi and Kandel 1987). The sexual revolution and the surge in drug use occurred simultaneously. In a large national sample of men and women between fifteen and twenty-one years old, 21 percent of those who had used no drugs were sexually active, compared to 45 percent of the marijuana users and 89 percent of those who had used illicit drugs other than marijuana (Yamaguchi and Kandel 1987). Alcohol and drug use has also been associated with unwanted sex. In a survey by Muehlenhard and Cook (1988), approximately one-fourth of the college students interviewed reported that while intoxicated they had had an experience with intercourse that they later wished they had avoided.

The association between alcohol and illicit drug use and the avoidance of condom use puts many people at risk for acquiring sexually transmitted diseases, the topic of the next section.

Sexually Transmitted Diseases

Sexually transmitted diseases are infections that affect the genital area (typically the vagina and cervix of women and the urethra of men) but that can also infect the soft tissue of the mouth in oral intercourse or the anus in anal intercourse. There are more than thirty sexually transmitted diseases, and one out of four Americans aged fifteen to fifty-five will contract at least one of these diseases during their lifetime (Planned Parenthood 1991b). Although sexually transmitted diseases are widespread, fear of contracting a sexually transmitted disease does not appear to have stopped sexual activity. In Murstein's (1989) survey of 430 undergraduate college students, none of the respondents reported that concern over sexually transmitted diseases had caused them to abstain from intercourse. However, Murstein did find that worry over contracting a sexually transmitted disease has led to more committed sexual relationships and to a tendency to restrict the number of sex partners.

Men, Women, and Sexually Transmitted Diseases

Sexually transmitted diseases are a concern for both men and women, but they pose a particularly serious problem for women. Most men who contract gonorrhea experience symptoms, such as a burning sensation at urination or a

BOX 6.6

Safer Sex Practices

It makes more sense to talk about "safer sex practices" than to adopt the more commonly used term, "safe sex practices." Short of abstinence, there is no 100 percent effective method of preventing the sexual transmission of AIDS and other diseases. The following precautions can lower, but not eliminate, the risk of acquiring a sexually transmitted disease.

Discussing Sex with Your Partner

Going with the flow and "letting sex happen" increases the risk of acquiring a sexually transmitted disease, such as AIDS. In contrast, having a discussion about sex before the initiation of intercourse in a relationship can be a wise choice. It is important to ask the partner whether or not he or she is infected with a sexually transmitted disease and to find out about the partner's past history. Has the partner used drugs intravenously or had intercourse with anyone who has used drugs intravenously? Has the partner had anal intercourse? In this discussion, condom use can be insisted upon.

Condom Use

Use of a latex condom lowers the probability that the human immunodeficiency virus (HIV) will be transmitted to an uninfected partner. However, condoms do not provide 100 percent protection. A study of condom use found that out of every 100 incidents of intercourse during which the condom was used, it broke or slipped off 15 percent of the time. In about 8 percent of the cases condoms broke or slipped off during intercourse and in 7 percent of the cases condoms slipped off during withdrawal at the end of intercourse (Trussell et al. 1992). The effectiveness of the condom can be increased by leaving a pouch at the end of the condom to catch the ejaculate, by withdrawing immediately after ejaculation, and by holding onto the condom during withdrawal after intercourse.

Nonoxynol-9

Partial protection against an HIV infection can also be gained by using a spermicide containing the ingredient Nonoxynol-9. It is important to read the list of ingredients to see whether a spermicidal foam, gel, or sponge contains this ingredient.

Avoiding Anal Sex

Sexually transmitted diseases are acquired much more easily through anal intercourse than through vaginal intercourse. Unlike the vagina, which contains a thick lining of cells, the anus is lined with a thin layer of cells that easily tear during anal intercourse. These small tears usually bleed and open up a route for infected semen to enter the bloodstream of the uninfected partner.

Avoiding Multiple Sex Partners

Having multiple sex partners increases the risk of acquiring a sexually transmitted disease. A person's own sexual history as well as that of the partner is important. A healthy-looking partner could be infected with a sexually transmitted disease acquired through a previous relationship.

Avoiding Casual Sex

Recreational sex with a new acquaintance puts a person at risk of acquiring a sexually transmitted disease. It is difficult to know the sexual history of a casual partner or to know whether or not they have used drugs intravenously, which would put them in a high-risk group for AIDS.

Avoiding Drug Use

The use of illegal drugs, even when taken orally, raises the risk associated with sex. Drug use increases the probability that sex will take place and also raises the risk that unsafe sex practices will be used.

Requiring the Partner to Have an AIDS Test

Some people now refuse to begin a sexual relationship until their partner has had a test for HIV. The HIV test detects antibodies to the virus that causes AIDS. Although this test is useful, a newly acquired HIV infection that has not had enough time to produce antibodies will not show a positive result on an AIDS test.

discharge from the penis, which alert them to seek medical attention. In contrast, 80 percent of women who contract gonorrhea are *asymptomatic,* meaning that they do not have any symptoms that are readily detectable by the infected person (Planned Parenthood 1989). If left untreated, gonorrhea, as well as a number of other sexually transmitted diseases, can create scar tissue that can result in sterility (Stephen et al. 1988). Often, women discover that they have become infected with either gonorrhea or syphilis only when these diseases reach an advanced stage or when a male partner reports having the disease, leading the woman to have a check-up at a clinic.

Now we turn to a closer look at AIDS. For a more complete discussion of sexually transmitted diseases, see Appendix B.

Acquired Immune Deficiency Syndrome

One sexually transmitted virus that has no early symptoms in men or women is HIV, the human immunodeficiency virus, which causes AIDS.

What Is AIDS?

The human immunodeficiency virus causes AIDS by attacking critical cells in the immune system, called CD4 cells. These CD4 cells are large, specialized white blood cells that coordinate the immune response of other white blood cells. White blood cells are important because they attack foreign bacteria and other pathogens (disease-causing substances) in the body. It is difficult to find a cure for AIDS because HIV is a *retrovirus*. A retrovirus infects a cell and alters the cell's genetic structure so that the infected cell becomes capable of replicating the virus. Thus the HIV virus turns the CD4 cell into an HIV virus factory that will eventually spew HIV viruses into the victim's blood system. In time, HIV kills the CD4 cell and the CD4 cell count in the HIV-infected person begins to drop. *AIDS,* acquired immune deficiency syndrome, develops when the immune system becomes so impaired that it is vulnerable to *opportunistic diseases.* An opportunistic disease is one to which the body normally has some resistance, but which flourishes when the immune system is not functioning properly (Cooper 1992). The Centers for Disease Control have identified 26 diseases that qualify an HIV-infected person for an AIDS diagnosis. In addition, a decline in CD4 cells to one-fifth the normal level produces an AIDS diagnosis (Navarro 1992). The average time from an AIDS diagnosis until death is one year (12.5 months) (Lemp et al. 1990). Several antiviral drugs, AZT and ddI, have been effective in delaying the onset of AIDS and prolonging life. However, because HIV is a virus that hides its genetic material inside human cells and mutates rapidly, HIV eventually becomes resistant to AZT and ddI.

Most researchers consider HIV to be fatal, and close to 100 percent of HIV-infected people are expected to develop AIDS and die (Berger 1990). However, there is some hope that some strains of the HIV virus many turn out to be less aggressive. At least six people have lived twelve years after acquiring an HIV infection without experiencing a deterioration of their health (Cowley 1993).

Latency Period

Following infection with HIV, there is typically a long *latency period* before AIDS develops. HIV has been called the "invisible epidemic" because people often acquire an HIV infection years before they are aware of having it. The latency period lasts an average of ten years, although a few HIV-infected people succumb to AIDS in several months and a few remain free of symptoms for twelve years before full-blown AIDS develops (Cooper 1992; Medley et al. 1987). During the latency period, the HIV-infected person can look perfectly healthy and have no symptoms, but still unwittingly pass the HIV virus on to unsuspecting sexual partners (Cooper 1992; Morgan and Curran 1986).

AIDS Related Complex

AIDS related complex (ARC) typically appears before the onset of full-blown AIDS. *ARC* usually includes night sweats, inexplicable weight loss of 10 pounds or more, swollen lymph nodes in the armpits or neck, fatigue, fever, and chills; these symptoms usually last several weeks and then recur. In addition, ARC can include chronic diarrhea or a cough that lasts too long to be associated with a simple flu. These symptoms do not mean that a person is infected with HIV and has developed ARC. There can be other causes. However, these symptoms alert a physician that an HIV test may be in order.

Incidence

AIDS has been called a *pandemic* because it is a worldwide epidemic (Cooper 1992). By the end of 1992 twelve million people worldwide had become infected with the HIV virus. Of these, two million have died of AIDS (Cooper 1992). In the United States, HIV infection has also spread quickly. The first AIDS case was diagnosed in the United States in 1981; and by June of 1993 over 1 million people in the United States were infected with HIV and 300,000 AIDS cases had been reported, of whom 150,000 had died (Cooper 1992; Mayer and Carpenter 1992; U.S. Department of Health and Human Services 1993b). Because the vast majority of those infected with HIV are sexually active, the United States stands poised for a major expansion of the AIDS epidemic.

HIV Transmission

HIV is not transmitted through casual social contact, such as eating at a table with an AIDS patient or having a conversation with one. The HIV virus is transmitted when the body fluids or the body tissue of an infected person come into contact with the blood system of an uninfected person (Capell et al. 1992). The three most common means of HIV transmission are through (1) sharing HIV-contaminated needles among intravenous drug users, (2) sexual contact using either anal or vaginal intercourse, and (3) transmission from mother to fetus during pregnancy. HIV is most commonly transmitted through infected semen or blood. However, HIV is also carried in other body products, including vaginal secretions and breast milk, which can transmit the virus (Cooper 1992; Kubler-Ross 1987).

AIDS has a unique history in the United States, where homosexual males and IV drug users were the first two large groups to become infected with HIV and to be identified. Today homosexual males and IV drug users are still the two largest categories of AIDS cases in the United States, and men make up the vast majority (87 percent) of AIDS cases. However, the picture changes when we take a world perspective. On a worldwide scale, HIV is primarily a heterosexually transmitted disease. In Africa, where the first cases of AIDS were diagnosed, most HIV infections are currently acquired through heterosexual transmission and half of the AIDS patients are women. Worldwide, one-third of the reported AIDS cases are women who acquired the disease heterosexually (Cooper 1992).

Growing Heterosexual Transmission

The sexual transmission of HIV in the heterosexual population is increasing. In 1983, less than 1 percent of AIDS patients acquired the HIV virus from a heterosexual partner. By the end of the 1980s, 4 percent of AIDS cases resulted from heterosexual transmission (Holmes et al. 1990). Nonetheless, many people still make the erroneous assumption that if they are not in one of the two major risk groups (gay males and intravenous drug users), they do not have to worry about AIDS. This assumption creates a false sense of security in some people. Today the fastest growing category of AIDS patients in the United States is women who have acquired HIV through heterosexual intercourse (Cooper 1992; Holmes et al. 1990).

Women account for 13 percent of all AIDS cases and for more than half (60 percent) of heterosexually transmitted AIDS cases in the United States (Ellerbrock et al. 1991; Guinan 1992). This increase in female AIDS cases represents both an increase in the heterosexual transmission of HIV and a broadening of the definition of AIDS to include more diseases that afflict women (Cooper 1992).

Elevated Risk for Women. There is growing evidence that the HIV virus is more efficiently transmitted from men to women during sexual intercourse than the other way around. Over one-third (37 percent) of women with AIDS became infected with HIV through heterosexual inter-

To have comfortable, healthy sex lives, we must educate ourselves about AIDS, sexually transmitted diseases, and safer sex practices.

course compared to only 2 percent of men with AIDS (Guinan 1992). The HIV virus enters the body more easily through the mucousal tissue of the vagina than through the skin of the penis (Cooper 1992; Mayer and Carpenter 1992). The major route for heterosexual transmission varies by social class. Low-income minority African-American and Hispanic women who have heterosexually acquired AIDS tend to have received the infection from a male sex partner who is an intravenous drug user (Holmes et al. 1990). The vast majority of IV drug users with AIDS are heterosexuals who are sexually active. The female sex partners of male IV drug users are at high risk for also acquiring an HIV infection (Ellerbrock et al. 1991). In contrast to lower-class women, white middle-class women with heterosexually transmitted AIDS tend to have acquired the disease from bisexual men (Holmes et al. 1990).

Homosexual Transmission

Lesbian women have very low exposure to the HIV virus because they are able to avoid anal and vaginal intercourse. Less than 1 percent of all AIDS cases are women who report that they have had sexual contact with other women. Of these lesbian women with AIDS, 95 percent are also IV drug users and the remaining 5 percent have received blood products through transfusions (Ellerbrock et al. 1991). Thus it is unlikely that these lesbian women acquired HIV from sexual activity. However, this does not mean that lesbian women are free of AIDS risk. HIV is present in vaginal secretions, menstrual blood, and breast milk; and lesbian women need to be concerned about the possibility of HIV transmission (Cooper 1992; Kubler-Ross 1987).

Gay men, on the other hand, are at high risk for contracting AIDS. The prevalence of multiple partners and anal intercourse among homosexual men increases their risk of acquiring an HIV infection. The tissue lining the anus has only a thin layer of cells so that anal intercourse easily creates small tears, which bleed. Infected semen can easily enter tissue of the passive sexual partner during anal intercourse. The response of the gay community to the AIDS epidemic has been to urge safer sex practices, such as condom use, monogamous relationships, or avoiding anal intercourse altogether. As a result, the HIV infection rate among the gay population in large urban areas has reached a plateau (Kelly et al. 1990; Martin et al. 1989). Gay men in small cities, where the incidence of AIDS is low, are far less likely than urban gays to use safer sex. Gay men in small towns are still using high-risk sexual practices, such as anal intercourse without condoms. Apparently, rural gay men feel that they are less likely than their urban counterparts to be exposed to HIV. The number of AIDS cases in small towns is expected to increase unless AIDS education programs urge rural inhabitants to use greater caution in sexual encounters (Calabrese et al. 1986; Kelly et al. 1990).

Entering a sexually exclusive relationship diminishes the probability of acquiring an HIV infection. Berger (1990) studied gay male couples who had lived together for at least one year and found that only half reported that they practiced safe sex and two-thirds (69 percent) did not use condoms at all. These men tended to believe that sexual exclusivity protected them from AIDS. Berger points out that many gay men in stable partnerships think that they do not need to use condoms because they reason that if the partner is infected with HIV, they have already been exposed. However, the risk of acquiring an HIV infection increases with the the number of sexual contacts a person has with an infected partner (Berger 1990). Also, an infected partner can become more infectious over time even though that partner is asymptomatic and looks perfectly healthy (Curran et al. 1988).

The spread of AIDS among homosexuals has fueled *homophobia*. Homophobia is fear and hatred of homosexuals. Although homophobia existed before the AIDS epidemic, in the minds of the public AIDS has become associated with homosexuality (Richardson 1988). Even though AIDS is not a disease of any one group, AIDS hysteria has led to increased discrimination against homosexuals. Homosexuals have been forced from their jobs, denied housing, and refused medical treatment in some cases. AIDS suffers need to be viewed with compassion, and the general public needs to understand that AIDS strikes all social groups, including women, children, and heterosexual men.

HIV and Other STDs

Many of those who are infected with HIV are also infected with other sexually transmitted diseases. These additional diseases increase the likelihood of the spread of HIV. For example, HIV-positive people who are also infected with herpes or syphilis are at increased risk of passing on the HIV virus to sexual partners. Herpes and syphilis tend to progress faster and are harder to treat in HIV-positive patients. In addition, herpes and syphilis create ulcerations in the genital area through which the HIV virus can easily pass to a sex partner. People infected with herpes who are also HIV-positive tend to shed more herpes virus than herpes sufferers who are HIV-negative (Minkoff et al. 1991). Genital ulcers increase the risk of transmitting HIV to a sexual partner.

High-Risk Sexual Behavior

Once the HIV virus enters either a homosexual or heterosexual population, high-risk sexual behavior exposes others to the possibility of contracting the infection. High-risk sexual behavior includes having sex with a stranger or casual acquaintance, having multiple sexual partners, having sex with a person who is at high risk for AIDS (such as an intravenous drug user or a male bisexual), and having either vaginal or anal intercourse without a condom. One would expect that those people who have at least one risk factor, such as multiple partners or a high-risk partner, would practice safer sex by using condoms. However, a number of studies have found that those who were at high risk for acquiring an HIV infection were not very likely to use safer sex practices (Cooper 1992). Baldwin and Baldwin (1988) found that college students who had a high number of partners over the past year (four or more) and who are thus at greater risk of acquiring an HIV infection, are no more likely to use condoms than those with few sexual partners.

Knowledge about AIDS does not seem to deter high-risk sexual behavior. However, *AIDS-worry* appears to be an important factor in changing sexual behavior in a more cautious direction. College students who report that they spend some time worrying about AIDS are far more likely than others to use condoms and avoid multiple partners (Baldwin and Baldwin 1988). There is probably a generalized tendency for people to be risk takers or risk avoiders (Zuckerman et al. 1976). People who regularly wear car seat belts are also likely to avoid casual sex and to use condoms consistently (Baldwin and Baldwin 1988).

AIDS in Men and Women

The pattern that AIDS takes differs in men and women. When an HIV-infected man's immune system begins to fail, the two most common opportunistic diseases that produce an AIDS diagnosis are Kaposi's sarcoma and pneumocystic pneumonia. *Kaposi's sarcoma,* sometime called simply Kaposi's, is a rare and deadly form of skin cancer that produces purplish spots on the skin. *Pneumocystic pneumonia* causes coughing, shortness of breath, and eventually respiratory failure (Cooper 1992; Kubler-Ross 1987). These two diseases occur less often in HIV-positive women. One of the first ailments acquired by HIV-positive women is repeated vaginal yeast infections. The yeast infections later appear in the throat (called thrush) and then move to the esophagus. Although men are subject to thrush, the yeast infection is less likely to be as pervasive and less likely to move to the esophagus in men. One of the most common causes of death in women with AIDS is *invasive cervical cancer,* which can spread quickly to other parts of the body (Cooper 1992). In 1993 the Centers for Disease Control added invasive cervical cancer to the list of diseases used to classify an HIV-infected person as having AIDS. This change is expected to double the number of reported AIDS cases among women (Navarro 1992). As more AIDS cases are diagnosed in women, AIDS will increasingly be recognized as a sexually transmitted disease among heterosexuals as well as homosexuals (Cooper 1992).

Review Questions

1. In what ways is alcohol and illicit drug use associated with sex?
2. Why are sexually transmitted diseases a particularly serious problem for women?
3. What is AIDS? What are the characteristics of HIV?
4. How is AIDS transmitted? Why is HIV more easily transmitted through anal rather than vaginal intercourse? Why is HIV more easily transmitted from men to women than vice versa? Why does having another sexually transmitted disease increase the risk of HIV transmission?
5. What activities represent high-risk sexual behavior?

Summary

1. There are four stages to the human sexual response: excitement, plateau, orgasm, and resolution.
2. Half of all women do not use contraception at first intercourse. Contraception is avoided because of sex guilt, denial, and embarrassment.
3. Dating couples in nonmonogamous dating relationships tend to use condoms, whereas couples in monogamous dating relationships tend to use the oral contraceptive.

4. Males tend to prefer contraception that can be used by women. Women prefer contraceptive methods that do not interfere with spontaneity and are easy to use.

5. Married couples use surgical sterilization and the oral contraceptive as their first and second choices of birth control.

6. Among married and cohabiting heterosexual couples, men tend to show more interest in initiating sex than women. Married couples who have found a purpose in life tend to have a satisfying sexual relationship.

7. Married men tend to complain about an inadequate frequency of sex, whereas married women tend to complain about an inadequate amount of foreplay. Sexual disenchantment can result from a decline in the intensity of love, stress, or habituation.

8. Men tend to have more extramarital sexual affairs than women. The extramarital sexual affairs of men tend to be primarily sexual in nature. Women tend to combine emotional and sexual involvement in their extramarital sexual affairs.

9. Sexual exclusivity is something to be negotiated between gay men. There is a trend toward committed relationships among gay couples in urban gay communities. Lesbian women tend to have partnerships that grow out of friendship and that are more committed than those of gay men.

10. There is a strong association between alcohol and illicit drug use and non-virginity, unwanted sexual experiences, and high-risk sexual behavior.

11. Women tend to be asymptomatic when they contract gonorrhea and many other sexually transmitted diseases.

12. HIV attacks the immune system, turning CD4 cells into virus factories. HIV infection has a long latency period during which the person looks healthy but can transmit HIV to a sex partner. The heterosexual transmission of AIDS is growing in the United States and is well established worldwide.

13. Low-income women with heterosexually transmitted AIDS tend to have acquired it from intravenous drug users; middle-class women tend to have been infected by bisexual men.

14. Homosexual transmission of AIDS in the United States is leveling off. Homophobia has increased in response to AIDS, although AIDS is not a disease of any one group.

15. AIDS-worry is associated with avoiding high-risk sexual behavior.

Key Words

Excitement Stage	Vasocongestion
Clitoris	Pre-ejaculatory Fluid
Neuromuscular Tension	Orgasmic Platform
Clitoral Hood	Sex Flush
Labia	Plateau Stage
Orgasm Stage	Resolution Stage
Refractory Period	Sexual Disenchantment
Novelty Effect	Cunnilingus
Fellatio	Sexual Orientation

Closed-Coupled
High-Risk Sexual Behavior
AIDS
Retrovirus
Latency Period
Pandemic
Homophobia

Open-Coupled
Asymptomatic
HIV
Opportunistic Diseases
ARC
AIDS-Worry
Kaposi's Sarcoma

Resources

Planned Parenthood
810 Seventh Ave.
New York, NY 10019
(212) 541-7800
Offers information on contraception, abortion, sexual health, and infertility.
Operates 900 centers with family planning services nationwide.

National STD Hotline
(800) 227-8922 (toll free), Monday through Friday 8 A.M. to 11 P.M. EST.
Provides general information regarding prevention, transmission, testing, and
treatment of all sexually transmitted diseases. Discusses risk assessment. Confidential.

Sex Information and Education Council of the United States (SECUS)
130 West 42nd St., Suite 2500
New York, NY 10036-7901
(212) 819-9770
Fax: (212) 819-9776
Resource center and library. SECUS develops, collects, and disseminates information pertaining to sexuality education issues, human sexuality related
research, and legislation.

World Health Organization
525 23rd St., N.W.
Washington, DC 20037
(202) 861-4346
Deals with international statistics on various sexual health issues including HIV
and AIDS. Publishes reports in English, Spanish, French, and Portugese.

CDC National AIDS Hotline (in English)
(800) 342-2437, 7 days a week, 24 hours

CDC SIDA Hotline (in Spanish)
(800) 344-7432, 7 days a week, 8 A.M. to 2 P.M. EST.

CDC TDD AIDS Hotline (for the hearing impaired)
(800) 243-7889, Monday through Friday, 10 A.M. to 10 P.M. EST.
The National Centers for Disease Control hotlines provide general information
regarding prevention, transmission, testing, and treatment of HIV and AIDS.

Also provide advice and information about related medical, legal, and therapeutic services. Discuss risk assessment. Refer callers to specific local organizations using the caller's zip code. Distributes publications on HIV and AIDS prevention and testing in several languages. Confidential.

American Venereal Disease Association
P.O. Box 1753
Baltimore, MD, 21203-1753
(301) 955-3150
Aims to reduce the incidence of sexually transmitted diseases. Publishes *Sexually Transmitted Diseases,* quarterly.

Herpes Resource Center (HRC)
P.O. Box 13827
Research Triangle Park, NC 27709
(919) 361-8488
Provides information and emotional support to people with genital herpes. Local chapters run monthly support groups. Publishes *Understanding Herpes,* periodic booklet, and pamphlets entitled *So Your Partner Has Herpes* and *Telling Your Partner.*

AIDS Action Council
2033 M St., N.W., Suite 802
Washington, DC 20036
(202) 293-2886
Provides information and education about AIDS, lobbies congress for research funding. Publishes *AIDS Action Update,* monthly, and *HIV Voting Record,* annually.

AIDS Task Force for the American College Health Association
University of Virginia
Department of Student Health
P.O. Box 378
Charlottesville, VA 22908
(804) 924-2670
Informs students about AIDS transmission.

National Gay and Lesbian Task Force
1517 U St., N.W.
Washington, DC 20009
(202) 332-6483
Advocates the elimination of prejudice based on sexual orientation, lobbies for gay rights and legislative reform. Publishes *National Gay and Lesbian Task Force Report,* quarterly.

Lesbian and Gay Caucus of Public Health Workers
708 Rockaway Beach Ave.
Pacifica, CA 94044
(415) 464-7906
Provides information on the health needs of homosexuals and strives to eliminate discrimination in health care workers. Publishes *AIDS Action Update,* monthly.

Marriage and Partnerships: Interpersonal Relationships

Lynn complains that she and her husband, Kevin, rarely talk about any-thing important. When she asks Kevin what he thinks about something, he gives short answers. When she presses him, he insists that he has nothing more to say. Last week when Lynn wanted to discuss the problems her sis-ter was having with her husband, Kevin did not reveal his opinions or feel-ings on the matter. Lynn sees Kevin as a closed book, difficult to "read," and even after years of marriage it seems that she is still trying to get to know him. However, there is one topic on which Kevin expresses himself: his job difficulties. Yesterday, when Lynn told Kevin that she had had a bad day, Kevin said, "So did I," and began to tell her about the trouble his boss had caused him. Lynn listened, as she always does, but felt that her worries had been ignored.

Kevin wishes that Lynn would not try to draw him into disputes among her relatives. Discussing family problems is not a form of compan-ionship he enjoys. He is tired in the evenings, and he gains a sense of togetherness when he and Lynn sit on the couch and watch television. He wishes that Lynn also found this form of companionship satisfying.

Kevin and Lynn express their feelings in arguments, but these outbursts often seem like "wheel-spinning" because the problems are rarely solved. Yesterday Kevin called Lynn an "overprotective mother" when she said that their son was too young to play football at the recreation center. Lynn retaliated by calling Kevin a "sports addict" who was more interested in sports than real life. Neither brought the discussion around to the pros and cons of football for eight-year-olds.

In spite of these occasional disagreements Kevin enjoys family life. He likes going to his young son's baseball games and taking the family out for pizza afterward. He sets aside time for the family and tries to avoid bring-ing home office work on the weekends. Although Kevin does not often attend church with the family, when he does attend he feels a sense of soli-darity with the family. Kevin seems committed to marriage, and he expresses this feeling by saying, "I'm not going anywhere. I plan to stay right here." Lynn appreciates Kevin's interest in spending time with the family as well as Kevin's sense of responsibility as a breadwinner. She is grateful that she is not pressured into full-time employment outside the home. Lynn particularly enjoys the times when both her relatives and Kevin's kin gather at their home for pot-luck dinners. (Interviews by author.)

There is good news about marriage. In a recent national study, more than half the married persons interviewed said that if they had it to do over again, they would marry the same person. On the down side, one in five spouses said that they would definitely not marry their current partner if they could marry again and an additional 25 percent said that they were not sure (Patterson and Kim 1991). What factors separate those who feel positive about their marriage from those who do not? In this chapter we examine sources of marital satisfaction, the influence of marriage on well-being, trends in marital happiness, marriage over the life cycle, the influence of gender on marriage, and marital roles. In addition to heterosexual marital relationships, gay and lesbian partnerships are explored.

Marital Quality

Social scientists make a distinction between marital quality, marital stability, and marital success (Glenn 1990). *Marital quality* refers to a partner's personal experience of satisfaction or happiness with a marital relationship. This term is often used interchangeably with the term "marital satisfaction." *Marital stability* indicates whether or not a couple has been able to avoid divorce. Marital quality and marital stability are different concepts: Some stable marriages have a low level of marital quality. *Marital success* combines the two concepts and refers to a marriage that both endures and has a high level of marital quality or satisfaction. Marital quality is multidimensional; a number of factors influence marital happiness. Couples may be satisfied with some aspects of their relationship and disappointed with others. For example, in the interviews above, Lynn appears to be disappointed with her husband's level of self-revelation but pleased with his commitment to spend time with the family. Factors that have been associated with marital quality include family ritual, spending time together, positive communication patterns, self-revelation, intimacy, commitment, and religious belief. These factors are discussed below.

Family Ritual

Family traditions and ritual are important sources of marital satisfaction, (Abbott et al. 1990; Curran 1983). These include cultural rituals, such as religious holidays spent with the family, which strengthen bonds with extended kin. Private family rituals, such as taking the children out for pizza as Kevin and Lynn did, camping with the family in the summer, or attending a baseball game together, are also an important source of marital satisfaction. The practice of having a sit-down family dinner, rather than eating individually in front of the television, has become a dying ritual in American families. Perhaps that is why Lynn particularly enjoys pot-luck dinners with extended kin. Planning and creating family events and repeating them so that they become rituals can increase marital satisfaction.

Spending Time Together

Couples who set aside time to spend in family activities tend to have higher marital quality than those who become overly wrapped up in individual activities. Couples often grow apart because they are involved in separate activities and have little time to spend together. A good way for a couple to improve their marital relationship is to take time to prioritize their activities and then eliminate those activities with low priority and substi-

Participating in family activities on a regular basis tends to increase marital satisfaction.

tute family activities (Stinnett and Defrain 1985). As mentioned above, Kevin made an effort to prioritize his activities, placing great value on family events.

Positive Communication Patterns

Communication patterns also affect marital quality. Couples who use positive communication patterns to discuss problems and who listen to each other's point of view with respect tend to have a high level of marital satisfaction (Robinson and Blanton 1993). Two positive communication patterns associated with marital satisfaction are discussing issues and avoiding cross-complaining.

Issues versus Personality. Happily married couples try to direct their conversation toward issues and avoid attacking personalities (Krueger and Smith 1982). An issue-oriented statement would be, "We rarely go out on the weekend. I would like to start getting a babysitter and going out on Saturday nights." In contrast, a personality-oriented statement would be, "You're just a couch potato who doesn't know how to have any fun." Addressing problems in a way that criticizes the partner's character is rejecting and puts down the partner's personality (Ting-Toomey 1983). When Kevin called Lynn "an overprotective mother" and she retaliated by calling him a "sports addict," they were attacking personalities rather than discussing issues.

Avoiding Cross-Complaining. Happy couples engage in less *cross-complaining* than unhappy couples. Cross-complaining occurs when one partner states a complaint and the second partner avoids addressing that issue and responds with a complaint about the first partner (Gottman 1982). In other words, cross-complaining involves responding to a complaint with another complaint. This pattern of interaction often leads to a downward spiral in which a series of complaints and defensive statements are made by both partners. Such a conversation is accompanied by increasing feelings of frustration and anger (Ting-Toomey 1983; Wilmot 1979). Note that Kevin and Lynn had a tendency to engage in cross-complaining.

Self-Revelation

In addition to the positive communication patterns discussed above, *self-revelation* affects marital satisfaction by creating feelings of closeness (Knapp 1984). Self-revelation refers to discussing personal information about oneself, including thoughts, feelings, and attitudes. Individuals rarely disclose very personal information to the entire family. Instead, self-revelation tends to take place in one-to-one interactions. Therefore, it is important for husbands and wives to spend some time alone together, apart from children and other relatives, in order to be able to talk privately (Pearson 1989; Krause 1983).

Discrepancies. Marital satisfaction tends to be high when the partners engage in similar amounts of self-revelation and low when one partner engages in more self-revelation than the other (Hansen and Schuldt 1984). In fact, the greater the discrepancy in self-revelation between the husband and wife, the lower their marital satisfaction. In the relationship between Lynn and Kevin, Lynn feels frustrated because Kevin reveals less about himself than she is willing to reveal about herself. In discrepant relationships the disclosing partner often feels frustrated and the

Figure 7.1
Marital Satisfaction by Level of Self-Revelation

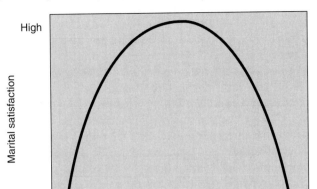

nondisclosing partner feels pressured, resulting in dissatisfaction for both partners (Davidson, Balswick, and Halverson 1983).

Upside-Down U-Curve. The relationship between self-revelation and marital satisfaction can be represented by an upside-down U-curve, with moderate levels of self-revelation producing the highest level of marital satisfaction. As Figure 7.1 shows, marital satisfaction tends to be low when very little self-revelation takes place (Davidson et al. 1983). Marital satisfaction then rises as self-revelation increases, but there comes a point of diminishing returns. When self-revelation is extremely high, marital satisfaction tends to decrease (Pearson 1989; Gilbert 1976). Why does marital satisfaction decrease with extremely high levels of self-revelation? High levels of self-revelation tend to be associated with criticism, lack of privacy, and asymmetrical power.

Criticism. Couples who engage in moderate levels of self-revelation tend to hold back some criticism of the partner. They exercise self-control and are in the habit of censoring statements that might be hurtful to each other. In contrast, partners who engage in very high levels of self-revelation tend to express whatever critical or disapproving thoughts pop into the mind. A partner needs to feel free to object to some aspects of the other's behavior, but excessive criticism becomes a burden to the relationship (Moss and Schwebel 1993). For this reason, moderate levels of self-revelation tend to produce high levels of marital satisfaction. In other words, the type of self-revelation influences marital satisfaction. Disapproval and criticism lower marital satisfaction (Schumm 1986). In contrast, positive communication that provides the partner with a source of self-esteem not only increases marital satisfaction but also tends to increase the overall quantity of communication in the relationship (Gilbert and Horenstein 1975). Partners with positive attitudes tend to encourage more talkativeness in their spouses.

Privacy. Moderate levels of self-revelation tend to maintain some individual privacy in a relationship. Privacy protects the partners from excessive tension and conflict. Frequent arguments can result when every feeling or thought is disclosed. Furthermore, privacy helps to maintain the focus of attention during conversation while avoiding interruption by a partner to talk about herself or himself (Pearson 1989).

Power. Husbands and wives differ in the amount of self-revelation they provide in a marriage; wives generally reveal more of themselves. This asymmetric pattern of self-revelation tends to provide men with greater power in the marriage relationship (Henley et al. 1990:400). On the other hand, when partners with low levels of power in a marriage withhold some information about themselves, they tend to achieve a more even balance of power in the relationship.

People in positions of power in organizations, such as administrators in a business, typically reveal very little personal information, whereas subordinates disclose much more personal information. Likewise, in a marriage relationship that is already marked by inequality, too much self-revelation on the part of the subordinate partner can further increase the power of the dominant partner (Sattel 1983). For example, when a wife reveals her intention to do something, her husband can object and tell her not to do it. In addition, when one partner discusses personal worries and concerns, the other partner can use that information later to influence decisions. For example, if one partner reveals that a friend called him or her "selfish," later, in a moment of anger, the other partner might say, "No wonder Susan said you are selfish. You won't even do this for me." Rubin's (1983) study of husband–wife interaction found that although wives had a need for intimacy, many were reluctant to reveal personal information to their husbands. As wives discussed their problems, husbands often participated in the conversation by giving advice and attempting to solve the problem. In this situation the wives felt that their husbands were trying to control their behavior. When wives revealed personal problems, they felt that their husbands became bossy and told them what to do (Rubin 1983). Yet, although wives experience their husband's advice as an attempt to exercise control, from the husband's perspective the conversation appears to be a normal problem-solving discussion. It seems natural to him to offer a solution when presented with a problem (Tannen 1990).

Intimacy

Intimacy refers to a feeling of togetherness, bondedness, or closeness (Sternberg 1986). An intimate relationship provides warmth and emotional support to the partners. The human need for intimacy is strong, and lack of intimacy is a major reason given by divorcing couples for breaking up the marriage. People in an intimate relationship have a lower rate of mental illness and overall better health than those in intimacy-deficient relationships (Moss and Schwebel 1993). Many couples report that intimacy tends to ebb and flow in their marriages. The periods of shared joy and closeness, such as childbirth or vacations, are interspersed with times of marital strain as problems arise (Robinson and Blanton 1993). As we see in the next section, being committed to the partnership helps couples weather the low points in marriage.

Commitment

Commitment, which involves the decision to maintain a love relationship over time, is closely associated with marital satisfaction (Sternberg 1986). People who expect to have a long-term relationship tend to exhibit greater attentiveness to the partner (Moss and Schwebel 1993). Committed couples report that the expectation their marriage will endure fortifies them and helps them over the rough spots. Couples who exhibit a high level of commitment are usually committed not only to each other but also to the institution of marriage. The feeling of security that commitment provides helps partners work together to solve their problems and renegotiate the relationship as changes in their life situation occu (Robinson and Blanton 1993).

Religious Beliefs

Religious belief and practice are strongly associated with marital satisfaction. Religious belief has been credited with giving couples emotional support that aids in coping with stress. Couples with religious beliefs report that attendance of religious services often provides inspiration to help them cope with family problems (Abbott et al. 1990; Bahr et al. 1982; Stinnett and Defrain 1985). In addition, religious orientation is related to other components of marital satisfaction, such as commitment and positive communication patterns (Schumm 1986).

All the above factors help marriage to provide emotional support for the partners. Marriage can substantially improve the well-being of the partners, as the next section points out.

BOX 7.1

Carol Mc
both th
riage
sou
th

Marriage and Well-Being

Marriage and well-being are closely associated (Coombs 1991; Lee et al. 1991). Married people generally have greater longevity and are more emotionally and physically healthy than those who are single. People who are divorced, widowed, or never married have substantially higher levels of alcoholism, suicide, and mental illness than those who are married. Although there is a paucity of data on Hispanic Americans, the relationship between marriage and well-being is strong for both whites and African Americans (Broman 1991; Taylor et al. 1990). There are two possible explanations for these apparent benefits of marriage: the selection hypothesis and the protection hypothesis.

The companionship and mutual care in marriage improves prospects for health and longevity of each partner.

Changing Marriage Practices Among the Bajju in Southern Nigeria

Kinney (1992) studied the past and present marriage practices of the Bajju of Southern Nigeria and found that marriages prior to the 1930s were diverse and complex. The typical marriage practice was polygyny, in which a man took plural wives. The first marriage was arranged by parents; betrothal often took place while the prospective bride and groom were young children. When the couple matured, the parents arranged a "marriage by capture." The girl was sent out to gather firewood or fetch water, and the groom and his age mates laid in waiting to "capture" her and take her to the groom's parents' house.

Second marriages involved individual choice for husbands and frequently took the form of "wife stealing." In wife stealing, a man forcefully captured a woman, with or without her consent. This could occur in a variety of ways. Women were sometimes captured in warfare and brought home as wives. More often, a man stole the wife of another man who lived nearby. Husbands worried about the possibility of losing a wife, so when a man went out with his wife or wives, he was always armed and walked behind them. Otherwise, he feared that he might turn around and find one of his wives gone. After the stolen wife had been with her captor for several days, she could decide whether to remain as the wife of her captor or to return home to her husband. If she stayed, the new husband would have to pay a bride price, which usually consisted of two or three chickens. Because stolen wives had the authority to decide whether or not to stay with the new husband, men used magical charms, such as leaves from the shea butter tree spread around the house, in an attempt to retain their wives.

A man whose wife was stolen could demand the return of the bride price, or chickens, which he had given to his wife's family. However, if he did not ask for the bride price to be returned, the woman remained married to him. In that case she had two husbands: the captor and the original husband. Many wives changed households from time to time, moving from the home of one husband to that of another. These wives practiced polyandry, or marriage involving plural husbands. Because their husbands typically practiced polygyny, in that

The Selection Hypothesis

The *selection hypothesis* argues that marriage and well-being are related because healthier people are selected into marriage. That is, people who have emotional or physical problems are probably less likely to take on the responsibility of marriage and are probably considered less desirable marriage partners than healthier people.

The Protection Hypothesis

The *protection hypothesis* holds that marriage provides some important protections against emotional and physical illness. The continuous companionship, emotional support, and interpersonal closeness provided by marriage act as a buffer against the stresses of daily living.

Both the selection hypothesis and the protection hypothesis probably play some role in explaining the relationship between marriage and well-being. However, after reviewing a number of studies, Smith (1989) concluded that far more evidence supports the protection hypothesis than the selection hypothesis. Married

they had plural wives, the Bajju marriage form was known as polyandrous polygyny.

Another way a marriage could occur was through the practice of the *levirate*, in which a man married the widow of his dead brother. Because Bajju kinship is patrilineal, with descent traced through the male line, the children belong to the husband's kin group. The widow who married her dead husband's brother could remain with her children and receive economic support from his family. If the deceased husband had several living brothers, the widow had a good deal to say about which one she married. After a period of mourning, one brother would send the widow a gift of tobacco through an intermediary. The widow asked who sent it; if she liked that brother, she accepted the gift and moved into his household. Otherwise, she sent the gift back and waited for the next brother to make a marriage offer.

During the 1930s Christianity became established in Nigeria and marriage practices of the Bajju began to change. The church frowned on plural marriage, and missionaries insisted that men send away all but one wife, separating many women from their children. Islamic influence at the national level led to the passage of laws requiring women to divorce one husband before marrying a second one.

Plural marriage for men continued to be legal under the influence of Islamic doctrine. However, the Christian establishment frowned on polygyny, and no man with more than one wife could hold an important position within the local church. Nonetheless, men have continued to take plural wives, and now only the younger, monogamous men hold influential church positions because older men typically have more than one wife.

Wives report that they are glad that now their husbands are discouraged by the church from taking a second wife. However, women have lost the freedom they had to move from the household of one husband to that of another husband. Knowing that a wife could leave gave husbands an incentive to keep their wives happy.

The Christian church prohibits a man who is already married from also marrying his dead brother's widow. Nonetheless, a surviving brother is still required to raise and economically support his dead brother's children. Thus the surviving brother has the traditional obligations of a brother without the benefit of the sexual and domestic services of the widow. From the widow's perspective, when all of her deceased husband's brothers are already married, she must leave her children and family home and seek a new mate elsewhere.

---

people are less likely than single people to become ill. The National Center for Health Statistics (U.S. Department of Health and Human Services 1988) found that married people experience fewer days of acute illness than those who are single. Moreover, once people become sick, they have a better chance of recovery if they are married. Married patients diagnosed with cancer tend to have higher survival rates than unmarried cancer patients (Goodwin et al. 1987). Because these studies investigated the onset of illness and recovery after the marriage began, the protection hypothesis is a better explanation for the association between marriage and well-being. However, although supportive marital relationships enhance well-being, unsupportive marital relationships can create stress in the lives of the partners.

Although marriage often offers some protection against stress and illness, it appears that the relative benefits of marriage are declining, as the next section discusses.

Trends in Marital Happiness

Married people consistently report that they are happier and more contented with life than all categories of single people, including those who are divorced, widowed, and never married (Coombs 1991; Lee et al. 1991). However, using data from the General Social Survey, which is based on a nationally representative sample, Lee and his colleagues (1991) discovered that attitudes toward being single have changed in a positive direction over the last two decades.

The Happiness Gap

In 1972 married women aged twenty-five through thirty-nine were four times more likely than single women of the same age to report that they were very happy. By 1989 this "happiness gap" between married and single women had diminished substantially. In 1989 40 percent of married women, compared to 31 percent of never-married women, reported that they were very happy. The diminished happiness gap can be attributed partly to an increasing percentage of young never-married women who report that they are very happy with their lives (Lee et al. 1991). Modern single women are more reluctant to take on the responsibilities of marriage and are becoming increasingly content to extend their singlehood.

The partial closing of the happiness gap is also attributable to declining marital happiness among young, married women, particularly those who are employed. Employed married women often face the stress of trying to find time for parenthood, household chores, and an intimate relationship with their husbands (Greeley 1989; Lee et al. 1991).

The happiness gap between married and single men also decreased during the 1970s and 1980s, but by a smaller amount than experienced by women (Lee et al. 1991). In 1972 married men aged twenty-five to thirty-nine were three times more likely than never-married men of the same age to report that they were very happy. By 1989 the happiness gap had diminished, so that 35 percent of married men reported that they were very happy compared to 19 percent of single men. Modern men have also become more comfortable with singlehood, but not as comfortable as modern single women.

One striking finding from Lee's (1991) study is that today never-married women are far more likely than never-married men to report that they are very happy. Apparently, young adult women find bachelorhood more attractive than do young adult men. This attitude may reflect the recognition on the part of young women that marriage and parenthood are typically combined with paid employment. Married women work a "second shift" of housecleaning, cooking, laundry, and child care when they return home from their jobs each day (Hochschild and Machung 1989). For a more complete discussion of marriage and work, see Chapter 8, Marriage, Work, and Power.

Next we examine the way gender influences performance of the roles of husband and wife.

Gender and Marital Role Interaction

Husbands and wives tend to approach marital interaction differently, partly because they have been socialized into separate gender roles. That is, the social definitions of maleness and femaleness influence how the husband and wife roles are enacted. Differences between husbands and wives have been found in their breadth of self-revelation and their display of empathy (Basow 1986; Fitz-patrick and Bochner 1981). In addition, ideal images of ourselves as men and women affect how we enact our husband and wife roles.

Breadth of Self-Revelation

Because women are socialized to recognize and label their feelings, wives tend to engage in more self-revelation than husbands (Basow 1986; Fitzpatrick and Bochner 1981). Wives typically provide a greater *breadth* of self-revelation than husbands. Wives reveal a wide range of personal information, whereas husbands tend to have a more narrow range of self-revelation, which often centers around discussing events related to their jobs (Bate 1988).

Males are socialized to relate less personally to others than are females (Jourard 1971; Rubin 1983). Men tend to describe as their best friends other men with whom they can discuss such topics as sports, gardening, cars, or the stock market. Unlike women, men rarely choose as best friends others with whom they can share private information, personal anxieties, or other feelings. In relationships with their girl-friends and wives, men tend to think that they are being intimate when they talk about the outside world or discuss their jobs. From a man's point of view, a career is part of the makeup of the "self," and he sees talking about his job as revealing him-self (Bate 1988). This often leads to female complaints that men are not being inti-mate and that they shy away from discussing their feelings. Nonetheless, men tend to disclose more of their feelings to their wives than to other people, including male friends. Lilian Rubin (1983) found that a substantial number of husbands named only one person, the wife, with whom they could discuss their worries and anxieties. In spite of these revelations by husbands, wives frequently consider the amount of male self-revelation to be inade-quate. In response, husbands often feel frustrated and con-fused by their wives' demands for expressiveness. Lilian Rubin quotes a husband who feels cor-nered by his wife's request for more intimate conversation:

> Karen complains that I don't talk to her, but it's not talk she wants, it's some other . . . thing, only, I don't know what the hell it is. Feelings, she keeps asking for. So what am I supposed to do if I don't have any to give to her or to talk about just because she decides it's time to talk about feelings? Tell me, will you; maybe we can get some peace around here (Rubin 1983:66).

Men confide more in their wives than in any other people. In other words, men's wives are usually their best friends.

The difference in levels of self-revelation between husbands and wives makes it difficult for couples to communicate successfully with each other. Psychologist John Gray (1992), who counsels couples with relationship problems, argues that when a man is upset, he often needs to be alone to work out his problems. A woman typically responds by wanting to nurture him and get him to talk. The man often sees her reaction as intrusiveness and finds it difficult to end the period of withdrawal while she hovers around him. Gray advises wives to back off and focus their attention on something else while the husband is withdrawn.

Empathy

Some social scientists maintain that the different approaches that men and women take toward self-revelation result in different levels of expressed empathy. According to Jourard (1971), one result of male socialization into the instrumental male gender role is that men often have difficulty empathizing with their wives. Because men in the traditional male role find it awkward to discuss feelings, they sometimes find it difficult to imagine how their partners feel. Mark Gerzon, in *A Choice of Heroes* (1982), observes that male specialization in the provider role encourages men to invest their time and energy in career rather than family. The wife's complaints of loneliness frequently go unnoticed by the husband. Gerzon points out that at the time a wife begins to bring up the topic of divorce, the husband often asks why the wife did not tell him earlier that she was unhappy. The wife typically answers that she did tell him, many times, but he did not hear her. Husbands often fail to pick up their wives' signals of distress.

In contrast, other social scientists argue that men are not less empathetic than women; they simply express empathy differently. Men often show empathy and support for a male friend by minimizing the friend's problems and assuring him that things will work out. When a man uses the same approach with his wife, she usually becomes upset and thinks that he does not understand her feelings (Gray 1992).

Gender, Marital Roles, and the Ideal Self

According to psychotherapist Karen Horney (1950) each of us carries in our mind an image of an *ideal self*, the self we would like to be. The ideal self is provided by culture, includes an ideal image of ourselves as men and women, and affects how we enact our husband and wife roles. Horney argues that these ideal-self images influence us through the *tyranny of the "shoulds."* The "shoulds" are strong and sometimes unreasonable demands on the self (Horney 1950). The ideal self exerts influence through guilt, which operates as self-punishment. Guilt is meted out by the ideal self when the person fails to live up to cultural demands and role expectations. In contrast, living up to an ideal-self image produces feelings of pride. Gender images form an important component of the ideal self and influence how men and women enact their husband and wife roles. One example is husband-centered migration patterns.

Husband-Centered Migration Patterns. The ideal self with its "shoulds" partly explains why married women are willing to defer to their husbands in decisions concerning migration. Many women derive an important part of their self-esteem from their image as "good wives" (Ferree 1991). For many women, being supportive of the husband's career ambitions is part of the ideal self. When the husband has a new job offer or promotion that would require the family to migrate, the wife tends to defer to her husband's wishes in deciding whether or not to pack up the family and move (Shihadeh 1991). The husband generally earns higher wages than the wife, and his income has a strong impact on the family's economic well-being. Thus his career often takes priority over the wife's career. In a Canadian-government-sponsored survey of over 2,600 families migrating to and from Alberta, Canada, Shihadeh (1991) found that migration decisions were made primarily by husbands. This pattern occurred even though wives often experienced negative consequences associated with the move. One-half of the wives in this study were in the labor force prior to the move. Many of the wives had difficulty finding employment after the move, and others took jobs at lower pay, so that in general wives had depressed earnings after the move. This is a concern because the migrating wife is in a diminished position for supporting herself and her children in the case of divorce or widowhood.

Shihadeh (1991) found that the wife's education, and thus her employability, had no effect on the decision to move. Well-educated employed wives were as likely as less-educated wives to follow their husbands. Furthermore, wives whose education or occupational status was superior to that of their husbands did not use these qualities to prevent the move. The factor of greatest importance in explaining the willingness of wives to give up their jobs and give up being near friends and family was traditional gender roles.

Gender roles played an important part in convincing women to migrate. Wives moved in order to follow their husbands, placing his career ambitions in the position of priority. The wives did not see the tension between migrating and staying put as a conflict between themselves and their husbands. Instead, they viewed the situation as producing tension between what is good for the marriage and what is good for the individual. Women have been socialized to put their marriages first, above individual preferences (Shihadeh 1991).

Review Questions

1. What is the difference between marital quality, marital stability, and marital success?
2. What factors are associated with marital satisfaction?
3. What positive communication patterns are associated with marital satisfaction?
4. Why does the relationship between self-revelation and marital satisfaction form an upside-down U-curve?
5. What is the relationship between marriage and well-being? What is the selection hypothesis? What is the protection hypothesis?
6. What is the happiness gap and why is it narrowing?
7. In what way does gender affect marital interaction? How do husbands and wives differ in self-revelation? What is the ideal self? How did gender affect marital migration patterns in the Canadian study?

Role Relationships in Troubled Marriages

When married people feel distressed about their lives, sometimes they seek the help and insight of a psychotherapist. In therapy, these people tend to focus on their individual feelings and pain. However, some social scientists believe that this approach may not be the most effective for people in troubled marriages. Maltas (1991) has criticized psychoanalysts, in particular, for focusing on the problems of the individual when a married person enters therapy. Such an approach overlooks the important influence of the marital relationship on the distress an individual is feeling. According to Maltas, we cannot easily understand the behavior of an individual marriage partner without understanding the role relationship the two partners maintain. In a role relationship, each partner feels some pressure to live up to the expectations of the other partner. Often the two roles fit together like two pieces of a puzzle. One type of role relationship common among married people seeking therapy is called the autonomous-partner and dependent-partner relationship.

Autonomous Partner and Dependent Partner

In the autonomous-partner and dependent-partner relationship, the marriage is characterized by the wife's need for closeness and the husband's need for distance. Often, the wife seeks therapy complaining of feeling rejected by her husband. The autonomous partner, typically the husband, experiences anxiety as he tries to maintain his autonomy (or independence) in a close marital relationship. His anxiety is experienced as a fear of losing his separate identity and being swallowed up by the wife. The autonomous partner, the husband, gives the appearance of self-sufficiency and acts as if the mate is not needed. However, he rejects and covers up his own dependency needs and withdraws from her. As a result, the wife often accuses the husband of avoiding communication and closeness.

The dependent partner, usually the wife, appears to have the opposite tendencies. She longs for closeness with her husband and is disappointed when he withdraws. The wife often feels that she has no independent existence outside the marriage relationship. She seeks merger with her husband while he attempts to maintain his independence. The wife experiences anxiety centered around her fear of being left alone. She is frightened by the prospect of her own independence and self-sufficiency and rejects her own autonomous urges. Rather than explore her own separate hobbies, friendships, and activities, which could provide her with a sense of independence, she centers her activities around those of her husband. Instead of becoming an autonomous person, she married a man whose strength and independence she could admire.

This kind of marriage becomes more satisfying when each partner begins to recognize and accept the rejected part of the self. As the wife begins to accept her need for autonomy and the husband accepts his dependency needs, the marriage tends to improve. When the wife recognizes her need for autonomy, she invests her time and energy in her own hobbies, friends, and work. Then the husband can begin to relax. At this point he often begins to recognize his dependency needs, which are filled by his wife. His efforts to draw her back into the relationship and her efforts to become autonomous offer some balance to the marital interaction (Maltas 1991).

Marital Stances and Marital Distress

Marriage partners often develop familiar ways, called *stances*, to enact their marital roles. These stances represent basic orientations toward the marriage relationship; spouses will gravitate to these stances over and over again as they enact their husband and wife roles. The following four stances often arise in stressful situations and tend to perpetuate marital distress.

Four of the most common stances taken by marriage partners when problems arise are the super-reasonable, the irrelevant, the placater, and the blamer stances (Goldenberg and Goldenberg 1980; Bandler, Grinder, and Satir 1976).

Super-Reasonable. The super-reasonable partner uses intellect and reason in discussions with the partner and ignores or brushes aside feelings. The partner taking a super-reasonable stance often speaks in a monotone devoid of emotion and is frequently accused by the other partner of being "like a machine" or "unfeeling."

Irrelevant. Partners who take the irrelevant stance change the subject to an unrelated topic when they become uncomfortable. For example, if one partner complains that the couple rarely goes out on weekends, the partner taking the irrelevant stance might respond by saying, "Did you remember to mail that letter that I gave to you this morning?" The person taking the irrelevant stance treats the complaint as if it had not taken place.

Placater. The placater seeks peace at any price and has the attitude, "Whatever you want is fine with me." This stance often develops when one partner has a strong interest in maintaining the relationship and fears alienating the partner. The placater rushes in to reduce tension by soothing an irritated partner or agreeing to the partner's requests. The placater often thinks that the marriage is working well because the couple rarely argues. However, gaining peace in the relationship often takes a toll in stress on the placater, who often feels that he or she is "walking on eggshells" in order to avoid upsetting the partner.

Blamer. The blamer does not address issues with a desire to discuss problems and attempt to solve them. Instead, the blamer accuses the partner when things go wrong. This stance displays toward the partner an attitude that seems to say, "You never do anything right."

Taking the stance of placater, blamer, irrelevant, or super-reasonable partner makes it unlikely that marital satisfaction will develop. All of these marital stances are fairly ritualized and tend to prevent closeness and intimacy from developing in a marital relationship.

Marital Stances Associated with Substance Abuse

Some of the above stances appear in marriages in which one partner is chemically dependent. For example, it is common for alcoholics to take the blamer stance, blaming their drinking behavior on the spouse, other family members, or the boss. In addition, chemically dependent partners and their spouses often use a pattern of shifting stances known as the "Karpman drama triangle," in which they rotate between victim, persecutor, and rescuer (Beattie 1987; Norwood 1985; Steiner 1974). The case study of Joe and Marianne, below, allows us to examine this pattern of marital interaction. Joe arrived home at midnight even though his wife, Marianne, had expected him to meet her for dinner at her sister's house. Joe never showed up for diner. When Marianne asked Joe where he had been, Joe told her that he had been drinking beer with the guys and lost track of time. What followed was an interaction in which both husband and wife shifted between the stances of persecutor, victim, and rescuer. This pattern develops when couples feel frustrated with marital problems that they seem unable to solve.

Marianne as Persecutor: I can't depend on you. You told me you would come to my sister's dinner party, but instead you went out drinking.

Joe as Victim: You're always getting in my face about something. When you criticize me for a little thing like having a few beers and losing track of time, it just makes me want to drink more.

Marianne as Rescuer: I don't mean to be so hard on you. I know that my sister's friends annoy you. Sit down and I'll fix you a cup of coffee and a sandwich.

Joe as Persecutor: It's a wonder that I come home at all. Any other man with a nagging wife like you would find another woman to spend his time with.

Marianne as Victim: I put aside a plate of dinner for you at my sister's house and I reheated it twice thinking that you would arrive at any minute. You always embarrass me in front of my family.

Joe as Rescuer: Here, honey, you go take a hot bath and relax and I'll bring you a glass of wine.

Joe and Marianne shifted between all three stances: victim, persecutor, and rescuer. The persecutor tends to elicit a victim response in the partner, and the victim position tends to pull the partner into the rescuer position. This is a common pattern in marriages in which one partner is engaging in substance abuse. However, this pattern can develop with any marital problem that goes unsolved. The victim, persecutor, rescuer sequence often begins to seem so familiar that children observing the marital interaction think, "Here we go again," when the marital argument begins. Taking up the persecutor, victim, rescuer stances results in "wheel-spinning," which leaves the partners feeling that their relationship is stuck in ongoing conflict. For a more complete discussion of marital communication, see Chapter 13, Communication and Conflict.

We now section look at the marital experience over the life cycle.

Marriage Over the Life Cycle

Several studies have found that marital satisfaction tends to fluctuate over the life cycle, forming a U-shaped curve (Rollins and Cannon 1974; Rollins and Feldman 1970). Newly married childless couples have high levels of marital satisfaction. As couples enter the childbearing and childrearing years, marital satisfaction declines by a small but significant amount (Belsky and Pensky 1988). Then when children leave home and couples enter the "empty nest" stage, marital satisfaction once again rises. This pattern holds for whites and African Americans (Broman 1991). However, there is insufficient data to determine the marital satisfaction pattern over the life cycle for Hispanic Americans.

Declining Marital Satisfaction in the Parenting Years

There are three major explanations for the small but important decline in marital satisfaction following the birth of a child: the life cycle squeeze, changes in marital power, and the husband's career commitment.

The Life Cycle Squeeze. Young married couples often experience a *life cycle squeeze,* which refers to problems surrounding the simultaneous launching of a family and a career (Coltrane and Ishii-Kuntz 1992). Although the young, childless, married couple may feel financially comfortable when both partners are working, financial strain usually sets in when children arrive. As the husband tries to establish his career, his income is lower than what it may later become. At this stage the couple are often trying to save money to purchase a home, and the added expense of children further tightens their budget. Participation of wives in the labor force is lowest in the early childrearing years, and this further diminishes the couple's earning potential. Later, as the children grow older, the wife is likely to return to work full time and the husband will probably have gained some seniority in his occupation, which diminishes the couple's financial hardship and insecurity. In addition to problems created by the life cycle squeeze, married couples are likely to experience a shift in power when children arrive.

Changes in Marital Power. During the childbearing and childrearing years the wife is most economically dependent on her husband. Her level of power in the relationship reaches a low point when she is raising children (Bergen 1991; Ferree 1991). Later, as the children grow older and leave the home, she is likely to be employed and gain more influence based on her economic contribution to the marriage.

Husband's Career Commitment. During the early-marriage years the husband usually devotes a great deal of time to his career. In these early childrearing years, money is usually tight, and the husband often feels pressured to work overtime. Many men feel that they have fulfilled a major part of their family-role obligation when they provide financially for their wives and children. In contrast, wives tend to think that companionship and romance are part of the husband's role obligation. These issues of companionship often create tension in the marriage as the husband devotes time to his career and the wife focuses attention on childrearing.

Comparing Parents to Nonparents

In the past, researchers have attributed the decline in marital satisfaction that follows childbirth to a damper effect that parenthood has on romance in marriage (Rollins and Cannon 1974; Rollins and Feldman 1970). However, it appears that the decline in marital satisfaction in the early years of marriage occurs whether or not the couple have children (MacDermid et al. 1990).

MacDermid and her colleagues (1990) studied married couples over the first two and a half years of marriage and compared couples who became parents during this period to couples who remained childless. Both parents and nonparents experienced a decline in marital satisfaction and diminished feelings of love for the partner over the first two and a half years of marriage. This declining marital satisfaction appears to be "normative" in that it is part of the natural process of moving out of the honeymoon stage and replacing an idealized view of the partner with a more realistic assessment of the partner's character. Thus, declining marital satisfaction tends to occur whether or not the couple have children. Furthermore, among those couples who become parents, satisfaction with marriage declined regardless of whether a child arrived soon after marriage or was born during the second year of marriage.

It appears that when children arrive, satisfaction with marriage declines only in certain areas of the marital relationship. When MacDermid examined specific aspects of marital satisfaction, differences between parents and nonparents appeared. Couples with children experienced more dissatisfaction with marital companionship and with the division of household labor than childless couples.

Household Labor. The greater dissatisfaction with the division of household labor experienced by married couples with children is probably the result of role shifts that occur in marriage after the birth of the first child. When a baby arrives, the total amount of necessary household labor greatly increases and more time must be spent in cleaning, laundry, and child care. In addition, the marital division of labor becomes more traditional, with the wife assuming a disproportionate share of household tasks. Allocating responsibility for child care and housework can become a major source of conflict in the marriage (Belsky and Pensky 1988; MacDermid 1990).

Companionship. The way married couples allocate their time also changes when they become parents. MacDermid (1990) found that after the birth of the first child, the amount of time married couples spent together in recreation declined. However, this did not mean that young parents avoided each other. In fact, couples who became parents engaged in more joint activities than did couples who were nonparents. Nonetheless, the nature of marital companionship changed. For young parents, family activities began to replace couple activities. Parents tended to spend their time together in child-related activities, such as shopping or child care, whereas nonparents spent more time in recreational, couple-oriented activities.

Some of the tensions that arise in marriage during the childbearing years result from the different ways in which the sexes view parenthood.

Wives have an easier time with the care of young children when their children are infants. By contrast, husbands find parenthood easier and more satisfying once their children have entered the toddler years.

Gender Differences in the Childbearing Years

Husbands and wives often react differently to the arrival of children. Husbands tend to experience the most difficulties in marital adjustment immediately following the birth of the first child. Moving from a dyadic (two-person) marital relationship to a three-person group in which the wife's attention is shared with a child is often problematic for husbands. In addition, couples tend to lament the loss of privacy that accompanies the birth of a child. However, as children enter the toddler years, husbands more readily embrace the parent role and find their relationships with children more satisfying and marital stress diminished (Crnic and Brown 1991).

In contrast, wives report that they feel less hassled when children are in their infancy than when children enter the preschool years. Wives who are mothers of preschoolers complain about the added time spent in housework "cleaning up messes" and the time spent in child-care hassles, such as the "struggle over bedtime" or "being nagged or whined to" by the child (Crnic and Booth 1991:1044). These preschool years are often a time when wives have a strong need for husbands to share child care and housework. Wives feel particularly burdened during this stage if they work outside the home.

Many of the strains of the early marriage and childbearing years can be reduced through delayed childbearing.

Delayed Childbearers

Coltrane and Ishii-Kuntz (1992) compared the marriages of couples who were late childbearers to the marriages of early childbearers. Late childbearers were defined as husbands who became fathers at age twenty-eight or older and wives who bore their first child at age twenty-five or older. Husbands who delayed fatherhood developed a more egalitarian marriage ideology than husbands who become fathers early in marriage. Husbands who postponed fatherhood were more likely to share in household labor and were particularly more willing to share in child care than husbands who become parents at a younger age. Husbands who were delayed parents were also better educated, which contributed to their egalitarian attitudes toward marriage. In addition, delayed fathers appeared to be more tolerant of the diminishing level of housework done by wives during the childrearing years. Wives of delayed fathers spent considerably less time in housework than wives of early fathers.

Delayed childbearing has other benefits for the wife. A wife who delays childbearing experiences a *role hiatus*, in which she takes a break between the daughter and mother roles and has time for employment before becoming a parent. Coltrane and Ishii-Kuntz (1992) argue that this role hiatus is valuable in promoting marital adjustment after the birth of a child. Delayed childbearing wives have time to focus on the marital relationship and to develop a taste for employment before becoming a parent. Delayed childbearing couples also postpone the shift toward a traditional division of labor that typically accompanies childbearing.

Launching Children

When married couples approach the "empty nest" stage, in which children will be launched, their marital relationship begins to change. This is a time when the couple begin to pull back toward each other, and attention becomes more focused on couple activities and concerns. This is also a stage when the couple move in the direction of combining companionship with autonomy or independence. The marriage partners begin to give attention to personal development in their own hobbies and careers. At first, the free time created by a diminished parenting role is likely to create anxiety and uncertainty as the spouses begin to explore what it is like to be a dyad, or couple again. Husbands, in particular, tend to appreciate the new focus of attention on the couple relationship; wives often find it difficult to adjust to a waning parental role (Aquilino and Supple 1991).

Hormones. Sociobiologists attribute the rise in marital satisfaction after the childrearing years to a change in hormone production in the husband and wife (Davis 1990). They point out that a man's level of androgen, or male hormone, is high when he is in his twenties, which is when men typically marry. As he enters middle age his androgen level declines. Sociobiologists argue that husbands become less aggressive and less dominant as their androgen level drops with age. Women also experience a decline in sex hormones as the estrogen level declines in middle age. Both men and women produce estrogen and androgen but in differing amounts. As the estrogen level in a middle-aged woman drops, her ratio of androgen to estrogen increases. Sociobiologists argue that women become more assertive as they age while at the same time their husbands are becoming more mellow. This hormonal explanation is more speculative than the other explanations for gender differences in marital satisfaction and has been criticized for reducing complex marital behavior to a simple biological explanation. For a discussion of midlife married couples with adult children living in the home, see Chapter 16.

Caregiving in Old Age

As couples age, one partner is likely to be faced with the challenge of caring for an ill or disabled spouse. Medical technology has increased life expectancy, and the number of elderly persons in the United States has grown. Over the last three decades the length of time that an ill or disabled elderly spouse must depend on the partner for care has also increased. Because husbands tend to become ill and die before their wives, women are more likely than men to fall into the caregiving role when they are elderly (Hoyert and Seltzer 1992).

Caregiving for a spouse tends to take a heavy toll on elderly wives. Caregiver-wives have lower levels of well-being than other wives; they are significantly more likely than noncaregivers to report poor health and depression. One explanation for this low level of well-being is the tendency for caregiving wives to become socially isolated. When a husband becomes ill, the wife tends to limit her social activities and abandon her membership in organizations outside the home, such as clubs. This occurs partly out of necessity and partly out of the wife's feeling of loyalty to the husband. Wife caregivers are further cut off from social life because they are significantly less likely to work outside the home than noncaregivers. As a result, wives who care for ill husbands are more homebound than noncaregivers (Hoyert and Seltzer 1992). Caregiving in a socially isolated situation puts strain on a marriage. Caregiving wives have more marital difficulties and report more disagreements with their spouses than noncaregivers (Hoyert and Seltzer 1992). Social scientists suggest that early intervention with spouse-caregivers would be useful in encouraging them to avoid social isolation by keeping up their friendships and outside activities.

Illness and Death of a Spouse

Husbands and wives respond differently to the terminal illness and death of a spouse. Smith (1989) found that men whose wives die suddenly have a higher death rate than men whose wives become ill and die gradually. Women typically play the caregiving role in marriage, and therefore men who abruptly lose their wives find it difficult to adjust. In contrast, men with chronically ill wives have time to make a gradual adjustment to the loss of a helpmate. On the other hand, Smith (1989) found that women run a higher risk of death when their husbands have a prolonged illness prior to death. Women tend to become both physically and emotionally exhausted caring for an ailing spouse.

Having examined heterosexual marriage relationships, we now turn to same-sex partnerships.

Same Sex Partnerships

Although legal marriage is not available to same-sex couples, they often form strong partnerships. Berger (1990) interviewed gay male couples who had lived together for one year or more and found that one-third would like to take part in a formal commitment ceremony, similar to a marriage ceremony, if such a ceremony were available to them. Same-sex partners lack many of the legal benefits provided by marriage. They are not allowed to file a joint tax return. The health insurance coverage of one person does not cover the partner in most cases. When one partner dies, the other is not eligible for survivor's benefits from Social Security. Even family health club memberships usually do not include the same-sex partner (Berger 1990; Quindlen 1992). The growing desire on the part of many same-sex couples to have their partnerships acknowledged as families is reflected in the terminology they use to describe their partners. Many same-sex couples have rejected the term "lover" because it fails to convey commitment and caring, and instead prefer the term "partner," which implies an ongoing relationship with substance (Berger 1990).

Changing Legal Rights

Same-sex partnerships are beginning to gain some of the legal rights currently enjoyed by married couples.

Domestic Partners. Some states, such as California, allow cohabiting homosexual and heterosexual couples to register with the state as "domestic partners." *Domestic partners legislation* has been passed in some major cities, such as San Francisco, in which the domestic partners of city employees are treated as spouses, in that they are covered under the city employee's health insurance. However, there are some limitations. These health benefits are available only to domestic partners who have lived together for six months or more. In addition, the legislation does not apply to employees of private companies. As domestic partners gain rights that were previously limited to married couples, the line between heterosexual marriage and same-sex cohabitation begins to blur to some extent.

Same-Sex Marriage. In 1993 the state of Hawaii took an important step toward legalizing same-sex marriages in the near future. Hawaii's State Supreme Court ruled in favor of three gay male couples who sued the state of Hawaii for denying them the right to marry. The court ruled that the state is engaging in sex discrimination, which violates Hawaii's state constitution. However, the court also invited the Hawaii state government to present arguments showing a compelling reason why the ban on same-sex marriages should be retained. This case will probably not be resolved for several years. However, if the Hawaii State Supreme Court decision remains unchanged and the ban on same-sex marriages is struck down, it is likely that at least some other states will recognize same-sex marriages (*Oakland Tribune* May 17 1993). It is possible that a number of same-sex couples could go to Hawaii to get married and then return to their home states with legal marriages.

We now examine the characteristics of same-sex relationships.

Social Norms and Same-Sex Relationships

Two important social norms that govern same-sex partnerships are the norms of androgyny and equality. (Berger 1990).

Androgyny. Both gay male and female lesbian partnerships offer some freedom to move out of the restrictions imposed by traditional gender roles (Reilly and Lynch 1990). Androgyny refers to a blending of characteristics associated with traditional male and female roles. The tendency in heterosexual partnerships to divide household chores along gender lines is missing in same-sex relationships. Same-sex partners negotiate the division of household labor, with each person choosing those jobs he or she enjoys the most or minds the least (Berger 1990; Reilly and Lynch 1990).

Equality. Gay male and female lesbian couples value equality. Same-sex partnerships involve two-earner couples, and partners are expected to be able to support themselves. Lesbians value equality in decision making and tend to have an equal say in decisions concerning vacations, leisure time, friends, and how to spend money (Reilly and Lynch 1990). In Eldridge and Gilbert's (1990) study of lesbian couples, those with greater equality experienced more satisfaction with the partnership. When one partner has superior earnings in a lesbian relationship, decision making tends to remain egalitarian. Thus lesbian relationships are able to accommodate two partners with different incomes (Reilly and Lynch 1990). The situation is different in gay male partnerships. Gay men also desire equality in their partnerships, but they experience more tension surrounding work and career issues than do lesbian women. A man's earning capacity is an important part of his identity, and gay men often experience relationship difficulties when one partner earns considerably more than the other. Unlike heterosexual social norms, which make the husband economically responsible for supporting his wife, gay men do not expect to support their partners. Thus, gay men tend to feel uncomfortable in a relationship in which one partner is supported by the other (Berger 1990; Blumstein and Schwartz 1983).

Commitment

A number of social scientists have observed that lesbian women usually have more committed partnerships than gay men (Davidson 1991; Leigh 1989). Eldridge and Gilbert (1990) found that, for lesbian women, commitment was strongly related to relationship satisfaction. For lesbian women, commitment usually includes sexual exclusivity, and lesbians are less likely than gay men to have sex with strangers or casual acquaintances (Leigh 1989). However, gay men tend to interpret the term "commitment" differently. In contrast to lesbians, gay men often view commitment and sexual exclusivity as separate issues. Many gay men reject the norm of sexual exclusivity because they feel that limiting sexual experiences to one partner would involve adopting the value system of the heterosexual world (Davidson 1991). As a result, a number of gay partners go out with people other than the partner, even when they live with the partner (Berger 1990). However, love relationships between gay men can be strong and ongoing, even though both partners may have sexual experiences with a variety of people.

Sexual freedom in gay male love relationships might be expected to produce jealousy. However, jealousy is considered less socially acceptable among gay men than among heterosexuals. Hawkins (1990) compared reports of jealousy among gay and heterosexual men and found that men in gay partnerships reported lower levels of sexual jealousy than men in heterosexual partnerships. Hawkins suggests that gay male partners, like heterosexual lovers, manage their emotions so as to bring them into conformity with social expectations in their community.

Not all gay male couples sanction multiple sexual relationships. The AIDS

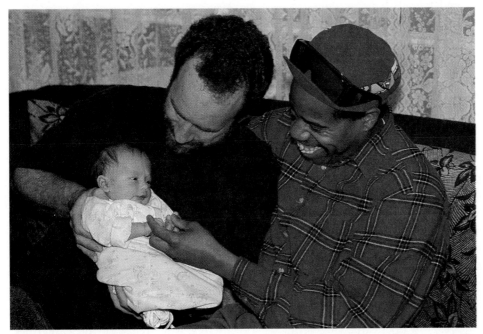

Although not legally recognized as marriage, some gay partnerships exhibit the traditional characteristics of monogamy, long-term commitment, and the desire to raise children.

epidemic has encouraged a growing number of gay men to establish monogamous relationships that emphasize commitment with sexual fidelity. Gay men in monogamous relationships report that they sometimes feel uncomfortable engaging in social activities with gay couples who adhere to the ideal of sexual freedom. Monogamous gay couples tend to choose as friends other gay couples who advocate sexual fidelity. Couples organizations that stress commitment and sexual exclusivity have been established in the gay community and are helpful in providing a network of friends for monogamous gay couples (Berger 1990).

Extended Kin

For some same-sex partnerships, relationships with kin can create strain. In Berger's sample of gay men in monogamous relationships, two-thirds reported that their relatives knew about their homosexuality and accepted their same-sex relationship. Nonetheless, some gay men find that their relationship with relatives is a primary source of tension. When parents and other relatives are unaware of the gay partner or disapprove of the gay relationship, a loyalty conflict often results. Sometimes one gay partner tries to hide the existence of the other partner and attends family holidays alone. This action generates resentment in the gay relationship (Berger 1990; Blumstein and Schwartz 1983).

Lesbians are less likely than gay men to reveal their sexual orientation to relatives or friends. Three-fourths of the lesbians in Eldridge and Gilbert's (1990) study reported that they had not disclosed their sexual orientation to the world at large. Half had not disclosed their sexual orientation to their fathers; one-third had not told their mothers; and two-thirds had not told their employers. Because lesbians often keep their sexual orientation secret, they are often less integrated into a supportive homosexual community than gay men. Many lesbian women have strong concerns about public disapproval and possible discrimination that could result from disclosing their sexual orientation. For the number of lesbians who are mothers raising children, this concern is heightened. The relative isolation of lesbian women leads them to place special emphasis on having a supportive and committed relationship with the partner.

Review Questions

1. What are the characteristics of the four marital stances: super-reasonable, irrelevant, placater, blamer?
2. How do the shifting stances of victim, persecutor, and rescuer operate when a couple has an unresolved problem?
3. Why does marital satisfaction tend to decline during the childrearing years? What differences appear between husbands and wives in the childrearing years? How does delayed childbearing affect marriage?
4. How does caregiving in old age affect wives, who are usually the caregivers? How does the death of a spouse affect husbands and wives?
5. In what ways are same-sex partnerships gaining some of the advantages currently associated with marriage?

6. What are the social norms of same-sex partnerships? What are some of the differences between gay male and female lesbian couples? What kinds of relationships do same-sex couples typically have with their kin?

Summary

1. Factors associated with marital satisfaction are family ritual, time spent together, positive communication patterns; self-revelation, and religious belief. Positive communication patterns; include discussing issues rather than personality and avoiding cross-complaining. Moderate levels of self-revelation tend to be associated with the highest level of marital satisfaction. The childrearing years often involve financial strain, husband career building, and a position of low power for the wife.

2. Married people tend to have higher levels of well-being than single persons.

3. The "happiness gap" between married and single people has been narrowing in recent decades.

4. Gender differences influence how people react to their marital roles. Wives tend to engage in more self-revelation than husbands.

5. Partners tend to gravitate to certain stances in times of stress. Unsolved problems are often accompanied by a shift between the victim, persecutor, and rescuer roles.

6. The marriage relationship changes over the life cycle, with small but significant declines in satisfaction with certain aspects of marriage occurring during the childbearing years. As children are launched, the marriage relationship once more gains primacy.

7. Same-sex partnerships stress equality and androgyny. Lesbian couples put more emphasis on sexual exclusivity, are less likely to reveal their sexual orientation to friends and relatives, and are more comfortable with unequal incomes than gay male couples. Relationships with extended kin can be a source of strain in same-sex relationships.

Key Words

Marital Quality	Marital Stability
Marital Success	Cross-Complaining
Self-Revelation	Intimacy
Commitment	Selection Hypothesis
Protection Hypothesis	Happiness Gap
Life Cycle Squeeze	Role Hiatus
Marital Stances	Super-Reasonable Stance
Irrelevant Stance	Placater Stance
Blamer Stance	Victim, Persecutor, Rescuer Stances
Domestic Partners Legislation	Androgyny

Resources

American Association of Marriage and Family Counselors
1100 17th St. N.W., 10th Floor
Washington, DC 20036
(202) 452-0109
Professional society for marriage and family therapists. Publishes *Family Therapy News,* bimonthly.

Association for Couples in Marriage Enrichment
P.O. Box 10596
Winston-Salem, NC 27108
(919) 724-1526
Holds retreats and marriage communication training courses. Promotes community services to foster successful marriage.

National Marriage Encounter
4704 Jamerson Place
Orlando, Fl 32807
(407) 277-8079
Runs weekend programs for married couples, organized by married couples and clergy. Holds retreats that encourage communication. Publishes *National Encounter Newsletter,* quarterly.

Mothers-in-law Club International
420 Adelberg Lane
Cedarhurst, NY 11516
(516) 295-4744
Works to solve problems between in-laws and to change the public image of the mother-in-law.

Mistresses Anonymous
P.O. Box 151
Islip, NY 11751
A self-help organization for women in relationships with married men.

Pro-Family Forum
P.O. Box 8907
Fort Worth, TX 76124
A Christian-oriented group concerned with strengthening the family. Runs seminars and workshops.
Publishes *The Family Educator.*

Part Three

Diversity in Families

Chapter

8

Marriage, Work, and Power

Sociologist Denise Segura interviewed Mexican-American wives who had recently come to the United States and were interested in seeking employment. Because working outside the home was at odds with the traditional Mexican female role for married women, husbands often offered resistance. One wife reported her husband's reaction after she acquired a job:

> *"Quit! Quit!" he says to me. "You don't need to work. You should be at home with the kids." So he puts it into my head that I have to quit. But I've got to stop thinking that. Pretty soon someone is going to look at my resume and say, "Wait a minute, this girl doesn't know what she wants!" And then I won't be able to get a good job because they won't trust me. (Segura 1988:26)*

Another wife interviewed by Segura described her husband's desire to be with her when she went into town:

> *My husband used to do everything for me. He took me to the doctor. He took me to the grocery store. He took me to school. He even spoke for me so that I didn't have to say anything. (Segura 1988: 25)*

This husband's desire to accompany his wife when she goes outside the home is part of an attitude of protectiveness that left the husband feeling uneasy when his wife wanted to seek employment. Yet, as Segura points out and as we shall see later in this chapter, Mexican-American immigrant wives do manage to exert their influence and convince their husbands that it would be beneficial for them to work outside the home.

(These quotations are from Denise A. Segura 1988. "Familism and Employment among Chicanas and Mexican Immigrant Women," pp. 24–31 in Margarita B. Melville, ed., Mexicanas at Work in the United States. *Houston: University of Houston, Mexican American Studies Program.)*

When Mexican immigrants come to the United States, they encounter a dominant culture in which the employment of married women is the norm. Over half of women and three-fourths of men age sixteen and over in the United States are in the labor force (U.S. Bureau of the Census 1994a, Table 615, p. 395). The *labor force* is defined as those who are employed and those looking for work. However, combining employment and family life can be challenging and often creates stress, particularly when the family contains young children. In this chapter we look at the trends in the employment of married women and discuss two-earner families. We examine the strain of combining work and family together with ways to reduce that strain. Finally, we explore theories that explain the relationship between employment and power in marital relationships. We begin by examining the overall pattern of employment in the United States.

Figure 8.1
Families in the Labor Force, 1940 to 1993

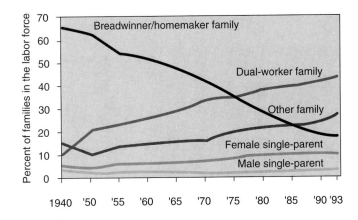

Note: "Other family" refers to families without a currently employed male breadwinner, including retired families and married couples in which only the wife is in the labor force..

Source: Dennis A. Ahlburg and Carol J. DeVita 1992. "New Realities of the American Family." *Population Bulletin*, Vol. 47, No. 2, Figure 10, page 25; U.S. Bureau of the Census 1994. Current Population Reports P20-477, *Household and Family Characteristics: March 1993*, Tables A and 15.

Husbands, Wives, and Work

The largest recent increase in labor force participation has taken place among married women. However, the modern family is not the only family in which women have engaged in economic production. In colonial American families of the seventeenth and eighteenth centuries, both husbands and wives worked on the farm producing crops, clothing, and other useful items, and the workplace and home were combined. In the nineteenth century the United States industrialized and most economic production moved outside the home. The husband–breadwinner, wife–homemaker family became the popular family form. In 1900, as the United States entered the twentieth century, only 6 percent of married women were employed (Skolnick 1991:107). As Figure 8.1 shows, in the 1940s the wife in the vast majority of families was a full-time homemaker. Before World War II (1941 to 1945) the wife's being employed indicated lower-class status and implied that the husband could not support the family. The working class strove to gain a "family wage," and in the 1950s many blue-collar factory workers were able to earn enough to support a wife who was a full-time homemaker and purchase a family home (Skolnick 1991:108)

The American family underwent a major transformation over the next 50 years. Women entered paid employment in large numbers when World War II created a labor shortage. Many wives returned home briefly at the end of the war, but by 1947 the employment of women equaled the wartime level and continued to grow (Skolnick 1991:108). Since 1960 the percentage of married women in the labor force has almost doubled (U.S. Bureau of the Census, 1994a, Table 626, p. 402). As Figure 8.1 shows, only one in five families today is a traditional family with a husband–breadwinner and a wife–homemaker.

Women entered the work force in large numbers during both world wars, when the industry of war created jobs but male labor was scarce. By the end of World War II, this was no longer a temporary measure but a new, increasing trend, with more and more women employed during peacetime. Today, a woman is a wife–homemaker in only 20 percent of American families.

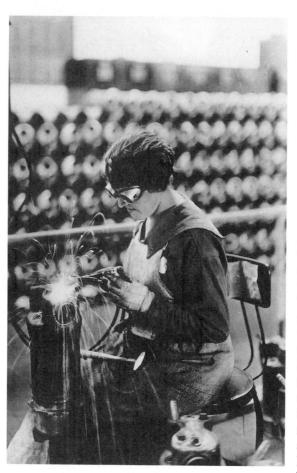

Employment Over the Life Cycle

Husbands and wives have a somewhat different pattern of participation in the labor force over the life cycle. The vast majority of women (70 percent) are in the labor force by the time they reach their early twenties, ages twenty to twenty-four. Female participation in the labor force gradually increases after age twenty, reaching a peak of 77 percent for women in their early forties. This means that approximately three-fourths of women will spend their midlife years in employment. In contrast, male participation in the labor force peaks at 94 percent when men are in their late twenties and remains high until men approach retirement (U.S. Department of Labor 1992, Table 3, p. 154).

Historically, African-American wives have been more likely than white wives to be employed because of the necessity of contributing to family income. In recent years both white and African-American women have tended to remain in the labor force when they have children. The family's need for income increases when children arrive, placing pressure on both parents to work outside the home. In fact, 60 percent of all married women in the United States with a child under age six are in the labor force (U.S. Bureau of the Census 1994a, Table 626, p. 402). Like men, the vast majority of women can expect to spend a significant portion of their adult years working outside the home. However, not all families benefit equally from the wife's employment, as we see in the next section.

The employment of the wife is particularly important to the economic well-being of the Mexican-American immigrant family, as we see next.

Working Wives among Mexican-American Immigrant Families

In traditional Mexican families the wife is a full-time homemaker who devotes her attention to caring for her family. When Mexican wives immigrate to the United States and seek employment, they frequently meet with resistance from their families. Segura (1988) interviewed 40 married and single Mexican-Ameri-

BOX 8.1   W o r l d   P e r s p e c t i v e s

Work and Family Life in Japan

The relationship between Japanese corporations and their male employees resembles a family relationship in that both parties display loyalty and a long-term commitment. Japanese men are expected to work for one firm during their lifetime. To look for a job in a different company is considered disloyal. Likewise, companies avoid laying off workers when the economy turns sluggish. About one in five Japanese male employees is in a career-track management or staff position with a salary that increases over his tenure at work. Japanese firms seek to cut costs elsewhere and save money by treating male and female employees differently. Even though women are as likely as men to hold a college degree, large corporations expect women to end their employment when they marry and have children. It is common for Japanese employers in large firms to ask women applicants whether or not they intend to quit work when they marry. Women who say "Yes" are more likely to be hired. Because employers expect women to be temporary employees, women are hired primarily for non–career-track, low-paying clerical jobs that lack opportunity for advancement. There is a self-fulfilling prophecy in which women must express a lack of career orientation in order to find a job and are treated like temporary employees when they show a lack of ambition. Only 7 percent of Japanese women employees are in career-track positions, and these tend to be women who have not married or borne children. Japan's Equal Employment Opportunity Law of 1985 prohibits sex discrimination in employment, but it carries no penalties. As a result companies still advertise for male employees for management positions (Brinton 1989; Brinton et al. 1991). When women do enter managerial positions they are likely to face sexual harassment (Holden 1992).

Women are further discouraged from entering managerial positions because of work conditions. In Japan the work week lasts six days, and Japanese managers are expected to be at their desks after their secretaries leave, often working until 10 o'clock at night. It is not unusual for a Japanese business manager to stay in the city overnight at a hotel that rents small sleeping cubicals so that he can avoid the commute home. The result is that women tend to raise children by themselves with little help from their husbands. Few Japanese mothers would seek management positions under these work conditions. In addition, husbands do not approve of wives working when they have young children. As the children grow older, Japanese women tend to return to work, but not at large firms. Midlife women tend to work in small businesses, which are typically family-owned. Here women earn only a fraction of the income that career-track managers receive in a large firm (Brinton 1989; Brinton et al. 1991).

One result of Japanese work conditions is that women are having fewer children. Both the difficulty of raising children alone and the necessity of forgoing motherhood in order to enter a management position have contributed to the declining birth rate. The Japanese birth rate has fallen to the point where the Japanese population is no longer replacing itself through natural increase (or births). As a result, workers from less developed countries have been drawn into Japan by the labor shortage. Japan, formerly one of the most culturally homogeneous societies in the world, now grapples with issues of cultural diversity, with its variety of religions, value systems, and lifestyles. Japanese society is experiencing tensions as women become disenchanted with marriage and motherhood under the current conditions of Japanese employment (Brinton 1989; Brinton et al. 1991). A recent survey found Japanese women to be less satisfied with life and more critical of men than American women (*The American Enterprise* 1992). The rapid pace of social change in Japan has created serious strains in family life.

can mothers who were recent immigrants enrolled in an employment training program in California. She found that wives who wanted to seek paid employment often came up against two traditional Mexican-American values: familism and patriarchy.

Familism. Mexican-American immigrant families bring the value of familism with them to the United States. *Familism* refers to values that place the needs of the family above the needs of the individual. When a wife wants to seek employment, her husband often appeals to her sense of loyalty to the family in order to change her mind. However, the Mexican-American husband's objections to his wife's employment tends to be limited to scolding.

Patriarchy. Mexican-American families are organized around the principle of patriarchy, and this also interferes with the wife's quest for employment. *Patriarchy* refers to male domination and female subordination and helps maintain male privilege at the expense of women (Segura 1988). Patriarchy among Mexican-American couples often takes the form of protection of the wife by the husband, as in the case at the beginning of this chapter in which the husband insisted on driving his wife when she wanted to go into town. Mexican-American husbands who are recent immigrants often attempt to maintain patriarchal control in the family by objecting to the wife's employment. However, Mexican-American immigrant wives often convince their husbands of the necessity of their employment by setting economic goals and urging the husband to adopt them.

When Mexican-American women do seek employment, they typically lack the language proficiency, education, and job skills necessary to secure well-paid employment (Ybarra 1988). They are disadvantaged in terms of income even when compared to Mexican-American men, who bring the same liabilities into the marketplace (Rodriguez 1988). Nonetheless, the wife's income is frequently essential if the family is to achieve upward mobility and attain a higher standard of living (Melville 1988).

For many families, a wife's income raises the standard of living from subsistence level to a better way of life. In Mexican-American families, this second income makes it possible to afford a nicer home or car and to send money to relatives still in Mexico.

Economic Goals

Segura (1988) found that Mexican-American immigrant wives were able to convince their husbands that their employment would be beneficial to the family by setting economic goals. The wives convinced the husbands to commit to these goals, which could be achieved only with the wife's earnings. The goals the wives set before entering the workforce fell into three categories, discussed below.

Basic Subsistence. One-third (35 percent) of the wives were concerned primarily with gaining employment in order to secure the basic necessities of life. A subsistence-level income was modestly defined because families compared their own economic condition to that of their relatives in Mexico, who were worse off.

Economic Betterment. Slightly over half (52 percent) of the women felt that their families had already attained a subsistence level of income and wanted a better way of life. These women hoped to rent a nice apartment, perhaps purchase a used car, and be able to send money home to relatives in Mexico. Segura calculated that to attain economic betterment the families would need an income between $18,000 and $29,000 a year.

Economic Security. Only a small fraction (13 percent) of the Mexican-American wives were currently seeking economic security, which involved obtaining a job with relatively high pay, job security, and advancement opportunities. However, nearly half hoped someday to attain economic security (Segura 1988).

Mexican-American wives have been successful in placing their participation in the workforce in the category of familism and emphasizing that their employment benefits the family.

Another group that faces challenges in combining work and family is African-American families.

The African-American Two-Earner Family

For African-American women, marriage and employment tend to go together. In fact, today African-American married women are more likely to be employed than unmarried African-American women. Historically, it has been necessary for African-American married women to work outside the home because of the precarious economic position of African-American men. Because the African-American wife's wages are often essential for the family to gain middle-class status, African-American men tend to be more approving of a wife's employment than either white men or Mexican-American men. However, the expectation that African-American married women will work outside the home and help support the family creates a heavy burden. Employed African-American wives report being less satisfied with family life than African-American wives who are not employed (Broman 1991).

African-American Men

Because many African-American middle-class families are the first of their extended kin to have risen above poverty, attaining middle-class respectability and success has a special meaning to black men. Being a good provider to the family and achieving steady employment are central to the self-image of African-

American middle-class men. The provider role is particularly important because many had fathers who were able to attain only irregular employment (Taylor et al. 1990). As with white marriages, marital roles that reverse the traditional American marriage pattern put a strain on African-American marriages. Employed African-American men with irregular employment who do most of the household chores report significantly lower levels of satisfaction with life than African-American men who perform less household work (Broman 1991).

Rewards and Costs of a Wife's Employment

Couples take the rewards and costs of the wife's employment into account when deciding whether or not to become a two-earner family. The rewards are related to the potential earnings of the husband and wife. Using a sample of married couples with their youngest child under age 18, Hanson and Ooms (1991) set out to discover how much the wife's earnings add to family income.

Rewards

Hanson and Ooms found that the economic advantage of the wife's employment varies with the husband's earnings.

Low-Income Families. The wife's earnings have the greatest impact on family income when the husband's earnings are low. Low-income husbands and wives tend to hold jobs that pay near the minimum wage, so that the wife's earnings increase family income by an average of 70 percent. In these low-income families, the wife's income is often crucial in preventing the family from slipping into poverty.

Once a wife in a low-income family becomes a mother, the economic benefits of her employment decrease. For women who work at minimum-wage jobs, the costs of child care and other work-related expenses eat up much of the income she produces. Child care can cost up to 25 percent of the wife's earnings in low-income families. For this reason, low-income families try to reduce the cost of child care by enlisting relatives to care for their children or by staggering their own work shifts so that the parents can provide their own child care (Hanson and Ooms 1991). When low-income couples are not able to obtain affordable child care through relatives, the wife tends to avoid paid employment.

Middle-Income Families. The benefit of the wife's earnings decreases as the husband's income rises. This is because wives in middle-income families typically earn far less than their mates. However, the wife's income is important because it is likely to make the difference between being a renter or home owner in middle-income families. Hanson and Ooms (1991) found that dual-earner families were more likely to own a home than single-earner families.

Costs

We cannot understand the economic benefits of the wife's employment by looking only at her earnings. When the costs of the wife's employment are taken into account, Hanson and Ooms (1991) found that the wife's earnings raise family income an average of 27 percent over the husband's earnings alone. The wife's employment creates added expenses for the family. Work-related costs include child care, meals eaten away from home, transportation, clothing and personal care, union dues, insurance, laundry service, social security, and other taxes. *Leftover income* is the income remaining after deductions have been made for taxes and work-related expenses. Approximately half of the wife's earnings are taken up by work-related expenses, so that her leftover income is approximately 50 percent of her earnings (Hanson and Ooms 1991).

Many social scientists have argued that we should be cautious and avoid considering the wife's work-related expenses to be only a cost of employment. Many of these expenses also constitute rewards of employment. The wife's clothing or a second car for commuting improves the family's standard of living and provides psychic rewards for the wife. The middle-income wife's earnings often allow her to purchase occasional lunches in restaurants, prepared food for the family, such as deli food and frozen entrees, and perhaps housecleaning services, all of which make life easier. In contrast, low-income families cannot afford to purchase these services to reduce the wife's work load at home. Therefore, the low-income working wife is most heavily burdened with a "second shift" of household labor at home (Hanson and Ooms 1991).

When the wife is employed outside the home, the question of how to divide household labor often comes up; this is the topic of the next section.

Household Labor

The ideal of gender equality has grown more popular in recent years, and most couples report that they believe household labor should be shared when the wife is employed (Thompson 1991). Husbands today take a greater role in child care than they did two decades ago, particularly when the wife works outside the home. However, husbands have made smaller changes in the area of housework. On the average, husbands are spending more time than they did two decades ago on only two chores: shopping for groceries and cleaning up after meals (Ferree 1991). Meanwhile, wives have adjusted to paid employment primarily by reducing their own household labor (Biernat and Wertman 1991). Since the 1960s all women, particularly employed women, have reduced the number of hours they spend in household chores.

How Is Household Labor Divided?

Household chores that have traditionally been labeled "women's work" tend to involve repetitive and frequently performed chores, such as cleaning and cooking, which typically take place inside the home. In contrast, men tend to perform those tasks that need to be done less often and that are performed outside the home, such as mowing the lawn and making household repairs. Grocery shopping appeals to men because it is an "outside" chore.

Although social scientists agree that, in general, wives do the majority of household chores, they disagree over the amount of inequity that actually exists in the division of household labor. When we look only at chores defined as "women's work," such as cooking, cleaning, and laundry, wives still perform most of the household labor (Coltrane and Ishii-Kuntz 1992; Thompson 1991,

1992). However, when we include work around the house that has traditionally been considered "men's work," such as yard work, paying bills, and household repairs, less inequality is found (Ferree 1991). An important survey on household labor that included both traditional male chores and traditional female chores is Ferree's study of two-earner marriages.

Ferree's Topology of Two-Earner Marriages

Ferree (1991) argues that although marriages have not become egalitarian, the degree of inequality in household labor has been exaggerated. She studied 382 two-earner couples in Connecticut. Both husbands and wives were asked about the amount of time they spent in household tasks, including cooking, cleaning, repairs, yard work, shopping, and bill paying. This list included tasks traditionally performed by men as well as tasks traditionally performed by women. Ferree arrived at the following topology of marriage relationships, based on the division of household labor in these marriages.

Drudge Wife. Almost one-third of the marriages were characterized by the "drudge wife," who performed most (more than 60 percent) of the household tasks while holding down a full-time job.

Semi-Housewives. One-fourth (24 percent) of the couples interviewed included a "semi-housewife" who worked part-time. Wives in these marriages worked less than thirty hours per week at paid employment and typically had young children in the home. Semi-housewives performed most of the household labor (67 percent) even though husbands put in an average of fourteen hours per week

Husbands spend more time than they did two decades ago on two household chores: shopping for groceries and cleaning up after meals. However, housework is still generally considered "women's work." The area of home life where husbands have more significantly increased their participation is child care.

on housework. The presence of young children in the home explains why heavy demands were placed on both the husband and wife to perform household tasks and bring in **income.**

Two-Housekeeper Couples. Over one-third (38 percent) of the couples were classified as "two-housekeeper couples" because the couple shared housework. These were the most egalitarian couples, with husbands performing 40 percent or more of the household chores. These two-housekeeper couples led Ferree to conclude that the division of household labor between husband and wife is more balanced today than in the past.

Cash-Paying Couples. The remaining 9 percent of the sample were "cash-paying couples" who together performed less than twenty hours of housework per week and purchased domestic services, such as laundry and housecleaning.

Changing Family Roles

Ferree (1991) compared her study to a similar one conducted in the mid-1970s and concluded that marriage relationships have become more equitable in the division of household labor. Ferree found that the proportion of drudge wives has remained relatively unchanged. However, the percentage of the most egalitarian marriages, two-housekeeper couples, has increased four-fold since the 1970s. Yet, only slightly over one-third of two-earner marriages involve two-housekeeper couples who approach an equal division of household labor.

Household Labor versus Total Labor

There is a good deal of debate over how much inequality exists in marriage. Some social scientists maintain that the marital division of labor is more equitable than Ferree's study, discussed above, and other studies indicate. These social scientists argue that there is a problem with examining only housework and child care to determine how labor is divided in marriage. Instead, they suggest looking at *total labor*, which includes both paid employment and household labor. Both paid labor, which produces family income, and household labor are important to the smooth functioning of the family (Bergen 1991). When we look at total labor, far less inequality exists in the marital division of labor. On the average, husbands work longer hours at paid employment than wives, while wives put in more hours in housework and child care (Bergen 1991). When we focus on total labor, many of the couples who were classified as semi-housewife couples in Ferree's topology of two-earner families appear to have a relatively egalitarian division of labor in marriage. Moreover, husbands who work fewer hours at paid employment tend to increase their participation in child care and other household labor (Coltrane and Ishii-Kuntz 1992). Perhaps some of the husbands in semi-housewife couples would prefer to be the parent who works fewer hours at paid employment and to increase the time spent at home caring for children and the household.

The Problem with Counting Hours

Another group of social scientists take a position that is the direct opposite of the one just discussed. These social scientists argue that the degree of inequity in the performance of household labor is actually larger than most studies indicate.

Counting the hours of housework can produce an underestimate of the wife's contribution to the family. These critics point out that household labor is qualitative as well as quantitative. In addition to the actual *time* they spend performing household tasks, wives spend time being *responsible* for the household: planning, coordinating, and thinking about meals and other household chores (Thompson 1991). It is usually the wife who must remember to take the meat out of the freezer to thaw so that dinner can be cooked. The concept of responsibility becomes particularly important when we examine child care.

Responsibility for Child Care

When it comes to performing child care, there is an important distinction between "parental responsibility" and "parental assistance" (Leslie et al. 1991). *Parental responsibility* consists of the remembering, planning, and scheduling that are involved in managing the daily lives of children. *Parental assistance* consists of providing physical child care without taking responsibility for planning.

Leslie (1991) surveyed dual-earner families and found that mothers tended to take responsibility for child care, whereas fathers "helped out," providing parental assistance. Fathers were rarely responsible for managing child-care activities. Women retain responsibility for children by anticipating needs and remembering schedules (Leslie et al. 1991). As a result, women experience more strain in their parental role than do men (Scott and Alwin 1989).

Perception of Fairness

Regardless of the definition of household labor used, studies show that employed wives generally do more housework than husbands. However, wives typically report that they consider the division of household labor to be fair. Only about one-third of wives report that they want the husband to do more housework (Thompson 1991). Employed wives use a number of strategies to arrive at a perception of fairness in the division of household labor.

Comparing Wives. Wives tend to compare their own time spent in housework to that of other wives, rather than comparing their own and their husband's contribution. For example, a wife might say to herself, "At least I don't have to iron shirts like Susan does" (Thompson 1991).

Comparing Husbands. Wives tend to compare their husbands' housework performance to that of other husbands, justifying the division of household labor by saying, "Well, he does more than most husbands" (Thompson 1991).

Labeling Work as "Nonwork. Wives frequently consider many of their tasks to be "nonwork" (Thompson 1991). This is particularly the case with running errands, such as dropping off the husband's shirts at the laundry or shopping for the children's clothes. Such tasks are so intertwined into their daily lives that women often do not label them as work.

Belief in Natural Gender Differences. Wives often legitimate the unequal division of housework by assuming that men are basically different from women. Some wives rationalize the husband's small contribution to household labor by thinking that he is incapable of doing a good job, or that he dislikes housework. However, although the husband's dislike for housework tends to excuse him, the wife's dislike rarely excuses her from the responsibility (Ferree 1991).

Thompson (1991) argues that employed wives who identify housework as labor that is important to the family, rather than as nonwork, are the ones best able to bargain with their husbands for a change in the distribution of household labor. In addition, wives who compare their own time spent in housework to that of their husbands are more likely to argue for change.

Nonetheless, wives are not the only ones who experience work–family conflict as they try to juggle paid employment, household chores, and child care. As we see next, both husbands and wives experience strain in trying to balance work and family roles.

Review Questions

1. What are the patterns of labor force participation among men and women? How has the pattern of labor force participation among married women changed since the colonial period?
2. What difficulties does the Mexican-American immigrant wife face in seeking employment? How is the Mexican-American immigrant wife able to convince her husband that she should seek employment?
3. What work patterns exist in African-American marriages?
4. In which families are the rewards of the wife's employment greatest? In which families are the costs of the wife's employment greatest?
5. How do husbands and wives differ in their contribution to household labor?
6. Describe the types of families included in Ferree's topology of two-earner families. Which is the most egalitarian family type? Which is the least egalitarian family type?
7. What psychological processes lead women to believe that the division of household labor is fair even though the wife performs most of that labor?
8. What is the difference between parental responsibility and parental assistance?

Work–Family Conflict

Balancing work and family life often creates stress in families. Over half of parents in dual-earner families report experiencing conflict between the demands of work and family (Hughes et al. 1992). This strain can take the form of negative mood spillover, role overload, or role conflict.

Negative Mood Spillover

In *negative mood spillover*, the problems and stress at work spill over and affect a person's ability to perform family roles. Work problems can lead a person to feel preoccupied, fatigued, and irritable at home. Spouses who experience negative mood spillover tend to agree with the statement, "When I am at home, I

BOX 8.2   Social Issues

Feminist Split Over Marriage Issues

Marriage is undergoing a profound restructuring as wives enter paid employment. The feminist movement has split over the issue of whether women should give priority to careers or to marriage and family life. *Humanistic feminists* argue that the quest for equality is paramount and women should pursue careers on par with men. According to these feminists, the family needs to make adjustments to accommodate the wife's career. Other feminists, called *gynocentric feminists,* maintain that women play a unique role in society as wives and mothers and that women need opportunities to cut back on paid employment so that they can give priority to their families (Bergen 1991). This debate is discussed below.

Humanistic Perspective

The humanistic feminists assume that women and men are basically alike and that women should seek the same rights and privileges that men hold. They urge women to compete with men for high-paying jobs. This humanistic feminist perspective has been important in helping women attain access to graduate schools and to well-paid professions. When Felice Schwartz (1989), writing in the *Harvard Business Review,* advised women with families to enter a "mommy track" of reduced work hours, humanistic feminists objected. Women who slow down their careers in order to spend more time with their families tend to be passed up for promotions and are often taken less seriously than men by upper management. In addition, a woman who slows down her career will be less able to support her family in the case of divorce than a woman who has kept pace with the men in her profession (Bergen 1991).

Other feminists have been critical of the humanistic perspective, pointing out that many assumptions made by humanistic feminists have created hardships for women.

Gynocentric Perspective

Gynocentric feminists oppose the position of the humanistic feminists. According to gynocentric feminists, women have historically played a unique role in society as the glue of family life. They argue that high-pressure careers have put women with families under stress. Professional women who work long hours tend to encounter high levels of role conflict because their schedules do not easily accommodate family needs (Guelzow et al. 1991). Gynocentric feminists argue that there is a need in the workplace for greater recognition of the special responsibility women bear in family life. The gynocentric perspective urges employers to be more considerate of working wives by providing flexible work schedules, family leave, on-site day care, part-time employment, and job sharing. All of these changes would make it easier to combine paid employment and family life. Moreover, if these options were available to both genders they would also be beneficial to husbands by allowing men the flexibility to become more involved with their families (Bergen 1991).

Backlash

In her book, *Backlash,* Susan Faludi (1991) has criticized both social researchers and the media for publicizing this debate over the role of women in American society. She sides with the humanistic feminists who want to protect equal opportunities for women. Faludi points out that the media have emphasized the role conflict and stress experienced by wives and mothers who are employed in the professions. She maintains that the unspoken message to young women is that equality in employment has brought trouble for women. According to Faludi, such research and media coverage represent a backlash against the women's movement and its quest for equality. In her view it sends an unfortunate message to women, implying that they should avoid seeking equality with men. Faludi worries that research and media attention to conflict in dual-career families will lead women to seek more traditional family roles and return to the home. Faludi maintains that the problems of working women are the result of too little equality, not too much equality. Women still bear primary responsibility for household chores and child care, and greater participation by husbands in household labor would ease the strain on women.

find myself thinking about work and not paying attention to my spouse" (Hughes et al. 1992:36). Such distractions make it difficult to be a relaxed, caring parent or spouse.

It is not unusual for the husband's distress over his job difficulties to contribute to emotional distress in wives (Rook et al. 1991). In fact, the husband's negative mood has been found to affect the well-being of wives adversely in terms of both psychological and physical health. Psychological symptoms in wives included nervousness, frightening thoughts, temper outbursts, and restlessness.

Rook (1991) accounts for the association between the husband's job difficulties and the wife's diminished well-being by using the *burden-of-care explanation.* The husband's job difficulties place caregiving demands on the wife. Wives often jeopardize their own well-being by ignoring their own needs in order to pay attention to the psychological needs of the husband. His distress elicits heightened levels of worry and concern on her part. As she begins to feel overburdened, she either tries harder to comfort him or withdraws from him. Wives who were sympathetic to their husband's job difficulties had more physical symptoms of stress than wives who had withdrawn to some extent from their husbands. Wives who had experienced recent marital discord had fewer stress symptoms than wives with harmonious marriages (Rook et al. 1991). Likewise, wives who feel overwhelmed by employment can also engage in negative mood spillover by bringing a bad mood home to burden the husband.

Role Overload

Role overload occurs when the duties required of a social role are greater than the energy and time available to perform those duties. The employed person filling the parent role often finds that there is not enough time in the day to help the child with homework, read a story out loud, take a child out to purchase a birthday present for an upcoming party, and volunteer in the child's classroom. Women, in particular, are likely to feel distressed because they compare themselves to their own mothers, who did all of these things and also had cookies and milk waiting when the children returned from school. The mother experiencing role overload generally fails to point out to herself that her own mother was not employed outside the home.

Role overload is experienced by both husbands and wives. Over one-third of men in the work force (36 percent) have children under age eighteen, and two-thirds of these fathers have wives who are employed. Fathers have become important in providing care for children (National Council on Family Relations Report, 1991, p.17). Almost three-quarters of American preschool children are cared for by the mother, father, or other relative (*Population Today* 1990, p. 5). Some fathers have substantial responsibility for child care because the husband and wife stagger their shifts so that one parent can remain at home with the children. Like mothers, fathers are also feeling the pinch of role overload.

Role Conflict

Role conflict occurs when the performance of one role, for example, a work role, makes it difficult to meet the obligations of other roles, such as the spouse role or parental role. Conflict between work and family roles tends to reduce marital quality, and considerable role conflict has been found among employed parents of young children (Hughes et al. 1992). Combining employment and parenting leaves couples with little time to focus on the marriage relationship. Both married women and married men with children tend to agree with the following statement: "Because of career demands, I find it difficult to be the kind of wife (husband) I'd like to be" (Guelzow et al. 1991). Work–family conflict is associated with a greater number of marital disagreements and with less marital companionship. Spouses who experience high levels of role conflict report that they confide in each other less and are less likely to share a joke or laughter than spouses with low levels of role conflict. Overall, conflict between work and family roles has a negative impact on the quality of marriage (Hughes et al. 1992).

In the next section we explore ways in which couples can reduce work–family conflict.

Strategies for Reducing Work–Family Conflict

There are five main ways in which couples attempt to reduce work–family conflict: role reduction, lowering standards for role performance, negotiating a reassignment of role duties, attempting to convince employers to change work conditions, and social redefinition.

Role Reduction

The primary strategy couples use to reduce work–family conflict is *role reduction*. Role reduction involves reducing responsibilities in major social roles. Wives tend to reduce their hours in paid employment as a strategy for diminishing work–family conflict. The necessity for working mothers to combine homemaking with employment probably accounts for the fact that one-fourth of employed married women work part-time compared to only 6 percent of employed married men (U.S. Department of Labor 1990:34).

Choice of Occupation. One common method of role reduction is for the wife to choose a female-dominated occupation, such as cashier, waitress, or nursery school teacher. Such jobs typically allow an employee to limit work to forty hours a week. A study of nurses revealed that they place greater importance on their domestic role than on their work role (Moore and Rickel 1980). Husbands tend to spend more hours at their jobs than do wives. Of husbands and wives who work full time, the median number of hours worked per week by married men is 45.4 hours compared to 40.8 hours for a married woman. This means that half of married men work 45.4 hours *or more* per week (U.S. Department of Labor, 1990, p.34). Male-dominated professions, such as law, tend to judge career commitment by the willingness to work long hours. Men in blue-collar occupations, such as factory work, also tend to work over 40 hours per week to gain overtime pay. Husbands employed in both professional and blue-collar work are attempting to fill the traditional male-role obligation of bearing primary responsibility for financially supporting the family. Employed mothers often seek occupations that allow them to make a sharp division between work and family life by not bringing work home and not being required to work overtime. However, the desire for limited work hours is not limited to mothers.

Fathers and Role Reduction. Fathers as well as mothers often desire a reduction in work hours in order to spend more time with their families. In a survey conducted for *Fortune Magazine*, almost the same percentage of fathers (37 percent) as mothers (41 percent) reported that their jobs interfered with family life (National Council of Family Relations 1991, p. 17). In a 1989 *Washington Post* poll, almost half of the fathers surveyed (48 percent) said that they had reduced their work hours in order to spend more time with their families and one-fourth (23 percent) indicated that they had turned down a promotion because it would have taken time away from the family (National Council of Family Relations Report 1991, p. 17).

Lowering Standards for Role Performance

Another method of role reduction is to lower standards of role performance, for example, by deciding that it is acceptable for the house to be dusty or for the dishes to be stacked in the sink and washed once a day. In addition, role strain can be reduced by developing legitimate excuses that allow a person to avoid performing a task. Working mothers often point out that their work and family responsibilities prevent them from becoming den mother or brownie leader. Likewise, working wives often limit the amount of time they spend driving an elderly relative on errands and look to relatives who are not employed or are employed part time to perform these tasks (Guelzow et al. 1991).

Negotiating Reassignment of Role Duties

Wives frequently attempt to reduce their own work–family conflict by convincing husbands to assume some household tasks that have traditionally been seen as part of the wife's role, such as grocery shopping. It is usually wives who initiate role sharing by negotiating with husbands as a means to reduce their own role overload (Volling and Belsky 1991). Wives have been more effective in inducing husbands to increase the amount of time they spend with children than in convincing husbands to take an increased role in housecleaning. Husbands tend to spend more time with children when wives are employed (Guelzow et al. 1991). Fathers who spend time with children often gain important personal rewards from an expanded father role.

Changing Work Conditions

A large number of both husbands and wives desire changes in the way paid work is organized in order to reduce work–family conflict.

Flexible Work Schedules. In a 1990 survey of Du Pont's 8,500 workers, over half (56 percent) wanted the option of a flexible work schedule to help them balance work and family obligations (National Council on Family Relations Report 1991). A flexible work schedule allows for variation in the hours at which a person must arrive at and leave the work site. For example, a flexible schedule might allow the husband and wife to stagger their work schedules so that one of them would be home when the children return from school. Parents in dual-career families who have flexible work schedules report significantly lower levels of marital, professional, and parental stress than those whose employers refuse to grant flexibility in work scheduling (Guelzow et al. 1991).

BOX 8.3   A Closer Look

Family Leave Policy

Diane McCourtney made history when she was fired from her job at Seagate Technology because she missed approximately half of her work days over a four-month period in order to care for her sick child. Within that time McCourtney's child had the flu, bronchial pneumonia, sinus infections, and two cases of pink eye. The child's day-care provider was not equipped to care for a sick child, and the one day care center in town that took sick children charged $103 per day, twice McCourtney's net take-home daily pay. McCourtney had an excellent work record for the eleven years she had been employed at Seagate Technology. After her firing, McCourtney filed for unemployment benefits with the state of Minnesota and was turned down. The state of Minnesota argued that unemployment benefits are paid only when workers loose their jobs through no fault of their own and that her absenteeism was her fault. McCourtney sued and was granted unemployment benefits when the Minnesota appellate court ruled that she had not engaged in any misconduct by taking days off from work to care for her sick child (Lewin 1991b).

The Family Leave Bill, passed in 1993, requires firms with fifty or more employees to provide twelve weeks of unpaid leave for family emergencies, including the illness of a child. In addition, companies are required to continue health benefits for the worker on leave and to guarantee that the employee can return to the same or a comparable job. Opponents of the Family Leave Bill argued that it would put a strain on employers and that only the well-off and middle class would benefit because the poor could not afford to take an unpaid leave (Feldman 1991). Still others feared that making it easier for mothers of young children to seek employment would result in more children being placed in day care (Gill 1993). On the other side of the argument, proponents of the Family Leave Bill maintained that it would allow workers to fulfill their family obligations and be good parents. Proponents argued that the fear of losing a job places great stress on families that depend on two incomes. Employment of married women is probably here to stay, and public policy that eases the strain on two-worker families will probably make strides toward improving the quality of family life.

Telecommuting. Some employers make life easier for employed parents by allowing telecommuting, in which work is performed at home on a computer and the information is then sent to the office though a modem, or telephone link, between the home computer and the main office computer.

Job Sharing. Employed parents who want to work part time sometimes engage in job sharing, in which two people split one job. For example, one worker might be in the office in the morning and the other after lunch.

Social Redefinition

When all else fails and the methods of reducing work–family conflict discussed above are not available, couples sometimes use *social redefinition* to reduce their feelings of stress. For example, some overworked couples tell themselves that there are more advantages than disadvantages to dual-earner families (Guelzow et al. 1991).

One type of family that is particularly likely to experience work–family conflict is the dual-career family, discussed next.

Dual-Career Marriages

Dual-career marriages are a special category of two-earner marriages. Careers are considered different from jobs, in that careers—such as medicine, law, architecture, and business management—usually pay higher salaries and require more education than jobs—such as secretarial or factory work. In addition, careers usually provide opportunities for advancement and personal development. A certain amount of commitment is required in careers, and the work often provides personal satisfaction.

Commuter Marriages

Because of the high level of commitment typical of a career, some couples develop *commuter marriages*. The partners maintain separate residences but spend time together as husband and wife on weekends or when their schedules allow. Commuter marriages arise when two people with careers in different cities marry or when only one partner relocates in order to take advantage of either a promotion or a new career opportunity. In a commuter marriage the couple makes an effort to maintain both careers because neither partner is expected to sacrifice a career for the mate. When suitable employment opportunities arise, often an effort is made to relocate so that the spouses can again share a household. Only a minority of dual-career marriages are commuter marriages because such marriages are difficult to maintain while the couple is raising children. Most dual-career marriages, like those discussed below, involve a common residence.

Pressure for the Wife to Continue Working

When a dual-career couple decides to have children, often both partners resume work soon after the birth. A partner who discontinues work misses out on promotions and falls behind in career advancement. Careers often require that a person keep up with new developments in the field, and a parent returning to work after raising a family often has to retrain in order to catch up. Furthermore, when a parent returns to work after taking time off to nurture preschoolers, there is no guarantee that the same job or an equivalent one will be available (Biernat and Wertman 1991). All these factors place pressure on parents to remain continuously employed.

"Telecommuting," or working at home and communicating with the office via modem, telephone, or FAX machine, is one way employed parents can reduce their work–family conflict.

Couples with Occupations of Equal Status

Biernat and Wertman (1991) interviewed 139 dual-career couples in which the wife was either an academic or businesswoman and both husband and wife held occupations of equal status. All these couples had minor children in the home. A number of strains existed in these dual-career marriages. When a wife has a career, she ceases to be a full-time "helpmate" in the home. In contrast, when a wife is a full time homemaker, she provides domestic services for her husband. By taking charge of cooking, cleaning, and laundry, the wife frees her husband to focus single-mindedly on his career. However, wives in professional careers devote far less time than full-time homemakers to domestic chores, primarily because wives with careers cut back on the amount of housework they perform. Husbands in dual-career families often must compete at work with men who have traditional wives who provide support services (Biernat and Wertman 1991). Wives often feel exhausted attempting to provide domestic support services for the husband and other family members while holding down a job outside the home.

Even though most husbands in dual-career marriages contribute to household labor, wives with high-status careers still perform the majority of household chores and child care. As a result, issues of power within marriage, the topic of the next section, have been of great interest to family researchers.

Theories of Work and Power

Family theorists who study patterns of work and marriage are generally interested in issues of power. There are two main types of power: influence and autonomy. *Power as influence* refers to the ability to influence the behavior of another person (Engels 1973, original 1884). When a husband convinces his wife to seek employment so that they can save money to purchase a home, he is exercising power as influence. Likewise, when a wife encourages her husband to share household chores and participate in child care, she is exercising her influence. Almost everyone can think of a time when they have tried to influence the behavior of a dating or marriage partner, for example, by attempting to convince a reluctant partner to go somewhere with you. If you succeeded, you were exercising power. Another type of power is *power as autonomy,* which refers to the ability to resist the influence of another person. When a wife declines to seek employment even though her husband urges her to do it, she is exercising the power of autonomy. Likewise, when a husband resists engaging in household chores even though his wife has requested it, he is also exercising the power of autonomy. That is, they are both resisting the influence of another person and making decisions for themselves (Sapiro 1986:258). Social scientists have attempted to determine the factors that provide one partner with more power than the other in a marriage. Three theories that attempt to explain power in relationships are conflict theory, exchange theory, and gender role theory, discussed below.

Conflict Theory

Conflict theory examines power and privilege in marital relationships and argues that power is derived from the resources a person possesses. Classical conflict theorists considered economic resources, such as income, to be the primary source of power (Engels 1973, original 1884). More recently, the concept of resources has been expanded to include the same resources that place a person in the social-class system—namely, income, educational attainment, and occupational status (Blood and Wolfe 1960). According to conflict theory, the partner with the most resources holds the greatest power.

The division of household labor is frequently used as an indicator of power in marriage. A number of studies have shown that wives with high earnings tend to do less housework than wives with low earnings (Coltrane and Ishii-Kuntz 1992). However, wives are rarely able to convince their husbands to take over more than a few of the household chores. Instead, wives tend to gain an equitable division of household chores by cutting back on their own contribution to housework and purchasing cleaning services, day care for children, and prepared food (Bergen 1991). Conflict theory explains this situation by pointing out that wives earn only about one-third of family income and are in a weak bargaining position in relation to their husbands. In terms of exercising power, employed wives are best able to exercise the power of autonomy and take steps to reduce the housework they perform. In contrast, employed wives are far less able to exercise the power of influence and convince their husbands to take on half the household chores. The diminished bargaining position of women develops in part because women are often economically disadvantaged in divorce and have an incentive to avoid it. Women's earnings are typically lower than their husbands'. Thus women are more likely than their former husbands to be impoverished following divorce.

Resistance to Change. Conflict theory uses a dominance–subordination model for relationships. In this model the dominant partner, usually the husband, seeks to maintain the status quo by resisting attempts by the subordinate partner to bring about change. Conflict theory depicts wives as pushing for change in marriage and at the same time taking actions that help maintain the status quo. Wives urge husbands to do more around the house, but when husbands object, wives tend to give in and stifle conflict. The desire to preserve harmony and retain their security in marriage is an important motivating force for wives who back off and do the household labor themselves (Komter 1989; Thompson 1992).

Critique. Safilios-Rothschild (1976, 1970) argues that the perspective taken by conflict theory, in which power is based primarily on income, occupation, and education, is too narrow. She maintains that *personal resources* are also important in providing power to a marriage partner. These include love, sex, companionship, affection, attention, intellectual stimulation, approval, emotional support, feeling needed, and personal services (such as doing laundry). Women often use these personal resources to make the balance of power in the relationship less skewed in the husband's favor. These other resources are taken into account by exchange theory, discussed below.

Exchange Theory

From the point of view of exchange theory, marriage is a relationship in which bargains are continuously negotiated and resources are constantly exchanged (Homans 1974). The resources exchanged include not only economic resources but also personal resources, such as love, sex, emotional support, and domestic services. The resources a partner receives constitute benefits of the marriage.

Exchange theory holds that partners weigh the benefits and costs of a relationship and tend to remain in a relationship when the benefits outweigh the costs (Ballard-Reisch and Weigel 1991).

Placing Value on Resources. Each spouse places a value on the resources offered by the partner. The person with the resources that are more valued by the partner holds the greater power (Safilios-Rothschild 1976, 1970). A wife who values her husband's companionship and affection may be willing to exchange her household labor in order to receive the emotional gratification he offers.

Alternative Resources. How high a value a partner places on a resource depends, in part, on how readily available that resource is from an alternative source. A husband may place a low value on the wife's companionship if that same resource is easily available from his buddies. Likewise, a middle-aged homemaker who has little education, few occupational skills, and faces sex discrimination in the job market may readily continue to offer domestic services to her husband, such as housekeeping and child care, even though he has withdrawn affection and engages in infidelity. He offers the economic resource of family support, which is not readily available elsewhere (Safilios-Rothschild 1976, 1970).

The Family Economy. A popular form of exchange theory focuses on "the family economy" and considers both housework and child care to be economically productive work. Household labor produces both products, such as meals, and domestic services, such as laundry. Households need both household labor and wage labor in order to survive. From the perspective of exchange theory, husbands exchange longer hours of wage labor for their wives' longer hours in household labor (Bergen 1991). Likewise, other researchers have found that husbands who

Both household labor and wage labor are essential to the smooth functioning of a family.

work fewer hours at paid employment tend to perform more housework and child care (Coltrane and Ishii-Kuntz 1992). From this point of view, exchange theory depicts marriage more equitably than conflict theory does. Exchange theory generally assumes that the resources offered by the husband (such as greater income and less household labor) are roughly equivalent to the resources offered by the wife (such as less income but more hours spent in child care and housework).

Critique. Critics of exchange theory argue that it is difficult to tell whether or not the labor which husbands and wives exchange is actually equivalent. Many women do not know exactly how much time they spend on housework (DeVault 1987). Housework is so thoroughly integrated into a woman's life that it is difficult for her to separate out and count the hours she spends in household labor (Ferree 1991). Furthermore, exchange theory has been criticized for its rational perspective, in which men and women are viewed as being able to keep a mental balance sheet of costs and benefits in a relationship. In contrast, a perspective that looks at the cultural, and less rational, aspects of power in a relationship is gender role theory.

Gender Role Theory

Expectations for the performance of gender roles are established in childhood as children are socialized (Ferree 1991). These expectations concerning gender roles are carried into adulthood and continue to influence behavior. Husbands are still expected to be the primary breadwinners, and wives are still expected to have primary responsibility for the family household (Bergen 1991; Ferree 1991). Even when holding full-time jobs, women still do most of the housework and child care (Ferree 1991).

Labor has different meaning to men and women. Men view labor as something distinct from the family. Women tend to take family needs into account when they allocate their productive time between paid employment and domestic services (Bergen 1991). Gender role theory argues that the possession of resources cannot explain the division of household labor because it fails to take into account the gender ideals that men and women hold.

Housework is considered to be "women's work" and closely associated with the social definition of womanhood. In her study of two-earner couples, Ferree (1991) found that women derive their self-image as "good wives" in part from the satisfactory performance of household labor. Wives who are concerned about the family having a "proper dinner" tend to spend more time on household tasks (Ferree 1991).

A marriage partner can influence a spouse's behavior by appealing to gender role expectations. When the husband holds high standards for housework, the time the wife spends in household labor increases. Husbands who care about having a "proper dinner" on the table when they return from work tend to have wives who spend more time on housework. Wives tend to attempt to live up to both their own standards and their husband's standards for running a household (Ferree 1991).

Whether or not a couple develops a traditional division of labor in marriage depends in part on whether or not they delay childbearing. Early childbearing tends to result in an early transition into traditional gender roles, whereas delayed childbearing tends to allow time for a nontraditional division of household labor to become established (Coltrane and Ishii-Kuntz 1992).

The strains currently created by work–family conflict will continue to create pressure for social change both in the workplace and at home.

Review Questions

1. What are negative mood spillover, role overload, and role conflict? How do they affect family life?
2. What are some strategies that people use to reduce work–family conflict? In what ways can work conditions be changed to reduce work–family conflict?

3. How do careers differ from jobs?

4. What are the characteristics of commuter marriages?

5. Why is there pressure for women to continue working after marriage? What strains exist in dual-career marriages?

6. How does conflict theory explain power in marriage? What is the critique of conflict theory?

7. How does exchange theory explain power in marriage? What is the critique of exchange theory?

8. How does gender role theory explain power in marriage?

Summary

1. The typical family today is the two-earner family. In general, the lower the husband's income, the greater the economic advantage of the wife's employment. However, the economic rewards of the low-income wife's employment greatly diminish when she becomes a mother.

2. A common pattern among Mexican-American immigrant families is for the wife to establish family goals that require her employment.

3. Married African-American women have traditionally been in the labor force. African-American men gain a sense of identity from the provider role. African-American husbands tend to participate in household labor more than white husbands.

4. Ferree's topology of two-earner families shows that some husbands have increased the time spent in household labor and that marriage tends to be more equitable than it was two decades earlier. Nonetheless, almost one-third of the wives were drudge wives who performed most of the household labor.

5. Women use a variety of strategies to create a perception of fairness in the distribution of household labor.

6. There is a difference between parental responsibility, which involves planning, and parental assistance in child care.

7. Strain from work–family conflict can take the form of negative mood spillover, role overload, or role conflict.

8. Strategies for reducing work–family conflict include role reduction, lowering standards of performance, negotiation over reassigning role duties, and changing work condition.

9. There are two types of power: influence and autonomy.

10. Conflict theory holds that power is derived from the resources a person possesses, with economic resources being most important.

11. Exchange theory holds that resources also include personal resources such as sex, love, and domestic services. The person with the resources most highly valued by the partner holds the greatest power. Resources tend to be highly valued when few alternatives are available.

12. Gender role theory argues that, as children, people are socialized to have gender role expectations. For many women, performing housework involves

living up to a cultural definition of womanhood. From this perspective, ideals concerning male and female behavior, rather than the possession of resources, are the more important determinant of power in marriage.

Key Words

Labor Force	Leftover Income
Familism	Patriarchy
Household Labor	Drudge Wife
Semi-Housewife	Two-Housekeeper Cole
Total Labor	Parental Responsibility
Parental Assistance	Work–Family Conflict
Negative Mood Spillover	Role Overload
Role Conflict	Role Reduction
Telecommuting	Social Redefinition
Dual-Career Marriage	Commuter Marriage
Power as Influence	Power as Autonomy
Conflict Theory	Economic Resources
Personal Resources	Exchange Theory
Alternative Resources	Family Economy
Gender Role Theory	Burden-of-Care Explanation

Resources

Equal Employment Opportunity Commission (EEOC)
1801 L St., N.W.
Washington, DC 20507
(202) 663-4900
(800) USA-EEOC (toll free)
Works to eliminate discrimination based on race, gender, religion, age, and disability in hiring, promotion, firing, and setting wages. Hears complaints and files lawsuits.

Women Employed
22 West Monroe, Ste. 1400
Chicago, IL 60603
(312) 782-3902
Works to improve employment opportunities for working women and advocates pay equity and parental leave policy. Publishes *Women Employed News,* quarterly newsletter, and *Workers and Families,* a monograph.

National Organization for Men
381 Park Ave. South
New York, NY 10016
(212) 686-MALE
Promotes men's equal rights with regard to alimony, child custody, battered

husbands, affirmative action, educational benefits, and veterans' benefits. Publishes *The Quest,* bimonthly newsletter.

Women's Research and Education Institute

1700 18th St. N.W., Ste 400
Washington, DC 20009
(202) 328-7070

A nonpartisan research institute affiliated with the congressional Caucus for Women's Issues, which suggests legislation on work, poverty, and day care. Publishes *The American Woman: A Report in Depth,* an annual report on the status of women.

National Congress for Men

2020 Pennsylvania Ave., N.W., Ste 277
Washington, DC 20006
(202) FATHERS

Promotes fathers' rights, divorce rights for men, and equality in child custody; and emphasizes the role of fathers in child development. Makes recommendations to Congress and runs educational programs. Publishes *Fathers for Equal Rights Newsletter.*

Women and Employment

601 Delaware Ave.
Charleston, WV 25302
(304) 345-1298

Seeks to improve employment opportunities and the economic position of women. Works for economic justice for low-income and minority women. Publishes: *Women and Employment News,* quarterly.

Women's Legal Defense Fund

200 P Street N.W., #400
Washington, DC 20036
(202) 887-0364

Provides legal counseling and engages in litigation on family law and issues of women's education and employment. Reports on U.S. Supreme Court decisions on women's employment and family law. Publication: *Women's Legal Defense Fund News,* quarterly.

Racial and Cultural Diversity Among Families

9

Dewayne, a ten-year-old boy living in the Appalachian mountains of Kentucky, describes his relationship with his parents:

> *My father grew up in Daisy, and my mother grew up on Turkey Creek. They went to school together. My mother's just about like any other mother. She does just about everything for me. She gets me up every morning. . . . Cleans up my bedroom. Fixes me things to eat. I like her a lot. My dad and I go hunting, work together. We build things. We're making a grease rack now, where he can work on his truck. We just about do everything together. . . . When I have problems, he'll help me. My family works hard. They feel good about it. . . . [but] I don't feel good about my dad working in the mines. He's been hurt five or six times. A big hook on a cable cut him right through the forehead. . . . He stayed in the hospital for two weeks. My mom doesn't like to talk about my dad getting hurt. The mountains are big and I feel good in them. I can go anywhere. Nothing bothers me up there except they [city people] are tearing them up with bulldozers—getting the coal out. . . . I don't like people from the cities. I don't like the way they talk and the way they dress. I just like seeing normal people around.* (Ewald 1985: 56)

The United States is rich with cultural diversity. Mountain families of Appalachia are one example of this cultural variation. The interview with Dewayne illustrates traditional gender roles and father–son bonding fostered among whites in the Appalachian mountains. Appalachian families also value social isolation and are distrustful of outsiders, whom they see as a threat to the land and to their way of life. Other racial and cultural groups also have family customs and issues specific to their culture. In this chapter we look at some of the diversity among families in the United States by examining mountain families of Appalachia, Hispanic-American families, African-American families, Mormon families who practice plural marriage, and Vietnamese-American families. These family systems share many of the attitudes and behavior patterns of the dominant culture. At the same time, each of these families has a cultural heritage that makes it distinctive.

We begin our examination of the diversity among families with a look at white families of Appalachia.

White Appalachian Families

The heart of Appalachia lies in Kentucky, West Virginia, and Tennessee, but the Appalachian region also reaches into parts of Virginia, Ohio, South Carolina, North Carolina, Alabama, and Georgia. The people of the Appalachian mountains, who are known as "mountain people" or "country people," are primarily descendants of English and Scots-Irish colonial settlers who migrated westward to the mountains of the frontier (Bryant 1981). Their relative isolation in the valleys of the Appalachian mountains has led to the development of a distinct mountain culture.

Relationship to the Land

Mountain Appalachian families rely primarily on farming or mining for their livelihood. Most families own their own farmland, but some families have become landless because their parents or grandparents sold the family farm to large land companies who speculated in strip mining and logging. Landless families rent land from relatives or from land companies (Bryant 1983). Settlements in mountain valleys, or "hollers" as they are called, are often named for small rivers, such as Kingdom Come Creek or Campbell's Branch. Mountain people value respect for the land, and much of the farming has traditionally been for subsistence rather than for sale to a distant market. Families typically keep a vegetable garden and animals such as chickens (Ewald 1985).

Coal mining has traditionally been the major source of employment. When the use of coal as a fuel in the United States declined, widespread unemployment in Appalachia threw many families into poverty. In recent years coal use has experienced a new national popularity and Appalachians have begun returning to the mines. However, in spite of the resurgence of mining in Appalachia, unemployment remains high and many families still rely on public assistance. In the interview at the beginning of this chapter, Dewayne views mining with mixed feelings. It provides employment for his father, but Dewayne worries that his father will be injured at work. Dewayne also resents mining as an intrusion of big business into his peaceful mountain environment.

Land Inheritance. Mountain people would like their children to continue farming and remain in the mountains. Nonetheless, parents rarely deed farmland to children outright because they fear that the children will sell the land and move away from the mountains. Instead, parents give permission to children to park their trailer on the parents' land. Before receiving parental land, children must go through a trial period of many years during which they demonstrate their intention to settle down in the mountains (Bryant 1983).

In the past, the ideal was for all sons to inherit land equally (Brown 1988). However, today children who move away to the cities are disinherited. In some families, all the sons have moved to towns and the daughters have inherited the land, farming it with their husbands (Bryant 1981). Women who inherit land gain considerable influence in their marriages (Brown 1988:75). The eldest child does not hold any advantage when it comes to inheriting land. In fact, the youngest child, who is known as the "baby" of the family, is often favored for inheritance. Parents are usually not ready to retire when the eldest child marries. The youngest child is left to care for aging parents after older siblings have married and moved out. By passing on the family land to the youngest child, parents gain some security in their old age (Brown 1988).

Family Size and Contraception

Mountain families are organized into nuclear family households of parents and children, and most families have traditionally been large. In isolated areas where few convenient birth control services are available, the typical household has six or more children; sometimes the children living at home range in age from

Although coal mining has provided much of their employment, Appalachian families respect farming as a way of life and often deed farmland to their children to insure that future generations will remain in their mountain communities and work the land.

infancy to age nineteen (Brown 1988). Babies are still born at home, and frontier nurses who practice midwifery are an important part of the medical delivery system, aiding mothers during labor and delivery (Breckinridge 1981).

In recent years state public-health agencies have established family planning clinics in rural Appalachia. In regions where family planning clinics are located, the number of children in each family has declined dramatically in recent years to two or three children per family. Appalachian women typically drop out of high school and marry by age eighteen. Women bear their children while in their late teens or early twenties. In one isolated eastern Kentucky county where family planning clinics are conveniently located, four out of five wives use some form of contraception and half of the women who rely on contraception have opted for female sterilization. Another one-fourth of the women use the birth control pill. The existing pattern in this extremely isolated region is for women to come to a clinic for sterilization within a year after their second birth. This means that the majority of women are in their twenties when they become sterilized. Mountain culture assigns responsibility for contraception to the woman, and women tend to opt for a contraception method that does not depend on male cooperation. Mountain families now view the ideal family as one with two children. They report that smaller families mean improved health for the mother and children, less economic hardship for the family, and the ability to place more emphasis on educating the children they have (Gairola et al. 1986).

Family Relationships

Appalachian culture exhibits a good deal of male dominance. The husband speaks for the family in public, and people who want to negotiate with the family speak to him. Men tend to control sexual encounters with their wives and are not expected to undergo the inconvenience of using condoms. In spite of the popularity of sterilization as a means of birth control, this option for limiting family size is not open to some wives. One wife reported that when she told her husband that she wanted no more children, he replied that such decisions were up to him (Brown 1988:75).

Women are expected to care for the family in the home, and most mothers do not work at paid employment (Gairola et al. 1986). In addition to cooking and tending the vegetable garden and animals, mothers clean up after children, particularly male children, just as Dewayne's mother picked up after him (Ewald 1985). Boys have a close relationship with their fathers centered around activities considered to be in the male domain, such as hunting and working on old cars. Daughters are expected to help their mothers with domestic chores.

Kin Networks

Relationships with kin are extremely important, and most of the network of people with whom mountain families associate are relatives who live nearby. Relatives visit frequently and provide such services as helping each other find work. A number of families rent farmland to a relative. Marriage frequently takes place within the larger kin group, and in Appalachia it is not unusual to marry a close relative, such as a cousin. In one Kentucky community known to its inhabitants as "the top of the mountain," Bryant found that almost everyone in that particular "holler" was related to everyone else (Bryant 1983). In another study of a mountain neighborhood with seventy-seven families, almost one-half (46 percent) of the marriages were between relatives. One out of five (21 percent) marriages were between second or closer cousins (Brown 1988:71). Extended kin form a tightly interwoven community around which many mountain families orient their lives.

Social Change

Such colleges as Berea College in Kentucky have been established to prepare mountaineers for modern employment, and a number of people utilize these opportunities. However, striving for upward mobility is often viewed askance by mountain families. People who take advantage of educational opportunities are often said to be getting "above their raising." That is, by seeking a more affluent lifestyle, they are sometimes seen as trying to be better than the family that raised them and better than other people in the "holler."

Another family that values traditional gender roles and extended family relationships is the Hispanic family.

Hispanic-American Families

Although customs vary among immigrant families from various Spanish-speaking countries, certain general themes run through Hispanic-American culture.

Courtship and Marriage

Courtship has traditionally been chaperoned in Hispanic culture, and the couple was required to secure permission from both sets of parents in order to marry. However, young people chafe at these traditional restrictions and some elope in order to escape parental oversight. After the wedding the young couple typically move in with the girl's parents, utilizing temporary *matrilocal residence,* until they can afford a home of their own. This arrangement fosters strong ties between a bride and her mother, and women retain a lifelong close relationship to their mothers and sisters (Queen et al. 1985). Furthermore, the situation in which the bride is surrounded by her kin affords the wife influence and high status in the family. In contrast, family systems that separate the wife from her kin diminish her influence (Nielsen 1990). Hispanic-American brides prefer to avoid living with their mothers-in-law, and usually the young groom is glad to be out from under the authority of his father. As the couple establish their own home, the husband becomes the patriarch, dominating the household as "jefe de la casa" (boss of the house) (Queen et al. 1985). However, even in patriarchal, or male-dominant, cultures women strive to gain influence, so that male dominance is never absolute (Kibria 1990a). The husband's dominant position is bolstered by the Hispanic ideal of machismo.

Machismo

Male dominance that involves pride in masculinity, honor in the husband-father's position as economic provider of the family, and a belief in a sexual double standard is known as *machismo* (Chavez 1988). The Hispanic-American family is hierarchal: wives are subordinated to husbands, the aged are influential and respected, and older children are dominant over younger children (Rivera-Martinez 1985). However, the degree of male dominance associated with machismo has been exaggerated. The wife has more influence in the family than the stereotype of machismo would lead us to expect. The wife has a good deal to say about the running of the household, although Hispanic-American women are more outspoken when they are alone with their husbands than they are in public (Gonzales 1980). The wife has a place of honor and respect in the family, and the importance of her position can be seen in the custom in which the husband takes his wife's family name and adds it to his own. If a man named Gonzales marries a woman named Martinez, his last name is Gonzales y Martinez after marriage. Likewise, the wife retains her maiden name and adds it to her husband's last name (Gallegos y Chavez 1980:75).

The sexual bravado that has been associated with machismo turns out to be more myth than reality (Gallegos y Chavez 1980). While the desire of husbands to have extramarital affairs is considered understandable, actual transgressions are considered risky. The unfaithful husband who brings home to his wife a sexually transmitted disease is scorned by the community. Fear of public disapproval puts a damper on the husband's willingness to engage in extramarital sexual activities (Madsen 1964). Moreover, some positive aspects of machismo have been overlooked until recently. A central aspect of machismo is the man's pride in financially supporting the family. Because fertility in Hispanic-American families is high, the main task of the wife involves caring for small children. Machismo helps to maintain the two-parent family and supports the role of the wife as a full-time mother and central figure in family relations (Gallegos y Chavez 1980:76).

Teen Pregnancy and Marriage

In rural areas of the American southwest, when a teenage Hispanic-American girl becomes pregnant both sets of parents become involved and force the couple to marry. The attitude of the girl's family is expressed in a frequently used New Mexico saying, "Ese bribon no va a burlarse de ti" (That rascal is not going to make a fool out of you.) (Gallegos y Chavez 1980). In spite of this pressure to marry, the couple generally adjust well to marital roles because early marriage is expected. As Hispanic Americans have migrated to urban areas, parental influence has diminished somewhat and the number of nonmarital births has increased. Nonetheless, for Hispanic Americans, teenage pregnancy is likely to lead to teen marriage.

Children

Traditionally, children are wanted, large families are expected, and impending births bring joy to the family. In the traditional Hispanic family, children are considered the "wealth of the poor" because parenting brings satisfaction to husbands and wives (Gonzales 1980). However, young marriage and childbirth is a path to poverty for many young Hispanic families. Hispanic-American women have lower high school completion rates than either African Americans or non-Hispanic whites (Forste and Tienda 1990). This tendency to drop out of high school is related to the cultural ideal of femininity, which makes homemaking the primary role of the woman and the wife the anchor of the family. It is less respectable in Hispanic culture for a married woman to work outside the home than in either African-American or non-Hispanic white culture. This curtailment of education brings economic hardship because half of all married Hispanic-American women find it financially necessary to enter the labor force by the time their children are in high school and they typically take low-paying jobs (Forste and Tienda 1990).

Women and Employment

In spite of the Hispanic cultural ideal that disapproves of married women working outside the home, employment of married Hispanic women is on the rise. However, the patterns vary among Hispanic groups. When a Mexi-

The Hispanic cultural ideal of femininity and emphasis on a woman's role in family life can put great pressure on those Hispanic-American women seeking an education. This can explain in part why Hispanic-American women have lower high school completion rates than either their African-American or white counterparts.

can-American wife in the southwestern United States enters the labor force, her employment status is likely to be permanent because her wages are needed to make ends meet. In contrast, more affluent Cuban wives in southern Florida tend to seek employment on a temporary basis and drop out of the labor force when the family's living conditions improve (Vega 1990; Kelly and Garcia 1989). Before entering the labor force, wives negotiate with their husbands and justify their employment in terms of improving the family's economic position. Nonetheless, when married women seek employment marital conflict is common. Violating the cultural ideal of the full-time homemaker takes a toll on women. There is some evidence that employed Hispanic wives are more vulnerable to depression than Hispanic homemakers (Vega 1990).

Social Change

Many Hispanic-American women feel that their interests lie in supporting Hispanic culture rather than in joining the women's movement. Hispanic women tend to feel that the women's movement is dominated by white middle-class women who have little in common with low-income Hispanic immigrants. A Hispanic-American woman often feels that because of ethnic discrimination "she must side with her man, who is daily fighting a hostile world" to gain employment and support a family (Gonzales 1980:93). In addition, supporting traditional Hispanic culture helps maintain the wife's central position in the family as a homemaker. However, some new Hispanic ideas about the family suggest that social change may be in the making. Young educated Hispanic feminists have raised in the Hispanic community new family issues that center around birth control, abortion rights, and the ability of women to determine the number of children they want to have (Gonzales 1980). These are issues that sharply divide young feminist Hispanics and older traditional women.

Familism

Familism, an important value in the Hispanic-American family, stresses the idea that the welfare of the extended family is of utmost importance and the needs of the extended family take priority over the needs of the individual. Most Mexican Americans tend to live near or with their kin, and they rely on extended kin for mutual aid (Keffe and Padilla 1987:130). Often the living arrangements come of necessity. The poor must depend on their relatives for help in difficult times. Men who lose their jobs often have to depend on relatives for job referrals. This mutual-aid network is an important part of the extended family. Even Hispanic Americans who have good incomes often live near relatives so that they can offer aid to those who have helped them in the past (Ramos and Ramos 1980.)

Another family system in which extended kin are important is the African-American family, as we will see in the next section.

Review Questions

1. How do Appalachian families earn a living and what economic hardships have they faced?
2. How do Appalachian mountain families handle inheritance?
3. What attitudes do Appalachian families have toward contraception and children?
4. How do relationships with extended kin affect the lives of Appalachian mountain people?
5. What customs surround Hispanic marriages?
6. What is machismo? How accurate is it to say that Hispanic husband–wife relationships are characterized by machismo?
7. What is the attitude of many low-income Hispanic families toward early marriage?
8. Why is familism important?
9. What social change is occurring in Hispanic families?

African-American Families

The family has been a source of strength to African Americans under adverse conditions that have included slavery and discrimination. This strength can be seen in patterns of childrearing, kin networks, and a number of other aspects of the African-American family.

Childrearing

Children are highly valued in African-American families. Like Hispanics, African Americans view "children as wealth," believing that children are important in adding enjoyment and fulfillment to life (Lewis 1989). The family not only shelters its own children but often provides a refuge for children of neighbors and relatives. Informal adoption is not unusual in the African-American community, where family ties often extend beyond blood relationships (Dore et al. 1990). In an informal adoption, the child of a relative or friend comes to live with a family and is treated as a natural-born child. Informal adoption has its roots in African culture and was a useful way of creating community responsibility for children in the United States.

Racial Socialization. African-American families play an important role in teaching children to cope with racism (Nobles 1981). Both mothers and fathers provide the child with *racial socialization*, preparing children to cope with discrimination in the larger society. Discrimination separates groups and allows the advantaged group to receive preferential treatment (Nobles 1981). Parents play an important role in encouraging African-American children to struggle and compete for jobs in an environment where prejudice and discrimination still exist (Taylor et al. 1990).

BOX 9.1 | World Perspectives

An African-American Folktale

Below is an African-American folktale that was told to children during slavery. It is still told to African-American children today:

A farmer hated the donkey on his neighbor's farm. To catch the donkey he dug a hole six feet deep, six feet long, and four feet wide. He lured the donkey into the hole and then began to shovel dirt on top of the donkey to bury him. But as each shovel full of dirt fell on the donkey, he shook it off, stamped it down, and rose above it. Each time the farmer threw another shovel full of dirt on the donkey, he again shook it off, stamped it down, and rose above it. The more the donkey tramped down the dirt, the faster the farmer shoveled. Pretty soon the trampled dirt was level with the ground. The farmer looked up, and in fright saw the donkey was level with him, and he took off running with the donkey close behind. *

This folktale is a story about spirit and character; it encourages African-American children to "rise above" discrimination and not let it discourage them. In the end, it was the mistreated donkey who prevailed and refused to be held down by prejudice. Although low-income African Americans face enormous obstacles to gaining middle-class status, the story encourages children to struggle and take pride in their efforts.

Makeba, a storyteller, adds, "The motif found in this story of discovering (an inner) strength while overcoming obstacles (in this case, a near-death experience) can be heard in stories told in the Black Church about the rebirth of Baby Jesus and the Phoenix. It also can be found in the stories that were told during the Civil Rights Movement. My great-grandma, Big Mama Alice, remembers hearing a similar story in her youth in the 1920s."

Awele Makeba, African-American storyteller and "Teller of All Tales," told this folktale at The Second Annual Ethnic Storytelling Festival at Diablo Valley College, February 26, 1992.

The Family as a Refuge. African-American families have been a haven of emotional support. Parents realize that their children face hardships in the world outside the family and tend to provide children with unconditional love. In unconditional love, the parent's love for the child is constant and is not made a reward for good behavior. This unconditional love gives children validation and respect, which help them to cope with prejudice in the outside world (Taylor et al. 1990).

Employment

African-American women have rarely had the choice of pursuing either employment or full-time homemaking. The societal tendency to undervalue the work of African-American men has meant low pay and high unemployment rates for them. The income of the African-American wife has been needed to make ends meet, and African-American women historically have worked outside the home (Aldridge 1989). Because the earnings of African-American men are often low, African-American wives and children contribute a larger portion of family income than do white wives and children (Taylor et al. 1990).

The Legacy of Slavery. It is often easier for African-American women than men to obtain employment. This is partly because African-American men and women have historically had different public images. African-American men were dehumanized under slavery by negative imagery (Young 1989). Today, white employers sometimes react with fear and rejection when deciding whether or not to hire a young-African American man. Young African-American men face "triple discrimination" based on race, gender, and age (Anderson 1989). In contrast to men, African-American women under slavery were were considered to have humane qualities that made them suitable as a "mammy" or nursemaid to take care of the white master's young children (Young 1989). These differing historical images have influenced current employers to prefer young African-American females as employees. Historically, African-American women could usually find domestic employment as maids while many African-American men went unemployed.

Socialization of Girls. Young African-American girls are typically raised to expect to work outside the home. African-American women were never viewed as purely ornamental. Young girls have been taught that hard work, good health, and education made them pleasing to God (Du Bois 1969; Young 1989). This expectation that women will work at paid employment has led African-American families to value education and hard work for both daughters and sons. In fact, young African-American women have been found to have higher educational aspirations than whites from similar backgrounds (Dore and Dumois 1990; Moore et al. 1986).

Kin Networks

An important source of strength in African-American families is the extended kin network of grandparents, aunts, uncles, cousins, and adult siblings. The importance of kinship is illustrated by the way African Americans choose people with whom to associate. The social networks of African Americans are typically made up primarily of kin, whereas the social networks of whites are likely to include a larger number of friends who are not relatives (Taylor et al. 1990). Among African Americans, kin networks also promote emotional well-being. African Americans who have a close relationship with a number of kinspeople report greater personal happiness than those who are somewhat isolated from kin (Ellison 1990). Extended kin are also important in providing housing in times of financial difficulty. African Americans are twice as likely as whites to live in extended-family households. Most African Americans who live with relatives are single mothers, and the rapid growth in the number of single-parent families since the 1970s has made assistance from kin particularly important (Taylor et al. 1990).

Helper Networks. African Americans tend to have more kin than nonkin in their informal helper networks (Chatters et al. 1989; Ellison 1990). *Helper networks* consist of people who exchange goods and services, such as financial aid, emotional support, and child care. African Americans have a *system of exchange* in which goods such as food, services such as babysitting, and financial support are traded among kin. The exchange system is characterized by *reciprocity*, an expectation that relatives who receive help will return the favor in the future. In the African-American community there is less obligation to reciprocate assistance offered by a friend than that offered by a relative (Ellison 1990). African Americans tend to have a larger network of relatives with whom to discuss problems and seek aid than do whites. In fact, African Americans with the largest helper networks are those with physical ailments. This situation illustrates the tendency for African-American kin groups to pull together to care for the sick and elderly (Chatters et al. 1989). In contrast, whites are more likely than African Americans to rely primarily on a spouse, rather than other relatives, for aid when problems arise in midlife (Chatters et al. 1989; Gibson 1982).

Among African Americans, friendships are frequently modeled on family relationships. In fact, the cultural tendency to feel particularly comfortable in kin relationships leads African-American families to turn nonrelatives into *fictive kin* by assigning them a family title, such as "Aunt," and treating them as family members (Dore and Dumois 1990). In contrast, whites are more likely to have a network of friends who are not given titles as relatives (Ellison 1990; Gaudin and Davis 1985).

Sources of Emotional Support

Lewis (1989) identified four major support networks for African-American mothers of young children: (1) extended kin networks of children, grandparents, aunts, uncles; (2) religious support networks in which members of a church provided emotional and material support; (3) friendship networks; and (4) current partners. In a national study, over three-fourths of African-American mothers reported that they had a strong network of supportive kin as well as a supportive current partner. Two-thirds were involved in a religious community that offered emotional support. However, less than one-fifth were involved in a large friendship network (Lewis 1989).

African Heritage

The strength of the extended kin network among African Americans today has its roots in African heritage (Nobles 1981). In traditional cultures along the western coast of Africa, women have an important economic role in farming, trading, and producing crafts. It was this region of Africa from which most African Americans originated. Women in western Africa are independent and control their own earnings (Sudarkasa 1981a; Young 1989). Some symbols of male dominance do exist in western Africa; for example, among the Asanti wives knelt before their husbands to show respect. However, motherhood is also venerated among the Asanti, and sons kneel in front of their mothers (Sudarkasa 1981b; Young 1989). The importance of motherhood is also evident in modern African-American families.

Current Migration Patterns

At the beginning of the twentieth century 90 percent of African Americans were living in the South. During the twentieth century African Americans migrated to northern and western cities in search of factory jobs, and this trend continued until 1970 (Lemann 1991). As factories shut down and moved overseas, northern cities lost their appeal to migrants. Over the last fifteen years there has been a reversal of this migration pattern. Today, more African Americans are returning to the south than leaving it (Lewis 1989). It is often stressful for African-

American women living in urban areas of the northeast to meet their employment and parental obligations. In urban areas there is a shortage of suitable African-American men to become partners for African-American women. African-American women living in the northeastern United States report more role strain than African-American women living in the south (Lewis 1989).

Marriage Rate

In recent decades there has been a decline in the expectation that African-American women will marry. Of those born in 1954, only 70 percent of African-American women are expected eventually to marry, compared to 90 percent of white women. It is significant that the vast majority of African-American women will eventually marry. However, almost one-third of African-American women face a shortage of potential partners because of the high rate of joblessness, incarceration and involvement with the criminal justice system, and high fatality rate among African American men (Taylor et al. 1990).

Misconceptions about the African-American Family

The news media have given the impression that the African-American two-parent family is a vanishing entity (Demos 1990). Over the past two decades African-American women have experienced a rising rate of singlehood, a rising divorce rate, a rising age at first marriage, and a dramatic increase in nonmarital childbearing. All of these trends have also characterized the white population, but to a lesser extent. Media commentators and social scientists often look at these trends and predict impending disaster for African-American families. This assumption about African-American families is frequently made without conducting personal interviews in order to find out how African Americans view their family experiences (Demos 1990). This "social problems approach" to the study of African-American families overlooks much of the reality of how low-income African-Americans live their lives.

African-American families, like many other families today, come in a variety of forms. Many low-income unmarried fathers are living with the mothers of their children even though they are not married. Many African-American children of single-parent homes not only have a relationship with their biological father but also describe this relationship as positive (Banks and Wilson 1989). Other African-American men act as fathers to their cohabiting partner's children from a previous relationship.

African-American women share the same attitudes toward marriage as the larger culture, even though they are less likely than other women to marry. However, that does not mean that African-American women lack close, satisfying romantic relationships. Tucker and Taylor (1989) analyzed data from the National Survey of Black Americans and discovered that a large number of African-American women are in nonmarital romantic relationships. The researchers found that over two-thirds of African-American women and men were either married or involved in a romantic relationship. The African-American women were evenly divided between marital and nonmarital romantic relationships. In contrast, a larger percentage of African-American men were married (Tucker and Taylor 1989).

This discrepancy between the marriage rates of African-American men and women partly results from a lopsided sex ratio. African-American women face a shortage of African-American marriage partners who are able to support a family. In addition, there is a greater tendency for African-American men to enter interracial marriages.

Nonmarital romantic relationships are prevalent among African Americans because the increasing economic marginality of many African-American men has meant that marriage is often not feasible (Taylor et al. 1990; Tucker and Taylor 1989). High rates of joblessness and sporadic employment have made it difficult for many African-American men to support a family. African-American men tend not to marry until they can fulfill the provider role. Being a "good provider" is an important part of male identity among working-class and middle-class African-American men (Tucker and Taylor 1989). Having a low income does not appear to deter the formation of romantic relationships. However, when an African American man has a low income, his economic marginality becomes a substantial barrier to moving from a romantic relationship to marriage (Tucker and Taylor 1989).

Another family system that has been influenced by its history is that of fundamentalist Mormons who practice plural marriage. We will discuss this family system in the section to come.

Review Questions

1. What are some important aspects of African-American childrearing?
2. What kind of work opportunities have African-American men and women had historically and in the present?
3. What is the role of extended kin in the African-American family?
4. What misconceptions exist concerning the African-American family?

Fundamentalist Mormon Families Practicing Polygyny

The Mormon church officially prohibits polygyny, the practice of one husband taking two or more wives. Nonetheless, a number of fundamentalist Mormon families living along the borders of Utah, Arizona, and Colorado practice polygyny. It is estimated that 50,000 people are in polygynous marriages in the western United States; the vast majority are Mormons who live in Utah (Lichfield 1991).

Historical Perspective

The prophet Joseph Smith founded the Church of Jesus Christ of Latter Day Saints, the Mormon church, in the 1830s. Mormon religion viewed polygyny— or "plural marriage," as the Mormons called it—as an important part of religious practice. Mormons believed that evidence of God's approval and blessing could be seen in the number of wives and children a man had. Plural marriage was also known as "celestial marriage" because it was considered to be morally

Is Polygyny Being Legalized in Utah?: The Case of Johanson v. Fisher

Vaughn Fisher already had two wives and five children when he married Brenda Thornton, a woman with six children by a previous marriage and who was dying of cancer. The Fisher family lives in the town of Hildale, whose population consists of a tightly knit fundamentalist Mormon community that practices polygyny. Hildale is located on the Utah–Arizona border, a convenient location in the 1940s, when police raided polygynous communities. Hildale families would escape police raids in one state by slipping across the border into the other state. Today police raids on polygynists have stopped and Hildale is a quiet community.

Vaughn Fisher took care of Brenda, his third wife, in the terminal stage of cancer while his two other wives took over the role of mother to Brenda's children, who ranged in age from three to seventeen. Before she died, Brenda, who was a member of the same Mormon fundamentalist sect as Vaughn Fisher, signed a will granting Fisher the right to adopt her children. The adoption was subsequently approved by the Utah Department of Social Services, which described the Fishers as an upstanding and religious family. Also giving their consent to the adoption were the Thornton children, the children's natural father, and the two remaining wives of Vaughn Fisher.

However, the adoption of Brenda Thornton's children was challenged in court by Brenda's half-sisters, Pat and Janet Johanson. One sister, a college administrator in Oregon, sought custody of the children. Brenda's sisters fear that polygynous marriages would be arranged for Brenda's daughters when they reached age sixteen or seventeen, as is the practice in this fundamentalist Mormon community. On the opposing side, arguing in favor of the polygynous Fishers, was the American Civil Liberties Union, which argued that the Fishers' right to practice polygyny is protected by the freedom of religion clause in the United States Constitution.

Judge Conder of the lower court stated that the only issue to be resolved in this case is whether or not the practice of polygyny, which is illegal in Utah and all forty-nine other states, disqualifies the Fishers from adopting the Thornton children. Judge Conder said that he did not consider polygynous couples to be immoral. In fact, both he and the two attorneys involved in the case had grandparents who had practiced polygyny. However, Judge Conder dismissed the Fishers' adoption petition, refusing to grant them an adoption hearing on the grounds that their practice of polygyny is illegal. Meanwhile, he granted temporary custody of the children to the Fishers while they appealed the case to the Utah Supreme Court.

In the historic decision of *Johanson* v. *Fisher* the Utah Supreme Court in 1991 overturned the lower court's decision stating that the civil rights of the Fishers could not be denied because they practiced polygyny. In this decision, which has profound implications for American family law, the Utah Supreme Court ordered the lower court to grant the Fishers an adoption hearing. In an interesting argument, the Utah Supreme Court compared polygyny to other illegal acts, such as fornication and adultery, which are not prosecuted by law enforcement officials. The Utah Supreme Court argued that people who engage in fornication and adultery do not lose their civil rights and neither should families who engage in polygyny (*Johanson* v. *Fisher* 1991: 3). The significance of the Utah Supreme Court decision in *Johanson* v. *Fisher* is that the decision goes a long way toward the *de facto* legalization of polygyny. The law prohibiting polygyny was not removed from the books, but the rights of polygynists have been substantially protected.

At the time of the Utah Supreme Court decision the Thornton children had been in the custody of the Fisher family for three years, and it is unlikely that the Fishers would be denied the right to adopt, especially when approval has been recommended by the Utah State Department of Social Services (Belkin 1989; *Johanson* v. *Fisher* 1991: 26).

superior to monogamy (Wyatt, Gary, 1989). The Mormons were persecuted and driven out of various settlements in the midwestern United States and eventually settled in Utah, where polygyny was practiced between 1852 and 1890. The elders of the church were particularly likely to have polygynous marriages: Brigham Young, Smith's successor, had twenty-six wives and fifty-seven children. (*Economist* 1988).

Mormonism was founded in the Victorian era of severe sexual restrictions, and polygyny shocked the population of the United States. Congress refused to grant statehood to Utah Territory until it banned plural marriage. When the Utah Mormons remained steadfast in their practice of polygyny, in 1887 Congress passed the Edmunds–Tucker Act, which dissolved the Mormon church as a legal corporation and confiscated its property. In response, the Mormon church relented and renounced polygyny in 1890, and plural marriage became illegal in the Utah in the same year. Congress then returned the Mormon church's property and granted statehood to Utah. However, some fundamentalists resented what they viewed as persecution based on religious beliefs. A number of fundamentalist sects of Mormons continued to practice polygyny secretly in small communities, such as Hildale and Colorado City.

Modern Polygyny

Beginning in the 1950s, Utah and Arizona adopted a "let live policy" regarding polygyny. There have been no arrests for the practice of plural marriage in either state since that time. The refusal of Utah and Arizona to arrest or convict polygy-

Although the letter of the law does not allow polygyny, polygynous Mormon families enjoy tolerance in Arizona and, especially, in Utah. Contrary to what one might assume about multiple marriage relationships, these Mormon families are characterized by high marital satisfaction.

nists has resulted in the "de facto decriminalization" of polygyny (Slovenko 1978). There is a distinction between *de jure* and *de facto* decriminalization of a behavior. *De jure* decriminalization of polygyny would involve changing the written law specifically to declare plural marriage legal. This has not occurred in any state of the union. On the other hand, *de factor* decriminalization means that the laws prohibiting polygyny remain on the books but are not enforced. The *de facto* decriminalization of polygyny is gradually creating a situation in which polygyny is treated as if it were legal in certain parts of the United States (see Box 9.2).

Why has Mormon polygyny continued to be practiced even though polygynists experienced persecution for many decades? Some social observers have argued that the importance placed on family life is an attraction to Mormonism, particularly to fundamentalist Mormonism. In fact, the emphasis on motherhood, large families, and missionary work has made the Mormon church one of the fastest growing denominations in the United States. Mormon polygyny has grown even though the official church position rejects plural marriage.

Modern Mormon Families

Large families are desired among Mormons, and an abundance of children is viewed as a sign of God's blessing. Family life is highly valued in the Mormon religion, and every Mormon man is advised to set aside Monday as "family home night." Mormon husbands are supposed to spend Monday evenings with their families in conversation and family problem solving (Wilkinson 1980). Mormon marriages appear to be happy; 81 percent of respondents in a Provo, Utah study described their marriages as "happy" or "very happy" (Miller, Richard, 1987). The high level of marital satisfaction has been attributed to the Mormon emphasis on family life and the high status granted to mothers. Mormon women are taught that parenting is a woman's most rewarding and fulfilling role (Miller, Richard, 1987).

Nonetheless, the Mormon family is patriarchal, with husbands having greater decision-making power than wives. Until the 1960s church doctrine prohibited married women from working outside the home. Mormon religion encouraged large families, and during the 1960s the birth rate in Utah was one of the highest in the industrialized world. However, in recent years the Mormon family has experienced some social change. Mormon wives are entering the labor force in increasing numbers, and the Mormon birth rate has declined. While the median number of children per family remained steady at 1.8 in the rest of the United States during the 1980s, in Utah it fell from 3.2 to 2.5 children per family. Most of this decline in Utah during the 1980s was accounted for by a dramatic decrease in the birth rate among Mormons, who make up 70 percent of the state's population (Robbins 1988).

The Mormon church has attempted to adjust to social change in the larger society by suggesting that women follow a "sequential family pattern" in which childrearing is followed by employment after the children have been raised. Today, Mormon church doctrine allows married women to work outside the home with the husband's approval. However, the husband must first determine that the mother's absence from the home during work hours will not harm the children (Iannaccone and Miles 1990). Although decision-making power is asymmetrical in the Mormon family, Mormon women are now experiencing some of the independence that comes with working outside the home.

Next we turn to the Vietnamese-American family which also values tradition.

Vietnamese-American Family

Of the Southeast Asian immigrants who have entered the United States since 1975, the vast majority have been Vietnamese. Nazli Kibria (1990a) has conducted extensive ethnographic research as a participant observer studying the family life of Vietnamese immigrants who arrived in the United States in the mid-1980s. She found these families to be coping with two major changes: downward mobility after immigration and the loss of the extended family as it had existed in Vietnam.

Downward Mobility

The immigrants studied by Kibria had not been able to maintain the middle-class status they had held in Vietnam. In the United States these families experienced *downward mobility,* which refers to movement to a lower social class. In Vietnam, the husbands had been middle-level government officials or had owned small businesses. In the United States they were working at low-paying, unskilled, service-sector or factory jobs. Thirty percent of the men studied by Kibria were unemployed, and two-thirds of the households had members who collected public assistance.

Women in Vietnam had worked at odd jobs, such as selling food and other goods at bazaars, or had participated in the family business. In the United States, women held low-paying service-sector jobs, such as working in restaurants. In spite of the family's loss of middle-class status in the United States and the husband's change in job status, women still felt economically dependent on husbands and feared that desertion by a husband would bring economic impoverishment (Kibria 1990a, 1990b).

Vietnamese Americans develop fictive kin, embracing Vietnamese immigrants who were previously distant relatives as new family members.

Gender Roles

In Vietnam, men were dominant and women were expected to follow the "three obediences." A woman was first under the authority of her father, then she was to submit to her husband, and when she became a widow, she was expected to obey her eldest son. However, there was a difference between the cultural ideal of the "three obediences" and the way people actually lived their lives. Patriarchy, or male dominance, was tempered by the active role taken by women in family life. The wife was the "noi tuong" or "home minister." She was responsible for managing the family budget, coordinating family schedules, and maintaining harmony in the home. In reality, family decision making was a joint process involving both the husband and wife. In addition, after a woman became a widow, her son consulted her before making decisions (Rutledge 1992).

The entry of women into the labor force in the United States is viewed by the family as a necessity that is tolerated rather than desired. Employment has given wives a new independence, and some Vietnamese immigrant men feel that they are losing control over their families. One man said that at home in Vietnam he could slap his wife and children to discipline them, but in the United States, if he slapped his wife, she might call the police (Rutledge 1992:124).

Reconstructing Extended Families

Vietnamese refugees left many of the husband's kin behind in Vietnam, which resulted in increased influence for the Vietnamese-American immigrant wife. In Vietnam the family practiced *patrilocal residence,* whereby the young bride moved into her husband's household. This meant that the young wife lived under the authority of her mother-in-law. However, because immigration often meant leaving aging parents behind, immigrant wives were typically free from the mother-in-law's authority. Kibria (1990a, 1990b) found that once in the United States, Vietnamese immigrants began the process of *reconstructing extended families* by adding new family members. Distant relatives with whom the family was unfamiliar in Vietnam were added to the family together with friends who were treated as *fictive kin.* Through this process of reconstructing extended families, the Vietnamese immigrant families developed large, complex households. The typical Vietnamese-American household studied by Kibria had seven members, and the largest contained nineteen people. Another study of Vietnamese-American families found that 55 percent of Vietnamese-American households contained extended kin or fictive kin, compared to only 6 percent of white families (Gardner, et al. 1985; Kibria 1990a).

Vietnamese immigrant wives played an important role in defining the family boundaries. Wives were influential in deciding who would be considered part of the family and who would not (Kibria 1990a). In Vietnam, families had practiced *patrilineal descent,* in which the family name and inheritance passed through the male line from father to son and the family associated primarily with the husband's relatives. However, in the United States the preference for the husband's relatives proved to be impractical because kin were often scarce. The wife often brought in some of her kin to be part of the extended family. Once the extended family had been reconstructed, Vietnamese-American women were able to turn to their own kin for support in conflicts with their husbands.

Patriarchy and Women's Influence

The Vietnamese family, like other Southeast Asian families, is *patriarchal,* with authority resting mainly in the male head of household. However, wives have some influence even in patriarchal family systems. Men and women negotiate the rules of male–female relationships in a process that Kibria (1990a) refers to as *bargaining with patriarchy*. However, the bargaining process in Vietnamese families is *asymmetrical* because the husband holds a position of greater power or influence.

Informal women's groups banded together to put limits on male authority and to protect women when they were in conflict with their husbands. The women did not directly challenge male authority but instead enlisted the help of their male relatives. At one informal meeting of neighborhood women observed by Kibria (1990a) one woman tearfully described taking her sister, Thu, to the hospital after her sister had been beaten by her husband, Chau. The other women discussed

---

Children of the "Boat People" Achieve in School

The "Boat People" were refugees who fled the social unrest of Southeast Asia (also known as Indochina) and settled in the United States in the 1970s and 1980s. These refugees were primarily Laotians, Vietnamese, and Chinese who had settled in Indochina. When these refugees came to the United States, they spoke very little, if any, English and were poorly educated. Children had lost a year or more of schooling while in refugee camps and had experienced the physical and emotional trauma of a lost home and relocation. These impoverished families moved into some of the poorest areas of America's cities and attended public schools that were known as the worst schools in the United States. There they excelled. A recent review of Indochinese children who attend school in five urban areas (Orange County, California; Houston; Seattle; Chicago; and Boston) shows that these children are excelling in both grades and achievement test scores. Three-fourths of the children attained a grade point average of B or better. In addition, in spite of the difficulties the children had with English, they scored above average in national achievement tests. The family has played an important role in the children's school success.

Parents played a crucial role in their children's school success even though most parents spoke little or no English. The parents could offer no assistance in teaching children any subject matter. What the parents did was create an environment favorable to learning. After dinner the table was cleared and school books spread out. The children worked together at the kitchen table, with the older children helping the younger ones. In fact, the more children in the family, the higher their grade point average was. Older children enhanced their own skills by helping younger children with homework. Parents aided this learning process by doing kitchen and household chores in the evening and freeing children's time for studies. Parents also read stories to younger children. Even when stories were read in the parent's native language, the child's grades tended to increase. Reading to children, regardless of the language, breaks down the barriers between home and school and encourages children to view reading as fun.

The values of Indochinese culture boosted children's grades. Unlike mainstream Americans, who value individualism and independent achievement, Indochinese families valued cooperation and family achievement. Older children took pride in the successes of younger siblings. Indochinese children also saw large differences between their own values and those of other Americans. When asked to check off characteristics on a list of characteristics that they felt separated them from other Americans, Indochinese children said other children were more interested in "fun and excitement" and "material possessions." But that does not mean that Indochinese children were unhappy. They took pleasure in successfully solving math and science problems.

Other studies of academic successes of Jewish immigrants, low-income African-American students in Chicago, and Japanese students after World War II have found that the family's role in creating an environment for learning in the home has been an essential ingredient of children's academic success. (Caplan, et al. 1992).

Chau's character, pointing out that he also hit the children, including a three-year-old. Various women said that they would talk to their husbands or brothers, who would then talk with Chau and tell him to stop beating his wife. Not long after the women's conversation, Chau found himself ostracized by both the women and their male relatives. He eventually left his family and moved to California, effecting an informal divorce. The informal women's group had been able to influence Thu's family situation.

Traditionalism

Immigrant Vietnamese are surrounded by the dominant American culture, which emphasizes gender equality. However, Vietnamese-American women have retained their traditional values emphasizing patriarchy, or male dominance, in the family. Kibria (1990b) argues that clinging to the traditional family is a rational choice for Vietnamese immigrant women. The family helps members cope with the disadvantages they face in dealing with the dominant culture. The extended family operates as a clearinghouse of information on how to cope with the schools and welfare system as well as information on where to obtain food and goods at bargain prices. This system of information exchange helps immigrants adjust to a new environment.

Vietnamese-American Parenting

When Kibria (1990a) studied recent immigrant Vietnamese-American families, she found that they feared the encroachment of mainstream American culture into their family life. They particularly worried that American values would erode parental authority and the value of *familism,* in which the needs of the family are placed above the needs of the individual (Kibria 1990a). Sometimes a role reversal takes place when parents need to deal with government authorities. Because children typically master English more quickly than their parents, they are often called upon to translate and act as intermediaries. In such situations a parent becomes dependent on a child's help, and the child's importance in the family is emphasized (Rutledge 1992).

Traditional Vietnamese culture, like other Asian cultures, emphasizes *filial piety,* which refers to the child's respect, obligation, and obedience toward parents. Filial piety continues into adulthood, and adult children are expected to support and care for their aging parents (Rutledge 1992). Parents are also concerned that their children might adopt the American value of individualism and put their own interests above those of the family. They worry that their children may begin to approve of dating, teen sexuality, and independent mate choice (Kibria 1990a). Marriages in Vietnam were arranged: A young man would typically pick out a girl whom he had met at ceremonial events and ask his parents to arrange a marriage (Rutledge 1992). This pattern is breaking down in the United States. Some Vietnamese parents complain that their teenage children secretly see teens of the opposite sex without the parent's approval (Kabria 1990a). Many Vietnamese-American parents hope to preserve their culture and pass it down to the next generation, but they fear that their children will be swayed by mainstream American values and cultural practices.

Review Questions

1. What is the history of Mormon polygyny?

2. What do we mean when we say that Mormon polygyny has experienced "*de facto* decriminalization"?

3. What kind of social change is taking place in the Mormon family?

4. In what way did Vietnamese-American families experience downward mobility?

5. How did Vietnamese-American families go about reconstructing the extended family in the United States?

6. In what ways do Vietnamese-American wives exert influence on their families in the United States?

Summary

1. White Appalachian families in mountain "hollers" rely on farming and mining for their livelihood. Parents wait to see if an adult child is committed to remain on the land before allowing that child to inherit the parents' farm. Public health clinics have increased the availability of contraception and reduced the birth rate. Mountain women tend to opt for sterilization as a means of birth control. Kin networks are strong, and intermarriage with relatives is not unusual.

2. Hispanic-American families tend to supervise the young during courtship. After marriage the young couple typically practice matrilocal residence, which gives the wife influence in the family. The degree of machismo (which refers to male dominance and the sexual double standard) in Hispanic families has been exaggerated, and wives do exercise influence in the home. Teen pregnancy and early marriage are common in Hispanic families, as they are in Appalachian families. Familism, the belief that the needs of the family take precedence over the needs of the individual, is strong in Hispanic families.

3. African-American parents engage in racial socialization, which helps to prepare children to function in a world that practices discrimination. The extended family is organized into an exchange network and is an important source of help for families. Close friends are often made into fictive kin, and the informal adoption of children is common. African Americans tend to have larger informal helper networks of relatives than whites. African-American women have historically worked outside the home. Today the migration pattern of African Americans is toward a return to the south. Misconceptions about African American families have led to the assumption that the African American family is disintegrating. In fact, many African Americans utilize cohabitation as an alternative family form.

4. The United States Congress tried to eliminate Mormon polygyny with the Edmunds–Tucker Act in the late nineteenth century. However, fundamentalist Mormons moved to the Utah borders and continued to practice plural marriage. Since the 1950s there has been a *de facto* decriminalization of

polygyny, or a "live and let live" policy. Mormons today have experienced a declining birth rate, and Mormon wives now enter the workforce when their children are old enough if the husband determines that the mother's employment will not have a harmful effect on them.

5. Vietnamese-American families are the most recent arrivals in the United States from Southeast Asia. They typically experience downward mobility. Extended families are reconstructed in the United States, with the wife's distant relatives and fictive kin being added to the family. These newly added kin enhance the wife's influence. Women bargain within the patriarchy system by forming informal women's groups and putting pressure on husbands and brothers to confront other men who use abusive behavior. The traditional family, with its strong kin network, acts as a clearinghouse of information for new arrivals.

Key Words

Hollers
Matrilocal Residence
"Jefe de la Casa"
Racial Socialization
Asanti
Celestial Marriage
De Facto Decriminalization of Polygyny
Downward Mobility
Patrilocal Residence
Asymmetrical Bargaining

Mountain People
Machismo
Familism
Fictive Kin
Polygyny
De Jure Decriminalization of Polygyny
Family Home Night
Reconstructing Extended Families
Bargaining with Patriarchy

Resources

Interracial Family Alliance
P.O. Box 16248
Houston, TX 77222
(713) 454-5018
Promotes acceptance of interracial families and solutions to problems unique to interracial families.
Publishes *Interracial Family Alliance Communique,* quarterly.

Minority Caucus of Family Services in America
34 1/2 Beacon St.
Boston, MA 02108
(617) 523-6400
Works to eliminate racism and acts as an advocate for minorities using social services.

Interracial and Intercultural Pride
1060 Tennessee St.
San Francisco, CA 94107
(415) 399-9111
Encourages well-being and positive child development in families with more than one ethnic heritage.

National Hook-Up of Black Women
5117 S. University Ave.
Chicago IL 60615
(312) 643-5866
Encourages black women in leadership positions in business, the professions, and community organizations. Publishes *Hook-Up News and Views*, quarterly.

Women for Racial and Economic Equality
198 Broadway, Room 606
New York, NY 10038
(212) 385-1103
A multiracial organization working to reduce race and sex discrimination in employment, child care, and wages. Promotes awareness of issues concerning feminism, homelessness, and world peace. Publishes *Women of the Whole World,* quarterly.

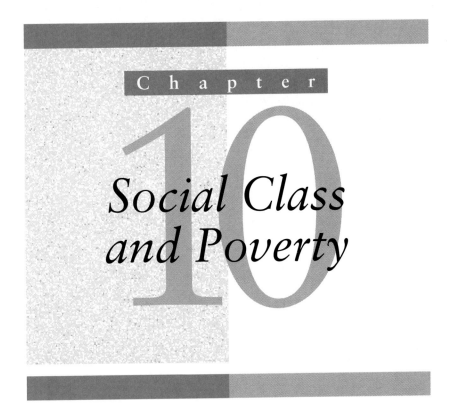

Chapter

10

Social Class and Poverty

The following is an excerpt from a study by Frank F. Furstenberg, Jr., of a Philadelphia public housing project:

The Projects are dangerous. Drug-related murders on the premises or in the immediate neighborhood have almost become routine. A guard house installed at the entrance of one of the neighboring buildings was immediately torn down, reputedly by drug dealers, who lounge at the entrance way to Lillie's building in search of customers. Lillie [an African-American mother on welfare] and her children use the back door and have learned to ignore the entreaties of dealers on the streets peddling their wares. Lillie's involvement with her building neighbors is minimal. "I don't know too many people here. . . . My kids—I basically don't let them go down and play. When I take them out, we all go together."

Leah, a longstanding resident of the projects, echoes many of the same sentiments about her neighbors and her neighborhood. Leah agrees with a member of her household who declares in a conversation, "You can live in the Projects but you ain't got to be like the Projects." When Leah was asked to draw a map defining the area where she travels, she responded: "I don't go nowhere around here. I don't know nobody. I don't want to know nobody." The fieldworker reports that in fact, Leah's acquaintance with her neighbors and neighborhood is much greater than she admits to, but her pretense of ignorance is an accurate expression of her feelings about the impoverished social world in and around the Projects. A sign of relatively low level of social integration in the Projects is that residents typically do not know the names of their neighbors, even some of those that they had dealings with on an occasional basis. Leah's attitude, like Lillie's, was to manage to survive until you can find a better place to live. (Furstenberg 1990:7–8)

Frank Furstenberg, Jr., and his team of associates (1990) interviewed mothers receiving welfare who were struggling to raise children in a West Philadelphia public housing project. Mothers such as Lillie spent a great deal of time in child management as a strategy for coping with a dangerous neighborhood. Child management involved confinement and chaperonage. In the process of trying to protect her family from drug dealing and violence, Lillie developed a fear and distrust of her neighbors, some of whom had become disabled by drug use. In the drug-abusing families of some of her neighbors, older siblings played the role of substitute parent. Mothers, like Lillie, were reluctant to entrust their children to the care of friends or neighbors in the housing project, and instead took direct responsibility for supervising their children.

Lillie made valiant efforts to protect her children from the dangerous conditions in the housing project. Nevertheless, as Lillie's children reach adolescence, they will be at risk for abusing drugs, joining a gang, dropping out of high school, and being involved in a teen pregnancy and out-of-wedlock birth. Why are the life chances of Lillie's children so bleak while a middle-class child can typically expect a much brighter future? In order to understand this puzzle we need to examine the American social class structure.

The American Social Class Structure

American society can be thought of as a layer cake, with the layers representing social class strata. Families, rather than individuals, are the units of social classes. Social scientists use income, wealth, power, and prestige to determine a family's social class position. By each of these measures, Lillie's family falls into the lower class. Lillie's *income* is provided by Aid to Families with Dependent Children (AFDC), also known as welfare, which leaves her family in poverty. *Wealth* refers to property owned, such as a family home, business, or stocks and bonds. Lillie, like most welfare mothers, has few valuable possessions and does not own her own home. *Power* refers to the ability to influence the lives of others and is generated by both wealth and occupation. As a welfare mother with few assets, Lillie is relatively powerless. *Prestige* refers to admiration and respect attached to an occupation; welfare mothers, who lack an occupation, fall near the bottom of the prestige ladder. As a short cut, the combination of the adult family members' income and occupation is usually considered a good indicator of social class position.

The social class position of college students is determined by their parents' income and occupation because college students are typically in a transitional low-income position. It would not be logical to consider a college student whose father is a corporation executive to be lower class even though that student works part time and has the same monthly income as a welfare mother. The college student will most likely be assuming a middle-class occupation and lifestyle after completing college. We now turn to a closer look at each social class. Although there are a number of ways to divide U.S. families into social classes, we use five main social categories: lower class (the poor), working class, middle class, upper-middle class, and upper class.

The Lower Class: The Poor

The poor, who are also known as the lower class, include mothers receiving welfare like Lillie and Leah; the homeless; a portion of the aged and disabled; the unemployed; and the working poor who perform low wage, low-skill jobs that do not pay enough to place a family above the poverty line. There were 37 million poor people in the United States in 1992, constituting approximately 14 percent of the U.S. population and 11 percent of U.S. families (U.S. Bureau of the Census 1993d: viii and Table 19, p. 113). Incomes of poor families fall below the poverty line, which in 1995 the U.S. Department of Commerce defined as an annual income of $15,150 for a family of four (National Archives and Records Administration 1995). This is the minimum amount the U.S. government considers adequate to cover the cost of housing, food, transportation and other basic necessities. As Table 10.1 shows, the United States has a larger percentage of poor persons than the United Kingdom, France, and a number of other European countries, which spend a large proportion of national income on social services for low-income families.

Michael Harrington in *The New American Poverty* (1987) points out that poverty can be seen as a "magnetic field." A number of American low-income working-class families are at risk of being drawn below the poverty line. Harrington considers these families to be "one recession, one illness, one accident away from being poor" (p. 111). Periodic lay-offs are a dreaded reality for many of America's low-income workers.

Poverty Rates in International Perspective	
Developed Countries	*Percent Poor*
Belgium	0.7%
Denmark	1.7
Germany	2.9
United Kingdom	6.4
Italy	8.0
France	9.0
United States	14.5
Greece	16.3
Spain	18.4
Developing Regions	
Latin America and the Caribbean	25.2
Middle East	33.1
Sub-Sahara Africa	47.8
South Asia	49.0

Sources: International Bank for Reconstruction and Development/World Bank 1993. *World Development Report, 1993,* Table 2.1, page 12. Oxford: Oxford University Press.

U.S. Bureau of the Census 1993d. Current Population Reports P60-168. *Poverty in the United States: 1992.* Washington, D.C.: U.S. Government Printing Office.

Eurostat 1990. *Poverty in Figures,* Table 3.1, page 23. Luxembourg: Office for Official Publications of the European Communities.

Fluidity

There is considerable movement in and out of poverty. Table 10.2 illustrates this fluidity. As the table shows, African Americans and Hispanics find it more difficult to exit poverty than whites. Only one out of six poor African-American adults (17.4 percent) and one out of seven (14.3 percent) poor Hispanic adults were able to leave poverty during a one-year period compared to almost one out of four poor white adults (23.3 percent). However, none of these groups made overall progress during this one year period because more people from each group entered poverty than left it.

The Working Poor

As the pie chart in Figure 10.1 shows, almost half of poor adults (48 percent) work at least part of the year. Many of these are *underemployed,* in that they work less than they would like to work. Many have less than full-time, year-round employment because the low-skill jobs they hold lack job security. Figure 10.1 shows the struggle involved in attempting to support a family on a low wage. Seventeen percent of poor heads of household work year round at full-time jobs. They hold low-income, low-skill jobs that do not provide an adequate income to support a family. A person working full time, earning $5 an hour for fifty-two weeks a year, without a vacation, would earn $10,400 a year before taxes, well below the poverty line for a family of four.

Moving In and Out of Poverty			
	Whites	*African Americans*	*Hispanics*
Number of adults* in poverty Jan. 1, 1991 (in thousands)	14,826	7,829	3,938
Exiting poverty between Jan. 1991 and Jan. 1992	3,454 23.3%	1,362 17.4%	563 14.3%
Entering poverty between Jan. 1991 and Jan. 1992	4,594 31.10%	1,375 17.5%	1,214 30.8%

* Age 18 or older
Source: U.S. Bureau of the Census, 1995a. Current Population Reports, P70-42, Table G.

Race, Ethnicity, and Poverty Rates

An important measure of poverty is the *poverty rate*. A poverty rate is the percent-age of families in a particular group that are poor. The bar graph in Figure 10.2 shows that African Americans, Hispanics, and Native Americans have much higher poverty rates than whites or Asians. Poverty rates are useful because they allow us to determine an individual's risk of being in poverty. A child born into a white fam-ily has a one in thirteen chance of being poor, whereas a child born to an African-

Figure 10.1
Who Are the Poor? Work Status of the Poor.

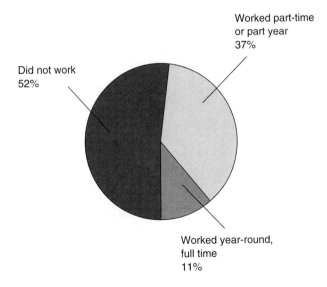

Did not work
52%

Worked part-time
or part year
37%

Worked year-round,
full time
11%

Note: All poor adults = 100 percent. Almost half of the poor work at least part time.

Source: U.S. Bureau of the Census 1993. Current Population Reports, P60-185, *Poverty in the United States, 1992,* Table 9. Washington, D.C.: U.S. Government Printing Office.

Figure 10.2

Poverty Rates for Families by Race and Ethnicity.

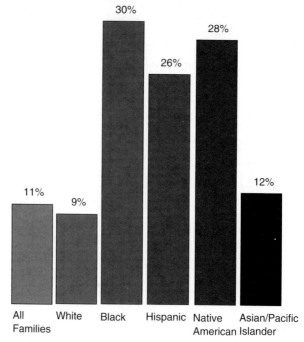

Note: Each racial or ethnic group = 100 percent. Poverty rates are highest among African Americans, Hispanics, and Native Americans.

Sources: U.S. Bureau of the Census, 1994. *Statistical Abstract of the United States, 1994,* Tables 49, 50, 51, and 53. Washington, D.C.: U.S. Government Printing Office. U.S. Department of Health and Human Services 1991, Public Health Service, *Health Status of Minorities and Low-Income Groups,* 3rd ed., Table 7. Washington, D.C.: U.S. Government Printing Office.

American family has a one in three chance of growing up in poverty. Children born into white families are more likely to grow up with a number of economic advantages, including parental economic subsidies while in college and a network of middle-class relatives who can offer aid in times of economic distress. In contrast, children from minority families are more often subject to economic hardship.

Age

Children and the elderly make up half of the poor. These are the age groups least able to care for themselves. Many of the remaining poor adults are parents who care for young children. Families with very young children are particularly likely to be in poverty. One out of every three children under age five lives in a poor family (U.S. Bureau of the Census 1990d). These are the children who represent the nation's future, yet the outlook for their future is not optimistic.

Poverty among those age sixty-five and over has been declining in recent years. The expansion of Social Security Insurance and Medicare health benefits has reduced poverty among the elderly by half in the last fifteen years (Rodgers 1986). Although this expansion of benefits has made life easier for the elderly, it has not put them on easy street. Many of the elderly are clustered just above the poverty line, with a meager standard of living (U.S. Bureau of the Census 1990d: 7). Social Security is funded through a payroll tax paid by both workers and employers. Those who are currently working pay for the Social Security and Medicare benefits of those who are retired. The United States needs a well-educated work force in the future so that the children of today can grow up to be productive adults. They will be the ones to pay the Social Security and Medicare benefits when current workers retire.

There are twice as many elderly women as elderly men represented among the poor (U.S. Bureau of the Census 1990d). This is partly because women live longer than men. Because many men become ill and die before their wives, often the family savings is spent on the husband's medical bills. The widow then finds herself in poverty in her last years.

The Feminization of Poverty

In order to understand the position of poor children in American society, we need to look at the *feminization of poverty*. The feminization of poverty refers to the growing tendency for poor families to be headed by women. Female-headed households, with no spouse present, constitute only 17 percent of all families, yet they account for more than half of the families in poverty (U.S. Bureau of the Census 1993c, Table 17; 1993d, Table 19). The association between mother-headed households and poverty can be seen in Table 10.3. As this table shows, the lower a family's income, the more likely the family is to be headed by a single mother. Lillie and her children, who were described at the beginning of this chapter, are an example of the feminization of poverty that can be found in all racial and ethnic groups. Mother-headed families represent over 75 percent of all poor African-American families, 43 percent of all poor Hispanic families, and 42 percent of all poor white families (U.S. Bureau of the Census 1993d, Table 19).

TABLE 10.3	Percent of Families in Each Income Group Which Are Headed by Women with no Husband Present			
Family Income	*All Families*	*White*	*African American*	*Hispanic**
Under 5,000	65%	55%	84%	59%
$5,000–$14,999	41	33	68	37
$15,000–$24,999	23	19	46	23
$25,000–49,000	13	11	31	13
$50,000 and up	5	4	12	7

*Hispanic origin may be either black or white.

Source: U.S. Bureau of the Census, 1993c. Current Population Reports P60-184, *Money Income of Households, Families and Persons in the United States: 1992.* Washington, D.C.: U.S. Government Printing Office, Tables 14 and 17.

As the column labeled All Families shows, of those families with an annual income under $5,000, 65 percent are headed by women with no husband present. As income increases, the percent of families headed by women with no husband present decreases. This holds for each racial or ethnic group shown. However, looking across each row, we see that within each income category African Americans are more likely than other groups to have families headed by women with no husband present.

In an era in which two incomes are usually necessary for a middle-class lifestyle, single mothers are at an economic disadvantage. In 1992, the median income for married-couple families was $42,064, more than twice the median income of $17,221 for families headed by women with no husband present (U.S. Bureau of the Census 1993c, Table 17). Women workers tend to be concentrated in low-paying occupations that lack opportunity for advancement. Families headed by single fathers have a median income of $27,821, which makes them far less economically disadvantaged than single-mother families (U.S. Bureau of the Census 1993c, Table 17).

The Underclass

At the bottom of the social class ladder we find a stratum that William Julius Wilson (1980) has termed the *underclass*, the most disadvantaged section of the poor. This subgroup of the poor consists of about 2 million people and represents those who have the greatest difficulty climbing out of poverty (Edsall 1990; O'Hare 1992). The underclass are primarily poorly educated mothers on welfare and single men who have typically not completed high school, have poor job prospects, and who often have no permanent address and stay with a sequence of relatives and friends. Wilson contends that the underclass are largely minorities who were concentrated in decaying inner cities, where factories have closed down and few opportunities for well-paid jobs are available. According to Wilson, being trapped and isolated in the inner cities has created hopelessness and a tendency to look to an underground economy of illegal activities to supplement income. Wilson (1987) points out that a number of public housing projects have become high crime areas.

Critique. Critics argue that the term "underclass" stigmatizes all the poor, which is a much larger group than the underclass (Edsall 1990). Including a high crime rate as a characteristic of the underclass creates the misleading perception that very poor families have a single set of values that reject the ethic of honesty and hard work. This assumption cannot explain why a number of children who grow up in very impoverished families get an education, work hard, and are able to move into the middle class. Other social scientists have argued that cultural values among the poor are actually heterogeneous rather than homogeneous (Furstenberg 1987b, 1990). Although some of the poor become involved in drug dealing, others—like Lillie, who was described at the beginning of this chapter—try to protect their children from drugs and crime, which they deplore. Lillie wants to give her children the best opportunities available, even though they now live in poverty.

In response to criticism, William Julius Wilson abandoned the term "underclass" and in its place began to use the more neutral term "ghetto poor" (Edsall 1990). Nonetheless, the term "underclass" is becoming entrenched and is widely used by the news media as well as by other social scientists. In fact, some social scientists have argued that poor Appalachian white families can also be described as members of an underclass (O'Hare 1992). These families also have few job opportunities because of the decline in mining and logging in rural areas. However, it may not be legitimate to include Appalachian white families in the underclass because they are typically landowners who own their own farms. In that sense they are less disadvantaged than propertyless renters in the inner cities. (See Chapter 9 for a discussion of white Applachian families.) Next

BOX 10.1   Social Issues

Tenant Board Screens Applicants for Public Housing

New York City is spending $5.1 billion over ten years to renovate older buildings into housing for homeless families. To qualify for this housing, a family must have been homeless and living in a city shelter for at lease three months. In one new social experiment, housing applicants must meet with a screening committee that includes current tenants who themselves were formerly homeless. This interview process was set up in an attempt to screen out drug dealers, who have made life miserable for tenants in other low-income public housing projects. Applicants are asked questions about their work history, how they became homeless, their plans for the future, and their history (if any) of drug use. Some applicants are married couples, but most are single mothers on welfare who have never worked and who have moved from their mother's overcrowded apartment to a city shelter. Only about one in seven applicants for housing is accepted by the tenant board (Rimer 1990).

When a Hispanic married couple applied to the tenant board, the husband described how he had begun to use heroin after leaving the Marines. He also explained that he had entered a methadone treatment program, saw his counselor regularly, and was looking for a job. The couple was accepted into the co-op.

Another applicant was the mother of two small, neatly dressed girls. She became homeless when she left a physically abusive husband. A tenant board member told the others that she had seen this woman in city shelters and that in spite of being homeless, she kept her children clean, took them to the park regularly and made sure that they were in bed by 8 P.M. The board member worried that if this woman did not find housing soon, she might become worn down and lose her energy. Her application was accepted. The applicants whom the board approved represented a variety of racial and ethnic groups (Rimer 1990).

Not all applicants met with board approval. When a board member asked another applicant about her family, she said that her brother was on drugs. The applicant then revealed that she had recently been robbed and lost a 35-millimeter camera, a VCR, a walkman, and three gold chains. She suspected that her brother had been the thief. The board members worried that if this woman were to live in the co-op, her brother might either move in with her or hang around her apartment. In addition, they wondered how a mother on welfare who had never held a job had been able to acquire the expensive items she listed. The tenant board rejected her application (Rimer 1990).

Critics arguing from various political positions have questioned the wisdom and fairness of the New York City housing plan for the homeless. Liberal critics argue that many homeless families are turned down because they don't meet standards of morality set by the co-op board, which values the desire to work or pursue an education. For drug-addicted applicants, the board looks for evidence of commitment to a drug rehabilitation program. Critics argue that the co-op board skims off the cream of the homeless population and leaves many desperately poor families on the streets. In response, the co-op board argues that it is attempting to create a safe environment in which to raise children. Poor families in the co-op hope to be able to live with dignity in a secure setting. Conservative critics argue that in spite of well-intentioned efforts to screen out potential problems, the homeless often bring drug abuse and crime into public housing projects. In response to complaints from public housing residents, New York City's Housing Authority announced plans in 1992 to decrease the number of apartments made available to the homeless (Fritsch 1992).

we look at those families whose incomes place them just above the poverty line: the working class.

Review Questions

1. How do social scientists determine a family's social class position?
2. What does Table 10.2 tell you about low-income workers?
3. What age groups are most likely to be poor? How has poverty among the elderly changed in recent years?
4. Which racial and ethnic groups have the highest poverty rates?
5. What is meant by the feminization of poverty?
6. Who are the underclass and why has the use of the term "underclass" been criticized?

Working Class

Members of the working class have incomes that fall above the poverty line but are less than approximately $25,000. Unlike the lower class, many of whom are unemployed, underemployed, or on public assistance, the working class often hold full-time jobs (Ehrenreich 1989). Working-class employment is characterized by low-skill manual labor in what are often called *blue-collar* jobs. The term "blue collar" evolved because factory and construction workers, who typi-

The pink-collar jobs of typist, waitress, and cashier offer less income than do blue-collar work, which is generally performed by men. This puts working-class women at a financial disadvantage.

cally got dirty on the job, wore colored work shirts rather than white dress shirts, which would have been difficult to wash clean. The working class also includes low-skill service workers, such as waitresses, typists, and sales clerks, who perform a service rather than produce a product. Many of these service jobs are performed by women and so have been tagged *pink-collar* work. Both blue-collar and pink-collar jobs tend to be dead-end occupations that offer low pay and require little education. However, many pink-collar jobs require more education but offer less pay than blue-collar jobs, which are typically filled by men (Tavris and Wade 1984). For example, the male worker on a loading dock often earns more than the secretary in the front office. Thus the division into male-dominated blue-collar and female-dominated pink-collar work puts women workers at a financial disadvantage.

The Organization of Work

The working class typically occupy jobs that offer hourly wages rather than annual salaries and provide low levels of economic security. Because blue-collar workers often experience layoffs, looking at hourly wages often gives a deceptively high estimate of annual income. Construction work tends to be seasonal, and factory workers lose work time when factory orders decline and when unions go out on strike (Rothman 1993). Working-class service jobs also pay a low hourly wage. Service jobs in retailing, such as sales clerks and counter clerks, often pay minimum wage or just over that amount.

Working-class jobs tend to be repetitive and monotonous. On an assembly line, work is divided into the smallest tasks, so that a factory worker might spend the entire workday screwing bolts into fenders. Workers have little or no sense of producing an entire product (Rothman 1993). Blue-collar and pink-collar jobs limit the worker's *autonomy*. Autonomy is the ability to make decisions that affect one's own life, and factory workers have very little say about the organization of their work (Rothman 1993). These workers follow the orders handed down by middle-class managers who hold authority (Ehrenreich 1989).

Working-Class Childrearing

Families tend to encourage character traits in children that will prepare those children for the kinds of jobs their parents hold. Working-class parents who have jobs requiring compliance to authority tend to stress obedience and conformity when raising children and often rely on physical punishment as a means of discipline (Kohn 1969; Volling and Belsky 1991). In modest-income families, the job is not a source of gratification in itself, but rather a means of earning a living. Life satisfaction is more likely to be derived from personal relationships in the family and among friends. Working-class parents are less involved in their work than parents with highly respected careers, and thus working-class fathers are not likely to bring home a briefcase full of work (Volling and Belsky 1991). Therefore, fathers with low-prestige occupations tend to spend more time with their children than fathers in high-prestige occupations (Levi-Shiff and Israelashvili 1988; Volling and Belsky 1991). In addition to childrearing, marriage patterns are affected by social class.

Fathers with high-prestige occupations are more involved in their work and, there-fore, spend less "quality time" with their children than do working-class fathers. Fathers in all social classes, however, are in transition as the social role of the father is changing.

Marital Interaction

In addition to influencing childrearing, social class is also associated with marital patterns. In the past, working-class couples tended to marry soon after leaving high school. Early marriage provided a way for young people to enter adulthood, escape from parental authority, and leave a crowded family home. However, today cohabitation tends to delay marriage in all social classes, including the working class.

Social class also affects patterns of marital interaction: Working-class couples often relate to one another in a style that is in some ways different from the style of marital interaction in the middle class. Krokoff and his colleagues (1988) compared blue-collar working-class couples in which the husband held a manual-labor job, such as factory work, to white-collar couples in which the husband held a middle-class office or professional job and found different patterns of marital interaction. Blue-collar husbands expressed more negative feelings and complaints to their wives than white-collar husbands. Krokoff and co-workers attribute this difference to the higher level of job distress and to the greater number of job-related problems reported by the blue-collar husbands. The blue-collar husband's stress on the job tended to spill over into the marriage in the form of a "negative mood." This negativity often had the effect of eroding marital companionship.

The pattern described above for husbands is reversed when we examine the behavior of wives. Blue-collar wives tended to express fewer complaints than white-collar wives. White-collar wives with marital grievances were quite vocal in their complaints (Krokoff et al. 1988). In contrast, blue-collar wives were reticent in voicing complaints to their husbands. This reluctance on the part of blue-collar wives to express dissatisfaction can be explained partly by the low expectations that blue-collar wives had for marriage. These wives tended to think that they were fortunate and had little room for complaint if the husband was a steady worker, did not drink heavily, and was not physically abusive. Blue-collar wives were more concerned with avoiding the economic hardship associated with divorce, desertion, alcoholism, or the husband's possible future unemployment than with other problems in the marriage (Krokoff et al. 1988; Rubin 1976).

Economic Pressure and Marital Quality. The low level of income in working-class families tends to create economic pressures that show up in marital tension. Lorenz and his associates (1991) found that couples who had difficulty making ends meet tended to experience diminished marital quality. Couples who said that they frequently had problems paying bills reported more marital quarreling than financially secure couples, and financially insecure couples more often reported that they had considered divorce. In addition, people in financially insecure marriages were more likely to report that within the past few weeks their spouses became angry, criticized them, made fun of their ideas, or threatened to do something that would upset them. In another study Lorenz (1991) asked married couples about their financial status and then videotaped them while they talked about the history and current status of their marital relationship. Couples experiencing financial difficulty expressed more hostility and less warmth in these videotapes than financially secure couples.

Gender and Marital Interaction. Lilian Rubin (1976), in *Worlds of Pain*, studied blue-collar couples and found that the pattern of interaction used when discussing problems often resulted in diminished marital satisfaction. Working-class husbands tended to use reason in approaching marital problems and considered a nonemotional approach to problem solving to be associated with masculinity. These husbands thought that taking feelings into consideration meant being weak, feminine, and childlike. This attitude often upset their wives. A pattern of discussing problems developed in working-class marriages in which the wife expressed her emotions, thinking that her feelings about the situation were an essential component of problem solving. The husband typically reacted by trying to "reason with her" while brushing her feelings aside. The wife's response was to become even more upset. This interaction often ended with the husband and wife feeling emotionally distant from one another and the husband defining the wife as "emotional" or "hysterical." Although this pattern also occurred in middle-class marriages, it was more pronounced in working-class marriages. Perhaps these experiences eventually lead to the pattern observed by Krokoff and co-workers (1988) in which blue-collar wives become somewhat reluctant to express complaints.

Economic Insecurity

Many working-class families have experienced economic insecurity as the American economy has changed over the last three decades. Beginning around 1960, the United States began emerging from an industrial economy based on factory production to a postindustrial economy characterized by information processing and services, such as computer programming. This process of deindustrialization continues today as U.S. factories close and relocate elsewhere. In today's postindustrial economy some working-class families experience *skidding* (Harrington

As American society wrestles with deindustrialization, the working class must be retrained for jobs in which they perform services rather than manufacture products.

1987). Skidding occurs when a worker is laid off and finds new employment at a lower wage. Workers who are skidding watch their *standard of living* decline. A standard of living is the style of life that a family is able to afford. Skidding workers often find that their rent and car payments become too expensive and that their wives have to enter full-time paid employment.

In the past, well paid, unionized, factory work provided a route to *upward mobility* for lower-class males. Upward mobility is movement to a higher social class. Unionized factory jobs required very little education and paid a *family wage,* a wage sufficient for a single breadwinner to support a family. Irish and Italian immigrants gained a foothold on the social class ladder by working in "smokestack industries," as the factories that belched smoke were called. Today the opportunities for upward mobility provided by U.S. manufacturing are drying up. The United States is undergoing the process of *deindustrialization*, in which factories are closing down and the economy is shifting from production to services. Factors associated with deindustrialization are the global economy, the technological revolution, and the emergence of a two-tier society (Ehrenreich 1986).

Global Economy. Deindustrialization began to accelerate as U.S. industry expanded into a *global economy* (Ehrenreich 1986). A global economy is an economy in which companies produce and sell their products in world markets. In a global economy U.S. workers find themselves competing with factory workers in third-world countries who earn only a few dollars a day. U.S. factories have been closing down in response to this competition. U.S. labor unions, which have kept wages high in the past, have recently lost some of their influence and membership. In 1992 only one in eight U.S. workers (private-sector wage and salary workers) held union membership (Frum 1993).

Technological Revolution. The *technological revolution* is also reducing the number of unionized factory jobs available in the United States (Wilson 1980).

Sea Coaling Families in Hartlepool, England

In the middle of the night when the tide is low, you can see father-and-son teams "sea coaling" along the coast near Hartlepool, England. A local coal processing plant discharges waste into the ocean, and at low tide coal is exposed along the beach among the seaweed. "Sea coalers" take a truck and shovels to the beach to gather coal, which they sell as cheap fuel. While the tide is out they can shovel about three tons of coal, which sells for about $40. Hartlepool, England, is a working-class town, but well-paid working-class employment has diminished in recent years as aerospace industries, steel mills, and coal mines have closed down throughout England (Powers 1992). On Hartlepool's waterfront abandoned docks and boarded-up factories are visible. Sea coalers are typically unemployed, and often the sons who accompany their fathers sea coaling are young teenagers who have dropped out of school (Horwitz 1992).

Professional occupations appear out of reach to England's working class, such as the children of sea coalers. Traditionally, English working-class boys have left school at age fourteen or fifteen and entered the mines or factories with their fathers. The social class system is rigid in England, offering little upward mobility into a higher social class. Education, which is a primary route to upward mobility in the United States, tends to reinforce class lines in England. Only one-third of England's students go on to college, which is half the rate of college attendance in Germany, France, and the United States. Educational opportunities are even more limited in Hartlepool, where only 4 students out of a graduating class of 150 will go to college (Horwitz 1992). The rest join the ranks of the working class or unemployed. Youths do not view themselves as having a possibility of moving into the professions and therefore see school as having little value or relationship to their lives. Young people are anxious to get out of school and "get on with their lives" and if possible work alongside their fathers. Despite the lack of employment opportunities for working-class jobs, the average Hartlepool youth drops out of school at age sixteen (Horwitz 1992).

England provides its families with a safety net of public assistance programs. All families are covered by a national health care system. In addition, an unemployed family with two children receives $160 a week, free rent, and free school meals. Jobs that are available in Hartlepool pay only approximately $150 a week, so a public assistance recipient loses money overall by taking one of these available jobs. Hartlepool has families who have received public assistance for a number of years; however, despite an unemployment rate approaching 20 percent, the crime rate in Hartlepool is low and murders are extremely rare (Horwitz 1992).

Sea coaling provides enough money to run a truck, which is a luxury in England. Few Hartlepool residents can afford a car or truck, which costs at least $10,000 to purchase. Nor can they afford gasoline at $4 a gallon. A number of Hartlepool residents lack a driver's license, and many families never leave the county. The relative isolation of Hartlepool's inhabitants has resulted in the development of a distinctive accent. Hartlepool residents would have a difficult time understanding the local accent of coal miners' families who live and work in a town 100 miles away. Some social scientists worry that England, with its rigid class system and poorly educated work force, will become the backwater of the European Economic Community. Some economists ask how England will be able to compete with Germany, France, and Sweden in the coming years if education and economic opportunity do not become more widespread (Horwitz 1992).

Modern machinery controlled by computers is replacing some factory workers. Computerized robots now weld automobile parts together on U.S. automobile assembly lines. Each robot replaces several human workers who previously performed the same job.

Two-Tier Society. As older factories have closed down, there has been a net loss of factory employment and an overall shift from production to service-sector jobs (Testa 1990). *Production jobs* involve the manufacture of goods such as steel and automobiles. *Service-sector jobs,* such as those in retailing and health care, involve performing services rather than producing goods. The service sector is becoming increasing split into two distinct parts, forming a *two-tier society* (Ehrenreich 1986). The first tier consists of low-paying, nonunionized, unskilled occupations, such as tending the cash register at a fast food restaurant or discount drug store. These jobs tend to be located in middle-class neighborhoods rather than in the ghetto (Wilson 1980, 1987). This low-paying segment of the service sector is experiencing the greatest growth. The other tier of the service sector includes professional services, which are highly skilled, well-paid occupations requiring considerable education. Careers in banking, law, medicine, science, and accounting are examples of professional services. This segment of the service sector is also growing. However, the working class typically lack the education needed to obtain these highly paid service jobs.

Shrinking Opportunity Structure

As the U.S. economy deindustrializes, young people from working-class families experience a shrinking *opportunity structure.* An opportunity structure refers to the number and type of job opportunities available in the economy. The loss of job opportunities is greatest for those who have not finished high school (Ortiz 1990). They now seek jobs at minimum wage in the service sector. Unlike the unionized factory jobs available in the past, these service-sector jobs often provide an income that is barely adequate to support a family.

The African-American Family

Deindustrialization has been particularly hard on African-American families (Lemann 1991, 1986). At the beginning of this century, the majority of African Americans lived in the south. Large-scale migrations northward began around 1918, during World War I, as job opportunities for African Americans opened up in war industries that produced munitions and ships (Norton 1985). The migrations continued during the first half of this century: One-fifth of the entire African-American population of the south left in the 1940s, during World War II. These job-seeking migrants moved to the northern and western cities, such as Chicago and San Francisco, where an African-American urban community had become established. These communities were segregated by race but integrated by social class. Because of housing discrimination, African Americans of all social classes, including doctors, clerks, teachers, and factory workers lived together in urban communities. The urban middle class and working class provided mutual aid to relatives who came from the south seeking work. Often an African-American family would house and feed a family member whom they had never met. An informal network of extended kin provided job referrals that helped ease the new migrants into northern factory jobs. African-American values stressed mutual aid. People were valued for the help they gave to others, particularly to relatives, rather than for the consumer goods they could display. Those with good jobs supported the migrants until they could find employment (Lemann 1986).

During the 1960s several major changes undermined this mechanism for upward mobility among African Americans. The 1960s was a decade in which deindustrialization began to accelerate. Northern factory workers were having diffi-culty finding jobs for their own sons, much less for migrants from the south. In addition, fair housing legislation was passed in the 1960s, opening up housing opportunities for middle-class and working-class African Americans. They left the inner city for the same reasons that whites left, namely, to find better housing, preferably a house with a yard in which their children could play (Lemann 1986). In addition, one more factor was complicating the northern migration of African Americans. The mechanization of agriculture in the south during the 1960s pushed African-American sharecroppers off the land, fueling migration. In 1950, 90 per-cent of cotton in the south was picked by hand. By 1970, only 4 percent was still hand picked. Whereas earlier migrants came north to seek their fortune and find a better job, many of the migrants of the 1960s were displaced agricultural workers (Harrington 1987). These migrants tended to be poorly educated and unfamiliar with the market economy of a large city. One and one-half million African Ameri-can migrants left the south during the 1960s only to find that the mechanism for upward mobility had broken down in the cities of the north and west. They became isolated in the inner-city ghettos, which tended to concentrate the African-Ameri-can poor into poverty neighborhoods (Lemann 1991, 1986).

One area in which the working class are particularly disadvantaged is in health care coverage.

Health Insurance Coverage

The working class are far less likely than the middle class to be covered by health insurance, and when they are covered, working-class families are more likely than middle-class families to experience a lapse in health care coverage. The working class are not typically eligible for such government entitlement programs as Aid to Families with Dependent Children, which provides medical care and income to impoverished children and their caretakers. Of those families whose income is above the poverty threshold but below two times that amount, only one-third are covered by health care insurance (U.S. Bureau of the Census 1990e). The precarious position of low-income working-class families some-times results in feelings of resentment toward poor families. Often working-class "nonpoor" families perceive themselves as no better off economically than those who are eligible for government assistance (Ehrenreich 1989).

Those families that are most likely to have health insurance have breadwinners with well-paid, stable employment. The U.S. Bureau of the Census followed fami-lies over a twenty-eight-month period and found that the vast majority (84 percent) of those families with a breadwinner who worked full time continuously over that period had continuous health care coverage. Three-fourths of these families gained their health insurance through an employer (U.S. Bureau of the Census 1990e). However, many of these middle-class workers with health care insurance worry that if they are laid off or change jobs they could lose their coverage. Working-class breadwinners often hold low-wage jobs that do not provide medical coverage. Because working-class families are more vulnerable to layoffs than middle-class families, the fear of losing the family's health insurance creates considerable anxi-ety. Almost half of the workers who experience unemployment or some other type of work interruption lose their health care coverage at least temporarily (U.S. Bureau of the Census 1990e).

In 1993 President Clinton presented to Congress a Health Security Act, which would provide universal health care coverage. Under the Clinton plan, the 32 million people who currently lack health insurance would be covered (U.S. Bureau of the Census 1994e). Universal coverage would significantly change the way health care is delivered. Currently, the uninsured tend to delay treatment until their illness reaches a crisis stage and requires expensive care in a hospital. The uninsured receive treatment at emergency rooms, and hospitals shift the cost of these services to health insurance companies by raising the price of hospital services for insured patients. In contrast, under the proposed universal health care plan, low-income workers would receive health care coverage through their place of employment. They would be encouraged to seek treatment at an early stage, when an illness is less expensive to treat. The proposed Health Security Act would provide health care security by eliminating the practice by insurance companies of "cherry-picking," in which the company can choose to insure only those who are most healthy. Now health insurance companies can cancel insurance or raise premiums when an insured worker or family member becomes seriously ill with a disease such as cancer. This has particularly been a problem for self-employed people who purchase private insurance and for employees of small companies that buy group insurance (*San Francisco Chronicle* 1993: A17). These two groups have little bargaining power with insurance companies. Undoubtedly changes will be made in the health care proposal as Congress debates the issue. Nonetheless, health care reform will remain an important social issue because of the insecurity many American families feel with regard to health care insurance.

The Changing Organization of Work

Those in the working class who are fortunate enough to find stable factory jobs often find that the nature of factory work is changing. In recent decades some factory work has been reorganized as *quality circles* have been introduced. Quality circles have been used by the Japanese and have become increasingly popular in U.S. factories over the last twenty years. In a quality circle, workers meet to discuss how to organize the workplace more efficiently and how better to produce the product. To some extent quality circles are worker self-management teams that blur the distinction between managers and workers. Workers are now expected to do more than take orders. Through quality circles, workers provide feedback on how production could be better organized. This change could affect the attitude of workers toward their jobs. Less personal stress on the job could have a positive effect on marital interaction patterns and will probably lead workers to encourage more creativity in childrearing. However, with the decline in factory jobs, only a small portion of the working class experience quality circles.

Next we turn to an examination of the more economically advantaged middle class.

Review Questions

1. What are the characteristics of working-class jobs?
2. Describe working-class childrearing.
3. How do the stresses of working-class jobs affect marital interaction?

4. How do working-class wives differ from middle-class wives in their marital communication?

5. What is meant when we say that the United States is a postindustrial economy experiencing deindustrialization?

6. What is a global economy and what impact does it have on U.S. workers?

7. What is meant by a shift from production jobs to service jobs in the U.S. economy? What do we mean when we say that the United States is becoming a two-tier society?

8. What is an opportunity structure and how has it changed for the working class in the United States?

9. What happened in the 1960s to slow upward mobility among African Americans who migrated from the south to the cities of the north and west?

10. Why were African Americans particularly disadvantaged by deindustrialization?

11. Why are so many families concerned about health care?

Middle Class

The middle class includes those families who earn incomes just above and below the median family income, which is currently $36,812 per year. (U.S. Bureau of the Census 1993d). A *median* is a midpoint, or fiftieth percentile, meaning that half the families in the United States earn $36,812 or more and half earn $36,812 or less. The lower end of the middle-class category begins at an annual income of around $25,000 (Wilkerson 1990). The middle class typically hold occupations in such areas as teaching, accounting, and bank management, which require more education than working-class jobs. Highly skilled blue-collar workers, such as electricians, are also included in the middle class. Many families maintain middle-class status only by combining the incomes of husband and wife (Ehrenreich 1986). Thus a single parent who is a file clerk would not have an income high enough for middle-class status, yet a married couple in which the husband has a blue-collar job as a carpenter and his wife has a pink-collar job as a file clerk would probably achieve middle-class status through their combined incomes. Notice in Table 10.4 that 86 percent of two-earner families in which both partners are full-time workers fall into the middle class or above. In contrast, two-thirds of single-mother families have incomes that place them below the middle class. Race and ethnicity also affect social class. As Table 10.5 shows, slightly less than half of African-American and and Hispanic families have incomes that place them in the middle class, compared to over two-thirds of white families.

Home Ownership

The middle class strive to be able to afford the major symbols of middle-class status: home ownership, a college education for their children, and family vacations. However, not all of the middle class can afford home ownership. An annual income of around $35,000 is required to purchase a median-priced home, which costs approximately $93,000, in the United States (Burkhardt 1990). Eligibility for home ownership varies with marital status, race, and ethnicity. When the U.S.

				Female-Headed Families, No Husband Present	Male-Headed Families, No Wife Present
Anual Income	*All Families*	*Married-Couple Families*	*Two-Earner Families**		
Below $25,000 (below middle-class)	32.4%	24.3%	14.0%	65.3%	36.1%
$25,000–$49,999 (middle class)	34.2	36.0	39.9	25.9	44.4
$50,000 and above (upper-middle class)	33.4	39.7	46.1	8.8	19.5
Total (percent)	100.%	100%	100%	100%	100%
Number of families (in thousands)	68,144	53,171	30,994	11,947	3,026
Median family income	$36,812	$42,064	$47,334	$17,221	$27,821

TABLE 10.4 — Family Structure and Inequality in Family Income: Percentage of Families in Each Income Group

*Includes both full-time and part-time workers.

Note: Figures for all groups are for 1992, except for two-earner families, which are for 1990.

Source: U.S. Bureau of the Census 1993d. Current Population Reports P60-184. *Money Income of Households, Families, and Persons in the United States: 1992,* Table 17, pages 52–64. Washington, D.C.: U.S. Government Printing Office.

U.S. Bureau of the Census 1991d, Current Population Reports P60-174. *Money Income of Households, Families, and Persons in the United States: 1990,* Table 19, page 90. Washington, D.C.: U.S. Government Printing Office.

Bureau of the Census compared family income to the median-priced home in the region in which each family lived, non-Hispanic white families were twice as likely as African-American or Hispanic families to have the income necessary to purchase a home in the region where they lived (U.S. Bureau of the Census 1991e). In addition, a larger percentage of married-couple families (69 percent) than single-parent families (13 percent) had an income adequate to purchase a median-priced home.

African Americans in the Middle Class

African-American families typically experience less economic security in the middle class than white families (Wilkerson 1990). The economic position of middle-class African American-families tends to be precarious because African Americans are likely to be new arrivals in the middle class and to have achieved middle-class status in their own lifetime. Middle-class African Americans often have relatives in pover-

| TABLE 10.5 | Race and Ethnicity and Inequality in Family Income: Percentage of Families Falling into Each Income Category | | | | |

Anual Income	All Families	White	African American	Hispanic	Asian and Pacific Islander
Below $25,000 (below middle-class)	32.4%	29.0%	56.9%	52.0%	28.7%
$25,000–$49,999 (middle class)	34.2	35.3	27.0	31.3	30.2
$50,000 and above (upper-middle class)	33.4	35.7	16.1	16.7	41.1
Total (percent)	100.%	100%	100%	100%	100%
Number of families (in thousands)	68,144	57,858	7,888	5,318	1,624
Median family income	$36,812	$38,909	$21,161	$23,901	$41,907

*Hispanic origin may be white or black.

Note: Figures for all groups are for 1992, except for Asian and Pacific Islanders, which are for 1991.

Source: U.S. Bureau of the Census 1993c, Current Population Reports P60-184. *Money Income of Households, Families, and Persons in the United States: 1992,* Table 17, pages 52–64. Washington, D.C.: U.S. Government Printing Office.

U.S. Bureau of the Census 1993a, *Statistical Abstract of the United States, 1993.* Washington, D.C.: U.S. Government Printing Office.

ty, and these kin often make requests for economic assistance. Family obligation is strong, and middle-class African Americans are frequently asked to help relatives who are behind in their rent or need car repairs. In contrast, white families have typically grown up in the middle class. In spite of family obligations, newly affluent African Americans have very little in the way of savings to share with relatives. The *median net worth* of whites is ten times that of African-Americans, $39,135 per family compared to $3,397 for African Americans. To find the median net worth, we take the total value of what is owned—such as a house, a car, equity in a business, or stocks and bonds—and subtract money owed—such as outstanding loans. Middle-class African Americans often lack the financial reserves needed to purchase a home or to subsidize a child's college education (Wilkerson 1990).

Upper-Middle Class

The upper-middle class are typically highly paid professionals, such as lawyers, doctors, anchorpersons, engineers, professors, financial managers, therapists, archi-

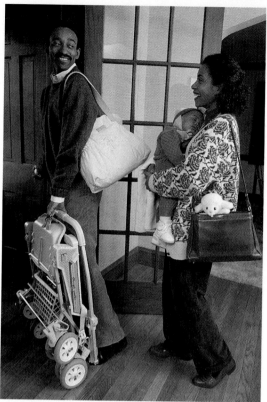

Many African Americans achieve middle-class status in their own lifetimes, rather than growing up in the middle class. As a result, they are often called on to help family members still in need.

tects, and scientists, as well as some government officials and corporation executives (Ehrenreich 1989). African Americans have experienced a substantial increase in the number of families with a breadwinner in a profession. During the 1970s and 1980s the number of African-American accountants, engineers, lawyers, computer programmers, managers, and administrators increased threefold (*Wall Street Journal*, May 6, 1992). Upper-middle-class professions are white-collar jobs that involve "mental work" rather than physical labor, pay a salary rather than an hourly wage, and offer a career path with promotion opportunities. Responsibility and initiative are encouraged in the professions, and autonomy is one of the rewards. Workers with autonomy can make some decisions that affect the pace of their work and the course the work takes (Rothman 1993).

The lifestyle of the upper-middle class often includes the ability to afford psychotherapy, fitness training, summer camp for children, and cultural activities. However, unlike those with inherited wealth, the professional middle class must work for a living. Very few of the upper-middle class own productive capital, such as a factory. Instead, economic status is based on education, as Table 10.6 shows, and requires at least a college degree. The "capital" of the upper-middle class is human capital: knowledge and skill. This capital cannot be bequeathed to children as land can be. Wealth must be renewed in each generation, so the upper-middle class puts an emphasis on education, deferred gratification, and self-discipline in raising their children. The upper-middle class are an insecure elite because the loss of a job means loss of wealth and class position. In the back of their minds there is a fear of a downward economic slide. Also feared are temptations toward hedonism and self-indulgence, which could undermine a person's work and lead to a loss of status (Ehrenreich 1989).

Separation from Lower Social Classes

The upper-middle class tends to live in a relatively insular social world composed of other members of their own social class. The most affluent of the middle class often use private rather than public services, such as private schools, private cars, and private clubs for recreation. They are likely to avoid riding the bus or taking their children to public parks where they could come into contact

TABLE 10.6	Does Education Pay Off?
Level of Education	*Average Monthly Earnings*
No high school diploma	$492
High school graduate (no college)	1,077
Some college	1,280
Associate college degree (two-year college degree)	1,672
Bachelor's degree	2,116
Master's degree	2,822
Doctorate degree	3,855
Professional degree (such as law or medicine)	4,961

Source: U.S. Bureau of the Census, *Statistical Brief* 1993, 93-7. "*Education: The Ticket to Higher Earnings.*" Washington, D.C.: U.S. Government Printing Office.

with the poor and homeless. Overhead skywalks remove upper-middle-class office workers from mingling with those on the streets of cities, who are likely to be people of color with lower incomes. Upper-middle-class families tend to withdraw their political support for public schools, parks, and transportation, which are the services on which the poor depend (Ehrenreich 1986:62).

Job Insecurity in Middle- and Upper-Middle-Class Families

Until recently a major distinction between working-class blue-collar jobs and middle-class positions was a higher level of job security for the middle class. However, economic insecurity has been creeping into middle-class families as midlevel corporation managers have experienced layoffs (*Forbes* 1993). Traditionally, industrial giants had many layers of managers and dominated U.S. industry. These large corporations were slow to respond when a competitor introduced a new product, and decision-making was cumbersome because of the number of managers involved. Today, U.S. corporations are *restructuring,* or reorganizing, to become more efficient. In this process they are *downsizing,* or becoming smaller, by eliminating layers of middle management. Restructuring is different from traditional layoffs. In the past layoffs were usually the result of a temporary recession, and workers expected to be rehired when the economy improved. However, in restructuring jobs are permanently eliminated and employees do not expect to be rehired (*Forbes* 1993). Middle-class breadwinners experience economic insecurity when they realize that individual management positions can be cut or the entire department in which they work can be eliminated from the corporate structure. It is not unusual for a laid-off executive

Corporate Restructuring Eliminates Middle-Class Jobs

The modern world has become an uncertain place for many corporate executives, engineers, and other professionals working for U.S. big businesses. Changes that make corporations more efficient and profitable also put some middle-class breadwinners out of work. U.S. business has restructured in the three ways described below, and by doing so corporations have eliminated a number of middle-class jobs.

Making Better Use of New Technologies

Many firms purchased computers in the 1980s but did not become more productive. The challenge of the 1990s is for businesses to utilize the new information technologies to become more efficient. K-Mart stores recently set up a computerized system for monitoring sales and inventory. This new system allows manufacturer Proctor and Gamble to restock K-Mart automatically with Crest toothpaste when inventories are low. The new computerized system eliminated middle managers who previously oversaw inventory and placed orders to suppliers. In addition, modestly paid workers who were previously hired to take inventory have lost their jobs (*Forbes* 1993).

Globalizing Operations

In the past it was thought that U.S. factory workers would lose jobs as U.S. corporations built plants out of the country but that well-paid middle-class jobs in such areas as research and development, management, marketing, engineering, and accounting would remain in the United States. Despite this expectation, many highly technical middle-class jobs have been transferred overseas. For example, the Irish government spent billions of dollars to upgrade Ireland's telephone system in order to attract telecommunications jobs. As a result, a California-based computer software company, Quarterdeck Office Systems, established an 800-number phone-answering operation in Ireland to answer customer questions. Irish employees now respond to complicated customer questions about how the software operates (O'Reilly 1992).

Gaining a Closer Relationship with Customers

A corporation's dominant position in a market can slip away within several years if they lose touch with the needs of their customers. Some corporations have become "top heavy," so that multiple layers of managers sometimes act as a barrier to vital communication with customers. For example, IBM continued to give top priority to the production of large mainframe computers in 1992 while their business customers were switching to personal computers (PCs) for their operations. As a result IBM lost sales along with part of its share of the computer market. IBM responded with massive worker layoffs and restructured to slim down its management staff (*Forbes* 1993; *Economist* 1992).

The challenge of the 1990s will be for the United States to hang on to both middle class and working class jobs while being able to compete in a global economy.

---

to spend half a year looking for another job and to wind up taking a job at lower pay with fewer benefits than the previous job (Stern 1992). The economic uncertainty that working-class families have traditionally faced now also plagues many middle-class families.

Upper Class

The upper class are typically business owners, upper-level corporation executives, and some professional service workers, such as doctors, whose incomes are substantially higher than those of the upper-middle class. A pediatrician who works for a health maintenance organization on a salary would fall into the upper-middle class, whereas a well-known surgeon would probably earn enough to be in the upper class. The upper class is divided into the lower-upper class, or "nouveaux riche" (translated "new rich"), who have recently acquired their wealth, and the upper-upper class, or "old rich," who have inherited family wealth. The old rich often look down on the new rich for what they see as their lack of refinement in manners and lifestyle. Like the upper-middle class, the upper class prefers to utilize private schools and private clubs, and the upper class are typically found in the most exclusive and expensive private institutions. Both subgroups of the upper class typically provide their children with access to country club membership and send their children to elite private colleges, where they can meet friends and future marriage partners. Upper-class children are expected to make a network of personal friends who will someday hold powerful positions in society and who can be of help in a later career.

Having glimpsed a picture of the social class structure, we now turn to an examination of some of the most vulnerable people in U.S. society: the homeless.

The Homeless

One segment of the poor cuts across age, race, ethnic group, and gender lines. They are the homeless, the most disadvantaged of the poor. Estimates of the number of homeless range from 500,000 (Rossi and Wright 1989) to 3 million (Kozol 1988; Pearce 1990).

Who Are the Homeless?

Many studies of homelessness have depicted the typical homeless person as a single individual, detached from family relationships (LaGory et al. 1991; Rossi and Wright 1989). Although this description is accurate for one segment of the homeless population, homeless families are often overlooked.

Cohabiting Couples. The use of a traditional definition of the family overlooks homeless cohabiting couples and fails to include the male partners of homeless single mothers in the count of homeless families. To correct this bias, the Birmingham Homeless Enumeration and Survey Project, which studied twenty-two homeless shelters in the Birmingham, Alabama, area, counted cohabitors as families. Using this definition of a family, over half of the people in the Birmingham shelters were there with a family member. Moreover, the majority of cohabitors had been together for one year or more (LaGory et al. 1991).

Mother-Headed Families. It is also easy to overlook, and thus undercount, mother-headed homeless families because they often attempt to appear invisible (Pearce 1990). Homeless mothers tend to rely on *hidden housing*, such as cars and abandoned buildings, and avoid homeless shelters if possible. They seek invisibility because they fear losing their children to the foster care system. Social service agencies are legally empowered to remove children from a parent who cannot offer adequate shelter and food. When homeless mothers lose their children to foster care, it is difficult to get them back. Loss of their children means that homeless mothers also lose their welfare income from Aid to Families with Dependent Children (AFDC). This situation is the "Catch 22" of homelessness (Pearce 1990). Loss of children and related welfare payments

BOX 10.4 · A Closer Look

Public Assistance Programs

When thinking about poverty programs, the Aid to Families with Dependent Children program, commonly known as welfare, immediately comes to mind for many people. However, a variety of public assistance programs are designed to provide a "safety net" that prevents certain segments of the population from becoming destitute. These programs are described below.

Aid to Families with Dependent Children

This program provides aid to dependent children and one parent caretaker. Only about 5 percent of AFDC families receive AFDC-UP (UP stands for unemployed parents). AFDC-UP provides welfare benefits to a parent with children and an unemployed partner, allowing the parents to remain together. The federal government provides the states with matching grants to fund AFDC and the Medicaid health care program for families on public assistance. The states then decide whether or not to include additional benefits, such as dental care and food stamps, for which they also receive federal matching grants. This is a *means-tested* program, meaning that it is available only to those with incomes below a specified level. AFDC, AFDC-UP, and Medicaid account for approximately 7 percent of federal social spending.

Food Stamps

Food stamps, a means-tested program, are provided to most AFDC recipients as well as to some of the working poor. Food stamp certificates may be used to purchase only food, not liquor, laundry detergent, or other nonfood grocery store items.

Women, Infants, and Children

This is a high-nutrient supplementary food program for nursing mothers and AFDC families with young children. WIC pays for a limited number of high-nutrient foods, such as milk, cheese, orange juice, cereals, and peanut butter. This is a means-tested program and together with the food stamp program accounts for approximately 1 percent of federal social spending.

Social Security

This is a social insurance program, funded from Social Security taxes paid for by current workers and their employers. Social Security combined with Medicare health benefits has been very effective in reducing poverty among the elderly. Those age sixty-five and over have the same poverty rate as people of working age. Social Security is a social insurance rather than a means-tested program, meaning that anyone who has paid into Social Security, even a millionaire, is entitled to receive benefits. Social Security and Medicare account for 35 percent of federal social spending.

Supplemental Security Insurance

This program offers income to the blind, disabled, and a portion of the aged and accounts for approximately 1 percent of federal social spending.

Half of the federal money spent on public assistance programs goes to Social Security payments, and another one-fourth goes to health and medical care expenditures. The last one-fourth is split between veterans programs, education, housing, and the other public assistance programs, such as Aid to Families with Dependent Children, listed above. Although many Americans complain about welfare (AFDC) expenditures, they go to support some of the most vulnerable people in society: children.

Source: U. S. Bureau of the Census, *Statistical Abstract of the United States, 1993,* Table 578.

---

makes it difficult for homeless mothers to find housing, yet without housing they cannot regain their children. Moreover, when homeless mothers voluntarily leave their children with relatives or voluntarily or involuntarily place their children in foster care, homeless families are undercounted. The mother is counted as a single homeless woman, and the children go into the foster care count.

One of the greatest challenges for homeless families with children is to provide them with continuity in their education. It is not unusual for a homeless child to attend four or five different schools in a single school year. Homeless children who have not yet been exposed to multiplication in math class at one school may arrive at a second school where the subject has already been covered. Other homeless children attend no school at all for months at a time (Asimov 1989; Stewart 1990). The disruption homelessness brings to the lives of children leads a number of social service workers to argue that foster care has advantages because it provides homeless children with stability. This attitude creates anxiety in homeless mothers.

Homeless Individuals and Their Kin

In addition to single mothers, the homeless population includes a large number of single men. Social scientists have asked why the extended families—the parents, siblings, adult children, or other relatives of these men—are not providing them with housing. The answers to this question fall into two categories: the social isolation perspective and the affiliation perspective.

The Social Isolation Perspective. Rossi and Wright's (1989) study of the homeless in Chicago found that a large number of homeless people had become socially isolated from their kin. These alienated homeless lacked an attachment to former friends and family. Many of the homeless men had lived with relatives before becoming homeless. The average homeless male had been unemployed for approximately four years and homeless for the last two of those years. This situation had probably drained the emotional and economic resources of kin, who eventually withdrew their support. After becoming homeless, most of these men lost touch with relatives (Rossi and Wright 1989:136).

The Affiliation Perspective. Although many homeless individuals appear to be isolated, it is easy for a social observer to overlook important social ties that the homeless do have. In the study of the homeless-shelter population in Birmingham, Alabama, two-thirds of the homeless reported that they occasionally saw relatives, visiting with a relative every two or three months. These relatives often lived in crowded housing and were not able to offer shelter to the homeless relative. However, the relatives did provide emotional support, including love and advice. Almost all (84 percent) of the homeless reported that they received some form of material support from relatives from time to time, such as money, food, clothing, transportation, or occasional shelter (LaGory 1991). However, because the homeless tended to have relatives who were also poor, these relatives did not have the financial resources that would allow them to offer permanent shelter.

It appears that there are many levels of family attachment among the homeless. Some of the homeless are socially isolated; others make periodic contact with their kin several times a year. Still others experience episodic homelessness: They live "doubled-up" with relatives and then become temporarily homeless when the strains of crowded living conditions become too great.

Explanations for Homelessness

There are two major explanations for homelessness: personal problems and structural conditions.

Because homeless families are constantly moving between shelters and makeshift housing, it is extremely difficult for the parents to hold down permanent jobs and for the children to attend school consistently. Thus, many homeless people feel unable to improve their lives.

Personal Problems. The *personal problems* explanation holds that the homeless suffer from a variety of personal afflictions that make it difficult for them to hold down a permanent job or maintain permanent housing. High rates of depression, mental illness, drug addiction, and alcoholism have been found in homeless populations (Elliott and Krivo 1991; LaGory et al. 1990; Rossi and Wright 1989). Critics of the personal problems explanation for homelessness point out that depression, alcoholism, and mental illness may be results as well as causes of homelessness. The homeless often feel hopeless and experience *economic defeatism*. Economic defeatism is the belief that one's life and economic situation will not improve (Mead 1989). Jonathan Kozol interviewed mothers living with their children in the crowded Martinique Hotel, a hotel for the homeless in New York City. One welfare mother living with her children in a single room of the hotel described her outlook on life as follows:

> After you're living here a while you begin to lose hold of your dream. You start to tell yourself that it's forever. "This is it. It isn't going to change. It can't get worse. It isn't going to get better." So you start to lose the courage to fight back. (Kozol 1988:33)

Kozol maintains that the homeless have to struggle against falling into depression, which can make it difficult to manage their lives.

Structural Conditions. Although personal problems are an important factor, they constitute only a partial explanation for homelessness. Personal problems tell us who is vulnerable to becoming homeless when certain structural conditions exist (Elliott and Krivo 1991). In contrast, the *structural conditions* explanation looks to the broader society for an explanation of homeless. Structural conditions refer to forces within the larger society which make it difficult for some families and individuals to find and maintain housing. Structural conditions that affect homelessness include a decline in the stock of low-cost housing, rising rents, deinstitutionalization of the mentally ill, and changes in the occupational structure.

Decline in the Stock of Low-Cost Housing. Each year the poor find fewer affordable housing units open to them. Those in poverty are renters rather than homeowners and, except for public housing, the construction industry does not usually build housing for the poor. They live in "hand-me-down" housing, which is often old, deteriorated urban housing, which the middle class abandoned as they moved to the suburbs. The poor also occupy old inner-city hotels, which became available for housing because travelers now stay at airport hotels or other new hotels (Harrington 1987:117–119). Recently, both of these sources of housing for the poor, older urban homes and inner-city hotel rooms, have become scarce. Some housing was abandoned due to lack of repair and the high crime rate in the inner city. Some units were burned by arson, and many units were converted into apartments and condominiums for the young married couples of the middle class who cannot afford to purchase a home in the suburbs where their parents live (Harrington 1987:117). The process by which the middle class renovates dilapidated housing previously used by the poor is called *gentrification*. The middle class now competes for this inner-city housing, in an effort to avoid long commutes from the suburbs and to find an affordable "fixer-up" house or newly renovated condominium to purchase.

Rising Rents. Rents have been increasing faster than incomes. Since 1970 the median monthly rent in the United States has risen more than the median monthly income of renters (Elliott and Krivo 1991). The families most at risk of becoming homeless are those that are "precariously housed." These are families who have been unable to pay their rent and have *doubled-up* by moving in with relatives or friends. There are nearly 2 million single-mother families who live doubled-up in the home of a relative (U.S. Bureau of the Census 1994b, page XIII).

Deinstitutionalization. The deinstitutionalization of mental patients accounts for many of the homeless. In 1955 over 500,000 mental patients were in public mental hospitals. Subsequent advances in drug therapy made it possible for many patients to be treated on an out-patient basis, and by 1979 over two-thirds of these had been released. However, the funding for out-patient mental health centers was not forthcoming, and very few urban mental health clinics were built to offer services to these released mental patients. This situation lead former Mayor Koch of New York City to say that the city had "its neighborhoods used as mental wards and its police officers used as orderlies" (Harrington 1987:102) Many former mental patients became bag ladies and single men living in single-room-occupancy (SRO) hotels, often alcoholic and alone.

Changes in the Occupational Structure. As we discussed earlier in this chapter, the number of well-paid factory jobs for poorly educated workers is declining. The potential marriage partners of many homeless single mothers are unemployed, impoverished, and unable to support a family. The feminization of poverty that accompanied deindustrialization has produced a growing number of homeless mothers with children. Likewise, many homeless men are unemployed or employed at occasional casual labor.

Review Questions

1. What are the characteristics of middle-class jobs? How do many families with modest-paying jobs achieve middle-class status?

2. How do middle-class jobs typically differ from working-class jobs?

3. Can all members of the middle class expect to achieve homeownership? Why or why not?

4. Why is the position of middle-class African American families more precarious than that of white families?

5. What jobs are typical of the upper-middle class?

6. Why are middle-class and upper-middle-class families experiencing economic insecurity?

7. Who is in the upper class? What is the difference between the lower-upper class and the upper-upper class?

8. Why are homeless families often undercounted?

9. Why do homeless mothers seek invisibility?

10. Why don't more homeless families move in with their kin?

11. Why is the personal problems explanation inadequate to explain homelessness?

12. What structural factors affect homelessness?

13. Why has a shortage of affordable housing for the poor developed?

Summary

1. The social class position of a family is based on wealth, power, and prestige, which are typically indicated by income and occupation.

2. Poverty is fluid: A number of families move in and out of poverty. Although the poor are often unemployed, underemployed, or on welfare, half of the poor work at some time during the year.

3. Poverty rates are higher among African-American, Hispanic, and Native American families than among white or Asian families.

4. There is a growing trend toward the feminization of poverty. Single mothers are particularly likely to be poor.

5. The bottom strata of the very poor in inner-city ghettos have been labeled the "underclass," a term that tends to stigmatize the poor.

6. The working class hold blue-collar and pink-collar jobs, tend to have manual labor jobs which involve taking orders, and raise their children to respect compliance to authority.

7. The working class tend to experience high levels of job stress; and this stress, along with the stress of financial worries, spills over into marriage. Blue-collar husbands tend to express more complaints to their wives than middle-class husbands. In contrast, working-class wives tend to be less willing to express complaints than middle-class wives.

8. Working-class families have been experiencing skidding, or downward mobility, because of deindustrialization. The entry of the United States into a global economy, the technological revolution, and the development of a two-tier society have all put a downward pressure on wages and created a shrinking opportunity structure for the working class. African-American families have been particularly disadvantaged by deindustrialization.

9. Not all middle-class families can afford to purchase a home. African-American families tend to have a less secure position in the middle class than white families.

10. Upper-middle-class professional families have jobs based on education and knowledge. They tend to opt out of using public services.

11. Middle-class and upper-middle-class families have experienced economic insecurity as U.S. corporations have begun restructuring.

12. The upper class has two layers, the lower-upper class, or newly wealthy, and the upper-upper class, who have inherited their wealth.

13. The most disadvantaged of the poor, the homeless, have experienced a shortage of affordable housing and often were doubled-up with relatives before becoming homeless. Many of the homeless are single men, some of whom are estranged from their kin.

14. Homeless families tend to be undercounted because of their desire for invisibility in order to avoid the foster care system. Cohabiting couples are often counted as single individuals rather than as families. When cohabitors are considered families, the majority of the homeless are in families.

Key Words

Social Class
Underemployed
Feminization of Poverty
Working Class
Pink-Collar Jobs
Skidding
Upward Mobility
Deindustrialization
Techological Revolution
Production Jobs
Opportunity Structure
Middle Class
Restructuring
Upper Class
Aid to Families with Dependent Children (AFDC)
Doubling-Up
Economic Defeatism
Gentrification
Industrial Economy

Lower Class
Poverty Rate
Underclass
Blue-Collar Jobs
Autonomy
Standard of Living
Family Wage
Global Economy
Two-Tier Society
Service Jobs
Quality Circles
Median Net Worth
Downsizing
Hidden Housing
Single-Room-Occupancy (SRO) Hotels
Personal Problems
Structural Conditions
Deinstitutionalization
Postindustrial Economy

Resources

Homeless Information Exchange
1830 Connecticut Ave., N.W., 4th Floor
Washington, DC 20009
(202) 462-7551
Provides information on homeless policies and services and compiles statistics on homelessness.
Publishes *Homewords*, quarterly newsletter.

Student Campaign Against Hunger and Homelessness
29 Temple Pl.
Boston, MA 11068
(617) 292-4823
Offers manuals and programs to assist students in reducing hunger. Publishes *Students Making a Difference,* monthly.

Children's Defense Fund
122 C Street, N.W.
Washington, DC 20001
(202) 628-8787
Advocates improvement in child welfare and child health. Collects information on the state of the nation's children. Publishes *CDF Child Youth and Family Futures Clearinghouse,* bimonthly, and *The State of America's Children,* annual.

Child Welfare League of America Research Center
440 First St. N.W., Ste. 310
Washington, DC 20001
(202) 638-2952
Collects information on teen pregnancy, Aid to Families with Dependent Children, young parents, child abuse and neglect, and adoption.

The Intimate World of the Family

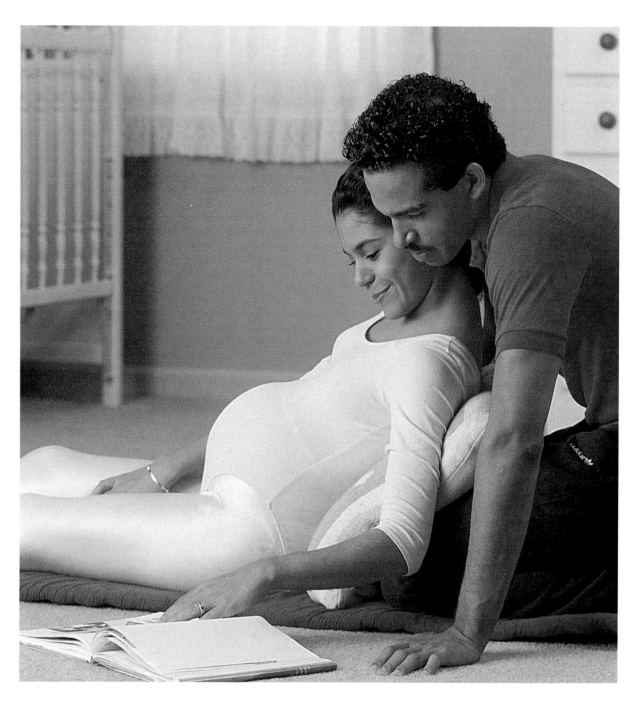

Pregnancy: Experiences and Choices

Anna and Gary had been married a year when she found out that she was pregnant. After feeling independent in her marital relationship, the changes in her body and life induced by pregnancy were now creating occasional pangs of insecurity that sometimes left Anna feeling somewhat childlike when she was with her husband. In the early part of pregnancy, Anna was glad to see that her breasts were enlarging, but she was often nauseous and excessively tired. Gary's complaints about their diminished sex life seemed like an irritation when she felt so uncomfortable.

Gary is pleased about the prospect of becoming a father. He likes it when Anna sleeps curled up with her belly to his back so that he can feel the baby kick at night. In spite of his excitement over the baby, Gary worries about his new financial responsibility. Their income will decline when Anna leaves work to take care of the baby. Anna feels some sadness about leaving her friends at work, and she is concerned that she might feel isolated at home after the baby is born. In addition, Anna is afraid that she might lose some of her influence in the marriage once she no longer brings in a paycheck. Gary also has concerns about the potential change in the couple's relationship which will probably occur after the baby arrives. In the past, Anna's income paid for special weekend getaways. Soon weekends will involve activities including the baby. Gary has occasional pangs of sadness when he realizes that the focus of Anna's attention will probably shift away from him. In spite of these worries, Gary wants to be a good father; and both he and Anna wonder about what kind of parents they will make.

Anna's changing body shape has a special attractiveness associated with pregnancy. She was grateful when she walked into her obstetrician's office and saw a poster on the wall featuring a nine-months-pregnant woman and a caption reading, "pregnancy is beautiful." Nonetheless, Anna wonders whether Gary still finds her as appealing. In spite of these worries, pregnancy has created new opportunities in their relationship. They recently began a Lamaze childbirth preparation class, which has brought them closer together and alleviated some of Anna's anxiety over labor and delivery.

The experiences of Anna and Gary are typical in that the couple have many of the hopes and anxieties normally associated with pregnancy. During pregnancy, couples must cope with the transition to a new stage in life as well as with the challenges associated with the pregnancy itself. Having a child, in addition to being a complex process, is one of the most important choices a couple can make. Pregnancy can be the first step to a rewarding experience with parenting, and it can also limit future opportunities, as in the case of teen pregnancy. Pregnancy can place strain on a partnership as well as promote couple bonding. However, pregnancy is not the only means by which people have a child. Adoption is an alternative, chosen mainly by those who are involuntarily infertile. In this chapter we explore the experience of pregnancy, childbirth, teen pregnancy, involuntary infertility and adoption, voluntary childlessness, substance abuse and pregnancy, and abortion. We begin by looking at the stages of pregnancy.

Stages of Pregnancy

Pregnancy is typically divided into three trimesters because the physiological changes in the body, attitudes, and level of comfort or discomfort in the course of a pregnancy roughly follow a three-stage pattern.

First Trimester (Months 1 to 3)

Despite the excitement and joy that pregnancy brings to many couples, many women find the physiological changes in their bodies disconcerting. Some of the first signs of pregnancy include tender breasts and the need to urinate frequently. Nausea and vomiting, known as "morning sickness," are common during the first trimester (first three months) of pregnancy. Contrary to its name, "morning sickness" does not necessarily occur in the morning, but can occur any time of the day. In addition, insomnia (difficulty sleeping), drowsiness during the day, mood swings, and feelings of dependency are common in early pregnancy. All of these reactions are normal responses to pregnancy. Many couples are startled by the discomfort many women feel in the first three months of pregnancy. Some couples think that if they truly want the pregnancy, the woman will be immune to morning sickness and will exude a glowing appearance of well-being. This erroneous assumption can lead to feelings of failure and self-doubt during the early months of pregnancy (Defries et al. 1985:6).

Ambivalence. Even when a pregnancy is planned and desired, a variety of unsettling emotions often arise. The couple typically experience *ambivalence*, which refers to holding two conflicting attitudes at the same time (Defries et al. 1985). On one hand, the possibility of parenthood creates a new source of identity and offers an opportunity for the new social role of parent to enhance self-esteem. On the other hand, both husbands and wives often experience anxiety over whether or not they will be good parents. Pregnancy tends to increase the pregnant woman's dependency on her partner (Defries et al. 1985). When the husband responds with reassurance and understanding and when the couple has had good marital communication before the pregnancy, the woman's fears are often allayed. Pregnancy is also a time when women often feel increasingly dependent on their own mothers, to whom they look for emotional support and reassurance (Defries et al. 1985). Family members become an important source of information on which aspects of pregnancy are normal, such as nausea in the early months, and which are a cause for concern, such as vaginal bleeding.

Men also experience anxiety during pregnancy as they wonder how the pregnancy and birth will affect their relationship with the partner. Many men keep their worries to themselves because they do not want to burden their wives who are experiencing morning sickness and increased emotional dependency. Men often feel some social isolation during the early months of pregnancy. They often find it awkward to express either their worries or their feelings of joy to friends or co-workers. Expectant fathers often fear that if they talk about their emotional reaction to the pregnancy, other men will see them as overly soft or sentimental (Grad et al. 1981).

Sexuality. Sexual activity tends to decrease during the first trimester of pregnancy (Defries et al. 1985; Pape 1982). Morning sickness and excessive fatigue are deterrents to sexual arousal. In addition, many men and women shy away from sex in a desire to protect the fetus from harm. Some women who have had previous spontaneous abortions (miscarriages) or who are experiencing vaginal bleeding may be advised by their doctors to avoid intercourse during the first trimester of pregnancy. However, under normal conditions intercourse presents no problem and can help create a special closeness during this time (Sarrel and Sarrel 1984). Discovering that it is safe to have sex often reawakens sexual interest in men who have backed off from sex during pregnancy.

Coping with sexual issues during pregnancy is especially difficult for husbands who develop the *madonna complex* when their wives first become pregnant. The madonna complex makes it difficult for some partners of pregnant women to become sexually aroused (Sarrel and Sarrel 1984). Men who experience the madonna complex tend to put lovers into one category and "good women" and mothers into another. In the minds of these men the wife shifts to the forbidden category of "mother" when she becomes pregnant. There is debate over whether or not a husband is more likely to engage in an extramarital affair when the wife becomes pregnant (Defries et al. 1985). However, there is no solid evidence to suggest that husbands of pregnant wives are any more likely to stray than other husbands (Sarrel and Sarrel 1984). One developmental task that husbands face during pregnancy is to integrate the images of wife, lover, and mother so that the mother of his child is also seen as a sexual being (Sarrel and Sarrel 1984). Today's cultural attitudes are changing, so that people are viewed as having a sexual nature over the entire lifecycle. The impact of the madonna complex has diminished as attitudes have shifted away from associating sex with youth and childlessness. The movement of divorced parents back into the dating arena has helped to change these sexual attitudes.

Second Trimester (Months 4 through 6)

During the second trimester of pregnancy, the fourth through sixth months, morning sickness tends to disappear and the pregnant woman experiences a greater feeling of well-being. However, as the woman watches her abdomen grow, both partners often begin to feel anxiety about areas of their lives they previously thought were conflict-free. Questions about their future roles as husband and wife and concerns over the woman's future career possibilities emerge. In addition, when the pregnancy becomes evident, some couples feel uncomfortable about this visible sign of their sexual relationship. At the same time, the pregnant woman's concern about sexual attractiveness often surfaces during the second trimester. As the woman's abdomen reminds the couple of the growing fetus, expectant fathers often have conflicting feelings about the new member of the family. On one hand, the realization that his wife's attention will soon be directed toward the new baby creates feelings of jealousy. On the other hand, fathers feel protective toward the fetus and often fear that sexual intercourse could bring on a miscarriage, a generally unfounded fear (Pape 1982).

Sexuality. Pregnancy can also be a time of elevated sexual pleasure. Many women experience enhanced sexual arousal during the second trimester because of vasocongestion (increased blood supply) in the pelvic area. In addition, the couple can relax because they do not have to worry about contraception to prevent pregnancy. The frequency of sexual intercourse tends to increase during the second trimester, but usually remains below pre-pregnancy levels (Defries et al. 1985;

Pape 1982). Many couples do not see the pregnancy as an inconvenience and instead view pregnancy as a chance to try out new sexual positions. Moreover, couples who find that intercourse seems awkward often increase their experimentation with oral sex and manual stimulation.

Third Trimester (Months 7 through 9)

After a relatively comfortable second trimester, the woman typically experiences an increase in physical discomforts in the last trimester of pregnancy, the seventh through ninth months. The growing size of the fetus and the pressure of the uterus on the woman's bladder lead to more frequent urination combined with occasional leakage of urine. This can be a disconcerting experience. In addition, some women feel fatigued, and many have difficulty finding a comfortable position when sitting or trying to sleep during the last month of pregnancy. In the last trimester, fears about labor and delivery surface, together with concern over the health of the infant (Vida 1982). Husbands also experience anxiety during the last trimester. Some expectant fathers are worried because they feel annoyed with their friends' children rather than drawn to them; such fathers wonder how they will react to their own child. In addition, husbands wonder if the mother-in-law will interfere with their own efforts to become acquainted with the child (Grad et al. 1981). Many couples cope with anxiety by intensive "nesting," in which they make plans for the infant's arrival, acquire baby equipment, and decorate the infant's room or sleeping area. Worries combined with discomfort tend to lead to a decrease in sexual activity during the last trimester of pregnan-

Expectant fathers and mothers may spend considerable time setting up a room for the infant and working extra hours before going on maternity or paternity leave, but much of the final trimester of pregnancy amounts to just waiting.

cy. In spite of anxieties over the birth process, by the ninth month of pregnancy both partners are usually anxious to move on to childbirth, which is described in the next section. (For diagrams depicting stages of pregnancy, labor, and delivery see the Appendix.)

Childbirth

Childbirth can create a strong parent–child bond, which sets the stage for positive parenting. Whether a child is born to a married couple or to a never-married mother, the experience of labor and delivery can be enhanced by childbirth preparation and the presence of a childbirth coach in the labor and delivery room.

Coached Childbirth

In the past, husbands were banished to the waiting room during labor and delivery and women in labor were sometimes treated like "frightened little girls" (Vida 1982). This demeaning situation failed to recognized the important role of

---

BOX 11.1   W o r l d   P e r s p e c t i v e s

The Couvade: A Multicultural Experience

The psychological experience of being the partner of a pregnant woman can be a powerful one. In many traditional societies the mother is not the only one who feels the discomfort of pregnancy and childbirth. Fathers go through the "couvade," in which they experience symptoms of pregnancy, labor, and delivery. The term "couvade" comes from the French word "couver," which means "to brood" or "to hatch." Men with pregnant wives have reported symptoms of morning sickness, including nausea, backache, occasional vomiting, bloating, and even labor pains at the time of birth (Bronstein 1984; Parke 1981).

The couvade is found South America, Africa, Europe, India, China, and many parts of North America, including Mexico, and in a number of Native American tribes including the Zuni, Chiricahua Apache, Havasupai, Papago, and Pawnee (Brian 1976; Kroeber 1948; Munroe and Munroe 1989). In many of these traditional societies, the couvade is linked to magical practices. Men who go to bed and experience labor pains are ritually acting as a decoy who draws away the attention of evil spirits believed to be able to harm the infant and mother. This leaves the mother free to deliver the baby in greater safety. Among the Erickala-Vandu of southern India, when the wife goes into labor the husband puts on women's clothing and make-up, including placing a red dot in the center of his forehead as women do. Then he retires to a cot in a dimly lit room where he experiences the pains of labor and delivery. After his wife gives birth, the child is washed and then placed beside the father on his cot (Parke 1981). The couvade is more than a mere charade: Husbands report that they end up exhausted after experiencing labor pains and they become quite sick from nausea earlier in pregnancy.

In the couvade, men identify with the mother and have a chance to act out the female role and express their femininity (Munroe and Munroe 1989). In fact, the couvade minimizes the differences between the sexes. The couvade also plays an important role in establishing the father's rights over the child (Brain 1976). By going through ritual suffering that parallels the pregnant moth-

families in the childbirth experience. Now it is becoming common for the mother to have a *childbirth coach,* such as a husband, boyfriend, or sister, who remains with her in the labor and delivery room. The job of the coach is to reassure the mother and help her focus on relaxation techniques. Having a partner or coach during delivery has important emotional benefits for the mother and newborn infant. A positive childbirth experience helps both mother and coach establish a strong bond with the infant. Mothers who had partners present to offer emotional support during childbirth touched, talked to, and smiled at their infants more than a control group of mothers who had no childbirth coach (Sosa et al. 1980). In addition, being present in the labor and delivery room promoted bonding between father and child. Fathers who are present at the birth of their children tend to be more involved in child care after the delivery (Nugent 1991). However, not all husbands are willing to enter the labor and delivery room, and many couples argue over the degree to which the father will participate in the birth. Some fathers do not view childbirth as a romantic experience and do not want to see their mates in pain. These fathers see childbirth as a private experience in the female realm. Sometimes the mother shares his feelings and seeks a family member or friend to stay with her during labor and delivery. In other cases a compromise is reached in which the father agrees to be present during labor but not delivery (Grad et al. 1981).

World Perspectives   CONTINUED

er's discomfort, a man makes clear to other members of society that he is indeed the child's father (Broude 1988). The couvade most often appears in societies in which mothers have great importance, such as societies that practice matrilocal residence, in which the married couple live near or with the wife's kin. Likewise, societies in which the mother and child sleep together after the birth also leave fathers feeling that they need to establish their claim to the child (Broude 1989).

Many men in modern western societies, including the United States, the United Kingdom, and Australia, go through a "couvade syndrome," which is less intense than the couvade experienced in traditional societies. A number of men attempt to change their appearance in some way during their wife's pregnancy by growing a beard or mustache or gaining weight. In the couvade syndrome men experience morning sickness, backache, vomiting, insomnia, irritability, headaches, and fatigue. These symptoms sometimes cause fathers to lose time at work when their wives are pregnant (Lewis 1986). It is estimated that the couvade syndrome affects 10 to 15 percent of all fathers in the developed world (Parke 1981). Often husbands feel better when a physician explains that the symptoms are a normal response to the wife's pregnancy.

Why is the couvade so widespread? Because men cannot become pregnant, they often feel cut off from the creative experience of pregnancy and childbirth. Bruno Bettleheim (1955) called this feeling "womb envy." In addition, in the last months of pregnancy most fathers experience some anxiety about the possible dangers that childbirth presents for the child and mother. Yet, the father lacks control over the birth process and often feels helpless. To complicate matters, the husband often allays the wife's anxieties by taking the role of "sturdy oak" on whom the wife leans for emotional support. Meanwhile, the husband avoids verbalizing his own worries. His anxieties are sometimes acted out physically as he begins to feel backache and stomach pain during the wife's labor and delivery (Lewis 1986). These men do not appear to be neurotic but instead are sympathetic to the wife's plight. Men in the United States who experience the couvade syndrome tend to be affectionate, have a positive attitude toward the wife's pregnant appearance, and enjoy sex during late pregnancy (Jackson 1987). The couvade syndrome allows involved fathers to participate vicariously in the pregnancy and birth experience.

Childbirth Preparation

In the 1950s it was common for women to receive a general anesthesia during childbirth. Women who receive anesthesia have little memory of the birth process. Other drugs to reduce pain or calm the mother during labor tend to diminish her alertness and diminish her ability to focus her attention. The newborn infant has a similar response. These reactions interfere with mother–child interaction after birth (Defries et al. 1985).

French obstetrician Fernand Lamaze popularized the idea that psychological preparation for childbirth could reduce the need for pain-killing drugs (Bing 1980). Like others before him, Lamaze noticed that women often experience a "cycle of fear and pain" in labor and delivery. He reasoned that fear caused a woman's muscles to tense, and tense muscles during childbirth caused pain. The onset of pain in turn increased the mother's fear. The result was a spiral of increasing fear and pain. To combat this cycle, Lamaze taught pregnant women relaxation exercises aimed at keeping other muscles limp while the uterus was tense with contractions. The main component of this childbirth method is breathing exercises that help to keep the mother calm (Walker et al. 1979).

Together with Lamaze, Bradley (1981) encouraged women to avoid pain-killing drugs during labor because these drugs also reach the fetus and can cause the baby to appear sluggish and unresponsive at birth. Both physicians argued that bonding with an infant is easiest with a responsive infant who is drug-free. Furthermore, a drug-free mother recovers more quickly after delivery and feels alert enough to enjoy her baby right away. Although "natural childbirth" without medication is a popular goal of middle-class women, working-class mothers take a more passive view and typically desire more medical intervention (Nelson 1983). Moreover, some women who prepare for childbirth and then ask for pain medication during labor wind up

The bonding time new parents spend with their infant is filled with emotion and a sense of awe. Some parents feel instantly bonded with their baby, whereas others require days to adjust to the new person in their lives.

labeling themselves as failures in childbirth. Childbirth practices need to take into account the various desires of women so that birth procedures do not induce guilt (Michaelson 1988). Furthermore, even when mothers require pain medication and are only partially alert, participating fathers can be involved with the infant right after birth. However, promoting a father's involvement with the infant is not a sufficient reason for the mother to take drugs if they are not necessary.

Promoting Bonding

Hospitals no longer routinely assume that it is necessary to separate the infant from the parents and place it in a hospital nursery following birth. Instead, an effort is usually made to keep parents and their new infant together (Vida 1982). Early contact between parents and infant promotes *bonding,* development of a strong emotional attachment. Hospitals promote bonding through *rooming-in,* placing the infant in a bassinet in the mother's hospital room. Some hospitals offer labor and delivery rooms that resemble a comfortable family bedroom, where a number of family members are allowed to be present at the birth. Some couples avoid a hospital setting by choosing a home birth.

Home Birth

Some couples choose a home birth in a nonmedical setting that does not put the mother in the role of a patient. The mother has the comfort of being surrounded by her family in a familiar setting, and older children have the opportunity to be part of the birth process by being with the mother. All in all, home birth represents a more relaxed and intimate experience within a family setting. However, there is also a downside to home birth. If an emergency develops, such as uncontrolled bleeding following delivery or the need to resuscitate the infant, time can be lost in the trip from home to the hospital. In addition, midwives who often attend mothers at home are not licensed to prescribe pain medication, and if the pain level is higher than expected, the mother does not have the option to receive pain medication at home. When a home birth is chosen, couples are advised to make contact with a hospital that has an anesthesiologist on twenty-four-hour duty in case an emergency develops (Stoppard 1986).

The Postpartum Period

The period following childbirth is called the *postpartum period.* After the birth, many a mother goes through a period of *postpartum depression* in which she feels "blue" for several days or weeks. About four out of five women experience at least a three-day period of the blues after childbirth (Defries et al. 1985:18). Depression can be experienced as a feeling of "ego depletion," a sense that additional burdens or stresses, even minor ones, are overwhelming (Defries et al. 1985:18). The depressed mother often wonders how she is going to meet the demands of motherhood, wonders why she sometimes cries without provocation, and occasionally feels that she is "falling apart." Fortunately, in most women the intensity of these feelings subsides in a few days.

Causes of Postpartum Depression

Postpartum depression has a variety of causes, which are physiological, psychological, and social.

Physiological Causes. The fact that symptoms of postpartum depression have been found in a variety of societies, including Tanzania, the West Indies, the United Kingdom, and the United States, points to physiological causes (Defries et al. 1985:18). Labor and delivery involve a significant change in a woman's hormonal levels. In addition, childbirth is followed by a disruption in sleep patterns as a mother wakes to feed a hungry infant every three or four hours. A sense of confusion can develop as days and nights blend together (Defries et al. 1985). Several days of discomfort from stitches following an episiotomy (the temporary surgical widening of the vaginal opening during childbirth) can also add to the blues.

Psychological Causes. Some feelings of depression are related to the mother's *body image* following childbirth. Body image is the perception of one's physical appearance and the negative or positive evaluation of that image. Some new mothers expect their bodies to return to the prepregnancy state immediately following childbirth. In reality, the shrinking of the uterus and abdomen is a slow process, which takes place over about six weeks. The hormones released by breastfeeding can help this process along. Sometimes the sight of a still-protruding stomach can lead a new mother to feel anxiety and to worry about what pregnancy and childbirth have done to her body. New mothers need to realize that it takes time for the body to adjust to the major physiological changes associated with childbirth.

Social Causes. In traditional societies pregnancy and childbirth were an event in which the extended family took an active interest. Today, mothers in small nuclear families often feel isolated, and this isolation has a tendency to accentuate the depression that often follows childbirth (Defries et al 1985). In addition, some new mothers feel a sense of loss of oneness with the infant which was experienced during pregnancy (Defries et al. 1985). Also, the focus of family attention switches from the pregnant mother to the new infant.

Sexuality

Childbirth is followed by a short period during which sexual intercourse is not recommended, usually about two weeks. It takes about two weeks for an episiotomy to heal fully, and there is some danger of infection in the two weeks following childbirth. After two weeks, the couple may have intercourse when they feel ready, as long as the intercourse is gentle. However, some doctors recommend a longer waiting period of a month to six weeks (Sarrel and Sarrel 1984).

Breastfeeding

In recent decades there has been a revival of interest in breastfeeding. Breastfeeding provides benefits to the infant. Breast milk is easier for an infant to digest than formula. The breastfed baby is held close to the mother's skin, feels her warmth, and hears her soothing heartbeat. In addition, there are benefits for the mother. Breastfeeding stimulates uterine contractions, which shrink the uterus to its normal size; and it promotes closeness between mother and child. Breastfeeding tends to suppress ovulation in the postpartum period but should not be relied on as a means of birth control (Mitchell 1981). On the downside, some women judge their adequacy as a mother on their success at breastfeeding. How a mother deals with the pressure to succeed at breastfeeding often depends on whether or not she has a family member, a friend, or a helpful hospital nurse who can support her and provide useful information (Defries et al. 1985). Some mothers who breastfeed choose to express milk into a baby bottle so that the father or another caretaker can feed the infant while the mother is away for short periods.

One group of people who experience special challenges during pregnancy are teenagers, who are discussed below.

Review Questions

1. How does the mother's level of comfort and discomfort change over the three trimesters of pregnancy?
2. What sexual issues arise during pregnancy? How do sexual issues change over the three trimesters of pregnancy?
3. What anxieties arise during pregnancy?
4. Why is it helpful to have a childbirth coach?
5. What is prepared childbirth? Why does prepared childbirth reduce the "cycle of fear and pain"?
6. In what ways is birth often organized differently today than in the past?
7. How can the birth experience promote bonding? What are the advantages and disadvantages of home birth?
8. What are the symptoms of postpartum depression? What are the causes of postpartum depression?
9. What are the advantages of breastfeeding?

Overview of Teen Pregnancy

About 1 million teenagers become pregnant each year (Roosa and Christopher 1990). Many of these pregnancies are unwanted, and the result is 400,000 teen abortions annually (U.S. Bureau of the Census 1994a, Table 112, page 85). Another half million of these pregnancies result in live births (U.S. Department of Health and Human Services 1993a, Table 11, p. 26). The remainder result in miscarriages. Of live births to teens, two-thirds (69 percent) are to unmarried mothers. Great concern has been expressed over childbearing by never-married adolescents. Teenagers who become unmarried parents often drop out of school, are at a disadvantage when it comes to finding a marriage partner, and face difficulty in finding employment.

Who Is at Risk?

Risk factors for teen pregnancy are those that decrease the age at first coitus and those that lead to less caution among teens who are sexually active. It takes con-

BOX 11.2	A Closer Look

Births

As Table 11.1 shows, for all racial groups combined, more than one in every four births (29.6 percent) is to an unmarried mother. Non-marital births are now prominent in each racial or ethnic group. Births to an unmarried mother constitute one-fifth of white births (21.8 percent), two-thirds of African-American births (67.9 percent), over half Native American births (55.3 percent), over one-third of Hispanic-American births (38.5 percent) and over one-tenth of Asian-American (or Pacific Islander) births (13 percent).

Births to teenage mothers are also becoming more common. For all racial and ethnic groups combined, 12.9 percent of all births are to teenage mothers. Teenage births are most common among African-Americans and Native Americans and least common among Asian-Americans and Pacific Islanders.

Hispanic-Americans have the highest birth rate (26 births per 1,000 population), partly because of the traditional female role in Hispanic culture and because Hispanic women tend to become mothers at a young age and have a long period of exposure to pregnancy.

The precent of babies with low birth weight gives us a rough indication of the mother's overall health and level of prenatal care. The percentage of low-birth-weight babies runs twice as high for African Americans (13.6 percent) as for the nation as a whole (7.0 percent). This reflects the high poverty rate among African-Americans.

TABLE 11.1			Births by Race and Ethnicity			
	All Races	White	African American	Native American	Hispanic*	Asian and Pacific Islander
Number of Births in thousands	4,094	3,241	682	39	623	145
Births to Unmarried Mothers						
Percent	29.6%	21.8%	67.9%	55.3%	38.5%	13.8%
Number in thousands	1,213	707	463	22	240	20
Births to Teenage Mothers						
Percent	12.9%	11.0%	23.1%	20.3%	17.2%	5.9%
Number in thousands	530	356	157	8	107	9
Birth rate†	16.3	15.4	21.9	18.3	26.7	18.2
Percent with low birth weight	7.0%	5.8%	13.6%	6.2%	6.1%	6.9%

*Hispanic origin may be either white or African American

†Number of births per 1,000 population.

Source: U.S. Department of Health and Human Services 1993. *Monthly Vital Statistics Report*, 42-3, Supplement. "Advance Report of Final Natality Statistics, 1991," Tables 23, 24, 25, 26, 27, 28, 29. Hyattsville, Maryland: U.S. Public Health Service.

siderable effort and motivation for a sexually active teen to avoid becoming pregnant. The teenagers who are most at risk for bearing a child out of wedlock are those in low-income families who grow up in single-parent homes, live in the inner cities, have friends who are sexually active, and perform poorly in school.

Socioeconomic Status. The risk of teen pregnancy is greatly increased if a teenager lives in poverty (Hogan and Kitagawa 1985; Murry 1991). Adolescents from low-income families and adolescents whose mothers have not finished high school are more likely than other teenagers to experience early sexual intercourse and exposure to pregnancy (Furstenberg et al. 1987a). Teenagers have three major pathways through which they can enter adult status. They can seek an education and employment; they can marry; or they can enter parenthood without marriage. For teenage women living in poverty areas, the *opportunity costs* of teen pregnancy are low. The prospects of marriage for these young women often appear bleak because their male partners have few job opportunities (Murry 1991). Likewise, such teens often feel discouraged about their own chances for occupational advancement. Under these conditions, teenagers often feel that they are giving up very little when they become pregnant.

Single-Parent Families. Teens who live in single-parent families are more likely than those from two-parent homes to be sexually active and thus exposed to pregnancy (Hogan and Kitagawa 1985; Murry 1991). Single parents sometimes have more difficulty than a pair of married parents in enforcing limits on adolescent sexual behavior. Furthermore, single-parent families are disproportionately represented among the poor, and low socioeconomic status is associated with teen pregnancy.

Social Networks. The National Survey of Children revealed that social networks strongly influence pregnancy risk. A *social network* is a group of friends or relatives with whom a person interacts frequently. Those fifteen- and sixteen-year-olds with several friends who had experienced sexual intercourse were far more likely than other teens to report that they had also experienced sexual intercourse (Furstenberg et al. 1987a).

Poor Academic Performance and Low Aspirations. Those teens who perform poorly in school and who have low educational and occupational aspirations are more susceptible to teen pregnancy than adolescents with high aspirations who do well in school (Hogan and Kitagawa 1985; Murry 1991). Teens who see the future as bright and expect to be successful in school and on the job tend to delay pregnancy.

Emotional Needs. Pregnancy for some teens is associated with feelings of dependency.

Although motherhood may satisfy certain emotional needs of teenage women, it can be an obstacle to education, employment, and marriage.

Such teenagers often experience conflict between wanting to nurture a child and wanting to be nurtured *by* a child. Often these two motivations for pregnancy are confused. For such young women, pregnancy often symbolizes a desire to be taken care of and mothered. Resolving this dilemma between dependence and independence is one of the central developmental tasks of adolescence (Lemkau 1988). In addition, in the minds of many teens, parenthood brings adult status.

Long-Term Consequences

The life chances of children born to unwed teen mothers are negatively affected by the mother's young age, her limited education, and her limited income. Such children are likely to grow up in poverty: Three-fourths of unmarried mothers receive some form of welfare assistance following the birth of the child (U.S. Bureau of the Census 1989b:14).

Longitudinal studies provide insight into the long-term consequences of teenage childbearing (Furstenberg et al. 1987b). A longitudinal study studies a single group of

---

BOX 11.3   S o c i a l   I s s u e s

Abstinence Only Programs

Success Express, a teen sex-education program funded under President Bush, attempted to reduce teen pregnancy by encouraging sexual abstinence. The Federal Office of Adolescent Pregnancy Programs funded Success Express and targeted low-income minority youth of junior high school age in the inner cities. The program consisted of six sessions that focused on building self-esteem, setting life goals, developing communication skills for saying "no" to sexual pressure, and learning the benefits of sexual abstinence, including avoidance of pregnancy and sexually transmitted diseases. An evaluation of the effectiveness of Success Express revealed that the program had failed to produce an increased level of sexual abstinence. Likewise, the program did not change the sexual attitudes of the participants. Roosa and Christopher (1990) concluded that federal money to prevent teen pregnancy was being spent on abstinence programs that did not work.

Roosa and Christopher (1990) compared the Success Express abstinence-only program to other programs that provide information on contraception and make referrals to birth control clinics. Those teens who participated in programs that emphasized contraception experienced a dramatically reduced teen pregnancy rate. Why then is not more attention and funding devoted to birth control education for minority inner-city poor youth?

Prejudicial Attitudes

Banks and Wilson (1989) argue that puritanical middle-class morality has prevented an expansion of programs that provide contraceptives to inner-city minority youth. "Americans opt to bury their heads in the Victorian sands of days gone by, hoping that youngsters will . . . abstain from sexual activity" (p.233). Some social scientists maintain that teen sexuality is too often viewed as problematic, even dangerous and disturbing (Chilman 1990; Maddock 1989). Concern over nonmarital teen pregnancy spills over into negative attitudes about teen sexuality in general. Chilman (1990) argues that teen sexual activity should be viewed as a normal stage in adolescent development rather than as a problem. Arguing from the same perspective, Banks and Wilson (1989) maintain that a commitment to the well-being of youth in the inner cities should involve working with local communities to improve and expand sex education programs that make contraception more readily available to teens.

There is considerable debate about whether or not children should be taught about sex and pregnancy at an early age. Some people disapprove of early sex education on the grounds that it encourages early sexual activity and teen pregnancy. Others feel it is crucial to give boys and girls the knowledge they need to make smart choices.

subjects at several intervals over a period of time. This study design allows the researchers to observe the effects of nonmarital childrearing on both mother and child. A longitudinal study of teen parenting in Baltimore followed the lives of 300 teenage mothers who were mostly African American and who became pregnant in the 1960s. These mothers were first interviewed when they were pregnant and again when their children were age five. Most recently, the mothers were interviewed when their children were teenagers. The majority of teenage mothers had managed to finish high school, leave welfare, and find a regular job. However, even with this progress under difficult conditions, the mothers were worse off economically than their peers from similar backgrounds who had been able to avoid teen pregnancy. Moreover, the mothers' struggle to overcome the disadvantages of poverty had taken a heavy toll on the children. High rates of school failure, delinquency, and teen pregnancy were found among the teenage children of these women. The problems faced by African-American unmarried teenage mothers, such as those in the Baltimore study, are explored below.

Explaining Racial and Ethnic Differences

As Table 11.2 shows, the tendency for teenage births to occur out of wedlock varies with race and ethnicity. The percent of nonmarital teen births is much higher among African Americans (97 percent) than among either whites (59 percent) or other racial groups (69 percent).

TABLE 11.2	Percent of Teenage Births that Are Out of Wedlock			
	Total	*White*	*African American*	*Other*
Total number of births to teens, in thousands	531	358	157	16
Number of out-of-wedlock births to teens, in thousands	368	211	146	11
Percent of births out of wedlock	69%	59%	92%	69%

Source: U.S. Department of Health and Human Services 1993. National Center for Health Statistics. *Monthly Vital Statistics Report,* Vol. 42. "Advance Report of Final Natality Statistics, 1991." Tables 15 and 16. Washington, D.C.: U.S. Government Printing Office.

African-American Teen Pregnancy

Social class, racial discrimination, and cultural factors all help explain why non-marital births are more common among African-American teens than other adolescents.

Social Class. African Americans are over-represented among the poor. In order to understand why so many African-American teenage births occur out of wedlock, it is necessary to understand the difficult economic position of the low-income unmarried teenage father (Brewer 1988). African-American males have an unemployment rate twice as high as that of white males. However, unemployment statistics include only those who are currently seeking employment. Many other young African-American males have become discouraged and are no longer looking for work. Only 54 percent of African-American males aged sixteen to sixty-four are in the labor force, compared to 78 percent of white males in this age group (Center for the Study of Social Policy 1991). This situation means that there is a shortage of employed African-American men who could support a family. The result is bleak marriage prospects for young, low-income, African-American women. Their limited marriage prospects have increased the likelihood that these women will form families through nonmarital childbearing as teenagers.

Discrimination. Young African-American males are stigmatized for their race, gender, and age. Anderson (1989) points out that many employers are fearful of young African-American men and therefore are reluctant to hire them. This discrimination against African-American men tends to influence the childbearing patterns of young African-American women. Using data from the National Surveys of Family and Growth Cycle, Murry (1991) compared sexual activity of African-American adolescents during the decades of the 1950s, 1960s, and 1970s. She found that during the civil rights movement of the 1960s, when hopes ran high for educational and occupational advancement of African Americans, female African-American adolescents tended to delay the onset of first coitus. However, when discouragement set in during the 1970s, the age at first coitus among African Americans declined. Youngsters who feel they have a stake in the future tend to make an effort to avoid pregnancy.

Cultural Ecology. Although social class explains much of the nonmarital pregnancy rate of African-American teens, it cannot offer a complete explanation. When researchers control for the the pregnant teen's family income and also for mother's educational level, African Americans still have a higher nonmarital birth rate than whites (O'Connell and Roders 1984). A portion of the African-American nonmarital pregnancy rate can be explained by *cultural ecology*. Cultural ecology refers to the social environment of the neighborhood in which a person lives. In his book, *The Truly Disadvantaged*, William Julius Wilson (1987) pointed out that low-income African-American families are becoming increasingly concentrated and isolated in the inner cities. This social isolation is a result of racial discrimination in both housing and employment (Meltzer 1986). Job opportunities in the inner cities are sparse, and inner-city dwellers are typically cut off from contacts with employed persons who could recommend them for a job (Wilson 1987). The cultural ecology of the inner city, including the school environment and sexual attitudes, raises the probability that teens will become pregnant.

Furstenberg and his colleagues (1987a) point out that school constitutes a major aspect of cultural ecology that affects teen behavior. They examined data from the National Survey of Children, which interviewed a nationally representative sample of fifteen- and sixteen-year-olds. African Americans who were in racially isolated classrooms tended to develop a set of social norms that lowered the barriers to teen nonmarital childbearing. A *racially isolated classroom* was defined as one in which 80 percent or more of the students share the same race. African-American adolescents in these racially segregated schools were eighteen times more likely than whites to expect parenthood to occur before marriage or at the same time as marriage. Whites were also typically found in racially isolated classrooms, although their schools tended to be located in in the suburbs. African Americans in racially segregated schools were more likely than suburban whites to have mothers who approved of cohabitation before marriage. The researchers conclude that racially isolated classrooms in poor neighborhoods present a social context in which nonmarital pregnancy is expected.

Attitudes Toward Sexuality. African-American sociologist Robert Staples (1982) described cultural differences between white and African-American teenagers, pointing out that African Americans have less puritanical attitudes toward sex than whites. African-American lower-class culture tends to be more open and accepting of sexuality than white culture, with both genders among African Americans being more willing to express a sexual interest in each other. As a result, African Americans report fewer problems with sex than whites both before and after marriage (Weinberg and Williams 1988).

Early First Coitus. African-American teens tend to begin sexual intercourse earlier than other groups and are therefore at greater risk of early parenthood. In one study of low-income African-American adolescents, over half (55 percent) of the boys and 18 percent of the girls had had intercourse by the age 13 (Banks and Wilson 1989:240). The National Survey of Children found that among fifteen- and sixteen-year-olds, African Americans are four times as likely as whites to have experienced sexual intercourse (Furstenberg et al. 1987a). Sexually active young teens run a high pregnancy risk because they typically do not have as much access to contraceptive information as do older teens (Moore et al. 1986). Furthermore, when African-American teenagers do give birth out of wedlock they are reluctant to give up the child to an adoption agency. Black families are strong and flexible, with grandmothers often helping out in child care. Therefore, African-American families are able to accommodate an unanticipated birth (Dore and Dumois 1990).

The pattern of nonmarital births among Mexican-American teenagers is somewhat different from that found among African-American adolescents.

Mexican-American Teen Pregnancy

Even though the majority of Hispanic teen births are out of wedlock, Hispanic females tend to be conservative in their sexual behavior. Aneshensel and her colleagues (1989) interviewed Mexican-American and non-Hispanic white female adolescents and found that Mexican-American teenagers are less likely than non-Hispanic whites to have have had sexual intercourse. However, when Mexican-American teens are sexually active, they are less likely than non-Hispanic whites to use contraception. In addition, once Mexican-American teens become pregnant they usually choose to give birth. Hispanics are less likely than either non-Hispanic whites or African Americans to end their pregnancies with abortion. These ethnic differences remained strong even when socioeconomic status was controlled.

Although adolescent pregnancy presents difficulties for young mothers, it also creates stress for young fathers, whose economic difficulties are the topic of the next section.

Economic Issues

The difficulty of finding employment that pays a family wage, a wage adequate to support a family, is the most serious problem facing low-income unwed teenage fathers. The Urban Poverty and Family Structure Survey project interviewed 2,490 fathers aged eighteen to forty-four living in inner-city poverty areas. Testa and his colleagues (1989) analyzed the results and found that employed fathers were twice as likely to marry the mother of their first child as fathers who were jobless. Furthermore, in the inner-city ghetto, women who had graduated from high school were considered more desirable mates than women who had dropped out of high school. This preference is probably related to the future earning power of female high school graduates (Testa et al. 1989). Employment and marriage appear to go hand and hand. The high rate of joblessness among inner-city males is closely related to the high rate of nonmarital births in these areas (Wilson 1980). Unemployment among African-American males has increased dramatically since the early 1970s and has paralleled the increase in mother-headed African-American families (Center for the Study of Social Policy 1991).

In spite of these economic difficulties, the image of the lower-class unwed father as one who abandons his children is more myth than realty. The African-American unwed father tends to be connected to his children either directly or indirectly through his relatives (Dore and Dumois 1990). In a study of 207 low-income African-American youth in mother-headed families, the majority reported that they had positive relationships with their fathers (Banks and Wilson 1989). Moreover, most described the relationship between their mother and father as positive regardless of the parent's marital status.

Involuntary Infertility

At the same time that some teenagers have to cope with the demands of parenthood at a young age, other couples seek pregnancy and are unable to attain it.

Involuntary infertility places great stress on couples who desire children. A couple's discovery of infertility usually marks a transition to a new status of childlessness, and this change in status involves considerable adjustment. Sabatelli and his colleagues (1988) interviewed fifty-two women and twenty-nine men at a Hartford, Connecticut, infertility clinic and found that the marriage relationship suffers when infertility is discovered and the frequency of intercourse for both men and women decreases, as does sexual satisfaction. Infertile spouses also tend to lose self-confidence. Married couples experiencing infertility often have stressful feelings, including sadness, depression, anger, confusion, desperation, and embarrassment. Infertile couples report exhaustion, distractability, moodiness, obsessive thoughts centering on children, and disorganized behavior (Valentine 1986). Being unable to conceive a child often produces the experience of "boundary ambiguity." The couple do not know where the boundaries of their family lie and do not know who is in and who is out of the family. As they attempt to become parents, they think about the child they wish they had. The child is "psychologically present but physically absent" (Burns 1987).

Adoption

Pregnancy is not the only way to become a parent; many infertile couples enter parenthood through adoption. In addition, some couples who have no difficulty with pregnancy expand their existing families by adding an adopted child. American couples adopt slightly over 100,000 American-born children each

---

BOX 11.4   A Closer Look

Challenging the Myth: Births to Unmarried Older Women

Slightly over a million babies are born to unmarried mothers each year. The stereotype of the unmarried mother as a teenager is partially true: 44 percent of unmarried mothers are age nineteen or younger. However, a growing number of unmarried mothers no longer fit this description. One-fourth of out-of-wedlock births are to women age 25 and over (U.S. Department of Health and Human Services 1993a, Table 23).

It is not only the poor and undereducated who become mothers without marrying. Seventeen percent of never-married mothers have some college education, and 6 percent are college graduates. (U.S. Bureau of the Census 1992a, Table 89). Many women are postponing pregnancy while they develop their careers. As a result, the first-birth rate has dramatically increased among women age 30 and over (McFalls 1992). Many women delay childbearing and then find themselves near the end of their childbearing potential. Some do not want to marry, and others have no prospective marriage partner. A growing number of these women are deciding to become mothers without a partner.

Births to unmarried professional women tripled during the 1980s (DeParle 1993). Currently, 8 percent of nonmarital births are to women who hold professional or managerial jobs (DeParle 1993).

The figures on nonmarital births can be misleading if we assume that all of these mothers are raising children alone. Many unmarried mothers are living with a partner at the time of birth. Nonmarital births to cohabiting partners are becoming increasingly common. Some of these children are actually living with both parents (DeParle 1993). Thus the trend toward nonmarital births affects a wide range of social classes, ages, and living arrangements.

year and an additional 9,000 children born outside of the United States. (U.S. Bureau of the Census, *Statistical Abstract of the United States, 1992,* Table 599). In half of all *domestic adoptions* (involving children born in the United States) the adoptive parents are relatives of the child. (U.S. Bureau of the Census, 1992a: Table 599). In many ethnic groups pressure is strong to keep children within the extended family.

Unrelated Adoptions

Adoptive parents who are unrelated to their adopted children account for the other half of domestic adoptions. The vast majority of these adoptions take place through public and private agencies. However, the waiting period at both public and private adoption agencies can be years for couples who want an infant or toddler. Some couples reduce their waiting time by seeking *independent adoptions* made through lawyers or doctors. There is some risk for couples who choose independent adoptions. The birth mother may decide to keep the baby even after the prospective adoptive parents have paid for medical expenses. In addition, independent adoptions have been criticized because the biological father is often ignored. In some cases biological fathers have gone to court to have the adoption overturned (Sullivan and Schultz 1990).

Interracial Adoption

The number of couples seeking to adopt an infant is far greater than the number of babies available for adoption. This is particularly the case for white couples. Over the last decade the decline in infants relinquished for adoption has been greatest among white unmarried mothers (Speer 1992). This situation has created a growing interest in interracial adoption. However, both African Americans and Native Americans have expressed concern over the possible loss of the child's racial and cultural identity in interracial adoptions. Therefore, many adoption agencies use a *three-tier adoption policy* in which the preferred placement of a child is with a relative. If no relative is available, same-race placement is sought. Placement with parents of another race is made if no same-race parents are available (Register 1991).

Foster-Adopt Programs

A recent innovation in adoption is *foster-adopt programs.* These programs place *children with special needs* with foster parents who are seeking to adopt a child. A child with special needs is any child who is difficult to place for adoption, such as an older child, a disabled child, or a child who has been sexually abused. The temporary foster care arrangement gives the foster parents and child a chance to get to know one another and allows the foster parents to find out what difficulties they may encounter in raising the child (Sullivan and Schultz 1990). If the parent–child relationship works out, the adoption is finalized. This program has been successful in placing many children who otherwise might not be adopted.

Foreign Adoption

The number of American-born infants available for adoption has diminished in recent decades as unmarried motherhood has gained social acceptance. Many couples now seek to adopt children from other countries. Foreign adoptions typically involve children from developing nations. In 1991 Romania provided the largest number of foreign-born children for adoption by U.S. parents (over 2,500 children), with Korea, Peru, Columbia, and India following in that order (U.S. Bureau of the Census 1992a, Table 599).

Foreign adoptions generally involve less waiting time than domestic adoptions. Nonetheless, processing paperwork can cause some delay. A child who is an infant when the adoption process begins may well be a toddler before he or she arrives in the United States (Register 1991). Considerations of health are important with foreign adoptions. However, acquiring a "healthy" foreign-born child may be a relative matter, and it is not unusual for such children to suffer from such correctable problems as undernutrition, parasites, or ear and skin infections. Older foreign-born children need some time to adjust to their new environment. They may engage in such behavior as hoarding food until they become accustomed to the abundance of food in their adoptive homes (Sullivan and Schultz 1990). (For additional information on adoption, see Chapter 12, Parents and Children.)

Voluntary Childlessness

While some childless couples expend a great deal of effort becoming parents through adoption, other childless couples drift into permanent childlessness. In

Although adoptive parents do not experience pregnancy and the birth of their children, they still feel a deep and complex attachment to them. If the couple has struggled with infertility, their opportunity finally to be parents may be all the more joyous.

fact, couples enter voluntary childlessness by two paths: conscious decision and extended postponement of childbearing. Some couples are aware of their discomfort with the idea of becoming parents and discuss their attitudes about childbearing and childrearing while dating. These couples explicitly communicate a conscious decision to remain childless. Other couples take a second route whereby they postpone childbearing until they no longer consider it desirable to become parents. In the second case, couples typically go through four stages on the road to childlessness (Benedek and Vaughn 1982).

Stage One. In the first stage the couple agree to postpone childbearing for a specific amount of time. They agree to wait until the conditions for childbearing improve. They decide to wait until their financial position improves, or until after they enjoy a honeymoon period, or until they work on emotional issues in their relationship, or until they become more established in their careers. At this stage they plan to have children at a later time.

Stage Two. In the second stage the couple postpone childbearing to an indefinite time in the future rather than to a specific date. They typically believe the issues that led to the original postponement are still concerns.

Stage Three. The third stage involves a change in thinking. Up to this time the couple have expected to have children someday. Now they become open to the possibility that they may never have children. They postpone the decision whether or not to have children until some time in the future.

Stage Four. In the last stage the couple reach the conclusion that they will not have children and either state this explicitly or behave as if the implicit decision has been made.

One serious condition affecting a number of women who do become pregnant is addiction to alcohol or drugs, the topic of the next section.

Review Questions

1. Who is at risk for teen pregnancy?
2. What are the long-term consequences of teen pregnancy?
3. What factors are important in explaining teen pregnancy among African Americans?
4. What factors are important in explaining teen pregnancy among Hispanics?
5. What reactions do couples go through when they experience involuntary infertility?
6. What types of adoption are available? Why do most adoption agencies use a three-tier adoption policy? What is the benefit of the foster-adopt program?
7. What are the stages couples typically go through when they drift into voluntary childlessness?

Substance Abuse and Pregnancy

Infants who are prenatally exposed to alcohol or illicit drugs, particularly crack cocaine, are increasing in number. The March of Dimes estimates that 11 percent of children born each year have mothers who used illegal drugs during pregnancy. This amounts to 375,000 drug-exposed infants born each year, 100,000 of whom have been prenatally exposed to cocaine (Firshein 1991). The General Accounting Office (GAO) of the U.S. Government estimates that 5 million women use illicit drugs and that most of these are in their childbearing years. According to the GAO, medical care, special education, and foster-home care for many of these children will cost billions of dollars (Firshein 1991).

Heavy exposure to alcohol during pregnancy can lead to *fetal alcohol syndrome,* which can result in facial deformities and neurological problems. Children who are exposed to illicit drugs also run the risk of acquiring a variety of other disabilities. Illicit drugs are illegal street drugs, such as cocaine. Prenatal exposure to either marijuana or cocaine impairs fetal growth. These infants tend to have shorter gestation periods, lower birth weights, shorter lengths, and smaller heads than drug-free babies. Marijuana increases the heart rate, blood pressure, and carbon monoxide levels in the the pregnant woman (Goldsmith 1990). Crack cocaine use by the mother can cause spasms in the fetal blood vessels, restricting the flow of oxygen and nutrients for lengthy periods of time (Staples 1991). In addition, the fetus can suffer strokes and seizures from prenatal exposure to cocaine, as well as the possibility of kidney, genital, intestine, and spinal cord malformation. Fetal health problems are exacerbated by the addicted mother's tendency to avoid seeking prenatal health care.

Additional problems appear when the drug-exposed child matures. The long-term effects of prenatal drug exposure include learning disabilities, short attention spans, and difficulty in concentration. As "crack babies" grow up, many will be learning disabled and need special programs in school. American society needs to come to grips with the consequences of having large numbers of drug-disabled children. Today's children are potentially the future engineers, inventors, and scientists who can help the United States compete with the Japanese and Germans in world markets. Investing in the future requires investing in the health of children.

Child Protective Services

Drug-exposed babies constitute the most difficult issue facing child welfare agencies (Besharov 1989). Because crack mothers resist treatment, "crack babies" face the possibility of abuse and neglect resulting from continued parental addiction. Parents addicted to illegal drugs tend to have abnormal mood states, including depression, which often result in poor parenting ability (Finnegan et al. 1981). Crack cocaine addiction is also associated with periodic episodes of violence (Staples 1991).

In light of this situation, Besharov (1989) recommends a three-step solution: (1) Provide hospitals with the legal power and financial resources to retain drug-exposed babies, (2) allow child protective services to ensure that drug-addicted parents who cannot provide adequate care for children do not have custody of those children, and (3) liberalize adoption procedures even if it means terminating parental rights of persistent drug-abusing parents. In a contrasting opinion, sociologist Robert Staples (1991) complains that many of the children placed in foster care are African American and they are often placed in homes of white foster parents. He maintains that the forcible removal of African-American children from their mothers is destructive to the African-American family. Staples argues that the foster care policy causes drug-addicted mothers to fear having their children taken away and therefore to avoid social services.

Inadequate Treatment Facilities

Adequate facilities for the treatment of drug abuse are not currently available. Women who request treatment are often told to call back later. In one drug treatment facility in Boston, 450 women who requested admission were told to call back later because the facility was temporarily full. Half never called back again. Such delays mean that rehabilitation programs cannot take patients at the time they are willing to enter treatment (Firshein 1991).

Drug Abuse and Fetal AIDS Exposure

Most drug-abusing females are sexually active (Staples 1991). Drug use diminishes the use of contraception so that drug abusers have a high exposure to pregnancy. In addition, crack cocaine users often also use heroin. Crack cocaine is a stimulant, and heroin, a depressant, is used to come down from a crack high. Because heroin addicts typically share needles, users run the risk of acquiring HIV, the virus that causes AIDS. Young drug-abusing women in their childbearing years risk acquiring HIV and passing it on to their children during pregnancy (Staples 1991).

The mothers discussed above are attempting to cope with drug addiction while raising drug-exposed children. The mothers discussed next are coping with the decision of whether or not to enter parenthood. In the next section we examine abortion, currently one of the most intensely debated topics in the social sciences.

BOX 11.5   **S o c i a l   I s s u e s**

The Criminalization of Illegal Drug Use During Pregnancy

District attorneys are increasingly charging with child abuse women who use illegal drugs while pregnant. In Rockford, Illinois, a mother was charged with involuntary manslaughter when her two-day-old child died. The mother had used cocaine shortly before delivery, and the drug caused complications in the placenta which deprived the infant of oxygen. A grand jury refused to indict the woman, and the case was dropped. However, the effort to impose criminal charges on pregnant drug abusers continues. In another case, six Colorado women were charged with use of a controlled substance and misdemeanor child abuse when their infants tested positive for illegal drugs at birth. The mothers were given probation combined with a drug treatment program and periodic drug tests. Under the terms of probation, if the mothers successfully completed a drug treatment program and remained abstinent from drugs during probation the charges would be dropped (Goldsmith 1990).

Proponents of criminalization point out that many women enter drug treatment only when they are faced with a choice between treatment and jail. Such threats of legal penalties have been successful in encouraging alcoholics with drunk driving convictions to seek treatment (Goldsmith 1990).

Opponents of criminal penalties for pregnant drug-abusing women argue that the fear of legal sanctions will discourage pregnant women from coming into clinics for prenatal care. They further argue that drug abuse is an illness and thus should fall within the domain of medical treatment rather than that of the courts (Goldsmith 1990).

Abortion

Abortions in the United States number 1.6 million each year (U.S. Bureau of the Census 1990a, Table 100, p. 71). The U.S. abortion rate (number of abortions per women in childbearing years) is far higher than that in other developed countries (Jones et al. 1988). This high abortion rate has been attributed to political opposition to birth control programs and insufficient delivery of contraceptive services, particularly to young women (Rodman 1991). The problem of inadequate contraceptive services extends to America's college campuses. The great majority of pregnancies experienced by unmarried college women each year are unplanned and unwanted, and 90 percent are aborted (Murray et al. 1989). Of sexually active college students, approximately 16 percent have had at least one abortion (Katz and Cronin 1980; Murray et al. 1989).

Contrary to popular mythology, teenagers are not the primary users of abortion. Women over age twenty account for three-fourths of all abortions. The typical woman who has an abortion is an unmarried adult rather than a young teenager. The median age for women who obtain an abortion is twenty-three (U.S. Bureau of the Census 1990a, Table 101, p. 71). Approximately half of women receiving an abortion had at least one previous live birth, and four out of ten had a prior abortion. African-American women are two and one-half times more likely than white women to terminate a pregnancy with an abortion (Kochanek 1990). A national opinion survey, the General Social Survey, revealed that African-American women are more approving of abortion than white women (Wilcox 1990). African-American women tend to be sympathetic toward women who choose abortion because they are poor or because they want no more children. This attitude pattern is reversed in men. African-American men are more disapproving of abortion than white men. This opinion is probably related to the traditional gender role attitudes held by a large number of African-American men as well as to the higher probability that African-American women will utilize abortion.

TABLE 11.3	Legal Abortions by Age	
Age	Number of Abortions (in thousands)	Percent Distribution
All ages	1,609	100%
Under 15	13	1
15–19	351	22
20–29	892	55
30 and over	353	22

Source: U.S. Bureau of the Census, Statistical Abstract of the United States, 1994, Table 112, page 85. Washington, D.C.: U.S. Government Printing Office.

Early Abortions

The vast majority of all abortions are "early abortions," which take place during the first trimester of pregnancy (U.S. Bureau of the Census 1994a, Table 112, p. 85). A simple abortion procedure known as *suction curettage* is typically used for these abortions. This is the predominant procedure used before the sixteenth week of pregnancy (Prager 1985). Suction curettage involves suctioning out the contents of the uterus with an aspirator and then gently scraping the uterine wall with a curette, a spoon-shaped surgical instrument. Suction curettage accounts for 96 percent of all abortions (Kochanek 1990).

Late Abortions

Only 4 percent of abortions are performed during the second trimester, months four through six, of pregnancy (Kochanek 1990). By the sixteenth week of pregnancy the placenta becomes securely attached to the uterus, and it is no longer safe to suction or scrape out the uterine contents. At this point either *saline induction* or *dilation and evacuation* are typically used as abortion methods. In a saline induction abortion, saline (salt water) is introduced into the amniotic sac, which holds the fetus. Saline is toxic to the fetus and stimulates uterine contractions so that a deceased fetus is delivered. In a dilation and evacuation abortion, the cervix, or opening to the uterus, is dilated and the fetus is removed. The women most likely to delay abortion and utilize these methods are teenagers and poorly educated women (Prager 1985).

Safety

Because of the relative safety of early abortions, such abortions carry a lower risk of death than carrying the fetus to full term. The risk of dying from complications associated with pregnancy and delivery is seven times higher than the risk of dying from an abortion performed in a medical facility (Cates et al. 1982). Overall, complications from abortions occur in less than 1 percent of all abortions. Early abortions using the suction curettage method have the highest level of safety, with complications occurring in only 3 out of every 1,000 abortions. Complications are more likely to occur in saline induction and dilation and evacuation abortions during the second trimester; these abortions result in complications in 1 out of 10 cases (Prager 1985). The most frequent abortion complication involves hemorrhaging and infection resulting from retention of fetal products (such as a piece of the placenta) in the uterus (Prager 1985).

Emotional Reactions

When a women freely chooses a legal abortion, serious negative emotional consequences are rare. Under these conditions of free choice, negative feelings such as depression, anxiety, and guilt sometimes arise before the abortion and diminish after the procedure. When the abortion is completed, the dominant feeling is typically a sense of relief (Lemkau 1988). Women who have a masculine gender role orientation and score high on measures of independence, confidence, and decisiveness tend to have relatively few problems following an abortion (Alter 1984). In addition, those who have a strong support network of family or friends tend to adjust well to abortion. A family support network is particularly important for the emotional adjustment of adolescents following an abortion, whereas the support of the sexual partner is more important for older women (Lemkau 1988).

BOX 11.6   S o c i a l   I s s u e s

Family Consent and Abortion

An important issue in the abortion debate concerns whether or not notification or consent of family members should be required when a woman seeks an abortion.

Parental Consent

Since the U.S. Supreme Court legalized abortion in its *Roe* v. *Wade* decision, a majority of states have enacted "parental consent" or "parental notification" laws (Worthington et al. 1989). Some of these states require parental notification before a minor can have an abortion; other states require parental consent. All states that require either parental notification or parental consent allow for *judicial bypass*, in which the minor can avoid informing her parents by going to court to seek the consent of a judge for the abortion.

Advocates

Advocates of parental consent legislation argue that parents have an important function of guidance in childrearing. Teenagers often think their parents will be angry if they find out about the pregnancy; in fact, many parents initially go through a period of anger. However, as the anger dies down, the majority of parents offer emotional support and assistance in decision making. Advocates of parental consent laws argue that too much emphasis has been placed on adolescent liberties and suggest that perhaps adolescents who become pregnant could benefit from parental oversight and limitations on their activities (Worthington et al. 1989).

Opponents

Arguing against parental consent legislation, Rodman (1991) maintains that a teen's voluntary disclosure of a pregnancy to parents is preferable to mandatory disclosure. A substantial number of teens report that they would use neither contraception nor abortion if they were required to inform their parents (Herold 1981). In a study of 477 cases of minors who sought judicial consent for an abortion, 10 percent came to court to appeal the parents' refusal to consent to an abortion and the other 90 percent felt that they could not talk over this matter with their parents. In all but 10 cases, the abortion was granted because the minor was judged mature enough to make the decision on her own. In 9 of the remaining cases, the court granted the abortion because it was thought to be in the young woman's best interest. In the single remaining case, the woman went out of state for an abortion. Judicial bypass did not prevent any of the 477 young women from having an abortion (Rodman 1991). Opponents of parental consent laws argue that such laws simply erect time-consuming hurdles to abortions that will most likely be performed anyway. Moreover, parental consent laws and the judicial bypass process tie up valuable court time (Rodman 1991).

Husband's Consent

A number of states have attempted unsuccessfully to pass legislation requiring married women either to notify or to gain the consent of their husbands before having an abortion. In a study of married women who recently had abortions, 89 percent of the women reported that they had informed their husbands and 11 percent had not (Ryan and Plutzer 1989). The women who did not inform their husbands about the abortion also kept the pregnancies secret from him. Three-fourths of the wives who were nondisclosers reported that they were having marital difficulties, and some of these pregnancies had resulted from an extramarital affair. Half of the noninforming women feared their husbands would pressure them to have the baby, thus trapping them in an unhappy marriage in which they would be financially dependent on the husband. Other nondisclosing women felt that their marriages would be jeopardized by disclosing the pregnancy and abortion.

The movement toward family consent legislation is a strong one which will continue to cause considerable debate.

Negative reactions in the aftermath of an abortion are more likely among women who are very young, deeply religious, or have experienced a recent breakup with a boyfriend. Women who originally wanted the pregnancy but were deserted by a partner and then reluctantly decided on abortion are prone to depression because they are also grieving for the loss of a relationship. Women who have the most difficult time adjusting to an abortion are those who were coerced into it by parents, a boyfriend, or husband. A post-traumatic stress disorder similar to that experienced by assault victims sometimes follows an undesired abortion (Lemkau 1988). This disorder includes fearfulness and withdrawal from social life.

Access to Abortion Is Diminishing

Access to abortion diminished during the 1980s even though abortion was legal. Over that decade the number of doctors performing abortions declined along with the number of medical students being trained in abortion procedures. Likewise, the number of hospitals offering abortions declined (Yoachum 1991). This trend was largely driven by a desire on the part of hospitals and medical personnel to avoid being picketed by right-to-life groups. In addition, some medical practicioners who offer abortion services have been harrassed and now fear for their own safety. In an effort to keep abortion available, in 1993 the U.S. Supreme Court let stand the trespass conviction in Kansas of a woman who tried to block the entrance of an abortion clinic in the case of *Tilson* v. *City of Wichita* (Savage 1993).

It appears unlikely that the landmark U.S. Supreme Court Decision, *Roe* v. *Wade,* which legalized abortion in 1973, will be overturned in the near future. Nonetheless, the nation's high court has allowed states to place some restrictions on abortion. In *Webster* v. *Reproductive Health Services* in 1989, the U.S. Supreme Court upheld a Missouri law requiring physicians to determine the viability of a twenty-week-old fetus before performing an abortion. This ruling effectively decreased the period of fetal development during which an abortion could be legally performed in Missouri. The Missouri law also banned the use of tax money to pay for abortions or abortion counseling. In addition, it prohibited public employees and publically funded hospitals from performing abortions except to save the life of the mother. Although these aspects of Missouri law were upheld, the U.S. Supreme Court stopped short of overturning *Roe* v. *Wade* (*New York Times* 1989a). In this case the high court established the *"undue burden" test* for evaluating the constitutionality of restrictions placed on abortion by the states. Justice Sandra Day O'Connor wrote that the states should "not impose an undue burden on a woman's abortion decision" (*New York Times,* 1989b). In other words, the current U.S. Supreme Court has forbidden the states to place restrictions on abortion that would make it excessively difficult for a woman to obtain an abortion. Nonetheless, the U.S. Supreme Court has been willing to allow the states to place more stringent restrictions on abortions for minors. In 1993, in *Barnes* v. *Mississippi,* the U.S. Supreme Court let stand a Mississippi law requiring the written consent of both parents, or the consent of a judge, for a woman under age eighteen to obtain an abortion. When the parents are divorced, the written consent of only one parent is required (Savage 1993).

The pro-choice side of the abortion debate gained an ally with the 1993 appointment to the U.S. Supreme Court of Justice Ruth Bader Ginsberg, an outspoken supporter of abortion rights. President Clinton, who holds a pro-choice position, may have opportunity to appoint another Supreme Court Justice, which makes the overturn of *Roe* v. *Wade* unlikely. Any future decline in access to abortion would probably result from antiabortion protests at abortion clinics and hospitals rather than from any action by the U.S. Supreme Court to overturn *Roe* v. *Wade*.

Pregnancy issues will have an important impact on shaping the family of the future. If legal abortion were no longer widely available and the level of sexual activity among teenagers remained the same, there would undoubtedly be a substantial increase in nonmarital pregnancies and early marriages. If *Roe* v. *Wade* is struck down or the availability of abortion greatly diminished, employed women would be faced with uncertainty as they planned their careers and tried to mesh marriage, childrearing, and work. Without the availability of abortion, the issue of the biological father's financial responsibility for offspring would probably become even more hotly debated. In addition, if drug-abusing women had no alternative but to carry their pregnancies to term, the number of prenatally drug-disabled infants and children would increase. On the other hand, the spread of the AIDS epidemic and the growing fear of AIDS may reduce the level of sexual activity outside of marriage so that the problems listed above many not be so severe. Moreover, a decline in the availability of abortion might have a dampening effect on sex outside of marriage and cohabitation.

Summary

1. Pregnancy is divided into three trimesters, each of which presents issues and challenges. It is generally safe to have sexual intercourse during pregnancy. Nonetheless, couples often need to work through their anxieties concerning sexuality during this time.

2. The postpartum period often brings a period of depression due to physical, psychological, and social causes.

3. Having a childbirth coach and preparing for childbirth through education enhance the childbirth experience.

4. Almost 1 million teenage pregnancies take place each year, and approximately two-thirds of teen births take place out-of-wedlock.

5. Adolescents who are most at risk for pregnancy are those from low-income families and single-parent homes who perform poorly in school, have friends who are sexually active, and are emotionally dependent.

6. African-American teenagers have a higher nonmarital pregnancy rate than either Hispanics or non-Hispanic whites. These teens are over-represented among the poor and experience discrimination in employment and housing. Many are concentrated in the inner cities, where attitudes encourage early coitus and teenagers expect childbearing to precede marriage.

7. Mexican-American teenagers are more sexually conservative in their behavior than either non-Hispanic whites or African-Americans but are more likely to give birth when they become pregnant.

8. Employment is a critical factor in determining whether or not a teen father will marry. An employed teen father is more likely than an unemployed teen father to marry the mother of his child.

9. Involuntarily infertile couples experience feelings of depression, anger, and confusion. Feelings of boundary ambiguity are common because they do not know whether the family will include a child.

10. Interracial and foreign adoptions are becoming more popular. Foster-adopt programs have been able to place children with special needs in adoptive homes.

11. Voluntarily childless couples usually drift into that position in a series of stages in which pregnancy is postponed.

12. Use of illicit drugs during pregnancy can have harmful effects on the fetus. Babies with addicted mothers are at risk for child abuse. The number of treatment centers is inadequate to meet the needs of drug-dependent pregnant women.

13. The typical woman who has an abortion is in her twenties. African-American women are two and one-half times more likely than white women to abort rather than give birth.

14. Early abortions, which account for 96 percent of all abortions, use the suction curettage method, which is considerably less likely to produce negative side effects than methods used in late abortions.

15. When a woman freely chooses to have a legal abortion, the emotional reaction is generally one of relief. Women who are coerced into abortion sometimes experience a post-traumatic stress disorder.

Key Words

Trimester
Madonna Complex
Postpartum Period
Opportunity Costs
Cultural Ecology
Racially Isolated Classroom
Children with Special Needs
Fetal Alcohol Syndrome
Suction Curettage
Dilation and Evacuation
Undue Burden Test
Pro-Life
Ambivalence

Coached Childbirth
Childbirth Preparation Home Birth
Postpartum Depression
Social Networks
Longitudinal Study
Three-Tier Adoption Policy
Foster-Adopt Program
Criminalization of Illegal Drug Use
   During Pregnancy
Saline Induction
Roe v. *Wade* Decision
Webster Decision
Pro-Choice

Resources

Planned Parenthood
810 Seventh Ave.
New York, NY 10019
(212) 541-7800
Offers information on contraception, abortion, sexual health, and infertility. Operates 900 centers with family planning services nationwide.

National Abortion Rights Action League (NARAL)
1101 14th St., N.W., Fifth Floor
Washington, DC 20005
(202) 408-4600
A pro-choice organization that supplies information to Congress, compiles statistics, and seeks to retain the right to legal abortions. Publishes *NARAL Newsletter*, quarterly.

Birthright
686 N. Broad St.
Woodbury, NJ 08096
(609) 848-1819
Hotline: (800) 848-LOVE toll free.
Promotes a pro-life agenda and helps women find alternatives to abortion, such as adoption. Has 540 chapters nationwide. Publishes *The Life-Guardian*, bimonthly newsletter.

American College of Nurse Midwives
1012 14th St., N.W., Ste. 801
Washington, DC 20005
(202) 347-5447
Nurse midwives, trained to deal with a normal birth, practice with the backing of an obstetrician. They refer the patient to an obstetrician if a problem develops.

Home Oriented Maternity Experience (HOME)
511 New York Ave.
Takoma Park
Washington, DC 20012
Provides information on home births.

La Leche International
9616 Minneapolis Ave.
Franklin Park, IL 60131
(414) 445-7470
Encourages mothers to breastfeed infants. Provides support and information on breastfeeding techniques.

American Academy of Husband-Coached Childbirth
P.O. Box 5224
Sherman Oaks, CA 91413
(213) 788-6662
Provides information and supports husband-coached childbirth.

Single Mothers by Choice
P.O. Box 1642
Gracie Square Station
New York, NY 10028
(212) 988-0993
Provides information to single professional women in their thirties and forties who want to have a child outside of marriage through birth or adoption. Publishes *SMC Newsletter*, twenty times a year.

Chapter 12

Parents and Children

On Saturday morning three four-year-olds sat digging in a sand box at a park, quietly making sand mounds to drive toy trucks over and to walk small doll-like characters through. Meanwhile, their parents sat reading newspapers, relaxing, and chatting on the park benches. The parents heard a commotion and looked up see the children throwing sand. Tim's father groaned but said nothing because he saw that Tim was not throwing sand at the other children; he realized children have an almost irresistible temptation to throw sand. James's mother walked over to her son and calmly explained that throwing sand was not a good idea. "The sand could accidentally hit another child in the face," she explained. Brian's mother promptly went over to him and slapped him, saying, "Don't be a wise guy." After some protest, the children sat back down, picked up their toys, and continued to dig and play in the sand.

R aising children is a challenging task because parents must both nurture children and guide their behavior. Parents often experience anxiety in deciding how to react to their children's behavior. Should parents punish children quickly after misbehavior, as Brian's mother did? Or should parents ignore misbehavior, realizing children often make mistakes, as Tim's father did? Or should parents react like James's mother and attempt to guide behavior by discussing the situation with the child? Each of these parents represents one of the parenting styles discussed below. In addition to parenting styles, in this chapter we explore the growing role of fathers in two-parent families, parenting in one-parent families, teenagers as parents, immigrant parents, parenting and employment, and adult children as caregivers for elderly parents. We begin our discussion of parents and children with a look at the ways parents socialize children.

Socialization and Parenting Styles

Socialization is the process by which a society passes on its behavior patterns, attitudes, values, and knowledge to the next generation. The family plays a key role in the socialization process as parents discipline their children. However, many parents feel uncomfortable with a discussion of discipline because they confuse discipline with punishment. *Punishment* is a reaction to the child's behavior which results in deprivation or pain. In contrast, *discipline* is a broad concept that encompasses the various ways parents guide the behavior and attitudes of children. Discipline as guidance lies at the core of a person's parenting style and involves a person's overall approach to parenting. At the beginning of this chapter Brian's mother, who slapped her son, was not the only parent who engaged in discipline. James's mother, who explained the consequences of throwing sand, was also guiding her child's behavior. Even Tim's father, who said nothing to his child in the sand box, was engaging in discipline as child guidance by implicitly allowing the behavior to take place. Let's look more closely at the parenting styles used by the three parents.

TABLE 12.1	Parenting Styles	
Permissive	*Authoritative*	*Authoritarian*
Few demands on child	Demands on the child and	Many demands on child
High responsiveness to child's needs and wishes	Responsiveness to the child in balance	Low responsiveness to child's needs and wishes
Child rights equal to adult rights	Child has fewer rights than adults	Child has very few or no rights
Low coercion	Moderate coercion	High coercion
Low inductive reasoning	High Inductive reasoning	Low inductive reasoning

Parenting Styles

Diana Baumrind (1983) has identified three basic parenting styles: permissive, authoritarian, and authoritative. Each of these parenting styles can be viewed as an analytical concept; in reality, many parents are eclectic and use elements of several parenting styles.

Permissive Parenting. In permissive childrearing, parents set few rules and therefore make very few demands on children. Tim's father was displaying permissive parenting when he said nothing after Tim threw sand in the park. In permissive parenting, the focus of parenting is on being responsive to the needs and wishes of children. Children are expected to regulate much of their own behavior. The rights of the child are seen as equal, or nearly equal, to those of adults.

The philosophy behind permissive parenting comes from the human potential movement in which unconditional acceptance and love for the child is seen as an important prerequisite for building the child's self-esteem (Baumrind 1983). However, children raised in permissive families tend to be low in self-control and self-reliance (Cool 1991). Because the parents often give in to the wishes of the child, families that use permissive childrearing have been described as giving the child a great deal of power in the family (Baumrind 1983).

Authoritarian Parenting. In authoritarian childrearing, parents set rigid rules for children and make strong demands for the child's compliance with these rules. Authoritarian parents display an attitude of "do it my way or else," and these parents do not believe it is necessary to be very responsive to the child's wishes. The emphasis in this parenting style is on obedience enforced through punishment. At the beginning of this chapter Brian's mother presented an example of authoritarian childrearing when she slapped her son. Children in authoritarian families are seen as having very few rights when compared to adults. As a result, the child has little input or influence on parental decisions (Baumrind 1983). Children raised in authoritarian homes tend to exhibit dependence and low levels of responsibility because they have not learned to make decisions on their own (Cool 1991).

Authoritative Parenting.   Authoritative parents attempt to balance parental demands and parental responsiveness to the needs of the child. Parents set firm rules for appropriate behavior and enforce those rules. However, parents foster individuality by encouraging children to make some decisions on their own. Both parents and children are seen as having rights that need to be respected. The emphasis in authoritative parenting is on discussing behavior with the child. Punishment is de-emphasized, but parents are willing to punish when a child willfully refuses to comply. In the opening vignette, James's mother used authoritative parenting when she explained to James why he should not throw sand in the sandbox. Authoritative parents tend to raise children who are independent and well adjusted (Baumrind 1983).

Consistency

Effective parental guidance is most often achieved when discipline is consistent (Nelson 1984). *Consistency* refers to a stable set of rules as well as to the parent's willingness to "follow through" on their directives to make sure the child complies. Authoritative parenting is the parenting style most likely to produce parental consistency. Unlike authoritative discipline, authoritarian discipline emphasizes punishment that is likely to be harsh. As a result, authoritarian parents often try to avoid using discipline, wait until tension has built up in the parent–child relationship, and then explode at a "last straw" incident (Dobson 1978). The result is often inconsistent discipline. Likewise, permissive discipline is often inconsistent because the parent frequently makes a demand and then responds to the child's feelings by withdrawing a demand (Lewis 1981). The use of inconsistent discipline by parents is associated with problems in the relationship between children and their peers. Children whose parents use inconsistent discipline tend to get into more fights with other children (Patterson et al. 1984; Bierman and Smoot 1991). Additional problems with authoritarian parenting are discussed below.

Problems with Authoritarian Parenting

Authoritarian discipline is associated with two serious problems: power struggles and interference with the development of a child's conscience.

Power Struggles.   Authoritarian parents rarely explain their decisions to the child. Instead, authoritarian parenting relies heavily on threats and punishments in order to control the child's behavior. This approach can lead to power struggles between parents and children in which a series of parental threats and punishments is followed by the child's resistance. In a power struggle the forbidden object or behavior looks increasing attractive to the child. This situation can spiral out of control as the parent–child relationship becomes increasingly punitive and hostile (McCord 1991). Authoritarian discipline fails to take into account the fact that young children often have a desire to please their parents. Parents can often gain children's compliance by a more positive approach, substituting requests for threats (Baumrind 1983). An emphasis on punishment not only creates power struggles but also can inhibit the development of the child's conscience.

The Development of Conscience.   The purpose of socialization is to encourage children to internalize social norms (social rules) and values and thereby develop a conscience. Once norms have been internalized, the desire to behave in socially acceptable ways comes from within the child rather than from a threat of external punishment. Children learn social norms most easily in a family environment that emphasizes warmth and affection (Liska and Reed 1985; Olson et al. 1990). Lewis

---

BOX 12.1   S o c i a l   I s s u e s

Listening to Children

Many situations arise between parents and children which do not call for correcting behavior. In these situations the child presents a personal problem that calls for the parent to listen. In his book, *Parent Effectiveness Training,* Thomas Gordon (1975) observed that many parents respond to their children's problems in a style their tends to cut short communication and that leaves the child feeling distressed. For example, when Jerome complained that his fourth-grade teacher did not like him, his father focused on trying to change Jerome's attitude rather than listening.

Some typical parental responses to Jerome's problem are given below. Gordon maintains that all of these parental reactions block communication and tend to close off the child's willingness to explain the problem further.

*   *Ordering, directing, commanding:* "You better try harder to get along with your teacher."
*   *Warning, admonishing, threatening:* "If you don't shape up I'll cause more trouble for you than your teacher does."
*   *Exhorting, moralizing, preaching:* "If you don't try to get along in school, you won't be able to get along on a job and you'll never amount to anything."
*   *Advising, giving solutions or suggestions:* "Your teacher is probably stressed out. Why not try to be more understanding?"
*   *Judging, criticizing, blaming:* "I'll bet you are goofing off in school and causing trouble for your teacher."

Gordon points out that an alternative to these responses is *active listening.* Active listening refers to reflecting back the message sent by the child without adding a message of your own. In *passive listening,* the listener is silent. However, in active listening, the listener speaks so that children know they have been heard, but the verbal response is a neutral one. Active listening involves *reflection,* in which the listener acts as a mirror and reflects back the message to the child by summarizing it. The listener may summarize either the content of the message or the feeling that seems to underlie the message. This method is self-correcting because children tend to object and clarify the problem if the parent has misunderstood. In the example of Jerome above, the parent could use active listening and say something such as:

*   *Reflecting content:* "You didn't like something that your teacher did."
*   *Reflecting feelings:* "You seem upset by the way the your teacher treats you."

The purpose of active listening is to encourage the child to talk more about the problem. However, a parent does not need to feel stuck in active listening with no other avenues of communication available. Once the problem has been defined through active listening, the parent can switch into a different mode of communication and, for example, offer advice. An active listening response to Jerome's problem might go like this:

Jerome: "Yeah, I didn't like it when Mrs. Johnson chose Russell to be the leader of our group."

Parent: "You were upset when Mrs. Johnson chose Russell."

Jerome: "Yeah. The teacher should have chosen me. I know a lot about our topic. Our group is reporting on American wildlife."

Parent: "You felt disappointed when she didn't choose you."

Jerome: "Yeah, but I guess Russell is all right. He does get along with the kids."

The idea behind active listening is that many children will "talk out" their problems and resolve their feelings if they have a parent or other person who is willing to listen in a neutral way. Active listening lets children guide the conversation toward the issues troubling them. Often the child feels better after simply being heard.

(1981) argues that *functionally superfluous control* inhibits the development of the child's conscience. "Functionally superfluous control" refers to parental discipline in excess of that required to gain the child's compliance. Often parents use threats of punishment when a mere suggestion would be sufficient to influence a child's behavior.

The process by which children internalize social norms can be understood through *attribution theory*. According to attribution theory, behavior is influenced by the sources to which we attribute our motivation. When discipline is harsh or excessive, children perceive control as coming from outside themselves and comply when they think they are under parental surveillance (Lepper 1982). When parental oversight is absent, self-control tends to disappear. In contrast, when parental control is mild, children are more likely to perceive themselves as wanting to comply with parental wishes. Because they perceive control as coming from within themselves, they are more likely to internalize social norms. Next we look at alternatives to harsh punishment.

Positive Parenting

Many parents use spanking even when they would rather avoid it because they have not had the opportunity to develop their parenting skills and learn alternative methods of child guidance (Straus 1991). Positive child guidance uses alternatives to spanking which include time-out, natural consequences, logical consequences, and creating a consensual environment.

Time-Out

Time-out is a particularly effective method of influencing the behavior of preschoolers. In *time-out,* the child who is hitting, throwing sand, or being disruptive is removed from the situation for several minutes. A bench or living-room couch is a good place to put the disruptive child. The aim of time out is not punishment, but rather to allow the child to calm down, regain self-control, and then return to the situation. When a child is disrupting dinner, two or three minutes on the couch in time-out will often be enough time to allow the child to see that the behavior is unacceptable and to return to the dinner table with a calmer attitude.

Natural Consequences

Natural consequences refers to allowing children to make their own choices and suffer the consequences of those choices (Dreikers 1972; Neville and Halaby 1984). For example, Sandy's mother reported that Sandy typically became jealous and sulky at her brother's and sister's birthday parties. Feeling left out when so much attention was directed toward her sibling, Sandy would announce that she did not want to be at the party and walk into the other room, Last year when Sandy had engaged in the same behavior, her mother had followed Sandy into the other room, tried to reason with her, and begged Sandy to return to the party. In contrast, this year Sandy's mother calmly ignored her exit from the party. She allowed Sandy to experience the natural consequences of her own behavior. Sandy missed out on having cake and ice cream and denied herself the companionship of the other children (Neville and Halaby 1984).

The natural consequences method works best when the child is not disrupting the activities of either the parents or other children, so that the only person who suffers negative consequences is the child. In addition, this discipline method is not designed to be used in situations in which the child's health or safety is in danger. Finally, not all situations have natural consequences that are unpleasant for the child. In this case the parent may need to create logical consequences.

Logical Consequences

Logical consequences are consequences that the parent creates and that grow logically out of the child's misdeed. The logical consequences method involves presenting the child with a choice of engaging in acceptable behavior or having limits placed on the unacceptable behavior (Neville and Halaby 1984; Samalin 1988). For example, either the child picks up his trucks or the mother will pick them up and put the trucks away until tomorrow; either the preschooler agrees to remain in the backyard or she must play in the house (Cool 1991); either the toddler refrains from throwing food or the mother will feed him. The advantage of logical consequences is that they flow logically from the problem behavior and attempt to solve the problem created by that behavior. Grounding a child for a week for any of the above actions would not be a logical consequence because of its severity and because it has little or no connection to any of these misdeeds. Logical conse-

quences avoid excessive punishment and help promote a positive relationship between parent and child.

Creating a Consensual Environment

McCord (1991) maintains that the compliance of children can be most effectively gained in a *consensual environment*, where the emphasis is on cooperation rather than on a power struggle between parents and children. In a consensual environment parents and children focus on meeting each other's needs. By responding to the needs and wishes of children, parents model cooperative behavior. In such an environment the parent

Sometimes being a parent simply means listening and letting our children know that their feelings are valid.

expresses feelings and uses reasoning to explain requests. For example, a parent might say, "If your superheroes remain on the living room floor, people might step on them and hurt their feet. Let's pick them up together so that the living room will look nice." In a consensual environment children have the opportunity to develop empathy with others and avoid focusing exclusively on themselves.

McCord (1991) maintains that a strong emphasis on punishment in childrearing is self-defeating. She points out that children's thought processes are influenced by the concepts provided by language. Children whose parents emphasize punishments and threats learn to think in "if . . . then" sequences: "If I don't pick up my toys, then I will be punished." According to McCord these children learn to focus on their own pains and pleasures, and this leads to an egocentric (or self-centered) view of the world. That is, in a punitive parent–child relationship children learn to ask themselves, "How will this situation affect me personally?" In an experiment, parents and their preschool children were randomly divided into an experimental group and a control group. Parents in the experimental group were trained to create a consensual environment. These parents were taught to respond to their children's wishes and to spend a period of time each day when they avoided making demands on their children. Children in the experimental group were more cooperative and complied with more of their parents' regular requests than did children in the control group, whose parents tended to use threats to influence their children's behavior (Parpal and Maccoby 1985). Children raised in a consensual environment tend to value independence and intellectual activity (Harrington et al. 1987; McCord 1991). In addition to the problems with harsh punishment discussed above, a punitive parental approach to childrearing can increase the likelihood that the child will have difficulty with peer relationships, which is the topic of the next section.

Relationships with Peers

Parenting style has an influence on the behavior of children. Parents who express warmth and are emotionally available to their children tend to have children with fewer behavioral problems than parents who are cold and rejecting (Kline 1991). In addition, the parent's disciplinary style is closely related to the ability of children to get along with their peers (Putallaz 1987). Parents who use *coercive discipline,* such as threats, yelling, and spankings, tend to have children who are less preferred by their peers as playmates (Bierman and Smoot 1991; Hart et al. 1990). In contrast, parents who use *inductive reasoning* to discipline their children tend to have children who get along well with their playmates (Hart et al. 1990). Inductive reasoning involves explaining to children how their behavior affects other people. For example, a parent using inductive reasoning might say, "When you call Bobby names, it hurts his feelings." In contrast, a parent who uses coercion would be more likely to say "Don't call Bobby names unless you want a spanking."

Discipline styles affect the development of a child's problem-solving skills. When a parent is coercive, the parent–child relationship often becomes "mutually coercive" so that the parent threatens the child and the child threatens the parent (Kline 1991). This parent–child relationship pattern spills over into peer relations. In contrast, children of parents who use inductive reasoning tend to take the feelings of other children into account when attempting to solve problems.

Hart (1990) and his colleagues studied parenting styles of parents of first- and fourth-grade children at two midwestern elementary schools. After parents were interviewed about their discipline style, children were presented with hypothetical situations, such as one in which a child used another child's bike without asking. The children were then asked how they would respond to these situations. Answer choices were categorized as shown in Table 12.2. There was general agreement among children that nonassertive responses would not be successful in solving the problem. However, the children were divided in their preference for unfriendly assertive versus friendly assertive responses. Children of coercive mothers tended to prefer unfriendly assertion (such as threatening to hit another child), which was often aggressive in nature. These children believed that a hostile strategy for resolving peer conflict would result in a positive outcome, in other words, they would get their way. Coercive parents do not typically use inductive reasoning to help children envision the consequences of their behavior. As a result, children of coercive mothers tended to think that unfriendly problem-solving strategies (such as commanding or threatening) would result in an effective solution to the problem.

In contrast, children of parents who used inductive reasoning in discipline preferred friendly assertive problem-solving strategies with their peers. These children felt that a friendly strategy would be successful in gaining what they wanted and in promoting positive peer relations. The internal emotional states of others are not readily visible to children, and parents can be important in interpreting emotional reactions. Inductive reasoning allows the child to envision the consequences of her or his actions by developing empathy with the feelings of another child.

Some caution should be used in interpreting these study results. It possible that in some cases the parent's coercive discipline may be a response to, rather than a cause of, a child's hostile behavior. The child's unfriendly assertive behavior may lead to both the child's difficulties with friends and the strong parental response (Bell and Chapman 1986).

Parents who use authoritarian discipline rely on coercion and rarely use inductive reasoning with children. Permissive parents use inductive reasoning; and when that strategy fails, these parents often abandon the effort to influence the child's behavior. Authoritative parents also use inductive reasoning to persuade children. However, when the child continues to resist parental directives, authoritative parents turn to coercion to enforce those directives.

There is a growing recognition that fathers as well as mothers have an important role to play in raising children. In the next section we examine fathers as parents.

TABLE 12.2	Problem-Solving Strategies
Strategy	*Example*
Unfriendly assertive	Saying in a mean voice, "Give me back my bike!"
Friendly assertive	Saying in a nice voice, "Please, give my bike back."
Unfriendly nonassertive	Giving a mean look without saying anything.
Friendly nonassertive	Stand there and not say anyting.

Source: Hart et al., 1990. "Children's Expectations of the Outcomes of Social Strategies: Relations with Sociometic Status and Maternal Disciplinary Styles." *Child Development* 61:127–137.

Review Questions

1. In what way is discipline distinguished from punishment?

2. Describe the major elements of permissive parenting. What are the drawbacks to this parenting style?

3. Describe the major elements of authoritarian parenting. What are the drawbacks to this parenting style?

4. Describe the major elements of authoritative parenting. What are the advantages of this parenting style?

5. Why would attribution theory argue that authoritarian parenting inhibits the development of conscience?

6. What is time-out and what is its purpose?

7. What are natural consequences and how do natural consequences differ from logical consequences?

8. How does a parent create a consensual environment?

9. What is the difference between inductive reasoning and coercion?

10. What impact does coercive childrearing have on a child's relationship with peers? Why does this outcome occur?

11. What impact does the use of inductive reasoning have on a child's relationship with peers? Why does this outcome occur?

The Growing Role of Fathers

The family can be seen as a social system in which family roles are interdependent. Each member of the family has an influence on the behavior of other family members. Mothers have traditionally been the primary caretakers of children and have a significant effect on their development. Currently, fathers are also coming to be seen as important in the social development of children (Lamb 1981; Nugent 1991). Today, a growing number of fathers are winning custody of children after divorce (Ahlburg and DeVita 1992). In 1992, 14 percent of all one-parent families with children under age eighteen were headed by fathers (Rawlings 1993, Table H). In fact, the father-headed one-parent family is the fastest growing family form (Ahlburg and DeVita 1992). In two-parent families, fathers are also taking a larger role in child care (McLeod 1993). The result of this growing prominence of fathers in child care has been a new emphasis on studying the relationships fathers have with their children.

Lamb (1986) identified three fathering styles that are evident when fathers become active in child care. Each fathering style represents a different level of involvement between fathers and children. *Accessible fathers* spent time doing chores near the child but did not often engage in one-to-one interaction. *Engaged fathers* spent time talking and playing with their children. *Responsible fathers* went beyond interacting with children and took responsibility for child care by making doctor's appointments and arranging for babysitters and day care. Today, 15 percent of families with preschool children have fathers who are the primary caretakers of these young children (McLeod 1993). These fathers fall into the responsible father category. Researchers are concerned with identifying the factors that predispose a father to become involved with his children.

Father–Child Involvement

A number of factors are associated with a father's willingness to spend time with his children. One of the most important factors is the father's gender role orientation (Volling and Belsky 1991). Fathers who are described as androgynous take a larger role in parenting than fathers with traditional masculine sex role characteristics (Palkovitz 1984). Androgynous fathers exhibit behavior associated with both the traditional male and traditional female gender roles. They are nurturant with children and also committed to their role as breadwinners. In fact, a new cultural image of the nurturant father is emerging in American society (Ahlburg and DeVita 1992). In the 1930s and 1940s fathers were depicted in cartoons in the *Saturday Evening Post* magazine as incompetent in the physical aspects of child care, such as changing diapers, and also ineffective in the social aspects of parenting, such as talking to the child's friends. This portrayal of fathers in cartoons as "bumblers" in the family sphere substantially declined during the 1970s at the same time women were increasing their participation in the labor force (LaRossa et al. 1991).

As the two-earner family has emerged, the number of hours mothers spend with children has decreased while the time fathers spend with children has increased (Demo 1992). The amount of time a father spends in child care is influenced by his attitudes. Fathers with child-centered attitudes tend to spend more time in child care than fathers with adult-centered attitudes (Volling and Belsky 1991). Moreover, fathers who are high in self-esteem report satisfaction with the child-care aspects of their parenting role, whereas fathers low in self-esteem often find caring for their children stressful. In addition, a father's job demands can limit the time he has available for parenting.

Marital Satisfaction and Fathering

A man's level of marital satisfaction also influences his parenting behavior. In a longitudinal study of 100 families who participated in the Pennsylvania Infant and Family Development Project, parents reported on their marriages during their first pregnancy, and when the child was three months, nine months, and three years of age (Belsky et al. 1991). Fathers who were experiencing marital difficulties spent less time with their children than fathers who felt satisfied with their marriages. In addition, fathers who began to doubt the wisdom of the marriage and whose love for their mates had declined over the course of the study behaved more negatively and intrusively toward their children than fathers who experienced more marital satisfaction. Children in these families displayed more disobedient behavior.

The association between marital dissatisfaction and negative parenting found among fathers did not show up among mothers. Women tended to compartmentalize family relationships by keeping separate the boundaries between the mother–child relationship and the marital relationship, at least while the marriage

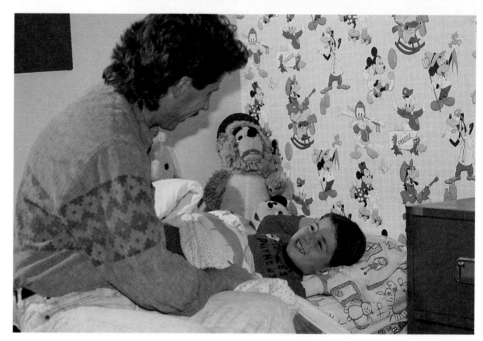

Fathers with high self-esteem experience more satisfaction with the child care aspects of parenting. Their sons, in turn, learn to associate fatherhood with pride and fullfilment.

was still intact (Belsky et al. 1991). In contrast, fathers had a more general pattern of relating to all family members. Either fathers were actively involved with both the wife and child or they were generally disengaged from both family members.

When both parents are employed, often neither parent has the option to leave child care to the other parent.

Balancing Parenting and Employment

In most families, mothers have primary responsibility for children even when they are employed full time. However, as children age, fathers tend to increase the time they spend in child care, particularly when the wife is working outside the home.

Balancing the demands of employment and family life is particularly challenging for parents; mothers and fathers both report that they experience conflict between their work and family roles. Parents of preschoolers and grade-school-age children frequently say their jobs interfere with family life (Guelzow 1991). Parents often feel the time they spend on their jobs prevents them from spending enough time with their spouses and children and interferes with getting things done around the house. Parents of young children also believe their family life interferes with their jobs. Parents report that, at times, family concerns make it difficult to concentrate at work. Furthermore, parents say the needs of young children sometimes make it hard for them to get to work on time (Guelzow 1991). For a further discussion of employment and parenting, see Chapter 8, Marriage Work, and Power.

When parents work, a major concern is finding quality child care for their children. As Table 12.3 shows, the majority of preschool children are cared for in a family home, their own or someone else's. In contrast, the majority of grade school and

TABLE 12.1	Child-Care Arrangements Used by Employed Mothers for Children under Age Five, Percent Distribution	
Care in the child's home		36%
By father		20
By other relative		11
By nonrelative		5
Care in another home		31
By relative		13
By nonrelative		18
Day care center/preschool		23
Kindergarten/grade school		1
Mother cares for child at work		9
Total		100%

Source: U.S. Bureau of the Census 1994, *Statistical Abstract of the United States, 1994,* Table 603, p. 386. Washington, D.C.: U.S. Government Printing Office.

junior high children, ages five to fourteen, utilize self-care (U.S. Bureau of the Census 1990a, Table 623). They are often called "latchkey" children because they stay at home after school and take care of themselves. The term "latchkey" arose because these children carry a house key to gain entry to the home in the afternoon. There is a great need for high-quality, supervised day care for children while their parents are at work.

Another family that experiences challenges in parenting is the one-parent family.

One-Parent Families

The number of one-parent families has grown substantially over the last two decades as the divorce rate has risen and the number of children born to unmarried mothers has increased. The vast majority (86 percent) of one-parent families are headed by single mothers (Rawlings 1993).

Single Parents and the Perceptions of Control

Single parents tend to feel pressured by the demands of employment and parenting (Dudley 1991). An important source of stress for single parents is the necessity of guiding or disciplining children. Machida and Holloway (1991) studied single mothers who were raising four-year-old children and found that issues of control were important in the mother–child relationship. Mothers who perceived themselves as being in control of the parent–child relationship had greater success in parenting than mothers who viewed the child as having significant control in the relationship. Mothers who felt "in charge" of the family tended to have children with higher self-esteem and fewer physical and psychological symptoms than mothers who felt they had less control over their children.

BOX 12.2   A C l o s e r L o o k

Description of General Trends

In 1993, one-fourth (26 percent) of all children lived in families headed by single parents. To arrive at this figure, look at the first block of bar graphs in Figure 12.1, labeled "All Races," and add together children in mother-headed families (23 percent) and children in father-headed families (3 percent). This block of bar graphs also shows that since 1960, children have been increasingly likely to live in one-parent families. In fact, the percentage of children living in both mother-headed families and father-headed families has tripled since 1960.

Racial and Ethnic Diversity

All groups for whom historical data are available

Percent of Children in Each Living Arrangement, 1960 to 1992

show a growing tendency for children to live in one-parent families. That trend is strongest among African Americans. In 1960, two-thirds (67 percent) of African-American children lived in two-parent families. By 1993, only one-third (35 percent) of African American chidlren were growing up in two-parent homes.

When we look only at the 1990s, Asian and Pacific Islander children (81 percent) were most likely to live in two-parent families; African-American children (35 percent) were least likely to live in two-parent families; and the percentages of Hispanic children (64 percent) and white children (77 percent) fell in between.

Note: Hispanics may be of any race.

Sources: U.S. Bureau of the Census 1994, Current Population Reports, P20-478, *Marital Status and Living Arrangements: March 1993,* Washington, D.C.: U.S. Government Printing Office, Table F, page XI.

U.S. Bureau of the Census 1991b, Current Population Reports, P20-450, *Marital Status and Living Arrangements: March 1990.* Washington D.C.: U.S. Government Printing Office, Table E, page 5.

U.S. Bureau of the Census 1991c, Current Population Reports, P20, *Asian and Pacific Islander Population in the United States, March 1990–91,* Washington, D.C.: U.S. Government Printing Office, Table 8, page 39.

Transition from a Two-Parent to a One-Parent Family

After divorce, the parenting style of the custodial parent affects the ease with which children make the transition from a two-parent to a one-parent family. When the parent–child relationship is warm and supportive and discipline is consistent, children tend to adjust well to living in a one-parent family (Skolnick 1991). Divorced parents who use an authoritative parenting style based on warmth and firmness tend to have children who exhibit social competence with low levels of peer conflict (Heatherington 1989; Machida and Holloway 1991). Likewise, a warm relationship with another adult, such as a noncustodial parent or grandparent, can ease the child's transition from an intact family to a one-parent family (Skolnick 1991).

Parenting Problems

Single parents often report that they have more discipline problems with boys than with girls. Single mothers raising young boys often attempt to regain control by using a restrictive and punitive parenting style characterized by giving orders and making threats (Heatherington et al. 1982; Kline 1991). In response,

Figure 12.1
Percent of Children in Each Living Arrangement, 1960–1993.

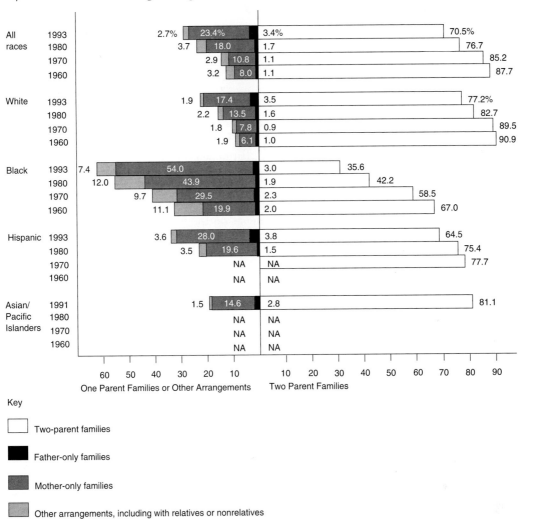

Key

☐ Two-parent families

■ Father-only families

▨ Mother-only families

▨ Other arrangements, including with relatives or nonrelatives

boys tend to use coercive strategies on their mothers, often giving orders and making threats (Block et al. 1988). Kline (1991) found that divorced mothers who experienced ongoing conflict with a former spouse tended to have more negative mother–son relationships than other mothers. This pattern of difficult parent–child relationships was particularly strong in mother-headed families with low socioeconomic status where economic strain is likely to be great.

Benefits of Growing Up in a One-Parent Family

There are some benefits to being a child of divorce. Children in one-parent families tend to be more androgynous than children in two-parent homes, experiencing less pressure to conform to rigid gender roles. Boys often need to learn to cook and iron clothes, and girls frequently need to seek a Saturday job to earn spending money. Children of single parents also exhibit greater maturity and a stronger sense of self-efficacy because they often have to cook and perform other tasks on their own (Lauer and Lauer 1991). In fact, the reaction of a child to divorce can be either negative or positive depending on the child's relationship with the custodial parent.

The Importance of the Noncustodial Father

Immediately following a divorce, the relationship children have with their fathers has an important effect on their sense of well-being. Regular visits with the noncustodial parent as well as with extended kin on both sides of the family is associated with optimism, better self-concepts, and higher levels of aspiration and achievement in school (Kline 1991). In contrast, children who feel that they have lost their relationship with the noncustodial parent tend to be depressed (Drill 1986). However, as the length of time following the divorce increases, the father's visits have less influence on the well-being of the child. Two years after divorce, neither the quality of the father–child relationship nor the amount of time a noncustodial father spends with his child appears to have an effect on the child's emotional adjustment (Kline 1991). The critical relationship for the child's postdivorce emotional adjustment appears to be with the custodial parent, who is usually the mother (Machida and Holloway 1991). However, after divorce the noncustodial father continues to play an important role in encouraging high educational aspirations and achievement.

Next we turn to couples who wish to become parents through adoption.

Adoption

Many married couples, as well as some single adults and some gay couples, desire to adopt a child. Over 2 million Americans report that they have contacted an adoption agency or a lawyer to inquire about adoption. Currently, 200,000 couples are seeking to adopt (Bachrach et al. 1991). However, only a small number of children are available. Only 4 percent of teenagers who give birth put their infants up for adoption. Those teens who release their children for adoption tend to have thought about their future and often have plans for education and employment (Donnelly and Voydanoff 1991). White and African-American women are equally likely to seek a child through adoption. White couples who adopt are typically well educated and affluent and adopt children who are unrelated to them. African-American couples who adopt are more likely to have a low income and low educational level and tend to adopt children who are already members of their extended family.

There are two main types of adoption, closed and open.

Closed Adoption

In a closed adoption, the birth mother does not meet the adoptive parents or have any identifying information about them. Adoption records are kept sealed at the courthouse so that the parties remain anonymous. Many adoptive parents believe this arrangement provides them with some protection against potentially intrusive attention from the birth mother.

Open Adoption

In an open adoption, the birth mother typically meets the birth parents and approves of them before relinquishing her child for adoption. Often the contact continues over time, with the adoptive parents periodically sending pictures of the child to the birth mother. In some cases, the adoptive parents are with the birth mother in the labor and delivery room and witness the birth of the child. In such cases, the birth mother often has visiting privileges so that she can watch the child grow up. Open adoption has advantages for the birth mother, who has a voice in choosing the adoptive parents and believes that she does not have to make a complete break with her child. And because the birth parent is known to the adoptive parents and child, the child does not grow up wondering about the birth parent.

Searching for Birth Parents

Most adoptions are closed, and some children of closed adoptions have a strong urge to find their birth parents and discover their biological roots. The Adoptee's Liberty Movement Association (ALMA), a national nonprofit organi-

Adopted children often have strong desires to locate their birth parents. Pictured here are the author, Robin Wolf (far right), her adopted daughter, Jennifer (center), and Jennifer's birth mother at an "I found" ceremony.

BOX 12.3   A   C l o s e r   L o o k

A Native American Adoptee's Family Reunion

A twenty-one-year-old Native American woman who was adopted by a white family explains what it was like to have her first reunion with her birth family at age twenty:

In searching through marriage and divorce records, I discovered my grandmother's address. I knocked at her door and said that I was looking for my birth mother. My grandmother jumped up and immediately knew who I was since my birth mother had been living with her when .she was pregnant. She went straight to the phone and started calling my natural family, urging them to rush to her house right away, but she did not tell them why. My grandmother did not want my birth mother to become too excited or upset and have an accident while driving. Hearing the urgency in my grandmother's voice, my birth family rushed to my grandmother's house thinking that there may have been a death in the family. I looked out the window and saw the first person to arrive. He was a handsome, dark, Native American man with straight, short black hair, about two years older than me. My grandmother explained that he was my brother, and he gave me a big hug saying, "Mom is going to be so surprised." By now I was standing on the sidewalk. Another car drove up, and my brother went to the car window to tell them who I was. First, a striking woman with long straight hair to her waist got out of the car and told me that she was my aunt. I looked in the car to see another woman crying, and watched my aunt and brother help her out of the car. The woman seemed too overcome with emotion to get out of the car on her own. My aunt took flowers from the woman's hands and gave them to me saying, "These are from your mother." My birth mother had brought the flowers assuming that the family had been summoned because of a death. After hugs and tears, we went inside to talk. That evening, we sat around comparing hands, knees, eyes, eyebrows, shoulders, and the difficulty we shared in finding blue jeans that fit. My birth mother and I not only had similar facial features, but we also had the same body shape.

Since meeting my other family, I have learned some aspects of being Indian. My other grandparents travel the pow wow circuit selling food out of a trailer. My first pow wow was the best one because I had never been around so many Indians or eaten Indian fry bread. There was something comforting about being around so many people who looked like me, and yet pow wow's seemed so different from the social world in which I grew up. My birth mother gave me a shawl which she had fringed herself. The shawl was for me to wear while learning native dances. My birth family also introduced me to Native American sweet grass, which is burned at ceremonials. In finding my family I have discovered that I have found some parts of myself. But my adoptive family, who raised me and encouraged me to go to college, are also important to me. In some ways I feel caught between two worlds. (Interview by author)

zation, was organized to help adoptees trace their birth parents. ALMA has members who have successfully searched for birth parents and birth children and who act as volunteer advisors in helping other members conduct a search. When a member finds the birth parent or birth child, the local chapter of ALMA usually holds a ceremony in which the member receives a large pin with the words "I found" on it. Although adoptees typically search for the birth mother only, they often discover an entire extended family. Next we discuss teenagers who become parents and experience strain in their parenting role.

Review Questions

1. What types of fathers tend to spend time with their children?
2. How do you explain the difference in parenting behavior of mothers and fathers in unhappy marriages?
3. What parenting style is associated with smooth parent–child relationships in single-parent families? What challenges do single mothers face in raising boys?
4. What are the advantages of growing up in a single-parent family?
5. How common is the desire to adopt a child? What is the difference between open and closed adoption?

Teenagers as Parents

The teenage birth rate is higher in the United States than in any other developed country. As discussed in an earlier chapter, the overall nonmarital birth rate among teenagers is rising. The birth rate among very young teenagers, ages ten to fourteen, increased by 33 percent during the 1980s (Nath et al. 1991).

As mothers, teenagers experience a special set of problems. Because they are in the process of identity formation, teenagers are likely to have an unstable identity. Their problem-solving skills are likewise incompletely developed. Teenagers often lack parenting skills and have limited knowledge of child development.

Children born to teenage mothers are at higher risk for developmental delays than children born to older parents (Whitman et al. 1987). An extended-kin support system can be important in preventing negative outcomes from teen parenting and in promoting a positive relationship between the teen mother and her child. Family support can take the form of *emotional support,* such as advice and empathy, or *instrumental support,* which involves providing income or services, such as babysitting, extra money, and help with housework. Because the majority of teen pregnancies are out of wedlock, the emotional support of a spouse is often missing. However, it is the level of overall family support rather than spousal support which appears to be crucial in the development of a child raised by a teenage mother (Nath et al. 1991).

Stress in Teen Parenting

Teenage mothers are "off-time" in their personal development because they are coping with the responsibilities of parenting while their peers are typically dating and enjoying a good deal of freedom and independence. This is often a stressful situation for the unwed teen mother. Teenage mothers appear to be more negative and less expressive with their infants than older mothers. Compared to older mothers, adolescent mothers exhibit lower levels of child acceptance, exhibit less positive affect (emotional expression), speak to their infants less often, spend less time demonstrating tasks to their toddlers, have more negative verbal interactions with their children, and are more punitive (Field 1980; Levine et al. 1985; McAnarney et al. 1986; Nath et al. 1991).

Parenting is often a source of conflict and insecurity for teenage mothers. Because help from relatives with child care is usually necessary if the teenager is to continue her schooling, the infant often develops a strong attachment to the grandmother and aunts. As a result, some teenage mothers report feeling left out when their infants seek out another relative, and teens often worry about whether or not their infants will recognize them as the mother (Apfel and Seitz 1991). Sometimes teen mothers feel competitive with their children in seeking the grandmother's attention. This feeling of jealously can resemble sibling rivalry when the infant receives toys and attention from the grandmother.

Teenage Parents and Their Mothers

Grandparents can offer a number of benefits to their children and grandchildren as babysitters, advisers to their daughters, and as surrogate parents. Apfel and Seitz (1991) studied inner-city African-American adolescent mothers who bore their children out of wedlock. These young mothers often relied on their own mothers' help in childrearing, and the presence of a grandmother often had a stabilizing effect on both grandchildren and young mothers. However, Apfel and Seitz found that many of the grandmothers studied were reluctant to take on the parenting role in middle-age. This was particularly true when the grandmother had a job that was important to her. "Early" grandmothers (median age thirty-two) were less willing than "on-time" grandmothers (median age forty-six) to take on the extra burden of childrearing associated with their daughter's birth. Apfel and Seitz identified four models of mother–grandmother relationships in families of unwed teens.

Parent Replacement Model. In this model the grandmother assumed responsibility for childrearing while her daughter played only a minimal parenting role. Ten percent of the families studied fell into this category. The grandmother's parenting role freed the daughter to finish high school or go to college, join the army, or get a job. As a result, the daughter was able to maintain a social life similar to that of her peers. Some grandmothers took on this role out of a desire to allow their daughters to gain an education or work experience; other grandmothers assumed the parenting role reluctantly when their daughters either abruptly or gradually abandoned their children. This model has the benefit of preparing the daughter to be self-supporting and reduces welfare dependency. The cost to the teen mother can be a low level of attachment with her child. In addition, the grandmother can feel deserted by her daughter if the daughter abandons the child.

Supplement Model. In this model the young mother and her mother share child care, often with the help of other family members, such as siblings. In a typical family the adolescent mother attends school until three o'clock and then comes home to take over childrearing duties. This was the most frequently used model and accounted for a little more than 50 percent of the families. These adolescent mothers were expected to sacrifice a good deal of recreational activity with peers. In fact, some grandmothers said they did not want to make life too easy for their daughters so that the daughter would take precautions against having a second child. This model has the advantage of allowing the mother and child to spend enough time together to establish a parent–child bond. However, the frustration of giving up activities with peers is a source of stress for the young mother.

Supported Parent Model. This model accounted for 20 percent of the families studied by Apfel and Seitz. Half of the young mothers in this category lived separately from their mothers, establishing a satellite household often in the same apartment building. Regardless of whether the teenage mother lived separately or with her own mother, the adolescent mother took full responsibility for child care. Frequent visits between mother and daughter were the hallmark of this model, and occasionally the grandmother provided babysitting. However, in this laissez-faire model, the daughter raises the child on her own and the grandmother engages in crisis intervention, temporarily offering help when the young mother becomes ill or has a problem. Often the mothers in this model were resistant to the grandmother's advice, and a number of the grandmothers worried about the quality of care the grandchild received. The benefit of this model is the development of a strong parent–child bond. The disadvantage lies in the low level of supervision provided by the grandmother.

Apprentice Model. In this model the adolescent mother took responsibility for child care under the watchful eye of the grandmother, who acted as a mentor. The grandmother helped her daughter develop parenting skills and confidence and then gradually relinquished control over childrearing as the young mother gained experience. The relationship between the adolescent mother and her own mother appeared to be positive because the grandmother acknowledged her daughter as the primary mother and saw herself as an advisor. This model accounts for only 10 percent of the families studied. Many adolescents in other family models were not willing to take on the apprentice role, and the birth of the baby exacerbated preexisting problems between mother and daughter. The researchers viewed the apprentice model as the family arrangement in which the young mother had the best chance to develop parenting skills.

Teen mothers are not the only parents to experience stress in childrearing. Immigrant parents also face special parenting problems, as we see in the following section.

Immigrant Parents

Parents who are recent immigrants face a special set of problems as they struggle to raise children in an alien culture. The mainstream society often holds expectations for children which are different from the ideals and values fostered in immigrant families. Children of immigrant parents often feel like marginal people who are involved in two cultures: the dominant culture as well as their parent's world.

Vietnamese-American and Mexican-American families represent two immigrant cultures.

Vietnamese-American Parents

Kibria (1990) studied recent immigrant Vietnamese-American families and found that they feared the encroachment of mainstream American culture into their family life. They particularly worried that American values would erode parental authority and the value of *familism*, in which the needs of the family are placed above the needs of the individual. Parents worried that their children

BOX 12.4   W o r l d   P e r s p e c t i v e s

Childbearing Among the !Kung of Africa's Kalahari Desert

The !Kung are hunters and gatherers who make their camps at water holes in Africa's Kalahari desert. They have a distinctive appearance; the men stand about 5 feet 2 inches tall, and the women less than 5 feet. Hunting and gathering was the means of subsistence that characterized all human societies more than 12,000 years ago, and the !Kung have continued this way of life into the present.

!Kung families spend a good deal of time on the move in the bush. Both men and women go on long foraging expeditions looking for roots, seeds, and other foods and often walk to distant camps to visit relatives. Hunting and tracking are an important aspect of the male gender role, and older boys accompany their fathers on hunting parties. Long before a boy reaches puberty, he develops important tracking skills. Boys can look at an animal print and the dung left behind and identify the species, tell its age by the size of the print, and look at the sand blown into the footprint to discover how many hours have passed since the animal was there. Girls also learn to recognize prints. Both boys and girls can identify from human footprints which member of the camp has recently passed by.

As children grow up, they learn that all relationships with both relatives and nonrelatives fall into one of two categories: joking relationships and avoidance relationships. With grandparents, children share a joking relationship that is relaxed, affectionate, and punctuated with laughter. Children also have joking relationships with people in their own generation. When these younger members of society are potential marriage partners, sexual joking of an explicit nature is common even between young children. Joking relationships include peers and grandparents but skip the parent's generation.

Children have an avoidance relationship with their parents and members of their parents' generation. Avoidance relationships are characterized by respect and reserve. Parents are warm with children, but children are expected to address their parents in a formal manner in contrast to the informal, familiar term of address used for their grandparents. The most restrictive avoidance relationship in !Kung society is created when a person marries and gains in-laws. Husbands and their mothers-in-law and wives and their fathers-in-law are expected to avoid talking directly to one another and communicate through a third-party intermediary.

!Kung children grow up to have a relaxed, unselfconscious attitude toward sexuality. Young children are not required to wear clothing, and children are expected to cover their genitals only when they enter their teenage years. !Kung parents sleep with their young children under the same blanket, and sexual relations between husband and wife take place while the child remains next to them. The preferred sexual position is the man-behind-woman-in-front with both partners lying on their side facing the fire. This position accommodates the family sleeping

would begin to approve of dating, teen sexuality, and independent mate choice. They were also concerned that their children might adopt the American value of individualism and put their own interests above those of the family. One woman told the interviewer that her sister-in-law's fifteen-year-old daughter, Mai, was suspected of seeing American boys. She described Mai's behavior as follows:

> . . . she was always playing on the streets, sometimes until late at night. And she didn't take care of her younger brothers and sisters, and didn't do any of the housework, instead always wanting money to go and buy the latest fashions (Kibria 1990a:19).

Many Vietnamese-American parents believed that American youth are selfish and do not show enough concern for their families.

arrangement, in which the child sleeps in front of the mother and the husband to the back of her. Children grow up familiar with the sex act and view sexuality as a natural part of life. Sex play is considered a normal part of childhood, and young children often go into the bush and pretend to have intercourse. Most childhood sex play is heterosexual, although homosexual experiences also occur. Homosexuality is not viewed with hostility in !Kung society; rather, it is looked at as a curiosity. In the process of childhood sex play, older children loose their virginity. In fact, virginity is not an important concept in !Kung society and is not valued at the time of marriage.

Although !Kung society considers childhood sex play normal, the !Kung do expect children to be born within marriage. The !Kung manage to confine most births to marriage by arranging marriages for children while they are still young. It is the job of parents to choose their child's future marriage partner, and children have no say in the matter. Soon after a girl is born, the parents of young boys begin to look her over as a potential mate for their sons. Traditionally, the marriage ceremony takes place when the girl is still a child, at about age ten or twelve. More recently, the marriage age has risen to about age 14. So the !Kung become parents as teenagers.

Arranged marriage creates a potential source of conflict between parents and their children. !Kung girls are brought up to be independent and often put up a protest when marriage is thrust upon them. When the marriage ceremony is to begin, the girl typically resists by kicking and screaming and sometimes has to be carried out of the hut on the back of a female relative to complete the ceremony. Often the marriage begins with a mock capture ceremony, in which the new husband carries away his protesting new wife. This struggle at the marriage ceremony shows that girls and women are a force to be reckoned with in the family. Approximately half of the girls put up such a fight that the new husband has difficulty sexually consummating the marriage and the parents relent and call off the marriage. When a marriage continues, the young husband settles down in the wife's camp for eight to ten years to prove his hunting skills before moving his bride to his parents' camp. The !Kung say that brides are too young to leave their parents soon after marriage.

Recently, the !Kung have been encouraged to send their children to school, but his effort has been largely unsuccessful. !Kung parents point out that it would be too expensive for them to purchase children's uniforms for school. However, the objections to school run deeper than this. The sedentary life of a school child runs counter to the nomadic life of the !Kung family. Parents worry that they would not be able to find enough food if they foraged in the area near the school. They would need to forage long distances from the schoolhouse and thus be separated from their children. Furthermore, parents fear that school attendance will disrupt the established pattern of social relationships in !Kung society. The !Kung have heard rumors about school children abandoning the traditional avoidance relationship with their parents and substituting a joking relationship. This lack of respect for elders is deeply troubling to !Kung parents (Lee 1984).

Hispanic-American Parents

Like Vietnamese-American families, Hispanic families emphasize familism. Hispanics retain an extended-family structure after immigrating to the United States. The *barrio,* a predominantly Hispanic neighborhood, provides a setting for kin to live in close proximity (Keefe 1987). The Hispanic extended family reaches beyond blood relatives. *Compadres,* or godparents, are treated as co-parents and are expected to establish a special bond with the child. Compadres are often close friends who become fictive kin, extending the family beyond the boundaries of blood kinship. Baptism, confirmation, and first communion formalize the compadre relationship. Compadres are expected to offer help and advice in times of trouble (Queen et al. 1985).

Childrearing and the Schools. In a study comparing children from a small town in northern Mexico to children of white non-Hispanic families in the United States, Martinez (1985) found that the socialization of Mexican immigrants did not prepare them well for competing in American schools. The Mexican mothers, who were less educated than Anglo mothers, held expectations for their children which were different from those of Anglo mothers. Hispanic children were taught to value cooperation rather than competition and, because of their strong identification with family, to think of achievement in terms of family achievement. In contrast, Anglo mothers encouraged individual achievement, competitiveness, and assertive behavior. Anglo mothers stressed inquiry and expanding devices, often using a question-and-answer format in which the mother asked the child to explain something. When the child finished the explanation, the Anglo mother asked for more information. This method of teaching is similar to that used in the American classroom (Laosa 1977). In contrast, Mexican mothers used nonverbal cues and gave more commands to their children than Anglo mothers. Mexican mothers responded more to their children's feelings, whereas Anglo mothers discussed information. These differences in socialization patterns put the Hispanic immigrant child at a disadvantage in school. For Hispanic children, there was a discontinuity between Hispanic socialization and expectations in the school setting, whereas Anglo children experienced continuity between their socialization and school experience.

Adult Children as Caregivers

Parents are caregivers for young children, but as parents move through the life cycle their relationship with children changes. For a discussion of parents and

Daycare workers perform many of the tasks formerly done only by parents now that American society is dominated by two-earner families and working single mothers.

unlaunched adult children, see Chapter 16. When people reach midlife they often find that they become caregivers to their own parents.

Medical technology has extended life expectancy, and the number of elderly persons in the United States is growing. As more people live to age eighty and beyond, the length of time an ill or disabled elderly person must depend on his or her children for care has also increased (Hoyert and Seltzer 1992). The job of caring for family members tends to fall to women, and daughters are more likely than sons to care for elderly parents. Likewise, the job of caring for a husband's elderly parents usually falls to his wife. Caregiving for an elderly parent results in a *role reversal*, in which social roles are swapped or reversed. In childhood, the parent is the caregiver to dependent offspring. In old age, the parent becomes dependent on the adult child's caregiving.

Sandwiched Generation

The modern midlife couple is likely to be in the *sandwiched generation,* raising children at the same time they are caring for disabled and aging parents. Many couples delayed childbearing in order to pursue their careers. These older parents find themselves wondering how they will be able to pay for their children's college education at the same time that their parents are becoming elderly and often need financial assistance. In addition, the emotional energy of midlife parents becomes divided between childrearing and elder care.

Stages of Caregiving

When a daughter provides care for a dependent elderly parent, the caregiving role rarely represents an abrupt change from her previous behavior. Instead, daughters tend to provide aid for aging parents long before the parents become dependent. Typically the daughter offers aid to a self-sufficient mother and gradually shifts into more caregiving as her mother becomes dependent (Walker and Pratt 1991).

Walker and Pratt (1991) compared midlife adult daughters who had self-sufficient mothers to midlife adult daughters with dependent mothers.

Self-Sufficient Mothers. Self-sufficient mothers were able to meet their own daily needs and were not dependent on their daughters for help with laundry, meal preparation, housekeeping, or personal care. Daughters primarily provided transportation and companionship for their self-sufficient mothers. These mothers had a mean age of seventy-five and many physical ailments that were not disabling.

Dependent Mothers. Dependent mothers had strong needs for help with shopping, errands, meal preparation, and housekeeping but relatively little need for personal care. The mean age of the dependent mothers was eighty-one, so these mothers were older than the group of self-sufficient mothers.

Continuity in the Caregiving Role

The caregiving role of a daughter with a dependent mother appears to be a continuation of a pattern established earlier, before the mother became dependent.

Daughters gradually increase their caregiving activities from taking the mother on shopping trips to providing some meal preparation and laundry assistance. The major difference between daughters of self-sufficient mothers and daughters of dependent mothers is the amount of time spent in caregiving. Daughters of dependent mothers spend more time giving aid than daughters with self-sufficient mothers. Both categories of daughters report that they take their parents shopping and that they spent about the same amount of money on aid to parents.

Strain in Caregiving

The National Survey of Families and Households, a nationally representative sample of over 13,000 respondents, provides insight into the role women play as caregivers for aging, ill, or disabled relatives. The caregiving role tends to put strain on a marriage. Adult daughters who provide care for an elderly parent report more marital difficulties than noncaregivers. Women who care for an elderly parent have more disagreements with their spouses and have higher levels of depression than noncaregivers (Hoyert and Seltzer 1992).

In spite of these difficulties, when adult daughters who care for a parent are compared to wives who care for ill husbands, adult-daughter caregivers have a higher level of well-being. Wives who care for ill husbands tend to become homebound and socially isolated. In contrast, adult daughters who provide care for parents tend to remain active in social activities outside the home. A daughter's place of residence also affects the amount of strain she experiences. Those daughters who lived separately from their aging and disabled parent had fewer marital problems and belonged to more social organizations than those who had an elderly parent living with them (Hoyert and Seltzer 1991).

Racial Differences in Caregiving

Deimling and his colleagues (1991) compared African-American and white families who provided care for an elder relative and found that the pattern of caregiving differed with race. African-American families are less likely than white families to involve the elderly relative in decisions about that relative's care. There are a number of possible explanations for this difference. First, African-American families tend to be larger and more diverse and rely on a greater number of relatives to provide elder care. The necessity of coordinating caregiving makes it difficult to bring the elderly person into the decision-making process. Second, a greater percentage of African-American elderly are widowed, divorced, or have no live-in partner. This means that care decisions are not often made within a marital dyad. The elderly tend to have greater input into decision making when the caregiver is a co-resident spouse. Third, African-American elderly are more likely to experience poor health than whites of the same age. The ravages of poverty and unstable work opportunities often take a toll on the health of the African-American poor. The greater role of relatives in decision making for the elderly in African-American families may reflect more severe health problems for African-American elderly.

Review Questions

1. What special stressors does an unwed teen mother face?

2. What four models of mother–daughter relationships did Apfel and Seitz find among unwed inner-city African-American teen mothers and their mothers? Which of the four models is most common and which do Apfel and Seitz believe has the best chance of developing the teen mother's parenting skills?

3. What kinds of problems do Vietnamese-American parents face?

4. How is the Hispanic-American family organized? What problems do Hispanic-American children face in school and how is this problem related to parenting?

5. What factors affect the well being of the adult-daughter caregiver? In what way are adult daughters with dependent mothers similar to and different from adult daughters with self-sufficient mothers?

6. How do African-American families differ from white families in their pattern of caregiving and why might this difference exist?

Summary

1. Parents using permissive parenting set few rules and make few demands on children. Authoritarian parents set rigid rules and make strong demands on children. Authoritative parents balance parental demands with the needs of the child.

2. Authoritarian parenting tends to result in power struggles and inhibits the development of conscience.

3. Methods of positive parental guidance include time-out, natural consequences, logical consequences, and creating a consensual environment.

4. Children whose parents used inductive reasoning tend to be preferred by their peers, unlike children whose parents used coercive discipline.

5. Fathers who are highly involved with their children tend to be androgynous, have high self-esteem, and tend to be satisfied with their marriages. Both parents find it difficult to balance employment and childrearing.

6. Single mothers who perceive themselves as being in control of their families tend to be successful parents. Single mothers experience more difficulty raising sons than daughters. There are benefits to growing up in a single-parent family.

7. Teen parents experience stress, and their mothers often offer aid using one of four models: parent replacement model, supplement model, supported parent model, or apprentice model.

8. Immigrant Vietnamese parents worry that their children will eventually devalue familism. Immigrant Hispanic children have values that are in contrast to the values put forth in the school.

9. With the extension of life expectancy, adult daughters increasingly find themselves in the role of caregiver to a parent. This role creates considerable strain.

10. Adult daughters tend to ease into a caregiving role with their parents, providing elder care before the parent becomes dependent. African-American families are less likely than white families to involve the elderly person in decisions about their care.

Key Words

Socialization	Discipline
Permissive Parenting	Authoritarian Parenting
Authoritative Parenting	Consistency
Power Struggles	Functionally Superfluous Control
Time-Out	Natural Consequences
Logical Consequences	Consensual Environment
Coercive Discipline	Inductive Reasoning
Instrumental Support	"Off-Time" Parenting
Parent Replacement Model	Supplement Model
Supported Parent Model	Apprentice Model
Familism	Compadres
Role Reversal	Sandwiched Generation

Resources

Adoptees Liberty Movement Association (ALMA)
P.O. Box 154, Washington Bridge Station
New York, NY 10033
(212) 581-1568
Provides assistance in searching for birth parents or birth children and has a computerized database for searches. Must be over eighteen years old to join. Publishes *ALMA Searchlight*, periodic newsletter; *ALMA Official Searcher's Guide* (book).

Adoption Triangle Ministries
P. O. Box 1860
Cape Coral, FL 33910
(813) 542-1342
Organization for adoptees, adoptive parents, and birth parents (adoption triangle). Holds discussion groups, workshops, and conferences. Publishes *Adoption Triangle Ministries,* a list of 200 search and support organizations.

American Mothers, Inc.
6843 Nashville Rd.
Lanham, MD 20706
(301) 552-2712
Seeks to strengthen motherhood; selects the American Mother of the Year; maintains a Hall of Fame of Mothers.

Big Brothers/Big Sisters of America
230 N. 13th St.
Philadelphia, PA 19107
(215) 567-7000

Adults volunteer to be a friend to a child from a single-parent home. Four hundred sixty groups nationally.

Children's Defense Fund
122 C St., N.W.
Washington, DC 20001
(202) 628-8787
Advocates improvement in child welfare and child health. Collects information on the state of the nation's children. Publishes *CDF Child Youth and Family Futures Clearinghouse*, bimonthly; *The State of America's Children*, annual.

Child Trends, Inc.
2100 M. Street, N.W., Ste. 610
Washington, DC 20037
Nonprofit organization promoting the well-being of children. Publishes *Facts at a Glance*, annual report.

Child Welfare League of America Research Center
440 First St. N.W., Ste. 310
Washington, DC 20001
(202) 638-2952
Collects information on teen pregnancy, Aid to Families with Dependent Children, young parents, child abuse and neglect, and adoption.

Gay and Lesbian Coalition International
P.O. Box 50360
Washington, DC 20091
(202) 583-8029
Strives to eliminate discrimination against gay parents and maintains a clearinghouse for information on parenting among gays and lesbians.

Grandparents Raising Grandchildren
P.O Box 104
Colleyville, TX, 76034
(817) 577-0435
Offers emotional support to grandparents who are raising their grandchildren.

Single Parents Resource Center
141 West 28th St., Ste. 302
New York, NY 10001
(212) 947-0221
Network of local single-parent groups and political advocacy for single parents' issues.

Toughlove International
P.O. Box 1069
Doylestown, PA 18901
(215) 348-7090
Network of over 2,000 weekly support groups for parents of problem teenagers. Publishes *Toughlove Notes*, quarterly.

Communication and Conflict

After dinner each night Janice found herself in the kitchen alone, doing the dishes, while her husband, Mark, sat in the recliner in the living room, reading the newspaper. She felt hurt and resentful because he did not participate in the kitchen cleanup, and she gave a loud, tired sigh when he left the kitchen. However, she said nothing to him about the dishes because she didn't want to appear to be a nag. Besides, she thought, if he loved her, he would come into the kitchen on his own and share the chores. Her resentment grew, and one night she walked into the living room and said, "You're so selfish. Who do you think I am, your maid? You never help with the dishes. You don't care how hard I work or how tired I am. In fact, you don't care about anyone except yourself."

Mark responded, "I don't see how you could be tired, you're just lazy. You have that easy job as a receptionist where all you do is talk on the phone all day. I'd hardly call that work. All you do is complain. Why should I want to help someone who is in such a foul mood?" Janice turned on her heel and walked out of the room. (Interview by author.)

Loving someone is not enough to produce a successful relationship. As Janice and Mark's situation illustrates, effective communication is also necessary to build a strong and intimate partnership. Communication is the connecting link between two people. Whether that link is a positive or negative one depends, in part, on the style of expression the partners adopt. Stating feelings, ideas, and needs can create experiences of bonding; or such statements can be the means by which we push each other away. Not only do we reveal ourselves and come to know another person through communication, we also depend on communication as the medium through which we attempt to resolve conflicts.

Effective communication does not guarantee that a conflict will be resolved. However, with many marriages ending in divorce, it is useful to explore the processes of communication and conflict resolution. Those couples who resolve conflict effectively increase their likelihood of having a successful marriage or partnership. In this chapter we explore the communication process, social theories that explain communication, styles of communication used in conflict situations, social roles and their impact on communication, and communication problems.

Communication

Communication patterns are key factors separating troubled couples from couples satisfied with their relationships (Aida and Falbo 1991; Rusbult et al. 1986; Ting-Toomey 1983). Communication style also predicts marital success. Couples who are satisfied with their communication at one point in time are likely to be satisfied with their marriages five years later (Markman 1981). In fact, communication is more important than the amount of leisure time spent together, family finances, or the sexual relationship in predicting marital happiness (Snyder 1979).

What exactly is communication? *Communication* is the process of sending and receiving messages. Communication is not a passive process: Messages must be interpreted by the recipient (Gordon 1975). The listener is actively involved in the communication process. In the case of Mark and Janice, Mark had to decode or interpret, Janice's message. Instead of asking for what she wanted—

Figure 13.1
Communication: Interpreting Messages

351

Chapter 13
Communication
and Conflict

namely, help with the dishes—Janice verbally attacked Mark's personality by calling him selfish. Mark interpreted her criticism as a sign that she doesn't appreciate him as a person.

One way to discern the impact of one's message on the other person is to utilize feedback. *Feedback* is a verbal or nonverbal response to a message. When Mark sent a message of his own, that message became feedback to Janice. Janice interpreted Mark's feedback as evidence that he didn't care about her feelings or needs. The way Janice expressed her grievance over the dishes diminished her chances of solving the problem and created animosity between her and Mark. Likewise, Mark's response created barriers to discussion. Thus their conflict emerged.

Nonverbal Communication

Words are not the only medium through which communication and conflict take place. In *nonverbal communication,* facial expressions, gestures, and behavior patterns send symbolic messages in two ways. Nonverbal communication can act as a message within itself, or it can frame a verbal statement. In the relationship between Janice and Mark, when Mark left the kitchen each night, Janice interpreted this nonverbal behavior to mean that Mark was insensitive to her feelings of exhaustion. Meanwhile, he simply saw himself as relaxing after a hard day's work. Nonverbal communication is easily misinterpreted, particularly when it acts as a message that is not accompanied by a verbal explanation.

Behavior associated with mastectomy provides another example of nonverbal behavior acting as a message to the partner. After a wife has a mastectomy, problems frequently occur when the husband holds back and does not sexually pursue her. The husband often assumes that his wife is not ready for sex soon after the surgery and feels that he is being considerate. The wife often interprets his waiting as a sign of sexual rejection. Nonverbal behavior is a form of communication often interpreted differently by two partners. The National Cancer Institute advises wives to let their husbands know when they are ready for sex after a mastectomy and for husbands to let their wives know they still find her attractive and desirable. Wives can also ask for this reassurance. The couple need to communicate openly about new and satisfying approaches to sex (National Institute of Health 1987:17).

BOX 13.1   World Perspectives

Nonverbal Communication in Cross-Cultural Perspective

Every culture has a pattern of nonverbal communication that carries important symbolism in the culture. These nonverbal communication patterns can easily be misunderstood by people from a different culture. Americans visiting Italy often find that Italians stand close while carrying on a conversation. Italians view this as a friendly gesture, but Americans often feel uncomfortable, sensing that their privacy and personal space has been invaded (Hall 1964). Likewise, the nonverbal communication of new immigrants from Asia can be easily misunderstood by other cultural groups. Korean immigrants who have opened small grocery and convenience stores in inner-city neighborhoods in Los Angeles follow the widespread Asian practice of avoiding eye contact when serving customers. To Asians, this form of nonverbal communication shows courtesy and respect (Crittenden 1991; Pyong Gap Min 1990). However, African-American customers who live near the Korean stores often view this nonverbal behavior as a sign of unfriendliness and social rejection.

Misunderstandings of communication patterns can create or aggravate real problems between cultural groups. In South Central Los Angeles, the site of riots following the 1992 acquittal of four policemen involved in the beating of African-American motorist Rodney King, communication problems between Koreans and African Americans exacerbated the deep racial tensions already present.

Many recently immigrated Koreans have opened family businesses in impoverished inner-city neighborhoods in the United States. In Korean-owned shops, family members typically comprise the entire staff. According to Korean tradition, the eldest son inherits the business, and all the children express their filial loyalty (loyalty of children to parents) by working in the family store (Choong Soon Kim 1989). The family typically speak their native tongue while working together and naturally engage in culturally familiar nonverbal communication as well.

Inner-city African Americans, who experience a high unemployment rate, have viewed Korean hiring practices as exclusionary. Thus relationships between the two groups were generally acrimonious (Herbert 1992; Hu 1992). The misinterpretation of the Koreans' avoidance of eye contact compounded these feelings of anger and bitterness among African Americans, who wanted to feel that they were being treated decently and respectfully by the owners of the shops they frequented. In the 1992 riots, Korean businesses were targeted and burned by African-American rioters. Koreans, who received little or no help from the police, armed themselves to defend their stores and themselves. Following the riots, community organizations began working to help Koreans and African Americans better understand each other's culture and communication patterns (Kang 1992).

Nonverbal communication can frame verbal statements and provide clues about how the other person views the relationship. The pace of the conversation, interruptions, body language, and touching can all help define the relationship between two speakers. When exploratory conversations are begun at the beginning of a male–female relationship, women often convey their interest in a man by working hard at helping the conversation along, often by filling in the conversation gaps with talk (Bate 1988). Once a male and female have become acquainted, a change in communication pattern typically occurs in which men guide the conversation to topics of interest to them. In this as in other situations, nonverbal communication can be important in establishing the context in which verbal communication occurs.

In the course of communicating, conflict, the topic of the next section, invariably arises.

Conflict

Conflict refers to the exchange of opposing messages. Most people want communication to do two seemingly contradictory things, namely, to produce a companionable feeling of togetherness and to provide a vehicle for expressing grievances. The difficulty in achieving both of these goals leads many people to avoid conflict by saying nothing when the partner says something that distresses them. This avoidance of conflict was recommended by marriage counselors fifty years ago. Marital conflict during the 1940s and 1950s was viewed as harmful to relationships, and marriage counselors advised couples to side-step around troublesome issues that might produce an argument (Bach 1970). Lewis Coser challenged this perspective in his book, the *Functions of Social Conflict* (1956), in which he suggested that conflict could be functional—that is, useful and even beneficial—by clearing the air, relieving tension, clarifying issues, and producing solutions. Blau (1964) continued this theme in the 1960s when he suggested that conflict can be "regenerative" when it produces new bargains and allows aspects of the relationship to be revised and made more rewarding. George Bach applied these ideas to marriage counseling in his book, *The Intimate Enemy* (1970). As the title implies, Bach argued that conflict was not only beneficial but also could produce intimacy and stronger feelings of love and bonding in a relationship. At this early stage of introducing marital conflict into marriage counseling, very few attempts were made to distinguish communication styles that could be harmful from those that could be beneficial. Bach made some effort in this direction when he suggested that as couples argued each partner could establish a "beltline." Couples would discover what kind of attacks were so hurtful as to be declared out of bounds or "below the beltline." These particular expressions of hostility would then be avoided by the couple in future arguments. Although this process appeared to work well in Bach's therapy practice, some couples who attempted the expression of hostility on their own watched their already troubled marriages flounder.

When we communicate, we connect and conflict with those around us. Theories of communication must take into account both of these processes as they examine the role communication plays in interpersonal relationships. In the next sections of this chapter we discuss theories that illuminate the dynamics of communication: exchange theory, conflict theory, and symbolic interaction theory.

Exchange Theory

According to exchange theory, people remain in relationships when the benefits outweigh the costs (Homans 1974). Many of the benefits and costs of a relationship are experienced through the process of communication. The benefits of a relationship can be tangible, such as income, or intangible and personal, such as expressions of empathy, warmth, and appreciation. Exchange theory explores how communication can provide the benefits—or the glue—that hold people together in family relationships. Benefits are found in the messages sent, such as expressions of appreciation and empathy, or in the style of communication used, such as expressing oneself in a way that shows respect for the partner. In addition, exchange theory looks at the costs of a relationship, which may include diminished self-esteem and emotional upset following hostile communication, "put-downs," and name-calling.

People sometimes remain in a relationship that has high costs (such as put-downs) if they feel they have few acceptable alternatives to that relationship (Safil-ios-Rothschild 1970). However, commitment to a relationship is most likely to grow out of the relationship benefits. Spouses who rate their partners high on the expression of warmth tend to be satisfied with their marital relationships. In other words, people who agree that their spouse is "loving and affectionate toward me" and "lets me know that s/he cares about me" tend to be happily married (Lorenz et al. 1991). One way a partner offers emotional support and warmth is through an expression of empathy and appreciation.

Empathy

The expression of empathy shows that one partner is trying to understand how the other partner feels.

Marriage and Empathy. Ting-Toomey (1983) found the expression of empathy to be an "integrative behavior" that draws couples closer together and that is strongly associated with marital satisfaction. In the case of Janice and Mark, described at the beginning of this chapter, Janice could have begun her discussion of sharing household chores with a statement of empathy, such as, "I realize you are tired when you arrive home from work and you look forward to resting and reading the newspaper." She then could have followed her expression of empathy with a discussion of household chores. In this context, a partner would be less likely to feel attacked and more likely to be willing to listen when problems are brought up for discussion.

Children and Empathy. Children who express empathy by recognizing and under-

Conflict is unavoidable. However, if a dialogue—even an angry dialogue—clearly communicates information, it can lead to increased understand for both people.

standing the emotions of their peers are sought out as friends more often than children who lack these skills (Burleson et al. 1992). Empathetic children possess "perspective-taking skills," the ability to describe another person's understanding of a situation even when one's own understanding of the situation is different. Perspective-taking is a foundation stone of friendship (Selman 1980). The child's ability to express empathy is related to the mother's communication style. Mothers who use positive communication patterns, such as reflective listening, with their children are more likely to have empathetic children. In *reflective listening,* the parent reflects back the content of the child's message by paraphrasing it, or the parent labels the emotion the child is expressing, by saying, for example, "You seem sad." Mothers who use reflective listening with children tend to have empathetic children who are evaluated positively by their peers (Burleson et al. 1992).

Appreciation

In addition to empathy, the expression of appreciation tends to bond people together and provides rewards for the partner. Stinnett found that the willingness to express appreciation is an important characteristic shared by strong families (Stinnett 1983; Stinnett and Sauer 1977). In strong families, marital partners helped their mates build a positive self-image by expressing appreciation for things the other person had done. These partners helped each other to feel esteem for themselves and, ultimately, to feel good about the relationship. People who agree that the partner "lets me know s/he appreciates my ideas and the things I do" tend to be satisfied with their marriages (Lorenz et al 1991). Stinnett (1983) points out that partners can strengthen their relationship by telling the partner one thing that he or she appreciates about that partner each day over the course of a week. Likewise, when a parent expresses appreciation for the actions taken by a child, the parent–child relationship becomes more rewarding for the child.

Next we turn to conflict theory, which focuses on the tensions that often arise in families.

Conflict Theory

We have explored some of the ways exchange theory focuses on the benefits exchanged through communication. In contrast, *conflict theory* points out that communication is often used to influence or dominate another person. To successfully influence the behavior of someone else is to exercise *power*. For example, men tend to interrupt women more than women interrupt men in conversation (Fishman 1983). Bate (1988) has argued that the tendency for men to interrupt women and guide conversation toward topics that interest them symbolically conveys dominance and control in communication. According to conflict theory, those with greater resources hold greater power and are in a better position to exert influence over their partners. In general, conflict theorists believe the most important resources are those that place a person in the social class hierarchy, such as income; wealth, including property ownership; educational attainment; and occupation. In dating and marriage relationships, men generally have more resources than women. Power is often displayed through aggressive communication that attempts to dominate and control the partner (Alberti 1978; Phelps and Austin 1987).

According to conflict theory, people give in to partners who threaten or give orders not because they lack communication skills but because they lack resources that provide them with power in a relationship. For example, according to conflict theory, many people give in to a partner's demands because they want to avoid a divorce and a diminished income, or because they fear domestic violence. They may fear being left alone and worry about the possibility of raising children as a single parent. Such worries can lead one partner to acquiesce in the other partner's exercise of power in the relationship.

Equal versus Traditional Partnerships

Aida and Falbo (1991) tested conflict theory by comparing two groups of married couples: "equal partners" and "traditional partners." Equal partners had similar earnings and therefore had a balance of financial resources and relatively equal power in the relationship. Each partner considered the other to be equally responsible for financial support of the family. In contrast, traditional partners had unequal financial resources and unequal power. In traditional partnerships, the husband had prime responsibility for providing the family with financial support. Aida and Falbo (1991) found that couples in these two types of marriages used different communication styles. Women in traditional marriages were more likely to use indirect strategies in problem solving, such as dropping hints and flattering. Women in equal partnerships were more likely to use an assertive approach, stating directly they wanted. The researchers concluded that because men in traditional marriages possess higher status, they simply assume they will get their way. Wives in traditional marriages make the opposite assumption and assume they are not likely to prevail. Therefore, wives in traditional marriages, in which resources and power are unequal, used indirect communication strategies to bolster their position in the relationship.

Symbolic Interaction Theory

Another theory that sheds light on the effect of communication on interpersonal relationships is *symbolic interaction theory*. Symbolic interaction theory states that social communication is accomplished through the use of symbols. The most common use of symbols is found in language. The way we use language as symbols affects the way in which we view reality (Sapir 1949; Whorf 1956). Forty years ago, adult women were frequently called "girls," and adult African-American men were often called "boys." These terms gave the impression that women and African-American men never fully matured into competent adults. The civil rights and feminist movements have pointed out that these labels affect the way we perceive women and African-American men. In addition, social scientists have, at times, been known to reveal their biases in the language they use in presenting research results. For example, some social scientists who study teen sexuality have labeled the behavior of sexually active female teenagers "promiscuous," while calling the same behavior in males "experimental" (Lips 1988). Such language implies that male sexuality is a normal part of growing up but female sexuality is immoral or perhaps even abnormal. A less biased approach is either to label both male and female sexual behavior "experimental" or to use the term "promiscuous" for both male and female sexual behavior. It is important to understand how dramatically these small changes in language can alter our thoughts, attitudes, and concepts of reality.

Communication and the Development of the Self

Communication, both verbal and nonverbal, plays an important role in the development of a person's identity. In family relationships, the words we choose to describe others and our nonverbal reactions to others affect the way family members define themselves and view reality. Both Charles Horton Cooley (1902) and George Herbert Mead (1934), who are known as symbolic interaction theorists, recognized that our self-concept develops through communication with others. A *self-concept* is an image that we hold of ourselves. We develop our self-concept through interpreting feedback that we receive from others. Charles Horton Cooley used the concept of *the looking glass self* to suggest that other people serve as a mirror, or looking glass, for our actions and conversations. We observe other people's reactions to what we say by watching their facial expressions and listening to their comments. We then evaluate our own behavior in terms of their reactions. Through this communication process, we develop either a positive image or a negative image of ourselves.

As with Cooley, the central focus of George Herbert Mead's symbolic interaction theory is the influence of social interaction on the development of the self. George Herbert Mead maintains that the self does not exist at birth. It develops through the process of interacting and communicating with others. George Herbert Mead maintains that the self has two related parts, the "I" and the "me." The "me" is the social part of the self, constituting the social identity of the individual. This includes social roles, such as student, son, employee, and best friend. The "I" is the conscious part of the self that is aware of the person's identity, or "me." The "I" is able to reflect on and think about the self, as when we say, "I'm proud of myself," "I controlled myself," or "I had a talk with myself." According to Mead, identity develops through social interaction during childhood as an individual gradually learns to "take the role of the other." In "taking the role of the other," people learn to anticipate the expectations of others and imagine how others view them. As people communicate with others around them and meet social expectations, they begin to develop a social identity. According to symbolic interaction theory, communication provides symbols through which we influence our perceptions of reality and develop our view of ourselves.

Next, we turn to communication styles that are commonly used when conflict arises.

Review Questions

1. Describe the process by which communication takes place. What is feedback? In what seemingly contradictory ways do people expect to use communication?

TABLE 13.1	Communication Styles	
Assertion	*Aggression*	*Nonassertion*
States feelings, wants, needs	States feelings, wants, needs	Avoids stating feelings, wants, needs
Direct	Direct or indirect	Silent or indirect
Chooses for oneself	Tries to choose for others	Allows others to choose for self
Displays respect for partner	Displays lack of respect for partner (sarcastic or demeaning)	Displays lack of respect for self
Owns feelings	Blames partner for feelings and behavior of self	Accepts blame for partner's feelings and behavior

2. In what ways can nonverbal communication be important in family relationships?

3. How have the attitudes of marriage counselors and social scientists toward marital conflict changed over the years?

4. How does exchange theory explain communication? What are some important rewards that are exchanged through communication?

5. How does conflict theory view communication? What evidence exists to support this theory?

6. According to symbolic interaction theory, how can language affect our perception of reality? What does George Herbert Mead mean by "taking the role of the other"? How does "taking the role of the other" influence a person's self-concept?

Communication Styles

Ideally, communication should allow intimate feelings to emerge from a relationship in which we also feel free to talk about problems, object to our partner's behavior, and initiate change. Herein lies the central dilemma of communication and conflict resolution with someone we love. How can we express grievances within an emotionally supportive communication environment? How can we blend love and conflict into a satisfying relationship? Janice and Mark, whose marital conflict was described at the beginning of this chapter, had little chance of success in resolving their conflict because of the communication style they chose. Successful solutions to problems require people to express their feelings and wants directly to the partner as well as to respond effectively to the partner's criticism.

It is useful to distinguish between three major communication styles commonly used to respond to a partner's grievance or to state a grievance of one's own. They are nonassertion, aggression, and assertion.

Nonassertion

Nonassertive communication involves not stating feelings, wants, ideas, and needs and, instead, withholding and suppressing them. In one case, Randy, a college freshman, and his friend had been accepted for a summer job at a mountain resort. They were excitedly discussing their summer plans when Randy's girlfriend walked up and overheard the conversation. She was upset and said:

> "When am I going to see you? Who will I spend the summer with?" Randy reassured her that she could come to visit on weekends. She continued to object, "What about during the week? I'll be miserable without you." Randy gave a heavy sigh and said, "You're right. I won't go. I'll get a job here for the summer." (Interview by author)

Nonassertion is a self-denying and passive form of communication (Alberti 1978; Baer 1976). Nonassertive people fail to speak up for what they want, or they do so in a hesitant way, allowing events to happen to them. In the above example, Randy is nonassertive when he agrees to give up his summer resort job in response to his girlfriend's objections. Nonassertive communication tends to be associated with three communication problems: gunnysacking, making the assumption of mind reading, and allowing the partner to define the situation.

Gunnysacking. Nonassertive communicators often engage in *gunnysacking* (Bach 1970; Galvin and Brommell 1986). They carry around a mental gunnysack into which they quietly stuff grievances while avoiding discussing those grievances with the other person. Eventually, the gunnysack fills up, and then a *last-straw incident* occurs. This last-straw experience is usually a small incident that creates one too many grievances to fit into the mental gunnysack. The gunnysack bursts and the person explodes in irritation, as Janice did, as we saw at the beginning of the chapter, when she walked into the living room to express her anger over cleaning up the kitchen alone. Afterward, the nonassertive communicator may feel embarrassed for becoming so angry over such a trivial incident, and this chagrin reinforces the tendency to withhold feelings and to continue gunnysacking in the future. Alternatively, nonassertive communicators may turn their feelings of resentment inward and experience a vague feeling of depression (Bloom et al. 1975).

Assumption of Mind Reading. Nonassertive communication may also involve the *assumption of mind reading*, which encourages withholding feelings and thoughts. Nonassertive communicators frequently have the feeling that if the partner truly loved them, the partner would know what the nonassertive person wants and would fill those needs (Satir 1972:52). At the beginning of this chapter, Janice assumed that if Mark loved her he would help with the dishes. In reality, a partner rarely knows what a person wants unless that person tells the partner, so the nonassertive person inevitably experiences disappointment. In fact, living with a nonassertive communicator can be a frustrating experience. This is especially true for the person who genuinely wants the partner to be happy in a reciprocal relationship in which the two partners meet each other's needs.

Definition of the Situation. Nonassertive communicators often allow the partner to define the situation. The *definition of the situation* refers to the perspective on the situation which is treated as representing reality (Thomas 1966). When a person defines the situation as one in which the nonassertive partner is to blame, often the nonassertive partner does not speak up and object. By not speaking up, nonassertive communicators allow the impression to remain that they have caused

Some partners assume that they do not have to explain to each other how they feel. This often leads to a breakdown in communication.

the problem. In the following case, John was on crutches with an injured foot. He phoned his girlfriend, Meagan, and asked her to drive downtown and pick him up, giving her detailed instructions on which streets to take. Meagan took a different route to the agreed-upon meeting place. While driving, she saw John attempting to run with his crutches. He opened the car door and began yelling at her:

> "I can't believe how stupid you are! You never do what I tell you to do. I walked a block to help you out so you could pick me up sooner. If you had gone the way I told you, you would have seen me! But no, you had to go around a different way and make me run on my hurt leg. Sometimes you really don't think!" Meagan didn't reply. Instead, she started to bite her lip and her eyes started to tear. (Interview by author)

Meagan felt hurt by John's definition of the situation, which saw her as the cause of the problem. However, she tacitly accepted the blame by refusing to offer her own definition of the situation. Nonassertive communication is not an effective means of problem-solving. When the nonassertive communicator declines to express feelings or grievances, problems in the relationship remain unresolved.

Unlike nonassertive communicators, who allow conflict to be resolved in a manner that does not meet their needs, aggressive communicators often get their way. However, aggressive communicators pay a high cost in terms of low relationship quality.

Aggressive Communication

Aggressive communication expresses feelings, wants, ideas, and needs in a way that attempts to dominate, control, and even humiliate the partner (Alberti 1978; Phelps and Austin 1987). In our example at the beginning of the chapter,

Janice was aggressive when she walked into the living room and called Mark selfish for not sharing the kitchen cleanup. Mark aggressively counterattacked when he told Janice that she was lazy. Communication theorists have identified four forms that aggressive communication typically takes: blaming, demeaning, making threats and giving orders, and coercive escalation.

Blaming. Aggressive communicators blame the partner for problems in the relationship and for their own misbehavior (Stets 1990; Zuker 1983:13). Blaming involves refusing to take responsibility for one's feelings, statements, and actions. In the case below, Katherine's husband complained that when he comes home, he frequently smells alcohol on his wife's breath. Katherine responded,

> Why should you care? You're hardly ever home. I'm the one who has to stay home alone with the kids all day. Besides, you don't offer me any emotional support, so the only thing to do is drink.

Katherine's refusal to take responsibility for her drinking behavior and her attempt to place the blame for her excessive drinking on her husband constitutes aggressive communication. One of the first steps in recovering from alcoholism is to begin to take responsibility for one's own behavior.

Demeaning. Demeaning shows a lack of respect for the other person and usually takes the form of name-calling, as when parents call their children "stupid" or "crazy." Name-calling is used to criticize and humiliate the partner in aggressive communication (Baer 1976:21). At the beginning of this chapter both Janice and Mark used pejorative names when they called each other "selfish" and "lazy."

Aggressive, demeaning statements are often used to control the other person's behavior. The National Family Violence Re-Survey revealed that over 99 percent of cases of physical violence began with verbal aggression (Stets 1990). It appears that violent partners attempt to control their mate's behavior first through verbal coercion, and when that fails they move on to physical violence. (We discuss domestic violence more fully in Chapter 14.)

Giving Orders and Making Threats. Attempts to control by giving orders, telling the partner what to do, and making threats are aggressive (Morton 1981:20). Statements that begin with, "You better not . . . ," "You should . . . " and "I'm warning you . . . " are typically aggressive in a relationship between equals. Pamela described her husband's response when she wore a sundress with a fitted bodice and a full skirt to a party:

> When we got home, Brian told me to take off the dress and never wear it again. I asked him if he was joking, and I told him that I would decide what I wear and don't wear. He grabbed me and said, "You'll wear what I tell you to wear, understand!" I very clearly understood. I nodded and said, "Okay. Okay." (Interview by author)

Aggressive communicators attempt to impose their definition of the situation on the partner. In the above example, Brian felt that Pamela was at fault for wearing a partially fitted dress that revealed her figure. He used demands and an implied threat to control her behavior. She reluctantly accepted his criticism and allow him to define the situation as one in which she was wrong.

Aggressive communicators often combine ordering, blaming, and demeaning into one message. After Semantha returned to college her husband complained:

Going back to college is another selfish, stupid idea of yours. You don't spend enough time with the kids as it is. And if you don't spend some time with me instead of with your books, I'm going to find someone who will spend time with me.

Name-calling has the effect of reinforcing the attempt to dominate. The self-worth of the demeaned person is called into question at the same time that the demeaned person is ordered to change behavior. The partners of aggressive communicators often have the feeling that if they just try harder to change and please the partner, approval and love will be forthcoming (Norwood 1985:20). What these partners often do not understand is that aggression is a communication style whose content may change without the communicator changing the pattern of communication. Changing to meet the aggressive communicator's demands does not necessarily end the aggression.

Even when a person is emotionally strong enough to stand up to the partner, aggressive communication can take a toll on the relationship, as the discussion of coercive escalation below shows.

Coercive Escalation. Aggressive communication is rarely effective in problem solving because it puts the partner on the defensive and is likely to produce *coercive escalation*. Coercive escalation refers to a string of attacks followed by counterattacks. Halford (1990) and his colleagues compared happily married couples to unhappily married couples and discovered that unhappy marriages were likely to be characterized by coercive escalation. In unhappy marriages, a negative comment about the partner was likely to produce a sequence of attack statements followed by counterattacks. Once begun, the negative exchange was very likely to continue. In contrast, happily married couples rarely engaged in coercive escalation. Happily married couples tended to avoid starting a negative chain of statements by avoiding the first aggressive statement that sets off coercive escalation. In addition, happily married couples tended to diffuse negative interchanges once they began. They were likely to follow an aggressive statement with a neutral statement rather than a counterattack (Halford 1990).

Some couples go back and forth between using nonassertive communication and aggressive communication. These couples tend to withdraw and avoid conflict and then are very likely to follow the pattern of coercive escalation when open conflict finally does erupt. Because these couples experience conflict as painful, they attempt to avoid it (Krokoff et al. 1988). Couples with this communication pattern carry a high risk of breaking up because they "never develop confidence that they can weather conflict together" (Krokoff et al. 1988:218). These high-risk couples avoid conflict and then get caught in a coercive escalation of attacks and counterattacks when open conflict begins.

It is unusual for aggressive communication to solve a problem in a way that satisfies both partners. After several rounds of attack and counterattack statements, the couple have usually moved the discussion so far away from the initial problem that they have often forgotten what the original issue was and, therefore, have little hope of resolving the problem. A more effective way to resolve conflict and retain positive feelings toward the other person is to use assertive communication.

Assertion

Our interactions with people are affected by the style of communication we use. A number of communication theorists argue that assertion is the communication style most likely to resolve a conflict successfully. In addition, assertive communication promotes a positive and supportive relationship. *Assertive communication* states feelings and wants directly, with honesty, and without depreciating other people (Alberti 1978:27; Morton et al. 1981:18). Many people are reluctant to assert themselves because they confuse assertion and aggression, and yet there are important differences between these two forms of communication. Assertion shows respect for the partner, whereas aggression is demeaning. Assertive communicators use "I" statements, own feelings, and take responsibility for their words and actions, whereas aggressive communicators blame their feelings and behavior on the partner. Perhaps most important, assertive communicators are willing to state grievances and request changes in the partner's behavior, but they realize that their partners are autonomous, self-directed individuals. Assertive communicators recognize that they cannot force change on the partner, even though change is strongly desired. The assertive communicator makes requests; the aggressive communicator attempts to grab power by giving orders and sometimes even by making threats.

Just as assertive communicators recognize the limits on their influence, they also refuse to hand over power to the partner by choosing to be nonassertive. In a relationship in which there are two assertive communicators, discussion takes place and grievances are expressed within an atmosphere of mutual trust and respect.

It is sometimes more difficult to be assertive with someone we love than it is to be assertive with a stranger, for example, one who has cut in front of the line at a store. We often fear that assertion will leave people we love hurt or angry and drive them away. While there are no guarantees that hurt or angry feelings in the partner will be avoided, assertive communication diminishes the risk of this outcome. Using some or all of the components of an assertive statement can help a person overcome reluctance to address problems in a relationship.

Components of an Assertive Statement

An empathetic assertive statement in a loving relationship typically has three components: a bonding statement, "I" statements, and a conclusion. These components are shown in Table 13.2.

Bonding Statement

Many people can overcome their reluctance to be assertive in a romance, a friendship, or a family relationship by beginning their assertion with a bonding statement. A bonding statement shows that a person values the relationship and wants the relationship to con-

When we can state our feelings and wants directly, we can constructively solve problems.

TABLE 13.2	Components of an Empathetic Assertive Statement	
Component	*Definition*	*Example: Janice's Option*
Bonding statement	Empathy statement, or statement that shows the relationship is valued	"I realize you are tired when you come home from work."
"I" statement	Statement of feelings and concerns	"But I'm tired too, and when I am here in the kitchen alone, I feel overworked, abandoned, and frustrated."
Conclusion statement	Asking for what you want OR saying "No," OR telling the partner what you plan to do	"I want us to share the clean-up job after dinner. I would like for both of us to stay in the kitchen until the dishes are done, the food is put away, and the kitchen is neat."

tinue (Zuker 1983:132). An example of a bonding statement is an expression of empathy. Empathy involves putting oneself in the other person's shoes and imagining what the situation looks like from the perspective of that person. However, empathy is not the same as sympathy. In *sympathy,* a person feels what the partner is feeling. One person hurts when the other person hurts. A person's identity becomes blurred with the partner's identity. *Empathy* is a distinct and separate experience from sympathy. In empathy, a person understands how the partner feels, but does not let that empathy erase her or his own feelings: "We don't necessarily have to agree with other people's viewpoints—we merely have to understand and accept those viewpoints as theirs. . . " (Zuker 1983). When people empathize, they are able momentarily to see the situation through the other person's eyes without losing sight of their own views and feelings.

"I" Statements

"I" statements express a person's thoughts and feelings from a personal perspective and usually begin with "I feel. . . ," "I wish. . . ," "I think. . . ," or "I want. . . ." Phrasing feelings in this way has been associated with direct and positive communication (Gordon and Snyder 1989). Such statements open a window into the speaker's thoughts and provide an opportunity for the other person to empathize with the speaker. In the case of Janice and Mark, at the beginning of this chapter, Janice could have reworded her complaint by saying, "When I get home from work I'm tired, too. When I'm in the kitchen alone, I feel overworked and abandoned." The focus of attention is on the speaker when "I" statements are used. Such statements are useful vehicles for working through conflicts because they reveal the speaker's thoughts without attacking the partner.

"I" statements can be useful in parent–child relationships. Instead of saying to a child, "Don't be lazy! Put your shoes on. You're going to make us late!" which makes accusations, a parent could use an "I" statement and say, "I'm worried that we may be late so you need to put your shoes on right away."

The expression of empathy helps to bond couples.

Using "I" statements will often diffuse tension that could lead to parent–child conflict. This does not mean that children will always respond as the parent desires. However, "I" statements encourage children to empathize with parents, and many children are thus motivated to help out.

Anger and Resentment. At the beginning of this chapter, we saw both Janice and Mark use "You" statements, criticizing each other's personality and calling motivations into question. "You" statements, such as, "You're so selfish, " or "You're just lazy," encourage counterattacks from the partner. As counterattacks emerge, the couple often become so caught up in the argument that they lose sight of the initial problem that started the argument in the first place.

In our case of Janice and Mark, Janice probably also feels resentful. Resentment can be expressed directly, for example, "I feel resentful when you walk out of the kitchen and I have to do the dishes alone." However, communication theorists disagree about the value of expressing anger and resentment in conflict resolution (Bach and Goldberg 1974; Green and Donnerstein 1983; Tavris 1982). It is often useful to keep expressions of resentment and anger in reserve, at least in the early stages of conflict resolution. Uncontrolled anger can take a discussion off the track and fog a person's vision, making it difficult to focus on the problem at hand and explore possible solutions. Furthermore, many conflicts can be resolved by focusing on the emotions that preceded the resentment and led to it, such as Janice's feelings of being tired, overworked, and abandoned. These earlier emotions, which preceded feelings of resentment, are likely to be the feelings with which a spouse or dating partner can empathize.

For some people, the expression of anger is an automatic response that sidesteps the difficult, but growth-producing, task of looking for the feelings that preceded and caused the anger. These people experience their emotions like a stone skipping across water. The stone lands briefly on earlier feelings (of being overworked and abandoned), but because the person does not focus on these feelings they are quickly lost to consciousness. The stone continues to skip through the emotional repertoire until it lands on anger, and that anger becomes the emotion expressed in the interaction. The partner often sees anger as a punitive and threatening emotion, and this creates emotional distance within the relationship.

Owning Feelings. Feelings can be disclosed in a way that encourages open communication or in a way that shuts off communication. Communication theorists point out that when people "own feelings," they take responsibility for their feelings and identify those feelings as coming from inside the self (Alberti et al. 1978:35; Phelps and Austin 1987:55). People who own feelings usually begin sentences with "I feel. . . ," rather than with "You make me feel. . . ." For example, if a speaker says, "You make me feel like a maid," the speaker is portrayed as a passive person, acted upon by the outside world. This statement conveys a sense of powerlessness in that the speaker views feelings as being caused by others. Rewording the statement to "I feel like a maid," makes it appear to both partners that the feelings were generated inside the speaker. This puts the speaker in charge of his or her own feelings.

The words people use affect their perception of the world around them (Sapir 1949; Whorf 1956). Likewise, the terms people choose to express their thoughts affect their self-perception (Beck and Burns 1979; Ellis 1973; Mischel 1973). For example, if Michelle, a college student, says to her dating partner, "When you call me an 'airhead', you make me feel stupid," she sees her partner as causing the feelings of stupidity. If she rewords the statement to say, "When you call me an 'airhead,' I feel stupid," Michelle gains ownership of her feelings. She now acknowledges that those feelings are generated within herself. She therefore has the flexibility to reevaluate her feelings and think, "Wait a minute. Why should I feel stupid? My partner was the one who was rude. Maybe I feel insulted instead of stupid." In this example, owning feelings allowed emotional experience to flow from one feeling to another. The benefit of owning feelings also extends to the partner. The partner can see the other person's reaction to the conversation without feeling blamed or threatened. Table 13.3 shows how statements can be reworded so as to take responsibility for one's feelings.

The Conclusion to an Assertive Statement

The last part of an empathetic assertive statement is the conclusion, which has three major uses: asking for what you want or need, saying "no" to a request, or stating what you plan to do.

TABLE 13.3	Perception of Feelings
"You" statements	*"I" statements*
Feelings will be perceived as caused by the partner	Owning feelings: Feelings will be perceived as arising in the self
You make me feel stupid.	I feel stupid.
You drive me crazy.	I feel frustrated and confused.
You hurt me.	I feel hurt.
You infuriate me.	I feel angry.
You ruined my life.	I feel like my life is falling apart.

Asking for What You Want. In the conversation at the beginning of this chapter, Janice should ask for what she wants by asking Mark to participate in the kitchen cleanup.

Saying "No" to a Request. For example, if one partner objects to the other partner's plan to spend next Friday night with friends, the partner who wants to see friends could say, "I realize you would like me to cancel my plans so I can be with you, and we do have a good time when we are out together [bonding]. But I haven't seen my friends in a long time, and I've missed them ["I" statements]. So I can't go out with you on Friday night [conclusion].

Stating What You Plan to Do. Recall the situation described earlier, in which Semantha returned to college and her husband complained that she spent more time with school books than with him. Semantha could respond assertively by saying "I know you have been lonely since I went back to college [empathy]. But my education is important to me, and I do need to study. But that doesn't mean I don't love you ["I" statements]. I plan to continue college and complete my degree, and what I want from you is your support and encouragement" [conclusion].

When constructing a conclusion to an assertive statement, it is always a good idea for speakers to ask themselves what they want from the other person and what they want to be the outcome of the assertive interaction. For example, it is more useful for a parent to say to a child, "It bothers me to have to step over these toys. I want them cleaned up before dinner," than for the same parent to complain, "This room is a mess! It looks like a pig lives here!" The second statement lacks a conclusion and fails to tell the child specifically what the parent wants. Because a conclusion to an assertive statement is based on the speaker's feelings and wants, one person's conclusion will be different from another person's, even though the problem addressed may be the same. Just as one person's wants and needs differ from another person's, so will their assertive statements differ. For example, if Janice is feeling overwhelmed by too much work, she would ask Mark to share the kitchen cleanup. On the other hand, if she feels satisfied with Mark's contribution to the marriage, but feels lonely in the kitchen, she might ask him to sit and talk with her in the kitchen while she does the dishes. What is important in making the assertion is for speakers to match their conclusion with their own personal feelings and desires.

The conclusion is important because it is the component that gives the assertive statement power. Without the conclusion, the "I feel" statements, such as "I feel abandoned," can sound like whining. The conclusion changes a whining statement into a powerful statement. It expresses the speaker's autonomy (independence and self-direction), ability to make decisions, and need to stand up for himself or herself. The conclusion focuses the discussion on problem solving. Without a conclusion, the partner recognizes a complaint but is left wondering how to solve the problem.

Next we will turn to an examination of conflict and family roles.

Review Questions

1. What is nonassertion and what are its disadvantages? What is gunnysacking and why do nonassertive communicators engage in it?
2. What is the assumption of mind reading and what impact does it have on a relationship? What is meant by the definition of the situation and how does

the situation tend to be defined in a relationship that includes a nonassertive communicator?

3. What is aggressive communication and what forms does it usually take? What is coercive escalation and why is it a problem?

4. What are the characteristics of assertive communication?

5. What are the components of an empathetic assertive statement? What is meant by "I" statements? What elements are included in the conclusion of an assertive statement? What is the value of having a conclusion to an assertive statement?

Conflict and Family Roles

In an unusual study of family conflict, Vuchinich (1987) took a video camera into the homes of fifty-two families and taped their dinner-table conversations. The sample contained all social classes as well as both African-Americans and whites, and urban and rural families. All families consisted of a mother, father, son, and daughter. Vuchinich recorded each conflict initiation statement made by a family member; such statements included accusations, insults, and disagreements. When another family member responded with an opposing statement, Vuchinich recorded that a conflict had occurred. He found that not all conflict initiation statements resulted in an argument. One-third, or 36 percent, of the conflict initiation statements were either ignored or followed by a nonconflicting response. Vuchinich argues that effective conflict management in families may involve striking a balance between, on the one hand, avoiding conflict by ignoring the initiator's statement and, on the other hand, challenging the conflict initiator's statement. In the families he studied there was a "one-third avoid to two-thirds fight" ratio between avoiding conflict and engaging in it.

BOX 13.2 — A Closer Look

Suggestions for Negotiating a Solution to a Conflict

1. Stick to the present problem. Avoid bringing in past grievances.

2. Be specific in stating your grievance. Avoid such statements as, "You always. . . " and "You never. . . ."

3. Use "I" statements to explain your position.

4. Empathize with your partner's position without losing sight of your own position.

5. Take responsibility for your feelings and behavior. Don't blame the partner for causing your feelings and behavior.

6. State what you want from your partner, for example, "What I would like is for you to let me finish what I have to say before you give your opinion."

7. Avoid giving orders, such as "You should. . . " or "You better do what I say."

8. Discuss your partner's behavior without discussing your partner's personality. "I was worried and upset when you came home at 2 A.M." is preferable to, "If you weren't so insensitive and irresponsible you wouldn't stay out so late."

9. Suggest alternative solutions. View your partner's position as a starting point for negotiation rather than as an immutable position.

Methods for Stopping Conflict

Vuchinich identified four methods family members used to stop conflict or to stop the sequence of opposition statements.

Submission. In submission, one person "gives in" and agrees with the other person. Submission has the disadvantage of causing a "loss of face," which can have a negative impact on a participant's self-image. Conflict was ended by submission in about one-fifth of the conflicts.

Compromise. Compromise involves finding a "middle ground" in which both parties give in to some extent. Compromise, the most complicated solution, requires the most effort; only 14 percent of the conflicts ended in compromise.

Withdrawal. In withdrawal, one person refuses to talk and sometimes leaves the room. Withdrawal is disruptive and implies that the group cannot sustain civil conversation. Only 4 percent of the conflicts ended in withdrawal.

Standoff. In a standoff, the combatants drop the subject and implicitly "agree to disagree." They simply move on to another topic of conversation. The standoff was the most popular option with the majority of conflicts, 61 percent, ending in this manner. The standoff avoids the difficulties and disadvantages of the other options.

Social Roles and Conflict

Vuchinich looked at the frequency with which each social role—mother, father, son, or daughter—initiated conflict. There was an overall egalitarian pattern of conflict initiation, with all family members exhibiting conflict initiation rights. Parents and children each initiated about half of the conflicts, and males were as likely to initiate

Sometimes our body language reveals as much as, or more than, our words. What can you tell about this couple's relationship from their nonverbal communication?

conflicts as were females. Mothers, sons, and daughters all received about the same number of conflict initiations. However, family members tended to avoid initiating conflict with fathers. Children initiated conflict with mothers twice as often as they initiated conflict with fathers. Fathers appeared to have superior status in the family; this status kept them more insulated from conflict attacks than other family members.

Mothers played an important part in conflict management. They took an active role in ending conflict by suggesting compromises and changing the subject of conversation when a standoff occurred. In other words, mothers initiated new, nonconflict topics of conversation at the end of an argument and kept the conversation flowing smoothly. Daughters were second only to the mothers in this peacemaker role. The females of the family encouraged the verbal combatants to drop the dispute and move on to new topics of conversation.

Next we turn to communication problems that are particularly troublesome in families and in romantic relationships.

Communication Problems

Certain communication problems are especially challenging for those who are confronted with them. In this section we explore four such problems: invalidation, indirect communication, manipulation and double messages.

BOX 13.3   **A Closer Look**

Responding to an Angry Family Member

There are three steps to an effective assertive response to anger: acknowledging the anger, listening to the complaint, and evaluating the criticism.

Acknowledge the Anger

Acknowledging another person's anger often calms the partner down by letting the partner know the angry complaint has been heard. The expression of a partner's anger is also an opportunity to set conditions for discussion of the grievance (Phelps and Austin 1987:161). For example, a person could say, "I realize you are angry, and I would like to discuss the problem with you. But I can't talk to you about it until you stop shouting."

Listen to the Complaint

Many people quickly refute a complaint before they have had a chance to hear and understand the grievance. A person needs to apply empathetic skills in order to understand the problem from the mate's perspective. A person can listen actively by paraphrasing the partner's complaint (Zuker 1983:132). For example, "I realize you are angry at me because I decided not to go to the dinner party at your mother's house." Listening actively and providing feedback lets the mate know the complaint has been heard.

Evaluate the Criticism

After a complaint has been heard and acknowledged, criticized partners should decide what part of the criticism they consider to be fair and valid and what part they feel is unfair and invalid (Baer 1976:23). By going through this sorting process, criticized partners can take responsibility for validly criticized behavior. For example, a partner could say, "I realize it caused you difficulty when I forgot to pick up the kids from day care. I won't forget in the future." Likewise, partners can assertively object to the portion of criticism that they feel is invalid and unfair. For example, "But I object to being called irresponsible. I am usually very responsible about taking care of the children's needs." Learning to respond effectively to anger takes much of the fear out of facing an angry person. Responding effectively and assertively to an angry family member can be useful in resolving family conflict.

Invalidation

Bloom (1975) points out that one goal in assertive communication is to preserve the dignity of both partners. She argues that every individual has assertive rights. The two most basic rights are

1. the right to be treated with respect, and
2. the right to have and to express your own feelings.

Both of these rights are at the core of the definition of assertion. The respect shown for the partner is what distinguishes assertion from aggression. Furthermore, without the right to express feelings there could be no assertion, because assertion is fundamentally self-expression.

Bloom points to a commonly used aggressive tactic in which the aggressive partner belittles the mate, thereby violating the mate's right to be treated with respect. When the demeaned partner objects, the aggressive communicator switches tactics and attempts to invalidate the partner's feelings by saying, "You're too sensitive," "You're overreacting," or "You shouldn't feel that way." *Invalidation* involves convincing partners that their feelings are not valid and should not exist or be expressed. Invalidation violates the demeaned partner's right to have and express feelings.

Bloom ran a series of assertiveness training groups in which clients talked about their difficulties with assertion over the week and received advice from the therapist and the group. Rachel was a plump, single woman who participated in one of Bloom's groups. She had gone to a party over the weekend. While she was standing at the dessert table eating a piece of chocolate cake, her friend Donna came up to her and said, "Rachel, you must be Weight Watchers worst failure" (p. 35). When Rachel objected to being teased about her weight, Donna replied, ". . . Sometimes I think you're too sensitive. . . . I'm sorry I hurt you, but you know . . . you really shouldn't feel that way" (Bloom 1975:35). Rachel's assertiveness training group came up with this hypothetical response to Donna's aggressive remarks:

> Donna, I don't like you to tease me. I know you apologized for it, but right now you're telling me to stop being so sensitive. I do have this sore spot, and I'm angry that you're telling me I shouldn't have it. . . . (Bloom 1975:36–37)

Rachel then went on to say that she wanted Donna to stop teasing her. Assertive communicators refuse to allow their feelings to be invalidated by others. Assertive communicators have the satisfaction of knowing that they have stated their opinions, stood up for themselves, and expressed their feelings and thoughts.

Indirect Communication

In indirect communication, speakers use hints and implied messages to state their thoughts. Unlike assertive communication which is direct and to the point, indirect communication consists of talking around the issue. Listeners must draw their own conclusions about the actual intent of the message; thus a good deal of room is left for an inaccurate interpretation.

Indirect communication can be nonassertive, as, for example, in the case of a woman who wants her new husband to spend more time with her son (his stepson). She says, "Justin has seemed so lonely lately." The husband could easily misinterpret her message and think that the boy needs friends his own age. When he responds, "That's a shame," but makes no offer to spend time with his stepson, the wife is likely to feel upset and angry. A more direct statement would be, "I would like for you and Justin to spend more time together. It would be nice if you would plan a specific activity to do with Justin." Indirect communication can also be aggressive. For example, if the wife said, "You sure don't seem to like kids," this would be an aggressive indirect statement.

To cope with the confusion caused by indirect statements, a person can ask for clarification. For example, the husband whose wife says, "Justin has seemed so lonely lately," could ask, "Is there something you would like me to do to help him feel less lonely?" Asking for clarification helps the partner to become more direct in stating needs and desires.

Manipulation

Manipulation involves indirect messages in a way that combines hints with an effort to control the partner's behavior. There is a hidden agenda in manipulation; the speaker has an unstated goal that she or he seeks to accomplish by manipulation. In manipulation there are two levels of messages: a verbal message and an underlying implied message that is not verbalized (Phelps and Austin 1987:130). The manipulator hopes the partner will respond to the implied message rather than to the spoken message:

> Jim and Susan were in the habit of shopping for food each afternoon before Susan cooked dinner. One afternoon in the grocery store, Susan said she wanted to cook chicken and vegetables for dinner that night. Jim objected, saying he did not like chicken and vegetables and wanted her to cook macaroni and cheese instead. Susan explained that she wanted to start having a healthier diet and did not want to cook macaroni and cheese. He responded, "Well then, I just won't eat." (Interview by author)

Jim's verbal declaration that he won't eat is emotionally dishonest and not meant to be taken at its face value. Jim hopes Susan will respond to his implied message: that he wants her to change the menu. One effective way to respond to manipulation is through what Phelps and Austin (1987) call counter-manipulation. In *counter-manipulation,* the partner responds only to the verbal message. The implied message is ignored. By responding in this manner, a person can avoid being manipulated through guilt:

> When Jim stated that he would not eat, Susan counter-manipulated by taking his statement at face value and saying, "All right." He escalated with, "I'm hungry. I haven't eaten since breakfast. But you go ahead and cook chicken and vegetables. I won't eat." She then asserted herself, saying, "I enjoy your company at dinner, but whether or not you eat is up to you. I'm concerned about my diet and I'm cooking chicken and vegetables." (Interview by author)

Jim did not eat that night, nor did he cook an alternative dinner for himself. Instead of feeling guilty and giving in, Susan followed through with her counter-manipulation by allowing Jim to experience the natural consequences of his decision not to eat, namely, that he had to contend with his hunger. *Natural consequences* are consequences that would naturally result from our decisions and behavior if no one else jumped in to save us from those consequences (Driekers 1972:61). Jim attempted unsuccessfully to manipulate Susan, and he found he had to face the consequences of his decision by either coping with his hunger or cooking a separate dinner for himself.

Double Messages

Double messages are two or more contradictory messages from a single person. The conflicting messages may be either two verbal messages or a verbal statement that conflicts with a nonverbal message, as when a person says, "I'm interested in what you're saying," in a flat, disinterested way while watching television. One problem double messages present for the listener is that no matter what course of action the listener takes, the partner cannot be pleased (Watzlawick 1968:77). People receiving conflicting messages often feel trapped, as if there were no way out, no acceptable choice open to them. For example, the child who is playing quietly across the room from his mother hears her say, "You're always off to yourself. You're so unfriendly." The child gets up and goes over to talk to the mother and then she snaps, "You're always under my feet. I can't get anything done with you here." Children who receive double messages are left feeling that they will be wrong no matter what they do. The way to cope with double messages is to comment on the fact that conflicting messages are being sent. This is difficult for children to do without special help. It is also difficult for battered women to do because their safety is a primary concern. However, in the following interview Laura, who had been periodically battered, stood her ground and pointed out to her partner that he had been sending double messages. Laura had been traveling with her boyfriend, Bill, who was a guitarist with a band. One night while she was watching her boyfriend's performance, he told her she should dance in order to encourage others to dance to his music. She danced with another man.

> At the break Bill came over to Laura and said, "What do you think you're doing? You're just cheap. Did you forget that you were with someone?" Laura snapped, "I was just doing what you asked." His voice became louder as he said, "I told you to dance, not to flirt with the guys. You know, just because I'm on stage doesn't mean I can't leave it [the stage] if I want to. Just give me a reason like you always do! [implied threat of violence] Laura retorted, "I don't like to dance by myself, if that's what you mean. So, I either dance with someone else or I don't dance at all!" Bill just sat there and looked at Laura. Something she said sunk in, and for a moment he realized what he was doing. He leaned over and kissed her and without saying a word, turned and joined the band. It was never brought up again and Laura stopped dancing, feeling that she really didn't enjoy it any more. (Interview by author)

Laura pointed out Bill's contradictory messages and stood up for herself. But the hint of violence limited her willingness to be assertive in the future, and she lost her interest in dancing.

Effective communication can improve the quality of a relationship as well as the self-esteem of the partners.

Review Questions

1. In Vuchinich's study of family dinner-table conversations, what methods of stopping conflict did families use? Which method was used most often?

2. In terms of the pattern of family conflict found in Vuchinich's study, in what way was the father role different from other roles in the family? What role did mothers and daughters play in conflict management?

3. What is invalidation? Give an example of invalidation.

4. What is indirect communication? Give an example of indirect communication?

5. What is manipulation? Give an example of manipulation.

6. What is counter-manipulation? Give an example of counter-manipulation.

7. What are double messages? Give an example of double messages.

Summary

1. Communication involves sending and receiving messages.

2. Conflict involves the exchange of opposing messages.

3. Exchange theory examines the rewards or benefits provided by communication, such as empathy and expressions of appreciation, as well as the costs, such as upset feelings after "put downs."

4. Conflict theory looks at how communication can be used to dominate and control others, thereby maintaining relationships of dominance and subordination.

5. Symbolic interaction theory looks at the way communication uses words as symbols to label our experience and influence our perception of reality.

6. George Herbert Mead points out that the "self" develops through the process of communication and social interaction.

7. Three communication styles commonly used in conflict situations are nonassertion, aggression, and assertion.

8. Nonassertive communication is passive. It frequently involves gunnysacking, makes the assumption of mind-reading, and allows the other person to define the situation.

9. Aggressive communication frequently involves blaming, demeaning, controlling through orders and threats, and coercive escalation.

10. Assertive communication directly expresses feelings, wants, and needs while respecting the other person.

11. The three components of an empathetic assertive statement are a bonding statement, "I" statements, and a conclusion.

12. Vuchinich's study of family dinner table-conversation found four commonly used methods for stopping conflict: submission, compromise, withdrawal, and standoff. Mothers and fathers differ in their use of these methods.

13. Communication problems include invalidation, indirect communication, manipulation, and double messages.

Key Words

Communication
Conflict
Empathy
Symbolic Interaction Theory
Gunnysacking
Assumption of Mind-Reading
Aggression
Assertion
Owning Feelings
Invalidation
Manipulation
Natural Consequences

Feedback
Exchange Theory
Conflict Theory
Nonassertion
Last-Straw-Incident
Definition of the Situation
Coercive Escalation
"I" Statements
Stonewalling
Indirect Communication
Counter-manipulation
Double Messages

Resources

Center for Nonviolent Communication
3229 Bordeaux
Sherman, TX 75090
(214) 893-3886
Helps people avoid communication patterns that can lead to verbally and physically abusive outcomes.
Publishes *Newsletter to Soulmates,* quarterly.

Children's Creative Response to Conflict Resolution
523 N. Broadway
P.O. Box 271
Nyack, NY 10960
(914) 358-4601
Runs workshops to help children live peacefully with others by learning to resolve conflict.

Conflict Resolution/Alternatives to Violence Training Center
P.O. Box 256
Ricker House
Cherryfield, ME 04622
(207) 546-2789
Trains people to use communication skills as an alternative to violence.

Global Learning
1018 Stuyvesant Ave.
Union, NJ 07083
(201) 964-1114
Offers workshops on developing conflict resolution skills.
Publishes *Gleanings,* newsletter.

National Marriage Encounter
4704 Jamerson Place
Orlando, FL 32807
(407) 277-8079
Runs weekend programs for married couples, organized by married couples and clergy. Holds retreats that encourage communication.
Publishes *National Encounter Newsletter,* quarterly.

Family Challenges

Chapter 14

Family Abuse and Violence

Laura's story: When I met Burt, he seemed like the nicest guy: attentive, interested in me, and easy to talk to. Our problems began at a party one night when Burt went off to another room to drink and get stoned. In the car on the way home, Burt grabbed my purse and dumped it out on the floor. He said he was looking for phone numbers of the guys who he said I had been flirting with. Then he accused me of wanting to sleep with several of the guys at the party. Any defense I tried to give resulted in him calling me a "guilty bitch." I was very frightened because I had never heard Burt get so angry. I curled up into a ball with my back to him as he ranted and raved. He pushed me against the door, banging my head against the window, and then turned me around to face him. He started pounding on the dashboard, saying how much he loved me and asking me how could I betray him. When I tried to tell him what really happened, he called me a liar.

I didn't want to see Burt again. But the next day while I was having lunch, Burt showed up with a large bouquet with a red ribbon around it. He begged me to forgive him, saying he wanted to make up for the horrible way he had treated me. Now I was confused. It was as though the other night had never happened, and the guy in the car had been another person. I decided to give Burt one more chance. Afterward, he was really sweet for a long time and I moved into his apartment.

We had been living together for several months when we got in a heated argument over his desire to have female friends in our apartment. I had told him I did not want him entertaining other women when I was at work, yet it had happened anyway the previous week. I said, "You can do what you want with your life, but I don't want to put up with it anymore. I'm leaving." Burt said nothing, but threw me down on the bed and started hitting me. I remember lying there wondering if he was going to break anything. When he was done, he fell to his knees and started crying. That was the only time I have ever seen him cry. He said, "Why did you make me do this to you?" and he left the apartment.

Instead of focusing on what he had just done to me, I only saw his tears and heard what he had said. I felt sorry for him and wondered what I had done to make him hit me. That night I went to bed feeling hurt and bewildered. One of the main reasons I didn't leave him was that I was afraid all those awful things he said about me were true, and that he was the only man that would ever love me. I thought to myself that if I had caused him to hit me, then I must also be able to make the relationship better.

After several more violent incidents, I moved out in a hurry, leaving my belongings behind. I later arranged to go to his apartment to pick up the rest of my things. When I got there he handed me a laundry basket containing my belongings. As I reached for it, he pulled it back slowly and turned it upside-down spilling its contents on the floor. I watched my stuffed animals, with holes in them and stuffing pulled out, and some clothes, torn into small pieces, fall to the floor. He said, "You owe me for the pain you've caused, and I'm going to take it out of your hide." I was terrified. He raised his arm to hit me but instead pushed me down on the bed, and I let him have sex with me. Afterward, I quickly straightened my clothes and ran out of the apartment door. Now I have an answering machine and I don't respond to his phone calls. (Interview by author.)

People expect to feel safe and nurtured in love relationships. However, romance and family relationships can be fraught with physical hazards. The United States is one of the most violent nations in the world, and courtship and family violence is now recognized to be a serious social problem (Barnes et al. 1991). *Violence* is an act committed with the intention of causing physical pain or injury. Using a nationally representative sample of over 3,500 couples, Straus and Gelles (1986) found that approximately one out of ten American wives and husbands experience violence at the hands of their spouses each year, ranging in intensity from a shove to an assault with a weapon. Three percent of wives report experiencing severe violence, which includes being hit with an object, beaten, kicked, or threatened with a knife or gun. These assaults often result in injury. Over one-third of women who are treated in emergency rooms have received their injuries at the hands of a husband or boyfriend (Barnes et al. 1991). Children are also likely to be targets of domestic violence. One out of every seven children has experienced physical discipline that goes beyond a simple spanking and includes being hit with a fist, belt, or stick. In fact, violence tends to spread through a family, so that both the spouse and children become targets.

In this chapter we explore physical abuse in marriage and dating relationships and physical and sexual abuse in parent–child relationships. We begin with courtship violence; then we look at the cycle of violence; explanations for violence, and factors associated with domestic violence. Next we turn to the case of battered men, the mitigation of domestic violence, elder abuse, and sibling violence. Finally, we examine the physical and sexual abuse of children in the family.

Battered Women

Although violence in a romantic relationship can claim either a male or a female victim, most research has concerned battered women. We look first at relationship violence targeted at women; then we turn to violence against men.

Courtship Violence

Violence in dating relationships is not unusual. One-fifth of female college students report that their partners have used physical force on a date. This force usually took the form of pushing or shoving. However, 4 percent had actually been battered by the clenched fists of a dating partner (Makepeace 1981). Between one-third and one-half of women who are battered by a dating partner report that they remained in the relationship after the first violent incident. Low self-esteem on the part of the victim, a belief that the violent partner will change, and fear of retaliation make it difficult for many women to escape violent dating relationships (Bird et al. 1991).

Severe violence does not usually begin during courtship. Acts of hitting or kicking are less likely to take place until after marriage or cohabitation has begun

(Burke et al. 1989). Bowker's (1986:8) national study of 1,000 violent relationships, sponsored by the National Institute of Mental Health, revealed that in three-fourths of the cases, violence began after marriage rather than during courtship. However, hints of potential violence are often present in the dating relationship. Many battered wives who looked back on their courtship days have recalled their mate's expressions of extreme anger. These angry outbursts, which Bowker referred to as "temper tantrums," usually stopped short of physical assault. In the interview at the beginning of this chapter, Burt displayed some early danger signals that warn of possible future violence. These include his excessive jealousy, his attempt to control Laura's behavior and limit the people to whom she may talk, his alcohol and drug abuse, and his anger toward her, which was expressed by hitting physical objects, such as the car.

Escalation. If physical attacks do occur prior to marriage, they are typically mild, for example, shoving or slapping. After marriage, these outbursts tend to escalate into more severe physical violence. Once the assaults begin, the level of violence typically escalates over time (Sonkin 1985:11). Giles-Sims (1983:52–53) studied women who entered a battered women's shelter after an average of five years of marriage or cohabitation. During the year prior to their entry into the shelter, 83 percent had been beaten and over half had been threatened with a knife or gun. For all but a few women, the beatings had become regular occurrences.

The Cycle of Violence

Violence in a relationship usually follows a pattern known as the *cycle of violence*. This cycle consists of three stages of social interaction that are associated with violence: (1) tension building, (2) the violent incident, and (3) contrition and courtship (Walker 1979; Wetzel and Ross 1983). This repetitive cycle, typical of both courtship and marital violence, contains the elements necessary to hook the victim firmly into the violent relationship. Laura and Burt are caught in a cycle of violence typical in abusive relationships. The stages of the cycle of violence are discussed below.

Tension Building. The violent incident is usually preceded by a period of tension building, when the violent partner, usually the man, appears to grow increasingly agitated. The battered partner feels she is "walking on eggs" in order to avoid upsetting him. In Laura's story, tension built up as Burt escalated his anger in the car after the party and Laura tried to soothe him by explaining her behavior. The tension-building stage consists primarily of verbal aggression: The violent partner engages in demeaning, blaming, and controlling communication directed at the partner. In Laura's case, Burt called her a "liar" and a "guilty bitch." In the tension-building stage, the violent person also attempts to establish tighter control over the partner by giving orders and attempting to limit the partner's freedom of action, for example, by telling the partner not to speak to certain people.

The Violent Incident. Tension finally builds to a climax of violent explosion. Severe violent attacks are more common than one might expect. Over one and a half million wives in the United States are beaten by their husbands in incidents of severe violence each year (Straus and Gelles 1986). The *trigger incident*, the argument that immediately precedes the violent attack, most often concerns either the male's complaints about the woman's domestic services, such as cooking and housekeeping, or issues of jealousy and possessiveness. In the study by Giles-Sims (1983:46) of violent marriages, 90 percent of the battered women cited the husband's jealousy as a serious problem in the marriage. In the interview with Laura, Burt exhibited extreme jealousy when he sent his friends to check on Laura at the party, when he searched her purse for phone numbers, and when he assumed she would arrange to be sexually unfaithful when she was out of his sight.

Contrition and Courtship. The first violent incident usually comes as a surprise to the victim. In fact, both partners typically experience initial feelings of shock, shame, and guilt (Dobash and Dobash 1979:95–96). Laura's shock was so great

---

BOX 14.1   S o c i a l   I s s u e s

Why Battered Women Stay

Why does a wife or cohabiting partner who has been beaten remain in the relationship? Once violence has occurred and the woman has threatened to leave, an insidious process called "denial" often interferes with her determination to end the relationship (Wetzel and Ross 1983). Denial involves not facing a frightening or unacceptable aspect of reality. Rarely does the battered woman deny that she has actually been hit or physically abused. The denial process is far more subtle. She will typically deny that her partner is a violent person and deny the likelihood that the violence will continue. Perhaps most importantly, she denies the danger to her own safety and well-being. A collusion of denial usually develops; both partners insist that the violent husband is not responsible for his behavior. Violence is often blamed on an outside factor, such as substance abuse, with the couple saying that the violence "was just the alcohol talking" and wouldn't have happened if the man had been sober. His behavior may also be excused because of a recent upset or depression, with the couple concluding that he would not have hit her "if he had been himself." This woman looks back on the excuses she made for her husband's violence;

> Four years after the first violent attack, I was still wondering how I could make the relationship better. I thought that if I could just learn not to yell so loud when I got mad, if I could avoid "getting in his face," things would be better and he wouldn't hit me. I would tell myself that it's just because he was hit when he was a kid and he couldn't help it. I must have found over a hundred good excuses for him, including his drinking, not to mention all the excuses he found for himself. (Interview by author)

Excuses concerning the violent partner's drug and alcohol abuse are extremely effective in encouraging the battered woman to remain with the violent partner. The battered woman does not want to believe the man she loves is actually violent in nature. She doesn't want to face the possibility that he may be violent for the rest of their lives together. She wants to hold onto the hope that someday he will quit drinking and the relationship will change. In her fantasy, she imagines the relationship will return to the loving, caring partnership she wants. The victim of battering sees the relationship in terms of how it could be rather than in terms of how it currently is (Norwood 1985).

Another way responsibility for violence is shifted away from the violent partner is by blaming the battered partner. This is a version of the old saying that "a woman does not get hit for nothing" (Dobash and Dobash 1979:96). The violent partner is likely to follow his apology with an explanation that presents the battered woman's actions as the cause of the violent incident. By focusing on her behavior and maintaining that she provoked the violence, he therefore is seen as merely overreacting to her questionable behavior. This is a seductive argument for the woman because, as he explains it, she is the one with the power to control his violence. She begins to think that if she changes her behavior, avoids talking to other men, and avoids upsetting him, the violence will end. In her desperate need to gain some control over her life and end the violence, she is often willing to accept the blame. This assumption gives the woman a false sense of power. Accepting blame becomes another form of denial used to excuse a violent person's behavior.

that she did not want to see Burt again. However, as the cycle of violence entered the contrition and courtship stage, Burt expressed remorse and convinced Laura to rethink her position and give him another chance. Following the first violent outburst, violent partners often feel genuinely guilty, promise it will never happen again, and beg for forgiveness.

During the contrition stage the violent partner experiences panic and anxiety and fears the mate will leave (Davidson 1978:26). To win her back, he takes the relationship into a courtship phase, in which he is attentive and charming, as Burt was when he brought Laura flowers and was "really sweet for a long time." The woman often establishes a pattern of leaving and returning in which her husband (or partner) goes after her, apologizes, pleads for forgiveness, promises it will never happen again, and begs her to come home. Dobash and Dobash (1979:144) found that 88 percent of the battered wives in their study had left their husbands at least once, only to return home when their mates became contrite.

To remain in an abusive relationship, the victim must *recommit* herself to the man and suppress her anger and hurt feelings (Wetzel and Ross 1983). Laura recommitted to the relationship when she decided to give Burt "one more chance." After the first violent incident, the woman usually acts on the assumption that the violence will never happen again. The abusive behavior is seen as being out of character and a "mere overreaction" to a provocative situation. "The first violent incident is played down, isolated, solved, defined as insignificant, and forgotten" (Dobash and Dobash 1979:96).

Normalizing Violence

Once recommitment takes place, the relationship continues in the cycle of violence as contrition gradually fades into tension building and the cycle is repeat-

Often, it takes more than physically leaving a violent partner to be safe from future violence. Here, battered women and their children participate in a workshop discussing how to recognize abusive relationships and avoid them in the future.

ed. As the violent episodes continue, the abusive person becomes less likely to apologize and try to win back the partner's affection. The violent partner begins to *normalize the violence* so that the violent behavior is no longer defined as deviant. The aggressive partner reinterprets the violence as an acceptable response to the other's unacceptable behavior (Wolf-Smith and LaRossa 1992). Blame for the violence shifts more firmly to the victim, and the perpetrator's remorse begins to diminish. At this point, the threat of severe retaliation for any attempt to leave is often sufficient to keep the victim in the relationship (Andrews and Brewin 1990).

Battered Men

Some social scientists have argued that men are not the only perpetrators of spousal violence and that battered husbands are often overlooked. Straus and Gelles (1986:470) asked husbands and wives to report violent acts they had committed during the past year and found that women were as likely to have hit their husbands as husbands were to have hit their wives. Twelve percent of husbands and 11 percent of wives used violence against their mates during a one-year period. It appears that husbands and wives are equally violent. However, the statistics in this study must be carefully interpreted. These figures were based on questions that asked whether or not particular violent acts, such as hitting, had been committed by a spouse during the previous year. Thus a husband who beat his wife once a month during the last year would be counted as one violent husband. If his wife took one punch in self-defense during the same year, she would be counted as one violent wife. The same would be true for a frequently violent woman matched with a nonviolent man. It would be a mistake to assume that there is a parity of violence in which physical fights in marriage are evenly balanced. Women, who typically endure the worst in a violent encounter, are more susceptible to injury because men usually get in the last blow (Gelles and Cornell 1985). Furthermore, many women report that their acts of physical aggression are used in self-defense in an ongoing assault (Saunders 1986). This is not to say that there are no men who are battered by women. These cases are in the minority, but the small number should not trivialize the pain experienced by men who are battered by women.

Next we look at explanations for domestic violence.

Explanations for Domestic Violence

There are four major explanations for domestic violence: psychological explanations, conflict theory, exchange theory, and gender role theory.

Psychological Explanations

Psychological explanations for violence against a partner focus on mental processes within the violent individual. The most frequently used psychological explanation for battering one's mate is the *lack of impulse control*. According to this theory, aggression is an impulse that must be kept under control by a strong ego or personality control center. Personality disturbances within the violent person weaken the ego. When anger and sudden violent impulses arise within the individual, the ego is overwhelmed and self-control is temporarily lost (Roy 1982: 44). Lending credence to this psychological explanation for violence are three factors observable in violent mates: behavior that exhibits paranoia, the Dr. Jekyll and Mr. Hyde syndrome, and emotional dependence (Wetzel and Ross 1983).

Paranoia. Paranoia is a fear that is greatly exaggerated and out of touch with reality. At the beginning of this chapter, Burt's fear bordered on paranoia when he suspected Laura had secretly arranged to sleep with other men at the party and when he further suspected she had hidden their phone numbers in her purse. Burt's suspicions lacked empirical evidence in support of their reasonableness. In violent partners jealousy often reaches the level of paranoia.

Dr. Jekyll and Mr. Hyde Syndrome. Some psychologists point to the *Dr. Jekyll and Mr. Hyde* syndrome to support their argument in favor of psychological disturbance as the cause of violence (Symonds 1978). At the beginning of this chapter, Burt who was at first calm and "easy to talk to," appeared to be transformed into a new, frightening personality when he entered his jealous rage. This shift from the gentle Dr. Jekyll to the frightening Mr. Hyde is one of the characteristics recounted by numerous victims of violent relationships. After the violence has passed and the violent person has returned to more normal behavior and demeanor, it often seems to the victim as if this calm, affectionate partner could not have performed the violent acts.

Emotional Dependence. Violent partners often exhibit a good deal of emotional dependence on their battered victims. As the interview below illustrates, the violent partner is often obsessed with maintaining the romantic relationship:

> Larry was holding a 45 magnum, pointing it at my head, as he told me, "If I can't have you, nobody else will either." I pleaded, "I don't want anyone else. Larry, please put the gun away. I promise I'll never leave." He put the gun away and said, "You better not because, if you do, I'll hunt you and you know that I'll find you." (Interview by author)

In partner violence there is a certain desperation that expresses an unwillingness to experience separation and aloneness or life without a particular partner.

Critique. Although a lack of impulse control can explain a minor portion of romantic violence, this explanation has some serious flaws. There is evidence that the typical batterer is not completely out of control during the violent incident. In fact, violent people are usually in control of many aspects of their behavior when aggression occurs. Violent husbands have been reported to wait until the children are asleep and carefully lock doors before beginning an assault. Furthermore, lack of impulse control is not usually a generalized personality characteristic that spreads to other relationships. In fact, Davidson (1978:26) found that 95 percent of the men he studied who had assaulted their wives had no prior criminal record, and half of the remaining 5 percent had a previous assault on their wives or girlfriends as their only criminal violation. These men were able to control their violence in most situations, and the only persons they were likely to assault were their mates. Lack of impulse control also fails to explain why some men walk out of the house when they feel they are losing control over their emotions while others stay to batter their wives. Probably only a small portion of wife battering can be fully explained by this psychological argument. In contrast to psychological explanations, conflict theory looks at violence as a way to gain power.

Conflict Theory

From the perspective of conflict theory, violence is used by a family member to maintain power over others. Power is the ability to influence the behavior of other people. In other words, according to conflict theory, violent partners use physical force to "get their way." Unlike psychological explanations which view aggression as an impulse within the personality which needs to be controlled, conflict theory views violence as a learned behavior associated with the desire to maintain a pattern of dominance and subordination. In support of conflict theory is evidence showing that violence is far more likely in male-dominant marriages than in egalitarian marriages (Coleman and Straus 1986).

Control Over Resources. According to conflict theory, the ability to exercise power is based on control of resources, such as money. The abusive partner often uses violence or the threat of violence to gain control of the family checkbook. Even when a woman is employed and bringing home a paycheck, the violent man usually takes control of her income. If a battered woman should decide to leave her partner, she would lack the cash to pay for a bus ticket or an apartment deposit. Violence becomes the ultimate resource in maintaining male domination and female subordination in marriage. In addition, if a battered wife threatens to leave, the violent partner often orders her to stay, backing up his demand with a threat (Bowker 1986:7).

Historical Roots. The use of violence to reinforce male authority in marriage goes back to Colonial America. English common law, the law in England's colonies, granted husbands the "right of chastisement," the right physically to punish an argumentative or disobedient wife. The "Rule of Thumb" allowed a husband to beat his wife as long as the stick he used was no thicker than his thumb (Miller 1975). As late as 1867 a husband's right to batter his wife was upheld by an appellate court in North Carolina (Straus and Gelles 1986:466).

Marital Decision Making. The subordinate position of the wife in violent relationships can be seen in marital decision making. In Bowker's (1986:6) study of 1,000 American battered wives, women reported that they prevailed in only one out of thirty arguments with their husbands in the first year of marriage. As time went on, the women felt they had become slightly more influential. During the year preceding the study, the women were successful in one out of eight arguments with their husbands. The battered women never knew whether an argument would erupt into violence or whether this would be one of the times they would win and get their way.

Sexual Property. From the perspective of conflict theory, violent husbands assume that they have acquired property rights over their wives; they view their wives as their sexual property (McCall and Sheilds 1986). The extreme jealousy of the violent mate and his attempt to isolate his partner socially are associated with his belief that the wife's place is in the home (Dobash 1979:90–91). If the woman remains near the home, her domestic services are available to her mate and she has few opportunities to be sexually unfaithful. Although battered women go out of the home to work, they are not expected to go out of the home to play or to socialize.

Critique. Although conflict theory is useful, it is not able to account for all violent situations in the family. Conflict theory has focused primarily on explaining wife battering and is far less able to explain why some husbands are battered by their wives. Likewise, sibling violence between two teenage brothers of equal size and equal power is also difficult for conflict theory to explain. Conflict theory has limited use in explaining irrational violence that grows out of mental illness or substance abuse. In contrast to conflict theory, both psychological theories and exchange theory, discussed below, are able to explain violence perpetrated by either gender.

Exchange Theory

In contrast to conflict theory, exchange theory avoids viewing relationships in terms of dominance and subordination. Exchange theory maintains that people are willing to engage in a particular behavior, such as violence, when the rewards outweigh the costs. This theory assumes that people are rational enough to weigh the costs and benefits of an action, even in the heat of emotion. Gelles (1983) developed the "exchange and social control theory" of violence; he argues that potentially violent mates often take into account the consequences of their behavior and pay attention to the level of *social control* in the environment. That is, they assess the probable response of the community before engaging in a violent act. Social control refers to efforts by the larger society to place limits on the behavior of its members. According to Gelles (1983), the level of marital violence will be high when social control over family behavior is weak. In contrast, negative sanctions by the police deter domestic violence by increasing the cost to the perpetrator. The cost of arrest includes lost time at work, the hassle of going through the court system, embarrassment if friends find out, and loss of self-esteem (Williams 1992).

Exchange theory argues that domestic violence is significantly curtailed when we as a society express our intolerance of it. If partners know that they face everything from humiliation among friends to incarceration, they will be less likely to commit violent acts.

Alternatives. Exchange theory is useful in explaining why battered women remain in abusive relationships. Exchange theory argues that a person, such as a battered woman, is likely to place a high value on resources offered by the mate, such as income, if there are few alternative sources from which to obtain those resources. Battered wives are likely to remain in a violent relationship when they have no other place to go and no alternative source of economic support. For this reason, violent husbands often threaten the wife's relatives if they offer her shelter and other aid.

When women have job skills that provide an alternative source of income and when shelters provide an alternative place for battered women to stay, then the violent mate must consider the possibility that the cost of violence will be the loss of his wife. In other words, exchange theory argues that the level of domestic violence is reduced when women have their own resources, which they can use to gain safety in the relationship.

Social Isolation. It is typical in violent marriages for the violent husband to attempt to isolate the battered wife socially (Wetzel and Ross 1983). When the battered woman is socially isolated, the violent partner becomes the main source of love, companionship, and emotional support. According to exchange theory, people remain in relationships when the resources offered by the partner, such as companionship and emotional support, are highly valued and when there are few alternative sources for obtaining those resources. When the battered wife weighs the costs and rewards of leaving the violent relationship, the loss of love and emotional support can seem like a heavy price to pay. In addition, those friends and relatives who could offer alternative friendship and encouragement have usually fallen by the wayside. Social isolation sometimes takes a direct form in which the violent husband forbids his wife to talk to her family, her friends, and especially other males. However, the process can also be subtle and indirect, with the violent person finding fault with his partner's friends and family and then making excuses to avoid seeing them.

Critique. Resources, costs, and rewards, the key concepts in exchange theory, are difficult to measure in a relationship. Therefore, it is difficult to ascertain the impact of costs and rewards on a person's behavior, except in a general way. Furthermore, exchange theory assumes that people weigh costs and rewards and make rational choices. Men who seek dominance, and who view dominance as a traditional male right, may not be very concerned with the costs of maintaining power. Likewise, a person who is emotionally unstable, or who abuses alcohol or drugs, may act before considering the consequences.

Gender role theory, discussed below, assumes that the behavior people often engage in is guided by images of maleness or femaleness, rather than by rational choices.

Gender Role Theory

Another way of explaining domestic violence is to look at both male and female traditional gender roles.

The Traditional Female Role. In the traditional female role, the woman is the nurturing and caregiving partner who subordinates her needs to those of her partner. Women who strongly adhere to the traditional female role often feel sorry for the partner and put the partner's needs above their own needs (Phelps and Austin 1985). The battered woman puts the contrite partner's need for forgiveness above her own need for safety. Women also have traditionally played the role of peacemaker in the family, and many battered women take it on themselves to solve the problem of violence by changing their own behavior and trying to avoid upsetting the violent mate.

The Traditional Male Role. In their study of domestic violence in Scotland, Dobash and Dobash (1979:89–90) argued that wife battering is an outgrowth of the traditional male role and its belief in male rights. In violent relationships, the male typically believes that he alone has the right to set the rules for the relationship and thus to set the rules for his wife's behavior. This is a contrast to many modern relationships, in which questions about who has responsibility for cooking and who will be allowed to maintain friendships with members of the opposite sex are negotiated as a variety of situations come up. In egalitarian relationships both partners participate in defining the relationship.

In violent relationships, a double standard typically exists: The violent man claims social freedom for himself while the wife must explain her social activities to him. In the violent relationships studied by Dobash and Dobash (1979:93–94), the men saw authority, independence, and freedom of movement as part of the prerogative of the male role, while expecting their wives to curtail their former social interests and social relationships.

The violent male who holds a traditional view of marriage often sees the modern wife as the one who provokes violence. From his perspective, when she violates his rules she has engaged in an act of aggression and he feels victimized (Davidson 1978). That is, when she stands up for herself, or enjoys a conversation with another man, or refuses to meet her husband's demands, he defines the situation as one in which she has been aggressive. This interpretation of her behavior as a personal assault on him increases the likelihood that he will use physical aggression in response (Giles-Sims 1983:32–33; Holting 1979:79).

Critique. Gender role theory does not explain why some men alter their traditional gender behavior to fit new circumstances. When the wife is employed, adjustments in the relationship are often made. Also, when the police make arrests in domestic violence situations, the violent partner may become reluctant to hit his wife. Exchange theory is more useful than gender role theory in explaining why a man who feels that he has traditional rights may decide that it is in his best interests not to insist on male prerogatives. Traditional gender roles do not explain all types of family violence, such as husbands who are battered by wives, siblings who abuse other siblings, or adult children who batter their elderly parents.

All of the social theories discussed above have some value in explaining domestic violence, but they also have limitations. Often a combination of theories is needed to explain the variety of situations in which family violence occurs. In the next section we examine factors associated with domestic violence.

Review Questions

1. How common is courtship violence?

2. Why would it be a mistake for a battered woman to assume that the violence will end?

3. What are the stages of the cycle of violence?

4. What usually happens in the contrition stage?

5. Why does the violent partner show less contrition after a number of violent incidents have taken place?

6. On what basis can the statement, "Wives are as violent as husbands," be questioned?

7. What are the psychological explanations for violence?

8. What are the shortcomings of the "lack of impulse control" explanation for violence?

9. How does conflict theory explain domestic violence? What are the weaknesses in that theory?

10. How does exchange theory explain domestic violence? What are the weaknesses in this theory?

11. What are the beliefs associated with the traditional female gender role and how do these beliefs prevent women from leaving violent relationships? What are the beliefs associated with the traditional male gender role and how do these beliefs encourage violent men to feel justified in using violence? What is the critique of the traditional gender role explanation for domestic violence?

Factors Associated with Domestic Violence

A number of factors have been associated with domestic violence. They are discussed below.

Substance Abuse

Numerous studies have noted the strong connection between substance abuse and partner battering. In the study by Giles-Sims (1983:47), 72 percent of the battered women cited the husband's alcohol abuse as a serious problem in the marriage. However, the causal relationship between substance abuse and violent behavior is not a simple one. On one hand, substance abuse can lead to violence by lowering inhibitions and increasing the likelihood that communication will be misinterpreted. On the other hand, people who want to use violence to vent anger often use alcohol or drugs beforehand to avoid taking responsibility for their violent actions (Dobash and Dobash 1979:96). Bowker (1986:15) points out that most men who batter their wives while in a drunken stupor also beat them while sober. Therefore, although substance abuse is associated with family violence, it would be a mistake to think that if the substance abuse ended, the problem of domestic violence would necessarily go away.

Children learn what they live. When children are the victims of violence, or are constantly exposed to violence in their homes, they learn to use violence as adults.

Violent Childhood

Being battered as a child tends to predispose a person to accept the use of violence as an adult. Children who either are physically abused or who observe physical violence are more likely to use violence as adults than are children who grow up in nonviolent homes (Renvioze 1978). (For additional discussion see the "Intergenerational Transmission of Violence" in the section on "Child Physical Abuse" in this chapter.)

Social Class

Although domestic violence occurs in all social classes, low-income couples are disproportionately represented in cases of reported partner battering (Gelles and Cornell 1985; Straus and Sweet 1992). In addition, families of blue-collar workers have higher rates of wife battering and child abuse than families of white-collar workers (Straus et al. 1980). Roy (1982: 23) studied 4,000 urban and suburban women who sought help at Abused Women's Aid in Crisis, a New York City battered women's shelter. Three-fourths of these women reported their abusive partners either were unemployed or were blue-collar workers who performed manual labor. Economic pressures on low-income families are associated with marital discord, and this conflict has the potential to erupt into violence. Nonetheless, there are probably more middle-class battered women than statistics from battered women's shelters indicate. Middle-class women tend to avoid shelters and often rely on relatives to shelter and aid them in times of crisis. A significant relationship between social class and domestic violence appears to exist, but it is a mistake to think domestic violence is limited to lower-class families.

Race

At first glance, race appears to be a factor associated with domestic violence against women. African-American couples have a higher rate of partnership violence than white couples (Straus and Smith 1990; Straus and Sweet 1992). However, this racial difference is probably largely accounted for by the fact that African Americans are overrepresented among the poor. African-American women are also overrepresented in battered women's shelters, which primarily serve low-income women.

Lockhart (1987) conducted a study to sort out the puzzle of social class, race, and wife battering. The study carefully controlled for both race and social class. Among the poor, African-American and white couples had the same level of domestic violence. However, among the middle class, the rate of domestic violence in African-American families was higher than that in white families. Lockhart concluded that because most African Americans have recently gained middle-class status, their hold this on newly attained economic position is tenuous, resulting in stress. Apparently, when African Americans become established in a higher social class position, the level of violence drops. Overall, upper-class African-Americans had the lowest rate of domestic violence, lower than that of upper-class whites (Lockhart 1987).

We should keep in mind that in all social classes, the majority of both African-American and white families reported no severe violence. It is a mistake to assume that because some families in a social class or racial group experience violence, all families in that social category do.

Status Differential

A status differential between partners increases the likelihood that violence will occur in the relationship. A status differential exists when one partner has a good deal more status than the other. Violence is least likely to occur in egalitarian relationships and most likely to occur when one spouse has greater status and power than the other. Husbands are more likely to batter housewives, who have low social status, than they are to batter employed wives (Straus, et al. 1980). Employed wives have financial resources and a position in the community, making it easier for them to move out of a violent home. Likewise, when the status differential is tipped in favor of the wife, and the husband has relatively low status, the probability of violence increases (O'Brien 1971). Bowker's (1986) national study of 1,000 battered wives found that violent husbands were less likely than their wives to have attended college. In other words, the greater the status differential between husband and wife, the greater the risk of violence.

Unemployment

Male unemployment and male financial dependency on a female partner appear substantially to increase the risk of domestic violence. Thirty-five percent of the battered women interviewed by Giles-Sims had partners who were unemployed at the time of the study, and 56 percent had mates who were unemployed at some time during the violent relationship. When a man lacks financial resources, Giles-Sims argues, violence becomes the "ultimate resource" he can use to convince a woman to give up her autonomy and grant him more power.

Mitigating Domestic Violence

Two factors are important in mitigating or reducing the amount of domestic violence and in making it easier for battered women to leave a violent relationship: shelters and police-initiated arrests.

Shelters

Battered women's shelters offer a safe haven to abused wives and their children who are escaping a violent environment. In 1985, the 1,150 shelters in the United States were estimated to house about one-eighth of the women who were escaping violent homes. The other battered women were housed by relatives and friends (Bowker 1986:43, 82). Because waiting lists for shelters are long, the typical length of stay is fifteen days, during which time the woman usually meets with a counselor to talk about her situation and makes future plans. Planning the future in an environment of personal safety is an experience many battered women have not had since the early days of their marriages. If the battered woman has decided to move out of a violent home, the counselor helps put her in touch with welfare services and helps her begin the search for an apartment. Within the shelter the isolation of the battered woman is broken, and she now has a chance to talk with other abused women and compare experiences. "Sheltering strikes at the heart of the batterers'

BOX 14.2   World Perspectives

Wife Battering by a Mother-in-Law: The Traditional Chinese Family

Not all battered wives live in fear of their husbands. In traditional Chinese society before the 1949 Communist revolution, the person most likely to batter a young wife was her mother-in-law. The young Chinese bride spent most of her time with her mother-in-law: The traditional Chinese family practiced patrilocal residence, in which the bride moved in with her husband's family. There the young bride was under the mother-in-law's thumb. The authority of the mother-in-law was far reaching, and she directed the activities of her daughter-in-law long after the younger woman had borne children. In fact, the mother-in-law made the major decisions about disciplining and raising her grandchildren. In times of famine, it was the mother-in-law who decided which, if any, of the wife's female children would suffer infanticide. Infanticide, the killing of children, took place through starvation in China.

Males were highly valued in traditional Chinese society, and family organization was patrilineal, with inheritance of the family farm and the family name passing through the male line from father to son. At birth, little girls were greeted with less joy because they would soon leave their parents' descent group to join their future husband's family. Sons, in contrast, would remain in the family household and take care of their aging parents (Freedman 1970). A new wife gained status when she bore a son who would carry on the family line. A woman's position in the family gradually improved as her sons grew older and she became revered as the mother of sons.

A mother had a closer relationship with her son than she had with her husband. Marriage was expected to be a distant and unemotional relationship. A husband was not expected to show affection to his wife outside of the sexual relationship. In fact, a husband was not expected to speak to his wife except to give her orders. Chinese marriage, like Chinese society, was strongly gender segregated: Husbands and wives were expected to avoid one another. Married couples could not work side by side in the fields, nor could they go to town to the market together. A woman's most emotionally intimate conversation with a highly valued male was found in the mother-son relationship, a relationship the mother prized and jealously guarded. The entry of her son's bride into the home presented a threat to the mother; she feared being displaced in her son's affections. (Wolf and Huang 1980).

The mother-in-law maintained her authority by physically disciplining her daughter-in-law. This is in contrast to the experience of a male. When a son married, he achieved adult status and it was no longer acceptable for his father to strike him (Ho 1989). Women, on the other hand, remained in an infantilized position and were physically disciplined in marriage by the mother-in-law. The more a mother-in-law physically punished her daughter-in-law, the more the daughter-in-law pressured her husband to leave his family home and set up a separate household. This effort of the daughter-in-law confirmed the mother's worst fears that the daughter-in-law would take away her son, and thus beating of the daughter-in-law escalated.

All of this has changed in the modern Chinese family. Women gained educational and employment rights after the Chinese Communist revolution in 1949. Today, the typical Chinese wife is employed, has her own pocket money, and is able to make important purchases for the family, such as buying a television. The modern Chinese wife has gained a good deal of independence from both her mother-in-law and her husband (Kejing 1993). In addition, China has instituted a one child policy, which requires families to have no more than one child. This policy has been difficult to enforce, particularly in rural areas and among families whose first birth is a female. The typical Chinese family today has two children, many fewer than the eight or nine children typical fifty years ago (Chen 1993) Young wives are less housebound and more independent than were their grandmothers, who had large families. In addition, there has been a decline in arranged marriage and a growing emphasis on romance between husband and wife (Holley 1991; Kejing 1993). All of these changes have raised the status of young wives in the family. Mothers-in-law, who are typically less educated than their daughters-in-law, are less likely to be employed and earn an income. They complain that their influence over their independent daughters-in-law is declining (Kejing 1993). The family system that supported physical abuse of daughters-in-law is changing as the husband becomes an ally to his wife and young women gain greater economic importance within the family.

isolation strategy by bringing women together" (Bowker 1986:86). Hearing about the behavior of other violent men gives her a perspective on her situation through which she often becomes less willing to take the blame for the violence.

Police-Initiated Arrests

It is unrealistic to expect a woman who has been battered and threatened with further abuse to file assault charges against her husband. However, when she is frightened and reluctant to take action, her husband's power increases and he is free to continue battering. To counteract this problem, some communities allow police to arrest the spouse when evidence of wife battering exists, without a formal complaint from the wife. In other words, a complaint is filed by the police rather than by the wife. Evidence suggests that such arrests tend to reduce future violent incidents in the relationship (Berk and Newton 1985).

Now we turn to the less obvious types of family violence: elder abuse and sibling violence.

Elder Abuse

A number of studies of elder abuse estimate that approximately 4 percent of elderly persons have been physically, emotionally, or financially abused by a relative, amounting to more than 1 million cases (Pillemer and Suitor 1988). This figure may represent only the "tip of the iceberg." The U.S. Congress House Select Committee on Aging (1985) estimated that 10 percent of the elderly are physically abused by a relative at some time in their old age.

Dependency

Dependency appears to be a key element in explaining elder abuse. Elder abuse is most likely to occur when the elderly parent becomes physically dependent on the adult child for care. A "role reversal" takes place in which the child becomes the caregiver, and this "generational inversion" places strain on the parent–child relationship. The probability of abuse is low when the elderly parent and child exchange services and help each other. However, when the adult child becomes a caregiver to a largely dependent parent, resentment often sets in and the probability of elder abuse rises (Pillemer and Suitor 1988). The situation becomes particularly explosive when the adult child is living with the elder parent. In a study by Pillemer and Suitor (1988), in over half of the cases of elder abuse the abusive relative was living with the elderly victim and was also financially dependent on the elderly person for housing. In such cases the caregiver often feels trapped in the caregiving role. Thus, both the physical dependency of the elder and the financial dependency of the abusive relative are associated with elder abuse.

Social Isolation

Social isolation of the elderly person increases the probability of abuse. An active network of social relationships for the elderly person acts as a protective factor. Friends, neighbors, and relatives who visit can ask questions when signs

When elderly persons lead active and independent lives, they are far less vulnerable to the family resentment that sometimes leads to abuse.

of abuse appear, can contact the police or court authorities, and can impose informal sanctions by registering their disapproval with the abusive person. In addition, knowing the elderly person has contact with other people and could report the abuse is a significant deterrent to abuse (Pillemer and Suitor 1988).

The Intergenerational Transmission of Violence

Many perpetrators of elder abuse were themselves physically abused as children. The child learned to be violent from the parent and when the parent becomes dependent, the pattern of violence reemerges, but the former battered child become the abuser (McCall and Shields 1986).

Legal Guardianship

Many social observers argue that the courts are too willing to assume that elderly persons are incompetent and assign legal conservatorship or guardianship of an elderly person to a younger relative. This action infantilizes the elderly person and robs that person of the right to make decisions that affect his or her life. Placing the elderly person under legal guardianship is often not warranted, for example, when the elderly person is mentally competent in a number of ways although not able to perform physical self-care. Such court action robs elderly persons of their civil rights and control over their property (Pillemer and Suitor 1988).

Sibling Abuse

The most common type of family violence is not child abuse or wife battering. The most frequent form of violence in the family involves the attack of one sibling on another (Straus, et al. 1980). Over one-half of siblings report that they have engaged in serious violence against a brother or sister which went beyond pushing, slapping, shoving, or throwing objects. One out of five siblings has beaten a brother or sister, amounting to 7 million cases of serious sibling abuse in the United States (Straus et al. 1980). However, Americans are usually tolerant of sibling abuse. The same people who react with shock and disgust when they discover child abuse perpetrated by a parent take a casual attitude toward violence initiated by a sibling. When they see a child hit a sibling, they often view the occurrence as natural, saying, "Kids will be kids." This attitude often blinds parents to sibling abuse when it takes place, and abuse is likely to be particularly severe when children are left home alone to care for themselves (Straus et al. 1980).

Sibling abuse tends to be associated with the age and gender of the child and with the overall level of family violence.

Age

The rate of sibling abuse is highest between preschool children and tends to decline with age. Almost all acts of violence against siblings, such as hitting and kicking, are typically prevalent at age three and decline as the child ages, reaching a low point in high school. However, in spite of the significant decline in sibling violence with age, about half of high school age siblings still occasionally hit or kick their brothers and sisters. The exception to this pattern involves threats with a weapon, which increase with age. High school students are far more likely than younger children to threaten a brother or sister with a knife or gun. One girl even reported that her brother's friends held her against a wall while her brother threatened her with an ice pick (Straus et al. 1980).

Gender

Gender also has an influence on sibling violence, with boys being more likely than girls to hit a sibling. Families with all daughters have lower levels of sibling violence than families with all boys. In fact, the presence of daughters in a family reduces the level of sibling violence. Also, boys with brothers engage in more sibling violence than boys who have only sisters (Straus et al. 1980).

Generalized Family Violence

Sibling abuse is most likely to occur in families already plagued by violence. Children who are hit by a parent are most likely to use serious violence against a sibling. In other words, violence tends to become generalized in the family, so that children with violent parents learn to settle disputes with physical force.

Child Physical Abuse

The home can be a dangerous place for a child. The family is supposed to be a safe haven, offering protection from the impersonal world outside. However, children are more likely to experience violence within the family than they are to be mugged by a stranger while walking down the street. The Congressional Report on Children, Youth, and Families (U.S. Congress 1990:6) found that over 2 million children are physically abused or neglected each year and reports of child abuse and neglect doubled during the 1980s.

The use of physical coercion to force compliance in children is common in American families. Over half (62 percent) of all children ages three to seventeen have parents who use some type of physical force on them. This figure includes acts ranging from shoving to assault with a knife or gun (Straus and Gelles 1986). Parents are more likely to use physical discipline on younger children than on older ones. Ninety-seven percent of parents of three-year-olds reported that they spanked, slapped, hit, or shoved their children, compared to one-third of fifteen- to seventeen-year-olds (Straus and Gelles 1986). These rates may not surprise many people because most Americans do not consider shoving or spanking children to constitute child abuse. However, 2 percent of American children experience "very severe violence," which includes parental acts likely to cause injury. Child abuse, or "very severe violence," includes being kicked, hit with a fist, beaten, or attacked with a knife or gun. This means that in a neighborhood of 100 children, on the average, 2 of those children are being physically abused with very severe violence each year.

Children can be exposed to violence both as targets and as observers. In fact, children who observe spousal violence are at risk of becoming victims of child abuse because violence against wives tends eventually to overflow into violence against children. Over half of the battered women in Bowker's (1986:8) study eventually saw their mates physically abuse their children. In no case did child abuse occur with the first incident, when the wife or live-in partner was battered. Children became involved over time as violence spread through the family.

The physical abuse of children tends to create emotional problems that extend into adulthood, such as low self-esteem and the tendency toward drug and alcohol abuse (Gelles and Cornell 1985). Likewise, children who observe the battering of a parent have been found to exhibit physical symptoms of emotional distress (Frosstrom-Cohen and Rosenbaum 1985).

The Intergenerational Transmission of Violence

Family violence tends to be transmitted from one generation to another. Children who are victims of violence as well as children who observe violence against other family members are at risk for becoming violent adults. Physically abused children and children who watch a mother being battered are more likely to use violence as adults than are children who grow up in nonviolent homes (Renvioze 1978).

Role Models. The intergenerational transmission of violence occurs through observation of family role models. According to social learning theory, children learn social roles by observing and imitating the behavior of others. Parents serve as *role models,* or examples of social behavior, unwittingly showing children images of adult behavior. In adulthood, formerly abused children reach into their memories and put these images of family behavior to work in creating their own social roles (Kruttschnitt 1987). When children experience family violence they incorporate a number of assumptions into their view of family life. By observing violence in adults, children discover that violence is rewarded by compliance with the violent person's demands. In addition, they learn that violence is considered an appropriate solution to family problems and an expected reaction to being frustrated by other family members (Dobash and Dobash 1979). Furthermore, family violence teaches children that it is the people who love them who are most likely to hurt them and that physical force appears justified when something is really important (Gelles and Straus 1979). These assumptions about family life, learned as a child, are carried into adulthood.

Males who either were beaten as a child or observed spousal violence are far more likely than those from nonviolent homes physically to abuse both their children and their wives in adulthood (Straus, et al. 1980). Likewise, female children from violent environments are more likely as adults to abuse children and to accept battering at the hands of a mate than are female children from nonviolent homes. In Giles-Sims (1983:45) study of violent partnerships, almost half of the battered women and three-fourths of the violent men either had been physically abused as children or had observed their fathers battering their mothers.

Children in violent families are often more than just casual bystanders who happen to observe the physical abuse of a parent. The study of marital violence by Dobash and Dobash found that children were sometimes roused out of bed at night by their fathers in order to "witness their mother's punishment as an additional degradation to her" (Dobash and Dobash 1979:151). In fact, purposely exposing children to marital violence is a theme that runs throughout studies of violent relationships.

The Effect of Violence on Boys

For the boy, the emotional experience of witnessing violence against his mother is often one of rage, helplessness, and divided loyalties; these feeling result in a special kind of emotional pain. As the child grows older, he is faced with the problem of deciding whether to defend his battered mother or to side with his violent father. This conflict is fraught with fear and guilt. On the one hand, he loves his mother and wants to protect her. On the other hand, he fears his father's wrath and worries that siding with his mother will lead to violence against him. Caught in a conflict of loyalties, the teenage boy commonly sides with the father in order to retain his affection and approval. Some boys imitate the father's behavior, and in some of the families studied by Davidson (1978:122) the teenage boys beat their mothers. After all, violent husbands usually tell their children that the mother has caused the violence and that the family would not have these troubles if the mother had behaved herself. The teenage boy's decision to identify with the violent father is a fateful one that predisposes him to violence in his adult years.

Mitigating Factors. Experiencing a violent family environment does not necessarily lead a child to a violent future. If the caretaking function is shared by household members other than the parents, such as a grandparent, uncle, or aunt, the child in a violent family is less likely to develop into a violent adult (Robins et al. 1975). This is particularly true if the relationship is affectionate and endures over a long period of time. Even when there is no third adult in the household, the presence of one nurturing adult, often the mother, provides a protective factor that tends to inhibit the development of later violent behavior in the child. This holds for both physically abused children and children who observe violence (Kruttschnitt et al. 1987:503).

A Second Definition of the Situation. The violent parent presents a definition of the situation in which the victim has caused the violence. However, children observe not only violent aggression but also the pain and suffering that are the effects of violence. Dobash and Dobash (1979:152–153) argue that mothers can be an important influence on sons by appealing to their sense of morality. Some battered wives tell their sons they should never treat their future wives in the way their mothers were treated. Such mothers can be a counteractive force, offering an alternative definition of the violent situation. This helps to insulate children from a violent future.

The Effect of Violence on Girls

Female children, as well as male children, have been reported to try to defend the mother and restrain the father (Davisdon 1978:122). This effort turns out to be a futile gesture that leaves the female child feeling powerless. Females who identify with the battered mother may come to see women as helpless and victimized. The attitude that women are powerless to stop violence in their lives, an attitude called *learned helplessness,* may later sap a woman's motivation to leave a violent male if she finds herself in a violent relationship as a adult (Walker 1977). As a result of this feeling of powerlessness, many female children who witness the battering of a mother experience bouts of depression (Frosstrom-Cohen and Rosenbaum 1985).

Child Sexual Abuse

One and a half million cases of child sexual abuse, including both molestation and incest, are reported to authorities each year (Gilbert 1988:3). Most of this abuse occurs within the context of the family. Based on interviews with a randomly selected sample of 900 adult women in San Francisco, Russell (1986) estimates that before they reach adulthood, 16 percent of all female children are sexually molested by a family member.

Effect on the Victim

When one or more children are elevated to the position of sexual partner in a troubled family, the change in status creates *role confusion* for the child. Role confusion refers to uncertainty about the expectations of one's social role. The parent or other relative treats the child, at least in sexual matters, as if the child were an adult or spouse (Summit and Kryso 1978). The child often has the feeling of growing up too quickly, not being a true child, and being somehow out of step and alienated from other children who lack these adult sexual experiences (Minuchin 1974).

Children who are victims of incest often have reactions similar to those of rape victims. They experience confusion, depression, crying, shame, and guilt (Nadelson and Sauzier 1986). This trauma can have long-term effects that last into adulthood. Sexual abuse disrupts a child's trust and affection for an important adult in her or his life. Confidence and trust are undermined, not only in the abusive relationship but also in the child's relationships with other family members. The experience introduces a secret the child feels obliged to keep, not only to protect himself or herself from retaliation but also to protect the other family members from the pain that the knowledge of molestation and infidelity would bring. The victim feels particularly burdened by this secret (Finkelhor, 1979:58–59). The guilt associated with this secret is especially strong if the child has experienced sexual pleasure during the incident (McFarlane 1978).

There appears to be a close association between the sexual abuse of female children and the tendency to become chemically dependent in adolescence. Chemical dependency refers to the abuse of alcohol or drugs. A study by Edwall and colleagues (1989) of 597 adolescent girls in drug and alcohol abuse treatment programs in five states revealed that about half of the girls had been sexually abused by a close family member. The low self-esteem, anxiety, depression, and guilt experienced by these victims of sexual abuse made them particularly susceptible to chemical dependency. Girls in this study who had been sexually abused also experienced a high incidence of physical violence directed against both themselves and their mothers. As Table 14.1 shows, within the group of chemically dependent female adolescents studied by Edwall, victims of sexual abuse were twice as likely as nonvictims to have grown up in a violent family. Abuse sometimes has the tendency to generalize in the family to include both violence and sexual abuse. The combination of sexual and physical abuse makes a girl particularly susceptible to chemical dependency in adolescence.

The Role of the Mother

The importance of the mother in preventing child sexual abuse comes to light when we observe the weak position of the mother in many families in which child sexual abuse occurs. The mother in most families plays the role of protector for daughters. Her presence and strength reinforce society's sexual code (Brown-

TABLE 14.1	Physical and Sexual Abuse of Chemically Dependent Adolescent Girls		
Family Sexual Abuse		*Victims*	*Nonvictims*
Girls beaten by family member		53%	24%
Other family member beaten by family member		51	26

Source: Adapted from Glenace E. Edwall, Norman G. Hoffmann, and Patricia Ann Harrison 1989. "Psychological Correlates of Sexual Abuse in Adolescent Girls in Chemical Dependency Treatment." *Adolescence* 24, Table 1, page 284.

Of the chemically dependent girls studied by Edwall and her colleagues, half (53 percent) of those who were sexually abused by a family member had also been beaten by a family member. In contrast, of the chemically dependent girls who were not victims of sexual abuse, slightly under one-fourth (24 percent) had been beaten by a family member. Therefore, sexual abuse tended to be associated with other physical abuse.

If children do not know how to talk about sexual abuse, or if their initial complaints are dismissed as untrue or imagined, they can be burdened for years with the dark secret of an abusive experience. Here, a psychologist uses a doll to help a young girl talk about the ways she has been inappropriately touched.

ing and Boatman 1977). In studies of families with father–daughter incest, the mothers were frequently depressed, incapacitated by illness or alcoholism, submissive to their husbands, physically abused by their husbands, or frequently absent from the home. These situations make it difficult for the mothers to provide any protection for the daughters (Becker and Coleman 1988; Finkelhor 1979:26). In a significant proportion of families in which incest takes place, the parent's marital conflict has resulted in an unpleasant or nonexistent sexual relationship between the husband and wife (Henderson 1972). In addition, in many of the families with child sexual abuse, the mother's relationship with the daughter who was the victim was strained and alienated (Finkelhor 1979).

The Victim Precipitation Argument Examined

For many years, a number of psychologists and social workers attributed child sexual abuse to *victim precipitation*. That is, they assumed the child behaved in a provocative manner toward the adult, thus causing his or her own victimization. Sigmund Freud offered a theory of childhood sexuality in support of this position when he argued that all children secretly fantasize about having sexual relations with the opposite-sex parent. Children who were victims of molestation or incest were believed to be acting out their sexual fantasies with an adult family member (Finkelhor 1979:24–26). Evidence to support this theory was found in the child's acquiescence to the sexual experience and his or her willingness to keep the experience a secret. This misguided theory of "victim precipitation" places the responsibility for child sexual abuse squarely on the shoulders of the child, thus blaming the victim.

More recently, psychologists and other social scientists have argued that the adult should take responsibility for setting the sexual rules of a relationship and for preventing child sexual abuse. Children often have difficulty resisting physical affection that turns into molestation when the molester is a trusted adult who is also an authority figure. The child has been taught to obey the commands of elders and to look to adults in the family to define socially appropriate behavior. To counter this adult dominance in sexual situations, recently developed sex education programs attempt to teach children to identify sexual abuse and to speak up when it occurs. Gilbert (1988:7) points out that effective sex education programs in elementary schools teach children that "they own their own bodies and that no one has a right to touch them in ways they do not like." Children are taught that sometimes a touch by an adult feels like "a bad touch," which is simply a touch that feels uncomfortable or "feels bad," such as a touch to the genitals. When they experience a bad touch children should demand that the molestation stop, and then inform their parents, a teacher, or some other adult. Such programs empower children to stand up for their right to live in a sexually safe environment.

Review Questions

1. What factors are associated with domestic violence?

2. Why is it reasonable to assume that statistics from battered women's shelters underestimate the amount of wife battering in the middle class?

3. Why should we question the statistics indicating that African-American families have a higher rate of wife battering than white families? What factor tends to confound these statistics?

4. What is meant by a status differential and how can a status differential encourage violence?

5. What factors have been effective in mitigating domestic violence? Why is it useful for a police officer, rather than the battered woman, to file a police complaint?

6. How common is child abuse?

7. How does the intergenerational transmission of violence take place? (How is violence transmitted from one generation to another?)

8. What special problems do boys experience when they witness violence against their mothers?

9. What mitigating factors can prevent the intergenerational transmission of violence?

10. What special problems do girls experience when they see their mothers battered?

11. In what way is the mother's role often significant in cases of sexual abuse?

12. What are the effects of sexual abuse on the victim?

13. What are the problems with the victim precipitation explanation for sexual abuse?

14. In what direction are sex education programs moving?

Summary

1. There are often signs during courtship of impending violence in a relationship, although courtship violence usually takes a mild form prior to marriage or cohabitation.

2. The battering of women forms a social pattern known as the cycle of violence; this cycle is played out in three stages: tension building, the violent incident, and contrition and courtship.

3. Domestic violence tends to escalate over time, and the contrition stage tends to diminish over time.

4. The psychological explanation for domestic violence attributes violence to a lack of impulse control, the Dr. Jekyll and Mr. Hyde syndrome, and dependency on the partner.

5. Conflict theory sees violence as an attempt to gain power in a relationship and thereby to create a relationship based on dominance and subordination.

6. Exchange theory argues that people will continue to be violent when the rewards outweigh the costs. Therefore, society needs to create costs for family violence.

7. Gender role theory explains domestic violence by looking at the traditional male gender role, with its belief in male rights, and the traditional female gender role, with its emphasis on peacemaking and putting the partner's needs first.

8. The lower class appears to have a higher rate of domestic violence, although the amount of middle-class violence is probably underestimated. The high representation of blacks in domestic violence populations is related to their overrepresentation in the lower class.

9. Domestic violence is related to substance abuse, a violent childhood, unemployment, and having a status differential in the marital or cohabiting relationship.

10. Women also batter men; however, there are problems in measuring the levels of male and female violence in marriage, and female violence against men is usually used in self-defense.

11. The mitigation of domestic violence can be partly accomplished though the establishment of battered women's shelters and by police-initiated arrests of violent partners.

12. Elder abuse, a serious problem, is most likely to occur when the adult batterer lives in the elderly person's home, is dependent on the elderly person for housing, and was a victim of child abuse.

13. Sibling abuse is the most common form of family violence and is related to other forms of violence in the family.

14. Growing up in a violent environment, both as an observer and as a victim, puts a the child at risk for the intergenerational transmission of violence.

15. The presence of a nurturing adult in the violent home can act as a protective factor, counteracting the long-term effects of a violent childhood.

16. Sexual abuse of a child destroys the child's trust in an important family relationship; has long-term effects, including a predisposition to chemical dependency in the teen years; and is more likely to occur when a strong mother figure is absent.

17. The victim precipitation argument claims that the child initiated the sexual abuse. This explanation does not take into account the cultural expectation of

obedience to parental demands and thus blames the victim. A new direction in sex education teaches children to demand that sexual abuse stop and to tell a responsible adult when it occurs.

Key Words

Violence
Tension Building
Contrition
Dr. Jekyll and Mr. Hyde Syndrome
Conflict Theory
Gender Role Theory
Role Model
Role Confusion
Cycle of Violence
Sexual Abuse

Trigger Incident
Paranoia
Psychological Theories
Exchange Theory
Status Differential
Intergenerational Transmission of
    Violence
Learned Helplessness
Victim Precipitation

Resources

Callers can find local hotlines in their phone books, appearing under such titles as RAPE, or from information operator. These hotline services are confidential, and although some are run by religious organizations, the general policy is not to discuss religion unless a caller wishes.

National Council on Child Abuse and Family Violence
1155 Connecticut Ave. N.W., Ste. 300
Washington, DC 20036
(202) 429-6695
Promotes public awareness of abuse of women, children, and the elderly.

National Coalition Against Domestic Violence
P.O. Box 18749
Denver, CO 80218-0749
(303) 839-1852
Gathers information on domestic violence and lobbies Congress for legislation.

National Network for Victims of Sexual Assault
P.O. Box 409
Ivy, VA 22945
(703) 671-0691
Links rape crisis centers, follows national and state legislation, and publishes a newsletter.

National Clearinghouse for the Defense of Battered Women
125 S. 9th St., Ste. 302
Philadelphia, PA 19107
(215) 351-0010
Offers encouragement to women imprisoned for killing their violent partners and advocates clemency for these women.

Women's Research Center
2245 West Broadway, Ste. 101
Vancouver, British Columbia
Canada, V6k 2E4
(604) 734-0485
Publishes articles on battered women, rape, and child sexual abuse.

Domestic Violence Coalition on Public Policy
2505 North Front St.
Harrisburg, PA 17110-1111
(717) 234-7353
(800) 53-PCADV
Coalition of organizations that help victims of domestic violence. Lobbies Congress on legislation related to domestic violence.

Center for Nonviolent Communication
3229 Bordeaux
Sherman, TX 75090
(214) 893-3886
Helps people avoid communication patterns that can lead to verbally and physically abusive outcomes. Publishes *Newsletter to Soulmates,* quarterly.

Conflict Resolution/Alternatives to Violence Training Center
P.O. Box 256
Ricker House
Cherryfield, ME 04622
(207) 546-2789
Trains people to use communication skills as an alternative to violence.

Samaritans
500 Commonwealth Ave.
Kenmore Square
Boston, MA 02215
Members volunteer to spend time with depressed and suicidal people. Publishes booklets.

Parents United
232 E. Gish Rd.
San Jose, CA 95112
(408) 453-7616
Provides assistance to individuals and families who have experienced child sexual abuse. Local chapters offer self-help groups. Has sponsored Sons United and Daughters United for childhood victims of sexual abuse. Publishes *PUN,* quarterly newsletter.

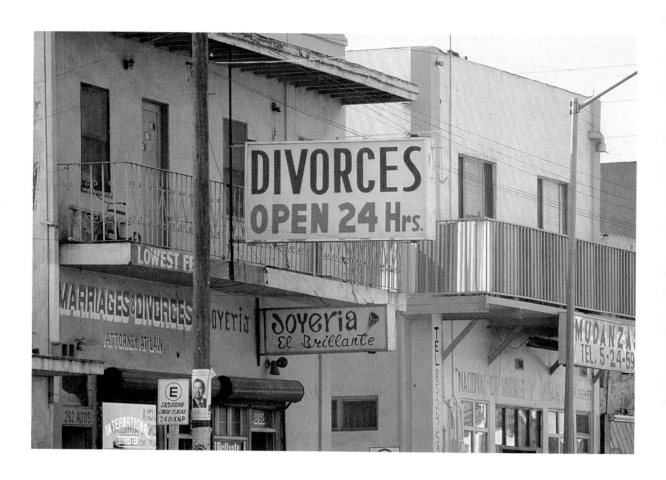

Chapter 15

Divorce

Jeff and Marie have been separated for a year, and their divorce has just become final. Marie has experienced a substantial drop in her income since becoming a single mother. Jeff's salary as an engineer provided a comfortable lifestyle, but now she supports her two children on her income as a secretary and child support payments from Jeff.

Marie has been worried about the upcoming summer because she cannot afford to put the children into a summer day camp program while she is at work and she doesn't want them to be left unattended at home. She asked Jeff to pay the summer camp expenses, but he told her he did not have the money. Marie knows Jeff has recently begun seeing another women and wonders if the expense of dating has made him reluctant to provide the extra money for the children's day camp.

Jeff believes most of his income goes to pay his basic expenses and to help support his children. When he picks up the children on the weekend, he often takes them for a haircut or shopping for shoes or other needed items. It seems to him that every time he goes to Marie's house they argue, usually over money. He also worries that Marie may have criticized him in front of the children. Lately, his stomach feels upset when he approaches her driveway and his visits with the children have diminished from once a week to once a month. Besides, Justine, the woman he has been seeing, needs a good deal of his time. If he spends less time with her, he is convinced she will break off the relationship. This divorce, intended to ease both Jeff's and Marie's lives and to end their unhappiness and difficulty, has created entirely new difficulties with which they must contend.

When divorced people face difficulties with their former spouses, do they think the "grass is always greener on the other side of the fence"? Not Jeff and Marie, who both acknowledge that life was also difficult when they were married. But divorce is not an easy solution. When they break the marital bond, a husband and wife often create a complicated new situation for themselves, especially when children are involved. In this chapter, we examine the complexities of dissolving a marriage, including the risk of divorce, reasons for divorce, adjustment to divorce, and child custody.

Trends

During most of American history, marriage was considered a lifelong commitment. In 1860, around the time of the Civil War, only 7,000 divorces occurred in the entire United States. Forty years later, in 1900, the number of divorces had slowly grown to 56,000 annually (Skolnick 1991; Arendell 1987). During the twentieth century, willingness to seek divorce accelerated. In the 1960s and 1970s, the divorce rate doubled before leveling off during the 1980s at over a million divorces annually (Glenn 1991). Today, half of all married couples experience a divorce, and demographers have estimated that two-thirds of those who enter into marriage in this decade will eventually divorce (Martin and Bumpass 1989). The median duration of marriage in the United States is currently seven years (U.S. Bureau of the Census, 1991a, Table

TABLE 15.1	Number of Divorces and Divorce Rates, 1900 to 1991	
Year	Number of Divorces	Divorce Rate
1900	56,000	0.7
1910	83,000	0.9
1920	171,000	1.6
1930	196,000	1.6
1940	264,000	2.0
1950	385,000	2.6
1960	393,000	2.2
1965	479,000	2.5
1970	708,000	3.5
1975	1,036,000	4.8
1980	1,182,000	5.2
1985	1,190,000	5.0
1990	1,175,000	4.7
1991	1,168,000	4.6
1992	1,215,000	4.8
1993	1,187,000	4.6

Note: The divorce rate is the number of divorces per 1,000 population.

Sources: World Almanac and Book of Facts, 1993. New York: Scripps Howard/Pharos Books, page 941.

U.S. Bureau of the Census 1993. *Statistical Abstract of the United States: 1992.* (112th ed.), Table 80, page 54. Washington, D.C.: U.S. Government Printing Office.

U.S. Department of Health and Human Services 1994. *Monthly Vital Statistics Report,* 42-13, Oct. 11, page 4.

133). Furthermore, divorce is no longer limited primarily to couples without children. One-fourth of American children currently live in a one-parent family, and over half of all children will witness their parents' divorce and spend some portion of their childhood in a one-parent home before they reach age eighteen (U.S. Bureau of the Census, 1994b, Table F; Bumpass 1984).

Explanation for the 1965 to 1980 Divorce Boom

Explanations for the dramatic rise in divorce in the late 1960s and 1970s include the following social trends: marital dissatisfaction, the declining wages of men, the employment of married women, extended life expectancy, and a decline in social support for marriage.

Marital Dissatisfaction. The increase in divorce in the late 1960s and 1970s may be due either to growing marital dissatisfaction or to an increased willingness to end an unhappy relationship. It is possible that levels of marital unhappiness have remained constant over the years. However, as divorce has became more acceptable, unhappy couples may have become more willing to end unsatisfactory marriages.

Alternatively, the rise in divorce could reflect growing dissatisfaction with marriage. Glenn (1991) examined data on marital happiness in the U.S. General Social Surveys, which have been conducted annually since 1972 using a nationally representative sample of adults age eighteen and older. He found that respondents have reported increasing levels of dissatisfaction with marriage since the early 1970s. Glenn attributes this growing disillusionment with marriage to the decline in the "ideal of marital permanence." Couples no longer expect that marriage will last until death. The expectation of divorce can produce a self-fulling prophesy. When people see divorce as a possibility, they become cautious about making the strong commitment and personal sacrifices that could strengthen their marriages (Gill 1993; Glenn 1991). Glenn (1991) argues that when people are in the habit of considering alternatives to their own marriages they begin to focus on the sources of irritation and dissatisfaction in the relationship. At the same time, people tend to overlook the ways a marital relationship meets their needs. Thus, according to Glenn (1991), freedom of choice creates a growing willingness to consider the option of divorce.

The Declining Wages of Men. Recent economic change in U.S. society has brought hardship to many marriages and increased the likelihood of divorce. The real wages of men have declined since 1960, creating economic insecurity and emotional strain. The availability of blue-collar factory jobs that pay a family wage has declined as factories have relocated to developing countries. The new high-technology industries in the United States offer jobs that pay only 68 percent of the wages offered by the declining "smokestack" factories, such as steel mills. Today one-third of white men and over one-half of African-Ameri-

When married women are earning their own income, they are not dependent on marriage for their financial survival and divorce is a less devasting option. Thus, women's participation in the workforce may be related to the rise in the divorce rate.

can men of family-building age, twenty to thirty-four years old, do not earn enough to support a family of four above the poverty line (Wilkie 1991). The deteriorating economic position of men has placed strain on marriages and made it necessary for many young wives and mothers to enter the labor force.

Employment of Married Women. The divorce boom of the 1960s and 1970s has also been attributed to the growing employment of married women since World War II (Ahlburg and DeVita 1992). Participation of wives in the labor force may promote divorce in two ways. First, employment offers women economic independence and an alternative to marriage. Second, Glenn (1991) argues that the paid employment of married women has increased the strains on marriage by creating conflict over how the roles of husband and wife are defined. As wives enter the labor force, disagreements over the division of household labor and child care become common (Booth, et al. 1984).

Extended Life Expectancy. As life expectancy has increased, marital partners have been challenged to undergo personal change as they move through the life cycle. In 1900, when the average person died at about the age of forty-eight, marriage involved a prolonged stage of childrearing (Skolnick 1991). Today, couples produce fewer children, combine paid employment with homemaking, and look forward to twenty-five or thirty empty-nest years. Each life stage requires adjustment in marriage.

Decline in Social Support for Marriage. Margaret Mead once said, "There is no society in the world where people have stayed married without enormous community pressure to do so" (quoted in Wallerstein and Blakeslee 1989:297). The sexual revolution of the 1960s and 1970s ushered in liberalized sexual attitudes and growing cohabitation. Unmarried people, including those who are separated or divorced, now have alternative sexual outlets. In the past, there was strong social pressure to limit sexual expression to marriage. By regulating sexuality, marriage provided sexual rewards not readily available elsewhere. As alternative sexual relationships have become possible, the institution of marriage has weakened.

No-Fault Divorce

In addition to the social change discussed above, divorce has become widespread partly because changes in divorce law have made divorces easier to obtain. In recent years, most states have changed from an adversarial divorce system to a no-fault one.

Adversarial Divorce System. In the *adversarial divorce* system, which was widely used in the past, one party had to prove the partner had committed adultery, cruelty, or some other wrongdoing in order to obtain a divorce. Most state laws made the assumption that marriage was a lifelong commitment unless misconduct had taken place. The adversarial divorce system frequently awarded alimony to the wife because the husband was expected to be responsible for his former wife's economic support. Partners hired lawyers and sometimes a private detective as well to bolster their positions in court. Divorce proceedings under this adversarial system inflamed existing conflicts between partners and added new ones. This heightened level of spousal animosity often resulted in emotionally distressed mothers who had difficulty caring for their children and fathers who backed away from seeing their children in order to avoid contact with the former spouse (Dudley 1991).

No-Fault Divorce System. In an effort to avoid the hostility associated with adversarial divorce, almost all states have adopted a *no-fault divorce* system in which "divorce on demand" is available (Kitson and Morgan 1990). In no-fault divorce couples can dissolve a marriage on the basis of incompatibility and neither partner is assumed to have "caused" the divorce. In many states, the partner's consent is not necessary for a divorce to be obtained. Thus, a divorce is easier to obtain today than it was in the past.

Mediation, now available in most states, also helps to reduce conflict. Under mediation, a court-appointed counselor helps a couple to agree on a divorce settlement rather than battle each other in court. The benefits of the new no-fault divorce system are a reduced level of spousal conflict and the promotion of an

---

BOX 15.1 · World Perspectives

Divorce in Saudi Arabia

Men and women do not have equal rights to divorce in the Muslim countries of the Middle East. Divorce in Saudi Arabia is a male prerogative that takes the form of "verbal repudiation." A husband can obtain a divorce by telling his wife two times that he is divorcing her. This right to "repudiate the wife" is unconditional, meaning the husband does not have to give formal reasons for the divorce or plead his case in a court of law. Divorce is a private act that takes place within the family, usually at home (Mernissi 1975; Minai 1981). A wife has no parallel right to divorce her husband unless that right was written into the marriage contract prior to marriage (Minai 1981). However, not all husbands end a marriage they consider unsatisfactory. Divorce brings social disapproval, and a wealthy husband is more likely to take a second wife than to divorce the first. Islamic law, which is based on the Quran (the bible of the Islamic faith), allows a man to have four wives if he can economically support them.

The custom in which a groom gives the wife a *dower* at marriage offers women some protection against divorce. The dower is money and gifts that the groom presents to the bride and her family at the time of the wedding. This is the opposite of a dowry, which is a custom in other cultures, where the bride's family presents money or gifts to the husband and his family. In the Middle East, the husband pays only part of the dower when he marries. The remainder is paid to the wife when and if her husband divorces

her. This divorce settlement money is supposed to provide for the wife's support, but in reality the amount is usually too small to maintain her for more than year. The divorced wife's family is expected to find her another husband during that time. However, older ex-wives have difficulty finding another spouse and experience economic hardship. Saudi Arabian men prefer young wives and often marry women who are about sixteen years old, putting older divorcees at a disadvantage in the marriage market (Minai 1981).

In a Saudi Arabian divorce, the custody of children goes to the father. Saudi Arabia, like other Islamic countries, practices *patrilineal descent,* through which children belong to the father's kinship group. Men remain in the family home with the children; the divorced wife returns to her parents home. During the first three months following divorce, women are not allowed to remarry. The divorced wife must remain chaste (free of sexual activity) during this time in order to see whether or not she is pregnant by her former husband. If she is, she has to turn over the infant to the husband after birth, although divorced mothers have visiting rights while they are nursing an infant. After the child is weaned, visitation for the wife is worked out informally between the former husband and wife. Many women try to revive their former husband's sexual interest after divorce so they can continue to visit their husband's household and maintain a relationship with

active role for noncustodial parents with their children (Dudley 1991; Buehler 1989). However, some states that have adopted no-fault divorce have also retained aspects of the adversarial system for settling property disputes and child custody questions.

In the last several decades, most states have also adopted a *principle of equity* in the division of property acquired during marriage. This change avoided some past abuses in which property, such as a family home or business, held only in the husband's name was awarded solely to the husband. However, the equal division of marital property often means that the family home is sold and the wife and children, as well as the husband, are forced to move (Weitzman 1990). This situation can be disruptive to the lives of children.

World Perspectives   CONTINUED

their children (Minai 1981).

The custom of *purdah* makes it difficult for Saudi Arabian women to find employment and support themselves after divorce. Purdah refers to the seclusion of women and is a form of gender segregation. Under purdah, women are forbidden to socialize with or work alongside men who are not family members (Ibrahim 1990a). To minimize social contact between the sexes, when women leave their homes they are required to wear a *chador,* a veil covering the head and held in front of the mouth, worn over a full-length robe reaching to the feet.

Purdah, or gender segregation, creates some jobs for women: Female teachers are needed in all-female schools, and female physicians are hired to treat women in medical clinics (Ibrahim 1990b). However, purdah closes many more jobs to women than it opens. For the Saudi Arabian woman who is lucky enough to find a job after divorce, getting to work can be difficult. Divorced women, like all Saudi Arabian women, are not allowed to drive. Employed women must either ask a male relative to drive them to work or hire a driver. In addition, Saudi Arabian women cannot easily take jobs that require travel. In order to obtain a passport, board an airplane, or stay in a hotel, a Saudi Arabian woman must either be accompanied by a male relative or have written permission from a male relative (Ibrahim 1990b).

During the Gulf War, Saudi Arabian women observed American women soldiers wearing pants and driving trucks. Some Saudi women were emboldened to stage a demonstration emphasizing their desire to be allowed to drive cars. Seventy well-educated Saudi women, property veiled in *chadors*, gathered in front of a Safeway grocery store in the city of Riyadh and drove in a caravan for about half a mile before they were arrested by the religious police. Saudi Arabia has two police systems, one civil and the other religious. Police who operate under The Committee for Commendation of Virtue and Prevention of Vice enforce religous practice and morality (Ibrahim 1990b). The protesting women were released by the religious police after signing a statement promising not to drive again. A strong backlash from Islamic fundamentalists caused a number of the women demonstrators to be fired from their jobs. Religious pamphlets labeled the protestors as prostitutes. However, the women protestors had the support of their families, and one woman's husband drove behind her in his car during the demonstration to offer moral support (Ibrahim 1990a).

Not all women are pushing for change in Saudi Arabia's dress code and prohibition of women drivers. Conservative women state that they are comfortable wearing the chador, or veil. Such women argue that the veil keeps them from being sexually harassed on the street, protects them from blowing sand, and provides them with privacy. Educated, upper-middle-class women who don the chador in public often wear European fashions such as high heels and short skirts when they remove the veil in the privacy of their homes. Many of these women are far more interested in gaining employment and divorce rights than they are in changing the traditional dress women wear in public (LeMayne 1990).

Who Runs the Highest Risk of Divorce?

Although divorce has become easier to obtain and more widespread, not everyone runs an equal risk of marital breakup. The risk of divorce is affected by age at first marriage, education, the presence of children, a prior nonmarital birth, parents' marital history, and race.

Age at First Marriage

The single most important factor influencing the risk of divorce is age at marriage. Those who marry as teenagers run a higher risk of divorce than those who marry in their twenties. Teenage brides and grooms tend to cut short their education which leaves them less prepared for employment than those who marry at an older age. Likewise, teen spouses often have limited experience with dating and independent living and thus have fewer opportunities to develop realistic expectations for adult marital roles. Married teenagers often feel isolated and left out of teen activities; this places stress on a marriage. The timing of their life events, including marriage and parenthood, is out of sync with their peers (Heaton 1991). People who enter their first marriage at a young age also carry a high risk of divorce in subsequent marriage. It may be young marriage interrupts the process of maturation and the impact of this deficit is long-lasting (White 1990).

Although some marriages begin early and last a lifetime, partners who marry young are at a higher risk of divorce, both in their first marriage and in subsequent marriage.

Education

The relationship between education and the risk of divorce is a complex one. That is, we are not able to say that the higher a person's educational level, the lower the divorce rate. In fact, those who have dropped out of high school and those who have dropped out of college have the highest divorce rate. Those who have completed high school and those who have completed four years of college are the least likely to divorce. Perhaps, persistence in pursuing an education is related to persistence in attempting to work out marital difficulties (Heaton 1991).

Presence of Children

Children tend to have a stabilizing effect on marriage, probably because their presence increases marital commitment. Childless couples have a higher divorce rate than couples with children (Heaton 1991). A first birth reduces the probability of divorce to "virtually nil" during the year following the birth (White 1990). The gender of children also influences the risk of divorce. Couples with one or more male children are less likely to divorce than couples with only female children. Because the father's role is more clearly defined for rearing sons, fathers of sons may feel more bonded to the family (Heaton 1991).

Premarital Birth

Women who have experienced a premarital birth run a higher risk of divorce than women who enter marriage childless. Premarital births tend to interfere with educational attainment, decreasing earning ability and making a woman less attractive as a mate. A premarital birth may also hinder the search for a suitable partner, thereby diminishing the probability of marital success. In addition, nonbiological parents may be less committed to the marriage and parenting role than biological parents, increasing divorce risk (Heaton 1991).

Socioeconomic Status

Couples of low socioeconomic status have a higher divorce risk than couples in the upper-income brackets. Low-income couples are more likely to possess a variety of characteristics that increase the probability of divorce, including low educational attainment, premarital pregnancy, and early marriage. In addition, an inadequate income puts a strain on the marital relationship, creating stress that shows up in marital disagreements (Krokoff 1987; Lorenz 1991).

Parent's Marital History

Adult children whose parents have divorced are at a greater risk of experiencing a divorce than are those from intact homes (Keith and Finlay 1988). Children of divorce often experience anxiety over romantic relationships and have greater difficulty trusting members of the opposite sex. The expectation of divorce can become a self-fulfilling prophesy.

Race

African Americans have a higher divorce rate than whites, but this has not always been the case (White 1990). In the past, African-American couples frequently separated without the benefit of divorce. However, as low-cost legal services became available to the poor, the divorce rate among African Americans increased. Currently, the cost of divorce still represents a hardship and African Americans remain separated longer than whites before obtaining a divorce (Arendell 1987).

Although racial differences in divorce rates appear to reflect in part the greater tendency for African Americans to be overrepresented in low income groups, social class does not explain all of the racial disparity in divorce rates. African Americans face a *sex-ratio imbalance* that also encourages divorce (White 1990). Guttentag and Secord (1983) argue that the divorce rate is influenced by the availability of alternative potential mates. When the number of unattached women is higher than the number of unattached men, men who divorce can be relatively confident that they will be able to form an alternative romantic relationship. Sociologist Robert Staples (1982) argues that the sex-ratio imbalance in the African-American community increases the probability of divorce. Educational and occupational attainment tends to be higher for African-American women than for African-American men, creating a situation in which African-American women experience a shortage of suitable partners. Likewise, the high unemployment rate among African-American men removes many of them from consideration as marriage partners. Well-educated, employed African-American men who divorce have a favorable position in the marriage market.

Review Questions

1. Describe the recent trends in the divorce rate.
2. How can you explain the rapid rise in the divorce rate during the 1970s?
3. How does no-fault divorce differ from adversarial divorce?
4. Who runs the highest risk of divorce?
5. Why is the divorce rate higher among African Americans than among whites?

Why Do People Divorce?

While the above section examined the social groups who run the highest risk of divorce, this section examines the dissatisfactions and conflicts that precipitate divorce.

Sexual Dissatisfaction and Extramarital Affairs

Disenchantment with the sexual relationship is often one factor contributing to divorce (McCann and Biaggio 1989; Sarrel and Sarrel 1984). In this case, the passion fades and the sexual relationship becomes habituated or boring. Waller-

BOX 15.2   A C l o s e r   L o o k

Explanation for Figure 15.1

In 1992 there were over 16 million currently divorced people in the United States. Figure 15.1 compares the number of divorced people* with the number of married people.† This figure illustrates the increase in the divorced population and the increasing prominence of divorced persons in American society over the last three decades. In 1960, there were only 35 divorced people for every 1,000 married people in the United States, and divorced people often felt unusual or out of place. By 1992, there were 152 divorced people for every 1,000 married people, and divorced people were a significant part of the American population.

The Growing Importance of the Currently Divorced Population

Explanation for Figure 15.2

Figure 15.2 shows that the ratio of divorced people to married people is highest in the black population. This is due to a high divorce rate and a low remarriage rate. Of the three groups shown, the ratio of divorced people to married people is lowest among Asians.

*Divorced people refers to those who are divorced but not remarried.
†Married people refers to both married and remarried people with spouse present.

Figure 15.2
Ratio of Divorced Persons per 1,000 Married Persons with Spouse Present, 1992

Figure 15.1
Ratio of Divorced Persons per 1,000 Married Persons with Spouse Present: 1960 to 1992.

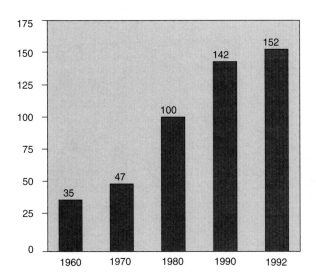

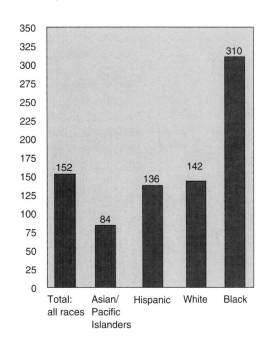

Sources: U.S. Bureau of the Census, Current Population Reports, P20-468, *Marital Status and Living Arrangements: March 1992,* U.S. Government Printing Office, Washington, D.C., 1992. Table D, page IX and page VII.

U.S. Bureau of the Census, Current Population Reports, P20-450, *Marital Status and Living Arrangements: March 1990,* U.S. Government Printing Office, Washington, D.C., 1991. Figure 2, page 2.

Sources: U.S. Bureau of the Census, Current Population Reports, P20-468, *Marital Status and Living Arrangements: March 1992,* U.S. Government Printing Office, Washington, D.C., 1992. Table D, page IX.

U.S. Bureau of the Census, Current Population Reports, P20, *Asian and Pacific Islander Population in the U.S.: March 1990–91.* U.S. Government Printing Office, Washington, D.C., 1991. Table 1, page 15.

stein and Blakeslee (1989) were surprised by the number of midlife people in their study who attributed their divorces to the declining sexual attractiveness of their mates. Many of these were men who subsequently married younger women. Wallerstein and Blakeslee (1989) argue that the physical changes in the partner's body remind spouses of their own mortality and the loss of sexual interest is in part brought on by a fear of aging.

One reason frequently cited for divorce is infidelity. However, it is often unclear whether the cause of divorce was dissatisfaction with the marriage or an attraction to an alternative partner. Many people who are contemplating divorce begin a liaison with another partner before announcing the desire for divorce (Wallerstein and Blakeslee 1989). This provides a cushion against loneliness following the separation and divorce. To the marriage partner, it looks like a betrayal, intensifying feelings of rejection and producing low levels of self-confidence and self-esteem. However, not all extramarital affairs lead to divorce (Patterson and Kim 1991).

Drifting Apart

Many divorced couples do not attribute their divorce to a specific precipitating event. It is far more common for divorced couples to report that they drifted apart. Sometimes two people marry who have different interests, religions, attitudes, or life goals and assume love will be able to smooth over these differences. As time passes, these differences become the source of arguments, and the strain can create emotional distance between the partners (Hunt and Hunt 1979). Even partners who begin marriage with similar interests find that much personal growth takes place outside of marriage, on the job or in other activities. At the beginning of a marriage, neither partner can predict what the other will be like twenty years later (Bohannan 1970). It is not unusual for couples to grow apart.

Substance Abuse and Domestic Violence

Substance abuse and domestic violence have long been associated with petitions for divorce. By the mid-nineteenth century most states had accepted cruelty as a ground for divorce; and women's groups, such as temperance organizations, campaigned against both excessive alcohol use and wife battering, which was often associated with it (Riley 1991). Today, substance abuse, including both alcoholism and drug addiction, and partner battering are still closely associated (Bowker 1986; Giles-Sims 1983). Either one can lead to divorce.

Economic Crisis

Economic crisis, such as unemployment of a spouse, can precipitate a marital breakup. Marriages that are unhappy but stable because they provide economic security are particularly vulnerable to economic crisis (Heaton and Albrecht 1991). Marital arguments increase when couples experience economic hardships (Lorenz 1991). In addition, the strain of unemployment substantially increases the risk of domestic violence (Giles-Sims 1983). Moreover, a couple's economic crisis frequently leads to the loss of housing and the necessity to double-up with relatives. Living with in-laws can place a marriage under strain.

Having looked at some of the practical reasons people end their marriages, we now turn to theories that explain why some couples remain together while others divorce.

Divorce Theories

Having discussed a number of aspects of divorce, we need to put some of this information into perspective. Two major social theories, exchange theory and conflict theory, can help explain why people divorce and also shed light on the period following divorce.

Exchange Theory

Exchange theory looks at the costs and benefits of choices people make and examines the available alternatives to those choices. Exchange theory is particularly useful for explaining why the probability of divorce declines as the duration of marriage increases. In general, the longer a couple are married, the greater the costs of marital break-up and the lower the benefits of being single. Couples accumulate property—such as a family home, car, boat, or family business—over the years, and it is costly to divide that property in a divorce. Likewise, couples make an emotional investment in children, and the emotional cost of being separated from children by divorce reduces the likelihood of marital breakup. Couples who have been together over a number of years have built up a common family history and have put in effort to achieve marital adjustment. The loss of this history and effort is another cost of divorce (Heaton 1991). Likewise, when attorney's fees associated with divorce are high, the attractiveness of divorce diminishes to some extent (White 1990).

Exchange theory also looks at alternatives to the current marriage in determining the costs and benefits of divorce. Couples who have separated are more likely to reconcile than divorce when the costs of divorce are high and when alternatives to the present marriage are unappealing. The benefits of being single decline as a person ages. Older individuals have a lower probability of finding an alternative mate in the marriage market (Thornton and Rodgers 1987). In addition, divorce may appear undesirable to a wife who is unemployed or has a low income and faces impoverishment after separation. Thus, costs and benefits operate in a context in which alternatives to the present marriage are examined.

While exchange theory looks at costs and benefits, conflict theory focuses on the distribution of resources.

Conflict Theory

Conflict theory looks at differences in power and well-being resulting from an unequal distribution of resources. This theory has been used to explain the differential impact of divorce on men and women, by examining how resources are distributed when divorce occurs. The unequal distribution of resources has an impact on the well-being of family members (Ferree 1990).

Husbands often have intangible resources that place them in a favorable position after divorce. A husband's education, professional license, retirement fund, and access to health insurance are all assets that are not typically divided in a divorce. Even though the wife may have sacrificed her education and career to work and support her husband through professional school, most judges have ruled that the wife cannot claim part ownership in his professional license or education.

Three-fourths of divorced women are employed and not dependent on public assistance. Of these employed women, nine out of ten work full time (Arendell 1987). Divorced women are at a disadvantage when they become the primary support of their families because they tend to have fewer resources, such as employment skills and education, for producing income. Because of their childrearing responsibilities, women rarely have the opportunity to pursue education and improve their employment skills after divorce. Most must rely on the employment skills they held during marriage. However, marriage does not prepare most women to earn an adequate living. Employed married women contribute only one-third of the total family income, primarily because women tend to be concentrated in low-paying, dead-end, pink-collar jobs, such as secretaries and waitresses (Teachman 1990). Furthermore, married women often interrupt employment to care for children, limiting their own career development. Divorced women who must support their families are at an economic disadvantage. However, divorced women who were employed during marriage fare better economically after divorce than women who were full-time homemakers (Arendell 1987).

Following a divorce, men tend to have more discretionary income to spend on recreation, food, and clothing than divorced women (Arendell 1987). Families headed by divorced women are less likely than other families to be covered by either publicly-funded or private health-care insurance. After divorce, child-care costs and health-care expenses tend to strain the budget of single mothers; therefore, they often economize by limiting the use of health care services (Arendell 1987). Thus, conflict theory focuses on the difference in resources possessed by men and women after divorce and how this difference affects their well-being. However, conflict theory does not adequately address the hardships experienced by divorced men, particularly custodial fathers. We now look at the economic impact of divorce on custodial parents and their children.

The Financial Impact of Divorce

Former spouses are not the only ones who must adjust to a new financial situation. The financial well being of children after divorce is closely tied to the economic fate of the custodial parent.

The Financial Position of Custodial Parents

The income of both men and women declines after divorce. However, the decline in standard of living tends to be particularly severe for custodial mothers, as was the case for Marie, described at the beginning of this chapter (Duncan and Hoffman 1985; Smock 1991).

The Impact of No-Fault Divorce. In her book, *The Divorce Revolution*, Lenore Weitzman (1985) argues that no-fault divorce produced unintended consequences that have created economic hardship for divorced women and their children. Weitzman points out that the no-fault divorce system makes the *assumption of self-sufficiency*, in which both the husband and wife are expected to be able to support themselves and be economically self-sufficient following divorce (Weitzman 1985, 1990). However, women generally earn a good deal less than men, and many divorced women are plunged into poverty or near poverty after divorce. Alimony has become a thing of the past in all but a few cases (Arendell 1987). The income transfer between former spouses following a divorce generally takes the form of child support.

Custodial Mothers. Women have the primary responsibility for child care after divorce, and 85 percent of one-parent families are headed by mothers. Most custodial mothers experience a dramatic decline in income following divorce. The U.S. Bureau of the Census reports in 1991 that married women with children who were living on a median income of $2,435 per month before separation from their husbands experience an average income decline to a median of $1,543 four months after separation. The income of these single mothers rises to a median of only $1,711 sixteen months after separation (Jost and Robinson 1991). In contrast, custodial fathers have an annual income averaging twice that of custodial mothers (Meyer and Garasky 1993).

The deteriorating economic position of children after divorce has become a serious national issue. The average child support payment in 1987, $2,710 per year, made up slightly less than one-fifth of the divorced mother's income (U.S Bureau of the Census 1991a, Table 617). Because the earnings of divorced mothers tend to be low, children often end up with too little money to provide for their needs (Arendell 1987; Weitzman 1990).

After divorce most custodial mothers experience a decline in their income. This puts children of divorce at financial risk, particularly when child support payments are late or go unpaid.

Custodial Fathers. Until recently, custodial fathers have largely been overlooked. However, single-father families now number more than 1 1/2 million, making up 15 percent of all single-parent families. The number of single-father families has tripled in the last two decades, reflecting an increasing willingness of judges to award physical custody of children to fathers (Meyer and Garasky 1993).

Child Support

The National Survey of Families and Households revealed that fewer than half of single mothers received any child support during the past year (Seltzer 1991). Parents with a child support award from the courts are more likely to receive child support than those without such awards. Of those custodial mothers with child support awards, three-fourths received some child support payments over the previous year (Meyer and Garasky 1993).

Single-father families are less likely than single-mother families to receive a child support award from the courts. In addition, single fathers who have received a child support award are even less likely than single mothers actually to collect child support from the noncustodial parent. This situation generally reflects the low income of the noncustodial mother (Meyer and Garasky 1993). However, the large number of single parents who receive inconsistent child support payments or no payments at all has led to congressional action.

In an attempt to remedy the problem of inconsistent or missing child support payments, the Family Support Act of 1988 provided for a system of automatically withholding wages of noncustodial parents whose child-support orders were being enforced by the state. Beginning in 1994, this provision expanded to allow all new child support awards to be deducted automatically from a noncustodial parent's paycheck. In addition, the law allows the government to attach the income tax returns of noncustodial parents who are delinquent in payments. Prior federal legislation allowed for wage withholding of parents whose former spouses received welfare (Jost and Robinson 1991; Seltzer 1991).

Studies of noncustodial fathers have revealed a connection between paying child support and visitation. Fathers who pay child support are more likely than nonpaying fathers to spend time with their children. Fathers who pay no child support have very little contact with their children (Furstenberg et al. 1983; Seltzer 1991). Although, we know very little about noncustodial mothers, the information available indicates that they tend to stay in touch with their children (Amato 1987; Fine and Kurdek 1992).

Divorced Parents and Poverty

The increase in divorce has contributed to the feminization of poverty, the growing impoverishment of women and their children. Female-headed families represent one-fourth of all families with children, yet they constitute over half (54 percent) of all poor families with children (U.S. Bureau of the Census 1993b, Table G; 1992c, Table 9). Divorce often results in sharp downward social mobility for women with children. The poverty rate among single-mother families runs 45 percent, compared to a 6 percent poverty rate for two-parent families and an 18 percent poverty rate for single-father families (Meyer and Garasky 1993; U.S. Bureau of the Census 1991a, Table 754). Although single-father families are less likely to live in poverty than single-mother families, the economic plight of all impoverished single parents and their children is a cause for concern.

Divorce creates financial hardships for many parents with young children. In addition, even women with grown children who have left home often find themselves in dire economic straits following divorce, as the next discussion of displaced homemakers shows.

Displaced Homemakers

Displaced homemakers are women age 35 and over who have been full-time homemakers for an extended period before divorce. The hallmark of the displaced homemaker is her lack of employment experience and skills. One out of five divorces involves women who have been married for fifteen years or more (Arendell 1987). Many of these are older women who settled into family life when marriage was considered to be a social contract in which the woman traded her child care and domestic services for lifelong economic support (Skolnick 1991). The economic hardship experienced by displaced homemakers is particularly severe.

Displaced homemakers make up a small but important segment of the population of single women who live alone in poverty (Arendell 1987). Welfare, which takes the form of Aid to Families with Dependent Children (AFDC), is not available to women with grown children. Likewise, child support payments from non-custodial parents typically end when children reach age eighteen. The displaced homemaker's economic hardship is likely to continue into old age. Divorce settlements do not usually award to women any interest in their former husband's pension plan. Furthermore, when a displaced homemaker enters paid employment, she is not likely to earn pension benefits because of the lengthy vesting requirement before a worker is eligible for pension payments (Arendell 1987).

Having looked at the financial adjustments faced by divorced people, we now examine emotional adjustment following divorce.

Emotional Adjustment to Divorce

Many couples find the period following separation and divorce a difficult one. They have made the decision to separate and divorce, and now a period of emotional adjustment is necessary. Adjustment to divorce is defined as being able to function adequately in daily responsibilities at work and home; being relatively free of symptoms of mental illness; and having established an identity that is separate from marriage to the ex-spouse (Kitson and Morgan 1990). People generally go through a series of stages as they gradually adjust to divorce.

Stages of Adjustment to Divorce

Judith Wallerstein and her colleagues (1980; 1989) identified three stages divorced persons go through as they adjust to their new life: the acute stage, transition, and stabilization.

The Acute Stage. The initial reaction to a deteriorating marriage and the decision to separate and divorce is often emotional upheaval. The acute stage of adjustment to divorce is characterized by bouts of anger and depression and feeling overwhelmed by the changes in one's life (Cauhape 1983, Wallerstein and Blakeslee 1989). This stage lasts from one to two years after separation, but in some individuals it can last longer. Areas of life in which recently divorced persons report significant difficulty are coping with loneliness, performing homemaking tasks, and functioning at work (Bloom et al. 1985). Family life is typically disorganized, with mealtimes and bedtimes for the children becoming erratic (Wallerstein and Kelly 1980). In addition, divorced persons report sexual dissatisfaction (Bloom et al. 1985).

For women, the acute stage is likely to be characterized by fluctuations in income and inconsistent child support payments, making financial worries a daily matter (Wallerstein and Blakeslee 1989). However, women are particularly adept at mobilizing a social support network that offers emotional support. Social networks of family and friends play a key role in facilitating adjustment to divorce, particularly for women (Kitson and Morgan 1990). In contrast men tend to rely on the spouse for intimacy and have fewer emotionally close relationships with relatives and same-sex friends. Thus, the loss of a spouse through divorce can mean severe loneliness for the divorced man (Wallerstein and Blakeslee 1989).

Transition. In the transition stage, which generally begins around a year and a half after separation, most people come to terms with the divorce and accept their new life as a single person. The chaos of the acute stage diminishes, and life settles into a routine. Many divorced people begin to see the transition stage as one that offers opportunities (Wallerstein and Blakeslee 1989). Some life changes that can characterize the transition stage are reestablishing relationships with old friends, going back to school, taking up a new hobby, focusing on physical fitness, changing jobs, establishing a new career, or beginning to look for a new partner. During this stage emotions can swing from exhilaration at being independent to great sadness over being alone (Cauhape 1983).

Restabilization. Restabilization, which generally begins three to five years after separation, is a stage of reclaiming oneself by establishing an identity separate from a relationship with the former spouse (Wallerstein and Blakeslee 1989). Detachment characterizes this stage: Divorced people report that the former spouse's remarks and behavior, which irritated them in the past, have lost the power to generate an emotional reaction. Many people remarry and reorganize their lives with a new spouse. Others begin to take being single in stride. However, Wallerstein and Blakeslee (1989) found winners and losers in divorce. Those who initially requested the divorce were far better adjusted and happier ten years after the divorce than those who initially resisted the divorce. For the partner who did not want the divorce, some leftover anger from the acute stage often spilled into the restabilization stage in the form of flashbacks and bitter memories.

Relationship with the Former Spouse

Divorce does not necessarily terminate a relationship between ex-spouses. In a study of couples two years after divorce (approximately three years after separation), Masheter (1991) found particularly low levels of well-being among those who experienced preoccupation with the ex-spouse. *Preoccupation* consists of obsessive thoughts of the ex-spouse that a person has difficulty getting out of his or her mind. The researchers also found that couples with children had less friendly contact and quarrelled more frequently than those without children. Former spouses who continued to quarrel experienced lower levels of well-being than those who got along well with their ex-spouses. Nonetheless, adjustment to divorce tended to improve with time. Two years after divorce (approximately three years after separation), a greater number of former spouses had friendly rather than hostile feelings toward their ex-spouses. Likewise, four out of five had low levels of preoccupation with the former spouse two years after the divorce.

Next we turn to the lives of children, which are also affected by divorce.

Review Questions

1. What are some factors that lead to marital conflict and precipitate divorce?
2. How does exchange theory explain the propensity to divorce?
3. How does conflict theory explain the diminished economic position of women following divorce?
4. What effect does divorce have on the economic position of custodial parents and their children? Why is divorce a particular economic hardship for custodial mothers?
5. How likely are custodial parents to receive child support and what recent legislation attempts to remedy this situation?
6. Who are displaced homemakers and what hardships do they face?
7. What are the stages of adjustment to divorce? What factors make adjustment to divorce difficult?

Children's Postdivorce Adjustment

Divorce has become so widespread that half of American children can expect to spend some time in a one-parent home before they reach age eighteen (Lauer and Lauer 1991). The transition from a two-parent to a one-parent family can be stressful.

Short-Term Difficulties

During the first two years following a divorce, children often have difficulty coping with this change in their lives. Divorce has been associated with problems in children's emotional, physical, social, and academic functioning.

Emotional and Physical Functioning. After parental separation children often experience anger and uncertainty about the future. Typical reactions of children to divorce include anxiety and depression accompanied by such symptoms as nightmares, bed-wetting, moodiness, temper tantrums, headaches, stomach aches, unusual fears, and problems in school (Kline 1991; Machida and Holloway 1991). For some children, this distress continues as long as two years after their parent's divorce (Lauer and Lauer 1991). Children of divorced parents tend to have more physical health problems than children from intact homes. Many of these health problems are believed to be associated with the stress of adjusting to divorce (Lauer and Lauer 1991). Younger children tend to have more difficulty adjusting to divorce than older children (Kline 1991).

Academic Problems. Children from divorce-disrupted families perform less well in school on the average than do children from intact homes. Both health problems and problems with classroom behavior contribute to these school difficulties. Children of divorce display symptoms of depression and anxiety in school, often appearing lethargic, inattentive, disruptive, or easily distracted (Kinard and Reinherz 1986; Machida and Holloway 1991).

Long-Term Consequences

The impact of divorce is likely to affect children in subtle ways well into adulthood. Adult children of divorce are more likely than those from intact families to experience a marital break-up of their own (Lauer and Lauer 1991). In their

---

BOX 15.3 — Social Issues

Should Unhappy Couples Stay Together for the Children?

A number of unhappily married couples think they should remain together for the sake of the children. However, many childhood problems that have been attributed to divorce are now thought to be the result of parental conflict regardless of whether the parents divorce or remain married (Skolnick 1991). Marital conflict has been associated with aggression, delinquency, and depression in children (Emery and O'Leary 1984; Shaw and Emery 1987). Disputing parents often model aggressive behavior or display withdrawal from conflict situations. Their children learn to respond to stress in a similar fashion (Kline et al. 1991). In fact, rates of depression and withdrawal are higher among adolescents from intact homes where parental conflict is prevalent than among children in divorce-disrupted families (Mechanic and Hansell 1989; Lauer and Lauer 1991).

Lauer and Lauer (1991) compared adult children from intact unhappy marriages to adult children from divorced-disrupted families. Those from intact unhappy families were more likely to divorce, had lower levels of marital happiness, and experienced more marital disagreement than those from divorce-disrupted families. Thus, remaining in an unhappy marriage does not necessarily benefit children.

Lauer and Lauer (1991) also found that adults from unhappy families (regardless of whether the family was an intact unhappy family or one disrupted by divorce) were more likely than those from intact happy families to currently be in an intimate relationship. The researchers suggest those from disrupted or unhappy families experience an "intimacy deficit," which makes it imperative for them to be in an intense relationship such as marriage, cohabitation, or steady dating.

Although adult children from divorce-disrupted homes tend to worry a great deal about the future success of their romantic relationships, they do not appear to have more relationship problems than any other group. The levels of self-esteem and social competence of adults with divorced parents are equal to those of adults from intact families (Lauer and Lauer 1991). However, anxieties and fears from childhood carry over into adult relationships. People from divorce-disrupted families appear to have doubts and anxieties about their current relationships, and their fears of breaking up sometimes become self-fulfilling prophecies. Lauer and Lauer (1991) suggest that one direction for counseling adult children of divorce is to help them become aware that these anxieties are a natural result of growing up in a divorce-disrupted family. Dealing with the anxiety may solve much of the problem.

book *Second Chances,* Wallerstein and Blakeslee (1989) used a longitudinal study to provide some insight into the long-term consequences of divorce. Children from divorce-disrupted families were followed for fifteen years, carrying the study into their adulthood. Wallerstein and Blakeslee found half of those from divorce-disrupted homes witnessed ongoing anger between their parents after the divorce. More than half felt rejected by one of their parents, and very few received financial help with college from their relatively affluent fathers. Almost half grew up to be self-deprecating, underachieving, and often angry adults. Women with divorced parents had difficulty trusting men and committing to relationships; men from divorce-disrupted homes had difficulty setting goals in life. Parental divorce also produces long-term consequences for marriage and childbearing patterns.

Early Marriage and Out-Of-Wedlock Births. A number of studies have shown that women from divorce-disrupted families are more likely to bear a child out of wedlock or are more likely to marry in their teens than women from intact families. However, these studies have been criticized for failing to control for social class. Women from families of lower socioeconomic class tend to exhibit higher levels of divorce, out-of-wedlock childbearing, and teen marriages than those from more affluent families.

Sleeper Effect for Girls. Mothers report that after divorce, sons have more health and behavior problems than daughters. However, studies are divided on whether boys suffer more postdivorce problems than girls (Kline 1991). Some researchers argue that the problems divorce creates for girls are less visible because girls are less likely to act out their distress in delinquent or disruptive behaviors. The impact of divorce has a *sleeper effect* on girls, an affect that shows up once they reach adulthood. Women from divorced-disrupted homes are far more likely to have their own marriages end in divorce than are men from divorce-disrupted homes (Machida and Holloway 1991; Stevenson and Black 1988).

Economic and Social Disruption

Recent research has begun to suggest that it may not be the divorce itself which presents problems for children, but instead the economic and social disruptions associated with divorce. When the family home must be sold as part of the divorce settlement, children often lose friends as they move out of their neighborhoods and change schools. Weitzman (1990) argues that divorce settlements that postpone the sale of the family home and allow children to remain in the same school and neighborhood go a long way toward alleviating some of the sources of stress experienced by children after a divorce. Another source of stress for children is the loss of income and downward social mobility that typically follows marital disruption. Mothers typically must work full time after divorce, and employment demands compete for the mother's time, energy, and attention.

Impaired Parenting Ability

Many parents have difficulty adjusting to singlehood following a divorce, and their personal problems can interfere with their ability to provide quality parenting for their children. Much of the negative impact of divorce on children can be explained by the custodial parent's impaired childrearing ability. One important factor that interferes with effective childrearing following a marital break-up is the parent's *self-absorption*. After divorce, parents often become preoccupied with their own emotional problems and responses. This inward focus diminishes a parent's ability to attend to the needs of the child (Kline et al. 1991; Wallerstein and Kelly 1980). Children in a stressful parent–child relationship often experience depression and anxiety.

Critique of the "Divorce Damages Children" Position

Critics of divorce studies point out that researchers often assume divorce will be damaging to children. This expectation often leads to some oversights in research design. Wallerstein and Blakeslee (1989), whose study was discussed above, have been criticized for failing to include in their study a control group of children from intact families (Lauer and Lauer 1991). The lack of a control group may have led to an exaggerated description of the long-term negative effects of divorce (Skolnick 1991). Perhaps adult children from intact homes have some of the same anxieties and difficulties as adult children of divorce. In addition, some of the negative impact of divorce on children may be the result of the stigma attached to divorced families by people outside the family. Some support for this position has been found in studies showing that the difference between children from divorced families and those from intact families has diminished since the 1950s. In recent studies, children of divorce appear to be only moderately more distressed than children from intact homes (Kulka and Weingarten 1979; Lauer and Lauer 1991). In fact, in some cases parental divorce can actually have a positive influence on children, encouraging them to be more self-reliant and self-sufficient (Lauer and Lauer 1991).

A major factor associated with distress in children is ongoing parental conflict following a divorce.

Divorce can be painful and confusing for children. Some of this negative impact can be reduced if they are reassured that they are still loved and that they are not at fault for their parents' separation.

Parental Conflict after Divorce

A major factor associated with distress in children after divorce is ongoing parental conflict following the divorce. In fact, social scientists have moved beyond seeing divorce as an event that by itself causes stress for children. Today, divorce is more apt to be viewed as one event in a long conflict process that began long before the divorce was finalized. The distress of children previously thought to be caused by divorce may actually be the result of parental conflict both before and after the divorce (Skolnick 1991). When divorced parents have a harmonious relationship following separation and divorce, children tend to make a smooth adjustment to living in a one-parent family. Children whose divorced parents get along well tend to have higher self-esteem and fewer behavior problems in school than children whose parents experience continuing conflict after divorce (Machida and Holloway 1991).

Continuing Parental Conflict

Kline (1991) conducted a longitudinal study that followed 154 children for two years after their parents filed for divorce. This study found that parents who had experienced high levels of conflict during marriage tended to have conflict-ridden relationships one year after divorce. Parental conflict affected children by diminishing the quality of the parent–child relationship. One year after divorce, parent–child relationships of mothers who were in conflict with their former spouses were characterized by less warmth and less empathy than mother–child relationships in divorced families where former spouses got along well. In addition, mothers in conflicted relationships modeled less ego control, for example,

---

S o c i a l   I s s u e s

Are Divorce Studies Biased?

Studies describing the effects of divorce on children tend to rely on reports from divorced mothers and teachers who describe the behavior problems of children after divorce. Amato (1991) suggests that these studies may be biased. He maintains that people expect children of divorce to have special problems and that these expectations affect their perception. In one study, Amato presented to college students a description of a twelve-year-old child. Half the students read about a child who had divorced parents; and the other half read the same description except that the marital status of the parents was not given. Students were then asked to describe the child from memory. Subjects who read stories about children of divorce remembered almost twice as many negative facts as did those who read stories about children whose family status was not given. Respondents tended to assume that, unless the divorced status was specified, the child was from an intact family.

Amato concludes that people recall information about children of divorce in a biased manner, remembering more negative information and less positive information about children from divorced families than about children from intact families. Amato suggests that respondents had a "schema" or "person prototype" depicting the child of divorce as a child with problems. They tended to recall information that fit this negative person prototype and overlook positive characteristics that were discordant with the prototype. The prototype acted as a "psychological anchor" in processing information, interpreting behavior and recalling information. Thus studies of the effect of divorce on children tend to be biased. The expectation that divorce will create problems for children tends to lead to reports of problems.

displaying less ability to control outbursts of temper. These mothers also tended to hold lower expectations for ego control in their children (Kline 1991). Parent–child relationships can also serve as a buffer against the negative effects of parental conflict when one parent is affectionate to the child in compensation for hostility expressed by the other parent (Kline 1991).

Triangulation

Divorced couples with children tend to quarrel more after divorce than do couples without children (Masheter 1991). *Triangulation,* in which children become enmeshed in loyalty conflicts, is often experienced by children with disputing parents. Children without siblings are particularly likely to feel pressured to take the side of one parent or the other (Lauer and Lauer 1991). The presence of siblings can be useful in deflecting some of the parental hostility that often follows divorce (Kline 1991).

One arrangement that has been shown to promote children's adjustment to divorce is joint custody, discussed in the next section.

Review Questions

1. What emotional, physical, and academic difficulties do children often experience after divorce?
2. What are the long-term consequences of divorce for children?
3. What criticism has been made of the belief that divorce damages children?
4. How does continuing parental conflict following divorce affect children?

Child Custody

In the past, most divorce cases resulted in *sole custody,* in which the child resided with one parent; in 90 percent of the cases this was the mother. The noncustodial parent, usually the father, had visitation rights. However, attitudes toward custody are changing, and currently all states offer the option of *joint custody,* in which former spouses share responsibility for raising their children. There are two types of joint custody: joint legal custody and joint physical custody (Kitson and Morgan 1990). In *joint legal custody,* the parents share decision-making authority: Each parent has a "say" in childrearing, sharing decisions concerning the child's health, education, and religious upbringing. However, when children reside with only one parent, joint legal custody is difficult to implement. In *joint physical custody,* the children actually have two residences. Instead of visits from the noncustodial parent, children are integrated into that parent's home, often having a bedroom where personal belongings can be kept. This frequent interaction with the children gives the noncustodial parent an opportunity to access their needs and informally to spend some discretionary income on haircuts, shoes, and other items that enhance the children's well-being (Dudley 1991). Joint physical custody is typically accompanied by joint legal custody (Kitson and Morgan 1990). Joint physical custody is rare, and 90 percent of the children of divorce reside with the mother. Parents who opt for joint custody often complain about the expense and logistical difficulties involved in providing two households for their children (Jost and Robinson 1991).

Joint physical custody, when voluntarily agreed upon by parents, has the advantage of promoting the child's adjustment to divorce. However, it is important to be cautious before concluding that joint custody is preferable in all cases. Joint physical custody is typically awarded when both parents request it. Thus, the existing sample of joint custody cases involves couples who get along well enough to work out the logistics of child-sharing (Kitson and Morgan 1990). Joint physical custody may be harmful if severe conflict continues between former spouses or when one spouse has been physically abused.

The Noncustodial Parent

The noncustodial parent is usually the father. There has been a great deal of interest in discovering the degree to which noncustodial fathers maintain a relationship with their children after divorce.

How Often Do Nonresident Fathers See Their Children?

Many noncustodial fathers have close relationships with their children and see them often. However, these involved fathers represent the minority rather than the majority of noncustodial fathers. A large number of divorced fathers have little or no contact with their children. In a broad sample of the American population, including all social classes, half the children of divorce had had no contact with the nonresident parent within the last year (Furstenberg et al. 1983). Using national

The noncustodial parent, most frequently the father, has to make a difficult adjustment when contact with the child is reduced to visits.

data, Seltzer (1991) found that less than one-third of children who live with their mothers see their fathers once a week (Seltzer 1991). Of those fathers who did not visit their children during the past year, 90 percent also had no telephone contact with their children. Furthermore, the amount of contact between the child and the nonresident father tends to decline with time after separation (Seltzer 1991).

Diminished contact with children tends to grow out of the father's emotional reaction to divorce. Noncustodial fathers often experience guilt over the family breakup and have a feeling of diminished competence in performing their parent role (Seltzer 1991). Like the father in the vignette at the beginning of this chapter, divorced fathers

---

BOX 15.5	A Closer Look

Absent Noncustodial Fathers

Dudley (1991) studied a sample of 255 divorced fathers and found that approximately one-third (84) had either no contact or infrequent visits with their children. These fathers had less than one overnight visit per month with their children. The fathers in this study had been divorced for an average of six years and had children under age eighteen. The four most common reasons the fathers gave for seeing their children infrequently are described below.

Former Spouse as an Obstacle

Thirty-three of the eighty-four low-contact fathers identified their former spouse as the major obstacle to frequent visits with children. They complained that their former wives interfered with visitation arrangements. Furthermore, many of these fathers believed that their wives had turned their children against them by expressing negative opinions of the father. Some of these fathers complained bitterly about the court system, which they believed was insensitive to their needs in failing to enforce or extend their visitation rights.

Father's Own Problems

Twenty-two fathers reported that personal problems, such as substance abuse, prevented more frequent contact with their children. Recovering substance abusers expressed a need for help in reestablishing lost relationships with children. Other fathers cited the time demands of their jobs or health problems as the reasons for diminishing contact with their children. Still others reported that they had girlfriends who demand-

ed their time. Unlike the first category of men, these fathers reported that their former wives were cooperative with child visitation, and they were content with the amount of time they spent with their children.

Children Growing Older

A third group of thirteen fathers had children in their late teens and reported that it was the child's decision to diminish contact. These teenagers wanted to spend time with their friends, and many had jobs that took up their time.

Long Distance

The last group of 12 fathers cited distance as the greatest obstacle to seeing their children more often. The average distance between fathers and their children in this group was 1000 miles. Unlike the three previous groups of fathers, who tended to have only minimal telephone contact with their children, these long-distance fathers stayed in touch by telephone immediately after the move, but this contact diminished over time. Fathers in this group tended to see their children for approximately one week over summer vacation.

The decline in contact between fathers and their children which frequently follows divorce occurs for a variety of reasons. Improving relationships between noncustodial fathers and their children will require addressing a variety of issues: the relationship between former spouses, the need for substance abuse treatment and follow-up counseling, the attitude of teenage children, and advice on how to stay close when great distances are involved.

often grieve because they feel they have lost their children. Noncustodial fathers report being particularly bothered because contact with children now takes the form of "visits" (Dudley 1991). Seltzer (1991) found that many fathers react to the pain of separation by avoiding their children, thereby facing fewer reminders of these "lost" children (Seltzer 1991).

Which Divorced Fathers Stay in Touch?

A number of factors affect the amount of contact fathers have with their children following divorce, including the socioeconomic status of the father, the marital status of both parents, and the age and gender of children (Dudley 1991). Fathers most likely to continue to see their children after divorce are those with higher levels of education and income and those with a steady income. Marital status also affects the frequency of a father's visitation after divorce. When a father has remarried and established a new family, the time demands of the new family frequently lead to fewer visits with his children by a previous marriage. Likewise, when a mother has remarried, the divorced father tends to decrease contact with his children. Some fathers believe that the parenting function is being fulfilled by the stepfather, and other fathers wish to allow the child to establish a firm relationship with the stepfather. The age and gender of the child also affect frequency of visits. Younger children, ages two to eight, tend to see the noncustodial father more than older children. Likewise, immediately after divorce, fathers are more likely to spend time with sons than with daughters. However, contact with both sexes equals out when the parents have been divorced for a year and a half or more (Dudley 1991).

Noncustodial Mothers

We have very little information on noncustodial mothers. However, the existing data suggest that noncustodial mothers tend to stay in frequent contact with their children. They tend to visit more often and remain more involved in the lives of their children than noncustodial fathers do (Amato 1987; Fine and Kurdek 1992).

As custodial and noncustodial parents marry, new family forms emerge. Co-parenting and forming stepfamilies are challenges that will be increasingly important in the future. For more information on remarriage and stepparenting, see Chapter 16.

Review Questions

1. What are the advantages of joint physical custody?
2. How important are frequent visits from the noncustodial father?
3. How often do noncustodial fathers see their children?
4. What factors are associated with frequent visits by noncustodial fathers?
5. Which divorced fathers stay in touch with their children?

Summary

1. In recent years most states have changed from an adversary divorce system to a no-fault divorce system.

2. Explanations for the divorce boom in the second half of the twentieth century include growing marital dissatisfaction, the declining wages of men, the employment of married women, extended life expectancy, and the decline in social support for marriage.

3. No-fault divorce has greatly lessened the adversarial aspects of divorce.

4. The risk of divorce is influenced by age at first marriage, education, duration of marriage, presence of children, out-of-wedlock birth, socioeconomic status, parent's marital history, and race.

5. Factors that sometimes precipitate a divorce include sexual dissatisfaction and extramarital affairs, drifting apart, substance abuse, domestic violence, and economic crisis.

6. Two prominent theories used to study divorce are exchange theory, which examines the costs, benefits, and alternatives of divorce, and conflict theory, which looks at the allocation of resources.

7. Women's standard of living tends to decline after divorce; many divorced women and their children become impoverished. A considerable number of custodial fathers are also impoverished.

8. People generally go through three stages in adjusting to divorce: the acute stage, transition, and restabilization.

9. The 1988 Child Support Enforcement Act encourages child support payments by allowing for wage withholding.

10. Children whose parents divorce experience both short-term and long-term negative consequences; but there are also benefits to growing up in a one-parent family.

11. Parenting is often impaired after a divorce, particularly when the former spouses continue to quarrel.

12. Mothers who perceive themselves to be in control of the parent–child relationship tend to have children who make a relatively smooth adjustment to divorce.

13. Joint physical custody among parents who voluntarily adopt this arrangement has had positive results.

14. Approximately half of nonresident fathers have little or no contact with their children. This is particularly the case if one spouse has remarried.

15. The influence of the noncustodial father diminishes with time after divorce.

Key Words

No-Fault Divorce	Adversarial Divorce
Sex-Ratio Imbalance	Exchange Theory
Conflict Theory	Principle of Equity
Assumption of Self-Sufficiency	Standard of Living
Displaced Homemaker	Preoccupation
Sleeper Effect for Girls	Self-Absorption
Triangulation	Joint Physical Custody
Joint Legal Custody	

Center for the Family in Transition
Building B, Ste. 300
5725 Paradise Dr.
Corte Madera, CA 94925
(415) 924-5750
A nonprofit center that conducts research on divorce, separation, remarriage, and child custody. Offers conflict mediation counseling.

Fathers for Equal Rights
P.O. Box 010847 Flagler Station
Miami, FL 33101
(305) 895-6351
An organization of parents and grandparents, especially fathers, involved in court custody cases. Educates the public on the importance of fathers in families. Publishes *Fathers Winning Child Custody Cases.*

Grandparents' and Children's Rights
5728 Bayonne Ave.
Haslett, MI 48840
(517) 339-8663
Clearinghouse of information on legislation related to grandparents' visitation rights.

Lesbian Mother's National Defense Fund
P.O. Box 21567
Seattle, WA 98111
(206) 325-2643
Reports on laws and judicial decisions that affect gay parenting and provides legal and emotional support for gay mothers in custody battles. Publishes *Mom's Apple Pie,* quarterly newsletter.

Mothers Without Custody
P.O. Box 27418
Houston, TX 77256
(713) 840-1622
Local self-help groups help individuals explore custody options. Offers support to parents of children kidnapped by an ex-spouse.

Stepfamily Foundation
333 West End Ave.
New York, NY 10023
(212) 877-3244
(800) SKY-STEP
Compiles information on stepfamilies. Publishes *Step News,* quarterly.

Chapter

16

Looking Forward: Emerging Trends and Future Potentials

Christopher was eight years old when his mother remarried. Now that Christopher is eleven, his stepfather, Jake, coaches his Little League baseball team. Jake played varsity baseball in high school, and he works with Christopher to improve his catching and batting skills. Christopher was never an outstanding ballplayer; sometimes the ball gets past him almost as often as he catches it. Nonetheless, he likes the attention from Jake, especially when he and his stepfather talk about game strategy and the batting lineup. Still, there are tensions between Christopher and his stepfather. Christopher complains that Jake is too strict in enforcing his mother's homework rules. His mother, a nurse, often works in the evenings. Jake insists that homework be completed before Christopher watches any television. On weekends, Christopher cannot go out in the neighborhood to play until his room is clean and Jake is satisfied that his chores have been finished. Christopher's mother occasionally suggests that Christopher call his stepfather "Dad." Christopher shrugs off his mother's suggestion, changes the subject, and continues to call him "Jake." Christopher likes to think of Jake as a "friend," although a demanding friend, rather than as Dad. This leaves Christopher free to have a special relationship with his biological Dad, Sam, whom he visits for two weeks every summer. Sam is curator of an art museum in a small suburban city. Like Sam, Christopher enjoys drawing. Unlike Jake, Sam seems laid back, jokes around with Christopher, and makes few demands. Things are relaxed when Christopher visits, and he is not asked to do chores. However, one evening Christopher overheard his Dad's live-in girlfriend complaining that Christopher left dirty dishes sitting around the apartment and didn't clean up after himself. His Dad defended him, telling her the visit was only for two weeks. That night his Dad ordered in pizza for Christopher, rented Christopher a video movie, and took his girlfriend out to dinner. Christopher resented this intrusion into his special time with his Dad. But his Dad seemed tense and Christopher did not want to start a argument with him. In spite of the occasional tensions, Christopher enjoys having two families; and on the whole, he likes both his Dad and his stepfather.

What issues will concern families in the twenty-first century? Four trends that are evident now and will probably be prominent in the future are remarriage and co-parenting after divorce, the emergence of stepfamilies as a major family form, the growing number of AIDS cases, and the increasing number of midlife parents with unlaunched adult children. Recent demographic shifts have both brought profound changes to American families and presented families with challenges for the future. The high divorce rate among couples with children will make it increasingly important to foster successful co-parenting relationships after divorce. Because most people who divorce also remarry, awareness of the importance of stepfamilies will grow and attempts to understand life in stepfamilies will increase. The AIDS epidemic may become more firmly established in heterosexual adult and teenage populations by the turn of the century, causing many people to rethink their approach to dating and sexual behavior. Moreover, many families will be faced with caring for an AIDS patient while coping with discrimination from the larger community. In addition, as the age at first marriage rises and the number of years spent in education grows, young adults are increasingly likely to live in their parents' home. Midlife couples can often look forward to one or more unlaunched adult children living with them, and many can expect to house a divorced adult child who returns home. We explore these trends in this chapter.

It is important to realize that the trends listed above illustrate the strength of families. Families rebuild after divorce, creating complex stepfamilies in which parenting is shared. Extended families are pulling together to nurture dying AIDS suffers. In addition, extended families are becoming increasingly important in housing adult children. Family life has remained important to Americans as they struggle to cope with social change. Let us turn now to divorce and co-parenting.

Divorce and Co-Parenting in the Future

It is widely recognized that divorce frequently brings economic and emotional hardships to family members, particularly children. In response, some social scientists have begun to urge that divorce be made harder to obtain.

Should Divorce Be More Difficult to Obtain?

Divorce frequently plunges women and children into economic hardship by creating single-parent families that live near or below the poverty line. The U.S. Bureau of the Census reported in 1991 that the median income of a woman with children drops an average of 37 percent within four months after separation from her husband. Over one-third (36 percent) of children whose parents have separated within the previous four months live in poverty. Moreover, divorce is likely to produce long-term economic hardship for women and children. The income of separated and divorced mothers remains 30 percent below the preseparation level sixteen months after the initial separation (Jost and Robinson 1991).

In response to the severe economic and emotional disruption experienced by children due to divorce, Americans are beginning to question the advisability of easy divorce. In a 1989 national Gallup poll, over half (54 percent) of adults and three-fourths (76 percent) of teenagers aged thirteen to seventeen said they thought divorce is too easy to obtain. The majority of the teenagers polled felt that most people who get divorced did not try hard enough to save their marriages (Jost and Robinson 1991). Many of these teenagers have a recent memory of their parents' divorce and have experienced the difficulties associated with attempting to maintain relationships with both parents, often under conditions of parental conflict.

In opposition, proponents of easy divorce point out that many marriages dissolve because of substance abuse, spousal abuse, or child abuse. Making divorce more difficult to obtain would only prolong the distress of those in abusive relationships. In addition, continued contact between former spouses may not be advisable when the marriage has been abusive.

Post-Divorce Relationships

A different approach is taken by some social scientists, such as Arlene Skolnick (1991), who point out that divorce is here to stay. Skolnick argues that new strategies for coping with divorce and co-parenting are needed. Social scientists are beginning to urge divorced partners from nonabusive relationships to put aside their hostility and cooperate in helping their children maintain a relationship with both parents. A new concept of *parenting coalitions* has arisen to describe a joint custody situation in which the families in the two households cooperate rather than compete in childrearing (Visher and Visher 1989). In parenting coalitions, the parents in each household make an effort to support the activities and decisions of the parents in the other household. Parents try to impose reasonably consistent household rules, but they also recognize that children are capable of adapting to a variety of situations with different rules, such as school, church, the homes of friends, and recreation activities.

Encouraging Fathering

Recently divorced fathers are often uncertain about their father role and make uneasy attempts to stay in touch with their children (Lund 1987). They often need support and encouragement in order to maintain the parent–child relationship (Seltzer 1991). Dudley (1991) points out that many fathers who would like more contact with their children are reluctant to seek expanded visitation for a number of reasons including conflict with the former wife and insufficient help in reconnecting with their children after entering recovery from substance abuse (Dudley 1991). Dudley maintains that professionals in the field of family relations should find ways to encourage and help fathers to remain active in the lives of their children. Of the 84 divorced fathers studied by Dudley who had only sparse contact with their children, one-fourth were currently attending a support group for nonresidential fathers. These groups allowed men to share their frustration over diminished contact with their children and focused discussions on problem solving as a way to facilitate increased father–child contact (Dudley 1991). Father support groups are likely to expand in the future, helping to bring about a social recognition of the importance of the father's role in the lives of both men and their children.

Regaining Confidence

Increasing attention has been paid to the elevated risk of divorce among adult children of divorce. However, in their study of adults from divorce-disrupted families, Lauer and Lauer (1991) found that the relationships of adult children of divorce are as high in quality as the relationships of adult children from intact families. The problem, according to Lauer and Lauer, is one of perception. Adult children of divorce tend to perceive themselves as having difficulty relating to others in a healthy way. Moreover, adults from divorce-disrupted families report that they are reluctant to trust others and make commitments. Lauer and Lauer attribute the high divorce rate among adult children of divorce to a crisis of confidence that becomes a *self-fulfilling prophecy*. In a self-fulfilling prophecy expectations affect the outcome. Here, anxiety over the possibility of divorce increases the probability of divorce. Lauer and Lauer (1991) argue that a partial solution lies in addressing this anxiety, which is experienced as a "fear of failure." Maintaining a satisfying marriage still requires communication and conflict-resolution skills. However, as adult children of divorce come to perceive themselves as competent in relationships, they can make strides toward reducing their own risk of divorce.

Remarriage

Early in this century, remarriage typically was preceded by the death of a marriage partner. In contrast, today most remarriages are preceded by divorce. Currently, 46 percent of marriages in any one year are a remarriage for at least one of the partners (U.S. Bureau of the Census 1994a, Table 140). Not everyone has the same probability of remarriage following a divorce, as the discussion below shows.

Factors that Affect Remarriage

Coleman and Ganong (1990) identified the following factors associated with the probability of remarrying after a divorce.

Age. The age of men does not influence their likelihood of remarriage. Middle-aged men bring their education and employment skills into the marriage as assets, and older men are likely to be settled in their careers and able to support a family. The situation is different for women, whose chances of remarriage decrease with

Almost half the marriages taking place every year are remarriages for at least one of the partners.

age (Coleman and Ganong 1990). Those least likely to remarry after divorce are women over age forty. This is probably because of the expectation that a remarriage will be cemented through childbirth. In over half of all remarriages, a child is born to the remarried couples (Wineberg 1990).

Children. Whether or not men have children does not influence their possibility of remarriage. Divorced men are unlikely to bring children to live with a new wife. The situation is different for women. As the number of her children increases, a woman's chance of remarrying decreases because a new husband typically takes on an additional economic burden. Those most likely to remarry after divorce are childless women under age twenty-five (Coleman and Ganong 1990).

Race and Ethnicity. Whites are more likely than African Americans to remarry after a divorce; Hispanics fall in the middle (Coleman and Ganong 1990). Hispanic women are likely to be Catholic, and the Catholic church frowns on divorce, making remarriage within the church difficult (Teachman 1986).

Employed African-American men are generally in a better position to remarry than employed African-American women because of the sex-ratio imbalance discussed in Chapter 5. The African-American woman who is least likely to remarry is the high school drop-out. Employment of both spouses is expected in the African-American community, and poorly educated women are the least able to help bring economic security to the family. Most middle-class African-American families depend on the wife's income to maintain their social class position.

Cohabitation and Remarriage

Couples appear to be cautious about remarriage immediately after divorce. The majority of couples who remarry do so only after cohabiting (Bumpass and Sweet 1989). African Americans cohabit considerably longer than whites before remarrying (Smock 1990). Cohabitation has the benefit of improving the economic status of divorced women because it brings another breadwinner into the household (Smock 1990).

Stepfamilies

Accompanying the high remarriage rate is a growing number of stepfamilies. Stepfamilies formed following divorce are known as *binuclear families* because the stepchildren often relate to parents and stepparents in two separate households. In contrast, stepfamilies formed following widowhood are called nuclear families because the surviving parent and new spouse share a single common residence. The vast majority of stepchildren have divorced parents and are members of two nuclear families. This is because widows and widowers tend to be considerably older than divorcees and thus are less likely to have young children living in the home.

Incidence

Thirty-five million adults and 13 million children presently live in stepfamilies, and each day 1,300 new stepfamilies are formed (Nelson and Levant 1991).

BOX 16.1 A Closer Look

What's a Stepfather to Do?

Stepfathers try to offer guidance to their stepchildren in an era when no road map for stepparenting exists (Nordheimer 1990). Men often enter remarriage with a "love will conquer all" optimism that causes stepfathers to assume that difficulties with stepchildren can be overcome by determination and effort (Lawson 1991). These hopeful stepfathers seem bewildered when the stepchildren display resentment toward the stepfather's new role in the family (Nordheimer 1990).

Men who marry divorced mothers sometimes feel like a knight rescuing his bride and her children from the hardships of life in a single-parent family. As part of this rescue effort, a number of stepfathers want to bring order to the household and subdue her unruly children. When the stepchildren resist his efforts, conflict arises. At this point, the wife typically intervenes, asking the new husband to back off. She is concerned about her children's adjustment to this major change in their lives and wants to go slowly. The stepfather feels double-crossed by his wife, who appears to side with her children (Nordheimer 1990).

The stepfather is not the only frustrated one in the new stepfamily. Many children hope their mother and father will get back together, and the mother's marriage to the new husband dashes these dreams. Often stepchildren will openly compare the stepfather to their biological father, who usually imposes few rules on them. Because their relationship with their children emphasizes fun rather than learning responsibility, noncustodial fathers are sometimes known as "Disneyland fathers." The stepfather becomes irritated when the stepchildren compare him with the fun-oriented biological father (Lawson 1991). For example, a child who watches an R-rated movie with a biological father may be forbidden to do so at home with his mother and stepfather. If no common ground on rules can be found in the two families, it sometimes helps to point out to children that every household has somewhat different rules. The parents in this household are committed to these rules. Part of growing up is learning to relate to different people in different situations.

In the face of difficulties with stepchildren, some stepfathers withdraw emotionally and spend more time alone. Others try to find a new approach to parenting. The most successful stepfathers are flexible and do not try to create a traditional nuclear family in which the father sets rules and enforces discipline (Nordheimer 1990). However, it is not easy for stepfathers to hang back. In fact, the common advice to let the wife take care of discipline may be biased toward middle-class white families. A number of moderate-income African-American stepfathers argue that their stepchildren have friends who live in single-mother households where teenagers often have a good deal of independence. These stepfathers often feel a need to set guidelines and reduce the influence of the stepchild's peers. Thus, advice to stepparents in one neighborhood with a low level of delinquent activity may not be applicable to stepparents who must contend with teen violence and drugs in their neighborhood (Nordheimer 1991).

Those stepfathers who weather these difficulties and bond with their stepchildren often gradually switch their allegiance away from their children by a previous marriage and toward their new wife and her children. A man's biological children who live with the former spouse often do not receive the same luxuries he provides for his new family. Moreover, remarried men, like other husbands, often leave their estates to their current spouse. This move tends to leave children from a previous marriage out in the cold as far as inheritance is concerned (Rosen 1990). One of the challenges of the future will be to blend families so that children feel free to have important relationships with both parents and stepparents. Parents also need to feel free to have bonded relationships with their biological nonresident children as well as with their stepchildren.

Approximately 40 percent of children currently being born will spend some time in a stepfamily before they reach age eighteen (Pill 1990). Official records underestimate the number of stepfamilies because only legally married partners with stepchildren are counted. In actuality, many people cohabit with divorced partners who have children. They play the role of stepparent but are not included in the official count (Smith 1990).

It is important to recognize that stepfamilies can take on a variety of forms (Coleman and Ganong 1990). Each type of stepfamily has special characteristics, which often arise out of its organizational structure. There are two major categories of stepfamilies: those with residental stepchildren and those with visiting stepchildren.

Stepfamilies with Residential Stepchildren

There are four types of stepfamilies with residential stepchildren: custodial mother–stepfather families, custodial father–stepmother families, dual stepparent families, and blended nuclear and stepfamilies. Each of these stepfamilies can be formed after either divorce or widowhood.

Custodial Mother–Stepfather Families. The most common type of stepfamily with residential stepchildren is one in which the mother has custody of her children and brings them into her remarriage. The relationship between a child and stepfather tends to be most positive when the stepparent becomes a substitute for the biological father. This situation is likely when the biological parent has little contact with the child or is deceased (Coleman and Ganong 1990; Seltzer and Bianchi 1988). Stepfathers are more likely than stepmothers to become a substitute parent because stepfathers usually live with their stepchildren.

Stepfathers tend to have more positive relationships with their stepchildren than stepmothers (Coleman and Ganong 1990). This is probably because stepfathers usually have daily contact with their stepchildren. Nonetheless, stepfathers experience some tension because the child's loyalty is divided between the biological father and the stepfather. As a result, stepfathers tend to view their stepfamilies less positively than do their wives (who are the biological parents) (Peek et al. 1988). See Box 16.1 for a further discussion of stepfathers.

Custodial Father–Stepmother Families. Father-headed one-parent families, constituting 2 1/2 percent of all families, are the fastest growing family type (Ahlburg and DeVita 1992). Many of these single fathers remarry and form stepfamilies. Following divorce, the courts still display a preference for mother-custody, particularly for young children. Fathers are more likely to obtain custody of adolescents than of young children, and of male than of female children. When fathers obtain custody, it is usually because the mother–child relationship was particularly conflictual or because the father had an especially close relationship with his children (Amato 1987). Although there are very few studies of this family type, there are indications that tension often exists between stepmother and stepchild. The special relationship between the father and child often leads the child to view the stepmother as an intruder (Amato 1987).

Dual–Stepparent Families. In dual-stepparent families, both husband and wife have children from a previous relationship who live with them. Dual-stepparent families have an advantage in that neither parent is consistently defined as the outsider. However, of the three stepfamily forms discussed above (stepmother, stepfather, and dual-stepparent families), relationships between children and stepparents have the greatest degree of emotional distance in dual-stepparent families (Coleman and Ganong 1990). This is perhaps a byproduct of the close relationship each parent has with her or his own biological children.

Blended Nuclear and Stepfamilies. About half of remarried couples have a child together, so that these families often contain the biological child of both parents as well as stepchildren. Some of these stepfamilies contain children who are "his," "hers," and "ours." In fact, these blended nuclear and stepfamilies can take on any of the three forms discussed above with the addition of a child from the new marriage. Those remarriages that are most likely to produce a birth are those in which the husband does not have children from a previous marriage.

Families with Visiting Stepchildren

Many people remarry a spouse who has children who visit on weekends.

Noncustodial Father–Stepmother Families. The most common type of family that has visiting stepchildren is one with a noncustodial father. The stepchildren usually reside in the home of their biological mother and visit with the father and stepmother on weekends and holidays. In these stepfamilies, wives (who are the stepparents) often complain about feeling left out of family interaction when their stepchildren visit (Smith 1990). Stepparents and stepchildren who reside separately tend to have a less close relationship than those who live together (Ambert 1986; Coleman and Ganong 1990).

Many stepmothers assume they must take on a nurturing, maternal role with their partner's children. When these efforts are met with rejection by the children, the stepmother often feels confused, hurt, and helpless. In this tense atmosphere, she is likely to have difficulty feeling love and affection for the stepchildren. Her response is often to feel shame and to try harder to be affectionate with the children. This often leads to a vicious cycle in which the children become more resistant (Smith 1990). Stepmothers tend to become discouraged with the stepmother–stepchild relationship over time (Coleman and Ganong 1990; Guisinger et al. 1989). Many stepmothers have found it easier to assume the role of friend rather than parent with stepchildren.

Noncustodial Mother–Stepfather Families. Very little research is available on remarried mothers who do not have custody of their children. However, on the whole, noncustodial mothers tend to be more involved with their children than noncustodial fathers. Noncustodial mothers visit more often with their children and remain more involved in the lives of their children than noncustodial fathers (Amato 1987; Fine and Kurdek 1992). Future research is needed to shed more light on this type of stepfamily.

Regardless of the form a stepfamily takes, stepfamilies tend to have characteristics that set them apart from intact nuclear families.

Characteristics of Stepfamilies

Stepfamilies tend to differ from traditional nuclear families in complexity, family boundaries, and social roles (Peek et al. 1988).

Complex Organization. Stepfamilies are typically more complex than nuclear families in that they usually involve a larger number of interpersonal relationships. Members of stepfamilies relate to noncustodial parents, ex–in-laws, and ex-spouses. This array of relationships with current and former family members requires good interpersonal skills, such as communication skills, in order to cope with potential conflicts (Peek et al. 1988).

Vague Boundaries. The boundaries that define who is in the family and who is outside the family are far less clear in stepfamilies than in families of first-married couples (Peek et al. 1988). Some stepparents complain that their spouses refer to the stepchildren as "his" children, or "her" children indicating that the stepparent belongs only partially to the family unit. In families in which the husband's children visit on weekends, stepmothers often complain that they are not accorded full membership in the family unit (Smith 1990). During the week, stepmothers are members of the family defined by a common residence. This family consists of the stepmother, her husband, and any children they have borne together. On weekends and holidays, the boundaries of the family unit change to include her husband's children from a previous marriage. Many stepmothers report that when their stepchildren visit, they feel like outsiders in their own home (Smith 1990). In addition, boundaries of stepfamilies sometimes actually change when child-custody arrangements are revised, changing the status of a stepchild from that of a resident to that of a visitor or vice versa.

Vague Social Norms. Stepfamilies tend to have fewer social norms (social rules) specifying what behavior is culturally expected of each family member (Peek et al. 1988). As a result, there is a good deal of *role ambiguity*, in which there are few guidelines delineating how a social role should be enacted. For example, should a stepchild who is older than a preschooler relate to the stepparent as a friend or as a parent? Are feelings of love expected to develop between stepchildren and stepparents? Our culture does not give clear answers to these questions. Therefore, members of stepfamilies must negotiate their roles in the family and create a relationship with the aid of few guidelines.

The stepmother's role in the stepfamily is particularly ambiguous. Her rights, responsibilities, and privileges are often not clear. Many stepmothers complain that although they have responsibility for their stepchildren—including cooking, shopping for them, and sometimes helping them with homework—they often lack the authority to set standards or discipline their stepchildren (Smith 1990). Stepmothers report that when the stepchildren visit, they sometimes feel lonely, displaced and excluded, and powerless (Smith 1990).

Because stepfamilies display the characteristics described above, they have been described as having low cohesion and high adaptability.

Cohesion

In traditional nuclear families (with two biological parents), children and parents often have strong emotional bonds, called *cohesion,* connecting them to the family. Cohesion is typically lower in stepfamilies than in traditional nuclear families (Pill 1990). Pill (1990) investigated stepfamily cohesion and found that wives and husbands tended to have different expectations. Wives tended to be satisfied with stepfamily life when cohesion was high. In contrast, the level of cohesion was not important in determining the husband's satisfaction with the stepfamily. Because wives were more likely than their husbands to have children from a previous marriage living with them, their feeling of connectedness with their children and the family was important to them. Perhaps men tend to be less concerned with emotional bonds and are able to tolerate a greater degree of separateness in a family without becoming dissatisfied with family life (Pill 1990).

When a stepfamily is newly formed, new social roles are negotiated. It's easiest to do this when each family member is willing to adapt to change.

A number of researchers have suggested that stepfamilies tend to function more smoothly if the bonds of connectedness (cohesion) are weaker. Families with too much cohesion experience fusion, with the members sacrificing separateness and individual autonomy. However, members of a family with too little cohesion become disengaged and uninterested in each other's lives (Pill 1990). A lower level of cohesion in stepfamilies than in traditional nuclear families may be functional. That is, because stepchildren continue to have contact with biological parents and participate in two households, low cohesion in stepfamilies reduces the potential for loyalty conflicts (Peek 1988). In other words, loose connections between members of stepfamilies may promote harmony.

Adaptability

Adaptability in families is the ability to change behavior patterns when new circumstances arise. Families must reorganize and adapt to change as children grow older and enter new developmental stages. Newly formed stepfamilies must also adapt, negotiate new social roles, and face issues of whether or not to express and accept love and bonding. Pill (1990) studied stepfamilies formed after divorce in which the parents had been married for two or more years. All of these families included an adolescent stepchild. Family members tended to be satisfied with stepfamily life when adaptability was high. In other words, families that adjust easily to change tend to be more comfortable with stepfamily life.

Next we turn to an issue that is often difficult for stepfamilies: discipline.

Discipline in Stepfamilies

Role ambiguity makes the discipline of stepchildren a challenging task and a source of potential conflict. Three ways stepparents handle discipline issues are discussed below.

Biological Parent as Disciplinarian. Stepparents often find that family life runs more smoothly when they turn discipline over to the biological parent. Among those who have recently remarried and become stepparents, a common pattern is for the stepparent initially to avoid taking an active role in disciplining stepchildren. In this case the stepparent's role becomes one of supporting the childrearing guidelines laid out by the biological parent (Fine and Kurdek). However, this method of handling discipline frustrates some stepparents, who feel it reinforces their position as an outsider in the family and emphasizes that the children are "his" or "hers" rather than "ours" (Berman 1982:14).

Compromise and Negotiation. In the process of compromise and negotiation, the parents work together, express their wishes for the children's behavior, prioritize their demands, and work on those guidelines which are most important. In one example, a stepmother felt that her stepdaughter was irresponsibly using money her father had given to her. She talked with her husband (the biological father) and worked out a compromise on the the amount of money to be given to the daughter as well as guidelines for spending the money (Ketover 1988:148).

Remaining Firm. In this method, the stepparent participates in disciplining the child and remains firm until the child complies. One stepmother believed that her husband's young children did not show respect for her or her home when they visited on the weekends. She was particularly bothered by their habit of eating in the living room, leaving a residue of crumbs and smudges. To solve the problem, she put their food on the kitchen table and stood by their chairs until they finished eating to prevent them from taking their plates, or hand held-food, to the other room. Eventually the children began to eat at the table without protest (Rowlands 1983:91).

The Age of Stepchildren

The age of stepchildren influences the kind of relationship that develops between children and their stepparents.

Stepfamilies with Preschoolers. The adjustment of both stepchildren and stepparents is easiest when the children are young, particularly when they are preschoolers. In these families the stepparent has a clearly defined role, namely, to nurture the children and look out for their safety. This mission provides the stepparents with authority over the children, and the stepparent often comes to be seen by the children as an integral part of the family (Smith 1990). Children age nine and under are much more accepting of stepparents than adolescents (Pill 1990).

Stepfamilies with Adolescents. Stepfamilies formed when the children are adolescents are often particularly stormy (Smith 1990). A natural tension develops in stepfamilies with adolescent children because the adolescent's personal developmental issues clash with concerns of the parent and stepparent. The adolescent is grappling with issues of separation and individuation. Teenagers are pulling away from being nurtured, controlled, or "parented." At the same time, parents in a new marriage are concerned with promoting cohesion and producing a collective identity (Pill 1990).

The special strains experienced by stepfamilies put remarriages at risk for redivorce.

Redivorce

Approximately half of all children whose parents divorce and remarry will watch a parent go through a second divorce (Coleman and Ganong 1990). A divorce in a remarriage is called a *redivorce*. The redivorce rate is 25 percent higher than the divorce rate for first marriages (Bumpass and Sweet 1989). Approximately half (49 percent) of first marriages end in divorce. Remarried women have a 54 percent divorce rate, whereas 62 percent of men's remarriages end in divorce (Pill 1990). At first glance, it may seem strange that men and women have different divorce rates for remarriage. This occurs because not all remarriages involve two divorced partners. A second marriage for one person may be a first marriage for the other partner. The redivorce rate is higher for men, probably because divorced women may have more financial incentive to remain in their remarriages than divorced men have to remain in theirs.

Explanations for Redivorce

Explanations for the high redivorce rate fall into the following two categories (White 1990).

"Kinds of People" Explanation. The first explanation looks at the "kinds of people" who divorce and remarry. Many people bring into a remarriage the same characteristics that raised the risk of divorce in the first marriage, for example, a low educational level. Moreover, divorced persons come into a remarriage after demonstrating that they are willing to use divorce as a means of settling marital disputes. The group with the lowest probability of divorce are educated men with postgraduate college training (such as lawyers and doctors). In addition, remarried men who bring their children from a previous marriage to live with them have a very low redivorce rate, particularly if this is a first marriage for the wife.

Family Dynamics Explanation. The second explanation focuses on family dynamics in stepfamilies. The presence of stepchildren often places special strains on a remarriage. Often the newly married couple are trying to solidify their marital bond at the same time that they are dealing with parenting issues (Pill 1990). However, couples who cope with the challenges of the early years of remarriage tend to have stable and rewarding family relationships. The first five years of remarriage carry the highest risk of redivorce. Half of remarriages end in the first five years, whereas only 20 percent of remarriages that have lasted ten years end in divorce (Pill 1990).

African Americans and Redivorce

African Americans have higher divorce and redivorce rate than whites. However, within each race, divorce and redivorce patterns differ for whites and African Americans. Among whites, the rate of divorce is higher for remarriages than for first marriages. However, among African Americans, remarriages are more stable than first marriages (Coleman and Ganong 1990). The lower divorce rate among remarried African Americans may reflect the tendency for second marriages to involve older, more economically secure partners.

Stepparents often establish close relationships with children, and when remarriages break up, they often wish to continue to see the children. The next section addresses stepparent–stepchild relationships following redivorce.

Relationships with Stepchildren after Redivorce

The states are beginning to establish policies and laws concerning stepparents' obligations for child support and stepparents rights in the areas of custody and visitation.

Child Support. Courts in some states have held that under certain conditions, stepparents are responsible for financially supporting their stepchildren after divorce. In the case of *Miller* v. *Miller* (1984), the New Jersey Supreme Court maintained that a stepparent can be required to pay child support when the following conditions are met:

1. the stepparent acted "in loco parentis" (in the place of the parent) by representing himself or herself to the community as the child's parent,
2. the child relied on the stepparent's income for support, and
3. the complete removal of the stepparent's income would have a detrimental effect on the child (Fine and Fine 1992).

This standard has been adopted in a number of other states. In other words, stepfamilies are increasingly being "normalized" by the courts, instead of being treated as an exceptional family form. As a result, stepfamilies are becoming subject to some of the same legal regulations faced by nuclear families.

Child Custody and Visitation. Several decades ago, stepparents had no legal grounds on which to argue for visitation or custody of a stepchild. Today this situation has changed, and now all fifty states allow third-party visitation. A third party is someone who is not the biological mother or father of the child. The third party who most often receives visitation rights is a grandparent. However, visitation rights have recently been extended to stepparents under the "third party" clause of state laws, and five states specifically grant stepparents visitation rights. In addition, twenty-five states allow third-party custody under certain conditions, and some stepparents have gained custody of stepchildren under these laws. In Wisconsin, legislation allows a stepparent custody of a stepchild when the biological parent is not a viable alternative; the more liberal Hawaii law allows a stepparent custody when it is in the best interest of the child (Fine and Fine 1992). Both legislatures and courts are beginning to recognize that families come in a variety of forms and that emotional attachment and commitment are important elements of the family.

Next, we examine a challenge that is facing an increasing number of families: the AIDS crisis.

Review Questions

1. What are the arguments surrounding the debate about making divorce more difficult to obtain?
2. What special problems are faced by fathers following divorce?
3. What factors affect the probability of remarriage?
4. How do Lauer and Lauer explain the high divorce rate among adult children of divorce?

5. In what ways do stepfamilies differ from traditional nuclear families? What kind of family organization promotes harmony in stepfamilies?

6. How do stepfamilies handle such issues as discipline?

7. In cases of redivorce, what changes are occurring concerning a stepparent's obligation to pay child support for stepchildren and the stepparent's rights to visitation and stepchild custody?

AIDS and the Family

In Chapter 6, we discussed the sexual transmission of AIDS and how the threat of HIV, the AIDS virus, may impact sexual partnerships and dating. Here we explore some of the larger social issues surrounding AIDS. AIDS, like other serious illnesses, affects the entire family. Elizabeth Kubler-Ross (1987) has said that in response to AIDS, the United States is being polarized into two groups: those who respond to the AIDS epidemic with offers of help and those "who judge, label, and denigrate" (Kubler-Ross 1987:318). With over a million people in the United States infected with HIV, the virus that causes AIDS, and 12 million people infected with HIV worldwide, a large number of families will be impacted by AIDS (Cooper 1992; Mayer and Carpenter 1992). The number of groups who run the risk of acquiring an HIV infection is growing, as the next section shows.

TABLE 16.1	AIDS Cases among Men and Women by Exposure Category	
Male Exposure Category (Total)	252,363	(100%)
Men who have sex with men	160,345	(64%)
Injection drug use	49,962	(20%)
Men who have sex with men and inject drugs	18,041	(7%)
Hemophilia/coagulation disorder	2,460	(1%)
Heterosexual contact	7,540	(3%)
Receipt of blood transfusion, blood component, or tissue	3,280	(1%)
Risk not identified	10,735	(4%)
Female Exposure Category (Total)	32,477	(100%)
Injection drug use	15,816	(49%)
Hemophilia/coagulation disorder	59	(less than 1%)
Heterosexual contact	11,638	(36%)
Receipt of blood transfusion, blood component, or tissue	2,104	(6%)
Risk not identified	545	(8%)

Source: U.S. Department of Health and Human Services, Centers for Disease Control and Prevention, "HIV/AIDS Surveillance Report," May 1993, Vol. 5, No. 1. Atlanta: Public Health Service, Tables 4 and 5.

Old and New AIDS Risk Groups

The two largest groups at risk for AIDS are homosexual males and intravenous drug users. Homosexual males make up the majority of new AIDS cases in the United States. Because of AIDS education programs and the promotion of safer sex practices in urban gay communities, the HIV infection rate among gay men has begun to level off. Intravenous drug users are the second largest AIDS risk group (Cooper 1992). These two major AIDS risk groups, homosexual males and IV drug users, tend to differ in race and social class as well as gender. Homosexual males with AIDS have been primarily middle class and white. In contrast, intravenous drug users with AIDS are largely low-income members of minority groups. A third risk group which is becoming prominent consists of the sexual partners of intravenous drug users. In fact, the fastest growing AIDS risk group is women who have acquired an HIV infection through heterosexual contact, mainly with partners who are IV drug users (Cooper 1992). As the number of HIV infected women grows, so does the number of infants who are born HIV-positive (Capell et al. 1992). In this section we explore all these risk groups, including homosexual men, but we place a special focus on groups who have only recently been identified as being at risk for AIDS, namely, women, minorities, the poor, and children of HIV-infected women.

BOX 16.2   World Perspectives

HIV Infection Worldwide

The first AIDS cases were identified in Africa, where now more than 7 million people are infected with HIV. In Africa and Asia, HIV is primarily a heterosexually transmitted disease. The number of AIDS cases among women in Africa is equal to the number of AIDS cases among men. Likewise, HIV infection is equally divided between men and women in India. In the United States, women represent the fastest-growing segment of the population who are HIV-positive. In another decade it is expected that the distribution of HIV between men and women in the United States will begin to resemble the African experience (Cooper 1992).

Figure 16.1
HIV Infections Worldwide

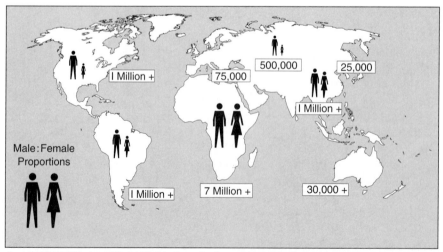

Source: United Nations World Health Organization, reprinted in Cooper 1992.

Homosexual Men and AIDS. AIDS issues have become a major focus of urban gay communities, and gay men have been active in political movements aimed at speeding the release of new drugs for AIDS treatment, gaining increased funding for AIDS research, and increasing services for AIDS patients. Even so, many partners of homosexuals with AIDS face discrimination. They frequently find that hospitals and social services are organized around a traditional definition of the family. Hospital rules allowing only family members at visiting hours often exclude partners of homosexuals (Levine 1991). Hospitals need to use a broader definition of the family to meet the needs of homosexual AIDS patients.

In response to the AIDS epidemic, gay communities have had to reconsider their social ideals. Sexual fidelity has been viewed as something to be negotiated between gay partners, and sexual exclusivity has largely been rejected in gay communities. However, as the AIDS epidemic advanced, some gay men began to question the ideology of guilt-free sex with multiple partners. Today an increasing number of gay men are establishing monogamous sexual partnerships (Berger 1990). Nonetheless, many gay men still date multiple partners, and tension has developed in the gay community between those who are HIV-negative and those who are HIV-positive.

Women and AIDS. While homosexual men have been identified for more than a decade as an AIDS risk group, women have only recently been recognized as having an AIDS risk. The number of women infected with HIV has increased rapidly over the last decade, primarily due to heterosexual transmission. In 1992, women made up 13 percent of all AIDS cases in the United States and were the fastest-growing group of AIDS suffers (Cooper 1992). Half of all women with AIDS became infected through intravenous drug use. Most of the rest were the sexual partners of male IV drug users (Ellerbrock et al. 1991). Most of the women who have contracted AIDS are low-income, minorities in the inner cities. Three-fourths of women who have AIDS are black or Hispanic (72 percent) and residents of large metropolitan areas (73 percent). Cities along the east coast are particularly likely to have a high concentration of AIDS cases. The highest AIDS rate for women in the United States is found in New York state, followed by the District of Columbia and Florida, in that order (Ellerbrock et al. 1991).

In spite of the growing number of women with AIDS, women often receive inadequate health care. Many health care workers do not have expertise in recognizing the symptoms of HIV infection in women (Mayer and Carpenter 1992). These symptoms often involve gynecological problems, including recurrent yeast infections, pelvic inflammatory disease, and ulcerations in the genital area (Cooper 1992). Women are less likely than men to receive an early AIDS diagnosis, and it is in the early stages when treatment with an antiviral drug, such as AZT, can be most effective. In addition, because many AIDS treatment clinics do not offer on-site gynecological services, female patients must be referred to a separate gynecology clinic for a second appointment. Because many HIV-infected women are poor, have a problem with transportation, and often have to arrange babysitting for a child at home, the organization of treatment delivery services creates a hardship for HIV-infected women. Women have also been excluded from much AIDS research. This is a disadvantage for two reasons. First, research projects provide AIDS patients with access to experimental drugs. Second, research on women would allow us to learn more about the course taken by HIV infection in women. Researchers have avoided including women in AIDS studies because they fear the woman may become pregnant while receiving treatment; researchers worry that experimental drugs may harm the fetus. These conditions have led some social observers to comment that women with AIDS are medically disadvantaged (Cooper 1992; Mayer and Carpenter 1992).

Minorities and AIDS. Minorities are overrepresented in impoverished neighborhoods where unemployment is high and intravenous drug use is evident. The high unemployment rate in the inner cities leaves minorities vulnerable to drug abuse. In addition, impoverished minority women are at risk for acquiring HIV through sexual contact with IV drug users (Ellerbrock et al. 1991; Holmes et al. 1990). Thus, the slow pace with which AIDS prevention programs have moved into the inner cities is a matter of great concern to urban minority civic leaders.

Rates of gonorrhea, syphilis, and AIDS are highest among low-income urban dwellers, and therefore are highest among African Americans and Hispanics. African-American women and Hispanic women have an incidence of AIDS which is thirteen times and eight times greater, respectively, than the rate for white women in the United States. Likewise, African-American men are ten times more likely than white men to be AIDS victims, and Hispanic men have an AIDS rate four times that of white men (Holmes et al. 1990). AIDS is now the leading cause of death among African-American women of reproductive age (fifteen to forty-four years old) in New York and New Jersey and is the eighth leading cause of death for all women of reproductive age in the United States (Ellerbrock et al. 1991). However, AIDS should not be thought of as an African-American or Hispanic disease: Less than 1 percent of any any racial or ethnic group is infected.

The Poor and AIDS. Intravenous drug users afflicted with AIDS are typically impoverished. Tuberculosis, which often attacks people with AIDS, is spreading through poor communities. In the crowded conditions of urban homeless shelters and low-income hotels, drug-resistant tuberculosis is becoming a serious public health concern (Castro et al. 1992). Bringing the spread of HIV under control will help slow the spread of tuberculosis. Banks and Wilson (1989) maintain that there is a strong need for additional clinics dispensing free condoms and for sex education programs promoting safer sex practices in low-income neighborhoods of the inner cities. Prevention programs are most successful when grassroots community involvement is sought by the agency providing the service.

Children and AIDS. As the AIDS epidemic spreads to women, children also become affected. AIDS affects children in three ways: They can become infected with HIV during fetal development; they can receive inadequate care because a parent is disabled by AIDS; or they can become orphaned when a parent with AIDS dies.

Most HIV-positive women are sexually active and in their reproductive years. When an HIV-infected woman gives birth, there is a one-in-four chance that she will have passed along the HIV-infection to her infant during pregnancy. Therefore, as the number of women with AIDS increases, so will the number of children with AIDS (Capell et al. 1992). An estimated 20,000 children are now infected with HIV, and an additional 2,000 HIV-positive children are born to HIV-infected mothers each year (Cooper 1992). In New York state, where AIDS rates are the highest in the United States, almost 1 percent (0.7 percent) of women who gave birth in 1988 tested positive for the HIV virus. In some areas of New York City the rate of HIV-positive women has reached 2 percent of those who gave birth in certain hospitals (Ellerbrock et al. 1991).

Unless a child with AIDS received the HIV infection from a blood transfusion, it is likely that the mother is also infected and may be showing AIDS symptoms. Many children who have AIDS belong to single mothers who provide the sole financial support for their families. These mothers are often too weak and exhausted to care for their dying infants and sometimes too afraid of social rejection and job loss to aggressively seek treatment for their children (Kubler-Ross 1987). Making matters even more difficult is the likelihood that mothers of AIDS babies are IV drug users who lack support from a husband, extended kin, or church to fall back on in a crisis (Kubler-Ross 1987). These children with AIDS need special help from public services.

AIDS is also creating a new group of orphans. AIDS has been called the "grandmother's disease" because it attacks women in the prime of their childbearing years, often leaving motherless children to be raised by their grandparents (Mayer and Carpenter 1992). In 1992, over 18,000 children had become orphaned by AIDS; this number is expected to exceed 80,000 by the year 2000 (Nicholas and Abrams 1992). Of those children whose mothers died of all causes in 1991, thirteen percent of children age twelve and under had mothers died of AIDS or an HIV-related disease (Michaels and Levine 1992). Most of these children belong to minority groups living in low-income communities (Michaels and Levine 1992). These are the children who are already vulnerable to poverty-associated risks, such as teen pregnancy, high school noncompletion, gang membership, and living in poverty as an adult.

Teenagers and HIV. The AIDS rate among teenagers is growing dramatically (Jurish 1992). It is estimated that between 1 million and 1.5 million people in the United States are infected with HIV, which causes AIDS. Although teenagers account for only 1 percent of diagnosed AIDS cases, the incubation period of AIDS typically is five years or more. One-fourth of AIDS patients are aged twenty

---

BOX 16.3   S o c i a l   I s s u e s

Should Dating Be Discouraged among High School Students?

Jurish and her colleagues (1992) argue that teenagers in high school are particularly vulnerable to contracting the AIDS virus and that the infection rate within this group will grow dramatically during the next decade. Jurich argues that AIDS-prevention programs are effective in altering sexual behavior only when people perceive themselves as susceptible to acquiring an HIV infection. The sense of invulnerability among young adolescents makes it difficult for them to take the AIDS message seriously. College students, on the other hand, appear to be more willing to change their sexual behavior in response to the AIDS threat.

The decade of the 1990s will be an interesting one to watch: Many of the elements of the 1970s sexual revolution may be reversed as the AIDS threat begins to loom large. As HIV infection makes its way through the heterosexual high school population, it is possible that the 1990s may witness two opposing strategies to curb AIDS. On one hand, high schools are likely offer more sex education courses, and more high schools may distribute condoms at clinics on the school campus. On the other hand, there may well be a move to discourage high school dating and encourage activities among groups of unattached persons. This possible trend would be compatible with the dramatic rise in the marriage age during the last two decades. An editorial in the *Journal of the American Medical Association* (July 1992: 520) recommends that teens be taught to protect themselves by avoiding sexual intercourse and waiting to choose a lifetime sexual partner. There may also be a move in the next decade to increase the driving age to eighteen in many states with the recognition that driving, the privacy of the back seat, and sex tend to go hand in hand. With the recognition of the connection between alcohol and drug use and unprotected sex, high schools may become sites for Alcoholics Anonymous and Narcotics Anonymous meetings after school. Many colleges already offer such meetings on campus.

to twenty-four, meaning that they originally acquired the HIV infection while in their teens (Ellerbrock et al. 1991; Jurish 1992). Teenagers tend to believe themselves to be invulnerable, which leads to risk-taking behavior. Even teens who are knowledgeable about the transmission of AIDS appear reluctant to modify their sexual behavior. Many adolescents continue to have unprotected sex even though they are aware of the risks involved (Jurich et al. 1992; Kegels et al. 1988). The family function of controlling sexuality diminished during the sexual revolution of the 1970s as teenagers began to make their own decisions regarding sex. It will be interesting to observe whether or not a power struggle will develop during the 1990s as the family and other social institutions, such as schools and churches, attempt to regain control over teenage sexual behavior (see Box 16.3). Meanwhile, during the next decade a growing number of families will be faced with a family member infected with HIV. In order to respond with compassion to AIDS sufferers and their relatives, it helps to see the impact AIDS has on the family, which is the topic of the next section.

Family Response to AIDS Victims

When a person falls ill with AIDS, the experience profoundly affects the emotional well-being of the entire family (Williams and Stafford 1991). Family members typically experience shock and denial, anger, guilt and blame, fear, and social isolation.

Shock and Denial. At first both the patient and family experience denial, wanting to believe that the family member is not dying. AIDS weakens the immune system: The AIDS patient dies of opportunistic diseases, usually within a year of diagnosis (Kubler-Ross 1987).

Relatives of AIDS patients frequently hear about the AIDS diagnosis at the same time that they learn that the HIV infection was acquired through either intra-

People diagnosed with AIDS need more care and support from their families than ever. When family members respond with denial or rejection, it only increases the inevitable suffering that AIDS brings.

venous drug use or sexual contact with a homosexual partner. Some men with AIDS report that when they told their parents they had AIDS, the first question from the parents was, "You're not gay are you?" (Kubler-Ross 1987). This lack of acceptance creates stress both for the AIDS sufferer and for the family. Their reluctance to reveal their sexual orientation makes some gay men reluctant to tell their families that they have AIDS.

Anger. When the diagnosis is accepted as accurate, anger sets in for both the patient and family. Angry patients often ask themselves, "Why me?" and sometimes take out their anger on their relatives. This places additional stress on the caretakers in the family. For relatives who are caretakers, fear, exhaustion, and anger occur together (Kubler-Ross 1987; Mayer 1988).

Guilt and Blame. Guilt is commonly experienced by parents who feel that they should have protected their adult child from exposure to the HIV virus while he or she was a teenager. Parents often blame each other for failing to prevent the infection (Serovich 1992). In addition, patients often feel guilty about the intravenous drug use or sexual contacts that exposed them to HIV infection (Kubler-Ross 1987).

Fear. AIDS patients fear being abandoned and rejected by family members. At the same time, family members often fear contagion and infection (Serovich 1992). Spouses and lovers, concerned that they may become infected through further sexual contact, worry about whether or not they should leave the relationship (Serovich et al. 1992). However, if sexual contact is not involved and precautions are taken, HIV is not likely to be passed from patient to caretaker. HIV is not transmitted through casual contact with AIDS patients (Serovich et al. 1992). In order for HIV to be transmitted, the body products (primarily blood and semen) or body tissue of the infected person must come into contact with the blood system of the uninfected person. The primary means of transmission are through sharing needles, sexual contact, and in utero transmission from the mother to the fetus (Schvaneveldt 1990). Further education is needed to allay fears on the part of both the families of AIDS suffers and the general public.

Social Isolation and Discrimination

The spouse of a cancer patient usually receives sympathy from a concerned community. Friends and neighbors are willing to lend a "listening ear" or occasionally to run errands. In contrast, when a person has AIDS, the family is likely to become increasingly socially isolated (Schvaneveldt 1990). For example, people may irrationally fear exposing their children to the uninfected members of the AIDS patient's family. This experience is not unusual for families of AIDS sufferers (Serovich 1992). If neighbors help out and occasionally shop for groceries for an AIDS patient, they typically leave the groceries outside the apartment door and avoid coming inside for a visit (Kubler-Ross 1987). In response to social shunning, patients who have visible signs of AIDS, such as facial lesions or weight loss, often isolate themselves (Kubler-Ross 1987).

Serovich (1992) found that families of AIDS victims had a strong reluctance to disclose the AIDS diagnosis to people outside the family. This attitude interfered with the ability of AIDS patients to secure counseling and other support services. Families of AIDS sufferers fear discrimination against the AIDS patient in housing and employment as well as discrimination against themselves (Serovich et al. 1992). Some of this fear is well founded: There have been cases in which close relatives of AIDS victims have been fired or otherwise forced to leave their jobs (Frierson et al. 1987). In spite of the stress faced by family members, most counseling services have focused on the AIDS patient rather than the relatives whose lives are also changed by the AIDS diagnosis (Williams and Stafford 1991). Serovich and his colleagues (1992) recommend the expansion of counseling and support groups that guarantee anonymity for family members of AIDS patients.

Discrimination. AIDS patients frequently report discriminatory treatment by the general public. Aids patients have reported that cab drivers have refused to drive them to the hospital and that barbers have declined to cut their hair, and relatives of AIDS patients have found that some funeral homes refuse to bury

AIDS victims (Kubler-Ross 1987). Ryan White, a fourteen-year-old hemophiliac from Kokomo, Indiana, who contracted AIDS from contaminated blood products used to produce a clotting factor for hemophiliacs, was a well-known victim of this kind of discrimination. Local parents went to court to prevent Ryan from attending school, and his family received hate mail (Kubler-Ross 1987). Similarly, when Elizabeth Kubler-Ross (1987) planned to build a hospice on her Virginia farm for 15 infants and children dying of AIDS, the neighbors collected a petition to prevent construction.

The mark of a compassionate society is how well it treats its most vulnerable members. It is important for Americans to work together to ease the suffering of those afflicted with serious health conditions rather than react out of fear.

We now explore a far less tragic form of familial care that is a growing demographic trend in midlife families: housing adult children who never left home or who are returning.

Review Questions

1. What groups have been identified as having an elevated risk of acquiring an HIV infection? What are some of the hardships experienced by these groups?
2. How do families with an AIDS patient typically respond to this crisis? What difficulties do they face?
3. In what ways have AIDS patients been discriminated against?

Unlaunched Adult Children

A growing number of "unlaunched adults" either remain in their parents' home after reaching adulthood or return home after a divorce or an unsuccessful attempt to establish a career. Almost half (45 percent) of midlife parents aged forty-five to fifty-four still have an adult child aged nineteen to thirty-four living in the home. Three-fourths of young unmarried adults aged nineteen to thirty-four live with their parents for at least some time after age nineteen. This new trend puts family living arrangements at odds with mainstream American values of independence and individualism (Aquilino and Supple 1992).

The American family follows a *neolocal residence* pattern in which young adults are expected to establish a residence separate from that of their parents. The presence of young adults in the home often creates strain. In the traditional American family, parents and their children have complementary developmental tasks as the children reach adulthood. On the one hand, children are expected to establish economic and emotional independence from parents. Parents, on the other hand, are expected to grapple with "letting go" and relinquishing control over children. Midlife is a time for parents to reestablish the primacy of the marital relationship while allowing the parental relationship to slip to a level of lower priority (Aquilino and Supple 1992). Parents expect to have opportunities for autonomy and self-development after their children leave home. Unlaunched adult children can interfere with these opportunities.

Parental Reaction to Co-Residence

Using a large national sample, Aquilino and Supple (1992) studied parents with children aged nineteen to thirty-four living in the home. The average age for unlaunched adult children was twenty-three, and the average age of parents was fifty-one. In spite of the traditional cultural expectation of independence in young adulthood, new social norms appear to be developing. Parents in this study tended to be well satisfied with the living arrangement that included adult children. In response to a question inquiring how well the co-resident living arrangement worked out for them, 70 percent of the parents chose 6 or 7 on a 7-point scale on which 1 represented "very poorly" and 7 represented "very well." Three-fourths of the parents reported having very enjoyable times with their adult child several times a month, and over two-thirds engaged in private talks with the adult child. Both mothers and fathers had more positive relationships with daughters than with sons living in the home and spent more enjoyable time with daughters. However, co-residence with adult children tended to work out better for mothers than for fathers. The frequency of shared activities, particularly housework, was an important factor in the mother's, but not the father's, satisfaction with the presence of an adult child in the home. Apparently, mothers appreciate the household labor provided by co-resident adult children.

Factors Promoting Adjustment to Co-Residence

Three factors strongly affected the parent's level of satisfaction with an unlaunched adult child living in the home: the presence or absence of the parent's own younger children in the home, the employment status of the unlaunched adult child, and the presence or absence of grandchildren in the home (Aquilino and Supple 1992).

Presence of Younger Children. Parents who had their own children under age eighteen still living in the home tended to report greater satisfaction with co-resident adult children than parents whose other children had been launched. The parents with other dependent children were not expecting to be free of childrearing responsibilities. They appreciated the help offered by a co-resident adult child, for example, chauffeuring a younger child to events.

Employment Status. Parents tended to be satisfied with adult children in the home as long as the adult child was either work-

Adult children are generally expected to "leave the nest." But when they continue to live with their parents, adult children can be helpful with housework and other essential activities.

ing, attending college, or going to a professional school. It appears that parents expected adult co-resident children to be on the road to economic independence but did not expect them to have already achieved independence. Only one in four co-resident adult children made room and board payments to parents. However, if the adult child was unemployed, the level of hostility expressed by the parents toward that child increased substantially. Parents of unemployed adult children reported frequent disagreements and arguments in the home. Apparently, parents were satisfied with the living arrangement as long as the adult child was making progress toward independence, but unhappy with the living arrangement if they failed to see this progress. Social class also affected parental attitudes. Highly educated fathers were much less satisfied with the co-resident living arrangement than working class fathers. Well-educated fathers tended to hold high expectations for independence and achievement in their children; working-class fathers tolerated a more gradual separation of the adult child from the family.

The Presence of Grandchildren. Many previously launched adult children return to the parental home after a divorce, often bringing grandchildren into the home. In the study by Aquilino and Supple (1992), both mothers and fathers were significantly less satisfied with the living arrangement when they shared their home with grandchildren. The resumption of parenting roles in relation to grandchildren caused considerable strain for grandparents, who expected to focus on their own autonomy, hobbies, careers, and self-development. Parents who had delayed childbearing and who were older tended to be less dissatisfied with the continuation of the parenting role. Perhaps these older parents did not feel that they needed to launch their children in order to experience things in life that they had missed out on because of early childbearing.

Changing Families/Strengthening Families

Family ties may appear to be weakening, yet families remain strong today. The high divorce rate has been seen as a weakness, but those who divorce tend to remarry and establish stepfamilies. Americans have not given up on marriage; rather, they seek more satisfying marital relationships. Some social scientists see another sign of family weakness in the recently declining marriage rate. However, this trend reflects a tendency to delay rather than reject marriage and can be seen as a positive sign. Young adults who wish to enter marriage and parenthood better prepared to support a family are extending their education and delaying marriage.

Cohabitation, although on the rise, does but not appear to be a rejection of family life. Cohabitation can be a temporary stage during which a couple can form a close intimate relationship without pressure from relatives to begin having children, or it can represent an adjustment to the economic uncertainty that makes marriage difficult. Nonetheless, cohabitation reveals a strong desire to form an emotional bond with another person.

Young adults are increasingly likely to live with their midlife parents, forming an extended family; this trend illustrates the strength of extended families and intergenerational ties. Furthermore, parents often come to the aid of young adults, divorced with children or struggling to establish careers, who are experiencing economic hardship. Thus families are becoming more complex and diverse. Perhaps it is in this interesting variation that families will display the strength to meet the challenges of a changing society.

In closing this book, we next turn to an overview of resilient families.

Resilient Families

Throughout this book we have discussed characteristics that make families strong or resilient and that help family members cope with the stress of everyday life. In addition, these characteristics are thought to have the potential to enhance the rewards of family life. The picture of resilient families drawn below is derived from theories and research findings presented in earlier chapters.

Viewing Love as Multifaceted

As Sternberg's theory of love tells us, love includes passion, intimacy or emotional connectedness, and commitment. Resilient couples foster all three aspects of love. They recognize the need to maintain emotional connectedness, and they realize that commitment lays a foundation that can help them endure difficult times in their marriage. Resilient couples also recognize the benefits of developing what Marks calls the "three-cornered self." That is, the partners retain their connection to the world outside the romance by keeping up their interests and friends. This helps to prevent them from becoming overly dependent on the romance and to maintain their individual identity as a separate person. At the same time, they devote time and attention to maintaining the love relationship (see Chapter 4, Falling in Love: Sexuality and Dating).

Keeping the Sexual Relationship Vital

In resilient families, the couples realize the importance of keeping the sexual relationship vital and satisfying. They keep the lines of communication open so that they are not reluctant to discuss their sexual needs, desires, and fantasies. Each partner takes into account the needs of the other, for example, by extending the period of foreplay to please the wife, or having sex more frequently to please the husband. When declining a sexual initiation by a partner, they explain why and often set a future time to have sex. Gay and lesbian couples also need to discuss and negotiate their sexual relationships (see Chapter 6, Sexuality).

Spending Time Together

Families can be strengthened by setting aside time to be together. Family rituals, such as family meals or family celebrations that take place periodically can create a sense of connectedness to the family. The inclusion of extended kin in some of these rituals places family members in a larger network of relationships that can provide emotional support in difficult times. Sometimes busy couples can benefit from following Stinnett's advice and prioritizing their activities so that additional family activities can be placed at a level of high priority (see Chapter 7, Marriage and Partnerships: Interpersonal Relationships).

Sharing Family Responsibilities

Two-earner families experience both the rewards of enhanced income and the costs of sometimes feeling overworked and stressed. Couples who cope well with employment and family life tend to be those who share child care and household labor. Two-earner families are fostering new androgynous gender roles in which breadwinning, parenting, and maintaining a household are part of both the male and female gender roles. At the same time there is a growing recognition that no single family form is superior; both two-earner families and breadwinner–homemaker families are valuable family forms. Two-earner families can be strengthened by flexibility in the workplace, such as family leave, flexible work hours, and job sharing, which makes it easier to combine employment with family life.

Pregnancy as a Bonding Experience

Resilient families view the experience of pregnancy as a joint effort, involving both husband and wife. Many wives feel increased dependence on their husbands during pregnancy and look to their husbands for reassurance. The husband's presence in the delivery room is comforting to the wife and promotes bonding between father and child. After the birth, many husbands may feel some jealousy over the need to share the wife's attention with the infant. Couples who communicate their needs and also offer each other emotional support find that the experience of pregnancy and birth can draw them closer together (see Chapter 11, Pregnancy: Experiences and Choices).

Authoritative Parenting

Resilient families use a parenting style that builds character while fostering individuality and self-esteem in children. Most child psychologists recommend an authoritative parenting style, in which parental demands and parental responsiveness are balanced. The parent allows children to make some decisions on their own, and yet the parent has a set of rules to guide the child's behavior. Such parents avoid authoritarian parenting, with its emphasis on rigid rules and obedience enforced through punishment. Likewise, authoritative parenting avoids excessive permissiveness, in which parents set few rules, guidelines are erratic or absent, and children regulate much of their own behavior (see Chapter 12, Parents and Children).

Assertive Communication

Resilient families use an assertive communication style in which they express their feelings, wants, and needs while also showing respect for the partner. These partners try to avoid aggressive communication that places blame on the partner, uses demeaning name-calling, and aims to gain control through giving orders and making threats. They also try to avoid nonassertive communication, in which feelings, wants, and needs are not expressed and the partner is often resented for not anticipating and fulfilling unexpressed needs (see Chapter 13, Communication and Conflict).

Nonviolent Conflict Resolution

Resilient families resolve conflict nonviolently. Violence is typically preceded by aggressive communication, in which blaming and name calling escalate into physical abuse. In contrast, nonviolent families often use a conflict-resolution pattern by which they identify the problem, state their opinions, listen to the partner's point of view, provide the partner with feedback, and then explore possible solutions. In resilient families, each partner seeks cooperation but recognizes that both partners are individuals and it is not desirable to attempt to control the partner's behavior with threats of physical force (see Chapters 13, Communication and Conflict, and 14, Family Abuse and Violence).

Easing the Divorce Experience for Children

In resilient families, when parents divorce they are aware that the relationship between the divorced parents will have a significant impact on the child. They try to avoid bringing the child into an ongoing conflict with the former spouse by denigrating the former spouse in front of the child and creating a loyalty conflict in which the child feels a need to choose between parents. The divorced parents also realize that the child needs to feel connected with the parents. Therefore, they make an effort to minimize self-absorption and preoccupation with the former spouse. As an aid in rebuilding their lives, divorced people can reestablish old friendships and make new ones, explore new activities, and maintain involvement with their children (see Chapter 15, Divorce).

These are some of the characteristics social scientists see as important in fostering strength and stability in families.

Review Questions

1. What developmental tasks do parents and children face when the children reach adulthood? How are these developmental tasks affected when unlaunched adult children live in the parental home?

2. What factors are associated with parental satisfaction with a living arrangement in which an adult child resides in the home?

3. What are the characteristics of resilient families?

Summary

1. The high incidence of divorce has led to debates over whether or not to make divorce more difficult to obtain. A number of social scientists have focused on finding strategies to make adjustment to divorce easier for children and parents.

2. Nearly half of all marriages are remarriages, and remarriages are less stable than first marriages for whites. The reverse is the case for African Americans. The probability of remarriage is affected by age, presence of children, education, and race.

3. Stepfamilies come in a variety of forms, each experiencing stresses related to the structure of its organization. Characteristics stepfamilies have in common are complex organization, vague boundaries, and vague social norms.

4. Stepfamilies tend to have low levels of cohesion and high levels of adaptability, which are functional for binuclear families.

5. Discipline can be a challenge for stepparents, who often choose between allowing the biological parent to be the disciplinarian, negotiating and compromising, or remaining firm.

6. Redivorce creates issues of child support, child custody, and visitation between the stepparent and former spouse.

7. In addition to the AIDS risk groups already recognized (homosexual males and IV drug users), AIDS risk is becoming a concern for women, minorities, the poor, children of HIV-infected women, and teenagers.

8. The families of AIDS sufferers often experience a range of responses, including shock and denial, anger, guilt and blame, and fear. Social isolation and discrimination place hardships on families of AIDS patients.

9. Midlife parents are increasingly likely to have an adult child living in the home. Parents tend to be satisfied with this living arrangement when they perceive the adult child as moving toward independence.

10. Parents are satisfied with adult children living in their home if the adult child is employed and does not bring grandchildren into the home, and if the parents still have younger children of their own at home.

11. Social scientists have pointed out that resilient families frequently have some or all of the following characteristics: they view love as multifaceted, develop intimacy through communication, spend time together, keep the sexual aspect of the marital relationship satisfying, share child care and household labor, view pregnancy as a joint experience, use authoritative parenting, foster assertive communication that shows respect for the partner, resolve conflict nonviolently, and attempt to promote the well-being of children when a divorce occurs.

Key Words

Self-Fulfilling Prophesy
Dual-Stepparent Families
Role Ambiguity
Adaptability
AIDS
Unlaunched Adult Children
Parenting Coalitions

Binuclear Families
Vague Boundaries
Cohesion
Redivorce
HIV
Neolocal Residence

Resources

467

Chapter 16
Looking Forward:
Emerging Trends and
Future Potentials

Stepfamily Association of America
215 Centennial Mall S., Ste. 212
Lincoln, NE 68508
(402) 477-7837
Establishes support networks of mutual help groups for people in stepfamilies.
Publishes *Stepfamilies*, quarterly, and *Learning to Step*, a manual.

Stepfamily Foundation
333 West End Ave.
New York, NY 10023
(212) 877-3244
(800) SKY-STEP
Compiles information on stepfamilies. Publishes *Step News*, quarterly.

Grandparents Rights Organization
555 S. Woodward Ave., Ste. 600
Birmingham, MI 48009
(313) 646-7191
Advocates grandparents' visitation rights after divorce.

United Fathers of America
415 N. Sycamore St., Ste. 207
Santa Anna, CA 92701
(714) 542-5624
Seeks equal rights for fathers in child custody. Provides education and monitors
legislation.

Aids Action Council
2033 M Street N.W., Ste. 802
Washington, DC 20036
(202) 293-2886
Lobbies Congress for funding for AIDS research and runs an education program
that provides information on AIDS. Publishes *AIDS Action Update*, monthly,
and *HIV Voting Record*, annually.

Aids Services and Prevention Coalition
23416 Highway 99, Ste. A
P.O. Box C-2016
Edmonds, WA 98020
(206) 778-6162
Monitors legislation related to AIDS and advocates education and prevention.
Publishes *ASAP News*, quarterly.

Names Project Foundation (AIDS Quilt)
2362 Market St.
San Francisco, CA 94114
(415) 863-5511

Sponsors a patchwork quilt in which families of AIDS victims memorialize their deceased family member. Publishes *The Quilt: Stories From the NAMES Project,* book.

Pediatric AIDS Coalition
1331 Pennsylvania Ave., N.W., Ste. 721-N
Washington, DC 20004
Advocates increased government funding for research and treatment of children with AIDS.

Mothers of AIDS Patients
1181 Field Dr., N.E.
Albuquerque, NM 87112-2833
(619) 544-0430
Assists in forming local support groups for families caring for AIDS patients. Publishes *Mother-to-Mother,* bimonthly newsletter.

National Minority AIDS Council
300 I St., N.E., Ste. 400
Washington, DC 20002
(202) 544-1076
(800) 544-0586
Gathers information on the effect of AIDS on minority communities and populations. Sponsors local discussion groups.

People with AIDS Coalition
31 West 26th St.
New York, NY 10010
(212) 532-0290
New York City hotline: (212) 532-0568
Free nationwide hotline: (800) 828-3280
Support network for people with AIDS. Provides a meals program, drop-in lounge, apartment referral, and public forums. Publishes *PWA Coalition Newsline,* monthly, and *SIDAhora* in English and Spanish, quarterly. Booklet also available: *Surviving and Thriving with AIDS.*

Sexually Transmitted Diseases

There are 12 million episodes of sexually transmitted diseases (STDs) each year. An episode involves one person with a single incidence of an STD. Some people contract more than one STD in a year and thus have more than one episode during that time. Two and a half million episodes of STDs occur among teenagers each year (Harlap et al. 1991). Sexually transmitted diseases vary in their ease of transmission. In general, women are more susceptible to infection than men. The Guttmacher Institute estimates that a single act of unprotected vaginal intercourse with a person infected with gonorrhea will result in infection 50 percent of the time for women and 25 percent of the time for men. The infection rate for chlamydia is estimated to be 40 percent for women and 20 percent for men in a single act of unprotected sex. Some STDs are equally easy for men and women to contract. These are genital herpes, with a 30 percent transmission rate, and genital warts, with a 10 percent transmission rate for a single unprotected act of vaginal intercourse (Harlap et al. 1991, Figure 6.). Continued intercourse with the same infected person increases the risk of transmission.

In the past, a sense of shame prevented many people from adequately discussing STDs or educating themselves about these diseases. The discomfort in talking about STDs made some people reluctant to have a medical exam or seek treatment when they experienced genital discomfort. Nonetheless, it is important for all sexually active persons to be informed about STDs and to monitor their sexual health in the same way they would show concern for any other aspect of their health. This is particularly important because so many STDs produce no symptoms in a number of people. Furthermore, early detection can be critical, even life-saving, for certain STDs. If you think that you just *might* have an STD, get it checked out by a medical practitioner and discuss it with your partner. The Centers for Disease Control recommend that while you are being treated for an STD you should refrain from sex while infectious, inform your partner, and use condoms to prevent future infection.

Further information on STDs can be gained by calling the following toll-free phone numbers:
Sexually Transmitted Disease National Hotline: 1(800) 227-8922
National AIDS Information Hotline:
1(800) 342-AIDS
1(800) 344-AIDS (for Spanish-speaking persons)
1 (800) AIDS-TTY (for hearing impaired persons)

AIDS

See Human Immunodeficiency Virus.

Bacterial Vaginosis

Bacterial vaginosis (VAJ-i-NO-sis) is caused by a number of different bacteria including Gardnerella and Mycoplasma.
Symptoms. Symptoms include a discharge that is usually grayish and frothy and may have an unpleasant odor.
Effects. Left untreated, these bacterial infections can lead to sterility.
Transmission. Transmission occurs through vaginal intercourse.
Treatment. Both partners are usually treated with antibiotics.

Chlamydia

The organism causing chlamydia (cla-MIH-dee-ah) infects approximately 4 million people per year. Chlamydia is the most frequently occuring STD and is of particular concern to health care practitioners because it is usually asymptomatic.
Symptoms. Seventy-five percent of people contracting chlamydia are asymptomatic (have no symptoms). When symptoms occur, they include a discharge from the penis or vagina, a burning while urinating, excessive vaginal bleeding, abdominal pain, nausea, fever, arthritis, or painful intercourse in women.
Effects. Chlamydia can produce an inflammation of the pelvic area, including the ovaries and the fallopian tubes, and ultimately can cause sterility. It also

can enter the urethra and cause a bladder inflection.
Transmission. Chlamydia is transmitted through vaginal and anal intercourse. During childbirth chlamydia can pass from the birth canal to the infant.
Treatment. Chlamydia is treated with antibiotics, in particular tetracycline. However, chlamydia often recurs if patients do not finish the course of treatment or do not take their medication consistently.

Cytomegalovirus

Symptoms. Cytomegalovirus (sigh-tow-MEG-a-low-VI-rus) (CMV) is less common than many other STDs. Often no symptoms occur, but when they do they include fatigue, nausea, diarrhea, and swollen glands.
Effects. Between 10 and 20 percent of mothers infected with CMV pass on the infection to their infants. Some infected infants suffer serious central nervous system damage. In adults, CMV can lead to loss of vision.
Transmission. Sexual intercourse, intimate sexual contact, needle sharing among IV drug users, and blood transfusions can transmit this disease. Many people infected with CMV suffer no symptoms, but CMV can unknowingly be passed to infants through breastfeeding and to a fetus during pregnancy.
Treatment. No successful treatment or cure exists.

Genital Warts

About 2 million men and women are infected with genital warts, and over half a million new cases are diagnosed each year. These warts are produced by the human papilloma virus (HPV).
Symptoms. Genital warts may be flat or look like miniature cauliflower florets. They can be found on the penis, vulva, cervix, in the urethra, anus, or occasionally in the throat. Although genital warts occasionally itch, they are typically asymptomatic. Genital warts often grow inside the body where they cannot be seen, and they can be transmitted by people who do not know that they are infected.
Effects. If they are not removed, genital warts can grow large enough to block the openings of the vagina, anus, or throat. Also, if untreated, warts can develop into precancerous growths on the cervix,

vulva, vagina, or penis.

Transmission. Genital warts are caused by a virus and spread through vaginal, anal, or oral intercourse.

Treatment. Treatment involves removing genital warts surgically by freezing, with acid, or with electric needles. They are sometimes treated with medication applied directly to the wart, which can be extremely irritating to uninfected skin. Also, women who have had HPV warts are advised to get regular pap smears at six month intervals following treatment.

Gonorrhea

There are approximately 1½ million cases of gonorrhea (gone-o-RHEE-a) each year. Eighty percent of women and 10 percent of men have no symptoms when they contract gonorrhea.

Symptoms. When symptoms do occur, gonorrhea can cause frequent, burning urination, discharge from the penis or vagina, or swelling of the vulva.

Effects. Left untreated, gonorrhea can lead to arthritis, heart problems, disorders of the central nervous system, and pelvic inflammation disease, which affects the uterus, ovaries, and fallopian tubes and can lead to sterility. During pregnancy, gonorrhea can cause stillbirth and premature delivery.

Transmission. Gonorrhea can be transmitted through vaginal or anal intercourse.

Treatment. Penicillin is usually effective in treating gonorrhea, but some strains have become resistant to penicillin and require other antibiotics. People infected with gonorrhea often are infected with chlamydia as well.

Herpes

Between 5 and 20 million Americans have genital herpes, and 500,000 new cases are diagnosed each year. Two viruses cause herpes: herpes simplex type 1 produces cold sores and fever blisters and is usually, but not always, located on the upper part of the body. It can, however, be passed to a partner's genital area through oral sex. Ninety percent of Americans are infected with herpes simplex type I. Herpes simplex type 2, called genital herpes, is typically located in the genital area.

Symptoms. Infection with herpes simplex type 2 results in a recurring red rash with clusters of white,

blistery sores located on the vagina, cervix, penis, mouth, anus, or anywhere the virus entered the body. Symtoms are a rash that burns and itches, swollen glands in the groin, fever, headache, general fatigue, and burning during urination.

Effects. Herpes can cause miscarriage or stillbirth during pregnancy. No cure is available, but medication can alleviate pain and shorten the healing process for sores.

Transmission. When herpes sores are present, they are highly contagious until they scab over and the scabs have fallen off. In addition, however, some herpes sufferers are contagious even when no sores are present. A partner's mucus membranes in the mouth, anus, vagina, penis, and eyes are particularly susceptible to infection. Thus transmission can occur during any sexual contact. Condoms should be used at all times, even between outbreaks, if a sex partner has herpes. However, condoms do not cover the entire genital area and cannot prevent transmission from sores on the vulva or skin around the genital area during an outbreak.

Treatment. The herpes virus is not curable. Once a person has it, he or she has it forever. Sometimes the virus is dormant, and other times the virus causes an outbreak of sores. Outbreaks can be aggravated by stress. The sores are often treated with acyclovir, but some people take acyclovir prophylactically.

Hepatitis B

Hepatitis is an inflammation of the liver. The hepatitis B virus can be transmitted through sexual intercourse, needle sharing, or blood transfusions. Approximately 200,000 cases of hepatitis B are reported each year; and there are an estimated 1 million carriers, many asymptomatic, who are infected with the virus and can pass it on to sexual partners. This type of hepatitis differs from hepatitis A, which is transmitted through food and water contaminated with fecal material. Outbreaks of hepatitis A often occur when sanitation is poor, such as in overcrowded conditions and during wartime.

Symptoms. During the most contagious phase of infection, hepatitis B has no symptoms. When symptoms occur they include loss of appetite, extreme fatigue, dark urine, light-colored stools, headache, fever, nausea, pain in the lower abdomen, and jaundice (a yellowish tint to skin and the white of the eye).

Effects. Nine out of 10 people treated for hepatitis B infection recover; but in those who do not recover, the disease can cause severe liver damage and death.

Transmission. Hepatitis B can be transmitted through body fluids, such as semen, during vaginal, anal and oral intercourse, as well as by kissing. IV drug use with unclean needles can also transmit the disease.

Treatment. Often the disease gradually disappears through the action of the immune system. Currently, there are no drugs that can cure hepatitis B, but a vaccine for prevention of this disease is available.

Human Immunodeficiency Virus

By June, 1993, 315,000 cases of acquired immunodeficiency syndrome (AIDS) had been reported to the U.S. Centers for Disease Control and Prevention (U.S. Department of Health and Human Services 1993c). It is estimated that at least 1½ million Americans are infected with the human immunodeficiency (im-mu-NO-dee-FISH-en-see) virus (HIV), the virus that causes AIDS. There is a difference between an HIV infection and AIDS. A person may be completely without symptoms or illness for as many as ten years after contracting HIV. It is only when severe symptoms present themselves that a person is diagnosed with AIDS.

Symptoms. When symptoms occur, they are at first called aids related complex (ARC). These symptoms can be fatal and include a "wasting" or weight loss from diarrhea and lack of appetite, fever, sweating, headaches, fatigue, coughs and colds that do not go away quickly, and thrush (candidiasis).

Effects. The HIV virus slowly attacks the immune system, rendering it vulnerable to serious "opportunistic" diseases. As the immune system falls victim to such diseases as pneumonia, tuberculosis, or cancer, the diagnosis is changed from ARC to AIDS.

Transmission. HIV can be transmitted when the body fluids (blood, semen, or vaginal fluids) of an infected person come into contact with the blood system of an uninfected person. Transmission takes place through anal, vaginal, or oral intercourse or sharing contaminated IV needles. In addition, HIV can be transmitted from mother to fetus during pregnancy and through breastfeeding.

Treatment. Drugs, such as AZT and antibiotics, are used to diminish the intensity of symtoms of ARC

and AIDS. There is no cure for an HIV infection, and it typically progresses toward death. For a more complete discussion of AIDS see Chapter 6, Sexuality, and Chapter 16, Looking Forward.

Molluscum Contagiosum

A quarter of a million cases of molluscum contagiosum (mo-LUS-kum con-tay-GEE-OH-sum) are reported each year.

Symptoms. The virus causes small pink or white polyp growths on the genitals or surrounding area.

Effects. Long-term effects are unknown.

Transmission. Sexual intercourse or other intimate contact with infected skin area can lead to transmission.

Treatment. Growths can be removed with chemicals or freezing, but the polyps may recur.

Pubic Lice

Pubic lice are tiny insects that look like crabs under a magnifying glass. These lice attach themselves to hair, including pubic hair, eyelashes, underarm hair, and eyebrows. Over 100,000 cases of pubic lice occur each year.

Symptoms. Intense itching is caused by the bites of the lice. Lice and clumps of eggs can be seen in body hair.

Effects. Reinfestation is common when all of those exposed to pubic lice are not treated.

Transmission. Sexual contact as well as contact with infested bedding, clothes, towels, or toilet seats can transmit public lice. All of these items should be cleaned when partners receive treatment.

Treatment. Over-the-counter medicated creams, lotions and shampoos are available to treat pubic lice. Pregnant women should consult their physician for a special medication.

Scabies

Scabies (SKAY-beez), small mites related to spiders, are too small for the naked eye to see. These mites burrow under the skin, causing irritation.

Symptoms. Intense itching and a red rash can appear on the genitals, between the fingers, on thighs, breasts, underarms, buttocks, or wrists.

Effects. If everyone who has been exposed to scabies is not treated at the same time, scabies can continue to be passed from person to person.

Transmission. Scabies can be transmitted sexually as well as through infested bedding, clothes, and towels. All of these items should be washed or dry-cleaned when the partners receive treatment.

Treatment. Treatment involves bathing thoroughly and applying over the body a cream that is available in drugstores.

Syphilis

Until the 1980s syphilis (SIFF-i-lis) was thought to be a disease of the past, but 100,000 cases of syphilis are currently reported each year.

Symptoms. Symptoms occur in three stages, which may be overlapping: In the primary stage, which occurs three to twelve weeks after infection, chancres (open sores that ooze clear liquid) appear on the genitals or infected area. In women, chancres that occur on the cervix may not be detectable without a medical examination. In the secondary stage, which occurs two weeks to six months after infection, a rash appears, often on palms of hands, soles of feet, or shoulders and back. After the secondary stage, syphilis enters a latent phase in which the disease becomes dormant for four years or longer. In the dormant phase the person is not contagious.

Effects. If left untreated, the dormant phase gives way to a tertiary stage, or "late stage." In the tertiary stage, syphilis again becomes active and affects the nervous system, heart, or brain, causing serious damage, even death.

Transmission. Syphilis can be transmitted when the virus is active, when chancres appear in the primary stage, when a rash appears in the secondary stage, and when internal organs are attacked during the tertiary stage. Syphilis is transmitted during vaginal or anal intercourse.

Treatment. Syphilis can be treated with antibiotics, but damage from the tertiary stage is usually permanent.

Trichomoniasis

Trichomoniasis, or "trich" for short, is a very common STD, with more than a million cases occurring each year.

Symptoms. There are often no symptoms, especially in women, but when symptoms occur they include a greenish-yellow discharge from the vagina or penis, itching, a musty genital odor, a frequent need for urination, irritation of the external genitals, and sometimes groin pain.

Effects. Trich can lead to an infection of the urethra and bladder.

Transmission. Trich is spread through vaginal or anal intercourse.

Treatment. Treatment involves both partners taking an antibiotic medication and using a condom during treatment.

Yeast Infection, or Candidiasis

Candidiasis (can-di-DYE-a-sis) is also known as a yeast infection or monilial vaginitis. It occurs when a fungus that occurs naturally in a healthy woman's vagina grows out of control. Under normal conditions the growth of yeast is usually limited by the vagina's natural acidity. Although a yeast infection is not usually transmitted sexually, it is sometimes transmitted to men through sexual contact.

Symptoms. Symptoms include a thick white vaginal discharge with a fishy order, and itching of the vulva, penis, or testicles. Yeast infections are called "thrush" when they appear in the throat, mouth, or tongue.

Effects. Candidiasis is uncomfortable, but it is treatable and is not usually associated with any long-term damage.

Transmission. Candidiasis is rarely transmitted sexually, but the symptoms can often be confused with an STD. Candidiasis is often brought on by the use of antibiotics, cortisone, or the oral contraceptive. When candidiasis is transmitted sexually, it is through vaginal, anal, or oral intercourse.

Treatment. Candidiasis is treated through antibacterial creams or suppositories, some of which are sold over the counter. In addition, prepared vinegar-and-water douches, available in drugstores, can be helpful. Some women with recurrent candidiasis find it beneficial to reduce their sugar intake and add yogurt containing live acidophilus to their diet.

References

Harlap, Susan, Kathryn Kost, and Jacqueline Darroch Forrest 1991. *Preventing Pregnancy, Protecting Health: A New Look at Birth Control Choices in the United States.* New York: The Alan Guttmacher Institute.

Planned Parenthood 1991a. *Herpes: Questions and Answers.* New York: Planned Parenthood Federation of America, Inc.

Planned Parenthood 1991b. *Sexually Transmitted Disease: The Facts.* New York: Planned Parenthood Federation of America, Inc.

Planned Parenthood 1990. *HPV and Genital Warts: Questions and Answers.* New York: Planned Parenthood Federation of America, Inc.

Contraception

Barrier Methods

Barrier methods of contraception place a physical barrier between the ovum and sperm. Some of these, such as the sponge and diaphragm, add a chemical contraceptive to the physical barrier.

Male Condom

The male condom is a thin sheath of latex or other material that is placed on the penis before intercourse.

How It Works. Condoms provide a mechanical barrier between sperm and the ovum. Some condoms are coated with spermicide, and this provides a small measure of additional protection.

Side Effects. No side effects are known, except for a small number of people who have an allergic reaction to the rubber substance from which the condom is constructed.

Advantages. Condoms provide some protection against STDs, although they do not provide complete protection. Only latex condoms, not those made of animal skin, provide some protection against the AIDS virus. Condoms are widely available.

Disadvantages. Condoms can slip off or tear during intercourse. The couple must interrupt foreplay so that the man can put the condom on. Animal skin condoms do not provide an effective barrier to the AIDS virus. Latex condoms are more effective in preventing the transmission of the AIDS virus; but users often have a false sense of security because condoms can tear, leak, or slip off.

Female Condom

The female condom is a thin sheath of polyurethane that unrolls into the vagina.

How It Works. The female condom is anchored by a ring to which the polyurethane sheath is attached.

Anatomy and Reproduction

Male Reproductive Anatomy

Sperm are produced in the testes (singular, testis) and travel along the vas deferens. Sperm then combine with semen, which is produced in the seminal vesicles and prostate glands. Next, semen enters the urethra and is ejaculated through the urinary opening. The ejaculatory pathway forms a continuous duct that connects the tip of the penis to the testes.

Female Reproductive Anatomy

The ovum ripens and then bursts out of the ovary in a process called ovulation. The ovum then travels down the fallopian tube, where it is likely to be fertilized by sperm. The fertilized ovum travels to the uterus and attempts to implant itself into the uterine wall. The unfertilized ovum (or the fertilized ovum that was not successful at implantation) passes out of the uterus through the cervix into the vagina, where it either disintegrates or passes out of the body.

Preventing Conception

Contraception prevents pregnancy by one of the following methods:

1. preventing ovulation (oral contraceptive or implant rods)
2. creating a mechanical barrier between sperm and ovum (condom, diaphragm, or sponge)
3. killing sperm (spermicidal foams or gels, the sponge or the diaphragm used with a spermicide)
4. preventing implantation of the fertilized ovum (interuterine device, or IUD)
5. thickening the cervical mucus, which traps sperm at the opening to the cervix (oral contraceptive or implant rods)

For a more complete explanation of how contraception works see Appendix A.

Figure 6.7
Male Reproductive System.

Figure 6.8
Female Reproductive System.

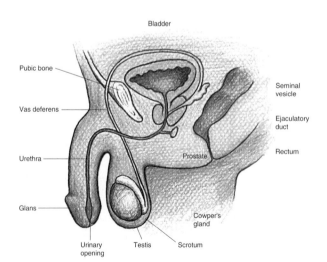

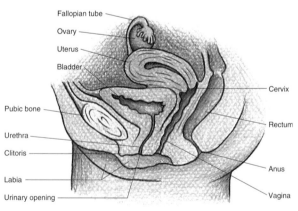

Source: Adapted from William H. Masters, Virginia E. Johnson, and Robert C. Kolodny 1986. *Masters and Johnson on Sex and Human Loving.* Boston: Little, Brown and Co.

This ring lies flat against the woman's vulva and remains outside the vagina. The condom provides a barrier between the man's penis and the vaginal wall. The man ejaculates into the female condom, and the condom is then withdrawn.

Side Effects. No side effects are known, except for a small number of people who have an allergic reaction to the polyurethane from which the condom is constructed.

Advantages. This condom provides women with greater control over contraception than the male condom provides. The degree of protection against STDs is unknown. However, because women are more susceptible than men to sexual transmission of HIV, it is hoped that the availability of the female condom may provide women greater protection against AIDS. Because the ring holding the polyurethane condom lies outside the female body and covers the vulva (the opening of the vagina), the female condom will probably also offer some protection against STDs, such as herpes, which can be transmitted through lesions on the vulva. In addition, the action of putting on the condom is controlled by the female, and the female can more easily insist that without a condom, no sex will take place.

Disadvantages. As with the male condom, foreplay must be interrupted in order to insert the female condom. In addition, male cooperation is still needed.

Sponge

The sponge is a polyurethane sponge containing nonoxynol 9, a spermicide. Thus the sponge is actually a barrier method combined with a chemical method. The sponge is inserted into the vagina and pressed up against the cervix prior to intercourse.

How It Works. The sponge forms both a mechanical and a chemical barrier against sperm.

Side Effects. A very small number of women using the sponge have experienced toxic shock syndrome. Some women have allergic reactions to the chemicals or to the material in the sponge. Heavy use of the sponge may result in vaginal lesions, which could increase the woman's susceptibility to STDs, including HIV.

Advantages. The sponge can be put in place before the sexual experience and can remain in place for twenty-four hours. Therefore it does not interfere with spontaneity in sexual activity. Intercourse may be repeated during the twenty-four-hour period without having to change the sponge. The sponge does not require a daily routine of pill taking. Nonoxynol 9 offers some protection against STDs unless the sponge is used so frequently that lesions occur. Because of the potential problem with vaginal lesions, it is unclear whether or not the sponge can act as a deterrent to transmission of HIV.

Disadvantages. The sponge must remain in place for six to eight hours after intercourse.

Diaphragm (Used with Cream, Gels, or Foam)

The diaphragm is a shallow cup of thin rubber or polyurethane stretched over a flexible ring. A spermicide cream (which kills sperm) is spread on both sides of the diaphragm, adding a chemical contraceptive. The diaphragm is inserted into the vagina and pressed up against the cervical opening to the uterus before intercourse.

How It Works. The diaphragm acts as a mechanical barrier, blocking the entry of sperm into the uterus. It also acts as a chemical barrier, catching and killing many sperm that manage to swim around the mechanical barrier.

Side Effects. No serious side effects are known. Some people have an allergic reaction either to the rubber substance used in the diaphragm or to the spermicide.

Advantages. There is no daily schedule of pill taking to which oral contraceptive users must adhere. Most women report no discomfort with its use. Spermicides containing nonoxynol 9 provide some limited protection against STDs, including HIV.

Disadvantages. The diaphragm must be inserted before intercourse and thus disrupts foreplay. It must remain in place six to eight hours after intercourse in order to make sure that sperm are dead. The diaphragm must be fitted by a medical practitioner, rechecked each year, and refitted if the woman's weight changes, if she gives birth, or, if she has an abortion. Some women find the diaphragm difficult to insert. Women with relaxed vaginal muscles cannot successfully use the diaphragm.

Cervical Cap

The cervical cap is similar to a diaphragm, only smaller. Like the diaphragm, the cervical cap is inserted into the vagina and fits over the cervical opening to the uterus. Spermicide placed in the cervical cap reduces the chance of pregnancy.

How It Works. The cervical cap acts both as a mechanical barrier, blocking the forward movement of sperm, and as a chemical barrier, killing sperm.

Side Effects. No serious side effects are known. Some people have an allergic reaction either to the rubber substance used in the cervical cap or to the spermicide.

Advantages. Many women find the cervical cap more comfortable than the diaphragm. Spermicides containing nonoxynol 9 provide some limited protection against STDs, including HIV.

Disadvantages. The cervical cap must remain in place six to eight hours after intercourse in order to make sure that sperm are dead. The cervical cap must be fitted by a medical practitioner. It can slip out of place during intercourse.

Chemical Methods

There are two types of chemical methods. Oral contraceptives and implants prevent pregnancy by interrupting ovulation. In contrast, spermicides operate by killing sperm.

Oral Contraceptives

People generally believe there is one kind of birth control pill; but in fact, there are two, each having different ingredients and side effects. The vast majority of women who use the oral contraceptive use the combined pill. Others use the mini-pill.

Combined Pill

The oral contraceptive combined pill contains two hormones, estrogen and progestin.

How It Works. The pill suppresses ovulation, preventing the release of the ovum.

Side Effects. Some side effects are nausea and unexpected vaginal bleeding. There is a small risk of a blood clot forming, which could be fatal if it were to reach the lungs, heart, or brain. Some other risks include gall bladder disease, high blood pressure, and liver tumors. Existing cancerous tumors tend to grow faster with the elevated estrogen level created by the oral contraceptive. Smoking is not advised while using the pill.

Advantages. The combined pill is very effective in preventing pregnancy. It allows the couple to avoid the inconvenience of interrupting foreplay to take care of contraception.

Disadvantages. The pill must be taken exactly according to instructions to provide maximum effectiveness. People who miss one or two pills are advised to use a back-up method of contraception until the next cycle of pills begins.

Mini-Pill

The mini-pill is like the combined pill, except that the mini-pill contains only progestin.

How It Works. Progestin causes cervical mucus to thicken, blocking the passage of sperm through the cervix and into the uterus. In addition, progestin interferes with ovulation.

Side Effects. Because the mini-pill contains no estrogen, most of the side effects associated with the oral contraceptive are avoided.

Advantages. The mini-pill allows the couple to be spontaneous in sexual activity. Health risks are reduced when compared to the combined pill.

Disadvantages. The mini-pill is less effective in preventing pregnancy than the combined pill. The mini-pill must be taken exactly according to instructions to be effective.

Implants

The contraceptive implant, commonly known as Norplant, consists of approximately six small rods about 1½ inches long and 1/8 inch thick. These are inserted under the skin of the underside of the upper arm and are not usually visible.

How does It Work?. Implant rods contain the hormones estrogen and progestin, and they slowly release these into the body over a period of years. These hormones interfere with ovulation and cause cervical mucus to thicken and form a barrier against sperm at the opening of the cervix.

Side effects. Side effects are the same as for the oral contraceptive. Smoking is not advised because it increases the likelihood of side effects.

Advantages. Norplant is effective for up to five years and allows spontaneity in sexual relations.

Disadvantages. The initial cost may be a burden, but when the cost is averaged over five years, it may actually provide a savings over the birth control pill.

Spermicides (Foams, Creams, Gels, and Suppositories)

Spermicides are foams, creams, gels, or suppositories that are inserted into the vagina before intercourse so that they cover the cervix.

How It Works. Spermicides form a chemical barrier that kills sperm before they enter the uterus.

Side Effects. No serious side effects are known, except that some people may have an allergic reaction that is sometimes eliminated by changing brands.

Advantages. Spermicides are sold over the counter and are readily available.

Disadvantages. Foreplay must be interrupted in order to insert the spermicide before intercourse begins. Care must be taken not to dislodge the spermicide before intercourse by such action as sitting or standing up. The spermicide needs to remain in place against the cervix. The "missionary position" with the man on the top is desirable in order to keep the spermicide in place. Suppositories require a waiting period after insertion before intercourse begins in order to allow the suppository to melt and spread.

Sterilization

Sterilization, including vasectomy and tubal ligation, involves surgery to create a permanent internal barrier to pregnancy.

Vasectomy

In male sterilization, called vasectomy, the tube that carries sperm is severed and tied off.

How It Works. A vasectomy involves surgically blocking the vas deferens, the tube that carries sperm, so that sperm cannot travel to meet and combine with semen. During intercourse, the man ejaculates semen that is free of sperm.

Side Effects. Surgery carries some discomfort fol-

lowing the procedure and a low risk of infection. Many men have the procedure performed on a Friday and can return to work on Monday.

Advantages. Sterilization is the most effective means of preventing pregnancy. It also allows for spontaneity in sexual activity.

Disadvantages. The surgery is not usually reversible, and some people who divorce and remarry may go through considerable expense in an attempt to have the surgery reversed. Couples should be sure that they want a permanent solution to contraception.

Tubal Ligation

Female sterilization, called tubal ligation, involves surgically severing and tying off the tubes that carry the ovum.

How It Works. In a tubal ligation, both fallopian tubes, which carry the ovum to the uterus, are surgically blocked so that the ovum is prevented from meeting with sperm.

Side Effects. Surgery carries some discomfort following the procedure and a low risk of infection. Women run a slightly elevated risk of a later hysterectomy.

Advantages. Sterilization is the most effective means of preventing pregnancy. It also allows for spontaneity in sexual activity.

Disadvantages. The surgery is not usually reversible, and couples should be sure that they want a permanent solution to contraception.

The Intrauterine Device

The intrauterine device (IUD) is a device inserted into the uterus by a medical practitioner.

How It Works. The IUD interferes with implantation of the fertilized ovum in the uterine wall. The IUD causes a mild inflammation, or irritation, of the uterine lining as well as uterine contractions, which interfere with implantation. In the "Copper 7" IUD, the copper also acts as a chemical barrier. Polyurethane strings hang down into the vagina so that the woman can check to make sure that the IUD is in place.

Side Effects. Some women complain of cramping and bleeding after insertion. Because of the strings extending into the vagina, the danger of infection is increased, and some women experience pelvic inflammatory disease (PID), which can lead to sterility by causing scar tissue to form in the fallopian tubes. In a very small number of cases the uterus has been perforated by the IUD.

Advantages. The IUD does not interfere with sexual spontaneity.

Disadvantages. The woman must check the strings to confirm that the IUD is in place, particularly after her menstrual periods. The availability of IUDs is limited due to lawsuits that have led some manufacturers to discontinue production.

Natural Methods

Withdrawal

Withdrawal involves the man removing his penis from the vagina prior to ejaculation.

How It Works. The man withdraws his penis toward the end of intercourse and ejaculates away from the vagina.

Side Effects. There are no known side effects.

Advantages. This is the simplest contraceptive method in that it does not require a visit to a physician or the purchase of equipment. It also involves no financial cost.

Disadvantages. The man must concentrate in order to withdraw and may not be able to control his ejaculation. In addition, fluid containing sperm are emitted before ejaculation in order to lubricate the vagina. These sperm can cause a pregnancy to occur.

Fertility Awareness, Calendar Rhythm

Fertility awareness involves calculating the expected time of ovulation and abstaining from intercourse on the days during which the woman can become pregnant. Calendar rhythm involves using a calendar and marking off the expected days when the woman could become pregnant.

How It Works. A menstrual cycle (or monthly cycle) runs from day one of the menstrual period to the last day before the next period. So the first step is to mark the first day of the woman's period on the cal-

endar and also to mark the estimated last day of her monthly cycle (the last day before the next period). The second step is to estimate when ovulation could take place. Ovulation occurs approximately fourteen days (between twelve and sixteen days) before her next period begins. Ovulation could take place on any one of these days. These days need to be marked on the calendar with a series of Xs. The third step is to subtract four days for sperm life. Place an S on the four days before the first X so that the days of sperm life immediately precede the days marking possible ovulation. The fourth step is to mark off days for ovum life. The ovum can live twenty-four hours. Therefore, using an O, mark off one day for ovum life and one extra safety day after the last X. All the days marked (with and S, X, or O) are days when intercourse is avoided. The other days are nonfertile days for that cycle length.

The woman must do the above calculations for both her longest and shortest cycles, because the day of ovulation depends on cycle length. The nonfertile days that occur within *both* the shortest and longest cycle can be considered nonfertile days when intercourse can take place.

Side Effects. There are no known side effects.

Advantages. On nonfertile days foreplay does not need to be interrupted to utilize a birth control device.

Disadvantages. Calendar rhythm has a high failure rate. Women who have irregular cycles cannot use the method. If the cycle length is different from that estimated, the calculation is thrown off and pregnancy can occur. Ovulation can occur at an unexpected time, particularly if the woman is sick or under stress. In rare instances a woman can ovulate twice in a month. In addition, abstinence can be frustrating.

Fertility Awareness, Mucus Method

The mucus method of fertility awareness involves abstaining from intercourse from the first day of the menstrual period until ovulation has occured and all ovulation mucus disappears. When the mucus method is combined with calendar rhythm the effectiveness of fertility awareness increases.

How It Works. Ovulation mucus appears approximately three days before ovulation; it is dense, opaque, and tacky in consistency. On the day of ovulation the mucus becomes clear and transparent and can be stretched like a rubber band. The day after ovulation the mucus begins to disappear. The woman abstains from intercourse from day one of the menstrual period until three days after cervical mucus disappears, monitoring her cervical mucus constantly.

Side Effects. No side effects are known.

Advantages. On nonfertile days, foreplay does not need to be interrupted to utilize a birth control device.

Disadvantages. The mucus method can fail because discharge from an infection can be mistaken for ovulation mucus. A woman can misread the mucus and not distinguish the actual day of ovulation. Abstinence can be frustrating.

Table B.1 gives failure rates for each of the contraceptive methods discussed.

References

Journal of the American Medical Association. 1992b, July 22. "Commentary." p. 520.

Journal of the American Medical Association. 1992a, July 22. "Editorial."

Hiatt, Jane and ETR Associates, Inc. 1986. *Birth Control Facts.* Santa Cruz, Ca.: Network Publications.

Planned Parenthood 1991c. *The Methods of Birth Control.* San Francisco: Planned Parenthood.

Planned Parenthood 1991d. *Ways to Chart Your Fertility Pattern.* New York: Planned Parenthood Federation of America, Inc.

Planned Parenthood 1989. *Facts About Birth Control.* New York: Planned Parenthood Federation of America.

U.S. Department of Health and Human Services 1990. *Contraception: Comparing the Options.* Washington, D.C.: U.S. Public Health Service.

Trussell, James and Kathryn Kost 1987. "Contraceptive Failure in the United States: A Critical Review of the Literature." *Studies in Family Planning,* Vol. 18, Table 11, page 271.

Table B.1 Contraceptive Failure Rates

	Lowest Expected Failure Rate	Actual Failure Rate
Chance (no contraception)	89	89
Periodic abstinence (rhythm)	—	20
Spermicides	3	25
Withdrawal	4	18
Cervical cap	5	18
Male condom	2	15
Female condom	Unknown	Unknown
Sponge	5	18
Oral contraceptive		
Progestogen only	0.5	3
Combined (estrogen		
and progestogen)	0.1	3
Diaphragm	5	18
Implant rods	0.2	0.2
Female sterilization	0.2	0.4
Male sterilization	0.1	0.15

Note: The "Actual Failure Rate" refers to the percent of couples who experience an accidental pregnancy during the first year of use if they use the method consistently. That is, these couples do not stop using the method for any reason. "The Lowest Expected Failure Rate" refers to the accidental pregnancy rate that would probably occur if the contraceptive method were to be used perfectly (consistently and correctly), during the first year, without stopping use for any reason.

Note: Women who have given birth have a higher failure rate with the sponge than women who have never been pregnant.

Sources:

James Trussell and Kathryn Kost, "Contraceptive Failure in the United States: A Critical Review of the Literature." *Studies in Family Planning*, Vol. 18, 1987, Table 11, page 271.

Editorial, *Journal of the American Medical Association*, July 22, 1992.

Commentary, *Journal of the American Medical Association*, July 22, 1992, p. 520.

Pregnancy and Childbirth

It is important for expectant mothers and their partners to be aware of the stages of pregnancy and childbirth so that they know what to expect during this experience. In addition, mothers and fathers who are aware of possible complications during pregnancy increase their chances of having a healthy baby.

Pregnancy

Pregnancy is a process that involves fertilization and implantation of the ovum, the emergence of the embryo into a fetus, and fetal development. In this section we trace pregnancy through conception and implantation and through three trimesters, each lasting approximately three months.

Conception and Implantation

On alternate months, one of the two ovaries releases an ovum in a process called *ovulation*. At ovula-tion the fingers of the fallopian tube move over the ovary to capture the released ovum. *Fertilization* of the ovum, in which the sperm penetrates the ovum and fuses with it, takes place within twenty-four hours after ovulation. After that point the ovum begins to disintegrate. Of the several hundred million sperm released during ejaculation, it is estimated that somewhere between several hundred and several thousand reach the fallopian tube. When a sperm penetrates the ovum, the ovum immediately releases a chemical substance that prevents the entry of additional sperm. Within several hours the fertilized ovum, now called a *zygote*, begins the process of cell division while it travels down the fallopian tube toward the uterus, a journey that takes about four days.

In the unusual instance in which two ovum are released and each is fertilized by a separate sperm, *dizygotic twins*, also called fraternal twins, are produced. Fraternal twins have no more genes in common than ordinary siblings. On the other hand, if the a single fertilized ovum splits completely apart

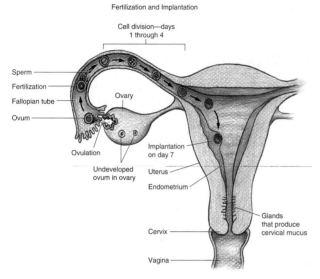

Fertilization and Implantation

Cell division—days 1 through 4

Sperm
Fertilization
Fallopian tube
Ovum
Ovary
Ovulation
Undeveloped ovum in ovary
Implantation on day 7
Uterus
Endometrium
Cervix
Glands that produce cervical mucus
Vagina

The First Trimester

Once the zygote is implanted, it will be called an embryo until the eighth week of pregnancy. As the embryo develops, an amniotic sac and a placenta are formed. An *amniotic sac* is a membrane that surrounds the embryo and fills with *amniotic fluid.* This fluid acts as a shock absorber and protects the embryo as the mother bends and moves about during her day. The *placenta* provides nourishment for the embryo by bringing the fetal blood system and maternal blood system next to each other. Nutrients, oxygen, and other substances from maternal blood cross over the cells in the placenta and enter fetal blood. Likewise, waste products such as carbon dioxide cross from the fetal blood into maternal blood. However, there is no mixing of the fetal and maternal blood systems. Pregnant women must be careful about the substances they put in their body because many can pass through the placenta into the fetal blood system. The placenta is attached to the embryo by the *umbilical cord.* This is a rope-shaped structure containing veins and arteries through which fetal blood travels to and from the placenta.

In the embryonic stage the internal organs begin to form. A rudimentary heart develops and begins pumping blood; the skeletal system, which includes a tail, is formed at this stage; the nervous system emerges as a simple "neural tube;" and the early development of other organs, such as the digestive system, begins. At the end of eight weeks, the embryo is known as a fetus and has that title until delivery. The eight-week fetus is approximately 1¼ inches long,

5 week embryo
1/2 inches long

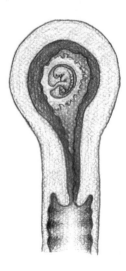

during cell division so that two separate but genetically identical cells are produced, the result is *monozygotic twins,* also known as identical twins.

After the zygote reaches the uterus, it floats in uterine fluid for several days. Then about seven days after fertilization the zygote's sticky outer layer of cells helps it to attach itself to the *endometrium,* the nutrient-rich uterine lining. Then the zygote begins to burrow into the endometrium, in a process called *implantation.* However, not all zygotes are successful at implantation. Some pass through the uterus and disintegrate. With implantation, the pregnancy is established and the zygote is now called an *embryo.* When implantation begins, it will be approximately another week before the woman expects her next period, so she does not know that she is pregnant.

Implantation does not always follow the pattern just described. Occasionally a zygote will become attached to the fallopian tube, where it does not have enough room to develop. Left unattended, this *tubal pregnancy* can result in either a miscarriage or a rupture of the fallopian tube. For this reason, when a tubal pregnancy occurs the embryo is surgically removed. Even more rare is a fertilized ovum that escapes outside the fallopian tube into the abdominal cavity and implants itself there. In this case a full-term pregnancy is possible, but the infant has to be delivered through surgery. Both tubal implantation and abdominal implantation are known as *ectopic pregnancies.*

weighs 1 ounce and has rudimentary arms and legs, which are developing.

Early in pregnancy, the ligaments in the pelvis begin to loosen and the mother may notice that her clothes do not fit even before she registers much weight gain. During this time, many women experience nausea, known as "morning sickness." Other signs of early pregnancy can include fatigue, frequent urination, tenderness in the breasts, and a darkening of the breast area around the nipples. These signs are not always present, but do occur in many women. It is essential for the woman who suspects that she is pregnant to have a pregnancy test and, if the result if positive, to go to a clinic to receive prenatal medical care. Over-the-counter pregnancy tests are available at drug stores and can be used at home. Many complications of pregnancy can be prevented by prenatal care that begins early and continues throughout the pregnancy.

As early as eight to ten weeks of pregnancy a physician can perform a test for genetic defects by using *chorionic villi sampling*. In this procedure a small part of the chorionic villi, which are projections from the placenta, are suctioned off and analyzed. Results can be obtained in only twenty-four hours, but the risk to the fetus is unknown.

As this first trimester ends, the pregnant woman is beginning to notice a small protrusion of her abdomen.

Second Trimester

The second trimester includes months four through six of pregnancy. As this trimester begins, the fetus is 3 inches long. In the next three months the eyes of the fetus become fully developed but remain closed and the fingernails begin to grow. During the second trimester many of the fetal organs, with the exception of the lungs, begin to function. The fetal digestive system becomes largely developed, and the fetus will urinate into the amniotic fluid. From this time on the amniotic fluid consists primarily of fetal urine.

The second trimester of pregnancy is particularly exciting. As the second trimester begins the fetal heartbeat can be detected when the mother receives her prenatal checkup. If the father accompanies her, he may be invited into the examination room to

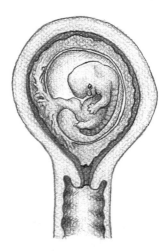

8 week fetus
1¼ inches long, ⅟₃₀ ounce

hear the heartbeat as well. The nausea experienced by many women earlier in pregnancy usually fades away during the second trimester and is replaced by a general feeling of well-being. Excitement increases when fetal *quickening* occurs. Quickening refers to the time when the mother first feels the fetus move. These movements can be felt in the fourth or fifth months of pregnancy. Because the fetus sleeps for periods of time, movement can often be detected when the fetus wakes up.

During the second trimester the total volume of maternal blood increases by 30 to 50 percent in order to handle the increased demands of the developing fetus for oxygen, nutrients, and the removal of waste products, such as carbon dioxide. Increased water retention can cause the mother's feet and ankles to swell. Many pregnant women try to avoid standing still for long periods of time to reduce the risk of fainting or developing varicose veins. Walking and lying down for brief periods during the day can improve the mother's sense of well-being.

When a pregnant woman is in her mid-thirties or older, or when there is a family history of genetic disorders, an *amniocentesis* can be performed to detect certain inheritable disorders. Amniocentesis, generally performed between the sixteenth and twentieth weeks of pregnancy, involves the withdrawal of a small amount of amniotic fluid for analysis. First *ultrasound* is used to provide a picture of the fetus and placenta without the use of x rays. The ultrasound picture locates the placement of the fetus in the amniotic sac. This reduces the risk that the fetus or placenta might be punctured during amniocentesis. Then an anesthetic is administered to the mother's abdomen. Finally, a hypodermic needle is placed through the abdomen, into the amniotic sac, and some amniotic fluid is withdrawn.

Amniocentesis allows many abnormalities in the chromosomes to be detected. For example, *Down syndrome* is associated with an extra, or third, chromosome in the twenty-first pair of chromosomes. Down syndrome is the most common cause of mental retardation and may also be associated with malformation of the heart and an increased risk of both infection and leukemia. In spite of these problems, many people experience a great deal of pleasure in raising children with Down syndrome.

The risk of Down syndrome increases with the age of the mother, and amniocentesis is primarily performed on women in their mid-thirties or older. As a byproduct of amniocentesis, the parents can also learn the sex of their child. Amniocentesis has been used to detect over fifty inheritable defects, including hemophilia, some muscular dystrophies, and cystic fibrosis.

Third Trimester

As the third trimester (months seven through nine) begins, the fetus is approximately twelve inches long and weighs 1 pound. Lanugo, a fine hair, covers the body of the fetus, but this hair will drop off toward the end of pregnancy. At this stage the fetus is growing eyelashes and the eyelids are separating. During the next three months it will gain approximately another 6¼ pounds and will double in length. This period of rapid growth may cause some discomfort for the mother because the fetus begins to put pressure on her bladder, making frequent urination necessary. Toward the end of pregnancy the growing fetus also presses up against the mother's diaphragm, making breathing somewhat difficult.

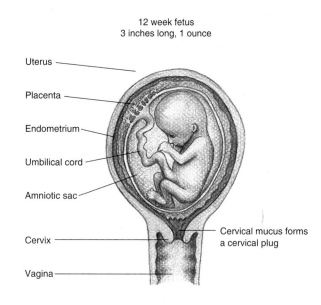

12 week fetus
3 inches long, 1 ounce

Uterus
Placenta
Endometrium
Umbilical cord
Amniotic sac
Cervix
Vagina
Cervical mucus forms a cervical plug

Complications of Pregnancy

Beginning prior to conception and throughout pregnancy, it is important for the mother to avoid substances that can be hazardous to the fetus. Substances that can pass from the mother to the fetus and cause harm are called *teratogens*. The first trimester is particularly critical to the development of a healthy fetus because the organs are formed during this trimester. The fetus can be exposed to teratogens when the pregnant woman smokes cigarettes, consumes alcohol, takes certain legal and illegal drugs, is exposed to hazardous environmental substances, or contracts certain viral infections or other diseases. The part of fetal anatomy affected by a teratogen is often determined by the stage in fetal development at which the teratogen is introduced. Organs being formed at the time the teratogen appears can be harmed.

Alcohol. Alcohol consumption during pregnancy, particularly heavy drinking, has been associated with *fetal alcohol syndrome*. Maternal alcohol consumption can result in minimal brain damage associated with learning disabilities or even in intellectual retardation. Children who experience fetal alcohol syndrome often exhibit facial malformation, which can include widely or unusually spaced eyes and small heads. Damage to the central nervous system can also occur.

Cigarettes. Cigarette smoking can interfere with oxygen delivery to the fetus, producing an increased risk of miscarriage and a risk of low birth weight at delivery. Low birth weight is a principal cause of infant mortality. In addition, cigarette smoking can damage fetal organs. Children whose mothers smoked during pregnancy also have an elevated risk of developing leukemia.

Prescription, Over-the-Counter, and Illegal Drugs. A number of both legal and illegal drugs can cause harm to the developing fetus. Many women and their partners do not realize that legal over-the-counter and prescription drugs can affect fetal development. Aspirin, antihistamines, and large doses of vitamins can be harmful, particularly during the first trimester of pregnancy. Women who think they might be pregnant should inform their physician before taking a prescription or over-the-counter drug. Illegal drugs, such as heroin and cocaine, can result in fetal addiction, and the addicted infant goes through drug withdrawal after birth. Addicted infants can experience fever, convulsions, and even death. In addition, a number of illegal drugs, such as cocaine, can cause premature total or partial separation of the placenta from the uterus. This can deprive the fetus of an adequate supply of oxygen and nutrients.

Environmental Substances. The fetus can be affected by contaminants in the environment that enter the pregnant woman's physiological system through breathing polluted air, drinking contaminated water, or eating food containing environmental hazards. Metals, such as mercury, can enter drinking water or the food chain (such as in shellfish) and sometimes affect brain development in the fetus. X rays are another environmental hazard that can harm the developing fetus. A woman who suspects that she is pregnant should let her dentist and doctor know her condition.

Toxemia. Eclampsia, also known as *toxemia,* is a complication of pregnancy that involves retension of protein in the urine, retention of an abnormal amount of fluid in the body, and hypertension. In the early stage of toxemia, which is known as *preeclampsia,* the treatment is usually rest and a reduction of salt in the diet. Only about 5 percent of women with preeclampsia develop full-blown toxemia, which can require hospitalization. This complication of pregnancy can be detected by a simple check for protein in the urine and a check for high blood pressure and fluid retention.

Rubella, AIDS, and Other Diseases. If the mother contracts rubella (also called German measles) during pregnancy, fetal development can be impaired. Blindness, deafness, or retardation can result in the developing fetus. In addition, the fetus can be harmed if the pregnant mother contracts any of a number of other diseases, including chicken pox, mumps, and HIV infection. The agents causing these diseases can pass through the placenta to infect the fetus. A mother who is HIV positive has one chance in four of passing on the virus to her developing fetus. However, the drug AZT has shown promise in reducing the risk that the fetus will acquire HIV from the mother.

Childbirth

Childbirth has three stages: labor, delivery of the infant, and delivery of the afterbirth.

Labor

Labor refers to contractions of the uterus that cause the cervix to dilate, or open, in preparation for the delivery of the infant. The cervix is the opening of the uterus into the vagina. During labor the cervix also experiences effacement, in which it thins out and becomes more flexible. As labor contractions begin, the *cervical plug* which is called the "show," is usually expelled. The cervical plug is a thick mucus that closes the cervix to help prevent fetal infection during pregnancy. The amniotic sac typically ruptures during labor or right before labor begins; when it does, it is called the "water breaking." Some of the fluid surrounding the fetus is released, and labor usually intensifies. If the amniotic sac breaks and labor does not begin with-

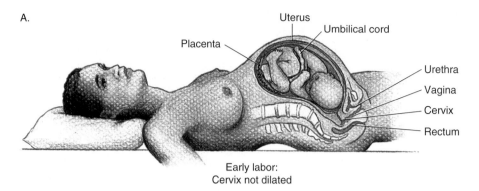

A.

Placenta

Uterus

Umbilical cord

Urethra

Vagina

Cervix

Rectum

Early labor:
Cervix not dilated

in twenty-four hours, labor is induced to prevent infection to the fetus through the ruptured amniotic sac. Labor for a first birth usually lasts twelve to sixteen hours.

At the beginning of labor, contractions of the uterus occur fifteen to twenty minutes apart, last only a few seconds, and might feel like mild indigestion. As labor proceeds, contractions gradually increase in intensity and duration and are closer together. The most intense part of labor comes right before delivery and is called *transition*. At this time, contractions typically last a minute and come two or three minutes apart. It is not unusual for the mother to feel disoriented, chilled, distressed, and sometimes even angry during this phase of labor. At the end of transition the cervix is fully dilated to 10 centimeters, approximately the width of a human hand, and delivery can begin.

Electronic fetal monitoring (EFM) is sometimes used during labor in order to record the fetal heart rate and the mother's uterine contractions. *External fetal monitoring* is conducted by sensors on straps placed around the mother's abdomen and can be used early in labor. *Internal fetal monitoring* can occur later in labor and involves placing an eletrode through the vagina into the uterus and attaching it to the fetal scalp. This type of fetal monitoring can take place after the cervix has become dilated and the amniotic sac has broken. A fetal monitor is often able to warn the medical staff of possible problems the fetus might be experiencing.

Delivery of the Infant

During labor the muscles of the uterus performed the work of contracting, and the mother was not asked to push. However, after the cervix is fully dilated *delivery* begins, and the mother bears down, or pushes, to help the uterine contractions move the baby through the cervix and down the birth canal, or vagina. Delivery usually takes approximately forty-five minutes. Some women find it a relief to be able finally to push and take an active role in the birth process. When the infant's head is visible, called *crowning*, and appears ready

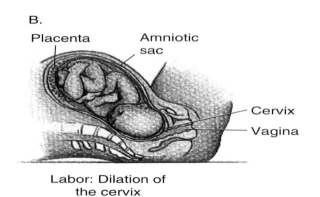

B.

Placenta   Amniotic sac

Cervix

Vagina

Labor: Dilation of
the cervix

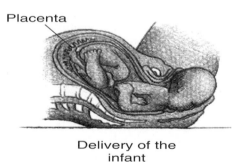

C.

Placenta

Delivery of the
infant

to move through the opening of the vagina, an *episiotomy* is usually performed by the physician. This is done with a local anesthetic and involves an incision to widen the vaginal opening to prevent tearing of tissue.

Complications of Delivery. Complications can necessitate delivery by *Caesarean section* rather than vaginal delivery. A Caesarean section involves the surgical removal of the fetus through the abdomen. Caesarean delivery can become necessary when problems occur, for example, when the infant experiences distress because the umbilical cord becomes kinked or wrapped in such as way as to endanger the flow of oxygen. The position of the infant during labor and delivery can be important. If the infant is in a lateral position, lying horizontally rather than vertically, delivery requires a Caesarean section. On the other hand, if the infant presents its buttocks rather than its head toward the cervix, a *breach birth* occurs. In this case the buttocks are delivered before the head, and care must be taken in the delivery of the head. Because of possible complications during delivery, home births have a somewhat higher infant mortality rate than hospital deliveries.

Delivery of the Afterbirth

Contractions continue after the infant is delivered. In the final phase of delivery the placenta separates from the uterine wall and is expelled. It is important for the *afterbirth*, which includes the placenta, umbilical cord, and amniotic sac, to be completely delivered so that no pieces remain which could cause infection.

References

Campbell, Neil A. 1987. *Biology.* Menlo Park, Calif: Benjamin/Cummings Publishing.

Defries, Zira, Richard C. Friedman, and Ruth Corn 1985. *Sexuality: New Perspectives.* Wesport, Conn.: Greenwood Press.

Mitchell, G. 1981. *Human Sex Differences.* New York: Van Nostrand Reinhold.

Tortora, Gerard J. 1989. *Principles of Human Anatomy.* New York: Harper and Row.

D.

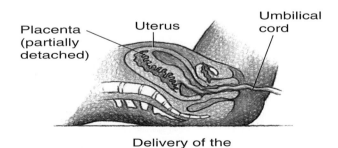

Delivery of the
afterbirth

Sexual Dysfunction

Sexual dysfunction refers to ineffectiveness in sexual activity. It includes the inability to perform a sexual act, as well as the inability to attain satisfaction from a sexual act. However, some critics point out that the term "sexual dysfunction" is often applied too widely and therefore sometimes labels sexual behavior that is within the normal range as dysfunctional. This criticism has been particularly applied to orgasmic dysfunction in women and premature ejaculation in men, which are discussed below.

Erectile Dysfunction (Impotence)

Erectile dysfunction refers to the inability to produce or maintain an erection firm enough to allow sexual intercourse to take place. This sexual dysfunction falls into two categories: primary and secondary erectile dysfunction. *Primary erectile dysfunction* is present when the male cannot sustain an erection long enough to have intercourse.

Some men with primary erectile dysfunction can maintain an erection during masturbation but not during intercourse. *Secondary erectile dysfunction* is far more common and describes a male who has had intercourse earlier in his lifetime, but currently cannot maintain an erection.

Secondary erectile dysfunction needs to be distinguished from the widespread, normal occasional inability to maintain an erection. Feeling tired or stressed can temporarily interfere with an erection. A man must have erectile difficulties at least one-fourth of the time before the condition can be termed a sexual dysfunction. Between 5 and 9 percent of males experience erectile dysfunction. In a number of cases a man's fears concerning sexual performance can become self-fulfilling prophesies by lowering the level of sexual arousal and thus can lead to the loss of an erection.

Erectile dysfunction can have a physiological cause. For example, illness, such as diabetes; an irregular blood flow to the penis; or some medications, such as some hypertensive drugs, can inhibit an erection. Psychological causes, such as depression, can also result in problems with erection. Some men experience erectile dysfunction only in certain circumstances. For example, some men can have an erection with an extramarital lover but not with the wife, and some men can produce an erection during masturbation but not when seeking coitus. In these cases the cause of erectile dysfunction is most likely psychological or social, as in the situation in which the romance has gone out of the marriage

Premature Ejaculation (Rapid Ejaculation)

There is disagreement over how to define premature ejaculation. The American Psychiatric Association considers it to be a lack of "reasonable voluntary control" over ejaculation. Others do not consider rapid ejaculation to be a problem if it does not interfere with sexual satisfaction of both partners. Premature ejaculation is generally considered a problem when the man ejaculates during foreplay or upon entry during coitus. While some women are understanding of this, others accuse their male partners of being selfish and withdraw from sex. Infrequent sexual activity tends to intensify the problem of premature ejaculation, and marital tension rises. However, some sexologists consider premature ejaculation to be a sexual dysfunction only when ejaculation takes place prior to vaginal entry and thus makes intercourse impossible.

A number of techniques have been suggested to prevent premature ejaculation. Frequent intercourse often helps delay ejaculation. Some couples have intercourse twice: the first time with rapid ejaculation and the second time with more leisurely intercourse. Other techniques include briefly stopping intercourse; having the woman squeeze the man's penis; or using the "valsalva maneuver," in which the man holds his breath and bears down as if having a bowel movement to delay ejaculation. Men using the last technique should alert their partners prior to using the maneuver.

Orgasmic Dysfunction (Anorgasmia)

Orgasmic dysfunction refers to consistently experiencing sex without an orgasm. Between 7 and 10 percent of all women never have an orgasm. However, many of these women enjoy sex, and their experience should be considered within the normal range of sexual response. Sexual excitement that does not lead to an orgasm can be very satisfying. Interpersonal problems arise when partners view themselves as failures because they feel unable to truly satisfy the partner and bring the partner to orgasm. The lack of an orgasm is not a problem for a woman or man who enjoys sex. As men age, some have difficulty reaching an orgasm. Men can also experience pleasure in sexual stimulation that does not have orgasm as the end result.

Orgasmic dysfunction, in which a sexually aroused person consistently has sex without an orgasm, should be distinguished from *hypoactive sexual desire*, which is difficulty in becoming sexually aroused. It is not unusual for long-term partners to have different levels of sexual desire. The less interested person is often said to experience hypoactive sexual desire. The person with less sexual interest can take the attitude Masters and Johnson call "be my guest," a situation in which sexual activity takes place without the expectation that both partners will be equally aroused or share a "his and hers orgasm." For the female, this involves intercourse if she is sufficiently lubricated, but without the expectation that she will have an orgasm. For the male, this involves stimulating the male partner to the point of erection and having intercourse without expecting him to have an orgasm. Otherwise, manual or oral stimulation can satisfy the more aroused partner.

Psychological factors can play a part in creating a tense situation during sex. For example, some women experience anxiety over trying to have an orgasm. Other women may have had a previous unpleasant experience with sex, such as childhood sexual abuse, making the sexual experience unpleasant. Therapy is often helpful in these cases.

Vaginismus

In vaginismus, the female has muscle spasms in the vagina; this makes penetration painful or even impossible. Vaginismus can result from fear of penetration when a woman has had a previous experience with painful intercourse, such as when a woman has a vaginal infection, has been raped, or fears intercourse for another reason. Treatment involves allowing the woman to experience penetration that is comfortable and during which she maintains control. Some couples use a position for intercourse in which the woman is on top to allow her to guide the experience of coitus.

Compulsive Sexual Behavior

The quest for sexual experiences becomes a sexual dysfunction when that desire is out of control, self-destructive, repetitive, and typically unsatisfying. Compulsive sexual behavior creates problems when it interferes with the formation of satisfying interpersonal relationships and when it interferes with a person's ability to function effectively at work or at home. Compulsive sexual behavior sometimes results from a need to find love and acceptance through sex or from a need to separate one's identity from that of a sexually restrictive parent.

Therapy can often be effective in uncovering issues that underlie compulsive sexual behavior. Sometimes a person avoids these issues by compulsively focusing on sex in a continuous way. There are very effective twelve-step programs, including Sex and Love Addicts Anonymous, for people with compulsive sexual behavior. These programs regard compulsive sexual behavior as a sexual addiction. Such programs provide a strong support network, which can help the person as it might with any other type of addiction.

References

Defries, Zira, Richard C. Friedman, and Ruth Corn 1985. *Sexuality: New Perspectives.* Wesport, Conn.: Greenwood Press.

Mahoney, E.R. 1983. *Human Sexuality.* New York: McGraw Hill.

Masters, William H., Virginia E. Johnson, and Robert C. Kolodny 1986. *Masters and Johnson on Sex and Human Loving.* Boston: Little, Brown.

Sarrel, Lorna J., and Philip M. Sarrel 1984. *Sexual Turning Points.* New York: Macmillan.

Schelp, Earl E. 1987. *Sexuality and Medicine.* Boston: D. Reidel Publishing Company.

Annotated Bibliography

Legend for term papers: The following annotations indicate term-paper topics and related bibliographical references.

A—Aging

F—*Fatherhood*
- F-1—Involvement in parenting
- F-2—Divorce and noncustodial parenting
- F-3—Unmarried fatherhood
- F-4—Pregnancy and birth

G—*Gender Roles*
- G-1—Socialization and childhood
- G-2—Relationships between men and women
- G-3—Feminism and gender theory
- G-4—Gender and violence
- G-5—Gender, work, and household labor

H—*Homelessness*

P—*Poverty*
- P-1—Economic conditions and social change
- P-2—One-parent families
- P-3—Men in poverty

R—*Race and ethnicity* (Additional references on race and ethnicity can be found under "P—Poverty.")
- R-1—African Americans
- R-2—Hispanic Americans
- R-3—Asian Americans
- R-4—Native Americans

S—*Sexuality*
- S-1—AIDS
- S-2—Sexual relationships in dating
- S-3—Sexual relationships in marriage
- S-4—Abortion
- S-5—Contraceptive use

S-6—Homosexuality
S-7—Rape and sexual abuse

S-2 Abbey, A. 1982. "Sex Differences in Attributions for Friendly Behavior: Do Males Misperceive Females' Friendliness?" *Journal of Personality and Social Psychology* 42: 830–838.

Abbott, Douglas A., Margaret Berry, and William H. Meredith 1990. "Religious Belief and Practice: A Potential Asset in Helping Families." *Family Relations* 39: 443–448.

R-4 Aberle, David F. 1951. "The Psychological Analysis of Hopi Life-History." *Comparative Psychology Monographs*. Berkeley: University of California Press.

Ahlburg, Dennis A., and Carol J. DeVita 1992. Population Bulletin 47 (2) *New Realities of the American Family*. Washington, D.C. Population Reference Bureau, Inc.

G-2 Aida, Yukie, and Toni Falbo 1991. "Relationships Between Marital Satisfaction, Resources, and Power Strategies." *Sex Roles* 24: 43–56.

G-2 Alain, Michel, and Yvan Lussier 1988. "Sex-Role Attitudes and Divorce Experience." *Journal of Social Psychology* 128: 143–152.

Alberti, Robert E., and Michael L. Emmons 1978. *Your Perfect Right: A Guide to Assertive Behavior*. San Luis Obispo, Calif.: Impact Publishers.

Alcoholism and Drug Abuse Week, "Addicts' Children Crushing Foster Care System." 3 (1) (May 1): 2.

Aldous, Joan, and Dumon Wilfried 1990. "Family Policy in the 1980s: Controversy and Consensus." *Journal of Marriage and the Family* 52: 1136–1151.

R-1 Aldridge, Delores P. 1989. "African-American Women in the Economic Marketplace: A Continuing Struggle." *Journal of Black Studies* 20: 123–128.

G-4 Allen, C., and M.A. Straus 1979. "Resources, Power, and Husband—Wife Violence," in M.A. Straus and G. Hotalling, eds., *Social Causes of Husband-Wife Violence*. Minneapolis, Minn.: University of Minnesota Press.

G-3 Allen, Katherine R., and Kristine M. Baber 1992. "Starting a Revolution in Family Life Education: A Feminist Vision." *Family Relations* 41: 378–384.

R-4 Allen, Paula Gunn 1986. *The Sacred Hoop*. Boston: Beacon Press.

S-4 Alter, R.C. 1984. "Abortion Outcome as a Function of Sex-Role Identification." *Psychology of Women Quarterly* 8: 211–233.

Amato, Paul R. 1991. "The 'Child of Divorce' as a Person Prototype: Bias in the Recall of Information about Children in Divorced Families." *Journal of Marriage and the Family* 53: 59–69.

Amato, Paul R. 1987. "Family Processes in One-Parent, Stepparent, and Intact Families: The Child's Point of View." *Journal of Marriage and the Family* 49: 327–337.

Ambert, Anne-Marie 1986. Being a Stepparent: Live-In and Visiting Stepchildren." *Journal of Marriage and the Family* 48: 795–804.

The American Enterprise 1992. "U.S. and Japanese Women." 3 (1) (Jan.–Feb.): 103–104.

Ammons, Paul, and Nick Stinnett 1990. "The Vital Marriage: A Closer Look." *Family Relations* 29: 37–42.

F-3 Anderson, Elijah 1989. "Sex Codes and Family Life among Poor Inner-City Youths." *Annals of the American Academy of Political and Social Science*

501: 59–78.

G-4 Andrews, Bernice, and Chris R. Brewin 1990. "Atributions of Blame for Marital Violence: A Study of Antecedents and Consequences." *Journal of Marriage and the Family* 52: 757–767.

R-2 Aneshensel, Carol S., Eve P. Fielder, and Rosina M. Becerra 1989. "Fertility and Fertility-Related Behavior Among Mexican-American and Non-Hispanic White Female Adolescents." *Journal of Health and Social Behavior* 30: 56–76.

R-1 Apfel, Nancy H., and Victoria Seitz 1991. "Four Models of Adolescent Mother—Grandmother Relationships in Black Inner-City Families." *Family Relations* 40: 421–429.

A Aquilino, William S., and Kalil R. Supple 1991. "Parent–Child Relations and Parental Satisfaction with Living Arrangements When Adult Children Live at Home." *Journal of Marriage and the Family* 53: 13–27.

Arafat, I., and Betty Yorburg 1973. "On Living Together Without Marriage." *Journal of Sex Research* 9: 21–29.

Arcus, Margaret E. 1992. "Family Life Education: Toward the 21st Century." *Family Relations* 41: 390–393.

Arendell, Terry J. 1987. "Women and the Economics of Divorce in the Contemporary United States." *Journal of Women in Culture and Society* 13.

Aries, Philippe 1962. *Centuries of Childhood: A Social History of Family Life.* New York: Vintage Books.

Asimov, Nanette 1989. "No School for Many of San Francisco's Homeless Kids." *San Francisco Chronicle*, Sept. 25.

Astone, Nan Marie, and Sara S. McLanahan 1991. "Family Structure, Parental Practices and High School Completion." *American Sociological Review* 56: 309–320.

Bach, George A., and Herb Goldberg 1974. *Creative Aggression.* New York: Doubleday and Co.

Bach, George R., and Peter Wyden 1970. *The Intimate Enemy.* New York: Avon.

Bachrach, Christine A., Kathryn A. London, and Penelope L. Maza 1991. "On the Path to Adoption: Adoption Seeking in the United States, 1988." *Journal of Marriage and the Family* 53: 705–718.

Baer, Jean 1976. *How to Be an Assertive (Not Aggressive) Woman in Life, in Love, and on the Job.* New York: Signet.

Bahr, H. W., S. J. Condie, and K. L. Goodman 1982. *Life in Large Families: Views in Mormon Women.* Washington, D.C.: University Press of America.

S-5 Baker, Sharon A., Stanton P. Thalberg, and Diane M. Morrison 1988. "Parents' Behavioral Norms as Predictors of Adolescent Sexual Activity and Contraceptive Use." *Adolescence* 23: 265–282.

Balakrishnan, T.R., K. Vaninadha Rao, Evelyne Lapierre-Adamcyk, and Karol Krotki 1987. "A Hazard Model Analysis of Covariates of Marriage Dissolution in Canada." *Demography* 24: 395–406.

S-5 Baldwin, John D., and Janice I. Baldwin 1988. "Factors Affecting AIDS-Related Sexual Risk-Taking Behavior Among College Students." *Journal of Sex Research* 25: 181–196.

Ballard-Reisch, Deborah S., and Daniel J. Weigel 1991. "An Interaction-Based Model of Social Exchange in the Two-Generation Farm Family." *Family Relations* 40: 225–231.

Bandler, R., J. Grinder, and V. Satir 1976. *Changing with Families.* Palo Alto,

Calif.: Science and Behavior Books.

Bandura, Albert 1973. *Aggression: A Social Learning Analysis.* New York: Prentice-Hall.

S-5 Banks, Ivan W., and Patricia I. Wilson 1989. "Appropriate Sex Education for Black Teens." *Adolescence* 24: 233–245.

S-3 Banmen, J., and N.A. Vogel 1985. "The Relationship Between Marital Quality and Interpersonal Sexual Communication. *Family Therapy* 12: 45–58.

G-1 Barak, Azy, Shoshana Feldman, and Ayelet Noy 1991. "Traditionality of Children's Interests as Related to Their Parents' Gender Stereotypes and Traditionality of Occupations." *Sex Roles* 24: 511–524.

S-1 Barnes, D.M. 1987. "Broad Issues Debated at AIDS Vaccine Workshop." *Science* 236: 255–257.

G-4 Barnes, Gordon E., Leonard Greenwood, and Reena Sommer 1991. "Courtship Violence in a Canadian Sample of Male College Students." *Family Relations* 40: 37–44.

S-7 Baron, L., and M. Strus 1987. "Four Theories of Rape: A Macrosociological Analysis." *Social Problems* 34: 467–489.

G-1 Basow, Susan A. 1980. *Gender Stereotypes.* Pacific Grove, Calif.: Brooks/Cole Publishing Co.

Bassuk, Ellen L. 1991. "Homeless Families." *Scientific American* 265 (Dec.): 66–73.

R-4 Bataille, Gretchen M., and Kathleen M. Sands 1984. *American Indian Women.* Lincoln: University of Nebraska Press.

G-2 Bate, Barbara 1988. *Communication and the Sexes.* New York: Harper and Row.

Bateson, Gregory 1971. "The Cybernetics of 'Self': A Theory of Alcoholism." *Psychiatry* 34: 1–18.

Bateson, Gregory, D. Jackson, J. Haley, and J. Weakland 1956. "Toward a Theory of Schizophrenia."

Baumrind, Diana 1983. "Rejoinder to Lewis's Reinterpretation of Parental Firm Control Effects: Are Authoritative Families Really Harmonious?" *Psychological Bulletin* 94:132–142.

Beattie, Melody 1987. *Codependent No More.* New York: Harper and Row.

Beck, P., and D. Burns 1979. "Anxiety and Depression in Law Students." *Journal of Legal Education* 30: 270–290.

S-7 Becker, Judith V., and Emily M. Coleman 1988. "Incest," in Vincent B. Van Hasselt, Randall L. Morrison, Alan S. Bellack, and Michel Hersen, eds., *Handbook of Family Violence,* pp. 187–206. New York: Plenum Press.

Belkin, Lisa 1989. "Custody Battle in Utah's Top Court Shines Rare Spotlight on Polygamy." *New York Times,* June 12, p. A16.

Bell, R.Q., and M. Chapman 1986. "Child Effects in Studies Using Experimental or Brief Longitudinal Approaches to Socialization." *Developmental Psychology* 22: 595–603.

Bellah, Robert, Richard Madsen, William Sullivan, Ann Swindler, and Steven Tipton 1985. *Habits of the Heart.* Berkeley: University of California Press.

Belsky, Jay, Lise Youngblade, Michael Rovine, and Brenda Volling 1991. "Patterns of Marital Change and Parent–Child Interaction." *Journal of Marriage and the Family* 53: 487–498.

Belsky, Jay 1990. "Parental and Nonparental Child Care and Children's Socioemotional Development: A Decade in Review." *Journal of Marriage and the Family* 52: 885–903.

Belsky, Jay, and Emily Pensky 1988. "Marital Change Across the Transition to Parenthood." *Marriage and Family Review* 12: 133–156.

Belsky, Jay 1988. "The 'Effects' of Infant Day Care Reconsidered." *Early Childhood Research Quarterly* 3: 235–272.

G-1 Bem, S. L. 1985. "Androgyny and Gender Schema Theory: A Conceptual and Empirical Integration," in T. B. Sonderegger, ed., *Nebraska Symposium on Motivation: Psychology of Gender*. Lincoln: University of Nebraska Press.

G-1 Bem, Sandra 1983. "Gender-Schema Theory and Its Implications for Child Development." *Signs* 8: 598–616.

G-1 Bem, S. L. 1981. "Gender Schema Theory: A Cognitive Account of Sex Typing." *Psychological Review* 88: 354–364.

Benedek, Elissa, and Richard Vaughn 1982. "Voluntary Childlessness," in Martha Kirkpatrick, *Women's Sexual Experiences,* pp. 205–222. New York: Plenum Press.

Bennett, Niel G., Ann Klimas Blanc, and David E. Bloom 1988. "Commitment and the Modern Union: Assessing the Link between Premarital Cohabitation and Subsequent Marital Stability." *American Sociological Review* 53: 127–138.

Bepko, Claudia 1985. *The Responsibility Trap: A Blueprint for Treating the Alcoholic Family*. New York: Free Press.

Berardo, Felix M. 1990. "Trends and Directions in Family Research in the 1980s." *Journal of Marriage and the Family* 52: 809–817.

G-5 Bergen, Elizabeth 1991. "The Economic Context of Labor Allocation: Implications for Gender Stratification." *Journal of Family Issues* 12: 140–157.

Berger, Peter L., and Hansfried Kellner 1964. "Marriage and the Construction of Reality." *Diogenes* 46: 1–13.

G-6 Berger, Raymond M. 1990. "Men Together: Understanding the Gay Couple." *Journal of Homosexuality* 19: 31–49.

G-4 Berk, Richard A., and Phyllis J. Newton 1985. "Does Arrest Really Deter Wife Battery? An Effort to Replicate the Findings of the Minneapolis Spouse Abuse Experiment." *American Sociological Review* 50: 253–262.

G-5 Berk, Sarah Fenstermaker 1985. *The Gender Factory: The Apportionment of Work in American Households*. New York: Plenum Press.

Berman, Claire 1982. *Step Families, Growing Reality*. New York: Public Affairs Committee, Inc.

Bernard, Jesse 1982. *The Future of Marriage*. New Haven: Yale University Press.

Berscheid, Ellen, and Elaine Walster 1974. "A Little Bit About Love," in T.L. Huston, ed., *Foundations of Interpersonal Attraction*. New York: Academic Press.

Besharov, Douglas J. 1989. "Children of Crack: Will We Protect Them?" *Public Welfare* 47: 6–11.

Bettleheim, Bruno 1955. *Symbolic Wounds*. Chicago: The Free Press.

Beutler, Ivan F., Wesley R. Burr, and Kathleen S. Bahr, and Donald A. Herrin 1989. "The Family Realm: Theoretical Contributions for Understanding Its Uniqueness." *Journal of Marriage and the Family* 51: 805–815.

Bierman, Karen Linn, and David L. Smoot 1991. "Linking Family Characteristics with Poor Peer Relations: The Mediating Role of Conduct Problems." *Journal of Abnormal Child Psychology* 19: 341–356.

G-5 Biernat, Monica, and Camille B. Wertman 1991. "Sharing of Home Responsibilities Between Professionally Employed Women and Their Husbands."

Journal of Personality and Social Psychology 60: 844–860.

F-1 Bigner, Jerry J., and R. Brooke Jacobsen 1989. "The Value of Children to Gay and Heterosexual Fathers." *Journal of Homosexuality* 17: 163–172.

Bing, Elizabeth 1980. *Six Practical Lessons for an Easier Childbirth*. New York: Bantam Books.

Bird, Gloria W., Sandra M. Stith, and Joann Schladale 1991. "Psychological Resources, Coping Strategies, and Negotiation Styles as Discriminators of Violence in Dating Relationships." *Family Relations* 40: 45–50.

Black, Claudia 1982. *It Will Never Happen to Me*. Denver, Colo.: M.A.C.

Blau, Peter 1974. *On the Nature of Organizations*. New York: Wiley.

Blau, Peter 1964. *Exchange and Power in Social Life*. New York: Wiley.

Block, Jeanne H., Jack Block, and Per F. Gjerde 1988. "Parental Functioning and the Home Environment in Families of Divorce: Prospective and Concurrent Analysis." *Journal of the American Academy of Child and Adolescent Psychiatry* 27: 207–213.

Blood, Robert O., and Donald M. Wolfe 1960. *Husbands and Wives*. Glencoe Ill.: Free Press.

Bloom, Bernard L., William F. Hodges, Michael B. Kern, and Susan C. McFaddin 1985. "Preventive Intervention Program for the Newly Separated: Final Evaluations." *American Journal of Orthopsychiatry* 55: 9–26.

Bloom, Lynn Z., Karen Coburn, and Joan Pearlman 1975. *The New Assertive Woman*. New York: Dell Publishing Co.

S-6 Blumstein, P., and P. Schwartz 1983. *American Couples: Money, Work, Sex*. New York: William Morrow.

Bohannan, Paul 1970. "The Six Stations of Divorce," in Bohannan, Paul, ed., *Divorce and After*, pp. 29–55. Garden City, N.Y.: Doubleday and Co.

G-6 Bologh, Roslyn W. 1992. "The Promise and Failure of Ethnomethodology from a Feminist Perspective." *Gender and Society* 6: 199–206.

Boorstin, Daniel J. 1989. *Hidden History, Exploring Our Secret Past*. New York: Vintage Books.

G-5 Booth, Alan, David R. Johnson, Lynn White, and John N. Edwards 1984. "Women, Outside Employment, and Marital Instability." *American Journal of Sociology* 90: 567–583.

G-4 Bowker, Lee H. 1986. *Ending the Violence*. Holmes Beach: Yale University Press.

F-1 Bozett, F.W. 1985. "Gay Men as Fathers," in S.M. Hanson and F.W. Bozett, eds., *Dimensions of Fatherhood*, pp. 327–352. Beverly Hills, Calif.: Sage.

F-4 Bradley, Robert A. 1981. *Husband-Coached Childbirth*. New York: Harper and Row.

Bradshaw, John 1988. *Bradshaw on the Family*. Health Communications.

Brain, Robert 1976. *The Last Primitive Peoples*. New York: Crown Publishers.

Brandon, Nathaniel 1980. *The Psychology of Romantic Love*. Los Angeles: J.P. Tarcher, Inc.

Bratter, Thomas E., and Gary G. Forrest 1985. *Alcoholism and Substance Abuse: Strategies for Clinical Intervention*. New York: Free Press.

Breckinridge, Mary 1981. *Wide Neighborhoods: A Story of the Frontier Nursing Service*. Lexington: The University of Kentucky Press.

P-2 Brewer, Rose M. 1988. "Black Women in Poverty: Some Comments on Female-Headed Families." *Journal of Women in Culture and Society* 13: 331–339.

G-5 Brinton, Mary C., Hang-Yue Ngo, and Kumiko Shibuya 1991. "Gendered Mobility Patterns in Industrial Economies: The Case of Japan." *Social Science Quarterly* 72: 807.

G-5 Brinton, Mary C. 1989. "Gender Stratification in Contemporary Urban Japan." *American Sociological Review* 54: 549.

R-1 Broman, Clifford L. 1991. "Gender, Work–Family Roles, and Psychological Well-Being of Blacks." *Journal of Marriage and the Family* 53: 509–519.

F-1 Bronstein, Phyllis 1984. "Differences in Mothers' and Fathers' Behavior Toward Children: A Cross-Cultural Comparison." *Developmental Psychology* 20: 995–1003.

Broude, Gwen J. 1989. "A Reply to Munroe and Munroe on the Couvade." *American Anthropologist* 91: 735.

Broude, Gwen J. 1988. "Rethinking the Couvade: Cross-Cultural Evidence." *American Anthropologist* 90: 902–911.

Brown, James S. 1988. *A Study of a Kentucky Mountain Neighborhood.* Berea, Ky.: Berea College Press.

Browning D., and B. Boatmen 1977. "Incest: Children at Risk." *American Journal of Psychiatry* 134: 69–72.

Bryant, F. Charlene 1983. "Family Group Organization in a Cumberland Mountain Neighborhood," in Allen Batteau, ed., *Appalachia and America,* pp. 28–47. Lexington: University of Kentucky Press.

Bryant, F. Charlene 1981. *We're All Kin: A Cultural Study of a Mountain Neighborhood.* Knoxville: University of Tennessee Press.

Buehler, C. 1989. "Influential Factors and Equity Issues in Divorce Settlements." *Family Relations* 38: 76–82.

Bumpass, Larry, L., James A. Sweet, and Andrew Cherlin 1991. "The Role of Cohabitation in Declining Rates of Marriage." *Journal of Marriage and the Family* 53: 913–927.

Bumpass, Larry, and James Sweet 1989a. "National Estimates of Cohabitation." *Demography* 26: 615–625.

Bumpass, Larry L., and James A. Sweet 1989b. "Preliminary Evidence on Cohabitation." *National Survey of Families and Households,* Working Paper No. 2. Madison, Wisconsin: University of Wisconsin, Center for Demography and Ecology.

Bumpass, Larry L. 1984. "Children and Marital Disruption: A Replication and Update." *Demography* 21: 71–82.

Burch, Thomas K., and Ashok K. Madan 1986. *Union Formation and Dissolution: Results from the 1984 Family History Survey.* Catalog No. 99–963. Ottawa: Statistics Canada.

Bureau of Labor Statistics: *See* U.S. Department of Labor.

Burek, Deborah M., ed. 1991. *Encyclopedia of Associations.* New York: Gales Research, Inc.

G-4 Burke, P., J. Stets, and M. Pirog-Good 1989. "Gender Identity, Self-Esteem, and Physical and Sexual Abuse in Dating Relationships," in M. Pirog-Good and J. Stets, eds., *Violence in Dating Relationships,* pp. 72–93. New York: Praeger.

Burkhardt, Susan 1990. "Golden Age Over?" *San Francisco Chronicle,* Oct. 29, pp. D1, D4.

Burleson, Brant R., Jesse G. Delia, and James L. Applegate 1992. "Effects of Maternal and Children's Social-Cognitive and Communication Skills on Children's Acceptance by the Peer Group." *Family Relations* 41: 264–272.

Burns, Linda Hammer 1987. "Infertility as Boundary Ambiguity: One Theoretical Perspective." *Family Process* 26: 359–372.

S-7 Burt, M.R., and B. L. Katz 1987. "Dimensions of Recovery from Rape: Focus on Growth Outcomes." *Journal of Interpersonal Violence* 2: 57–82.

S-7 Burt, M.R. 1980. "Cultural Myths and Support for Rape." *Journal of Personality and Social Psychology* 38: 217–230.

G-2 Buss, David M. 1989. "Conflict Between the Sexes: Strategic Interference and the Evocation of Anger and Upset." *Journal of Personality and Social Psychology* 56: 735–747.

S-3 Byers, E. Sangra, and Larry Heinlein 1989. "Predicting Initiations and Refusals of Sexual Activities in Married and Cohabiting Heterosexual Couples." *Journal of Sex Research* 26: 210–231.

S-1 Calabrese, L.H., B. Harris, K.A. Easley, and M.R. Proffitt 1986. "Persistence of High Risk Sexual Activity Among Homosexual Men in an Area of Low Incidence for Acquired Immunodeficiency Syndrome." *AIDS Research* 2: 357–361.

Campbell, Neil A. 1987. *Biology*. Menlo Park, Calif.: Benjamin/Cummings Publishing.

Canape, Charlene 1986. *Adoption: Parenthood Without Pregnancy*. New York: Henry Holt and Company.

Cancian, Francesca M., and Steven L. Grodon 1988. "Changing Emotion Norms in Marriage: Love and Anger in U.S. Women's Magazines Since 1900." *Gender and Society* 2: 308–342.

Cancian, Francesca M. 1987. *Love in America: Gender and Self Development*. Boston: Cambridge University Press.

S-1 Capell, Frank J., Duc J. Vugia, Virginia L. Mordaunt, et al. 1992. "Distribution of HIV Type 1 Infection in Childbearing Women in California." *American Journal of Public Health* 82: 254–256.

R-3 Caplan, Nathan, Marcella H. Choy, and John K. Whitmore 1992. "Indochinese Refugee Families and Academic Achievement." *Scientific American*, Feb. pp. 36–42.

Carlson, Elwood 1986. "Couples without Children: Premarital Cohabitation in France," in Kingsley Davis with A. Grossbard-Schechtman, eds., *Contemporary Marriage: Comparative Perspectives on a Changing Institution*. New York: Russell Sage Foundation.

S-2 Carroll, J.L., K.D. Volk, and J.S. Hyde 1985. "Differences Between Males and Females in Motives for Engaging in Sexual Intercourse." *Archives of Sexual Behavior* 14: 131–139.

Caspi, Avshalom, and Glen H. Elder 1988. "Emergent Family Patterns: The Intergenerational Construction of Problem Behavior and Relationships," in Robert Hinde and Joan Stevenson-Hinde, eds., *Understanding Family Dynamics*. New York: Oxford University Press.

Cassidy, Margaret L., and Gary R. Lee 1989. "The Study of Polyandry: A Critique of and Synthesis." *Journal of Comparative Family Studies* 20: 1–11.

S-1 Castro, Kenneth G., Ronald O. Valdiserri, and James W. Curran 1992. "Perspectives on HIV/AIDS Epidemiology and Prevention from the Eighth International Conference on AIDS." *American Journal of Public Health* 82: 1465.

S-4 Cates, Willard, Jr., Fack C. Smith, Roger W. Rochat, and David A. Grimes 1982. "Mortality from Abortion and Childbirth." *Journal of the American Medical Association* 248: 192–196.

Cauhape, Elizabeth 1983. *Fresh Starts: Men and Women After Divorce*. New York: Basic Books.

P-2 Center for the Study of Social Policy 1991. "The 'Flip-Side' of Black Families Headed by Women: The Economic Status of Black Men," in Robert Staples, ed., *The Black Family: Essays and Studies,* pp. 117–123. Belmont, Calif.: Wadsworth.

A Chatters, Linda M., Robert Joseph Taylor, and Harold W. Neighbors 1989. "Size of Informal Helper Network Mobilized During a Serious Persona! Problem among Black Americans." *Journal of Marriage and the Family* 51: 667–676.

R-2 Chavez, Leo 1988. "Settlers and Sojourners: The Case of Mexicans in the United States." *Human Organization* 47: 95–108.

R-2 Chavira, Alicia 1988. "'Tienes Que Ser Valiente' Mexicana Migrants in a Midwestern Farm Labor Camp," in Margarita B. Melville, ed., *Mexicanas at Work in the United States,* pp. 64–74. Houston: University of Houston, Mexican American Studies.

Cherlin, Andrew J. 1993. "Nostalgia as Family Policy." *Public Interest* 110: 77–91.

Cherlin, Andrew J., Frank F. Furstenberg, Jr., P. Lindsay Chase-Lansdale, et al. 1991. "Longitudinal Studies of Effects of Divorce on Children in Great Britain and the United States." *Science* 252 (June 7): 1386–1389.

Cherlin, Andrew 1981. *Marriage, Divorce and Remarriage.* Cambridge: Harvard University Press.

5-2 Chevan, Albert 1990. "Hispanic Racial Identity: Beyond Social Class." Paper presented to the Annual Meetings of the American Sociological Association, Aug., Washington, D.C.

S-5 Chilman, Catherine S. 1990. "Promoting Healthy Adolescent Sexuality." *Family Relations* 39: 123–131.

G-1 Chodorow, Nancy 1978. *The Reproduction of Mothering.* Berkeley, Calif.: University of California Press.

G-1 Chodorow, Nancy 1974. "Family Structure and Feminine Personality," in Michelle Z. Rosaldo and Louise Lamphere, *Woman, Culture, and Society,* pp. 43–66. Stanford, Calif.: Stanford University Press.

R-1 Clark-Nicolas, Patricia, and Bernadette Gray-Little 1991. "Effect of Economic Resources on Marital Quality for Black Couples." *Journal of Marriage and the Family* 53: 645–656.

Clayton, Richard R., and Harwin L. Voss 1977. "Shacking Up: Cohabitation in the 1970s." *Journal of Marriage and the Family* 39: 273–283.

S-2 Cobliner, W. Godfrey 1988. "The Exclusion of Intimacy in the Sexuality of the Contemporary College-Age Population." *Adolescence* 23: 99–114.

G-4 Coleman, Diane H., and Murray A. Straus 1986. "Marital Power, Conflict and Violence." *Violence and Victims* 1: 139–153.

Coleman, E. 1983. "Sexuality and the Alcoholic Family," in P. Golding, *Alcoholism: Analysis of a World-Wide Problem,* pp. 413–420. Boston: MTP Press Ltd.

Coleman, Marilyn, and Lawrence H. Ganong 1990. "Remarriage and Stepfamily Research in the 1980's: Increased Interest in an Old Family Form." *Journal of Marriage and the Family* 52: 925–940.

G-5 Coltrane, Scott, and Masako Ishii-Kuntz 1992. "Men's Housework: A Life Course Perspective." *Journal of Marriage and the Family* 54: 43–58.

G-5 Colwill, N. L., and H. D. Colwill 1985. "Women with Blue Collars: The Forgotten Minority." *Business Quarterly* 48: 87–93.

Commonweal 1991. "Little Girls Dying: An Ancient and Thriving Practice." Vol. 118 (Aug. 9): 481.

Cool, Lisa Collier 1991. "Loving Limits." *Child* 6:104–107.

Cooley, Charles Horton 1902. *Human Nature and the Social Order*. New York: Scribner's.

Coombs, Robert H. 1991. "Marital Status and Personal Well-Being: A Review of the Literature." *Family Relations* 40: 97–102.

S-1 Cooper, Mary H. 1992. "Women and AIDS." *Congressional Quarterly Researcher* 2(48) (Dec. 25): 1123–1139.

Coser, Lewis A. 1956. *The Functions of Social Conflict*. New York: Free Press.

Cott, Nancy F. 1977. *The Bonds of Womanhood: "Women's Sphere" in New England 1780–1835*.

R-1 Cottingham, Clement 1989. "Gender Shift in Black Communities." *Dissent* 36: 521–525.

G-2 Cowan, Connell, and Melvyn Kinder 1985. *Smart Women, Foolish Choices*. New York: Clarkson Potter.

S-1 Cowley, Geoffrey 1993. "The Future of AIDS." *Newsweek*, March 2, pp. 46–52.

Crapo, Richley H. 1990. *Cultural Anthropology: Understanding Ourselves and Others*. New York: Dushkin.

R-3 Crittenden, Kathleen S. 1991. "Asian Self-Effacement or Feminine Modesty?" *Gender and Society* 5: 98–117.

F-1 Crnic, Keith A., and Cathryn Brown 1991. "Mothers' and Fathers' Perceptions of Daily Hassles of Parenting Across Early Childhood." *Journal of Marriage and the Family* 53: 1042–1050.

F-1 Crouter, Ann C., M. Perry-Jenkins, T. Huston, and S.M. McHale 1987. "Processes Underlying Father Involvement in Dual-Earner and Single-Earner Families." *Developmental Psychology* 23: 431–440.

Cuber, John, and Peggy Harroff 1966. *Sex and the Significant Americans*. Baltimore: Penguin Books.

Curran, D. 1983. *Traits of a Healthy Family*. Minneapolis, Minn.: Winston Press.

S-1 Curran, J.W., H.W. Jafe, A.M. Hardy, W.M. Morgan, R.M. Selik, and T.J. Dondero 1988. "Epidemiology of HIV Infection and AIDS in the United States." *Science* 239: 610–616.

Current Population Reports: *See* U.S. Bureau of the Census.

S-6 Curry, H., and D. Clifford 1986. *A Legal Guide for Lesbian and Gay Couples*. Berkeley: Nolo Press.

S-6 Curtis, Richard F. 1986. "Household and Family in Theory on Inequality." *American Sociological Review* 51: 168–183.

Daniel, Peggy Kneffel, and Carol A. Schwartz 1993 and 1994. *Encyclopedia of Associations*. Detroit: Gale Research, Inc.

S-1 Davidson, Alan G. 1991. "Looking for Love in the Age of AIDS: The Language of Gay Personals, 1978–1988." *Journal of Sex Research* 28: 125–137.

Davidson, B., J. Balswick, and C. Halverson 1983. "Affective Self-Disclosure and Marital Adjustment: A Test of Equity Theory." *Journal of Marriage and the Family* 45: 93–102.

G-4 Davidson, Terry 1978. *Conjugal Crime: Understanding and Changing the Wifebeating Pattern*. New York: Hawthorn Books.

Davis, Keith E., and Holly Latty-Mann 1987. "Love Styles and Relationship Quality: A Contribution to Validation." *Journal of Social and Personal Relationships* 4: 409–428.

S-7 Davis, R.C., and L.N. Friedman 1985. "The Emotional Aftermath of Crime and Violence," in C.R. Figley, ed., *Trauma and Its Wake: The Study and Treatment of Post-Traumatic Stress Disorder*, pp. 90–111. New York: Brunner/Mazel.

Davis, Susan 1990. "Ruled by Hormones?" *San Francisco Examiner* Oct. 28, pp. D13–D14.

S-5 Day, Randal D. 1992. "The Transition to First Intercourse Among Racially and Culturally Diverse Youth." *Journal of Marriage and the Family* 54: 749–762.

Dechter, Aimee R., and Frank F. Furstenberg, Jr. 1990. "The Changing Consequences of Adolescent Childbearing: A Comparison of Fertility and Marriage Patterns Across Cohorts." Paper presented to the Annual Meetings of the American Sociological Association, Aug. 11–14, Washington, D.C.

G-6 Deckard, Barbara Sinclair 1983. *The Woman's Movement.* New York: Harper and Row.

Defries, Zira, Richard C. Friedman, and Ruth Corn 1985. *Sexuality: New Perspectives.* Westport, Conn.: Greenwood Press.

Degler, Carl N. 1981. "Family Membership in Plymouth Colony," in Mel Albin and Dominick Cavallo, *Family Life in America: 1620–2000*, pp. 3–13. St. James, N.Y.: Revisionary Press.

Degler, Carl N. 1980. *At Odds: Women and the Family in America from the Revolution to the Present.* New York: Oxford University Press.

A,R-1 Deimling, Gary T., and Virginia L. Smerglia 1992. "Involvement of Elders in Care-Related Decision: A Black/White Comparison." *Family Relations* 41: 86–96.

Deitz, Steven, and Jane Parker Hicks 1989. *Take These Broken Wings and Learn to Fly.* Tuscon: Harbinger House.

S-6 Dell, A.P., and M.S. Weinberg 1978. *Homosexualities: A Study of Diversity Among Men and Women.* New York: Simon and Schuster.

S-5 D'Emilio and Freedman 1988. *Intimate Matters: A History of Sexuality in America.* New York: Harper and Row.

F-1 Demo, David H. 1992. "Parent–Child Relations: Assessing Recent Changes." *Journal of Marriage and the Family* 54: 104–117.

R-1 Demos, Vasilkie 1990. "Trend Analysis of Black Family Studies in JMF." *Journal of Marriage and the Family* 52: 603–612.

DeParle, Jason 1993. "Big Rise in Births Outside of Wedlock." *New York Times,* July 14, pp. A1 and A14.

G-5 DeVault, M. 1990. "The Problem with Housework: The Problem That (Still) Has No Name," in L. Kriesberg, ed., *Research in Social Movements, Conflict, and Change.* Greenwood, Conn.: JAI.

G-4 Dobash, R. Emerson, and Russell Dobash 1979. *Violence Against Wives.* New York: Free Press.

G-4 Dobash, R. Emerson, and Dobash, R.P. 1977. "Love, Honour, and Obey: Institutional Ideologies and the Struggle for Battered Women." *Contemporary Crisis* 1: 403–415.

Dobson, James 1978. *The Strong-Willed Child.* Wheaton, Ill.: Tyndale House Publishers.

Dodson, Fitzhugh 1971. *How to Parent.* New York: Signet/New American Library.

Donnelly, Brenda W., and Patricia Voydanoff 1991. "Factors Associated with Releasing for Adoption among Adolescent Mothers." *Family Relations* 40: 404–410.

Donovan, John E., and R. Jessor 1985. "The Structure of Problem Behavior in Adolescence and Young Adulthood." *Journal of Consulting and Clinical Psychology* 53: 890–904.

P-2 Dore, Martha M., and Ana O. Dumois 1990. "Cultural Differences in the Meaning of Adolescent Pregnancy."*Families in Society: The Journal of Contemporary Human Services* pp. 93–101.

Dornbusch, S.M., J.M. Carlsmith, S.J. Bushwall, et al. 1985. "Single Parents, Extended Households, and the Control of Adolescents." *Child Development* 56: 326–341.

Driekers, Rudolf 1972. *Coping with Children's Misbehavior.* New York: Hawthorn Books, Inc.

Drill, R. L. 1986. "Young Adult Children of Divorced Parents: Depression and the Perception of Loss." *Journal of Divorce* 10: 169–178.

DuBois, W.E.B. 1969. "The Damnation of Women," in Darkwater, *Voices from within the Veil.* New York: Schocken.

F-2 Dudley, James R. 1991. "Increasing Our Understanding of Divorced Fathers Who Have Infrequent Contact with Their Children." *Family Relations* 40: 279–285.

P-2 Duncan, Greg J., and Hoffman, Saul D. 1985. "A Reconsideration of the Economic Consequences of Marital Disruption. *Demography* 22: 485–498.

Durkheim, Emile 1966 (original 1897). *Suicide.* New York: Free Press.

Easley, Margaret J., and Norman Epstein 1991. "Coping with Stress in a Family with an Alcoholic Parent." *Family Relations* 40: 218–224.

Economist 1992. "IBM: Hardware and Tear." Vol. 325 (Dec. 19): 61–62.

Economist 1988. "Polygamy Under Seige." Vol. 306 (Jan. 30): 20–21.

P-1 Edsall, Thomas B. 1990. "The 'Underclass' Term Falls from Favor." *Washington Post,* Aug. 13.

S-7 Edwall, Glenace, Norman Hoffman, and Patricia Harrison 1989. "Psychological Correlates of Sexual Abuse in Adolescent Girls in Chemical Dependency Treatment." *Adolescence* 94: 279–288.

Edwards, John N. 1989. "The Family Realm: A Future Paradigm or Failed Nostalgia." *Journal of Marriage and the Family* 51: 816–818.

Ehrenreich, Barbara 1989. *Fear of Falling: The Inner Life of the Middle Class.* New York: Pantheon Books.

Ehrenreich, Barbara 1986. "Is the Middle Class Doomed?" *New York Times,* Sept. 7, pp. 44ff.

S-6 Eldridge, Natalie S., and Lucia A. Gilbert 1990. "Correlates of Relationship Satisfaction in Lesbian Couples." *Psychology of Women Quarterly* 14: 43–62.

S-1 Ellerbrock, Tedd V., Timothy J. Bush, Mary E. Chamberland, and Margaret J. Oxtoby 1991. "Epidemiology of Women with AIDS in the United States, 1981 through 1990." *Journal of the American Medical Association* 265 (June 12): 2971–2975.

H Elliott, Marta, and Lauren J. Krivo 1991. "Structural Determinants of Homelessness in the United States." *Social Problems* 38: 113–131.

Ellis, Albert 1992. "What Is Sexual Disturbance?" *The Humanist* 52: 45–47.

Ellis, A. 1973. "Rational-Emotive Therapy," in A. Corsini, ed., *Current Psychotherapies.* Itasca, Ill.: Peacock.

R-1 Ellison, Christopher G. 1990. "Family Ties, Friendship, and Well-Being Among Black Americans." *Journal of Marriage and the Family* 52: 298–310.

Emery, Robert E., and K. Daniel O'Leary 1984. "Marital Discord and Child Behavior Problems in a Non-Clinic Sample." *Journal of Abnormal Child Psychology* 12: 411–420.

Engels, Frederick 1977 (reprint). *Socialism: Utopian and Scientific.* Westport, Conn.: Greenwood Press.

Engels, Frederick 1973 (original 1884). (Eleanor Burke Leacock, ed.) *The Origin of the Family, Private Property, and the State.* New York: International Publishers.

R-4 Euler, Robert C., and Henry Dobyns 1971. *The Hopi People.* Phoenix: Indian Tribal Series.

Ewald, Wendy 1985. "A Testimony to Love: The Children of Appalachia." *Psychology Today* 19 (5): 52–60.

G-6 Faludi, Susan 1991. *Backlash: The Undeclared War Against American Women.* New York: Crown Publishers.

Farber, Bernard 1987. "The Future of the American Family: A Dialectical Account." *Journal of Family Issues* 8: 431–433.

Feldman, Margaret 1991. "Public Policy Interest Rising." *National Council on Family Relations Report,* 36 (Dec.): 8.

Fernandez, Roberto M., and David Harris 1991. "Social Isolation and the Underclass." Paper presented to the Annual Meetings of the American Sociological Association, Aug.

G-5 Ferree, Myra Marx 1991. "The Gender Division of Labor in Two-Earner Marriages: Dimensions of Variability and Change." *Journal of Family Issues* 12: 158–180.

G-6 Ferree, Myra Marx 1990a. "Beyond Separate Spheres: Feminism and Family Research." *Journal of Marriage and the Family* 52: 886–884.

G-6 Ferree, Myra Marx 1990b. "Feminism and Family Research." *Journal of Marriage and the Family* 52: 866–884.

Field, T.M. 1980. "Interactions of Preterm and Term Infants with Their Lower- and Middle-Class Teenage and Adult Mothers," in T. Field, S. Goldberg, D. Stern, and A. Sostek, eds., *High-Risk Infants and Children.* New York: Academic Press.

S-4 Figueira-McDonough, Josefina 1989. "Men and Women as Interest Groups in the Abortion Debate in the United States. *Women's Studies International Forum* 12: 539–550.

G-1 Filene, Peter G. 1986. *Him/Her/Self: Sex Roles in Modern America.* Baltimore: Johns Hopkins University Press.

Fine, Mark A., and David R. Fine 1992. "Recent Changes in Laws Affecting Stepfamilies: Suggestions for Legal Reform." *Family Relations* 41: 334–340.

Fine, Mark A., and Lawrence A. Kurdek 1992. "The Adjustment of Adolescents in Stepfather and Stepmother Families." *Journal of Marriage and the Family* 54: 725–735.

S-7 Finkelhor, David, and A. Browne 1985. "The Traumatic Impact of Child Sexual Abuse: A Conceptualization." *American Journal of Orthopsychiatry* 55: 530–541.

S-7 Finkelhor, David 1979. *Sexually Victimized Children.* New York: Free Press.

Finnegan, Loretta P., Susan M. Oehlberg, Dianna O'Malley Regan, and Martha E. Rudrauff 1981. "Evaluating of Parenting, Depression, and Violence Profiles in Methadone Maintained Women." *Child Abuse and Neglect* 5: 267–273.

Firshein, Janet 1991. "Growth in Drug-Exposed Infants Demands Response." *Independent Living* 3 (March): 23.

Fisher, B. 1987. *Rebuilding: When Your Relationship Ends.* San Luis Obispo, Calif.: Impact Publishers.

Fisher, Helen 1987. "The Four-Year Itch." *Natural History* 10: 12–16.

G-2 Fishman, Pamela 1983. "Interaction: The Work Women Do," in Barrie Thorne, Cheris Kramarae, and Nancy Henley, eds., *Language, Gender and Society,* pp. 89–102. Rowley, Mass.: Newbury House.

G-2 Fitzpatrick, M. A., and A. Bochner 1981. "Perspectives on Self and Other: Male–Female Differences in Perceptions of Communication Behavior." *Sex Roles* 7: 523–535.

Flint, Jerry 1993. "These Are the Good Old Days." *Forbes* 151 (1) (Jan. 4): 60–61.

G-2 Flowers, Blaine J. 1991. "His and Her Marriage: A Multivariate Study of Gender and Marital Satisfaction." *Sex Roles* 24: 209–221.

Fogel, Robert William 1989. *Without Consent or Contract, The Rise and Fall of American Slavery.* New York: W.W. Norton.

Forbes 1993. "Annual Report on American Industry." Vol. 151(1) (Jan. 4): 94–180.

Frazier, Franklin E. 1939. *The Negro Family in the United States.* Chicago: University of Chicago Press.

Freedman, Maurice 1970. *Family and Kinship in Chinese Society.* Stanford: Stanford University Press.

Freud, Sigmund 1974 (original 1925). "Some Psychical Consequences of the Anatomical Distinction Between the Sexes," in *The Standard Edition of the Complete Psychological Works of Signumd Freud,* vol. 19. London: Hogarth Press and the Institute of Psycho-Analysis.

Freud, Sigmund 1960 (original 1924). *A General Introduction to Psycho-analysis.* New York: Washington Square Press.

S-1 Friedland, G.H., and R.S. Klein 1987. "Transmission of the Human Immun-odeficiency Virus." *New England Journal of Medicine* 317: 1125–1135.

S-1 Frierson, R.L., S.B. Lippman, and J. Johnson 1987. "AIDS: Psychological Stresses on the Family." *Psychosomatics* 28: 65–68.

H Fritsch, Jane 1992. "New York Agency Cuts Apartments for the Home-less." *New York Times,* Aug. 19, p. A1.

G-4 Frosstrom-Cohen, Barbara, and Alan Rosenbaum 1985. "The Effects of Parental Marital Violence on Young Adults: An Exploratory Investigation." *Journal of Marriage and the Family* 47: 467–472.

Frum, David 1993. "Union Rules." *Forbes* 151: 88.

Furstenberg, Frank, Jr. 1990. "How Families Manage Risk and Opportunity in Dangerous Neighborhoods." Paper presented to the Annual Meetings of the American Sociological Association, Aug., Washington, D.C.

R-1 Furstenberg, Frank F., Jr., S. Philip Morgan, Kristin A. Moore, and James L. Peterson 1987a. "Race Differences in the Timing of Adolescent Intercourse." *American Sociological Review* 52: 511–518.

P-2 Furstenberg, Frank F., Jr., J. Brooks-Gunn, and S. Philip Morgan 1987b. *Adolescent Mothers in Later Life.* Cambridge: Cambridge University Press.

Furstenberg, Frank F., Christine Winquist Nord, James L. Peterson, and Nicholas Zill 1983. "The Life Course of Children of Divorce." *American Sociological Review* 48: 656–668.

S-2 Gagnon, John N., and William Simon 1987. "The Sexual Scripting of Oral Genital Contacts." *Archives of Sexual Behavior* 16: 1–25.

S-5 Gairola, Gerry A., Donald L. Hochstrasser, and Lorraine E. Garkovich 1986. "Modern Contraceptive Practice in Rural Appalachia." *American Journal of Public Health* 76: 1004–1008.

R-2 Gallegos y Chavez, Ester 1980. "Northern New Mexico Women: A Changing

Silhouette," in Anulfo D. Trejo, ed., *The Chicanos,* pp. 67–80. Tuscon: University of Arizona Press.

Galvin, K.M., and B.J. Brommell 1986. *Family Communication, Cohesion, and Change.* Glenview, Ill.: Scott, Foresman.

R-3 Gardner, Robert W., Bryant Robey, and Peter C. Smith 1985. "Asian Americans: Growth, Change and Diversity." *Population Bulletin* 40 (4) (Oct.).

Gargan, Edward A. 1991. "Ultrasonic Tests Skew Ratio of Births in India." *New York Times,* Dec. 13, p. A12.

Garrison, Jayne 1992. "Experts Glum as New Drugs for AIDS Flop." *San Francisco Chronicle,* Feb. 2, pp. A1, A10.

R-1 Gaudin, James M., and Katheryn B. Davis 1985. "Social Networks of Black and White Rural Families: A Research Report." *Journal of Marriage and the Family* 47: 1015–1020.

R-4 Gayford, Jasper J. 1975. "Wife Battering: A Preliminary Survey of 100 Cases." *British Medical Journal* 1: 194–197.

Geertz, Armin W., and Michael Lomatuway'ma 1987. *Children of Cottonwood.* Lincoln: University of Nebraska Press.

Gehorsam, Jan 1990. "Women Unhappily Find That It's Still a Man's World." *The Contra Costa Times,* Dec. 3, p. 4D.

G-4 Gelles, Richard J., and Claire Cornell 1985. *Intimate Violence in Families.* Beverly Hills, Calif.: Sage.

G-4 Gelles, Richard J. 1983. "An Exchange/Social Theory," in D. Kinkelhor, R.J. Gelles, G.T. Hotaling, and M.A. Straus, eds., *The Dark Side of Families: Current Family Violence Research,* pp. 151–165. Beverly Hills, Calif.: Sage.

G-4 Gelles, Richard J., and M.A. Straus 1979. "Determinants of Violence in the Family: Toward a Theoretical Integration," in W.R. Burr, R. Hill, F.E. Nye, and I.L. Reiss, eds., *Contemporary Theories About the Family.* New York: Free Press.

R-1 Genovese, Eugene D. 1974. *Roll, Jordan, Roll: The World the Slaves Made.* New York: Pantheon.

S-5 Gerrard, M. 1987. "Sex, Sex Guilt, and Contraceptive Use Revisited: The 1980s." *Journal of Personality and Social Psychology* 52: 975–980.

F-1 Gerzon, Mark 1982. *A Choice of Heroes.* Boston: Houghton Mifflin Company.

R-1 Gibson, Rose C. 1982. "Blacks at Middle and Late Life: Resources and Coping." *Annals of the American Academy of Political and Social Science* 464: 79–90.

S-7 Gilbert, Niel 1991. "The Phantom Epidemic of Sexual Assault." *Public Interest* 103: 54–65.

S-7 Gilbert, Niel 1988. "Teaching Children to Prevent Sexual Abuse." *Public Interest* 93: 3–15.

Gilbert, Shirley J. 1976. "Self-Disclosure, Intimacy and Communication in Families." *The Family Coordinator* 25: 221–230.

Gilbert, Shirley J., and D. Hornenstein 1975. "The Communication of Self-Disclosure: Level versus Valence." *Human Communication Research* 1: 316–322.

G-4 Giles-Sims, Jean 1983. *Wife Battering: A Systems Theory Approach.* New York: The Guilford Press.

Gill, Richard T. 1993. "Family Breakdown as Family Policy." *Public Interest* 110: 84–91.

Gill, Richard T., and T. Grandom Gill 1993. "A New Plan for the Family." *Public Interest,* 111: 86–94.

Glass, Shirley P., and Thomas L. Wright 1992. "Justifications for Extramarital Relationships: The Association Between Attitudes, Behaviors, and Gender." *Journal of Sex Research* 29: 361–387.

Glazer, Nathan 1991. "The Lessons of New York City." *Public Interest* 104: 37–49.

Glenn, Norval D. 1991. "The Recent Trend in Marital Success in the United States." *Journal of Marriage and the Family* 53: 261–270.

Glenn, Norval D. 1990 "Quantitative Research on Marital Quality in the 1980s: A Critical Review." *Journal of Marriage and the Family* 52: 818–831.

Glenn, Norval D., and Charles N. Weaver 1988. "The Changing Relationship of Marital Status to Reported Happiness." *Journal of Marriage and the Family* 50: 317–324.

Glick, Paul C. 1989. "Remarried Families, Stepfamilies, and Stepchildren: A Brief Demographic Analysis." *Family Relations* 38: 24–27.

R-1 Glick, Paul C. 1988a. "Demographic Pictures of Black Families," in Harriette P. McAdoo, ed., *Black Families.* 2nd ed. Beverley Hills, Calif.: Sage.

Glick, Paul C. 1988b. "Fifty Years of Family Demography: A Record of Social Change." *Journal of Marriage and the Family* 50: 861–873.

Glick, Paul C., and Graham B. Spanier 1980. "Married and Unmarried Cohabitation in the United States." *Journal of Marriage and the Family* 42: 19–30.

Glick, Paul C., David M. Heer, and John C. Beresford 1963. "Family Formation and Family Composition: Trends and Prospects," in Marvin B. Sussman, ed., *Sourcebook in Marriage and the Family,* 2nd ed., pp. 30–40. Boston: Houghton Mifflin.

Goldenberg, Irene, and Herbert Goldenberg 1980. *Family Therapy: An Overview.* Monterey, Calif.: Brooks/Cole.

Goldman, Noreem, Charles F. Westoff, and Charles Hammerslough 1984. "Demography of the Marriage Market in the United States." *Population Index* 50: 5–25.

Goldscheider, Frances K., and Linda Waite 1987. "Nest Leaving Patterns and the Transition to Marriage for Young Men and Women." *Journal of Marriage and the Family* 49: 507–516.

Goldsmith, Stephen 1990. "Prosecution to Enhance Treatment." *Children Today* 19, (5) (July–Aug.): 13.

Goleman, Daniel 1992. "After Kinship and Marriage, Anthropology Discovers Love." *New York Times,* Nov. 24, pp. C1, C12.

Goleman, Daniel 1990. "Death of a Sex Life: In Therapists' Offices Today, the Big Dark Secret is Lack of Desire." *Health* 22: 53–57.

R Gonzales, Juan L., Jr. 1992. *Racial and Ethnic Families in America.* Dubuque, Ia.: Kendall/Hunt Publishing Co.

R-2 Gonzales, Sylvia Alicia 1980. "The Chicana Perspective: A Design for Self-Awareness," in Arnulfo D. Trejo, ed., *The Chicanos,* pp. 81–100. Tuscon: University of Arizona Press.

G-4 Goode, W. 1971. "Force and Violence in the Family." *Journal of Marriage and the Family* 33: 624–636.

Goodwin, J.S., W.C. Hunt, C.R. Key, and J.M. Samet 1987. "The Effect of Marital Status on Stage, Treatment, and Survival of Cancer Patients." *Journal of the American Medical Association* 258: 3152–3130.

S-3 Gordon, Sol, and Craig W. Snyder 1989. *Personal Issues in Human Sexuality.* Boston: Allyn and Bacon.

Gordon, Thomas 1975. *Parent Effectiveness Training.* New York: Signet.

Gottman, J.M. 1982. "Emotional Responsiveness in Marital Conversations." *Journal of Communication* 32: 108–120.

Gove, Walter R., and Hee-Choon Shin 1989. "The Psychological Well-Being of Divorced and Widowed Men and Women." *Journal of Family Issues* 10: 122–144.

F-4 Grad, Rae, Deborah Bash, Ruth Guyer, Zoila Acevedo, Mary Anne Trause, and Diane Reukauf 1981. *The Father Book: Pregnancy and Beyond.* Washington, D.C.: Acropolis Books Ltd.

G-5 Greeley, Andrew 1989. "The Declining Morale of Women." *Sociology and Social Research* 73: 53–58.

Green, Russell G., and Edward I. Donnerstein 1983. *Aggression: Theoretical and Empirical Reviews.* New York: Academic Press.

G-5 Greenstein, Theodore N. 1990. "Marital Disruption and the Employment of Married Women." *Journal of Marriage and the Family* 52: 657–676.

Greshof, Dorine 1990. "Fighting Over Tompkins Square Park: Homelessness and the Control of Public Space." Paper presented to the Annual Meetings of the American Sociological Association, Aug. 11–14, Washington, D.C.

Gross, A.E. 1978. "The Male Role and Heterosexual Behavior." *Journal of Social Issues* 34: 87–107.

Groth, N. 1978. "Guidelines for Assessment and Management of the Offender," in A.W. Burgess, A.N. Groth, L.L. Holstrom, and S.M. Sgrol, eds., *Sexual Assault of Children and Adolescents.* Lexington, Mass.: Lexington Books.

G-5 Guelzow, Maureen G., Gloria W. Bird, and Elizabeth H. Koball 1991. "An Exploratory Path Analysis of the Stress Process for Dual-Career Men and Women." *Journal of Marriage and the Family* 53: 151–164.

S-1 Guinan, Mary E. 1992. "HIV, Heterosexual Transmission and Women." *Journal of the American Medical Association:* 268 (4) (July 22): 520–521.

Guisinger, Shan, P. Cowan, and D. Schuldberg 1989. "Changing Parent and Spouse Relations in the First Years of Remarriage of Divorced Fathers." *Journal of Marriage and the Family* 51: 445–456.

Guttentag, Marcia, and Paul Secord 1983. *Too Many Women? The Sex Ratio Question.* Beverly Hills, Calif.: Sage.

Hagedorn, John M. 1990. "De-industrialization, Neighborhoods, and Contemporary African-American Gangs." Paper presented to the Annual Meetings of the American Sociological Association, Aug., Washington, D.C.

S-2 Hajcak, Frank, and Patricia Garwood 1988. "Quick-Fix Sex: Pseudosexuality in Adolescents." *Adolescence* 23: 755–760.

Halford, W. Kim, Kurt Hahlweg, and Michael Dunne 1990. "Cross-Cultural Study of Marital Communication and Marital Distress." *Journal of Marriage and the Family* 52: 487–500.

Hall, Edward 1964. *The Silent Language.* New York: Viking.

R-1 Hall, Elaine J., and Myra Marx Ferree 1986. "Race Differences in Abortion Attitudes." *Public Opinion Quarterly* 50: 193–207.

Hansen, Jeffrey E., and W. John Schuldt 1984. "Marital Self-Disclosure and Marital Satisfaction." *Journal of Marriage and the Family* 46: 923–932.

G-5 Hanson, Sandra L., and Theodora Ooms 1991. "The Economic Costs of Two-Earner, Two-Parent Families." *Journal of Marriage and the Family* 53: 622–634.

Harlap, Susan, Kathryn Kost, and Jacqueline Darroch Forrest 1991. *Preventing Pregnancy, Protecting Health: A New Look at Birth Control Choices in the United States.* New York: The Alan Guttmacher Institute.

S-5 Harold, E.S., and J.E. McNamee 1982. "An Explanatory Model of Contraceptive Use Among Young Single Women." *Journal of Sex Research* 18: 289–304.

Harris, Scott 1991. "Two Moms or Two Dads—and a Baby." *Los Angeles Times,* Oct. 20, pp. A1, A26, A27.

Harrington, David M., Jeanne H. Block, and Jack Block 1987. "Testing Aspects of Carl Rogers's Theory of Creative Environments: Child-rearing Antecedents of Creative Potential in Young Adolescents." *Journal of Personality and Social Psychology* 52: 851–856.

P-1 Harrington, Michael 1987. *The New American Poverty.* New York: Penguin.

S-6 Harry, Joseph 1990. "A Probability Sample of Gay Men." *Journal of Homosexuality* 19: 89–104.

Hart, Craig H., Gary W. Ladd, and Brant R. Burleson 1990. "Children's Expectations of the Outcomes of Social Strategies: Relations with Sociometic Status and Maternal Disciplinary Styles." *Child Development* 61: 127–137.

Hatfield, E. 1988. "Passionate Love and Companionate Love," in R. Sternberg and M. Barnes, eds., *The Psychology of Love,* pp. 191–217. New Haven: Yale University Press.

Hatfield, Elaine, Jane Traupmann, Susan Sprecher, Mary Utne, and Julia Hay 1985. "Equity and Intimate Relations: Recent Research," in William Ickes, ed., *Compatible and Incompatible Relationships,* pp. 91–117. New York: Springer-Verlag.

Hatfield, Elaine, and Richard L. Rapson 1987. "Passionate Love: New Directions in Research." *Advances in Personal Relationships* 1: 109–139.

Hauser, Robert M., and Douglas K. Anderson 1989. "Post-High School Plans and Aspirations of Black and White High School Graduates: What Has Changed Since the Mid-1970s?" *Center for Demography and Ecology, Working Paper N. 89–15.* Madison: University of Wisconsin.

S-6 Hawkins, Robert O. 1990. "The Relationship Between Culture, Personality, and Sexual Jealousy in Men in Heterosexual and Homosexual Relationships." *Journal of Homosexuality* 19: 67–84.

F-1 Heath, Douglas 1976. "Competent Fathers: Their Personalities and Marriages." *Human Development* 19: 26–39.

Heatherington, E. Mavis 1989. "Coping with Family Transitions: Winners, Losers, and Survivors." *Child Development* 60: 1–14.

Heatherington, E. Mavis, Martha Cox, and Roger Cox 1982. "Effects of Divorce on Parents and Children," in M. Lamb, ed., *Nontraditional Families,* pp. 233–288. Hillsdale, N.J.: Erlbaum.

Heaton, Tim B. 1991. "Time-Related Determinants of Marital Dissolution." *Journal of Marriage and the Family* 53: 285–295.

Heaton, Tim B., and Stan L. Albrecht 1991. "Stable Unhappy Marriages." *Journal of Marriage and the Family* 53: 747–758.

Henderson, J. 1972. "Incest: A Synthesis of Data." *Canadian Psychiatric Association Journal* 17: 299–313.

G-2 Hendrick, Clyde, Susan Hendrick, Franklin H. Foote, and Michelle Slapion-Foote 1984. "Do Men and Women Love Differently?" *Journal of Social and Personal Relationships* 1: 177–195.

G-2 Hendrick, Susan S., and Clyde Hendrick 1992. *Romantic Love.* Newbury Park: Sage.

G-2 Hendrick, Susan, Clyde Hendrick, Michelle Slapion-Foote, and Franklin H.

Foote 1985. "Gender Differences in Sexual Attitudes." *Journal of Personality and Social Psychology* 48: 1630–1642.

F-3 Hendricks, Leo E. 1988. "Outreach with Teenage Fathers: A Preliminary Report on Three Ethnic Groups." *Adolescence* 23: 711–720.

G-2 Henley, Nancy M., Mykol Hamilton, and Barrie Thorne 1990. "Womanspeak and Manspeak: Sex Differences and Sexism in Communication, Verbal and Nonverbal," in Sheila Ruth, *Issues in Feminism,* pp. 394–406. Mountain View, Calif.: Mayfield.

Herbert, Solomon J. 1982. "Why African-Americans Vented Anger at the Korean Community During the L.A. Riots." *The Crisis:* 99: 5–6.

S-6 Herdt, Gilbert 1987. *The Sambia: Ritual and Gender in New Guinea.* New York: Holt, Rinehart and Winston.

Herold, E.S. 1981. "Contraceptive Embarrassment and Contraceptive Behavior Among Young Single Women." *Journal of Youth and Adolescence* 10: 233–242.

Heslin, R., T.D. Nguyen, and M. L. Nguyen 1983. "Meaning of Touch: The Case of Touch from a Stranger or Same Sex Person." *Journal of Nonverbal Behavior* 7: 147–157.

Hiatt, Jane, and ETR Associates, Inc. 1986. *Birth Control Facts.* Santa Cruz, Calif.: Network Publications. *Journal of the American Medical Association* 1992. "Editorial," vol. 250, July 22.

Hill, Karen 1991. *Research Centers Directory.* New York: Gale Research, Inc.

Hill, Robert B. 1990. "Social Policy and the Status of Young Black Males." Paper presented to the Annual Meetings of the American Sociological Association, Aug., Washington, D.C.

Hirschl, Thomas A. 1990. "Homelessness: A Sociological Research Agenda." Paper presented to the Annual Meetings of the American Sociological Association, Aug. 11–14, Washington, D.C.

Ho, David Y.F. 1989. "Continuity and Variation in Chinese Patterns of Socialization." *Journal of Marriage and the Family* 51: 149–163.

Hobart, Charles W. 1987. "Parent-Child Relations in Remarried Families." *Journal of Family Issues* 8: 259–277.

G-5 Hochschild, A., and A. Machung 1989. *The Second Shift: Working Parents and the Revolution at Home.* New York: Viking.

P-2 Hogan, Dennis, and Evelyn Kitagawa 1985. "The Impact of Social Status, Family Structure, and Neighborhood on the Fertility of Black Adolescents." *American Journal of Sociology* 90: 825–855.

Holden, Ted 1992. "Revenge of the Office Ladies." *Business Week* 3274 (July 13): 42.

Holley, David 1991. "A Sexual Revolution in China." *Los Angeles Times,* May 27, p. A1.

S-1 Holmes, King K., John M. Karon, and Joan Kreiss 1990. "The Increasing Frequency of Heterosexually Acquired AIDS in the United States, 1983–1988." *American Journal of Public Health* 80: 858–863.

G-4 Holting, G.T. 1979. "Facilitating Violence: Why Intimates Attribute Aggression," in M.A. Straus and G. Holting eds., *Social Causes of Husband-Wife Violence.* Minneapolis, Minn.: University of Minnesota Press.

Homans, George 1974. *Social Behavior: Its Elementary Forms.* New York: Harcourt, Brace, Jovanovich.

Homans, George C. 1961. *Social Behavior: Its Elementary Forms.* New York: Harcourt, Brace and World.

Horney, Karen 1973 (original 1926). "The Flight from Womanhood," reprinted in J. B. Miller, ed., *Psychoanalysis and Women.* Baltimore: Penguin Books.

Horney, Karen 1950. *Neurosis and Human Growth.* New York: W.W. Norton and Co.

Horwitz, Tony 1992. "Working Class Culture Erodes Britain's Rank in a Unified Europe." *Wall Street Journal,* Feb. 11, pp. A1, A10.

Hostetler, John A. 1989. *Amish Roots: A Treasury of History, Wisdom and Lore.* Baltimore: Johns Hopkins University Press.

Hostetler, John A. 1980. *Amish Society.* Baltimore: Johns Hopkins University Press.

A Hoyert, Donna, and Marsha Mallick Seltzer 1992. "Factors Related to the Well-Being and Life Activities of Family Caregivers." *Family Relations* 41: 74–81.

R-3 Hu, Arthur 1992. "Us and Them: An Asian Take on L.A." *The New Republic* 206 (June 1): 12–13.

Hughes, Diane, Ellen Galinsky, and Anne Morris 1992. "The Effects of Job Characteristics on Marital Quality: Specifying Linking Mechanisms." *Journal of Marriage and the Family* 54: 31–42.

Hunt, Morton M. 1974. *Sexual Behavior in the 1970s.* New York: Dell Publishing.

Hunt, Morton, and Bernice Hunt 1979. *The Divorce Experience.* New York: McGraw Hill.

Hymowitz, Carol, and Michaele Weissman 1978. *A History of Women in America.* New York: Bantam.

Iannaccone, Laurence R., and Carrie A. Miles 1990. "Dealing with Social Change: The Mormon Church's Response to Change in Women's Roles." *Social Forces* 68: 1231–1250.

Iber, Frank Lynn 1991. *Alcohol and Drug Abuse as Encountered in Office Practice.* Boca Raton, Fla.: CRC Press.

Ibrahim, Youssef M. 1990a. "Saudi Women Take Driver's Seat in a Rare Protest for the Right to Travel." *New York Times,* Nov. 7, p. A18.

Ibrahim, Youssef M. 1990b. "Saudi Tradition." *New York Times,* Nov. 7, p. A18.

Jackson, Sonia 1987. "Great Britain," in Michael E. Lanb, ed., *The Father's Role: Cross Cultural Perspectives,* pp. 29–57. Hillsdale, N. J.: Lawrence Erlbaum Associates.

S-2 Jacoby, Arthur P., and John D. Williams 1985. "Effects of Premarital Sexual Standards and Behavior on Dating and Marriage Desirability." *Journal of Marriage and the Family* 47: 1059–1065.

Jankowiak, William R., and Edward F. Fischer 1992. "A Cross-Cultural Perspective on Romantic Love." *Ethnology* 31: 149–155.

S-6 Jay, K., and A. Young 1979. *The Gay Report: Lesbians and Gay Men Speak Out About Their Sexual Experiences and Lifestyles.* New York: Summit Books.

Jessor, R., and S.L. Jessor 1977. *Problem Behavior and Psychosocial Development.* New York: Academic Press.

R-1 Jewell, Sue K. 1988. *Survival of the Black Family: The Institutional Impact of U.S. Social Policy.* New York: Praeger.

Johanson v. *Fisher* 1991. WL 42632 (Utah) 1991 Utah Lexis 23; 157 Utah Advance Report 26.

S-5 Jones, E.F., J.D. Forest, S.K. Henshaw, J. Silverman, and A. Torres 1988. "Unintended Pregnancy, Contraceptive Practice and Family Planning Services in Developed Countries." *Family Planning Perspectives* 20: 53–67.

Jost, Kenneth, and Marilyn Robinson 1991. "Children and Divorce." *Congressional Quarterly Researcher* 1 (5): 351–363.

Jourard, Sidney 1971. *The Transparent Self.* New York: Van Nostrand.

Journal of the American Medical Association 1992a. "Commentary," vol. 250 (July 22).

———— 1992b. "Editorial," vol. 250, July 22.

S-1 Jurich, Joan A., Rebecca A. Adams, and John E. Schulenberg 1992. "Factors Related to Behavior Change in Response to AIDS." *Family Relations* 41: 97–103.

Jurich, Joan A. 1989. "The Family Realm: Expanding Its Parameters." *Journal of Marriage and the Family* 51: 819–822.

Kagan, Jerome 1964. "Acquisition and Significance of Sex Typing and Sex Role Identity," in M. S. Hoffman and L. W. Hoffman, *Review of Child Development Research*, pp. 234–263. New York: Russell Sage.

Kagan, Jerome, Barbara Hosken, and Sara Watson 1961. "Child's Symbolic Conceptualization of Parents." *Child Development* 32.

Kahn, Joan R., and Kathyrn A. London 1991. "Premarital Sex and the Risk of Divorce." *Journal of Marriage and the Family* 53: 845–855.

R-3 Kang, Connie 1992. "Koreans Confront a Need for Change." *Los Angeles Times*, Nov. 16, p. JJ6.

Katz, J., and D. Cronin 1980. "Sexuality and College Life." *Change* 3: 44–49.

Katz, Michael B., and Mark J. Stern 1981. "Fertility, Class and Industrial Capitalism: Erie County, New York, 1855–1915." *American Quarterly* 33: 63–92.

Katz, P.A., and S. Boswell 1986. "Flexibility and Traditionality in Children's Gender Roles." *Genetic, Social and General Psychology Monographs* 112: 105–147.

Katzer, Jeffrey, Kenneth H. Cook, and Wayne W. Crouch 1991. *Evaluating Information.* New York: McGraw Hill.

R-2 Keefe, Susan E., and Amado M. Padilla 1987. *Chicano Ethnicity.* Albuquerque: University of New Mexico Press.

Kegels, S.M., N. Adler, and C. Iwrin 1988. "Sexually Active Adolescents and Condoms: Changes Over One Year in Knowledge, Attitutdes, and Use." *American Journal of Public Health* 78: 460–461.

Keith, V.M., and B. Finlay 1988. "The Impact of Parental Divorce on Children's Educational, Marital Timing, and Likelihood of Divorce." *Journal of Marriage and the Family* 50: 797–809.

R-2 Kellam, Sheppard, et al. 1982. "The Long-Term Evolution of the Family Structure of Teenage and Older Mothers." *Journal of Marriage and the Family* 44: 539–554.

S-2 Kelly, Jeffrey A., Janet S. St. Lawrence, Ted L. Brasfield, L. Yvonne Stevenson, Yolanda E. Diaz, and Allan C. Hauth 1990. "AIDS Risk Behavior Patterns Among Gay Men in Small Southern Cities." *American Journal of Public Health* 80: 416–418.

R-2 Kelly, Patricia F., and Anna Garcia 1989. "Power Surrendered, Power Restored: The Politics of Home and Work Among Hispanic Women in Southern California and Southern Florida," in L. Tilly and P. Guerin, eds., *Women and Politics in America.* New York: Russell Sage Foundation.

Kennedy, Janice H. 1985. "Childrearing Attitudes in Appalachia Today: A Preliminary Look." *Psychological Reports* 56: 677–678.

Kephart, William M. 1987. *Extraordinary Groups: An Examination of Unconventional Life-Styles.* New York: St. Martin's Press.

Kessler, R.C., and J.A. McRae 1981. "Trends in the Relationship Between Sex and Psychological Distress: 1957–1976." *American Sociological Review* 46: 443–452.

Ketover, Pearl 1988. *Step Mothering, Another Kind of Love: The Way to Happiness and Success as a Stepmother.* Los Angeles: Forman Publishing, Inc.

Khoo, Siew-Ean 1987. "Living Together as Married: A Profile of De Facto Couples in Australia." *Journal of Marriage and the Family* 49: 185–191.

R-3 Kibria, Nazli 1990a. "Power, Patriarchy, and Gender Conflict in the Vietnamese Immigrant Community." *Gender and Society* 4: 9–24.

Kibria, Nazli 1990b. "Migration and Vietnamese Refugee Women: Women's Status and Women's Traditionalism." Paper presented to the Annual Meetings of the American Sociological Association, Aug. 11–15, Washington, D.C.

R-3 Kibria, Nazli. "Vietnamese-American Families: A Review and Formulation of a Research Agenda," in R. L. Taylor, ed. *Minority Families in the United States: A Comparative Perspective.* New York: Prentice-Hall.

R-3 Kim, Choong Soon 1989. "Attribute of 'Asexuality' in Korean Kinship and Sundered Koreans during the Korean War." *Journal of Comparative Family Studies* 20: 313–320.

Kinard, E.M., and H. Reinherz 1986. "Effects of Marital Disruption on Children's School Aptitude and Achievement." *Journal of Marriage and the Family* 48: 285–293.

Kinsey, A., C. Martin, and P. Gebhard 1953. *Sexual Behavior in the Human Female.* Philadelphia: W.B. Saunders.

Kinsey, A.C., W. Pomeroy, and C. Martin 1948. *Sexual Behavior in the Human Male.* Philadelphia: W.B. Saunders.

S-6 Kite, M.E., and K. Deaux 1987. "Gender Belief Systems: Homosexuality and the Implicit Inversion Theory." *Psychology of Women Quarterly* 11: 83–96.

Kitson, Gay C., and Leslie A. Morgan 1990. "The Multiple Consequences of Divorce: A Decade Review." *Journal of Marriage and the Family* 52: 913–924.

Kitzinger, Sheila 1980. *The Complete Book of Pregnancy and Childbirth.* New York: Alfred A. Knopf.

Klein, Dianne 1992. "Fatherhood Beyond Ozzie and Harriet." *San Francisco Chronicle*, July 5, "Sunday Punch," p. 3.

Kline, Marsha, Janet R. Johnston, and Jeanne M. Tschann 1991. "The Long Shadow of Marital Conflict: A Model of Children's Postdivorce Adjustment." *Journal of Marriage and the Family* 53: 297–309.

Knapp, Mark L. 1984. *Interpersonal Communication and Human Relationships.* Boston: Allyn and Bacon.

Kochanek, Kenneth D. 1990. "Induced Terminations of Pregnancy: Reporting States, 1987." National Center for Health Statistics, *Monthly Vital Statistics Reports* 38 (9) Supplement, Jan. 5., Washington, D.C.: U.S. Government Printing Office.

Kohlberg, Lawrence 1969. "Stage and Sequence: The Cognitive-Developmental Approach to Socialization," in David A. Goslin, ed., *Handbook of Socialization Theory and Research*, pp. 347–480. Chicago: Rand McNally.

Kohlberg, Lawrence 1966. "A Cognitive Developmental Analysis of Children's Sex-Role Concepts and Attitudes," in Eleanor E. Maccoby, *The Development of Sex Differences*. Stanford, Calif.: Stanford University Press.

Kohn, Melvin 1969. *Class and Conformity: A Study in Values*. Homewood, Ill.: Dorsey.

G-2 Komter, A. 1989. "Hidden Power in Marriage." *Gender and Society* 3: 187–216.

S-7 Koss, Mary P., and Barry R. Burkhart 1989. "A Conceptual Analysis of Rape Victimization." *Psychology of Women Quarterly* 13: 27–40.

S-7 Koss, Mary P., Christine A. Gidycz, and Nadine Wisniewski 1987. "The Scope of Rape: Incidence and Prevalence of Sexual Aggression and Victimization in a National Sample of Higher Education Students." *Journal of Counsulting and Clinical Psychology* 55: 162–170.

Kotler, Pamela, and Deborah Lee Wingard 1989. "The Effects of Occupational, Marital, and Parental Roles on Mortality: The Alameda County Study." *American Journal of Public Health* 79: 607–611.

H Kozol, Jonathan 1988. *Rachel and Her Children: Homeless Families in America*. New York: Fawcett Columbine.

G-5 Krause, N. 1983. "Conflicting Sex-Role Expectations, Housework Dissatisfaction and Depressive Symptoms Among Full-Time Housewives." *Sex Roles* 9: 114–1125.

S-1 Kreiss, J., E. Ngugi, and K. Homes 1992. "Efficacy of Nonoxynol 9 Contraceptive Sponge Use in Preventing Heterosexual Acquisition of HIV in Nairobi Prostitutes." *Journal of the American Medical Association* 268 (July 22): 477–482.

Kroeber, A.L. 1948. *Anthropology, Race, Language, Culture, Psychology, and Prehistory*. New York: Harcourt, Brace.

G-2 Krokoff, Lowell J., John M. Gottman, and Anup K. Roy 1988. "Blue-Collar and White-Collar Marital Interaction and Communication Orientation." *Journal of Social and Personal Relationships* 5: 201–221.

Krueger, D. L., and P. Smith 1982. "Decision-Making Patterns of Couples: A Sequential Analysis." *Journal of Communication* 32: 121–134.

Kruttschnitt, Candace, David Ward, and Mary Ann Sheble 1987. "Abuse-Resistant Youth: Some Factors That May Inhibit Criminal Behavior." *Social Forces* 66: 501–519.

Kruttschnitt, Candace, Linda Heath, and David Ward 1986. "Family Violence, Television Viewing Habits and Other Adolescent Experiences Related to Violent Criminal Behavior." *Criminology* 24: 201–233.

S-1 Kubler-Ross, Elizabeth 1987. *AIDS: The Ultimate Challenge*. New York: Macmillan.

Kulka, R.A., and H. Weingarten 1979. "The Long-Term Effects of Parental Divorce in Childhood on Adult Adjustment." *Journal of Social Issues* 35: 50–78.

Kurdek, Lawrence A. 1991a. "The Relations between Reported Well-Being and Divorce History, Availability of a Proximate Adult, and Gender." *Journal of Marriage and the Family* 53: 71–78.

S-6 Kurdek, Lawrence A. 1991b. "Correlation of Relationship Satisfaction in Cohabiting Gay and Lesbian Couples: Integration and Contextual, Investment, and Problem-Solving Models." *Journal of Personality and Social Psychology* 61: 910–922.

S-6 Kurdek, Lawrence A. 1988. "Relationship Quality of Gay and Lesbian Cohabiting Couples." *Journal of Homosexuality* 15: 93–118.

S-6 Kurdek, Lawrence A., and P.J. Schmitt 1986. "Relationship Quality of Partners in Heterosexual Married, Heterosexual Cohabiting, and Gay and Lesbian Relationships." *Journal of Personality and Social Psychology* 51: 711–720.

H LaGory, Mark, Ferris Ritchey, and Kevin Fitzpatrick 1991. "Homelessness and Affiliation." *Sociological Quarterly* 32: 201–218.

H LaGory, M., F. Ritchey, and J. Mullis 1990. "Depression Among the Homeless." *Journal of Health and Social Behavior* 31: 87–101.

F-1 Lamb, Michael 1986. "The Changing Roles of Fathers," in Michael Lamb, ed., *The Father's Role: Applied Perspectives.* New York: Wiley-Interscience.

F-1 Lamb, Michael E., ed. 1981. *The Role of the Father in Child Development.* New York: Wiley.

Lampe, Phillip 1987. *Adultery in the United States.* Buffalo, N.Y.: Prometheus Books.

Laner, Mary Riege 1989. *Dating: Delights, Discontents, and Dilemmas.* Salem, Wis.: Sheffield Publishing Company.

Laosa, L.M. 1977. "Inequality in the Classroom: Observation Research on Teacher–Student Interaction." *Aztlan* 8: 51–67.

F-1 LaRossa, Ralph, Betty A. Gordon, Ronald J. Wilson, Annette Bairan, and Charles Jaret 1991. "The Fluctuating Image of the 20th Century Father." *Journal of Marriage and the Family* 53: 987–997.

Lasch, Christopher 1977. *Haven in a Heartless World.* New York: Basic Books.

Lauer, Robert H., and Jeanette C. Lauer 1991. "The Long-Term Relational Consequences of Problematic Family Backgrounds." *Family Relations* 40: 286–290.

Lavee, Yoav, and David C. Dollahite 1991. "The Linkage between Theory and Research in Family Science." *Journal of Marriage and the Family* 53: 361–373.

Lawson, Annette 1988. *Adultery: An Analysis of Love and Betrayal.* New York: Basic Books.

Lawson, Carol 1991. "Where Stepparents Are Understood." *New York Times,* May 30, p. C1.

Lee, Gary R., Karen Seccombe, and Constance L. Shehan 1991. "Marital Status and Personal Happiness: An Analysis of Trend Data." *Journal of Marriage and the Family* 53: 839–844.

Lee, John Alan 1973. *The Colors of Love: An Exploration of the Ways of Loving.* Toronto: New Press.

Lee, Richard B. 1984. *The Dobe !Kung.* New York: Holt, Rinehart, Winston.

S-5 Leigh, Barbara C. 1990. "The Relationship of Substance Use During Sex to High-Risk Sexual Behavior." *Journal of Sex Research* 27: 199–213.

S-3 Leigh, Barbara Critchlow 1989. "Reasons for Having and Avoiding Sex: Gender, Sexual Orientation, and Relationship to Sexual Behavior." *Journal of Sex Research* 26: 199–209.

Leigh, Geoffrey K., Thomas B. Holman, and Wesley R. Burr 1984. "An Empirical Test of Sequence in Murstein's SVR Theory of Mate Selection." *Family Relations* 33: 225–231.

Leigh, Julia Hood 1990. "Is Monogamy a Myth?" *Health* 22: 66–69.

P-1 R Lemann, Nicholas 1991. *The Promised Land: The Great Black Migration and How it Changed America.* New York: Alfred A. Knopf.

P-1 R Lemann, Nicholas. 1986. "The Origins of the Underclass." *Atlantic* 257 (June): 31–55.

LeMayne, James 1990. "Some Saudi Women Push for Changes." *New York Times,* Dec. 8, p. 8.

S-4 Lemkau, Jeanne P. 1988. "Emotional Sequelae of Abortion." *Psychology of Women Quarterly* 12: 461–472.

S-1 Lemp, George F., Susan F. Payne, Dennese Neal, Tes Temelso, and George W. Rutherford 1990. "Survival Trends for Patients with AIDS." *Journal of the American Medical Association* 263: 402.

S-1 Lenaghan, D.D., and M.J. Lenaghan 1987. "AIDS and Education: The Front Line of Prevention." *The Futurist* 21: 17–19.

Lepper, M., G. Sagotsky, J. Dafoe, and D. Greene 1982. "Consequences of Superfluous Social Constraints: Effects of Nominal Contingencies on Children's Subsequent Intrinsic Interest." *Journal of Personality and Social Psychology* 42: 51–65.

G-3 Lerner, Gerda 1986. *The Creation of Patriarchy.* New York: Oxford University Press.

G-5 Leslie, Leigh A., Elaine A. Anderson, and Meredith P. Branson 1991. "Responsibility for Children: The Role of Gender and Employment." *Journal of Family Issues* 12: 197–210.

S-1 Levine, Carol 1991. "AIDS and Changing Concepts of Family," in Dorothy Nelkin, David P. Willis, and Scott V. Parris, eds., *A Disease of Society: Cultural and Institutional Responses to AIDS.* Cambridge: Cambridge University Press.

Levine, L., C.T. Garcia-Coll, and W. Oh 1985. "Determinants of Mother–Infant Interaction in Adolescent Mothers." *Pediatrics* 75: 23–29.

F-1 Levy-Shiff, Rachel, and R. Israelashvili 1988. "Antecedents of Fathering: Some Further Exploration." *Developmental Psychology* 24: 434–440.

S-6 Lewin, Tamar 1991a. "Disabled Woman's Lesbian Partner is Granted Right to be Her Guardian." *New York Times,* Dec. 18, p. A26.

Lewin, Tamar 1991b. "A Mother's Job: Major Court Battle Started with a Sick Child." *San Francisco Examiner,* Sunday Punch, March 17, p. 6.

F-1 Lewis, Charlie 1986. *Becoming a Father.* Philadelphia: Milton Keynes.

Lewis, C.C. 1981. "The Effects of Parental Firm Control: A Reinterpretation of Findings." *Psychological Bulletin* 90: 547–563.

R-1 Lewis, Edith A. 1989. "Role Strain in African-American Women: The Efficacy of Support Networks." *Journal of Black Studies* 20: 155–169.

Lewis, Oscar 1964. *Five Families: Mexican Case Studies in the Culture of Poverty.* New York: John Wiley and Sons.

Lichfield, John 1991. "A Career Woman Embraces Polygamy." *San Francisco Examiner,* April 25, p. A19.

Liebowitz, M. 1983. *The Chemistry of Love.* Boston: Little, Brown, and Company.

Limerick, Patricia Nelson 1987. *The Legacy of Conquest; The Unbroken Past of the American West.* New York: W.W. Norton.

Lips, Hilary M. 1988. *Sex and Gender.* Mountain View, Calif.: Mayfield Publishing Co.

Lisitzky, Gene 1966. *Four Ways of Being Human.* New York: Viking Press.

Liska, Allen E., and Mark D. Reed 1985. "Ties to Conventional Institutions and Delinquency: Estimating Reciprocal Effects." *American Sociological Review* 50: 547–560.

R,G-4 Lockhart, Lettie L. 1987. "A Reexamination of the Effects of Race and Social Class on the Incidence of Marital Violence: A Search for Reliable Differences." *Journal of Marriage and the Family* 49: 603–610.

R,G-4 Lockhart, Lettie L. 1985. "Methodological Issues in Comparative Racial Analyses: The Case of Wife Abuse." *Social Work Research and Abstracts* 21: 35–41.

Lorenz, Frederick O., Rand D. Conger, Ronald L. Simon, and Les B. Whitbeck 1991. "Economic Pressure and Marital Quality: An Illustration of the Method Variance Problem in the Causal Modeling of Family Processes." *Journal of Marriage and the Family* 53: 375–388.

Loseke, Donileen R. 1991. "Reply to Murray A. Straus: Reading on 'Discipline and Deviance.'" *Social Problems* 38: 162–166.

S-4 Luker, Kristin 1984. *Abortion and the Politics of Motherhood*. Berkeley: University of California Press.

F-2 Lund, Mary 1987. "The Non-Custodial Father: Common Challenges in Parenting after Divorce," in Charlie Lewis and Margaret O'Brien, eds., *Reassessing Fatherhood: New Observations on Fathers and the Modern Family*, pp. 212–224. Beverly Hills, Calif.: Sage.

G-1 Lynn, David 1966. "The Process of Learning Parental and Sex-Role Identification." *Journal of Marriage and the Family* 28: 466–470.

Maccoby, Eleanor E., and Carol N. Jacklin 1974. *The Psychology of Sex Differences*. Stanford, Calif.: Stanford University Press.

G-3 MacDermid, Shelly M., Joan Jurich, Judith A. Myers-Walls, and Ann Pelo 1992. "Feminist Teaching: Effective Education." *Family Relations* 41: 31–38.

G-2 MacDermid, Shelly M., Ted L. Huston, and Susan M. McHale 1990. "Changes in Marriage Associated with the Transition to Parenthood: Individual Differences as a Function of Sex-Role Attitude Changes in the Division of Household Labor." *Journal of Marriage and the Family* 52: 475–486.

Machida, Sandra, and Susan D. Holloway 1991. "The Relationship Between Divorced Mothers' Perceived Control Over Child Rearing and Children's Post-Divorce Development." *Family Relations* 40: 272–278.

Macklin, Eleanor D. 1978. "Nonmarital Heterosexual Cohabitation: A Review of Recent Literature." *Marriage and Family Review* 1: 3–12.

R,P-3 MacLeod, Jay 1987. *Ain't No Makin' It*. Boulder, Colo.: Westview Press.

Madanes, Cloe 1984. *Behind the One Way Mirror: Advances in the Practice of Strategic Therapy*. San Francisco: Jossey-Bass Publishers.

Madsen, William 1964. *Mexican-Americans of South Texas*. New York: Holt, Rinehart and Winston.

Mahoney, E.R. 1983. *Human Sexuality*. New York: McGraw Hill.

H Main, Thomas J. 1986. "The Homeless Families of New York." *The Public Interest* 85 (Fall): 3–21.

G-4 Makepeace, James M. 1981. "Courtship Violence Among College Students." *Family Relations* 30: 97–102.

Malamuth, C. L., and S. W. Cook 1984. "Aggression Against Women: Cultural and Individual Causes," in N. M. Malamuth and E. Donnerstein, eds., *Pornography and Sexual Aggression*, pp. 19–52. Orlando, Fla.: Academic Press.

Malinowski, Brnislaw 1922. *Argonates of the Western Pacific*. New York: Dutton.

Maltas, Carolyn 1991. "The Dynamics of Narcissism in Marriage." *Psychoanalytic Review* 78: 568–581.

Markman, H.J. 1981. "Prediction of Marital Distress: A Five-Year Follow-Up." *Journal of Consulting and Clinical Psychology* 49: 760–762.

Marks, Stephen R. 1989. "Toward a Systems Theory of Marital Quality." *Journal of Marriage and the Family* 51: 15–26.

Martin, John D., Garland E. Blair, Robert Nevels, and Joyce H. Fitzpatrick 1990. "A Study of the Relationship of Styles of Loving and Marital Happiness." *Psychological Reports* 66: 123–126.

S-1 Martin, J.L., M.A. Garcia, and S.T. Beatrice 1989. "Sexual Behavior Changes and HIV Antibody in a Cohort of New York City Gay Men." *American Journal of Public Health* 79: 501–503.

Martin, Teresa Castro, and Larry L. Bumpass 1989. "Recent Trends in Marital Disruption." *Demography* 26: 37–52.

S-1 Martinelli, Leonard 1987. *When Someone You Know Has AIDS.* New York: Crown.

R-2 Martinez, Marco A. 1985. "Toward a Model of Socialization for Hispanic Identity," in Pastora San Juan Cafferty and William C. McCready, *Hispanics in the United States.* pp. 63–85. New Brunswick, N.J.: Transaction Books.

Martinson, Brian C., and Larry L. Bumpass 1990. "The Impact of Family Background on Premarital Births Among Women Under 30 in the United States." *National Survey of Families and Households Working Paper No. 9.* Madison: Center for Demography and Ecology, University of Wisconsin.

Marx, Karl 1967 (original 1867). *Capital.* New York: International Publishers.

Masheter, Carol 1991. "Postdivorce Relationships between Ex-Spouses: The Roles of Attachment and Interpersonal Conflicts." *Journal of Marriage and the Family* 53: 103–110.

Masters, William H., Virginia E. Johnson, and Robert C. Kolodny 1986. *Masters and Johnson on Sex and Human Loving.* Boston: Little, Brown.

S-1 May, R.M., and R. M. Anderson 1987. "Transmission Dynamics of HIV Infection." *Nature* 326: 137–142.

S-1 Mayer, Kenneth H., and Charles C.J. Carpenter 1992. "Women and AIDS." *Scientific American* 266 (March): 218.

S-1 Mayer, R. 1988. "Not in My House," in Ines Rieder and Patricia Ruppelt, eds., *AIDS: The Women,* pp. 20–23. San Francisco: Cleis Press.

R,F-1 McAdoo, J.L. 1981. "Black Father and Child Interactions," in L.E. Gary, ed., *Black Men,* pp. 135–150. Beverley Hills, Calif.: Sage.

McAnarney, Elizabeth R., R.A. Lawrence, H.N. Riccuiti, J. Polley, and M. Szilagyi 1986. "Interactions of Adolescent Mothers and Their One Year Old Children." *Pediatrics* 78: 585–590.

McAnarney, Elizabeth R., and Corrine Schreider 1984. *Identifying Social and Psychological Antecedents of Adolescent Pregnancy.* New York: William T. Grant Foundation.

S-7 McCahill, R. W., L.C. Meyer, and A. M. Fischman 1979. *The Aftermath of Rape.* Lexington, Mass.: Lexington Books.

McCall, George J., and Nancy M. Shields 1986. "Social and Structural Factors in Family Violence," in Mary Lystad, ed., *Violence in the Home: Interdisciplinary Perspectives,* pp. 98–123. New York: Brunner/Mazel, Inc.

McCann, Joseph T., and Mary Kay Biaggio 1989. "Sexual Satisfaction in Marriage as a Function of Life Meaning." *Archives of Sexual Behavior* 18: 59–72.

McChesney, Kay Young 1989. "Absence of a Family Safety Net for Homeless Families." Paper presented to the Annual Meetings of the American Sociological Association, Aug., San Francisco.

McCord, Joan 1991. "Questioning the Value of Punishment." *Social Problems* 38: 167–179.

McCromick, N.B. 1979. "Come-Ons and Put-Offs: Unmarried Students' Strategies for Having and Avoiding Sexual Intercourse." *Psychology of Women Quarterly* 4: 194–211.

McFalls, Joseph A., Jr. 1992. "Reproductive Roulette: Women Who Delay Childbearing." *USA Today Magazine* 121 (2570) (Nov.): 69–71.

McFarlane, K. 1978. "Sexual Abuse in Children," in J.R. Chapman and M. Gates, eds., *Victimization of Women*. Beverly Hills, Calif.: Sage.

McKinney, Carol V. 1992. "Wives and Sisters: Bajju Marital Patterns." *Journal of Comparative Family Studies* 31: 75–87.

McLanahan, Sara S., and Larry Bumpass 1988. "Intergenerational Consequences of Family Disruption." *American Journal of Sociology* 93: 130–152.

McLeod, Ramon G. 1993. "More Dads Being Mr. Moms." *San Francisco Chronicle*, Sept. 22, p. A2.

Mead, George Herbert 1934. *Mind, Self, and Society: From the Standpoint of a Social Behaviorist*. Charles W. Morris, ed. Chicago: University of Chicago Press.

P-2 Mead, Lawrence M. 1989. "The Logic of Workfare: The Underclass and Work Policy." *The Annals of the American Academy of Political and Social Science* 501: 156–169.

Mead, Margaret 1966. "Marriage in Two Steps." *Redbook* 127: 48–49, 85–86.

Mead, Margaret 1963. *Sex and Temperament*. New York: Dell.

Mechanic, D., and S. Hansell 1989. "Divorce, Family Conflict and Adolescents' Well-Being." *Journal of Health and Social Behavior* 30: 105–116.

S-1 Medley, G.F., R.M. Anderson, L. Cox, et al. 1987. "Incubation Period of AIDS in Patients Infected Via Blood Transfusion." *Nature* 328: 719.

Meisler, Andrew W., and Michael P. Carey 1991. "Depressed Affect and Male Sexual Arousal." *Archives of Sexual Behavior* 20: 541–554.

P-2 Meltzer, Milton 1986. *Poverty in America*. New York: William Morrow.

R-2 Melville, Margarita 1988. "Mexican Women in the U.S. Wage Labor Force." *Mexicanas at Work in the United States*. Houston: University of Houston, Mexican American Studies.

Menken, Jane, James Trussell, Debra Stempel, and Ozer Babokol 1981. "Proportional Hazards Life Table Models: An Illustrative Analysis of Sociodemographic Influences on Marital Dissolution in the U.S." *Demography* 18: 181–200.

Mernissi, Fatima 1975. *Beyond The Veil: Male–Female Dynamics in a Modern Muslim Society*. New York: John Wiley and Sons.

Merton, Robert K. 1968. *Social Theory and Social Structure*. New York: Free Press.

S-7 Meyer, C.B., and S.D. Taylor 1986. "Adjustment to Rape." *Journal of Personality and Social Psychology* 50: 1226–1234.

F-1 Meyer, Daniel R., and Steven Garasky 1993. "Custodial Fathers: Myths, Realities, and Child Support Policy." *Journal of Marriage and the Family* 55: 73–89.

Meyerding, J., and J. James 1977. "Early Sexual Experiences as a Factor in Prostitution." *Archives of Sexual Behavior* 77: 31–42.

S-1 Michaels, David, and Carol Levine 1992. "Estimates of the Number of Motherless Youth Orphaned by AIDS in the United States." *Journal of the American Medical Association* 268: 345.

Michaelson, Karel L. 1988. "Childbirth in America: A Brief History and Contemporary Issues," in Karen L. Michaelson, ed., *Childbirth in America*, pp. 1–33. Mass.: Bergin and Garvey Publishers.

Miller, Brent C., and Tim B. Heaton 1991. "Age at First Sexual Intercourse and the Timing of Marriage and Childbirth." *Journal of Marriage and the Family* 53: 719–732.

G-1 Miller, C.L. 1987. "Qualitative Differences Among Gender-Stereotyped Toys: Implications for Cognitive and Social Development in Girls and Boys." *Sex Roles* 16: 473–487.

G-3 Miller, Jean Baker 1976. *Toward a New Psychology of Women*. Boston: Beacon Press.

Miller, John C. 1966. *The First Frontier: Life in Colonial America*. New York: Dell.

Miller, Richard 1987. "Trends in Marital Happiness in Provo, Utah: 1955–1983." *Sociology and Social Research* 71: 294–297.

S-5 Miller, W. 1986. "Why Some Women Fail to Use Their Contraceptive Method: A Psychological Investigation." *Family Planning Perspectives* 18: 27–32.

S-7 Miller, W., A.M. Williams, and M.H. Bernstein 1982. "The Effects of Rape on Marital and Sexual Adjustment." *The American Journal of Family Therapy* 10: 51–58.

R-3 Min, Pyong Gap 1990. "Problems of Korean Immigrant Entrepreneurs." *International Migration Review* 24: 436–455.

Minai, Naila 1981. *Women in Islam: Tradition and Transition in the Middle East*. New York: Seaview Books.

S-1 Minkoff, Howard L., and Jack A. DeHovitz 1991. "Care of Women Infected with the Human Immunodeficiency Virus." *Journal of the American Medical Association* 266 (Oct. 23): 2253–2257.

Minuchin, Salvador 1984. *Family Kaleidoscope*. Cambridge, Mass.: Harvard University Press.

Minuchin, Salvador 1974. *Families and Family Therapy*. Cambridge: Harvard University Press.

R-2 Mirande, A. 1979. "A Reinterpretation of Male Dominance in the Chicano Family." *Family Coordinator* 28: 473–479.

Mischel, W. 1973. "Toward a Cognitive Social Learning Reconceptualization of Personality." *Psychological Review* 80: 252–283.

G-1 Mischel, Walter 1970. "Sex-Typing and Socialization," in Paul H. Mussen, ed., *Carmichael's Manual of Child Psychology*, pp. 3–72. vol. 2, New York: Wiley.

G-1 Mischel, Walter 1966. "A Social-Learning View of Sex Differences in Behavior," in Eleanor E. Maccoby, ed., *The Development of Sex Differences*, pp. 56–81. Stanford Calif.: Stanford University Press.

Mitchell, G. 1981. *Human Sex Differences*. New York: Van Nostrand Reinhold.

S-4 Mohr, James 1981. "The Great Upsurge of Abortion, 1840–1880," in Mel Albin and Dominick Cavallo, *Family Life in America, 1620–2000*, pp. 119–130. St. James, N.Y.: Revisionary Press.

Montgomery, Marillyn J., Edward R. Anderson, E. Mavis Hetherington, and W. Glenn Clingempeel 1992. "Patterns of Courtship for Remarriage: Implications for Child Adjustment and Parent–Child Relationships." *Journal of Marriage and the Family* 54: 686–698.

R-2 Moore, Joan, and Mary Devitt 1989. "The Paradox of Deviance in Addicted Mexican American Mothers." *Gender and Society* 3: 53–70.

R-1 Moore, K.A., M.C. Simms, and C.L. Betsey 1986. *Choice and Circumstance: Racial Differences in Adolescent Sexuality and Fertility.* New Brunswick, N.J.: Transaction Books.

G-2 Moore, L. M., and A. U. Rickel 1980. "Characteristics of Women in Traditional and Non-Traditional Managerial Roles." *Personnel Psychology* 33: 317–322.

S-1 Morgan, W.M., and J.W. Curran 1986. "Acquired Immunodeficienty Syndrome: Current and Future Trends." *Public Health Reports* 101: 459–465.

Morton, Jody C., Cheryl A. Richey, and Michele Kellett 1981. *Building Assertiveness Skills.* St. Louis: C.V. Mosby.

S-5 Mosher, William D., and Christine A. Bachrach 1987. "First Premarital Contraceptive Use: United States, 1960–82." *Studies in Family Planning* 18: 83–95.

Moss, Barry F., and Andrew I. Schwebel 1993. "Marriage and Romantic Relationships, Defining Intimacy in Romantic Relationships." *Family Relations* 42: 31–37.

Moynihan, Daniel P. 1965. *The Negro Family: The Case for National Action.* Washington, D.C.: U.S. Government Printing Office.

S-2 Muehlenhard, Charlene L., and Lisa C. Hollabaugh 1988. "Do Women Sometimes Say No When They Mean Yes? The Prevalence and Correlates of Women's Token Resistance to Sex." *Journal of Personality and Social Psychology* 54: 872–879.

S-2 Muehlenhard, C.L., and Stephen Cook 1988. "Men's Self-Reports of Unwanted Sexual Activity." *Journal of Sex Research* 24: 58–72.

S-7 Muehlenhard, Charlene L., Dabra E. Friedman, and Celeste M. Thomas 1985. "Is Date Rape Justifiable? The Effects of Dating Activity, Who Initiated, Who Paid, and Men's Attitudes Toward Women." *Psychology of Women Quarterly* 9: 297–310.

G-2 Muehlenhard, C. L., and R. M. McFall 1981. "Dating Initiation from a Woman's Perspective." *Behavior Therapy* 12: 682–691.

Muller, Robert L. 1990. "Dowry Deaths." *Wall Street Journal,* Aug. 24, p. A4.

Munroe, Robert L., and Ruth H. Munroe 1989. "A Response to Broude on the Couvade." *American Anthropologist* 91: 730–735.

S-2 Murnen, Sarah K., Annette Perot, and Donn Byrne 1989. "Coping with Unwanted Sexual Activity: Normative Responses, Situational Determinants, and Individual Differences." *Journal of Sex Research* 26: 85–106.

Murphy, Kim 1990. "Saudis Blame U.S. for Growing Social Chasm." *Los Angeles Times,* Nov. 23, p. A1.

Murphy, M. J. 1985. "Demographic and Socio-Economic Influences on Recent British Marital Breakdown Patterns." *Population Studies* 39: 441–460.

R-1 Murray, Charles 1984. *Losing Ground: American Social Policy.* New York: Basic Books.

S-5 Murray, Joan, S. Marie Harvey, and Linda J. Beckman 1989. "The Importance of Contraceptive Attributes Among College Students." *Journal of Applied Social Psychology* 19: 1327–1350.

R-1 Murry, Velma McBride 1991. "Socio-Historical Study of Black Female Sexuality: Transition to First Coitus," in Robert Staples, *The Black Family: Essays and Studies,* pp. 73–87. Belmont, Calif.: Wadsworth.

S-2 Murstein, Bernard I., Michelle J. Chalpin, Kenneth V. Heard, and Stuart A.

Vyse 1989. "Sexual Behavior, Drugs, and Relationship Patterns on a College Campus Over Thirteen Years." *Adolescence* 24: 125–140.

Murstein, Bernard I. 1987. "A Clarification and Extension of the SVR Theory of Dyadic Pairing." *Journal of Marriage and the Family* 49: 929–933.

Murstein, Bernard I. 1986. *Paths to Marriage.* Beverly Hills, Calif: Sage.

Murstein, Bernard I. 1980. "Mate Selection in the 1970s" *Journal of Marriage and the Family* 42: 777–792.

Murstein, Bernard I. 1970. "Stimulus-Value-Role: A Theory of Marital Choice." *Journal of Marriage and the Family* 32: 465–481.

G-4 Nadelson, Carol, and Maria Sauzier 1986. "Intervention Programs for Individual Victims and their Families," in Mary Lystad, ed., *Violence in the Home: Interdisciplinary Perspectives,* pp. 153–168. New York: Brunner/ Mazel.

Napolitane, Catherine, and Victoria Pellegrino 1977. *Living and Loving After Divorce.* New York: Rawson Associates.

Nath, Pamela S., John G. Borkowski, Thomas L. Whitman, and Cynthia J. Schellenbach 1991. "Understanding Adolescent Parenting: The Dimensions and Functions of Social Support." *Family Relations* 40: 411–420.

Nathanson, C.A. 1984. "Sex Differences in Mortality." *Annual Review of Sociology* 10: 191–213.

National Center for Health Statistics: *See* U.S. Department of Health and Human Services.

National Council of Family Relations 1990. N.C.F.R. Presidential Report, *2001: Preparing Families for the Future.* Minneapolis, Minn.: Bolger Publications/ Creative Printing, Inc.

National Council on Family Relations Report, 1991. "Fatherhood Topic of Hearing." *National Council on Family Relations Report* 36 (Dec.): 17.

National Institutes of Health 1987. *Mastectomy: A Treatment for Breast Cancer.* Publication No. 87-658. Bethesda, Md.: U.S. Government Printing Office.

S-1 Navarro, Mireya 1992. "More Cases, Costs and Fears Under Wider AIDS Umbrella." *New York Times,* Oct. 29, pp. A1, B2.

G-3 Neilsen, Joyce McCarl 1990. *Sex and Gender in Society: Perspectives on Stratification.* Prospect Heights, Ill.: Waveland.

Nelson, Gerald E. 1984. *The One-Minute Scolding.* Boulder: Shambhala Publications.

Nelson, Margaret K. 1983. "Working-Class Women, Middle-Class Women, and Models and Childbirth." *Social Problems* 30: 284–291.

Nelson, Wendy P., and Ronald F. Levant 1991. "An Evaluation of a Skills Training Program for Parents in Stepfamilies." *Family Relations* 40: 291–296.

Neville, Helen, and Mona Halaby 1984. *No-Fault Parenting.* New York: Facts on File Publications.

New York Times 1989a. "Participants in Missouri Case Expect More Battles." July 4, p. 9.

New York Times 1989b. "Excerpts from Court Decision on the Regulation of Abortion." July 4, pp. 10–11.

S-2 Newcomer, Susan, and J. Richard Udry 1985. "Oral Sex in an Adolescent Population." *Archives of Sexual Behavior* 14: 41–46.

S-1 Nicholas, Stephen W., and Elaine J. Abrams 1992. "The 'Silent' Legacy of AIDS: Children Who Survive Their Parents and Siblings." *Journal of the American Medical Association* 268: 3478.

G-3 Nielsen, Joyce McCarl 1990. *Sex and Gender in Society: Perspectives on Stratification.* Prospect Hills, Ill.: Waveland.

R-4 Niethammer, Carolyn 1977. *Daughters of the Earth.* New York: Macmillan.

Nirenberg, Ted D., John P. Wincze, Sudhir Bansal, Michael R. Liepman, Mindy Engle-Friedman, and Ann Begin 1991. "Volunteer Bias in a Study of Male Alcoholics' Sexual Behavior." *Archives of Sexual Behavior* 20: 371–380.

S-5 Nix, Lulu Mae, Alfred B. Pasteur, and Myrtice A. Servance 1988. "A Focus Group Study of Sexually Active Black Male Teenagers." *Adolescence* 23: 741–751.

R-1 Nobles, Wade W. 1981. "African-American Family Life: An Instrument of Culture," in H.P. McAdoo, ed., *Black Families,* pp. 77–86. Beverly Hills, Calif.: Sage.

Nofziger, Margaret 1976. *A Cooperative Method of Natural Birth Control.* Summertown, Tenn.: The Book Publishing Company.

F-2 Nordheimer, Jon 1990. "Stepfathers: The Shoe Rarely Fits." *New York Times,* Oct. 18, pp. C1, C6.

Norton, Arthur J., and Jeanne E. Moorman 1987. "Current Trends in Marriage and Divorce among American Women." *Journal of Marriage and the Family* 49: 3–14.

R-1 Norton, Eleanor Holmes 1985. "Restoring the Traditional Black Family." *New York Times Magazine,* June 2.

Norwood, Robin 1971. *Women Who Love Too Much.* New York: Pocket Books.

F-1 Nugent, J. Kevin 1991. "Cultural and Psychological Influences on the Father's Role in Infant Development." *Journal of Marriage and the Family* 53: 475–485.

Nye, F. Ivan 1988. "Fifty Years of Family Research." *Journal of Marriage and the Family* 50: 305–316.

Oakland Tribune 1993. "Gay Marriages Spark Debate Over Legal Issues." May 17, pp. A1, A10.

G-4 O'Brien, J.E. 1971. "Violence in Divorce-Prone Families." *Journal of Marriage and the Family* 33: 692–698.

O'Connell, M., and C.C. Rogers 1984. "Out-of-Wedlock Births, Premarital Pregnancies, and Their Effect on Family Formation and Dissolution." *Family Planning Perspectives* 16: 157–162.

R-1 O'Hare, William P., Kelvin M. Pollard, Taynia L. Mann, and Mary M. Kent 1991. *African Americans in the 1990s. Population Bulletin* 46 (1). Washington, D.C.: Population Reference Bureau.

P-1 O'Hare, William 1992. *Can the Underclass Concept Be Applied to Rural Areas?* Washington, D.C.: Population Reference Bureau.

R-4 O'Kane, Walter Collins 1970. *Sun in the Sky.* Norman: University of Oklahoma Press.

G-3 O'Kelly, Charlotte G., and Larry S. Carney 1986. *Women and Men in Society.* Belmont, Calif.: Wadsworth.

Olson, Sheryl L., John E. Bates, and Kathryn Bayles 1990. "Early Antecedents of Childhood Impulsivity: The Role of Parent–Child Interaction, Cognitive Competence, and Temperament." *Journal of Abnormal Child Psychology* 18: 317–334.

O'Reilly, Brian 1992. "Your New Global Work Force," *Fortune* 126 (13): 52-66.

Ortiz, Vilma 1990. "Latinos and Industrial Change in New York and Los Angeles." Paper presented to the Annual Meetings of the American Sociological Association, Aug. 11–14, Washington, D.C.

G-3 Ortner, Sherry B., and Harriet Whitehead 1981. "Accounting for Sexual Meanings," in Sherry B. Ortner and Harriet Whitehead, *Sexual Meanings*, pp. 1–28. Cambridge: Cambridge University Press.

G-3 Ortner, Sherry B. 1974. "Is Female to Male as Nature is to Culture?" in Michelle Z. Rosaldo and Louise Lamphere, *Woman, Culture, and Society*, pp. 67–88. Stanford, Calif.: Stanford University Press.

G-3 Osmond, Marie Withers, and Barrie Thorne 1993. "Feminist Theories: The Social Construction of Gender in Families and Society," in Pauline G. Boss, William J. Doherty, Ralph LaRossa, Walter R. Schumm, and Suzanne K. Steinmetz, eds., *Sourcebook of Family Theories and Methods: A Contextual Approach*, pp. 591–623. New York: Plenum Press.

F-1 Palkovitz, Rob 1984. "Parental Attitudes and Fathers' Interactions with their 5-Month-Old Infants." *Developmental Psychology* 20: 1054–1060.

Pape, Rachel Edgarde 1982. "Female Sexuality and Pregnancy," in Martha Kirkpatrick, *Women's Sexual Experiences*, pp. 185–197. New York: Plenum Press.

F-1 Parke, Ross D. 1981. *Fathers*. Cambridge: Harvard University Press.

Parpal, Mary, and Eleanor E. Maccoby 1985. "Maternal Responsiveness and Subsequent Child Compliance." *Child Development* 56: 1326–1344.

Parsons, Talcott 1964. *The Social System*. Glencoe, Ill.: Free Press.

Parsons, Talcott, and R. F. Bales 1955. *Family, Socialization, and Interaction Process*. Glencoe, Ill.: Free Press.

Patterson, G.R., T.J. Dishion, and L. Bank 1984. "Family Interaction: A Process Model of Deviancy Training." *Aggressive Behavior* 10: 253–267.

Patterson, James, and Peter Kim 1991. *The Day America Told the Truth*. New York: Prentice-Hall.

Pear, Robert 1992. "Number of Poor in U.S. Is Highest Since 1964." *San Francisco Chronicle*, Sept. 4, p. A1.

P-2 Pearce, Diane 1978. "The Feminization of Poverty: Women, Work and Welfare. *Urban and Social Change Review* 11: 1–2.

Pearce, Diana 1990. "The Herstory of Homelessness." Paper presented to the Annual Meetings of the American Sociological Association, Aug. 11–14, Washington, D.C.

Pearson, Judy C. 1989. *Communication in the Family*. New York: Harper and Row.

Peek, Charles W., Nancy J. Bell, Terry Waldren, and Gwendolyn T. Sorell 1988. "Patterns of Functioning in Families of Remarried and First-Married Couples." *Journal of Marriage and the Family* 50: 699–708.

Pepe, Margaret V. and T. Jean Byrne 1991. "Women's Perceptions of Immediate and Long-Term Effects of Failed Infertility Treatment on Marital and Sexual Satisfaction." *Family Relations* 40: 303–309.

S-6 Peplau, L.A., and S. L. Gordon 1983. "The Intimate Relationships of Lesians and Gay Men," in E. R. Allgeir and N.B. McCormick, eds., *Changing Boundaries: Gender Roles and Sexual Behavior*. Palo Alto, Calif.: Mayfield Press.

Perper, Timothy 1985. *Sex Signals: The Biology of Love*. Philadelphia: I.S.I. Press.

Petersen, Lyle R., Carol R. White, and the Premarital Screening Study Group 1990. "Premarital Screening for Antibodies to Human Immunodeficiency

Virus Type I in the United States." *American Journal of Public Health* 80: 1087–1090.

Phelps, Stanlee, and Nancy Austin 1987. *The Assertive Woman*. San Luis Obispo, Calif.: Impact.

Phelps, Stanlee, and Nancy Austin 1985. *The Assertive Woman*. San Luis Obispo, Calif.: Impact.

Pill, Cynthia J. 1990. "Stepfamilies: Redefining the Family." *Family Relations* 39: 186–193.

A Pillemer, Karl, and J. Jill Suitor 1988. "Elder Abuse," in Vincent B. Van Hasselt, Randall L. Morrison, Alan S. Bellack, and Michel Hersen, eds., *Handbook of Family Violence*, pp. 247–270. New York: Plenum Press.

P-1 Piven, Frances Fox, and Barbara Ehrenreich 1987. "Workfare Means New Mass Peonage." *New York Times*, May 30, pp. 15ff.

Planned Parenthood 1991a. *Herpes: Questions and Answers*. New York: Planned Parenthood Federation of America.

Planned Parenthood 1991b. *Sexually Transmitted Disease: The Facts*. New York: Planned Parenthood Federation of America.

Planned Parenthood 1991c. *The Methods of Birth Control*. San Francisco: Planned Parenthood Federation of America.

Planned Parenthood 1991d. *Ways to Chart Your Fertility Pattern*. New York: Planned Parenthood Federation of America.

Planned Parenthood 1990. *HPV and Genital Warts: Questions and Answers*. New York: Planned Parenthood Federation of America.

Planned Parenthood 1989. *Facts About Birth Control*. New York: Planned Parenthood Federation of America.

S-5 Pleck, Joseph H., Freya L. Sonenstein, and Leighton C. Ku 1990. "Contraceptive Attitudes and Intention to Use Condoms in Sexually Experienced and Inexperienced Adolescent Males." *Journal of Family Issues* 11: 294–312.

S-5 Pleck, J.H., F.L. Sonnenstein, and S.O. Swain 1988. "Adolescent Males Sexual Behavior and Contraceptive Use: Implications for Male Responsibility." *Journal of Adolescent Research* 3: 275–284.

Popcorn, Faith 1991. *The Popcorn Report*. New York: Doubleday.

Popenoe, David 1992. "The Controversial Truth: Two-Parent Families Are Better." *New York Times*, Dec. 26, p. 21.

Popenoe, David 1988. *Disturbing the Nest: Family Change and Decline in Modern Societies*. New York: Aldine De Gruyter.

Population Today 1990. "The State of U.S. Children." 18 (5).

Power, Eileen 1975. In M.M. Postan, ed., *Medieval Women*. Cambridge: Cambridge University Press.

Powers, Charles 1992. "English Town Crash-Lands as Plant Shuts." *Los Angeles Times*, Nov. 1, pp. D3, D7.

Prager, Kate 1985. "Induced Terminations of Pregnancy." National Center for Health Statistics, *Monthly Vital Statistics Report* 34 (4) Supplement (2), July 30.

Putallaz, M. 1987. "Maternal Behavior and Children's Sociometric Status." *Child Development* 58: 324–340.

Queen, Stuart A., Robert W. Habenstein, and Jill S. Quadagno 1985. *The Family in Various Cultures*. New York: Harper and Row.

Quindlen, Anna 1992. "Evan's Two Moms." *New York Times*, Feb. 5, p. A23.

R-2 Ramos, Reyes, and Martha A. Ramos 1980. "The Mexican American: Am I

Who They Say I Am?" in Arnulfo D. Trejo, ed., *The Chicanos*, pp. 49–66. Tuscon: University of Arizona Press.

Ramu, G.N. 1991. "Changing Family Structure and Fertility Patterns: An Indian Case." *Journal of Asian Studies* 26: 189–206.

Rawlings, Steve W. 1993. *Household and Family Characteristics: March 1992*. U.S. Bureau of the Census. Current Population Reports, P20-467. Washington, D.C.: U.S. Government Printing Office.

Redekop, Calvin 1989. *Mennonite Society*. Baltimore: Johns Hopkins Press.

Register, Cheri 1991. *Are Those Kids Yours? American Families with Children Adopted from Other Countries*. New York: Free Press.

S-6 Reilly, Mary Ellen, and Jean M. Lynch 1990. "Power-Sharing in Lesbian Partnerships." *Journal of Homosexuality* 19: 1–29.

Reiss, Ira L. 1980. *Family Systems in America*. New York: Holt, Rinehart, and Winston.

Renvioze, Jean 1978. *Web of Violence: A Study of Family Violence*. New York: Routledge and Kegan Paul.

S-1 Richardson, Diane 1988. *Women and AIDS*. New York: Metheun, Inc.

G-3 Richgels, Patricia B. 1992. "Hypoactive Sexual Desire in Heterosexual Women: A Feminist Analysis." *Women and Therapy:* 12: 123–135.

S-1 Richwald, Gary R., Garland R. Kyle, Michele M. Gerber, Donald E. Morisky, Alan R. Kristal, and Joan M. Friedland 1988. "Sexual Activities in Bathhouses in Los Angeles County: Implications for AIDS Prevention Education." *Journal of Sex Research* 25: 169–180.

Riley, Glenda 1991. *Divorce: An American Tradition*. New York: Oxford University Press.

H Rimer, Sara 1990. "A 'Homeless Co-op Board' as Tough as Park Avenue." *New York Times,* Aug. 15, p.B2.

S-5 Rindskopf, K.D. 1981. "A Perilous Paradox: The Contraceptive Behavior of College Students." *Journal of College Health* 30: 113–118.

Ringheim, Karin 1990. "The Structural Determinants of Homelessness: A Study of Eight Cities." Paper presented to the Annual Meetings of the American Sociological Association, Aug. 11–14, Washington, D.C.

Risman, Barbara J., Charles T. Hill, Zick Rubin, and Letitia Anne Peplau 1981. "Living Together in College: Implications for Courtship." *Journal of Marriage and the Family* 43: 77–83.

R-2 Rivera-Martinez, Carmen 1985. "Hispanics and the Social System," in Pastora San Juan Cafferty and William C. McCready, *Hispanics in the United States,* pp. 195–214. New Brunswick, N. J.: Transaction Books.

Robbins, Jim 1988. "Fertility Rate in Utah is Off Amid Slump." *New York Times,* Dec. 29.

Robins, Lee N., Patricia West, and Barbara L. Jerjanig 1975. "Arrests and Delinquency in Two Generations: A Study of Black Urban Families and Their Children." *Journal of Child Psychology and Psychiatry* 16: 125–140.

Robinson, Linda G., and Priscilla W. Blanton 1993. "Marital Strengths in Enduring Marriages." *Family Relations* 42: 38–45.

R-4 Robles, Annette 1992. *State of Native American Youth Health*. Indian Health Service, Division of General Pediatrics and Adolescent Health. Washington, D.C.: U.S. Government Printing Office.

P-2 Rodgers, Harrell, Jr. 1986. *Poor Women: Poor Families*. New York: M.E. Sharpe, Inc.

Rodgers, Joseph Lee, and David Rowe 1990. "Adolescent Sexual Activity and

Mildly Deviant Behavior, Sibling and Friendship Effects." *Journal of Family Issues* 11: 274–293.

S-4 Rodman, Hyman 1991. "Should Parental Involvement Be Required for Minors' Abortions?" *Family Relations* 40: 155–160.

R-2 Rodriguez, Julia E. Curry 1988. "Labor Migration and Familial Responsibilities: Experiences of Mexican Women," in Margarita B. Melville, ed., *Mexicanas at Work in the United States,* pp. 47–63. Houston: University of Houston, Mexican American Studies.

Rollins, Boyd C., and Kenneth L. Cannon 1974. "Marital Satisfaction Over the Family Life Cycle." *Journal of Marriage and the Family* 36: 271–284.

Rollins, Boyd C., and Harold Feldman 1970. "Marital Satisfaction Over the Family Life Cycle." *Journal of Marriage and the Family* 32: 20–28.

G-1 Romer, N., and D. Cherry 1980. "Ethnic and Social Class Differences in Children's Sex-Role Concepts." *Sex Roles* 6: 245–263.

G-5 Rook, Karen, David Dooley, and Ralph Catalano 1991. "Stress Transmission: The Effects of Husbands' Job Stressors on the Emotional Health of Their Wives." *Journal of Marriage and the Family* 53: 165–177.

S-2 Roosa, Mark W., and F. Scott Christopher 1990. "Evaluation of an Abstinence-Only Adolescent Pregnancy Prevention Program: A Replication." *Family Relations* 39: 363–367.

Rosen, Jan. M. 1990. "Shielding Children After Remarriage." *New York Times,* Sept. 22, p. A32.

Rosenberg, Charles E. 1973. "Sexuality, Class and Role in Nineteenth Century America." *American Quarterly* 25: 131–153.

Rosenfelf, Seth 1992. "Passions Raised by Herpes Lawsuit. What Legal Duties Associated with Sex?" *San Francisco Chronicle,* Feb. 2, pp. A1, A10.

G-5 Ross, Catherine E. 1987. "The Division of Labor at Home." *Social Forces* 65: 816–833.

H Rossi, Peter H., and James D. Wright 1989. "The Urban Homeless: A Portrait of Urban Dislocation." *The Annals of the American Academy of Political and Social Science* 501: 132–142.

R-1 Rothman, Robert A. 1993. *Inequality and Stratification; Class, Color, and Gender.* Englewood Cliffs, N.J.: Prentice-Hall.

Rowlands, Peter 1983. *Love Me, Love My Kids.* Los Angeles: Continuum Publishers.

G-4 Roy, Maria 1982. *The Abusive Partner: An Analysis of Domestic Battering.* New York: Van Nostrand Reinhold.

G-2 Rubin, Lilian B. 1983. *Intimate Strangers: Men and Women Together.* New York: Harper and Row.

Rubin, Lillian B. 1976. *Worlds of Pain: Life in the Working-Class Family.* New York: Basic Books.

Rusbult, C.E., D.J. Johnson, and G.D. Morrow 1986. "Impact of Couple Patterns of Problem Solving and Distress and Nondistress in Dating Relationships." *Journal of Personality and Social Psychology* 50: 744–753.

S-7 Rush, Florence 1980. *The Best Kept Secret: Sexual Abuse of Children.* New York: McGraw-Hill.

S-7 Russell, D. 1986. *The Secret Trauma: Incest in the Lives of Girls and Women.* New York: Basic Books.

S-7 Russell, D.E.H. 1984. *Sexual Exploitation: Rape, Child Sexual Abuse, and Workplace Harassment.* Beverly Hills, Calif.: Sage.

Russianoff, Penelope 1981. *Why Do I Think I Am Nothing Without a Man?*

New York: Bantam.

R-3 Rutledge, Paul J. 1992. *The Vietnamese Experience in America*. Bloomington: Indiana University Press.

S-4 Ryan, Barbara, and Eric Plutzer 1989. "When Married Women Have Abortions: Spousal Notification and Marital Interaction." *Journal of Marriage and the Family* 51: 41–50.

Sabatelli, Ronald M., Richard L. Meth, and Stephen M. Gavazzi 1988. "Involuntary Childlessness." *Family Relations* 37: 338–343.

Safilios-Rothschild 1976. "A Macro Micro Examination of Family Power and Love: An Exchange Model." *Journal of Marriage and the Family* 38: 355–362.

Safilios-Rothschild 1970. "The Study of Family Power Structure: A Review 1960–1969." *Journal of Marriage and the Family* 32: 539–543.

Samalin, Nancy 1988. *Loving Your Child Is Not Enough*. New York: Penguin Books.

Sandefur, Gary D., Sara McLanahan, and Roger A. Wojtkiewicz 1989. "Race and Ethnicity, Family Structure, and High School Graduation." *Center for Demography and Ecology. Working Paper No. 89-27*. Madison: University of Wisconsin.

Sapir, Edward 1949. "Selected Writings of Edward Sapir" in David G. Mandelbaum, ed., *Language, Culture, and Personality*. Berkeley: University of California Press.

Sapiro, Virginia 1986. *Women in American Society*. Palo Alto, Calif.: Mayfield.

A Sarrel, Lorna J., and Philip M. Sarrel 1984. *Sexual Turning Points: The Seven Stages of Adult Sexuality*. New York: Macmillan.

Satir, Virginia, and M. Baldwin 1983. *Satir Step by Step: A Guide to Creating Change in Families*. Palo Alto, Calif.: Science and Behavior Books.

Satir, Virginia 1972. *Peoplemaking*. Palo Alto, Calif.: Science and Behavior Books.

G-2 Sattel, J. 1983. "Men, Inexpressiveness, and Power," in R. Thorne, C. Kramarae, and N. Henley, eds., *Language, Gender and Society*. Rowley, Mass.: Newbury House.

G-4 Saunders, Daniel 1986. "When Battered Women Use Violence: Husband-Abuse or Self-Defense." *Victim and Violence* 1: 47–60.

Savage, David G. 1993. "Abortion Law Survives Appeal to High Court." *San Francisco Chronicle*, Nov. 16, pp. A1, A15.

Scanzoni, John 1989. "Review of *Understanding Family Policy*." *Journal of Marriage and the Family* 51: 838–839.

Scanzoni, John, Karen Polonko, Jay Teachman, and Linda Thompson 1989. *The Sexual Bond: Rethinking Families and Close Relationships*. Newbury Park, Calif.: Sage.

Scanzoni, John 1987. "Families in the 1980s: Time to Refocus Our Thinking." *Journal of Family Issues* 8: 394–421.

G-5 Scarr, Sandra, Deborah Phillips, and Kathleen McCartney 1989. "Working Mothers and Their Families." *American Psychologist* 44: 1402–1409.

Schelp, Earl E. 1987. *Sexuality and Medicine*. Boston: D. Reidel Pulishing Company.

Schenk, J., H. Pfrang, and A. Rausche 1983. "Personality Traits Versus the Quality of the Marital Relationship as the Determinant of Marital Sexuality." *Archives of Sexual Behavior* 12:31–42.

Schoen, Robert, and John Wooldredge 1989. "Marriage Choices in North Carolina and Virginia, 1969–71 and 1979–81." *Journal of Marriage and the Family* 51: 465–481.

Schumm, Walter R. 1986. "Marital Quality Over the Marital Career: Alternative Explanations." *Journal of Marriage and the Family* 48: 165–168.

Schvaneveldt, Jay D., and Margaret H. Young 1992. "Strengthening Families: New Horizons in Family Life Education." *Family Relations* 41: 385–389.

S-1 Schvaneveldt, Jay D., Shelley L.K. Lindauer, and Margaret H. Young 1990. "Children's Understanding of AIDS: A Developmental Viewpoint." *Family Relations* 39: 330–335.

G-5 Schwartz, Felice 1989. "Management Women and the New Facts of Life." *Harvard Business Review* 67: 65–76.

Schwieder, Elmer, and Dorothy Schwieder 1975. *A Peculiar People: Iowa's Old Order Amish.* Ames: Iowa State University.

G-5 Scott, J., and D.F. Alwin 1989. "Gender Differences in Parental Strain." *Journal of Family Issues* 10: 482–503.

S-4 Scott, Jacqueline 1989. "Conflicting Beliefs about Abortion: Legal Approval and Moral Doubts." *Social-Psychology Quarterly* 52: 319–326.

Searight, H. Russell, and William T. Merkel 1991. "Systems Theory and Its Discontents: Clinical and Ethical Issues." *The American Journal of Family Therapy* 19: 19–31.

R-2 Segura, Denise A. 1988. "Familism and Employment Among Chicanas and Mexican Immigrant Women," in Margarita B. Melville, ed., *Mexicanas at Work in the United States,* pp. 24–32. Houston: University of Houston, Mexican American Studies.

Selman, R.L. 1980. *The Growth of Interpersonal Understanding: Developmental and Clinical Understanding.* New York: Academic Press.

F-2 Seltzer, Judith A. 1991. "Relationships Between Fathers and Children Who Live Apart: The Father's Role after Separation." *Journal of Marriage and the Family* 53: 79–101.

F-2 Seltzer, Judith, and S. Bianchi 1988. "Children's Contact with Absent Parents." *Journal of Marriage and the Family* 50: 663–677.

S-1 Serovich, Julianne M., Kathryn Greene, and Roxanne Parrott 1992. "Boundaries and AIDS Testing: Privacy and the Family System." *Family Relations* 41: 104–109.

F-2 Shaw, Daniel S., and Robert E. Emery 1987. "Parental Conflict and Other Correlates of the Adjustment of School-Age Children Whose Parents Have Separated." *Journal of Abnormal Child Psychology* 15: 269–281.

G-5 Shihadeh, Edward S. 1991. "The Prevalence of Husband-Centered Migration: Employment Consequences for Married Mothers." *Journal of Marriage and the Family* 53: 432–444.

S-2 Shotland, R. Lance, and Jane M. Craig 1988. "Can Men and Women Differentiate Between Friendly and Sexually Interested Behavior?" *Social Psychology Quarter* 51: 66–73.

S-7 Shotland, R. Lance, and Lynne Goodstein 1983. "Just Because She Doesn't Want to Doesn't Mean It's Rape: An Experimentally Based Causal Model of the Perception of Rape in a Dating Situation." *Social Psychology Quarterly* 46: 220–232.

S-7 Siegel, Judith M., Susan B. Sorenson, Jacqueline M. Golding, M. Audrey Burnam, and Judith A. Stein 1989. "Resistance to Sexual Assault: Who Resists and What Happens?" *Journal of Public Health* 79: 27–31.

Sidorowicz, L., and C. Lunney 1980. "Baby X Revisited." *Sex Roles* 6: 67–73.

Simon, Robin W., Donna Eder, and Cathy Evans 1992. "The Development of Feeling Norms Underlying Romantic Love among Adolescent Females." *Social Psychology Quarterly* 55: 29–46.

Skolnick, Arlene 1991. *Embattled Paradise: The American Family in an Age of Uncertainty.* New York: Harper Collins.

Slovenko, Ralph 1978. "The De Facto Decriminalization of Bigamy." *Journal of Family Law* 17: 297–308.

Smith, Barbara Clark 1985. *After the Revolution.* New York: Pantheon Books.

Smith, Daniel Scott, and Michael S. Hindus 1975. "Premarital Pregnancy in America, 1640–1971: An Overview and Interpretation." *Journal of Interdisciplinary History* 5: 537–570.

Smith, Donna 1990. *Stepmothering.* New York: St. Martin's Press.

A-4 Smith, K. 1989. "When Death Does Us Part: The Differences Between Widows and Widowers." *Psychology Today* (Nov.).

S-7 Smith, Ronald E., Charles J. Pine, and Mark E. Hawley 1988. "Social Cognitions About Adult Male Victims of Female Sexual Assault." *The Journal of Sex Research* 24: 101–112.

Smith, Selwyn M., and Ruth Hanson 1975. "Interpersonal Relationships and Child Rearing Practices in 214 Parents of Battered Children." *British Journal of Psychiatry* 127: 513–525.

Smith, Suzanna, and Bron Ingoldsby 1992. "Multicultural Family Studies: Educating Students for Diversity." *Family Relations* 41: 25–30.

Smith, Tom W. 1990. "The Polls—A Report: The Sexual Revolution." *Public Opinion Quarterly* 54: 415–435.

R-1 Smock, Pamela J. 1990. "Remarriage and Cohabitation among Previously Married Women: Race Differentials and the Role of Educational Attainment." *National Survey of Families and Households. Working Paper No. 31.* Madison: Center for Demography and Ecology, University of Wisconsin.

Snyder, K.K. 1979. "Multi-Dimentional Assessment of Marital Satisfaction." *Journal of Marriage and the Family* 41: 813–823.

G-4 Sonkin, Daniel Jay, Del Martin, and Lenore Auerbach Walker 1985. *The Male Batterer: A Treatment Approach.* New York: Springer.

Sorrentino, Constance 1990. "The Changing Family in International Perspective." *Monthly Labor Review* 113 (March): 41–56.

Sosa, R., M.D. Kennell, M. Klaus, S. Robertson, and J. Urrutia 1980. "The Effect of a Supportive Companion on Perinatal Problems, Length of Labor, and Mother–Infant Interaction." *The New England Journal of Medicine* 303: 597–600.

South, Scott 1991. "Sociodemographic Differential in Mate Selection Preference." *Journal of Marriage and the Family* 53: 928–940.

Spanier, Graham B. 1983. "Married and Unmarried Cohabitation in the United States, 1980." *Journal of Marriage and the Family* 45: 277–288.

Spector, Ilana P., and Michael P. Carey 1990. "Incidence and Prevalence of the Sexual Dysfunctions: A Critical Review of the Empirical Literature." *Archives of Sexual Behavior* 19: 389–408.

P-2 Speer, Tibbett L. 1992. "Why Single Women Keep Their Babies." *American Demographics* 14: 9–10.

G-2 Sprecher, Susan 1992. "How Men and Women Expect to Feel and Behave in

Response to Inequity in Close Relationships." *Social Psychology Quarterly* 55: 57–69.

S-2 Sprecher, Susan, Kathleen McKinney, Robert Walsh, and Carrie Anderson 1988. "A Revision of the Reiss Premarital Sexual Permissiveness Scale." *Journal of Marriage and the Family* 50: 821–828.

R-1 Stack, Carol 1974. *All Our Kin: Strategies for Survival in a Black Community.* New York: Harper and Row.

Stack, Steven, and James H. Gundlach 1992. "Divorce and Sex." *Archives of Sexual Behavior* 21: 359–367.

G-5 Stafford, Rebecca, Elaine Backman, and Pamela Dibona 1977. "The Division of Labor Among Cohabiting and Married Couples." *Journal of Marriage and the Family* 39: 43–57.

G-5 Stanley, Sandra C., J.G. Hunt, and L.L. Hunt 1986. "The Relative Deprivation of Husbands in Dual-Earner Households." *Journal of Family Issues* 7: 3–20.

R-1 Staples, Robert 1991. "Substance Abuse and the Black Family Crisis: An Overview," in Robert Staples, ed., *The Black Family: Essays and Studies,* pp. 257–267. Belmont, Calif.: Wadsworth.

R-1 Staples, Robert 1985. "Changes in Black Family Structure: The Conflict Between Family Ideology and Structural Conditions." *Journal of Marriage and the Family* 47: 1005–1013.

R-1 Staples, Robert 1982. *Black Masculinity.* San Francisco: The Black Scholar Press.

Statistical Abstract of the United States: See U.S. Bureau of the Census.

G-3 Steinem, Gloria 1992. *Revolution from Within.* Boston: Little, Brown and Company.

Steiner, Claude M. 1974. *Scripts People Live.* New York: Grove Press.

R-1 Stephen, Elizabeth H., Ronald R. Rindfuss, and Frank D. Bean 1988. "Racial Differences in Contraceptive Choice: Complexity and Implications." *Demography* 25: 53–70.

Stephen, Timothy D. 1985. "Fixed-Sequence and Circular-Causal Models of Relationship Development: Divergent Views on the Role of Communication in Intimacy." *Journal of Marriage and the Family* 47: 955–963.

Stern, Gabriella 1992. "White-Collar Workers Face Tougher Time After Their Layoffs." *Wall Street Journal,* Aug. 24, p. A1.

Sternberg, Robert J., and M.L. Barnes, eds. 1988. *The Psychology of Love.* New Haven: Yale University Press.

Sternberg, Robert J. 1986. "A Triangular Theory of Love." *Psychological Review* 93: 119–135.

Sternberg, Robert J., and S. Grajek 1984. "The Nature of Love." *Journal of Personality and Social Psychology* 47: 312–329.

G-4 Stets, Jan E. 1990. "Verbal and Physical Aggression in Marriage." *Journal of Marriage and the Family* 52: 501–514.

G-4 Stets, Jan E., and Maureen A. Pirog-Good 1989. "Sexual Aggression and Control in Dating Relationships." *Journal of Applied Social Psychology* 19: 1392–1412.

G-1 Stevenson, M.R., and K.N. Black 1988. "Parental Absence and Sex-Role Development: A Meta-Analysis." *Child Development* 59: 793–814.

H Stewart, Jocelyn 1990. "In Search of Roots: Homelessness Strains the Students—and the Schools." *Los Angeles Times,* April 28, pp. B1, B4.

Stinnett, N., and J. Defrain 1989. "The Healthy Family: Is It Possible?" in M.

Fine, ed., *The Second Handbook on Parent Education,* pp. 53–74. New York: Academic Press.

Stinnett, N., and J. Defrain 1985. *Secrets of Strong Families.* New York: Berkley.

Stinnett, N. 1983. "Strong Families: A Portrait," in D. Mace, ed., *Toward Family Wellness.* Beverly Hills, Calif.: Sage.

Stinnett, N., and Sauer, K.H. 1977. "Relationship Characteristics of Strong Families." *Family Perspective* 11: 3–11.

S-1 Stone, Katherine M., and Herbert B. Peterson 1992. "Spermicides, HIV, and the Vaginal Sponge," *Journal of the American Medical Association* 268 (4), July 22, pp. 521–523.

Stoppard, Miriam 1986. *Dr. Miriam Stoppard's Pregnancy and Birth Book.* New York: Villard Books.

Straus, Murray A., and Stephen Sweet 1992. "Verbal/Symbolic Aggression in Couples: Incidence Rates and Relationships to Personal Characteristics." *Journal of Marriage and the Family* 54: 346–357.

Straus, Murray A. 1991. "Discipline and Deviance: Physical Punishment of Children and Violence and Other Crime in Adulthood." *Social Problems* 38: 133–152.

G-4 Straus, Murray A., and C. Smith 1990. "Violence in Hispanic Families in the United States: Incidence Rates and Structural Interpretations," in M.A. Straus and R.J. Gelles, eds., *Physical Violence in American Families: Risk Factors and Adaptations to Violence in 8,145 Families,* pp. 341–367. New Brunswick, N.J.: Transaction.

G-4 Straus, Murray A., and Richard Gelles 1986. "Societal Change and Change in Family Violence from 1975 to 1985 as Revealed by Two National Surveys." *Journal of Marriage and the Family* 48: 465–479.

Straus, Murray A. 1985. "Family Training in Crime and Violence," in A.J. Lincoln and M.A. Straus, eds., *Crime in the Family,* pp. 164–185. New York: Thomas.

G-4 Straus, Murray, Richard J. Gelles, and Suzanne K. Steinmetz 1980. *Behind Closed Doors: Violence in the American Family.* Garden City, N.Y.: Anchor Books.

G-5 Sudarkasa, N. 1981a. "Female Employment and Family Organization in West Africa," in F.C. Steady, ed., *The Black Woman Cross-Culturally.* Cambridge, Mass.: Schenkman.

R-1 Sudarkasa, N. 1981b. "Interpreting the African Heritage in Afro-American Family Organization," in H.P. McAdoo, ed., *Black Families,* pp. 37–53. Beverly Hills, Calif.: Sage.

Sullivan, Michael R., and Susan Shultz 1990. *Adopt the Baby You Want.* New York: Simon and Schuster.

S-6 Sullivan, Ronald 1992. "Judge Says Lesbian Can Adopt Companion's Child." *New York Times,* Jan. 31, p. B1.

Sullivan, Thomas J. 1992. *Applied Sociology: Research and Critical Thinking.* New York: Macmillan.

Summit, R., and J. Kryso 1978. "Sexual Abuse of Children: A Clinical Spectrum." *American Journal of Orthopsychiatry* 48: 237–251.

Surra, Catherine A. 1990. "Research and Theory on Mate Selection and Premarital Relaitonships in the 1980s." *Journal of Marriage and the Family* 52: 844–865.

Surra, Catherine A. 1987. "Reasons for Changes in Commitment: Variations by Courtship Type." *Journal of Social and Personal Relationships* 4: 17–30.

Sweet, James A., and Larry L. Bumpass 1987. *American Families and House-holds.* New York: Russell Sage Foundation.

Swidler, Ann 1980. "Love and Adulthood in American Culture," in Neil J. Smelser and Erik H. Erickson, eds., *Themes of Work and Love in Adulthood*, pp. 120–147. Cambridge: Harvard University Press.

G-4 Symonds, M. 1978. "The Psychodynamics of Violence-Prone Marriages." *American Journal of Psychoanalysis* 38: 213–222.

P-2 Tanfer, Koray 1987. "Patterns of Premarital Cohabitation among Never-Married Women in the United States." *Journal of Marriage and the Family* 49: 483–495.

G-2 Tannen, Deborah 1990. *You Just Don't Understand.* New York: Ballantine Books.

Tapper, Nancy 1980. "The Women's Subsociety among the Shahsevan Nomads of Iran," in Jane I. Smith, *Women in Contemporary Muslim Societies,* pp. 374–398. London: Associated University Press.

G-1 Tauber, M. 1979. "Sex Differences in Parent–Child Interaction Styles in a Free-Play Session." *Child Development* 50: 981–988.

G-3 Tavris, Carol, and Carole Wade 1984. *The Longest War: Sex Differences in Perspective.* New York: Harcourt Brace Jovanovich.

Tavris, Carol 1982. *Anger: The Misunderstood Emotion.* New York: Simon and Schuster.

R-1 Taylor, Robert Joseph, Linda M. Chatters, M. Belinda Tucker, and Edith Lewis 1990. "Developments in Research on Black Families: A Decade Review." *Journal of Marriage and the Family* 52: 993–1014.

Teachman, Jay D. 1990. "Socioeconomic Resources of Parents and Award of Child Support in the United States: Some Exploratory Models." *Journal of Marriage and the Family* 52: 689–699.

R-1 Teachman, Jay 1986. "First and Second Marital Dissolution: A Decomposition Exercise for Whites and Blacks." *Sociological Quarterly* 27: 571–590.

Teays, Wanda 1991. "The Burning Bride: The Dowry Problem in India." *Journal of Feminist Studies in Religion* 7: 29.

Tennov, Dorothy 1980. *Love and Limerence: The Experience of Being in Love.* New York: Stein and Day.

R-4 Terrell, John U., and Donna M. Terrell 1974. *Indian Women of the Western Morning.* New York: The Dial Press.

Testa, Mark 1990. "Joblessness and Absent Fatherhood in the Inner-City." Paper presented to the Annual Meetings of the American Sociological Association, Aug. 11–14, Washington, D.C.

R-1 Testa, Mark, Nan Marie Astone, Marilyn Krogh, and Kathryn M. Neckerman 1989. "Employment and Marriage Among Inner-City Fathers," in W.J. Wilson, ed., "The Ghetto Underclass: Social Science Perspectives." *Annals of the American Academy of Political and Social Science* 501: 79–91.

P-1 Teti, Douglas M., Michael E. Lamb, and Arthur B. Elster 1987. "Long-Range Socioeconomic and Marital Consequences of Adolescent Marriage in Three Cohorts of Adult Males." *Journal of Marriage and the Family* 49: 499–506.

Thobaben, Robert G., Donna M. Schlagheck, and Charles Funderburk 1991. *Issues in American Political Life.* New York: Prentice-Hall.

Thomas, W.I. 1966. *Thomas on Social Organization and Personality.* (Morris Janowitz, ed.) Chicago: University of Chicago Press.

G-3 Thompson, Linda 1992. "Feminist Methodology for Family Studies." *Journal of Marriage and the Family* 54: 3–18.

G-5 Thompson, Linda 1991. "Family Work: Women's Sense of Fairness." *Journal of Family Issues* 12: 181–196.

G-5 Thompson, Linda, and A. Walker 1989. "Gender in Families: Women and Men in Marriage, Work and Parenthood." *Journal of Marriage and the Family* 51: 845–871.

G-2 Thornton, Arland 1989. "Changing Attitudes Toward Family Issues in the United States." *Journal of Marriage and the Family* 51: 873–893.

Thornton, Arland, and Willard L. Rodgers 1987. "The Influence of Individual and Historical Time on Marital Dissolution." *Demography* 24: 1–22.

Tiesel, Judy Watson, and David H. Olson 1992. "Preventing Family Problems: Troubling Trends and Promising Opportunities." *Family Relations* 41: 398–403.

Ting-Toomey, Stella 1983. "An Analysis of Verbal Communication Patterns in High and Low Marital Adjustment Groups. *Human Communication Research* 9: 306–319.

Tortora, Gerard J. 1989. *Principles of Human Anatomy.* New York: Harper and Row.

S-5 Trussell, James, David Lee Warner, and Robert A. Hatcher 1992. "Condom Slippage and Breakage Rates." *Family Planning Perspectives* 24 (1):20–26.

S-5 Trussell, James, and Kathryn Kost 1987. "Contraceptive Failure in the United States: A Critical Review of the Literature." *Studies in Family Planning* 18: 237.

R-1 Tucker, M. Belinda, and Robert Joseph Taylor 1989. "Demographic Correlates of Relationship Status among Black Americans." *Journal of Marriage and the Family* 51: 655–666.

Tuller, David 1993. "Uninfected Gays Suffering, Too." *San Francisco Chronicle*, March 19, pp. A1, A4.

U.S. Bureau of the Census 1993a. *Statistical Abstract of the United States: 1993.* Washington, D.C.: U.S. Government Printing Office.

———— 1993b. Steve W. Rawlings, Current Population Reports, P20-467. *Household and Family Characteristics March 1992.* Washington, D.C.: U.S. Government Printing Office.

———— 1993c. Current Population Reports, P60-184. *Money Income of Households, Families and Persons in the United States: 1992.* Washington, D.C.: U.S. Government Printing Office.

———— 1993d. Current Population Reports, P60-185. *Poverty in the United States: 1992.* Washington, D.C.: U.S. Government Printing Office.

———— 1992a. *Statistical Abstract of the United States: 1992.* Washington, D.C.: U.S. Government Printing Office.

———— 1992b. Current Population Reports P20-468, *Marital Status and Living Arrangements: March 1992,* Washington, D.C.: U.S. Government Printing Office.

———— 1992c. Current Population Reports P60-181, *Poverty in the United States, 1991.* Washington, D.C.: U.S. Government Printing Office.

———— 1992d. *Statistical Brief, 1992.* No. 91-15. "Housing of Single-Parent Families." Washington, D.C.: U.S. Government Printing Office.

———— 1991a. *Statistical Abstract of the United States: 1992.* Washington, D.C.: U.S. Government Printing Office.

———— 1991b. Current Population Reports P20-450. *Marital Status and Living Arrangements: March 1990.* Washington, D.C.: U.S. Government Printing Office.

———— 1991c. Current Population Reports, Series P-20, *Asian and Pacific*

Islander Population in the United States, March 1990–91. Washington, D.C.: U.S. Government Printing Office.

———— 1991d. Current Population Reports, P60-174, *Money Income and Poverty Status in the United States: 1990.* (Advance Data from the March, 1990, Current Population Survey.) Washington, D.C.: U.S. Government Printing Office.

———— 1991e. *Statistical Brief* 91-4. "Does Education Pay Off?" Washington, D.C.: U.S. Government Printing Office.

———— 1991f. *Statistical Brief,* 91-14. "Who Can Afford to Buy a House?" Washington, D.C.: U.S. Government Printing Office.

———— 1990a. *Statistical Absract of the United States 1990.* Washington, D.C.: U.S. Government Printing Office.

———— 1990b. Current Population Reports, P20-444, *The Hispanic Population in the United States: March 1990.* Washington, D.C.: U.S. Government Printing Office.

———— 1990c. Current Population Reports P20-447. *Households and Family Characteristics: March 1990 and 1989.* Washington, D.C.: U.S. Government Printing Office.

———— 1990d. Current Population Reports, P60-168, *Money Income and Poverty Status in the United States: 1989.* (Advance Data from the March 1990 Current Population Survey.) Washington, D.C.: U.S. Government Printing Office.

———— 1990e. *Statistical Brief,* 9-90. "Health Insurance Coverage: The Haves and Have-Nots." Washington, D.C.: U.S. Government Printing Office.

———— 1989a. Current Population Reports, P23-163, *Changes in American Family Life.* Washington, D.C.: U.S. Government Printing Office.

———— 1989b. Current Population Reports, P70-14, *Characteristics of Persons Receiving Benefits from Major Assistance Programs.* Washington, D.C.: U.S. Government Printing Office.

———— 1989c. Current Population Reports, P20-441, *Households, Families, Marital Status and Living Arrangements: March 1989, Advance Report.* Washington, D.C.: U.S. Government Printing Office.

———— 1989d. Current Population Reports, P20-442. *The Black Population in the United States: March 1988.* Washington, D.C.: U.S. Government Printing Office.

———— 1989e. Current Population Reports, P23-159, *Population Profile of the United States, 1989.* Washington, D.C.: U.S. Government Printing Office.

———— 1989f. Current Population Reports, P23-162, *Unmarried Couple Households in 1988.* Washington, D.C.: U.S. Government Printing Office.

———— 1989g. Current Population Reports, P23-150, *Population Profile of the U.S., 1984–85.* Washington, D.C.: U.S. Government Printing Office.

———— 1989h. Current Population Reports, P23-162. *Studies in Marriage and Family.* Washington, D.C.: U.S. Government Printing Office.

———— 1988. *Statistical Abstract of the United States: 1988.* Washington, D.C.: U.S. Government Printing Office.

———— 1960. *Statistical Abstract of the U.S.: 1960.* Washington, D.C.: U.S. Government Printing Office.

U.S. Congress 1990. *Congressional Report on Children, Youth, and Families.* Washington, D.C.: U.S. Government Printing Office.

U.S. Congress Subcommittee on Human Resources and Intergovernmental Relations 1989. *Medical and Psychological Impact on Abortion.* Washington, D.C.: U.S. Government Printing Office.

U.S. Department of Health and Human Services 1993a. Centers for Disease Control and Prevention, National Center for Health Statistics. *Monthly Vital Statistics Report* 42 (3), Supplement, Sept. 8. Publication No. (PHS)93-1120, "Advance Report of Final Natality Statistics, 1991." Washington, D.C.: U.S. Government Printing Office.

———— 1993b. Centers for Disease Control and Prevention, National Center for Health Statistics. *Monthly Vital Statistics Report* (6), "Births, Marriages, Divorces, and Deaths for June 1993." Washington, D.C.: U.S. Government Printing Office.

———— 1993c. Centers for Disease Control and Prevention, National Center for Health Statistics. *HIV/AIDS Surveillance Report* 5 (2). Washington, D.C.: U.S. Government Printing Office.

———— 1990. Centers for Disease Control and Prevention, National Center for Health Statistics, Public Health Service. *Vital Statistics of the United States: 1988* 1, "Natality." Department of Health and Human Services Publication No. (PHS) 90-1100. Washington, D.C.: U.S. Government Printing Office.

———— 1990b. *Contraception: Comparing the Options.* Washington, D.C.: U.S. Government Printing Office.

———— 1988. National Center for Health Statistics. *Vital and Health Statistics,* 10 166. Department of Health and Human Services Publication No. 88-1594. Washington, D.C.: U.S. Government Printing Office.

———— 1989. National Center for Health Statistics. *Monthly Vital Statistics Report* 38 (3), "Advance Report of Final Natality Statistics, 1987." Washington, D.C.: U.S. Government Printing Office.

U.S. Department of Labor 1992. Bureau of Labor Statistics. *Employment and Earnings,* 39 (1) (Jan.) Washington, D.C.: U.S. Government Printing Office.

———— 1990. Bureau of Labor Statistics. *Employment and Earnings* 37 (11) (Nov.). Washington, D.C.: U.S. Government Printing Office.

———— 1989. Bureau of Labor Statistics. *Handbook of Labor Statistics,* Bulletin 2340. Washington, D.C.: U.S. Government Printing Office.

Valentine, Deborah P. 1986. "Psychological Impact of Infertility: Identifying Issues and Needs." *Social Work in Health Care* 11: 61–69.

Vander, Arthur J., James H. Sherman, and Dorothy S. Luciano 1990. *Human Physiology: The Mechanisms of Body Function.* New York: McGraw-Hill.

R-2 Vega, William A. 1990. "Hispanic Families in the 1980s: A Decade of Research." *Journal of Marriage and the Family* 52: 1015–1024.

Vida, Judith E. "The Developmental Crisis of Pregnancy," in Martha Kirkpatrick, *Women's Sexual Experiences,* pp. 199–204. New York: Plenum Press.

F-2 Visher, E.B., and J.S. Visher 1989. "Parenting Coalitions After Remarriage: Dynamics and Therapeutic Guidelines." *Family Relations* 38: 65–70.

G-1 Vogel, Dena Ann, Margaret A. Lake, Suzanne Evans, and Katherine Hildebrandt Karraker 1991. "Children's and Adults' Sex-Stereotyped Perceptions of Infants." *Sex Roles* 24: 605.

F-1 Volling, Brenda L., and Jay Belsky 1991. "Multiple Determinants of Father Involvement during Infancy in Dual-Earner and Single-Earner Families." *Journal of Marriage and the Family* 53: 461–474.

Voydanoff, P. 1990. "Work and Family Life," in National Council on Family Relations, *2001: Preparing Families for the Future,* pp. 12–13. Minneapolis, Minn.: National Council on Family Relations.

G-2 Vuchinich, Samuel 1987. "Starting and Stopping Spontaneous Family Conflicts." *Journal of Marriage and the Family* 49: 591–601.

A Walker, Allexis J., and Clara C. Pratt 1991. "Daughters' Help to Mothers: Intergenerational Aid versus Caregiving." *Journal of Marriage and the Family* 53: 3–12.

G-4 Walker, L.E. 1979. *The Battered Woman.* New York: Harper and Row.

G-4 Walker, L.E. 1977–1978. "Battered Women and Learned Helplessness." *Victimology* 2: 535–534.

Walker, Morton, Bernice Yoffe, and Parke H. Gray 1979. *The Complete Book of Birth.* New York: Simon and Schuster.

R-1 *Wall Street Journal* 1992. "Many Voices: Diversity of Leaders Reflects Changes in Black America; Professionals, Artists Add Clout." May 6, pp. A1,A8.

Wall Street Journal 1990a. "End of An Era in Wales." Sept. 19, p. A18.

Wall Street Journal 1990b. "The '80s Merger Mania Applies to Families, Too." Feb. 20, p. B1.

Wallace, Anthony F.C. 1981. "Childhood, Work, and Family Life in a Nineteenth Century Cotton Mill Town," in Mel Albin and Dominick Cavallo, *Family Life in America: 1920–2000,* pp. 169–184. St. James, N.Y.: Revisionary Press.

Wallerstein, Judith S., and Joan B. Kelly 1980. *Surviving the Breakup: How Children and Parents Cope with Divorce.* New York: Basic Books.

Wallerstein, Judith, and Sandra Blakeslee 1989. *Second Chances: A Decade After Divorce.* New York: Tricknor and Fields.

Walsh, Joan 1990. "Asian Women, Caucasian Men: The New Demographics of Love," in *Image. San Francisco Examiner,* Dec. 2, pp. 11–17.

Watzlawick, Paul 1968. In Don D. Jackson, ed., *Communication, Family and Marriage: Human Communication,* vol. 1. Palo Alto, Calif.: Science and Behavior Books.

Wegscheider, Sharon 1981. *Another Chance: Hope and Health for the Alcoholic Family.* Palo Alto, Calif.: Science and Behavior Books.

R-1 Weinberg, Martin S., and Colin J. Williams 1988. "Black Sexuality: A Test of Two Theories." *Journal of Sex Research* 25: 197–218.

Weinrich, Janes D. 1987. *Sexual Landscapes.* New York: Charles Scribner's Sons.

Weiss, Richard J. 1991. "Effects of Antihypertensive Agents on Sexual Function." *American Family Physician* 44: 2075–2082.

Weiss, Robert S. 1979. *Going It Alone: The Family Life and Social Situation of the Single Parent.* New York: Basic Books.

P-2 Weitzman, Lenore 1990. "Women and Children Last: The Social and Economic Consequences of Divorce Law Reforms," in Sheila Ruth, *Issues in Feminism,* pp. 312–335. Mountain View, Calif.: Mayfield.

P-2 Weitzman, Lenore 1985. *The Divorce Revolution: The Unexpected Social and Economic Consequences for Women and Children in America.* New York: Free Press.

G-1 Weitzman, Lenore 1975. "Sex Role Socialization," in Jo. Freeman, ed., *Women: A Feminist Perspective.* Palo Alto, Calif.: Mayfield.

Wetzel, James R. 1990. "American Families: 75 Years of Change." *Monthly Labor Review* 113 (March): 4–12.

G-4 Wetzel, Laura, and Mary Anne Ross 1983. "Psychological and Social Ramifications of Battering." *The Personnel Guidance Journal* (March): 423–427.

White, James M. 1987. "Premarital Cohabitation and Marital Stability in

Canada." *Journal of Marriage and the Family* 49: 641–647.

White, Lynn K. 1990. "Determinants of Divorce: A Review of Research in the Eighties." *Journal of Marriage and the Family* 52: 904–912.

F-2 White, Lynn K., D. Brinkerhodd, and A. Booth 1985. "The Effect of Marital Disruption on the Child's Attachment to Parents." *Journal of Family Issues* 6: 5–22.

Whitman, T.L., J.G. Borkowski, J.G. Schellenbach, and P.S. Nath 1987. "Predicting and Understanding Developmental Delay of Children of Adolescent Mothers: A Multi-Dimensional Approach." *American Journal of Mental Deficiency* 92: 40–56.

Whorf, Benjamin L. 1956 (original 1941). "The Relation of Habitual Thought and Behavior to Language," in *Language, Thought, and Reality*, pp. 134–159. Cambridge: The Technology Press of M.I.T.; New York: Wiley.

S-4 Wilcox, Clyde 1990. "Race Differences in Abortion Attitudes: Some Additional Evidence." *Public Opinion Quarterly* 54: 248–255.

R-1 Wilkerson, Isabel 1990. "Middle-Class Blacks Try to Grip a Ladder While Lending a Hand." *New York Times*, Nov. 26, pp. A1, A13.

P-2 Wilkerson, Margaret B., and Jewell Handy Gresham 1989. "The Racialization of Poverty." *The Nation* 249: 126–132.

P-1 Wilkie, Jane R. 1991. "The Decline in Men's Labor Force Participation and Income and the Changing Structure of Family Economic Support." *Journal of Marriage and the Family* 53: 111–122.

Wilkinson, Melvin 1980. "The Influence of Family Size, Interaction and Religiosity on Family Affection in a Mormon Sample." *Journal of Marriage and the Family* 42: 297–304.

S-1 Williams, Jane, and William B. Stafford 1991. "Silent Casualties: Partners, Families, and Spouses of Persons with AIDS." *Journal of Counseling and Development* 69: 423.

S-6 Williams, John D., and Arthur P. Jacoby 1989. "The Effects of Premarital Heterosexual and Homosexual Experience on Dating and Marriage Desirability." *Journal of Marriage and the Family* 51: 489–497.

Williams, Linda B. 1990. "Marriage and Decision-Making: Inter-Generational Dynamics in Indonesia." *Journal of Comparative Family Studies* 21: 55–66.

Williams, Linda B., and William F. Pratt 1990. "Wanted and Unwanted Childbearing in the United States: 1973–88." National Center for Health Statistics, *Vital and Health Statistics, Advance Data* 189 (Sept. 26). Washington, D.C.: U.S. Government Printing Office.

R-2 Williams, Norma 1990. *The Mexican American Family: Tradition and Change*. Dix Hills, N.Y.: General Hall, Inc.

Wilmot, W. W. 1979. *Dyadic Communication: A Transactional Perspective*. Reading, Mass.: Addison-Wesley Publishing Co.

P-2 Wilson, James Q. 1993. "The Family-Values Debate." *Commentary* 95: 24–31.

P-1 Wilson, William Julius 1987. *The Truly Disadvantaged: The Inner City, the Underclass, and Public Policy*. Chicago: University of Chicago Press.

P-1 Wilson, William Julius 1980. *The Declining Significance of Race*. Chicago: University of Chicago Press.

Wineberg, Howard 1990. "Childbearing after Remarriage." *Journal of Marriage and the Family* 52: 31–38.

Winter, David 1973. *The Power Motive*. New York: Free Press.

Wolf, Arthur P., and Chien-shan Huang 1980. *Marriage and Adoption in China, 1845–1945*. Stanford: Stanford University Press.

G-4 Wolf-Smith, Jane H., and Ralph LaRossa 1992. "After He Hits Her." *Family Relations* 41: 324–329.

World Almanac and Book of Facts, 1993. New York: Scripps Howard/Pharos Books.

World Bank 1993. *World Development Report, 1993*. Washington D.C.: The International Bank for Reconstruction and Development, and Oxford University Press.

World Health Organization 1993. *Weekly Epidemiological Record* (Jan. 15). Geneva: World Health Organization.

S-4 Worthington, Everett L., David B. Larson, Malvin W. Brubaker, Cheryl Colecchi, James T. Barry, and David Morrow 1989. "The Benefits of Legislation Requiring Parental Involvement Prior to Adolescent Abortion." *American Psychologist* 44: 1542–1545.

R-1 Wyatt, Gail Elizabeth 1989. "Reexamining Factors Predicting Afro-American and White American Women's Age at First Coitus." *Archives of Sexual Behavior* 18: 271–298.

Wyatt, Gail E., Stefanie D. Peters, and Donald Guthrie 1988a. "Kinsey Revisited, Part I: Comparisons of the Sexual Socialization and Sexual Behavior of White Women Over 33 Years." *Archives of Sexual Behavior* 17: 201–239.

R-1 Wyatt, Gail E., Stefanie D. Peters, and Donald Guthrie 1988b. "Kinsey Revisited, Part II: Comparisons of the Sexual Socialization and Sexual Behavior of Black Women Over 33 Years." *Archives of Sexual Behavior* 17: 289–332.

Wyatt, Gary 1989. "Mormon Polygyny in the Nineteenth Century: A Theoretical Analysis." *Journal of Comparative Family Studies* 20: 13–20.

S-2 Yamaguchi, Kazuo, and Denise Kandel 1987. "Drug Use and Other Determinants of Premarital Pregnancy and Its Outcome: A Dynamic Analysis of Competing Life Events." *Journal of Marriage and the Family* 49: 257–270.

Yancey, George, and Sarah Berglass 1991. "Love Styles and Life Satisfaction." *Psychological Reports* 68: 883–888.

R-2 Ybarra, Lea 1988. "Separating Myth from Reality: Socio-Economic and Cultural Influences on Chicanas and the World of Work," in Margarita B. Melville, ed., *Mexicanas at Work in the United States*, pp. 12–23. Houston: University of Houston, Mexican American Studies.

G-4 Yllo 1984. "The Status of Women, Marital Equality, and Violence Against Wives: A Contextual Analysis." *Journal of Family Issues* 5: 307–320.

Yoachum, Susan 1991. "Access to Abortion Begins to Disappear." *San Francisco Chronicle*, June 27, pp. 1, A4.

R-1 Young, Carlene 1989. "Psychodynamics of Coping and Survival of the African-American Female in a Changing World." *Journal of Black Studies* 20: 208–221.

Zelnick and Kantner 1972. "The Probability of Premarital Intercourse." *Social Science Research* 1: 335–345.

P-2 Zick, Cathleen D., and Ken R. Smith 1991. "Marital Transitions, Poverty, and Gender Differences in Mortality." *Journal of Marriage and the Family* 53: 327–336.

Zimmerman, Shirley L. 1988. *Understanding Family Policy: Theoretical Approaches*. Newbury Park, Calif.: Sage.

Zuker, Elaina 1983. *Mastering Assertiveness Skills, Power and Positive Influence at Work*. New York: AMACOM.

Zuckerman, M., R. Tushup, and S. Finner 1976. "Sexual Attitudes and Experience: Attitude and Personality Correlates and Changes Produced by a Course in Sexuality." *Journal of Consulting and Clinical Psychology* 44: 7–19.

Zuska, Joseph J., and Joseph A. Pursch 1988. "Long Term Management," in Stanley E. Gitlow and Herbert S. Peyser, eds., *Alcoholism: A Practical Treatment Guide*, pp. 98–123. Philadelphia: Grune and Stratton.

Glossary

AIDS: Acquired immune deficiency syndrome, a disease in which the immune system becomes so impaired that it is vulnerable to opportunistic diseases.

AIDS Latency Period: The period of time following infection with HIV before symptoms occur.

AIDS-Worry: Worrying about becoming infected with HIV and becoming ill with AIDS.

Androgyny: Choosing and combining traits associated with maleness and femaleness.

ARC: AIDS Related Complex: A group of symptoms that typically appear before the onset of full-blown AIDS.

Asymmetrical Relationships: Relationships in which one partner holds a position of greater power or influence.

Asymptomatic: A state in which symptoms are not readily detectable by the infected person.

Autonomy: Independence and self-direction.

Bargaining with Patriarchy: Negotiating or influencing the rules of male–female relationships in a patriarchal family.

Bias: Systematic error in social research.

Biculturalism: Participating in two cultures.

Blamer Stance: Accusing the partner rather than addressing the issues with a desire to discuss problems and attempt to solve them.

Burden of Care: When the distress of one family member evokes a caregiving response and heightened levels of worry in another family member.

Clitoral Hood: A piece of skin that covers the clitoris during sexual arousal.

Clitoris: A small nub containing sensitive nerve endings which is located on the edge of the labia.

Cognitive Development: The process of maturation in which the manner of processing information changes.

Cognitive Developmental Theory: A theory that explains learning in terms of the child's age and stage of cognitive development.

Cohabitation: Two unmarried adults living together in a sexual relationship.

Commitment: A decision to maintain the love relationship.

Commuter Marriage: Marriage in which the partners maintain separate residences but spend time together as husband and wife on weekends or when their schedules allow.

Companionate Love: A strong and enduring affection that is more peaceful and comfortable than romantic love.

Concept: An abstract term that describes certain aspects of reality.

Conflict Theory: A theory that holds that power and privilege are derived from the resources a person possesses.

Constant: A factor that does not change.

Control Group: In an experiment, the group that does not receive the experimental treatment.

Control Variable: A third variable, or test variable, that is introduced to see whether or not it explains the relationship between the first two variables.

Correlation: A relationship between two variables so that they vary together.

Cross-Complaining: A verbal exchange in which one partner states a complaint and the second partner avoids addressing that issue, responding with a complaint about the first partner.

Cunnilingus: Oral–genital sex in which the partner uses the lips and tongue to stimulate the female clitoris and outer portion of the vagina.

De Facto: A situation that exists in fact but is not mandated by law.

De Jure: A situation that is mandated by law.

Demographic Trend: A change in population characteristics.

Demography: A field of study that gathers statistics on major milestones of life such as births, deaths, marriages, and divorce.

Dependent Variable: The variable the study hopes to explain.

Domestic Partners Legislation: Legislation passed in some cities which treats cohabiting partners of city employees as spouses, in that they are covered under the city employee's fringe benefits, such as health insurance.

Dominant Group: The group with power over subordinant groups in society.

Double Standard: The belief that sexual activity is acceptable for males but not for females.

Downward Mobility: Movement to a lower social class.

Dysfunction: A social institution's failure to fill its social functions.

Dysfunctional Family: A family that exhibits rigid social roles and does not adequately meet the needs of its members.

Endogamy: The tendency to marry within one's own social group.

Erection: Vasocongestion of the penis, clitoris, and often the nipples during sexual arousal.

Exchange Theory: A theory that maintains that behavior is influenced by the cost and benefits of taking a particular action.

Excitement Stage: The first stage of sexual arousal in which vasocongestion and neuromuscular tension occur.

Exogamy: The tendency to marry outside one's own social group.

Experiment: Research involving manipulation of one variable while trying to control other variables.

Experimental Group: In an experiement, the group that receives the experiemental treatment.

Expressive Demonstration of Love: Expression of love that emphasizes verbal expression of love and emotional closeness.

Expressive Role: Social role that stresses nurturance and emotional expression.

Extended Family: A family that includes kin who extend beyond the nuclear family.

Familism: A social value that places the needs of the family above the needs of the individual.

Family: Two or more people related by blood, marriage, or adoption who share a common residence.

Family Economy: A family as a small economy that needs both wage labor and household labor in order to survive. From this view, household labor is productive work.

Family Wage: A wage sufficient to support a family.

Fatuous Love: A form of love that involves commitment and passion without intimacy.

Fellatio: Oral–genital sex in which the penis is licked or sucked.

Feminization of Poverty: The growing tendency for poor families to be headed by women.

Fictive Kin: Nonrelatives who are treated as kin and often assigned a family title, such as Aunt or Uncle.

Field of Eligibles: The pool of people available for marriage.

Filial Piety: Respect, obligation, and obedience toward parents; this is an ideal in Asian cultures.

Function: A task contributing to the maintenance and continuation of society.

Functional Family: Family that allows for flexible, shifting roles and open communication, and that meets most of the needs of the members.

Functionalism: See *Structural-Functional Theory.*

Gender Constancy: The recognition that gender is a permanent characteristic, not subject to change.

Gender Role Theory: The theory that holds that expectations for the performance of gender roles established in childhood continue to influence adult behavior.

Gender Schema: A set of general characteristics that a person views as being central to a particular gender.

Gender Segregation: The tendency for males and females to be separated into different social activities, such as different jobs.

Gender Stratification: A social system that evaluates and rewards the work of males and females unequally.

Global Economy: An economy in which goods are produced and sold in world markets.

Group Marriage: The marriage of two or more men to two or more women.

Happpiness Gap: A difference in reported happiness: Single women report being happier than married women.

Helper Networks: People who exchange goods and services, such as financial aid, emotional support, and child care.

High-Divorce-Rate Society: A society in which divorce is widespread, socially acceptable, and easily available.

High-Risk Sexual Behavior: Behavior that increases the possibility of exposure to sexually transmitted diseases, such as AIDS.

HIV: The human immunodeficiency virus, which causes AIDS.

Homeostasis: The stability of a social system.

Homophobia: Fear and dislike of homosexuals.

Hypothesis: A prediction about how two or more variables are related.

Idealization: Exaggerating desirable characteristics and minimizing unattractive traits.

Ideal Marriage Form: The preferred form of marriage in a particular society.

Ideal Self: The self we would like to be.

Identification: A strong emotional attachment to another person and a desire to be like that person.

Identification Shift: A shift in identification from the mother to the father experienced by boys around age six or seven.

Identification Theory: A theory that explains socialization through identification.

Ideology: A set of beliefs or cultural ideals.

Independent Living: Living in a residence separate from that of one's parents or relatives.

Independent Variable: The explanatory variable.

Industrial Society: A society based on factory production.

Instrumental Demonstration of Love: Expression of love by having sex and providing economically for the family.

Instrumental Role: Social role emphasizing rationality and goal-orientation.

Interview: A process in a survey whereby a researcher asks questions and records the respondent's answers.

Intimacy: Feelings of closeness, connectedness, and support.

Intimacy Need Fulfillment: A stage in Reiss's wheel theory in which partners have a feeling of closeness and confide in each other.

Invasive Cervical Cancer: A form of cancer that can be associated with AIDS in women and that can spread quickly to other parts of the body.

Irrelevant Stance: Changing the subject to an unrelated topic when a partner becomes uncomfortable in a conversation.

Issue of Separation: An issue faced by adolescent girls, according to Chodorow, in which they face the problem of separating their identity from that of the mother.

Job Structure: The types of jobs that are available.

Kaposi's Sarcoma: A form of skin cancer, sometimes associated with AIDS, which produces purplish spots on the skin.

Labia: The outer portion or lips of the vagina.

Labor Force: Those who are employed or looking for work.

Latency Period: See *AIDS Latency Period.*

Leftover Income: Income remaining after deductions for taxes and work-related expenses have been made.

Life-Cycle Squeeze: A stage in the life cycle in which two time-consuming developmental tasks occur at the same time, as in simultaneously launching a family and a career.

Loss of Self: The inability to recognize one's inner wants and desires.

Love as Self-Development: A love ideology that emphasizes self-development and individualism for both partners.

Love as Self-Sacrifice: Love that emphasizes fulfilling the needs of the partner over one's own needs.

Love Ideology: A set of beliefs or cultural ideals related to love.

Machismo: Male dominance involving pride in masculinity, honor in the husband–father's position as economic provider of the family, and a belief in the sexual double standard.

Marital Quality: A partner's personal experience of satisfaction or happiness with a marital relationship.

Marital Stability: Marital continuity in that divorce is avoided.

Marital Stances: Familiar ways to enact their marital roles, to which spouses gravitate in stressful situations.

Marital Success: A marriage that both endures and has a high level of marital quality or satisfaction.

Marriage: A sexual relationship between two adults who cooperate economically; marked by a ceremony or ritual that is publically recognized as changing the social status of the partners involved.

Marriage Squeeze: A situation in which one gender experiences a shortage of potential marriage partners of the appropriate marriage age.

Median: A midpoint or fiftieth percentile.

Median Age at First Marriage: The age at first marriage which refers to the midpoint or fiftieth percentile.

Meidung: An Amish term meaning to shun.

Monogamy: Marriage of one man to one woman.

Mutual Dependency: A stage in Reiss's wheel theory in which the partners cooperate in doing things together and come to depend on each other.

Negative Mood Spillover: When problems and stress at work affect a person's ability to perform his or her family role.

Neuromuscular Tension: A physiological change in which energy or tension builds up in the nerve endings and muscles throughout the body. This occurs during sexual arousal.

Novelty Effect: A increase in sexual interest accompaning a new experience.

Nuclear Family: A family consisting of two generations, parents and children.

Operationalize a Variable: To find a concrete procedure for measuring a variable.

Opportunistic Disease: A disease against which the body normally has some resistance, but which flourishes when the immune system is not functioning properly.

Orgasm Stage: A stage in sexual arousal in which sexual tension rises to a peak and is discharged through orgasm.

Orgasmic Platform: A change in the vagina during sexual arousal in which the vagina experiences vasocongestion and narrows.

Overgeneralization: The assumption that behavior and attitudes found in one group or situation can also be found in groups or situations with different social characteristics.

Pandemic: A worldwide epidemic.

Parental Assistance: Providing physical care to a child without taking responsibility for planning.

Parental Responsibility: Remembering, planning, and scheduling involved in managing the daily lives of children.

Passion: The erotic or motivational component of love that involves physical attraction and physiological arousal.

Patriarchal Authority: Authority resting mainly in the male head of household.

Patriarchy: A pattern of male domination and female subordination that maintains male privilege at the expense of women.

Patrilineal Descent: The family name and inheritance are passed through the male line from father to son, and the family associates primarily with the husband's relatives.

Patrilocal Residence: The bride moves into the household of her husband and his family.

Personal Resources: Personal assets or services valued by the partner in a relationship, such as companionship or sex.

Plateau Stage: A stage in sexual arousal characterized by a sensation of heart pounding, heavy breathing, and elevated blood pressure.

Placater Stance: Seeking to reduce tension in the relationship by soothing an irritated partner or agreeing to the partner's requests.

Pneumocystic Pneumonia: A form of pneumonia, sometimes associated with AIDS, which causes coughing, shortness of breath, and eventual respiratory failure.

Polyandry: Marriage of one wife to two or more husbands.

Polygyny: Marriage of one man to two or more wives.

Population: The entire category of people being studied.

Positive Reinforcement: Social rewards that communicate approval.

Postindustrial Family: An urban family that is shaped by the need for higher education and career development.

Postindustrial Society: A society organized around information processing, advanced technology, and service jobs.

Poverty Rate: The percentage of a particular group who are poor.

Power: The ability to influence the lives of others and also to resist the influence of others.

Preejaculatory Fluid: A small amount of fluid emitted from the Cowper's gland prior to ejaculation.

Prestige: Admiration and respect.

Protection Hypothesis: The hypothesis stating that marriage and well-being are related because marriage provides some important protections against emotional and physical illness.

Questionnaire: A written set of questions in a survey.

Racial Endogamy: The tendency to marry within one's own race.

Racial Exogamy: The tendency to marry outside one's own race.

Racial Socialization: Preparing minority children to cope with discrimination in the larger society.

Random Sample: A sample in which each respondent has an equal chance of being selected.

Rapport: Feeling at ease and free to talk to a certain other person.

Reciprocity: The expectation that those who receive help will return the favor in the future.

Reconstructing Extended Families: Adding new family members to the extended family, such as distant relatives or fictive kin.

Refractory Period: A period of time following orgasm during which another erection and orgasm are impossible.

Reliability: The ability of a measuring device to produce consistent results in more than one measurement on the same person.

Representative Sample: A sample in which the characteristics of the population are accurately reflected.

Reserve Labor Force: A category of people who are drawn into employment when there is a labor shortage.

Resolution Stage: A stage following orgasm in which sexual intensity gradually subsides and muscle tension is replaced by relaxation.

Resources: Assets that provide a person with power.

Respondent: Person who is interviewed in a survey.

Response Rate: The percentage of people in a sample who agree to participate in the study.

Retrovirus: A virus that infects a cell and alters the cell's genetic structure so that the infected cell becomes capable of replicating the virus.

Rite of Passage: A ceremony marking the young male's change in status from boyhood to manhood; grants the young male full entry into adult male culture.

Role Conflict: A condition that occurs when the performance of one role—for example, a work role—makes it difficult to meet the obligations of other roles, such as the spouse role or parental role.

Role Hiatus: A break in time between assuming certain social roles, such as a break between the roles of daughter and mother.

Role Model: Someone with whom a person identifies and whose behavior is imitated.

Role Overload: A condition in which the duties required of a social role are greater than the energy and time available to perform those duties.

Role Reduction: Reducing responsibilities in major social roles.

Romantic Love: An intense, erotic attraction and yearning that idealizes the partner.

Romeo and Juliet Hypothesis: Hypothesis stating that when parents express opposition to a romance, the romance grows stronger.

Sample: A limited number of cases selected from a population.

Schema: A mental structure through which a person processes information.

Scientific Method: A procedure for designing a study, systematically collecting data, and analyzing results.

Second Shift: Unpaid labor in the home performed by employed women.

Selection Hypothesis: The hypothesis that marriage and well-being are related because healthier people are selected into marriage.

Self-Revelation: Sharing personal information about oneself.

Selfish Standard: Preference for a marriage partner less experienced than oneself.

Serial Monogamy: Marriage to more than one marriage partner in sequence.

Sex Flush: A reddening of the skin resembling measles which occurs in some people during sexual arousal.

Sexual Disenchantment: Boredom with the sexual relationship.

Sexual Harassment: Remarks and behavior, such as sexual advances, that create a hostile working environment for women.

Sexual Orientation: The preference for same-sex or opposite-sex partners.

Sexual Revolution: A change in social attitudes in which sex outside of marriage is considered more acceptable.

Social Cohesion: Integration with a group that provides a sense of unity with its members.

Social Functions: See *Functions*

Social Institutions: Social organizations such as the family, government, or corporations.

Social Learning Theory: A theory that explains socialization in terms of observation, imitation, and reinforcement.

Social Network: A group of people with whom a person interacts on a face-to-face basis.

Social Redefinition: Redefining a social situation in order to reduce feelings of stress, for example, telling oneself that there are more advantages than disadvantages in a particular situation.

Social Structures: The social institutions and behavior patterns of a society.

Social System: A set of interdependent parts so that one part has an impact on other parts.

Social Theory: An explanation for how societies operate which uses a set of concepts that label behavior.

Spurious Relationship: When two variables are related but one did not cause the other.

Stimulus-Value-Role Theory: Murstein's theory of mate selection in which a couple moves through three stages in selecting a mate: the stimulus stage, value stage and role stage.

Structural-Functional Theory: A theory that examines social relationships, asking how they contribute to the maintenance and stability of society.

Structures: See *Social structures*.

Subfamilies: A family housed in a dwelling of another family.

Subordinate Group: A group with less power than the dominant group.

Super-Reasonable Stance: The use of intellect and reason in discussions with the partner; ignores or brushes aside feelings.

Superstructure of Ideology: A set of values that supports and justifies the superior power position of the dominant group.

Survey: A set of standardized questions asked to a sample of people.

System of Exchange: A system in which resources such as food, services such as babysitting, and financial support, are given and the recipient is obligated to return the favor at a later date.

Systems Theory: A theory that views society as a set of interdependent parts.

Three-Cornered Self: Marks's theory depicting the "self" as a triangle with three corners—the partnership corner, the inner corner, and the outside corner— each corner representing a separate identity within the individual.

Token Resistance: A "sexual script" that holds that a woman's role is to behave in a resistant manner, even when she wants to have sex.

Traditional Female Gender Role: A social role that includes such traits as passivity, nurturance, helpfulness, and submissiveness.

Trial Marriage: Cohabitation as a stage in the mate-selection process, located between dating and marriage, that allows couples to test their compatibility prior to marriage.

Triangular Theory of Love: Sternberg's theory stating that love has three components: passion, intimacy, and commitment.

Two-Component Theory of Emotions: Stanley Schachter's theory that any emotion, including romantic love, has two components: physiological arousal and an interpretation of that physiological response.

Tyranny of the "Shoulds": Horney's term for strong and sometimes unreasonable demands on the self.

Underclass: The most disadvantaged subgroup of the poor, consisting of about 2 million people who have the greatest difficulty climbing out of poverty.

Underemployed: Those who work less than they would like and have less than full-time, year-round employment.

Validity: Accuracy of measurement; the extent to which research measures what it set out to measure.

Values: Broad, vague, ideological positions such as a commitment to career or religious beliefs.

Variable: Something that can have more than one value.

Vasocongestion: A state that occurs when the penis and testes of the man and the clitoris and breasts of the woman become engorged with blood.

Victim, Persecutor, Rescuer Stance: An interaction pattern in which both partners shift between the stances of persecutor, victim, and rescuer in response to problems in the relationship.

Vital Marriage: An ideal form of marriage characterized by "heroic sacrifices" for the benefit of the partnership and a consuming interest in the romantic relationship.

Wealth: Property owned, such as a family home, business, or stocks and bonds.

Wheel Theory: Reiss's theory maintaining that a person goes through four stages when falling in love: rapport, self-revelation, mutual dependency, and intimacy need fulfillment.

Withdrawal-Integration Hypothesis: The hypothesis stating that as people fall in love, they tend to withdraw from their social network of friends.

Women as Part of Nature: A theory tracing male dominance and female subordination to women's biological reproductive functions.

Acknowledgments

HarperCollins thanks the copyright holders for permission to reprint the following excerpts from copyrighted materials.

Box 2.1 adapted from May P. Koss, Christine A. Gidyez, and Nadine Wisniewski. 1987. "The Scope of Rape: Incidence and Prevalence of Sexual Aggression and Victimization in a National Sample of Higher Education Students." *Journal of Consulting and Clinical Psychology,* **55** (2):167. Copyright 1987 by the American Psychological Association. Adapted by permission.

Quote in Chapter 3 from Sandra Lipsitz Bem. 1983. "Gender Schema Theory and Its Implications for Gender-Aschematic Children in a Gender-Schematic Society." *Signs* 8:612. Copyright (c) 1983 by the University of Chicago Press. All rights reserved. Reprinted by permission.

Figure 4.1 adapted from Susan Sprecher, Kathleen McKinney, Robert Walsh, and Carrie Anderson. 1988. "A Revision of the Reiss Premarital Sexual Permissiveness Scale." *Journal of Marriage and the Family,* 50:825 (Fig. 1). Copyright 1988 by the National Council on Family Relations, 3989 Central Avenue NE, Suite 550, Minneapolis, MN 55421-3921. Reprinted by permission.

Figure 4.2 adapted from Ira L. Reiss. 1980. *Family Systems in America,* 3rd edition. Copyright (c) 1980 by Holt, Rinehart & Winston, Inc. Reproduced by permission of the publisher.

Figure 4.3A and B from Stephen R. Marks. 1989. "Toward a Systems Theory of Marital Quality." *Journal of Marriage and the Family,* **51**:15–26. Copyright 1989 by the National Council on Family Relations, 3989 Central Avenue NE, Suite 550, Minneapolis, MN 55421-3921.

Reprinted by permission.

Box 5.1 based on Norma Williams. 1990. *The Mexican-American Family: Tradition and Change.* Reprinted by permission of General Hall, Inc.

Figure 5.1 adapted from Bernard K. Murstein. 1987. "Feedback: A Clarification and Extension of the SVR Theory of Dyadic Pairing." *Journal of Marriage and the Family,* **49**:931. Copyright 1987 by the National Council on Family Relations, 3989 Central Avenue NE, Suite 550, Minneapolis, MN 55421-3921. Reprinted by permission.

Figure 5.2 Adapted from Valerie K. Oppenheimer. 1988. "A Theory of Marriage Timing." *American Journal of Sociology,* **94**:579. Copyright 1988 The University of Chicago Press. Reprinted by permission.

Figure 8.1 from Dennis A. Ahlburg and Carol J. DeVita. 1992. "New Realities of the American Family." *Population Bulletin,* **47** (2): 25 (Fig. 10). Reprinted by permission of the Population Reference Bureau.

Quotes in Chapter 8 from Denise A. Segura. 1988. "Familism and Employment Among Chicanas and Mexican Immigrant Women." In Margarita B. Melville (ed.). 1988. *Mexicanas at Work in the United States,* pp. 24–31. Reprinted by permission of the University of Houston Mexican American Studies Program and the author.

Quote in Chapter 8 based on Myra Marx Ferree. 1991. "The Gender Division of Labor in Two-Earner Marriages: Dimensions of Variability and Change." *Journal of Family Issues,* **12**:158–180. Reprinted by permission of Sage Publications, Inc.

Quote in Chapter 9 from Wendy Ewald. 1985. "Testimony of Love." *Psychology Today* (May):56. Copyright (c) 1985 Sussex Publishers, Inc.

Quote in Chapter 9, African American folktale as told by Awele Makeba at the Second Annual Ethnic Storytelling Festival, Diablo Valley College, February 26, 1992. Used by permission.

Quote in Chapter 10 from Frank Furstenberg, Jr. 1990. "How Families Manage Risk and Opportunity in Dangerous Neighborhoods." Published in Julius Wilson (Ed.). 1992. *Sociology and the Public Agenda,* pp. 237–238. Reprinted by permission of Sage Publications, Inc.

Quote in Chapter 12 from Nazli Kibria. 1990. "Power, Patriarchy, and Gender Conflict in the Vietnamese Immigrant Community." *Gender and Society,* **4**:9–24. Reprinted by permission of Sage Publications, Inc.

Table 12.2 from Craig H. Hart, Gary W. Ladd, and Brant R. Burleson. 1990. "Children's Expectations of the Outcomes of Social Strategies: Relations with Sociometric Status and Maternal Disciplinary Styles." *Child Development,* **61**:127–137. Copyright (c) The Society for Research in Child Development, Inc. Reprinted by permission.

Table 14.1 adapted from Glenace E. Edwall, Norman G. Hoffmann, and Patricia Ann Harrison. 1989. "Psychological Correlates of Sexual Abuse in Adolescent Girls in Chemical Dependency Treatment." *Adolescence,* **24**:284 (Table 1). Reprinted by permission of Libra Publishers.

Name Index

Mothers. *See also* Parents
 financial impact of divorce on, 425
 noncustodial, after divorce, 437
 role of, in child sexual abuse, 403-404
Mountain people, 230
Mucus method, for contraception, 481-
 482
Mutual aid, in Amish families, 47
Mutual dependency, as stage of falling in
 love, 104

Name-calling, 363, 364
Native Americans, 76-78
Natural consequences, 375
 parenting and, 326-327
Natural methods, of contraception, 481-
 482
Nature, argument of women as part of in
 gender inequity, 76
Negative mood spillover, in work-family
 conflict, 215-216
Negotiation, 370
 by parents, discipline in stepfamilies
 and, 452
Neolocal residence, 462
Net worth, median, 275
Neuromuscular tension, 144
The New American Poverty Harrington),
 257
No-fault divorce, 415-417
 financial impact of, 425
Nonassertive communication, 361-362
Noncustodial fathers, 336
Nonoxynol-9
 in safe sex, 160
Nonverbal communication, 353-354
Normalizing the violence, 386-387
Norplant, for contraception, 479-480
"No" statement, as conclusion to
 assertive communication, 369
Novelty effect, sexuality and, 152
Nuclear families, 25
Nurturance, female role and, 63
Nurturing, in traditional family, 6

Observation
 in social learning theory, 64
 unstructured, as method of data collec-
 tion, 41
Occupational structure, changes in, as
 explanation for homelessness,
 283
Occupations, couples with equal status
 in, 220
"Off time" parenting, 339
Old age, caregiving in, 192-193
Open adoption, 337
Open-coupled relationships, 157
Opportunistic disease, Acquired Immune
 Deficiency Syndrome as, 161
Opportunity costs, 301

Opportunity structure, shrinking in
 working class, 270
Oral contraceptives, 479
Oral-genital sex, 90
Ordering behavior, in aggressive
 communication, 363-364
Orgasmic dysfunction, 492
Orgasmic platform, 145
Orgasm stage
 of human sexual response, 145
 physiologic changes during, 145
*The Origins of the Family, Private Property
 and the State* (Engels), 79
Overgeneralization, 78, 125
Over-the counter drugs, as complication
 of pregnancy, 487
Ovulation, 483
Owning feelings, as "I" statement com-
 ponent of assertive communica-
 tion, 368

Pandemic, 162
Paranoia, as psychological explanation
 for domestic violence, 388
Parental assistance, in child care, 212
Parental responsibility, in child care, 212
Parent Effectiveness Training (Gordon),
 325
Parenting, 321-346
 adoption and, 336-338
 after divorce, in future, 443-445
 authoritarian, 323
 authoritative, 324
  to maintain resilient family, 466
 balancing with employment, 332-333
 consensual environment and, 327-
 328
 consistency in, 324
 impaired, as long-term difficulty for
 children after divorce, 431-432
 influence of on relationships with
 peers, 328-329
 logical consequences and, 327
 marital satisfaction and, 331-332
 natural consequences and, 326-327
 permissive, 323
 positive, 326
 problems of, in single-parent families,
 335
 single-parent families and, 333, 335-
 336
 socialization and, 322
 styles of, 323-324
 time-out as tool for, 326
Parenting coalitions, 444
Parent replacement model, unwed teens
 and, 340
Parents
 adult children living with, 462-465
 birth, adoption and, 337-338
 compared to nonparents, 189-190

custodial, financial impact of divorce
 on, 425
Hispanic-American, 343-344
immigrant, 341-344
marital history of, as risk factor of
 divorce, 419
single, as indicator of cohabitation,
 132-133
teens as, 339-341
 mothers and, 340-341
 stress and, 339-340
Participant observer, 41
Partnerships, equal versus traditional, in
 conflict theory, 358
Passion, as component of love, 103
Patriarchy, 12, 79
 in Mexican-American families, 206
 Vietnamese-American women and,
 247-249
Patrilocal descent, of Vietnamese-
 American families, 247
Patrilocal residence, 12-13
 of Vietnamese-American families, 247
Peers, influence of on parenting,
 328-329
Permanence, expectation of in tradition-
 al family, 6
Permissive parenting, 323
Persecutor, as marital stance in
 substance abuse, 188
Personal problems, as explanation for
 homelessness, 282
Personal resources
 in conflict theory, 221
 in exchange theory, 49
Phenylethylamine (PEA), 102
Pheumocystic pneumonia, 166
Physical abuse, 400-402
Physical functioning, as short-term diffi-
 culty for children after divorce,
 429-430
Pie chart, 24
Pink-collar jobs, 265
Placater stance, as stance in marital dis-
 tress, 187
Placenta, 484
Plans, statement of, as conclusion to
 assertive communication, 369
Plateau stage, of human sexual response,
 144-145
Police-initiated arrests, role of in mitigat-
 ing domestic violence, 397
Polyandry, 10-11, 12-13
 fraternal, 12-13
Polygyny, 11
 legalization in Utah of, 243